Princeton in the Nation's Service

Recent titles in
RELIGION IN AMERICA SERIES
Harry S. Stout, General Editor

Princeton in the Nation's Service

Religious Ideals and Educational Practice, 1868–1928

P. C. Kemeny

New York   Oxford
OXFORD UNIVERSITY PRESS
1998

Oxford University Press

Oxford New York

Athens Auckland Bangkok Bogotá Buenos Aires
Calcutta Cape Town Chennai Dar es Salaam Delhi Florence
Hong Kong Istanbul Karachi Kuala Lumpur Madras
Madrid Melbourne Mexico City Mumbai Nairobi Paris São Paulo
Singapore Taipei Tokyo Toronto Warsaw

and associated companies in
Berlin Ibadan

Published by Oxford University Press, Inc.
198 Madison Avenue, New York, New York 10016
Oxford is a registered trademark of Oxford University Press, Inc.

Library of Congress Cataloging-in-Publication Data
Kemeny, Paul Charles.
Princeton in the nation's service: religious ideals and educational practice,
1868–1928 / P. C. Kemeny.

Includes bibliographical references and index.
ISBN 0-19-512071-X
1. Protestant churches—Education—United States—History—19th century—Case studies.
2. Protestant churches—Education—United States—History—20th century—Case studies.
3. Church and college—United States—History—19th century—Case studies.
4. Church and college—United States—History—20th century—Case studies.
5. Princeton University—History. I. Title. II. Series: Religion in America series (Oxford University Press)
LC621.K45 1998
378.749'65—dc21   97-35710

1 3 5 7 9 8 6 4 2

Printed in the United States of America
on acid-free paper

For Betsy

Acknowledgments

No one writes a book alone. So it is one of the true joys of completing one to be able to acknowledge in print my gratitude to those who advised, assisted, and encouraged me. I am especially thankful for the enthusiasm and encouragement of my dissertation committee. James H. Moorhead, under whose direction this work began at Princeton Seminary, patiently encouraged me to clarify my argument. Jane Dempsey Douglass gave my study a careful reading and challenged me to explore the original sources in their larger historical context. John F. Wilson graciously pushed me to reexamine the assumptions that I brought to the study. I am also thankful to George M. Marsden for reading the manuscript and offering helpful suggestions at how to refine my line of inquiry. For the encouragement, inspiration, listening ear, and refreshing doses of sarcasm I also want to thank Greg Bezilla, Henry Warner Bowden, Darryl Hart, Brad Longfield, Dan Sack, and Bruce Springsteen. I am also thankful for the year of affiliation with the Center for the Study of American Religion at Princeton University when I revised this for publication. Bob Wuthnow, the Friday workshops, and numerous afternoon coffees with friends proved to be invaluable in helping me clarify my thinking. I am also grateful for the excellent editorial suggestions offered me by Tom Wisneski and Jane Bailey. I am also thankful to Bob Alderink, and, at Oxford University Press, Cynthia Read, Jessica A. Ryan, and Carole Berglie for helping to guide the manuscript through the publication process.

I also want to express my sincere appreciation for the help offered me by the library staffs at both Princeton Seminary and Princeton University. At Speer Library, William O. Harris helped me dig out previously untapped sources and offered me endless encouragement, Douglass Denné and Raymond Cannata likewise kept an eye out for helpful sources and listened patiently to my latest stories about life in Princeton in the nineteenth century, and Kate Skrebutenas, reference library par excellence, helped me obtain through inter-library loan those few books not possessed by one of the libraries in Princeton. At the Seeley G. Mudd Manuscript Library, Ben Primer, Nanci Young, Daniel Linke, and Monica Ruscil were not only supportive during the dark days of archival research but also proved to be first-class sleuths in tracking down material in the university's vast archival holdings. Ellen Sherry and the staff at the Manuscript Room in Firestone Library likewise made my research as productive and enjoyable as possible. The library staffs at Columbia Seminary, Harvard University Archives, the New Jersey Historical Society, the Lawrenceville School, and Westminster Seminary also graciously helped me track down useful sources.

I am eternally grateful for my family. My mother and my father, who passed away before he could see this work completed, as well as my brothers and in-laws at different times and in different ways expressed a supportive interest in my work and graciously accepted my evasive answers about how the project was going. I am also thankful for one particular humbling inquiry of my sister-in-law who, when she asked me how my "little paper" was going, helped me keep the project's importance in proper perspective. I am grateful too for my daughter Helen whose unbridled enthusiasm and joyful disposition provided perfect study breaks from the tedium of research and writing. I am also thankful that she resisted the temptation to play with that cool-looking laptop computer on my desk or the dining room table. My greatest debt of gratitude goes to my wife, Betsy, whose love, patience, and support is a true blessing.

April 1998
P. C. Kemeny

Contents

Princeton in the Nation's Service

Introduction

Princeton versus Harvard: this 1886 "battle of the Titans," as one reporter described it, was not an athletic contest, and more was at stake than college pride. At a wintry February meeting of the Nineteenth Century Club at the American Art Gallery in New York City, a "large and fashionable" audience gathered to hear two combatants debate the question, "What place should religion have in a college?" Specifically, the question concerned the role of religious instruction and worship in collegiate education. Princeton College President James McCosh represented the denominational college and his counterpart at Harvard College, Charles W. Eliot, the neutral or nondenominational institution. Each president read his paper with a politeness befitting the Victorian sensibilities of the audience, yet beneath the decorum lay two very different understandings of the nature and role of religion in American collegiate education. McCosh had history on his side, but Eliot had the future on his.[1]

"Nearly all the older colleges, such as Harvard, Yale, and Princeton," McCosh explained, "were founded in the fear of God, with the blessing of heaven invoked; they gave religious instruction to the students, and had weekly and daily exercises of praise and prayer to Almighty God." Compulsory religious instruction and worship, McCosh insisted, were essential to the intellectual and moral well-being of students—America's future leaders—and so, ultimately, to the welfare of the nation. Princeton, as with many other institutions established before the Civil War, was officially a nondenominational college chartered in 1746 to serve the general public. In reality, however, Princeton, was a de facto denominational college that met the educational needs and upheld the intellectual ideas of Presbyterians and the larger Protestant community. Because the older American colleges promoted a nonsectarian Protestantism, which would not give offense to any evangelical denomination, McCosh reasoned, they upheld the faith of most Americans and performed a public service. At Princeton, this traditional approach was still readily evident in the late nineteenth century. Nine professors taught English Bible to each academic class; seniors also took required courses in Ethics and Evidences for Christianity; all students participated in mandatory daily chapel services, as well as Sunday morning and evening services. But many of these older colleges, as they attract "a greater and more varied constituency of teachers and students," McCosh complained, are "abandoning" the traditional place of religion "till now little is left." The state universities, founded after the Civil War, he observed, "make no profession of religion." "[B]eing troubled in dealing with the various sects—Christian and Jewish, Catholic and Protestant," McCosh contended, these schools have found it "easiest

3

to give up all religious services of a systematic kind." Yet Princeton's president did not expect to see an "attempt to drive religion out of the college." As he had explained to an international gathering of Presbyterian church leaders two years earlier, "I have noticed that some of our *Secularists* in America do not wish the question started. They would let the old American customs, the Bible and prayers first, and finally all discipline disappear, without anyone noticing it."[2] McCosh and his colleagues at Princeton not only remained firmly committed to continuing these traditional religious practices at their school but also hoped that by drawing the public's attention to this ominous trend at Harvard and a few other institutions they could prevent additional colleges and universities from abandoning conventional religious commitments.

By contrast, Eliot, the leading architect of the modern American research university, championed the ideal of the "unsectarian" college where religious instruction and worship were voluntary. Because the United States had no established church and was becoming "more and more heterogeneous as regards religion," Eliot reasoned, the university that aspired to serve the nation's educational interests could not privilege the peculiar beliefs of one particular group. "To all denominations," Harvard's president insisted, "the College must be *just*, and it must be careful not to wound the susceptibilities of any." Voluntary religious education, Eliot explained, provided the most equitable means for offering religious education while respecting the diversity of faiths represented in the student body.[3] In 1885, Eliot had made religious instruction in the undergraduate curriculum elective courses. In the spring of 1886, the innovative Eliot made all chapels service at Harvard optional.

Conventional Interpretations

Within a generation after the 1886 McCosh-Eliot debate, Princeton had adopted a position toward religion quite similar to the one advocated by Harvard's president. Despite the dogmatic commitment of McCosh and his colleagues to evangelical Protestantism's role in collegiate education, traditional evangelical practices and values had been almost entirely eliminated in Princeton's transition from the College of New Jersey into a major research university. By 1917, for example, the faculty and trustees had dropped the two mandatory terms of apologetics and natural theology, as well as the elective courses in these fields from the curriculum. They had also compressed the three required terms of ethics into one elective course. They even replaced the four years of obligatory Bible instruction with upperclass elective courses. After fundamentalists' attacks on the theological modernism of the university's sole Bible instructor, Lucius H. Miller, forced him to resign in frustration in 1917, despite a supportive faculty resolution and the trustees' commitment to academic freedom, Bible courses were dropped altogether from their place as a regular part of the curriculum. By this time, the administration had made chapel services practically a voluntary activity: students had to attend at least half of the Sunday morning services each academic year. Other important signs evidenced the end of evangelical Protestantism's dominance over the affairs of the university in the early twentieth century. After he became president of Princeton in 1902, Woodrow Wilson ended the practice of making inquiries into the theological orthodoxy of prospective faculty members to ensure they would fit into the community. In addition, in order to qualify for Carnegie Foundation pension funds in 1906, Wilson persuaded the Board of Trustees to declare Princeton officially a nondenominational institution. That same year, the trustees reduced from twelve to eight the number of seats on its board designated by charter for clerics. They also eliminated scholarships designated for preministerial candidates and the sons of Presbyterian ministers. In perhaps the most sensational illustration of the demise of evangelicalism's privileged position on campus, President John G. Hibben, to the consternation of many conservative Presbyterians, refused to allow the evangelist Billy Sunday to hold a revival service on campus in 1915. After recalling the time when, as an undergraduate, President McCosh cancelled classes in order to allow D. L. Moody to hold revival services at the college, one dismayed alumnus asked, *"Is Princeton Christian?"*[4] Many of this aging alumnus' contemporary critics of Princeton in particular and American universities in general answered his question with a resounding negative.

Conventional interpretations of the history of American higher education, if they devote any attention to the subject at all, attribute the demise of traditional evangelical interests and practices at colleges and universities such as Princeton to the corrosive results of secularization. To be sure, such interpretations are not entirely misguided when they point to the destructive consequences that the grand educational and intellectual changes of the late nineteenth and early twentieth centuries had on established educational commitments and conventions.

In the decades after the Civil War, American higher education, as conventional interpretations observe, underwent a dramatic transformation. In 1885, James McCosh, though welcoming many of the advances in collegiate education in his day, warned Princeton's Board of Trustees that "a great crisis in the higher education of America has now come." While the occasional cause of McCosh's anxiety was the abandonment of compulsory religious education and the expansion of the elective system, the efficient cause was, as Richard Hofstadter later described in his formative essay, the revolution that reshaped American higher education between the Civil War and World War I. The statistical growth of higher education in this period illustrates that sweeping changes were taking place when McCosh and Eliot debated the merits of traditional religious education. While the general population grew an estimated 375 percent between 1870 and 1920, the percentage of eighteen- to twenty-one-year-old students enrolled in colleges or universities increased even more (480 percent), as did the number of college degrees (520 percent), the number of professors (875 percent), and the number of colleges and universities (from 563 to 1,040). Such changes were in part a reaction against the failures of what had been characterized as the antebellum "discipline and piety" philosophy of higher education. The Yale Report of 1828 canonized this vision of the nature and purpose of collegiate education. The aim of a college education, the report stated, was to foster piety, to equip students with a basic body of knowledge, and to discipline the powers of students' minds—namely, affection, understanding, and will, according to the tripartite faculty psychology of the day. In the late antebellum period, anti-intellectual attitudes common to the Jacksonian Age, the diminished correlation between a college degree and worldly success, a corresponding decline in the percentage of youths attending colleges, and the failure of the nation's college-educated leaders to resolve the slavery crisis peacefully opened a gap between colleges and American society. After the Civil War, a young and restless generation of educators grew increasingly dissatisfied with the old-time college's ability to produce only gentlemen well versed in Scottish commonsense philosophy, conversant in dead languages and literatures, and merely familiar with some natural science. As the failures of American higher education before the Civil War revealed, the nation desperately needed leaders trained to meet efficiently the real and pressing economic, political, and social problems of the day. Consequently, many educators revolted against the educational status quo associated with the antebellum college. An even more critical force driving this educational revolution was academic specialization. "The conflict between a Jacksonian distrust of privileged elites and the advance of specialization," John Higham argues, "was resolved by widening immensely the opportunity to specialize and restricting the opportunity to dominate." According to Higham, an institutional "matrix of specialization" emerged in the postbellum period that not only created a decentralized democracy of specialists but also, when combined with the university's teaching functions, enabled the university to gain widespread support in a culture that regarded egalitarianism and pragmatism as virtues. In the late nineteenth century, specialization helped to foster a "culture of professionalization," in which experts with Ph.D. degrees replaced amateurs as teachers, new scholarly disciplines emerged (most notably in the nascent social sciences) to explore previously unknown frontiers of human knowledge, and new academic associations and publications were organized to distribute the latest scholarship and to cultivate self-conscious professional identities. The university also served as the seminal institution for burgeoning new professions outside the academy, such as business and journalism, which offered the expanding middle class greater opportunities for financial success and social authority.[5]

The dislocation of colleges from the rest of American society in the late antebellum period provided educators after the Civil War with an opportunity to experiment by adapting selective elements of the German university to the American college. Specifically, German universities provided educational reformers with examples of new scholarly methods, a high appreciation of academic freedom, and, most important, a university model for higher education itself. After the Civil War, two new visions of higher education emerged. The first concentrated on the search for new knowledge and placed elite groups of scholars conducting specialized research at the heart of the university. This wave of academic reform began in the mid-1870s and received institutional form in

1876 with the founding of the Johns Hopkins University—the Göttingen of Baltimore. This type of pure research university initially lacked undergraduate colleges and, because of perceptions of elitism, was not as popular as the second reform movement, which promoted a more utilitarian and vocational vision of higher education. Harvard under Eliot and Cornell University, established in 1868 with Andrew D. White as president, led this movement, which eventually came to dominate the great state universities that had been created by the Morrill Act of 1862.[6] As Johns Hopkins, Harvard, Cornell, and other emerging universities responded to new needs for scientific expertise or professional preparation, older colleges attempted to incorporate, often awkwardly, elements of one or both new visions of higher education into their traditional programs. Established evangelical interests and practices, according to conventional interpreters, were abandoned because they conflicted with educational advancements and new standards made popular by the revolution in higher education.[7]

At the same time as American higher education was experiencing a revolution, many American Protestants in the Gilded Age were stricken with a spiritual crisis. Darwinism and the higher criticism of the Bible sabotaged Victorians' beliefs in God's providential design of creation and in the accuracy and authority of the Bible. The intellectual sources guiding Darwinism and higher criticism, scientific naturalism and historicism, respectively, challenged both revealed religion and natural theology by undermining the traditional two-tiered Protestant worldview taught in most college curricula. On a philosophical level, positivism and German idealism subverted the intellectual hull of Scottish commonsense realism upon which the deck and masts of the dominant educational, moral, social, and theological views of the day were built. Positivism subverted natural theology and moral philosophy by limiting human knowledge exclusively to that which could be obtained through empirical observation of phenomena. Idealism made the mind an active agent in constructing human knowledge, not an objective recipient of direct sensory experience of reality, and opened the door for reconstructing a theology based upon experience or ethics. A few iconoclasts in the late nineteenth century, such as Robert G. Ingersoll, the John the Baptist of American agnosticism, made a career of torpedoing the conventional faith of many Americans. Other Victorians saw their faith quietly slip below the waterline. John Dewey, for example, lost his boyhood faith while teaching public school in Oil City, Pennsylvania. "I've never had any doubts since then," he later recalled, "nor any beliefs."[8] While many conservative Protestant thinkers in the late nineteenth century actively opposed positivism and idealism, they were fighting a losing battle.

The unbelief that had infected a few Victorians in the late nineteenth century had become an epidemic on the college campus in the early twentieth. According to one 1916 survey of America's leading scientists, for instance, slightly more than a quarter affirmed belief in a God who answered prayer while more than half expressed disbelief and the remainder were simply unsure.[9] Given the decline of orthodox belief in academic circles and the general revolution in higher education, compelling students who were preparing to meet the chal-

lenges of the twentieth century to study archaic evangelical beliefs in mandatory Bible and apologetic courses made no more sense than requiring them to
study alchemy. Consequently, many distinctively evangelical interests and practices disappeared on campuses in the early twentieth century. As one observer
recently concluded, "In almost every way imaginable the new university under-
cut the traditional values of Christian higher education in America."[10]

The Neglected Public Dimension and a New Interpretation

Despite the demise of traditional evangelical concerns and customs, however,
historians have overlooked important ways in which religion still thrived on
American campuses in the early twentieth century. At Princeton in the 1920s,
for example, religion continued to dominate the interests of many in the university. Contrary to the opinions of some of the university's older alumni and conservative Presbyterian supporters, a special committee on the religious life of
the university reported to the Board of Trustees in 1927 that "Princeton has
been and is in fact today a *Christian* University." The university's administrators, anxious to provide a prominent place for the religious education of students, constructed an enormous, two-million-dollar Gothic chapel at the heart
of the campus in 1928. They also hired a chaplain to oversee the religious life of
the university. That same year the university hosted a conference on the role of
religion in collegiate life, which attracted nearly 200 college and university
presidents, professors, and officials from private boarding schools and various
religious organizations. Throughout much of the decade, the Philadelphian Society, Princeton's Y.M.C.A., flourished. In the 1924–1925 academic year, for
instance, students held weekly Sunday evening meetings; organized fifty discussion groups for freshmen; enrolled 300 upperclassmen in faculty-led discussion groups; solicited more than $27,000 from over 1700 donors for the campus
ministry; raised another $45,000 to support the society's mission in China,
Princeton-in-Peking, which had recently taken over responsibility for a Department of Sociology and Political Science in Peking University; conducted En-
glish-language classes for immigrant communities living in Princeton; and organized summer camps in Bay Head, New Jersey, and West Chester,
Pennsylvania, for some 400 urban youths. Moreover, many members of the
faculty, including a number of prominent scientists, eagerly sought to promote
Christianity. The distinguished biologist Edwin G. Conklin, for example, lectured and published widely on the harmony between theism and evolution.[11]
This brief review of some of the activities and interests at Princeton in the 1920s
suggests that the relationship between religion and modern higher education in
the early twentieth century was more complicated than has been assumed.

Historians of American religion and of higher education, even recent revi-
sionists, have typically neglected or frequently undervalued the ways in which
Protestant beliefs and practices continued to play a crucial role in higher education in the early twentieth century. This study challenges conventional interpre-

tations by arguing that at one representative institution, Princeton University, Protestant interests were not abandoned but rather modified to conform to the intellectual and educational values of the modern university. The expansion of the university's public or civic mission in the late nineteenth and early twentieth centuries, and the concurrent decline of evangelical Protestant cultural hegemony, fueled this modification. This study explores not only the dramatic changes in the role of religion in collegiate education but also the persistence of Protestant values at Princeton between 1868, when McCosh became president, and 1928, when President John G. Hibben and his colleagues attempted to resolve once and for all the place of religion within a university devoted to serving the educational needs of a nation that was increasingly pluralistic in its religious beliefs and practices. In brief, this study examines what happens to a religious institution when it broadens its civic mission while attempting to preserve its religious identity in a growing religiously diverse environment. By adapting religion to more modern intellectual standards and educational values, Princeton, like many other private colleges and universities, continued to attempt to preserve the mainline Protestant character of American society for another generation despite the "second disestablishment" of Protestantism in the 1920s.

Protestant efforts to mold American life and thought through higher education have a history as old as the nation itself. After the formal disestablishment of the church in the late eighteenth and early nineteenth centuries, Protestants sought to Christianize America through voluntary means such as revivals, reforms, and education. In this early national period, first Jeffersonians and later Whigs considered education the crucial means to preserving democracy. However, the Whiggish conception of higher education rejected the Jeffersonian insistence on a strict separation of religion and civic life and maintained that the young nation needed a common set of values, nonsectarian Protestant moral values, in order to avoid the social turmoil associated with the French Revolution. This Whiggish view thrived in the ensuing cultural hegemony of postdisestablishment Protestantism and shaped educational leaders' understanding of the relationship between higher education and American society. Throughout much of the nineteenth century, upholding the religious ideals of the pan-Protestant community and meeting the educational needs of the nation were inseparable aims. In other words, educators conceived of the civic purpose of higher education in religious terms. Courses in moral philosophy, for instance, were first introduced into the college curriculum in the late eighteenth century, in order to harness the more constructive forces of what Henry F. May has termed the conservative "didactic" form of the Enlightenment and at the same time to counter the destructive skeptical and revolutionary elements of the European Enlightenment. Such courses, as historians have observed, not only harmonized the truths derived from the classical curriculum with those revealed in the Bible but also tried to shape the conscience of the nation's future leaders and ultimately the moral fabric of American society. Courses in Bible and Evidences for Christianity, mandatory chapel services, and voluntary religious activities nurtured the evangelical Protestant faith of students and sought to infuse American culture with evangelical values. Historians have not given ample attention to what was actually taught through these courses and activities and, more important, how nineteenth-century Protestant theology provided a unifying center to the entire educational endeavor. Because the Scottish philosophy and prevailing Baconian method gave both sides of the curriculum an irrefutable scientific character, the curriculum, many educators believed, transcended sectarian differences while fostering a broadly Protestant worldview. Institutions also employed a variety of formal or informal practices, such as orthodoxy tests for hiring faculty and stipulations requiring a certain number of clerics on the board of trustees, designed to safeguard the evangelical character of the institutions. Evangelical Protestantism, despite denominational differences, dominated American culture throughout the nineteenth century; as one British observer of American life, Lord James Bryce, commented in 1888, "Christianity is understood to be, though not the legally established religion, yet the national religion." Thus, because evangelical Protestantism was the de facto national religion, it was the unofficial but established religion for a large portion of American higher education throughout much of the nineteenth century. By shaping the intellectual, moral, and spiritual character of the nation's future leaders, American colleges, including Princeton, played a critical part in advancing the Christian character of American culture.[12]

Beginning in the late nineteenth century but especially in the early twentieth, colleges and universities began to distinguish between their public and religious purposes. Educational institutions no longer identified their religious commitment with their public function because the old-stock Protestant denominations' efforts to preserve their hold on American life and thought were weakening and colleges and universities were broadening their civic mission. While many educators had doubts concerning the intellectual credibility of the evangelical faith, as conventional interpretations observe, it was the growing cultural pluralism of the nation that made evangelicalism increasingly sectarian and therefore disparate with higher education's civic function. At the same time, colleges and universities were broadening their public mission by providing American society more practical and profitable forms of knowledge through more utilitarian curricula, professionalization of the faculties, and development of graduate and specialized research programs. Consequently, formal policies and informal strategies designed to preserve an institution's evangelical character became hindrances not merely to the institution's educational advancements, as conventional interpreters have noted, but ultimately to higher education's expanded civic purpose. This study recovers the changing public rationale for higher education in the early twentieth century and examines its impact on religious beliefs and practices in higher education. In a nation that was increasingly heterogeneous in its religious beliefs and practices, state and denominational institutions emphasized their public and ecclesiastical commitments, respectively, and thereby could more easily serve the educational needs of either the general public or a particular religious community. By contrast, private, nondenominational colleges and universities struggled to preserve their religious identities and at the same time to broaden their civic function without appearing to betray the public interest—a commitment for which such institutions had originally been founded—for the sake of a specific religious community.

In the 1920s, as a result of the massive influx of non-Protestant immigrants, the growth of cities and industry, and the divisions within the Protestant house, Protestantism experienced a "second disestablishment" in American culture and lost its place as the national religion. Even so, there were moments in this decade, such as the crusade to preserve Prohibition legislation and the united Protestant opposition to Al Smith's 1928 presidential campaign, when mainline Protestants appeared to maintain their old power.[13] Mainstream Protestants, moreover, continued to presume their custodianship of American society and still dominated many important institutions and organizations in American culture. In many colleges and universities, most notably private, nondenominational institutions, educators did not abandon the religious purpose of higher education but modified it to conform to the university's public mission. Educators, in short, widened the Whiggish conception of higher education. The persistence of this widely shared understanding of the purpose of higher education helps to explain the sources of both the changes and the continuities in religion in the university in the early twentieth century. Institutions not only abolished those practices designed to guard the distinctly evangelical character of the old-time college and adapted religion to modern science and new educational ideals but also attempted through these adjustments to provide the increasingly diverse nation with a unifying and integrative national religion. Consequently, mainstream Protestants continued to function, or at least still attempted to serve, as the custodians of American culture and remained firmly entrenched in many of the nation's most influential educational institutions despite the "second disestablishment." These modifications also made fundamentalists and, to a lesser degree, many cultural modernists outsiders to many modern universities in the early twentieth century. By the mid-twentieth century, however, the new fusion of civic and religious purposes became increasingly difficult to maintain in light of the nation's growing cultural and intellectual pluralism.[14]

One Institution

An examination of the history of Protestantism at one institution can reveal the changes and the continuities that religion played in American higher education in the late nineteenth and early twentieth centuries by focusing on everyone who inhabited the college campus during the period in question and by uncovering often overlooked primary sources. General surveys typically emphasize the lead actors in the drama of religion in American higher education, such as college presidents. These surveys also depend heavily upon printed primary sources, which are invaluable insofar as they usually express what the administration officially wanted its supporters to believe was taking place on campus. A study devoted to one institution can analyze not only the actions of these prominent figures but also those of other, typically ignored members of the drama.

The entire cast—the professors who taught and wrote about the faith, the trustees who guided the university, the alumni and other members of the university's community who supported or resisted change, and the students who sat through hundreds of hours of Bible classes and chapel services—can be fully explored. Moreover, a wealth of neglected primary sources—the correspondence, diaries, lecture notes, and papers of presidents, professors, students, and trustees; the papers of the Y.M.C.A. and other student organizations; campus newspapers and other student publications—can be dissected in order to recover what was, and was not, actually happening on campus. Whereas general surveys excel at delineating the grand forces reshaping American religion and higher education— such as Darwinism, the higher criticism of the Bible, academic specialization, and professionalization—an examination of one institution can recover the human agents involved in this period of transition. Furthermore, by keeping the critical developments and events of the institution in their larger educational context through comparisons of what was happening at other colleges and universities, an examination of one representative institution can shed light on the entire history of Protestantism's role in American collegiate education. An analysis of the changes and continuities in religion that considers not only official pronouncements but also actual practices both inside and outside of the classroom can more fully recover the complexity of religion's role in higher education and higher education's role in a changing American culture.

Princeton

An examination of the history of religion at Princeton University provides an excellent case study of Protestantism's changing role in collegiate education in the late nineteenth and early twentieth centuries. Developments in Protestantism's place in collegiate education at Princeton are representative of those at many other American colleges and universities. Religion at Princeton, as at many other institutions in the late nineteenth century, enjoyed a principal role in undergraduate education throughout McCosh's presidency. At the same time, Princeton, along with Cornell, Johns Hopkins, Harvard, Michigan, and Yale, was in the vanguard of the university movement. While the German university model resulted in the creation of specialized research universities and the vocational or professional training model of higher education produced new state universities, Princeton resisted the wholesale embrace of either model. Instead, Princeton, like many other private and denominational institutions, selectively engrafted elements of each into the older antebellum model of collegiate education. Because Princeton tried to preserve, sometimes militantly, the traditional place of religion while attempting to transform the college into a university, and thus advance its public mission, it was also typical of many private institutions, such as Yale, and especially denominational institutions, such Lafayette. Princeton, in fact, served as a role model for many private and church-related colleges and universities. McCosh, for example, regularly spoke to leaders of

Presbyterian higher education, served as an unofficial consultant for Presbyterian and other denominational college presidents, and educated more than one hundred college presidents and professors in his twenty years at Princeton. During the administrations of Woodrow Wilson and John G. Hibben, Princeton, like other institutions, took radical steps to advance its public mission by improving its standing as a research university. By 1930, Princeton stood among the top twenty research universities that were receiving the lion's share of research funding from foundations and industry. While distinctly evangelical concerns and practices ended during this period of radical transition, traditional Protestant interests resurfaced in new forms and in other places on campus. These changes made Princeton less representative of denominational colleges than it had been in the nineteenth century. For the same reasons, however, Princeton was more representative of private colleges and universities in the twentieth century. In his 1947 study of Protestantism's role in higher education, Merrimon Cuninggim placed Princeton at the front of the movement, which had emerged in the 1920s, to preserve a role for Protestantism in America's colleges and universities. A study of Princeton during this period offers a window onto the changes and continuities in Protestantism's role in American collegiate education, as well as onto the critical changes in the public mission of higher education in the late nineteenth and early twentieth centuries.

An examination of the place of Protestantism in collegiate education at Princeton in the late nineteenth and early twentieth centuries also sheds new light on not only the relationship between mainstream Protestantism and one of the nation's most influential cultural institutions, the American university, but also upon how they responded to the questions of cultural diversity and assimilation. When Protestants enjoyed cultural hegemony during the nineteenth century, Princeton, like most other colleges and universities, was a de facto Protestant institution. In the twentieth century, Wilson, Hibben, and their colleagues continued to insist, like their predecessors, that Protestantism was indispensable to the public good and that civic institutions, like universities, served public interests when they sought to cultivate the Protestant faith of students. To be sure, mainline Protestants could tolerate a certain amount of religious heterogeneity, but the need for social order and stability demanded cultural uniformity. The religious controversies of the 1910s and 1920s at Princeton threatened the unity of the institution and ultimately the university's religious mission. Princeton's administration attempted to assimilate diversity and resolve dissent by centralizing the university's program of religious education in a new bureaucratic structure. As evidenced in the fundamentalist-modernist controversies in the northern Presbyterian church, mainstream Protestant churches responded to the threat of fundamentalism in the same way. By accommodating Protestantism to the modern university, Princeton's leaders, like their peers at many other private institutions, continued to attempt to fashion the moral outlook of American society. Consequently, despite the "second disestablishment" of mainstream Protestantism in the 1920s, Princeton, like many other colleges and universities, remained a de facto Protestant institution and mainstream Protestants continued to play an influential role in American culture for another generation. As part of the mainstream Protestant establishment, Princeton graduates in the sixty years under consideration had an influence over American culture disproportionate to their numbers. A brief review of these alumni reveals an impressive list of figures who shaped not only American Protestantism but also American politics, literature, business, and arts and sciences from the late nineteenth through the mid-twentieth century and, in certain respects, even until today. Among the significant ecclesiastical leaders to graduate in this period were the conservative Presbyterian theologian B. B. Warfield; the first secretary of the intercollegiate Y.M.C.A. Luther D. Wishard; the organizer of the Student Volunteer Movement Robert P. Wilder; the evangelical Presbyterian churchman and educator Charles R. Erdman; the Presbyterian missions leader Robert E. Speer; the liberal and later neo-orthodox Episcopal theologian and Soren Kierkegaard scholar Walter Lowrie; the neo-orthodox theologian, ecumenical leader, and president of Union Theological Seminary (New York) Henry P. Van Dusen; and the secretary-general of the World Council of Churches and civil rights activist Eugene Carson Blake. In American political life, Princeton produced, most notably, the twentieth-eighth president of the United States, Woodrow Wilson; eight U.S. senators, including H. Alexander Smith from New Jersey; twenty-six members of the U.S. House of Representatives; seven state governors, including Illinois governor and two-time Democratic presidential candidate Adlai E. Stevenson; the undersecretary general to the League of Nations and president of the Rockefeller Foundation and the General Education Board Raymond B. Fosdick; Secretary of State John Foster Dulles; Secretary of Defense James V. Forrestal; twenty-nine U.S. ambassadors, including George Kennan, ambassador to the Soviet Union; two U.S. Supreme Court Justices; and six-time socialist presidential candidate Norman Thomas. Among the literary figures who attended Princeton at this time were the novelists Booth Tarkington, Jesse Lynch Williams, F. Scott Fitzgerald, and Henry Van Dyke Jr., who was also an important figure in the northern Presbyterian church and the U.S. ambassador to the Hague; the dramatist Eugene O'Neill; and the literary critic Edmund Wilson. Business leaders who graduated in this period included the copper mining giant Cleveland H. Dodge, the president of International Harvester Cyrus H. McCormick Jr., the financiers Moses Taylor Pyne and Robert Garrett, the industrialists John D. Rockefeller III and Laurence Rockefeller, the publisher Charles Scribner, and the advertising executive Ivy Lee. Among the notable scholars to be educated at Princeton in this period were the paleontologist William Berryman Scott, the psychologist James Mark Baldwin, the director of the American Museum of Natural History Henry Fairfield Osborn, art historian Allan Marquand, the mathematician Henry B. Fine, the Wordsworth scholar George M. Harper, the astronomer Henry Norris Russell, and the historian E. Harris Harbison. Without attributing, for example, American cold-war or post-cold-war foreign policy to John Foster Dulles's undergraduate experience at mandatory chapel services or locating the source of the present-day Protestant Consultation on Church Union in Eugene Carson Blake's undergraduate membership in the Y.M.C.A., an examination of religion at Princeton tells us a great deal about the religious milieu in which some of the nation's most influential figures were educated. A study of religion at Princeton, moreover, reveals a great deal about the nature of mainstream Protestantism. The Protestant establishment, as William R. Hutchison argues, consisted not only of the seven denominations that dominated the Federal Council of Churches in the early twentieth century but also a personal network of familial, social, and old-school tie relationships among mainstream Protestant leaders.[15] An examination of religion at Princeton involves an exploration of this personal network. Finally, a study of Princeton University during this period fills a major lacuna in its institutional history.[16]

Outline of Study

The following chapters try to uncover the changes and continuities in Protestantism's role in collegiate education at Princeton in particular and in American higher education in general. Chapter 1 examines the harmonious relationship, predicated upon the evangelical Protestant hegemony over American culture in the late nineteenth century, between upholding the religious ideals of Protestants and serving the nation's educational interests. During the presidency of James McCosh (1868–1888), mandatory evangelical Protestant religious instruction and worship continued to enjoy a central role in collegiate education because they provided an important counterweight to the traditional liberal arts curriculum and prepared students to uphold the nation's religious, moral, and political standards. McCosh and his colleagues also attempted to advance Princeton's civic mission by transforming the college into a university. In particular, they enlarged the institution's educational mission through the professionalization of the faculty and academic specialization. They also attempted to expand the institution's mission by increasing the student body. To finance these improvements, they looked beyond the Presbyterian church for support. In spite of efforts to maintain traditional religious ideals and practices, the advancements achieved through professionalization and specialization began to alter traditional ways through which Princeton fulfilled its religious mission. Chapter 2 explores these developments. Chapter 3 reviews the emergence of a conflict during the presidency of Francis L. Patton (1888–1902) between the institution's religious heritage and its public purpose as doubts surfaced about the intellectual credibility of the evangelical faith, misgivings appeared concerning traditional practices intended to protect the institution's Protestant character, and suspicions grew about the suitability of the college's traditional educational philosophy. Chapter 4 surveys Woodrow Wilson's reconfiguration of the institution's dual mission during his presidency (1902–1910). As expressed in his famed sesquicentennial address, "Princeton in the Nation's Service," and later in his inaugural address, "Princeton for the Nation's Service," Wilson stressed in a new way the institution's mission as a public institution. Consequently, Wilson undertook a variety of educational reforms to enable the university to meet the nation's educational needs more effectively. The religious aspect of Princeton's heritage, however, was altered, not forsaken, to conform to the institution's new public orientation. In liberal Protestantism, Wilson found a religion that conformed to the prevailing scientific naturalism and historicism. Wilson also abolished all practices that were considered sectarian through measures such as changing mandatory religion classes into electives, dropping informal orthodoxy tests for prospective faculty members, and reducing the number of clerics on the Board of Trustees. Although these dramatic changes produced little conflict during Wilson's presidency, they were a source of constant controversy during John G. Hibben's administration (1912–1932). Chapter 5 assesses these controversies and the major reevaluation of the nature and role of religion within collegiate education that they precipitated at Princeton in 1928. Fundamentalists in the university community encouraged the administration to secularize the undergraduate program—abandon Bible instruction and eliminate mandatory chapel services. The liberals in the administration, however, refused to forsake the university's Protestant mission. In fact, they proved to be the true conservatives. As a result of the reappraisal of 1928 and the completion of the new university chapel, the administration attempted to preserve the religious unity of community by assimilating diversity and dissent. Princeton centered the university's program of religious education in its new chapel and under the auspices of the newly created Dean of the Chapel. The reevaluation also established the groundwork for the eventual introduction of the academic study of religion in the college curriculum in the following decades. An epilogue briefly reviews the subsequent history of Protestantism at Princeton and examines the forces that led to the final "disestablishment" of Protestantism at Princeton and other private colleges and universities. Throughout the study, I do not pretend to resolve all the difficulties between religious and civic commitments in the history of religion in American higher education. Instead, I strive to preserve the ambivalence, tension, and increasing complexity between them with the hope of fostering better-informed and more judicious reflections upon the contemporary place of religion in American higher education.

Chapter 1

Education and Religion in the
Nation's Service, 1868–1888

"Can the oversight of the religion and morals of the young men, long kept up in American Colleges," President James McCosh asked an international audience of Presbyterian leaders in 1884, "be maintained any longer?" "Three-fourths to nine-tenths" of America's colleges, McCosh observed, earnestly "continue to profess religion." But state institutions, he noted, "scarcely profess to keep up any religion" lest they "offend" any religious minority. Some of the nation's larger colleges also find it "vain" to give religious instruction to students. Yet the absence of religious education in "our secular institutions," according to McCosh, was not the only problem facing American higher education. To avoid "the Infidelity" now evident in some parts of American higher education, many denominations were establishing their own institutions. Yet, in McCosh's estimation, the academic quality of their faculties was so low that these institutions actually injured the cause of religion. "The time is over," the brusque Scotsman insisted, "when men are to be appointed to our College chairs simply because they are pious or loud in their orthodoxy." Unless Christian institutions have a faculty "equal in ability and scholarship" to the leading colleges and universities, the nation's best students "will, in spite the efforts of ministers, flock to the Secular Colleges, which will then control them, and may use the intellectual life which they possess to the worst of purposes." To McCosh, his colleagues at Princeton, and many peers at other institutions, parents and students should not have to choose between scholarship or orthodoxy. When Charles W. Eliot, president of Harvard College, accepted an invitation to debate the role of religion in collegiate education two years later before the Nineteenth Century Club in New York City, McCosh welcomed the opportunity to present a case for preserving evangelical religion's place in the halls of the nation's leading academic institutions.[1]

At Princeton, evangelical ideals and practices helped the institution fulfill its dual purpose of meeting the nation's need for educated leaders and, as the college's first president termed it, serving as a "Seminary of vital Piety as of good Literature."[2] Many in the late nineteenth century believed that traditional evangelical convictions and customs were essential to the entire educational endeavor and ultimately for the advancement of the Christian character of the nation. This chapter first will examine the harmonious relationship between Princeton's religious purpose and civic missions. McCosh's debate with Eliot provides an excellent starting point for such an examination because his eloquent apologia for the traditional role of Protestantism in collegiate education contrasts sharply with Charles Eliot's understanding of the role of religious education. Although Harvard had achieved many of the educational advances that McCosh sought for Princeton, such as a distinguished Ph.D. program, Harvard was also leading the movement to make religious education entirely voluntary—the very trend McCosh sought to arrest. This chapter, second, will explore the nature of the religion that McCosh believed that students should learn in the classroom and chapel services. Third, in order to appreciate fully why McCosh and other educators in his day sought to advance the cause of religion in American education, this chapter will examine the impact of evangelical Protestant hegemony over American culture on American higher education in the nineteenth century. This chapter, fourth, will analyze the place of religious instruction and worship in McCosh's "discipline and piety" philosophy of higher education. This chapter, finally, will review what was actually taught to the nation's future leaders in the compulsory courses and chapel services.

The Role of Evangelical Religion in Collegiate Education

"I approach the discussion of this difficult question," Eliot began his presentation at the Nineteenth Century Club, "with the sincerest diffidence." As he looked across the nation's educational landscape from the banks of the Charles River, Eliot (1834–1926) discerned three types of American colleges: the denominational, the "partially denominational," and the "undenominational." The denominational college, according to Eliot, stood under the complete control of one ecclesiastical body; only church members were appointed to the trustees and to the faculty; students were drawn from the denomination's secondary schools; and financial aid was given exclusively to church members. Such schools left little doubt as to the place of religion. "Each teaches," he explained, "its own religious faith and its own forms of worship to all its students with the ardor of full conviction, and with no intention or pretense of tolerating any other religious opinions or practices." While Eliot believed that denominations certainly had the right to operate their own colleges, he also held that such institutions could only represent the educational interests of one particular community. Furthermore, Eliot criticized denominational schools for perpetuating racial, social, and political distinctions. Since Harvard was located in an urban area characterized by deep divisions between Protestants of English descent and Irish Catholics and other more recent ethnic Catholic immigrants, Eliot was more than familiar with the threat that ethno-religious differences and prejudices posed to civic harmony. Eliot also condemned church-related schools for perpetuating theological divisions in the "Christian house." In addition, he charged that these schools failed to "yield the best fruits of real culture—namely, openness of mind, liberality of sentiment, and breadth of sympathy." Protesting that "plants which have been so much sheltered often prove not to be too hardy," Eliot concluded that denominational institutions failed to prepare its graduates to live in the modern world.[3]

The "partially denominational" college, in Eliot's estimation, was the most common type of American institution. Because of the need to attract more students and donors as well as competition from other institutions, Eliot explained, denominational institutions became partially denominational colleges. The loosening of ecclesiastical ties naturally led to a remarkable diversity in the role that religious instruction and worship played in the partially denominational schools. At one extreme, many colleges held neither Sunday services nor gave religious instruction in their curricula; at the other extreme, many schools not only had obligatory Bible courses and chapel meetings but also arranged revivals and pressured students to become church members. Ironically, some of the most conservative partially denominational institutions did not require the students in their scientific schools to participate in compulsory classes and services. "Whether such scientific students," sarcastically mused the former chemistry professor, "were thought to be in no need of such discipline, or to be hopeless subjects of it, I must leave it to others to determine." To Eliot, the chief weakness of the partially denominational college involved religious education. For some parents a partially denominational college practiced too much religion; for other parents, too little.[4]

The third type of college, Eliot believed, possessed the greatest number of assets and the fewest liabilities. Harvard, Eliot's ideal "undenominational" institution, balanced its civic mission with an increasingly socially and religiously diverse community with a largely voluntary program of religious education. Harvard did not maintain its own church but encouraged students to attend the church in which they were raised or another one to their liking, and even paid the pew rentals in six different churches in the area for this purpose. Ministers from five different denominations led daily chapel on a rotating basis; Catholics, high-church Anglicans, and Jews were excused on petition. Religious instruction of "an exegetical or dogmatic character," Eliot explained, could not be offered because it would "compromise the impartiality of the institution." However, since Americans agreed upon the importance of morality and Victorian interests in righteousness transcended denominational differences, Eliot reasoned that undenominational institutions should offer ethics courses. The nondenominational college, however, faced two obstacles: first, the college could lose the "support and confidence" of some ecclesiastical bodies; and second, a disadvantage that especially annoyed Eliot, "[h]asty or bigoted people" would charge that the neutral college "is Godless, like the constitution of the United States." However, the college that was "friendly but neutral toward all religious organizations" enjoyed distinct advantages: it could protect the religious opinions of all members of the university community and encourage students to make mature decisions about their religious affiliations. By assimilating religious diversity through an ecumenical, though predominately Protestant, program of voluntary religious education, Eliot believed Harvard produced in its graduates a "wholesome catholicity of mind" befitting the institution's public mission to a religiously heterogeneous nation. Eliot concluded by offering three principles that he believed could be practiced in all three types of colleges despite their differences: they could foster an attitude of respect for religion, encourage students to attend church services, and exhibit "the same serious, candid, truth-loving spirit" in the study of religion as they did in history, natural science, or philosophy.[5]

Responding to Eliot's presentation, McCosh observed, "Of late years a great change is going on in many of our American colleges as to the place allotted to religion." McCosh went on to explain: "Nearly all the older colleges, such as Harvard, Yale, and Princeton, were founded in the fear of God, with the blessing of heaven invoked; they gave religious instruction to the students, and had weekly and daily exercises of praise and prayer to Almighty God. But some of them, as they became larger and had a greater and more varied constituency of teachers and students, found a difficulty in carrying out this thoroughly, and are abandoning one position after another, till now little is left."[6]

Moreover, in light of the dramatic growth of public and private universities after the Civil War, McCosh suspected that the problems facing religion in higher education were even worse than the general public probably knew. Having defended the traditional role of evangelicalism in American collegiate education within Presbyterian circles for several years, McCosh was now taking the issue to the general public with the hope of rallying support to reverse the trend. The greatest threat to the evangelical purpose of American higher education, McCosh warned, was not a frontal attack on the value of chapel or Bible classes. "So far as I can see," he charged, "there will be no attempt to drive religion out of the college, but it looks as if some were preparing to let it die out." While Eliot discerned three types of American colleges, McCosh saw only two: "Those which give an important place to religion, having prayer and praise and religious instruction; and those which virtually and actually take no serious interest in divine things."[7]

The Presbyterian minister offered two reasons for "retaining" the traditional practices. First, religiously trained college graduates had a positive influence upon the nation. Observing that ministers, doctors, lawyers, and other college-educated leaders were able to raise the "general intelligence of the people, stimulate their enterprise, [and] elevate their tastes and even their manners," McCosh posed the question, "May they not also exercise a mighty influence, by their example and their teachings, on the morals and piety of their districts?" McCosh and other advocates of American republican ideals believed that virtue in citizens, especially in their leaders, was the key prerequisite for a healthy society. The only way to guarantee a stable and enduring presence of virtue among the nation's leaders was if they had an active Christian faith. Consequently, colleges had to foster an evangelical faith among the nation's future leaders because the Christian character of American society depended upon it. According to McCosh's diagnosis, the abolition of mandatory religious instruction and worship was only a symptom of a deeper illness in many colleges and universities—a grave departure from the civic mission of American higher education.

Christianity, he observed, "has had a mighty influence in stimulating and in forming modern civilization," and he pointed to the arts, architecture, and literature as evidence. Abandoning compulsory religion threatened the Christian character of American society. When students learn that they have souls and thus a responsibility before God and that "God is good and gave His son to die for us," McCosh explained, they are compelled to do good. In short, the abandonment of religion, McCosh believed, removed "one of the vital forces which have [*sic*] given life and body to our higher education." Harvard's motto, *Pro Christo et Ecclesia*, McCosh observed, symbolized the central and historic role that religion has played in American higher education.[8]

In addition to exerting a beneficial influence on American society, McCosh asserted that compulsory religious instruction had an equally positive influence on the very lives of students. Colleges, he believed, typically formed students' character for life, something parents, "anxious about the welfare of their children," expected institutions to do. "All true Christians," McCosh explained, "believe that faith in God and Saviour is the most potent force which can be brought to bear upon the young, to lift them above themselves, and above the selfish and sensual world." Students who had been properly trained under the "inspiring power" of compulsory religion, McCosh insisted, had their character so transformed that they devoted "themselves to high ends, which they have followed through life, and diffused around a happy, perhaps a holy, influence." In addition to character formation, colleges had to be ready to answer that one question that McCosh believed all students asked sometime during their college days: "Is life worth living?" Neither agnosticism nor the ordinary college curriculum could satisfactorily answer this question. Its answer, McCosh insisted, lay elsewhere: "Faith in God and Christ and spiritual truth can see that life is worth living, places before us glorious ends and useful works, and sets the young man forth on a life of self-sacrifice, of love and benevolence." Religion needed a "clear and unmistakable" place within college education; otherwise McCosh feared that students would think it was a "farce."[9] The stakes were too high to allow seventeen-year-olds to participate voluntarily in their religious education. A destructive Civil War had left a deep sectional rift and deeper racial divisions in America. The influx of millions of immigrants from Europe and elsewhere, coupled with industrialization and urbanization, produced previously unknown social problems. Radical advancements in science created unheralded hopes for social progress, as well as secular threats to traditional beliefs. Instead of abandoning the compulsory religious education of students, McCosh reasoned, the best interests of both students and the nation should compel colleges now more than ever to try to nurture an evangelical faith in the nation's future leaders. Many in the late nineteenth century believed that the Christian character of the nation rested upon its college-educated leaders. A heavier burden rested upon the shoulders of the teachers of these future leaders. Clearly, this was a burden that McCosh took seriously.

Many, in McCosh's opinion, were shirking their responsibilities and duties. McCosh believed the decline of religion in American colleges derived from two factors: "from the desire of young men to be freed from all restraints, and from the growing indisposition of young Professors to take any charge of the morals of young men." After noting that Harvard students recently had petitioned to abolish required attendance at daily prayers in order to make the service a matter of sincerity and not duty, McCosh wryly asked if "such a motive [would] secure attention to other branches—say mathematics?" Abandoning compulsory religion because of the irresponsibility of students was simply wrongheaded in McCosh's estimation since such a move would cut students off from the most "beneficent power" that could enable them to live moral lives. College administrators who abolished religious education had forsaken their duty not only morally but intellectually. Religious education, McCosh insisted, was essential to combatting the dangers implicit in the growth of specialized knowledge: "A mere savant in a college may be a narrow-minded man," McCosh explained, but nothing "will enlarge these men's minds so effectively as belief in the grand truths of religion." McCosh's definition of liberal education included not only training in the classical curriculum but also exposure to the spiritual realities that give life meaning. McCosh's simple solution to these problems was to hire professors who had spiritual gifts for teaching religion. If American universities failed to fulfill their religious responsibilities necessary for the civic well-being of the nation, he concluded, then the churches would have to take up the work through campus ministries.[10]

Protestant Modernism versus Evangelical Protestantism

Not only did McCosh assign a different role to religion in collegiate education than Eliot but he also had a rather different understanding about the type of religion that should be taught to students in classes and chapel. This critical difference became obvious at the end of the evening at the Nineteenth Century Club, when Eliot brusquely suggested that he meant something very different by the term religion than did McCosh. "While he respected the doctor's beliefs," the *New York Times* reported Eliot as saying, "he should be sorry to have his own sons taught them."[11] Apparently, others at Harvard shared Eliot's sentiment. The following fall at Harvard University's 250th Anniversary, Oliver Wendell Holmes read a poem that referred to the "dry creed" of Calvinism taught at Princeton. McCosh became so infuriated that he left the celebration early to return to Princeton.[12]

Despite McCosh's suggestion to the contrary, Eliot believed that colleges should teach religion, but that this religion should have a more modern orientation than McCosh's evangelicalism. Eliot was a lifelong member of the Unitarian Church, which was an important precursor to and participant in a burgeoning effort in the late nineteenth century to adjust traditional faith to modern culture. By the early twentieth century, Protestant liberalism or modernism came to represent in general terms three loosely defined sets of ideas: the adaptation of religious ideas to contemporary intellectual developments, the immanence of God in nature and human history, and, correspondingly, the belief that society was slowly moving toward the realization of the kingdom of God.[13] Although typically reserved about his own theological beliefs, Eliot's conception of the nature of the religion that colleges should teach was in line with these modernist ideas. If one recognized that "there is no separating God from nature, or religion from science, or things sacred from things secular," Eliot argued, then "the truth-loving spirit of the sciences" could teach "some just conception of the Transcendent Intelligence."[14] Eliot's theological liberalism appealed to the hopeful temper of the Gilded Age more than McCosh's Calvinism did. After the destruction of the institution of slavery in the Civil War and the numerous technological advancements made in the late nineteenth century, many Americans were increasingly optimistic about the continual progress of humankind and American society. Eliot was convinced that religion had a future in American collegiate education so long as it was a religion that conformed to the intellectual standards established by modern science.

By contrast, McCosh believed that American colleges and universities simply could not allow students to graduate without a "knowledge of God and Christ." He rejected Eliot's contention that the so-called denominational and partially denominational colleges "impose religious opinions" upon the "susceptible" minds of their students. Of the 300 American institutions of higher learning with which he had some familiarity, McCosh insisted, all "inculcate religion without interfering with any one's conscience." The "prayers and praises" offered in these schools were of "a thoroughly catholic (in the true sense of the term) character."[15] Eliot's definition of a truly catholic religion consisted of a philosophical theism at least sympathetic to, if not identical with, the burgeoning movement to modernize Protestantism, while for McCosh a truly catholic religion meant broadly evangelical Protestantism. The Scottish preacher believed, as he told the Presbyterian Alliance three years earlier, that no "student passes through our College without being addressed from time to time, in the most loving manner, as to the state of his soul." While inviting popular preachers to campus was an useful way of stimulating students' interest in divine things, the most effective means for combatting the destructive effects of agnosticism was positive religious instruction: "Agnosticism will disappear like a cloud when the true light shines."[16] Although McCosh agreed with Eliot that theism could be taught through the humanities and sciences, he considered this method alone to be insufficient. Since evangelical Protestantism was the most catholic version of Christianity and since it answered students' most personal questions, formed their character, and prepared them to shape the nation's moral character, it seemed not merely reasonable to McCosh and many in his generation but even necessary to compel students to take part in constructive religious instruction and worship.

Despite the evangelical character of nineteenth-century Protestantism, as well as the role that it had played in the history of American higher education, McCosh's defensive posture betrayed his lionhearted rhetoric and suggests that he was genuinely nervous about the future of the revivalistic religion in collegiate education. By 1886, liberalism was beginning to challenge the dominance of evangelicalism in many Protestant ecclesiastical circles. For instance, when Edwards Amasa Park retired in 1881 from Andover Seminary, originally founded as a conservative rival to Unitarian Harvard, the institution became a bastion of the new "Progressive Orthodoxy," much to the consternation of conservative Congregationalists. Modernism was also making inroads among northern Presbyterians but with more limited success. In 1874, the popular Chicago Presbyterian preacher David Swing had been driven from the denomination by a young Princeton Seminary graduate for espousing certain liberal ideas about the nature of the Bible and doubting the very possibility of propositional truth as expressed in the Westminster Standards. In the very year that McCosh and Eliot debated, the faculties of Princeton Seminary and Union Seminary in New York were in the midst of a debate over the value of the higher criticism of the Bible. At the same time, more conservative southern Presbyterians were caught up in a controversy surrounding the dismissal of James Woodrow (1828–1907) from Columbia Seminary for simply attempting to harmonize evolution and theism.[17]

Although American Protestantism was overwhelmingly evangelical at this time, in the more independent circles of higher education, liberal Protestantism was enjoying a more welcoming reception. The emerging research universities in the late nineteenth century have typically been portrayed as secular institutions. Such portraits, however, have little basis in reality.[18] Eliot, for instance, clearly had no intention to eliminate the religious sensibilities of students at Harvard. In fact, a liberal Protestant religion actually played a central role within many of the institutions leading the revolution in higher education. Harvard was not alone in this regard. When the opening exercises of Johns Hopkins University in 1876 included an address by the agnostic T. H. Huxley but no invocation by a minister, the institution came to represent, according to conventional wisdom, the archetype secular university. Yet President Daniel C. Gilman not only advocated the teaching of religion in higher education but conceived of the entire university enterprise as an extension of his liberal Protestant commitments. In an address before Harvard's Phi Beta Kappa chapter in 1886, Gilman professed that the university should be "a place for the maintenance of religion, not . . . by forcing assent to formulae, or by exacting conformity to appointed rites, but by recognizing every where the religious nature of man, considered individually, and the religious basis of the society into which Americans are born."[19] At the same time, liberal Protestantism was gaining popularity at smaller but equally prestigious private colleges, such as Dartmouth and Bowdoin; at major private universities, such as Chicago; and at many of the great midwestern land-grant universities.[20]

Yet in 1886, evangelical Protestantism still dominated the vast portion of American higher education. At Yale College, for instance, evangelical convictions and customs remained the established religion. Even at those universities among the first to establish programs in *Religionswissenschaft*, such as Boston University and New York University, these courses often had distinctly Christian apologetic purposes.[21] While Princeton might have been among a minority in the ranks of elite, private colleges and universities, its commitments and practices were representative of not only denominational institutions but also many private ones. For a wide network of officially denominational and more loosely affiliated Presbyterian colleges, moreover, Princeton served as a role model. Princeton educated more than 115 college professors and presidents during McCosh's tenure. McCosh regularly addressed Presbyterian and other denominational educators. His extant correspondence is filled with letters advising other educators on educational and religious matters. By defending the traditional role of religious instruction and worship in collegiate education in his debate with Eliot, McCosh was simply defending the traditional mission of the vast portion of American higher education.[22]

Protestant Hegemony and Collegiate Education

McCosh's, and by extension Princeton's, commitment to the preservation of the established evangelical purposes and practices of collegiate education stood upon two pillars. The first involved his understanding of the religious character of American society and the relationship of the college to society, particularly as reflected in the founding purpose and nature of the College of New Jersey. The second concerned his philosophy of higher education. Both pillars supported the prominent place of evangelical Protestantism in the life of Princeton. Charles Eliot's views on the first issue again provide a useful background for fully appreciating those of McCosh.

In a genuinely national university, according to Eliot, "justice" dictated that religious instruction and worship be voluntary because America was a religiously heterogeneous nation. Eliot contended that the religious composition of Harvard's undergraduate student body, faculty, and Board of Overseers reflected this religious diversity. Harvard College was "so divided among the various religious communions that no denomination has any approach to a majority, and that nearly every variety of religious faith, from Roman Catholic to Israelite through all shades of Protestantism, is represented among them." This diversity, he added, would only continue to increase in the future as the population of New England became more religiously heterogeneous and as Harvard attracted more students from different parts of the nation. In sharp contrast to most denominational and partially denominational colleges, he insisted, "the unsectarian college is the most useful type in a country where there is no established church, and no single denomination numerically, socially, or morally dominant." "Now, an institution of higher education, which aspires to draw its students from the whole nation and *to be of service to the whole nation*, must pursue the same policy of toleration which the Constitution imposes on the national legislature."[23] The national university had to foster religious beliefs while promoting tolerance for religious diversity.

The nation's growing religious pluralism in the late nineteenth century and higher education's historic commitment to the religious education of its students provided a new challenge to educators aspiring to build national universities. Eliot hoped to assimilate the nation's growing diversity into a common culture. Philosophical theism, or proto-modernism, Eliot believed, could assimilate the nation's theological diversity, which often fell along ethnic and racial lines, by transcending doctrinal peculiarities. Much like McCosh, Eliot hoped to train the future leaders of a culturally diverse nation under one theological canopy. Whether in Harvard's student body or the nation as a whole, Eliot stood confident that philosophical theism had universal appeal because of its compatibility with the engine of science that was driving the nation's progress.

Whereas Eliot saw boundless religious pluralism in America, McCosh believed that, since "the great body of the people profess to be Christians," America was a Christian nation.[24] The majority of the nation's older colleges, he observed, had been established by Christians. Most of these institutions, he added, stood under "the influence of religious denominations," while remaining technically nondenominational schools. He pointed to Princeton as one such nondenominational, but de facto Presbyterian, institution. Because these institutions propagated in both the classroom and chapel services a broadly evangelical Protestant faith without "sectarian peculiarities," most of these older colleges were, by his definition, truly nonsectarian in character.[25] At McCosh's nonsectarian college, the student body was overwhelmingly Protestant in character; all but five of the 115 fifteen students who graduated in June of 1886 were Protestant.[26] From McCosh's perspective and experience at Princeton, meeting the educational needs of the nation and advancing the evangelical faith and worldview of the vast majority of Americans were identical endeavors.

However, McCosh was not unaware of the nation's religious diversity and the potential problem that pluralism posed for the future of religion in higher education. He complained to the Nineteenth Century Club that some of the great land-grant universities "make no profession of religion." With Protestant, Catholic, and Jewish students on campus, these universities abandoned compulsory religious education.[27] The nominal religion programs at some colleges and universities, he asserted in an earlier address, were "fast becoming mummies." "Sooner or later," he believed, "there will arise some iconoclast to declare that it is of no use keeping up these images when there is no belief in the gods they represent, and he will have a considerable amount of support in the secular press when he denounces the profession of religion as hypocrisy and pretense." Worse than lukewarm religion, in McCosh's opinion, was the propagation of false religion. He complained with sectarian disdain, ironically in the pages of the *Catholic Presbyterian*, that few evangelicals preached in the chapel at Cornell University, but "a discourse by the rationalistic Jew, Dr. Adler" had been recently heard, and students had even petitioned to have the agnostic Robert Ingersoll invited to lecture.[28]

While McCosh believed that a broadly evangelical Protestantism represented the faith of most Americans, he still recognized that not all students shared his religious beliefs. Like Eliot, McCosh's views of religion's role in higher education had establishmentarian tendencies. Eliot wanted to assimilate religious diversity into a common culture through a program of voluntary religious education that taught a more modern Protestantism. McCosh also wanted to convert religious outsiders. But if he could not assimilate diversity, McCosh also recommended a policy of religious toleration. He wanted to respect religious minorities without compromising the religious scruples of the evangelical majority. As a former dissenting minister who helped found the Free Church of Scotland, McCosh adamantly defended "the rights of conscience possessed by parents and by students." The "conscience clause" permitted students with variant faiths to be excused from chapel services, thereby safeguarding the religious principles of those students who stood outside the canopy of evangelicalism. McCosh was also drawing upon his own experience at Queens University, a state institution where he had taught for sixteen years. The Belfast college, which enrolled both Catholics and Protestants, McCosh insisted, "never had a difficulty" encouraging respect for religious diversity among students.[29]

McCosh's belief that evangelicalism was essential to higher education rested on the prevailing Protestant conviction that Christianity was the only foundation for a healthy civilization. This conviction reflected the evangelical Protestant hegemony of American culture. Throughout the nineteenth century, evangelicals Protestants dominated American educational, religious, political institutions and shaped the larger intellectual ideals and social values of the nation. After the formal separation of church and state in 1791, religious interests had been forced to find new ways to influence American society. "This influence," John F. Wilson observes, "consisted generally of a suffusion of Christian values and goals into society, but more specifically of concerted actions on behalf of particular projects." Christians employed moral persuasion and voluntary agencies as the primary means to transform the nation into a "Christian Commonwealth." By the Civil War, comments Winthrop S. Hudson, "the ideals, the convictions, the language, the customs, the institutions of society were so shot through with Christian presuppositions that the culture itself nurtured and nourished the Christian faith."[30] This antebellum public religion, or "republican Protestantism," was dominated by white evangelical Protestants and their ideals.

In the 1880s, the 9 million members of the major Protestant denominations numbered an estimated 18 percent of the general population but exerted a disproportionate influence over American society. While America always had been religiously pluralistic, the increase in immigration of non-English-speaking people from countries without strong Protestant churches made many Americans, and many Protestants in particular, more conscious and even more uneasy about the nation's growing religious heterogeneity. Between 1870 and 1920, the general population rose from nearly 40 to 106 million, with immigration providing the single largest source for this increase. Recent studies reveal that the Catholic population grew from slightly over 1 million in 1860 to almost 16 million in 1916 and the Jewish population expanded from roughly 250,000 in 1880 to 1 million in 1900. Immigration, combined with the growth of cities and industries, threatened to undermine evangelical Protestant cultural homogeneity. At the same time, scientific naturalism and historicism threatened the evangelical Protestant intellectual consensus. Between the 1880s and 1920s, the confluence of these forces began to undermine evangelical Protestant hegemony. By the 1930s, Protestantism as the de facto public religion had experienced a "second disestablishment."[31] In retrospect, Eliot appears to have been more attuned than McCosh to these grand forces changing the nation of American society.

Yet the transition from Protestant America to pluralistic America had hardly begun when McCosh and Eliot squared off over the role of religion in 1886. Six years after their debate, Associate Justice David J. Brewer articulated the traditional Protestant perception of the nature of American society in a unanimous decision of the Supreme Court in which he declared outright that America was "a Christian nation."[32] The custodial duty of Protestantism was just coming into question, and state-supported public education was among the first areas to be challenged. The pressures undermining Protestant hegemony in public education were much clearer than in higher education, where the independence or private status of institutions complicated matters. Before the Civil War, individual Protestants and some denominations had wholeheartedly supported the creation of public schools as an excellent means for educating youths in basic knowledge and common civic values. A few Protestants, however, such as Princeton College trustee and Princeton Seminary professor Charles Hodge, had unsuccessfully opposed these efforts on the grounds that public schools could not adequately teach distinctly Protestant beliefs without violating the separation of Church and State.[33] By the 1880s, Catholic, Jewish, agnostic, and nonreligious parents began to contest not only the compulsory participation of their children in readings from the King James Bible but also what they perceived as state financing of Protestant public education.[34] In response, many Protestants defended the traditional character of public education. For example, Charles Hodge's son and successor as both a trustee of the college and professor at the seminary, A. A. Hodge, argued that the vast majority of Americans who were Christians had the constitutional right and moral duty to demand that public schools uphold their beliefs and morality. "The system of public schools must be held to the claims of Christianity," the younger Hodge insisted, "or they must go, with all other enemies of Christ, to the wall."[35] While Protestantism remained firmly entrenched as the nation's public religion during McCosh's presidency, the cultural and religious landscape was beginning to change rapidly and dramatically. Between 1880 and 1920, as Robert T. Handy has recently argued, "the informal hegemony that the Protestant movement had long held over American religious and cultural life by its numerical pluralities and the power of its organizational network was weakened."[36]

The cultural hegemony of Protestantism fostered what has been described as the Whiggish conception of higher education. Whiggery was not only a political party in the mid-nineteenth century but also a larger cultural tradition with distinctive political and social ideas.[37] Whigs treasured self-determination and opposed British tyranny, cherished personal liberty and fought intemperance, valued scientific freedom and resisted Catholic dogmatism and superstition.

After the Revolutionary War and the disestablishment of the church and in light of the excesses manifested in the French Revolution, Whig political leaders and ordinary citizens alike assumed that the young republic could not survive without shared moral and social values. Next to religious conversion, education was believed to play an important role in promoting these common values, particularly as evidenced in the exponential growth of newspapers, literary societies, lecture circuits, and especially Horace Mann's "common schools." Like the Jeffersonians in the late eighteenth century, Whigs in the earlier nineteenth century valued education for its civilizing function. Unlike Jeffersonians, who wanted a strict exclusion of religion from public life, Whigs advocated the teaching of nonsectarian, Protestant values through education. Colleges, according to the Whiggish conception of higher education, played a central role in shaping the moral fabric of American society. Colleges trained not only the nation's teachers but also its political and religious leaders. The culminating and unifying point of this training came in the senior-year capstone course in moral philosophy. The task of the instructor of this course, typically a minister and the college president, "was to shape and instruct an American public conscience, to create an ethical frame of mind that would direct a new nation seeking a moral as well as political identity in a changing world."[38] Colleges set nonsectarian moral, political, and social standards by which all Americans, or at least white citizens, could be assimilated into a common culture.[39] Both Eliot and McCosh drew upon this Whiggish conception of higher education. Both wanted colleges to infuse the national culture with religious values. They differed, however, over what type of Protestantism served the nation's interests most effectively. McCosh espoused the more traditional or conservative position that evangelicalism represented a truly nonsectarian religion. Eliot wanted to broaden the theological parameters of the national religion; he wanted philosophical theism, or proto-modernism, to define American society's moral outlook.

McCosh's appeal to the prevailing Whiggish conception of higher education was also compatible with the founding purpose of Princeton College. New Side Presbyterian ministers and laypeople, who favored vital piety over the doctrinal precision of their Old Side rivals, established the college amid the first Great Awakening and an ecclesiastical schism (1741–1758). In order to receive approval for their charter from the Anglican colonial governor, the founders appealed to the Fundamental Concession of 1664, which granted religious freedom to the people of the colonies and pledged to offer students "free and Equal Liberty and Advantage of Education" in the "learned Languages, and in the Liberal Arts and Sciences . . . notwithstanding any different Sentiment in Religion."[40] The founders, therefore, were not concealing their religious interests by giving the nondenominational institution a broad purpose because they did not clearly distinguish between its civic and religious missions. This sentiment was expressed in one of the earliest publications of the college. Princeton, one of the first trustees wrote in 1764, was "originally designed for the promotion of the general interests of christianity, as well as the cultivation of human science."[41] Affirming the religious beliefs, values, and worldview of the larger pan-Protestant community and serving colonial interests were virtually identical tasks. The founders, moreover, had a special interest in preparing candidates for the Presbyterian ministry, as the first president, Jonathan Dickinson (1688–1747), explained before the opening of the college: "The great & chief design of erecting the College, is for the Education of pious & well qualified Candidates for the Ministry, that vital Piety may by that means be promoted in our Churches. . . . But then, we are by our Charter obliged to admit without Distinction, those of any & of every religious Profession to the Privileges of a liberal Education, thus submitting to the Laws and Orders of the College. This is a natural Right than cant be justly denied to any."[42] In short, under the rubric of the officially broad purpose, the founders intended to uphold the true religion of Protestantism while teaching the liberal arts in order to prepare students for public service and especially the ministry.[43]

However, in the 120 years between the college's opening and McCosh's inauguration, it had not always been easy to preserve this dual heritage. In its first twenty years, the college succeeded both in attracting students from throughout the colonies and in preparing students for the ministry.[44] When John Witherspoon (1723–1794) became president in 1768, he not only led Princeton through the turbulent years of the Revolutionary War but also harmonized a traditional Presbyterian faith with the moderate Scottish Enlightenment under the sacred canopy of republican patriotism. Tension, however, was the hallmark of the presidency of Samuel Stanhope Smith (1751–1819), Witherspoon's successor and son-in-law. Critics within the college community questioned, for example, whether moral philosophy, as a science grounded in natural reason and not in special revelation, posed a latent threat to the Christian faith and whether the college could train ministers and statesmen with equal success. These doubts only seemed to be confirmed by a suspicious fire that destroyed Nassau Hall in 1802; a rebellion in 1807 by students who claimed, in the language of republicanism, that they were opposing the tyranny of the college administration; and a decline in the number of students who entered the ministry. Princeton, in the eyes of many trustees, had departed from its original mission.[45] Two subsequent developments reversed this trend. The first development came in 1808, when several Presbyterian ministers closely associated with the college made plans to create a theological seminary in order to meet the church's need for more ministers. Smith pleaded for the creation of a college-related divinity school, but this proposal proved unsatisfactory because such a school would have been under the independent authority of the college's self-perpetuating board and therefore under the influence of the college's questionable orthodoxy. After three years of discussion, the church negotiated a close but informal relationship with the college. The college agreed to allow the seminary to build its own facilities on campus and to use the college facilities during the period of construction. The college further agreed to handle the seminary's finances, to divert endowment funds designated for ministerial candidates to the seminary, and not to hire a theology professor so long as the seminary remained in Princeton.[46] The college continued to exhibit a special interest in preparing students for the ministry, but now it expressed this interest by preparing them for the seminary. The second development came in 1812 when, after a major turnover on the board, Smith was forced to retire in 1812 by those trustees who rejected "Smith's version of the Witherspoon synthesis, with its supreme commitments to the moral philosophy of the Enlightenment and to the promotion of science" in favor of the more pious side of Witherspoon's legacy and thus assigned "a much larger role for evangelistic religion and the promotion of the church."[47] When Ashbel Green (1762–1848) was elected president, the original balance between the college's civic and religious mission was reestablished. Green said as much in his own history of the college when he insisted that Princeton "was intended, by all the parties concerned in its founding, to be one in which *religion* and *learning* should be *unitedly cultivated*, in all time to come."[48] Green may have actually understated the role that the church played in the affairs of the college. Under Green and his successors, James Carnahan (1775–1859), president from 1823 to 1854, and John Maclean Jr. (1800–1886), president from 1854 to 1868, Presbyterian interests enjoyed the central place in the life of the college.[49]

When James McCosh (1811–1894) came to Princeton in 1868, the college's leaders remained firmly committed to offering, as his immediate predecessor described it, "*a thorough, liberal, and a christian education.*" This commitment had been nourished for decades by the dominant Whiggish conception of higher education and Protestant cultural hegemony. The trustees made their commitment to the civic and religious mission of Princeton clear to McCosh at his inauguration. Charles Hodge, speaking as the senior member of the Board of Trustees, told the new president that he was expected to preserve the "true religion" that had dominated the institution in past generations. Students, he believed, "should be made to feel that the eternal is infinitely more important than the temporal, the heavenly than the earthly." The trustees, moreover, "earnestly desired" that no conflict between the "twin daughters of heaven," religion and science, should ever be taught in the college. The retiring president reminded McCosh that the charter charged him with overseeing the entire curriculum, including religious instruction: "For these the Laws make him personally responsible, and in so doing they accord fully with the aim of the pious and excellent men who laid the foundation of our College, and sought thereby to promote the cause of our blessed Redeemer and the welfare of our race, by the erection of an Institution for the advancement of *true religion and sound learning*." In complete agreement, McCosh responded that the college "has had a religious character in time past, and it will be my endeavor to see that it has the same in time to come."[50]

Although McCosh inherited a situation in which the college's civic and religious mission coexisted harmoniously, the college was not formally an ecclesiastical institution. McCosh affirmed Princeton's standing as an independent institution and did so for theological reasons. According to his doctrine of the church, the formal management of colleges was not among the "spiritual functions" of any ecclesiastical body. "Happily," said the Presbyterian minister, most Presbyterian schools were "not under the General Assembly or any Church courts, whose province, as it appears to me, is to execute the laws of the kingdom of Christ, and not to appoint professors of classics or of mathematics." But he did approve a more informal influence. "Presbyterian colleges," McCosh observed, "are, however, under the control of trustees, ministers, and laymen, who are mostly, though not all, Presbyterians, and who secure that the teaching shall be moral and religious."[51] McCosh was not alone in his appreciation of this form of influence. William C. Roberts (1832–1903), a long-time trustee at the college and later president of Lake Forest College, believed that it was part of the "great mission" of the Presbyterian church to oversee informally the "great cause of higher education, not, for the purpose of supplying her own pulpits merely, but also to supply the professions, and affirm liberal education to all who may desire it for its own sake."[52] What was true for Presbyterian colleges in general was true for Princeton College in particular. Though "not officially connected with any denomination," McCosh told the trustees that Princeton "may be considered as in a general way under the patronage of the Presbyterian Church."[53]

McCosh's understanding of Princeton's status as a formally nondenominational, but de facto Presbyterian, college was shared by his contemporaries in both the college and the Presbyterian church. John Maclean, while maintaining that the college was founded with a "catholic spirit" that freed it from both church and state control, also acknowledged that the institution had "merited and received the countenance and favor" of the Presbyterian church. In 1877, he emphatically insisted that *the promotion of true religion and sound learning was the aim of all concerned in laying the foundations of the College of New Jersey.*[54] Presbyterians, especially those who graduated from Princeton College or Seminary, considered the college to be the leading Presbyterian college in the nation. This helps to explain why so many Presbyterian educators looked to Princeton for direction. The *Presbyterian*, a weekly published by theological conservatives in Philadelphia, a stronghold of Old School Presbyterians, paid close attention to the affairs of the college. One particularly proud alumnus in 1886, for example, praised Princeton, "the first Presbyterian College of the land," and concluded his review of its educational achievements with the prayer, "Long live Princeton College . . . a bulwark of sound classical learning, of true philosophy and of pure religion."[55]

Leaders of Princeton not only agreed with McCosh's understanding of Princeton as a de facto Presbyterian institution but also shared his traditional Whiggish conviction about the civic value of established Protestant convictions and practices in collegiate education. Investments in nonsectarian colleges, contended another long-time trustee, Jonathan F. Stearns (1808–1889), paid dividends in more than just the lives of individual students. "The opportunity of impressing Christian truth upon the minds of those who shall hereafter occupy posts of influence in the State and the secular professions," said the Presbyterian pastor, "is one which must repay tenfold all the expense which the Church must incur in taking these institutions under her patronage."[56] A year before McCosh debated Eliot, the young Latin professor Andrew F. West (1853–1943) told readers of the *North American Review* that he found the abandonment of obligatory instruction and worship to be "the most dangerous element" of all the trends reshaping collegiate education.[57] Presbyterians within the college's larger community of support applauded McCosh for defending in his debate with Eliot those colleges that maintained a "definite place" for "the religion of Christ." "If we read all the signs aright," the *Presbyterian* warned, "there is to be a serious struggle to keep our institutions of learning from becoming *paganized*, or at least standing in the attitude of neutrality in the contest between error and truth."[58]

Princeton professors and trustees, however, were not oblivious to the problem that religious pluralism posed for traditional Protestant religious interests and customs. Moral philosophy professor Lyman Atwater, like McCosh, deplored the growing trend among state institutions to eliminate compulsory instruction and worship in order to remove any "taint of sectarianism" in the name of the separation of church and state. Fortunately, in Atwater's opinion, private schools were free to uphold unabashedly the cause of "Christo et Ecclesiae."[59] At least one Princetonian, however, recognized that the future course of traditional Protestant higher education was threatened less by disagreements over whether chapel should be compulsory than by the growing religious heterogeneity of the nation. In a 1886 commentary in the *New Princeton Review* on a federal bill proposing the creation of a national university, an anonymous author argued that such an institution would lead, as Jeffersonians had wanted a century earlier, to the complete disestablishment of religion in public education. "[T]heists and atheists, believers, infidels and heathen, Christians and Jews, Catholics and Protestants" would protest the teaching of religious opinions contrary to their own in such a national institution. "Social justice," consequently, would dictate that the only workable solution would be "absolute silence on religious questions." To the author, such a solution was untenable, since religiously informed presuppositions, primarily metaphysical and epistemological ones, molded the "philosophical basis" of each academic discipline. Philosophy, ethics, jurisprudence, political and social science "can be conceived of and treated from only a theistic or from an atheistic point of view. . . . Teleology must be acknowledged everywhere or be denied everywhere." Religious pluralism, therefore, imperiled evangelicalism's role in higher education by coercing students and professors to adopt a seemingly neutral, but actually atheistic, perspective on their academic pursuits.[60] Yet this examination of the first principles of science stands out as an exception. During McCosh's tenure, Princetonians remained supremely confident that the sciences would only confirm belief in theism so long as scientists adhered to an open-minded inquiry of the evidence.

In the debate between Eliot and McCosh, the religious mission of American higher education was at stake. The presidents of Harvard and Princeton represented two competing understandings of religion's role in higher education in the late nineteenth century. At one level, the issue dividing these rival visions arose from different understandings of the religious composition of the nation. To Eliot, America was a religiously diverse nation. For McCosh, evangelical

Protestantism predominated. Theologically, they held opposing views on what constituted a genuinely catholic faith. Eliot insisted that a philosophical theism, or proto-modernism, was inclusive. McCosh maintained that a broad evangelicalism represented the faith of most Americans. Consequently, these presidents differed over whose religion was genuinely nonsectarian and therefore appropriate for a national institution to promote. Still, these men's different opinions about whose faith was truly nonsectarian should not obscure the vast areas of agreement between their alternative visions. Despite significant theological differences, both Eliot and McCosh were advocating a form of Protestantism. Moreover, while they differed over how best to cultivate students' religious sensibilities, they remained committed to the religious education of students. Finally, as educators at Harvard and Princeton and elsewhere had done for decades, both presumed that the moral welfare of the nation depended heavily upon the moral character and, consequently, the religious training of its leaders.

The "Discipline and Piety" Philosophy of Education

"I see in the newspapers that obligatory attendance at prayers has been abandoned at Harvard, and all religious instruction given up," McCosh told the trustees in February 1885. This was an "ominous fact," McCosh warned, given the number of students at the school and the institution's prominence in American higher education. An "equally significant" fact, he pointed out, was that Harvard's president was advocating that students be given the complete freedom both to choose their own studies and to govern themselves.[61] Both facts, McCosh correctly perceived, sprang from the same utilitarian philosophy that was gaining popularity in higher education. This philosophy fashioned the entire curriculum into a democracy of equals and gave students the freedom to specialize in new fields even to the exclusion of those subjects traditionally considered a prerequisite for all liberally educated gentlemen. The elective system came to symbolize the spectacular advancements as well as some objectional consequences of the revolution in American higher education in the last quarter of the nineteenth century. "The American university, as it emerged at the end of the nineteenth century," Alexandra Oleson and John Voss conclude, "was Charles W. Eliot's elective principle writ large."[62] In February 1885, the year before their confrontation over the role of religion in collegiate education, the Nineteenth Century Club had hosted a debate between Eliot and McCosh on the value of the elective principle in collegiate education. "I mean not only to defend, but to fight for what I believe to be a fundamental principle with this college," McCosh told the trustees about the upcoming debate, "that what is great and good in the past is to be retained along with the new in the obligatory studies."[63] McCosh suspected that the fight over the elective system would last for years and expected Princeton's trustees, professors, and alumni to enter the fray.

Taking the affirmative position, Eliot argued that a genuine university best served the public interest by offering its students freedom of choice in studies, academic honors, and self-government. Since it would take forty years to cover all the available undergraduate courses, Eliot drolly suggested that students could take only part of the curriculum. Except for courses in English composition, French or German, and a few lectures on chemistry and physics, Harvard undergraduates in 1885 enjoyed the freedom of selecting their own course of study, though Harvard's overall curriculum comprised only "liberal" or "pure" disciplines. The elective system, according to Eliot, worked so well not only because students diligently pursued those subjects in which they had an aptitude and a vocational interest but also because, compared to the elementary and homogeneous prescribed classical curriculum, the elective system raised the level of instruction of the entire institution. No subject possessed such "supreme merit" as to deserve the attention of all students.[64] In the late nineteenth century, the nation needed science, technology, and professional expertise to compete successfully in an expanding economic marketplace. In Eliot's estimation, the classical curriculum was simply obsolete. The elective system appealed to the anti-elitist, individualistic, and pragmatic values of the day. The elective system, moreover, enabled the university to fulfill its civic function by meeting the pressing needs of the day for practical knowledge free from ancient superstitions. Although there were no true universities in America, "only aspirants to that eminence," Eliot believed that the elective system was the key means toward realizing that ideal. Eliot also believed that the elective system helped fulfill the "moral purpose" of a university's policy: "to train young men to self-control and self-reliance through liberty."[65]

"I am as much in favor of progress as President Eliot," McCosh began his three-point response to Eliot, "but I go on in a different, I believe a better way [*sic*]. I adopt the new, I retain what is good in the old." The Princeton philosopher suggested that a university possessed two "essential powers or properties." One power was to ensure that students were in class, as parents expected, and not off ice skating. The second power was to require students to take sacrosanct courses in Princeton's educational trinity: "We in Princeton believe in a Trinity of studies: in Language and Literature, in Science, and in Philosophy." In language reminiscent of the 1828 Yale Report, McCosh argued that these courses formed the foundation for all other knowledge and disciplined students' reasoning faculties and consciences. Eliot and other educators in the late nineteenth century attacked the traditional curriculum not only as impractical but also as elitist for it provided the nation's leaders with a common body of knowledge and a shared set of moral principles. McCosh deplored the elective system not because of its democratic nature and appeal but because it threatened to destroy the common intellectual property that had bonded the nation's leaders into a community of discourse. Without this shared property, intellectual differences, divisions, and misunderstandings imperiled the harmony of civic life. A university, McCosh contended, should give its students what is "best" and not such "fictitious and pretentious" courses as "French Plays and Novels," as Harvard offered. "If this be the modern education," McCosh quipped, "I hold that the old is better."[66]

Yet, McCosh did not oppose the elective system per se. In addition to required courses in the "cardinal studies," McCosh argued, a true university should prudently allow students to take a judicious number of elective courses. McCosh saw the expansion of human knowledge and the creation of specialized disciplines as a positive development and considered the elective system as the best means to introduce students to these fields. An unregulated elective system, however, ran the danger of turning a student into a "jack of all trades and master of none." The classical curriculum coupled with a moderate elective system kept a "good college curriculum" in "an organic whole" and enabled the university to train well-rounded gentlemen capable of meeting the nation's pressing needs. This, McCosh insisted, was the critical difference between Princeton and Harvard. To clinch his argument, McCosh appealed to one of the traditional goals of higher education: the preparation of a learned clergy. What a tragedy it would be, McCosh suggested, for a college junior to receive the divine call "to preach the gospel of salvation" but be unable to enter the ministry because he failed to study Greek as a freshman.[67]

McCosh agreed with Eliot's final point: a university should encourage the self-government of students. He disagreed, however, on how this goal should be accomplished. While Eliot described the *in loco parentis* policy as an "ancient fiction," McCosh believed that, just as the classical curriculum disciplined students' mental powers, the *in loco parentis* policy developed their moral qualities. These alternative approaches arose from different perspectives on human development and human nature. First, when McCosh looked at the student body, he saw a group of boys. By contrast, Eliot saw young men. Consequently, McCosh treated students like children while Eliot treated them as adults. Second, the Calvinist McCosh not only taught the doctrine of total depravity to students but was convinced that they practiced it; the Unitarian Eliot had a more sanguine view of human nature and was not as disturbed as McCosh by student misbehavior. According to McCosh, parents did not expect colleges to permit their children to desecrate the Sabbath or visit dancing saloons, and thus prevention through restraint was a better policy than *post facto* punishment (although the litany of penalties recorded in the faculty minutes suggests that he was not adverse to the latter).[68]

McCosh's theology informed more than just his commitment to the *in loco parentis* policy. It provided a unifying center for his entire philosophy of higher education and, along with the Whiggish conception of higher education and Protestant cultural hegemony, served as a major pillar upon which traditional Protestant concerns and practices rested. Educational and theological orthodoxy in the nineteenth century went hand in hand. McCosh's administration, according to conventional interpretations, represented the persistent presence of the antebellum "discipline and piety" educational philosophy amid the postbellum revolution in higher education.[69] Although McCosh was not the educational paleoconservative that conventional portraits suggest, educational and theological orthodoxy at Princeton certainly correlated, based on common assumptions that all truth was God's truth and that any person of common sense could discern that truth. The college curriculum, McCosh believed, should maintain a delicate balance between secular and sacred knowledge. The classical liberal arts curriculum contained that body of knowledge derived from natural revelation and learned through natural reason. The English Bible classes taught that body of higher truths divinely revealed in special revelation. The natural theology courses endeavored to preserve the harmonious relationship between these two great realms of truth. Fastidious adherence to the Baconian method guaranteed that the entire enterprise was a scientific one, transcending sectarian doctrinal differences. For McCosh and many in his generation, the Christian character and progress of American society rested upon a balanced familiarity with both secular and sacred truth.

Whereas Princeton's classical curriculum formed an intellectual solar system, McCosh alleged that in Harvard's unrestrained elective system "everything is scattered like the star dust of which worlds are formed."[70] McCosh believed that unregulated academic specialization jeopardized more than the unity of knowledge. In 1886, McCosh further argued that by removing the study of "the holy Scriptures" from the curriculum, Harvard was "taking away the sun from our sky, leaving us only the lesser lights like those of the stars."[71] By eliminating the mandatory study of sacred knowledge, he believed, Harvard would produce intellectually "one-sided" graduates. McCosh saw in the rise of the practical and instrumental forms of knowledge that appealed to Americans' growing confidence in science and technology another equally ominous trend. The unregulated elective system aided the growth of atheism since it allowed students to avoid studying moral philosophy, a circumstance that in turn promoted, maybe unintentionally, philosophical materialism. McCosh feared that when "students are instructed only in matter they are apt to conclude that there is nothing but matter." For McCosh, Eliot's scheme ultimately imperiled the Christian character of American civilization. "Our colleges," McCosh believed, "should save our promising youths, the hope of the coming ages and ages," by teaching them that they have souls, "with lofty powers of reason and conscience and free will," which can enable them to know both "the secrets of nature" and God. Parents needed to know, he insisted, what educators of Eliot's ilk proposed to do with their children. "They are to teach them Music and Art, and French Plays and Novels, but there is no course in the Scriptures—in their poetry, their morality, their spirituality." He sarcastically explained, "The wise leaders of the new departure do not propose to fight against religion . . . but they are quite willing to let it die out, to die in dignity," a kind of passive euthanasia. The elective system, moreover, eliminated the compulsory study of Greek. "The Churches of Christ will do well to look to this new departure," McCosh suggested, "for they may find that they have fewer candidates for the office of the ministry." But more was at stake than a decline in the number of students prepared to enter graduate work at a seminary. The elective system, in short, endangered the religious mission of American higher education. "I fear," he added, "that the issue will be an unfortunate division of colleges into Christian and infidel." He hoped the "crisis" precipitated by the abandonment of religious instruction at Harvard would arouse such opposition throughout the nation that the "evil" could be averted in other colleges.[72]

Conservative Presbyterians, predictably, celebrated the "strong and wise" views expressed in McCosh's "very able reply" to Eliot.[73] Princeton students, or at least the editors of the *Princetonian*, favored their system over Harvard's, which, they condescendingly observed, attracted a "certain class" of students who wanted to get through college quickly to get "an early start in their specialty."[74] Criticizing Harvard's elective system and Eliot's educational utilitarianism had become something of a cottage industry among Princeton professors in the mid-1880s. In the most eloquent defense of Princeton's system, Andrew F. West argued that Eliot's elective system was "unsound" in theory because it did not fulfill the purpose of education, which he described as lifting students out of their ignorance of themselves and the world. According to the young Latinist, this herculean task could be achieved only though mental discipline and teaching only the most valuable kinds of knowledge. McCosh's faculty also shared his commitment, at least in principle, to the *in loco parentis* supervision of student life. Mental and moral discipline, according to West, were the "preconditions and products of genuine education." "He who has them not is in the worst sense uneducated." Nothing less than the Christian character of American democracy, West argued, was dependent upon having "genuinely" educated leaders. "What our society needs," he concluded, "is a large number of trained, enlightened men, the only sure guarantee for an enlightened public opinion."[75]

Cultivating Virtue in the Nation's Future Leaders: Compulsory and Voluntary Religious Education

"There is much talk in certain quarters of the importance of giving in the English Bible in Colleges," McCosh observed in his farewell address to the Princeton community in 1888. "Let me tell those who are recommending this to us," he added, "that this has always been done in Princeton. We are not ashamed, neither Professors nor students, of the gospel of Jesus Christ."[76] McCosh and many of his colleagues at Princeton and at other institutions in the late nineteenth century were equally committed to using chapel services and the other courses in the institution's program of religious education to nurture an evangelical faith in students and to provide them with a Protestant worldview that would serve them well throughout their lives. To McCosh and other educators, clerics, and interested laypeople, mandatory religious education served as a barometer to a college's or university's commitment to its historic religious mission. No subject or activity in collegiate education played a more important role in cultivating virtues in the nation's future leaders, thus safeguarding the Christian character of the nation, than the program of religious education. McCosh's defensive posture suggests that foundational commitments upon which religious education rested were under attack. McCosh, like many of his peers in other colleges, had no interest in surrendering to this dangerous trend.

The Protestant worldview that had dominated antebellum American collegiate education was founded on Scottish commonsense realism. Although romanticism had provided an alternative for some intellectuals before the Civil War, Henry F. May observes, "At least until the Civil War, and in some places long after, the Common Sense philosophy reigned supreme in American colleges, driving out skepticism and Berkeleyan idealism, and delaying the advent of Kant."[77] Postbellum Princeton, which had been a bastion of the Scottish philosophy since Witherspoon's administration in the late eighteenth century, was one such institution where the tradition still prevailed. McCosh's reputation as "the leading thinker and champion of sound philosophy in the United Kingdom," the *New York Observer* reported, played a prominent part in his election to Princeton.[78] "I am devoting my declining life to two objects," McCosh confided to a correspondent in the summer of 1879. The first was to "build up Princeton College." The second was to prevent philosophy in America from reaching the "state it has come to in England."[79] For McCosh, as Princeton's president and the last great champion of Scottish realism, the two goals were inseparably intertwined. McCosh attempted to conserve the basic epistemological and metaphysical commitments of the Scottish philosophical tradition by advancing a mediating position between the extremes of French sensationalism and German idealism.[80] Scottish commonsense realism, armed with the Baconian method, expounded the philosophical foundations and implications of the perspicuity and immutability of truth in every field of human inquiry. Science, it was believed, not only aided society's progress with technological advances but also served a higher "doxological purpose" by pointing out the divine benevolence revealed in the providential design of every aspect of the natural world. Protestant intellectuals also constructed a moral philosophy, as distinguished from theological ethics, which was based on supernatural revelation. Moral philosophy, or moral science as some termed it, provided an ethical system that transcended sectarian peculiarities, using scientific principles in an introspective examination of the "moral sense." This "moral sense" was one of the prerational first principles of the Scottish philosophy. Even theology was regarded as a science. The task of theologians was simply to codify the facts of the Bible into a taxonomic whole using the Baconian method as the keystone of their hermeneutic. Natural theology safeguarded the concord between the natural and supernatural by corroborating the truths revealed in Scripture with the hard facts of science. Although belief in God was not among the first principles of the commonsense philosophy, apologetics demonstrated the reasonableness of theism with the aid of both natural and moral science.[81]

As the southern states were being reconstructed in the aftermath of the Civil War, the Protestant worldview that had dominated academia in postbellum America was being ravaged by an intellectual revolution. By 1913, George Santayana, the scion of the Harvard philosophy department, observed, "The present age is a critical one and interesting to live in. The civilization characteristic of Christendom has not disappeared, yet another civilization has begun to take its place. We still understand the value of religious faith. . . . On the other hand the shell of Christendom is broken."[82]

In addition to the revolution restructuring American higher education, the intellectual credibility of the evangelical Protestant theology and worldview came under attack. For some intellectuals, questions about the veracity of the Bible raised by higher criticism made belief in God untenable. For others, Darwinism produced the same result. As important as these intellectual developments were, the principal cause for the demise of evangelical Protestantism was the collapse of Scottish realism. Behind scientific Darwinism and the Higher Criticism of the Bible rose philosophical positivism and historicism, which undermined the foundations of Christian belief. The "spiritual crisis" of the Gilded Age made agnosticism intellectually and morally compelling for many intellectuals.[83] McCosh and his colleagues at Princeton were well aware of these pressures. Indeed, McCosh feared, as he privately told Princeton alumnus John DeWitt, that his philosophy was being "crushed" between the German idealist school, the materialistic school of Alexander Bain, and the agnostic school of Herbert Spencer.[84] In a day marked by tumultuous intellectual change, McCosh and his colleagues sought to defend and to perpetuate the Scottish philosophy and the traditional Protestant faith through religious instruction and worship that had guided many of the nation's leaders for decades.

In 1868, Princeton students were fed, Eliot might add by force, a full diet of religious instruction. In addition to his courses in psychology and the history of philosophy, McCosh taught English Bible; Charles W. Shields (1825–1904) offered natural theology, Christian evidences, and science and religion courses; and Lyman Atwater (1813–1883) taught moral philosophy and political economy as well as logic and metaphysics.[85] At the winter meeting of the Board of Trustees in 1883, McCosh demanded that the trustees create a "School of Philosophy equal or superior to any in the country" in order to enhance Princeton's standing as a bulwark of the Scottish philosophy. Atwater's death nine days later made McCosh's demand all the more urgent. When he thought the board was dragging its feet, McCosh threatened to resign. Three new professors were soon added to the philosophy department. Alexander T. Ormond (1847–1915), a McCosh disciple, was hired as Professor of Logic and Mental Science, Alexander Johnston (1848–1889) as Professor of Jurisprudence and Political Economy, and Francis L. Patton (1843–1932), the Professor of the Relation of Science and Philosophy to the Christian Religion at Princeton Seminary, as a lecturer in ethics in 1884, and as the Professor of Ethics the following year.[86] The specific purpose of religious instruction and worship was to nurture virtue among the nation's future leaders. The only way to cultivate an enduring virtuous character, McCosh and other educators believed, was to promote an evangelical faith among students. The Christian faith required both intellectual and spiritual grounding because good theology and righteous living went together. The ethics and political economy classes taught students their personal and public duties; the English Bible classes taught students basic Christian doctrines and Bible content; and the natural theology and science and religion courses defended the intellectual credibility of Christianity against an emerging array of detractors. Worship services helped order students' spiritual priorities on a daily basis. Erroneous views of the nature of moral obligations, the Bible, or science threatened to subvert a sound theology and ultimately to jeopardize the Christian health of American society.

The nation needed virtuous leaders and the purpose of Patton's ethics classes was to help provide them. Patton did not impartially present the strengths and weaknesses of various ethical systems, but tried to convince students that they were inherently moral creatures endowed with an intuitive moral sense who were obliged to do the good they discerned through reason or learned through special revelation. He championed the same moral perspective of the Scottish philosophers as Lyman Atwater did. Unlike his predecessor, however, Patton was more sensitive to current developments in the field and sought to repudiate the ethical systems of idealists and utilitarians.[87] Patton defined his subject as "the *Science* which deals with the character and conduct of a Free Agent in relation to an Obligatory Ideal."[88] Ethics was a science because it was based upon natural reason, not supernatural revelation. And because it was viewed as a science, according to conventional wisdom, Patton's ethics courses transcended narrow doctrinal differences.

Patton began his lectures by first establishing the psychological and then the metaphysical aspects of the "Categorical Imperative Ought" by reviewing and repudiating those moral theories that denied the *a priori* character of this intuitive first principle. Utilitarian ethicists, such as J. S. Mill (1806–1873), Patton asserted, were "Universalistic Hedonists" because they made the end of all conduct the greatest happiness for the greatest number. Accordingly, they failed to account for the source of moral obligation. Evolutionary ethicists, such as Herbert Spencer (1820–1903), relativized all moral imperatives by making them a result of the evolutionary progress of social life.[89] The emerging array of alternative ethical systems, according to Patton, ultimately reduced personal morality to utilitarianism because they were constructed on flawed psychological and metaphysical presuppositions. In the end, Patton insisted, the idea of obligation is an intuitive, an "ultimate psychological fact," and the word "Ought" represented "the ethical Atom."[90]

Patton's moral "physics" ultimately rested upon the metaphysics of theism. To expound this metaphysical foundation, Patton turned to Immanuel Kant (1724–1804), who, as he put it, correctly recognized the "intuitive character" of this moral imperative. Although he appreciated Kant's exposition of the moral imperative's intuitive nature, he complained that even Kant ultimately surrendered to the spirit of utilitarianism. Kant's key categorical imperative, "'Act only on that maxim whereby thou canst at the same time, will that it should become a universal law [sic],'" Patton believed, was in the final analysis subjectivism because it "emanated from no source higher than my own will and looked to no moral system outside." The only legitimate foundation for moral obligation, Patton taught students, was theism: "I feel that I ought. I also believe in God. If God exist [sic], and I am a subject of his moral government, it is only natural that he should give me a moral nature and that moral law should issue from that nature, which after all is only the law of God." As moral philosophers had taught American students for generations, Patton instructed his students that God had endowed them with a conscience that enabled them to know intuitively what was right and what was wrong. Moreover, the very workings of nature revealed the pattern of God's moral law, for God had created it. The nation, Patton taught, needed leaders who would base their influential decisions, not upon economic or political expediency, but upon these decisions' congruity with what their consciences' taught them was intrinsically right. Though they might be more self-conscious of the moral law because of their college training, students were not unique in living in the presence of the moral imperative. The self-evident presence of the moral imperative, Patton taught, had a "universal application."[91] Students, like the average American citizen, had no way to escape this ever-present witness to what was right or wrong. So long as a consensus existed about the scientific character and intellectual credibility of Scottish philosophy's first principles, this was an ethical system upon which the Christian character of American culture could be advanced.

The aim of the moral imperative, Patton told students, was the *summum bonum*. "Why ought I to do Right?" he asked. "No satisfactory answer can be given other than that the idea of Right carries with it that of moral obligation."[92] As opposed to a teleological ethical theory, which held that an action was right if it promoted some end that was intrinsically good, the Presbyterian minister taught, like the earlier nineteenth-century moral philosophers, a deontological ethical theory that held that an action was obligatory if that action was good. That an action's end may be personally or publicly beneficial did not necessarily make it right. "Right," Patton explained, "is that which is in accordance with the nature of God [i.e., goodness]."[93] "Rightness" and "Goodness," in Patton's analysis, could not be subordinated one to another but rather had to be "coordinated"; the means to the highest good had to be morally congruent with the end. For these reasons, Patton explained, both Utilitarianism and "Christian Altruism" were defective because they rested moral obligation on the end.[94] One knows what is right, Patton said, through "experience, induction, [and] revelation." As a person gained experience by judging actions, a person became more aware of moral laws, and over time could draw moral generalizations.

Given the perspicuity of truth, Patton argued, "There is no reason why a revelation cannot show what we know intuitively."[95] Basic moral truths discerned through introspection were also disclosed in special revelation. Almost parenthetically, the Old School Presbyterian minister reminded students that the Scriptures taught "that man's chief end is to glorify God." The teaching of reason and supernatural revelation, Patton contended, did not conflict at this point because glorifying God and the *summum bonum* were identical. The moral obligation to do the *summum bonum* glorified God and promoted the welfare of others and society. In addition, the *summum bonum* had beneficial consequences for the moral agent him or herself. The "Good," he told students, had an end also within individuals but it differed from the Utilitarian notion of personal happiness. It was a moral perfection that a person gradually achieved through "the embodiment of the Moral Law in our nature and life."[96]

Patton's ethics courses taught students their personal moral duties. Alexander Johnston's courses in political economy and jurisprudence taught students their public duties as individuals in relation to society.[97] Previously, Lyman Atwater had taught political economy as part of moral philosophy. Now Johnston was teaching both jurisprudence and political economy as separate courses. When these fields were part of the old moral philosophy course, the college authorities believed, they were taught on the basis of theologically neutral principles. As separate classes, Johnston's political economy and jurisprudence courses, just like Patton's ethics courses, simply extended this allegedly nonsectarian and scientific enterprise. Academic specialization and professionalization precipitated this division of labor and further separated religious interests from these disciplines. No one considered the division of labor a threat to Princeton's commitment to the religious education of its students. Johnston's personal character and the congruity between his teaching with that of Atwater also made this segregation possible.

Johnston was a pious elder at the First Presbyterian Church in Princeton and an activist in the temperance movement. A self-taught "professional-amateur" historian and a founding member of the American Historical Association in 1884, Alexander won immediate fame with his first work, *History of American Politics* (1878), which gained wide usage as a college textbook by such professors as Frederick Jackson Turner at the University of Wisconsin. Yet Princeton hired Johnston in 1883 to teach not history but the related fields of jurisprudence and political economy.[98]

Johnston, like Atwater, was an ultra-Jeffersonian who taught students traditional republican values of individualism, federalism, and laissez-faire economics.[99] Unlike his predecessor's course, Alexander's required class in political economy had little to say about moral law and its relationship with public life. Johnston's course was basically a sweeping review of various theories of the state's origins and its functions. He prefaced the entire discussion with a perfunctory lecture on the "divine" theories of the origin of the state. The only "immediately" established state, according to Johnston, was the Jewish theocracy: "The voice of God called it. The hand of God guided it. The wrath of God has scattered it and it is not." The mediate theory, as "held by most devout men nowadays," maintained that "people are the source of authority because the Creator implanted in them" "social instincts" to establish laws and governments. This "social instinct" was a fruit of the "moral order of the universe" implanted by "a personal God" manifested in the "law of nature." This lecture, however, stood unrelated to the five other theories of the origin of the state that he outlined in the remainder of his lectures on political economy and jurisprudence.[100] While much of Johnston's work was congruous with the old-time moral philosophy course, it was one further step removed from theological ethics. This shift reveals how the boundaries between religious and secular interests were constantly being renegotiated in the face of new educational pressures in the late nineteenth century. On the one hand, the breakdown of the antebellum moral philosophy course into its constitutive parts expanded the older Christian Enlightenment perspective through the creation of new disciplines such as political economy. On the other hand, the older Christian Enlightenment perspective was diluted as these new disciplines slowly muted, in the name of scholarly objectivity, the interpretive framework from which it had risen. Johnston's colleagues did not see the breakdown of the moral philosophy course as a compromise of Princeton's religious mission. Instead, they viewed it as an academic advancement that helped Princeton better fulfill its civic mission. Upon Johnson's premature death at the age of forty in 1889, Patton eulogized that Princeton had lost "one of the most brilliant and successful teachers," who "represented a type of man that we could wish to see in all the colleges of the land." "Only a man of Christian faith," Patton concluded, could "fill his vacant place or take up with profit to us the work that he leaves incomplete."[101]

While the ethics and political economy courses provided the nation's future leaders with a personal moral compass and a map to the traditional republican values for public life, no subject at Princeton proved more critical to sustaining the evangelical Protestant faith of students than Charles W. Shields' six courses in natural theology and science and religion. The struggle between science and religion in the late nineteenth century endangered the intellectual credibility of the evangelical faith that Princeton taught students. This struggle, Shields told students, was of interest to more than philosophers living in an ivory tower, for the nation needed leaders who could defend the scholarly reliability of Christian supernaturalism against the growing menace of secular naturalism: "As lawyers, physicians, clergymen, [and] scholars in every walk of life" students would face a growing number of "intellectual temptations." "You will be taking sides," he cautioned, "in the great battle between the knowledge and faith of the time; and it rests with you now to determine, in these preliminary trials, whether you shall hereafter be found among the mere bigots and charlatans of your day, or ranked as lovers of truth and benefactors of mankind."[102] Posed in this way, Shields left little doubt as to where he thought the more intelligent students should stand. Shields and many in his generation believed that if science sabotaged or supplanted the evangelical faith of the nation's future leaders evil would inevitably spread, public virtue would retreat, and the Christian character of American culture would be endangered.

As the intellectual foundation of the nation's "established" religion began to crack in postbellum America, no one welcomed the challenge of defending the harmony of science and religion with more confidence than Shields. Shields had the perfect Princeton pedigree for his position. A maternal descendent of one of the original trustees of the college, Shields graduated from the college and the seminary and pastored the prestigious Second (Old School) Presbyterian Church of Philadelphia where Ashbel Green had served before becoming the college's president. His brief treatise on the harmony of science and religion, *Philosophia Ultima* (1861), had won praise from the editors of the *Biblical Repertory and Princeton Review*.[103] Academia was clearly Shields's lifelong ambition. In order to free him from the pastorate, where he had longstanding personality conflicts with some in his congregation, several wealthy friends created a professorship at his alma mater where they thought he could be of better use to the church.[104] Shields insisted to President Maclean that he designate his position the "Harmony of Science and Religion" to which the Board added the adjective "Revealed" as if the subject matter needed to be clarified.[105] It was the first professorship in an American college devoted specifically to the subject.

Although William Paley's *Natural Theology* (1802) and Bishop Joseph Butler's *Analogy of Religion* (1736) were somewhat dated, Shields told students, he believed these two staples of the antebellum natural theology course were still useful as a "mental gymnastic" and, more important, as a defense against the arguments of atheists.[106] Paley had proposed, on universally accepted "principles of knowledge," a probablistic argument for the existence of God. "The proof," he explained, "is not a conclusion which lies at the end of a chain of reasoning" but "an argument separately supplied by every separate example," whose cumulative result is to make it exceedingly probable and therefore convincingly reasonable to believe in God. After finding a watch and examining its design, according to the classical teleological argument, one could conclude that there had to have been a watch designer. In the same way, a careful examination of the design in nature suggested the likely existence of a Grand Designer. After an extensive survey of the design evident in animals, vegetation, and, most important, human beings, Paley concluded that the "multitudes of proofs" offered strong support for belief in the existence of the God revealed in the Bible.[107] Butler's *Analogy* likewise offered a probablistic argument for theism. He presented empirical evidence in a series of arguments that drew out analogies between natural and divine revelation to support strongly the conclusion that God existed. The "fact," for instance, that virtue was rewarded and vice punished in this life provided analogical evidence, Butler reasoned, that both would likewise be rewarded and punished, just as Scripture teaches, in the life to come. Yet Butler went one step further than Paley; he presented proofs for the truthfulness of revealed religion. He pointed to miracles and fulfilled prophecy as factual evidence that left the sinner "absolutely without excuse" for unbelief.[108] For at least one student, however, Shields's lectures dispelled his interest in natural theology more than it eradicated atheism. Blair Lee (1857–1944), a member of the Class of 1880, complained in letters to his parents that he found Paley "abstruse" and Butler the "dryest stuff." The professor's "Christian gentleness," as Lee described it, earned these courses the reputation of being "easy."[109] Shields's real interest lay in his own course on science and religion.

Shields devoted his academic career to slowly developing the ideas expressed in the 1861 essay that had first brought him to the attention of his mentors at Princeton. This work was largely an attempt to overcome the threat that positivism presented to Scottish epistemology, "doxological" science, moral philosophy, and even the very possibility of a theology based on supernatural revelation.[110] In the effort to conserve Protestant orthodoxy in the face of the Comtean challenge, Shields stood among the judicious conservatives in British and American Protestant academic circles who redoubled their philosophical and theological commitments with slight modification.[111] The purpose of his science and religion course, Shields told students, was to reunite science and religion as they once were "so compactly joined in

Christian philosophy and scholastic culture." The growing hostility between science and religion as well as the "multiplicity of intellectual pursuits," Shields believed, had created the need for a new discipline within the community of scholars. His position, in the "Philosophical Faculty as distinguished from a Theological Faculty," sought to resolve the conflict not through Christian apologetics, which "attempts to render science tributary to orthodoxy," but through the founding of a "Christian science" that strove "to make essential Christianity helpful to science." The conflict was an abnormal state, Shields insisted, but could be rectified through a philosophy that integrated scientific truths insofar as they related to revealed truths and vice versa.[112]

The "great battle" of his day, Shields told students, pitted the "two rash knights" of science and religion against one another.[113] Shields was not alone in this assessment. In the wake of Charles Darwin's *Origin of Species* (1859), many educators, scientists, and philosophers, most notably John Draper in *History of the Conflict between Religion and Science* (1874) and Andrew D. White in *A History of the Warfare of Science with Theology in Christendom* (1896), portrayed the relationship between science and dogmatic theology as one of conflict.[114] No development in nineteenth-century science posed a greater danger to Shields's work than Darwinism. By offering a compelling and thoroughly naturalistic explanation of the appearance of design in nature, Darwin had so destroyed "the proof value of design" that "its plausibility fizzed away like air from a leaky balloon."[115] Shields discerned four popular misunderstandings of the relationship between science and religion that had turned the old friends into antagonists. "1st. The Extremists, who would render science and religion hostile and exterminant. 2d. The Indifferentists, who would leave them separate and independent. 3d. The Impatients or Eclectics, who would combine them prematurely and illogically. 4th. The Despondents or Sceptics, who would abandon them as contradictory and irreconcilable." Shields found all four misconceptions present in the sciences of anthropology, astronomy, geology, psychology, sociology, and theology. In anthropology, for example, Shields contended that extremists among the scientists, such as Ernst Haeckel of Jena, held to the anthropocentric error that the work of Jean de Lamarck and Charles Darwin had overturned any intellectual credibility for the conviction that humankind was made in the image of God. In light of modern geological discoveries, Shields argued, some skeptics among the religionists, such as Friedrich Schleiermacher, "pronounced the Hebrew cosmogony unscientific, and relinquished the task of harmonizing it with modern geology."[116] Although Shields characterized science and traditional nineteenth-century Protestantism as antagonists, he planned to resolve their conflicts.

Once the two "exhausted and bleeding warriors" had "fought their way into a recognition of each others' truth and virtue," Shields asserted, they would "clasp hands as friends who had but mistaken themselves for foes." Shields told students the conflict could be solved through the "umpirage" of philosophy. The "Ultimate Philosophy," which Shields proposed for this task, was tethered between the extremes represented by the Positivism of Auguste Comte and the

Absolutism of Georg F. W. Hegel. Shields, like McCosh, appreciated the empiricism of positivism, but found positivism wanting because its nescience rendered supernatural revelation irrelevant. Absolutism, on the other hand, rightly recognized the intuitive character of knowledge but ultimately supplanted supernatural revelation with its "fancied omniscience." These two philosophies, Shields concluded, "are true in what they affirm" and "false only in what they deny." Shields hoped to demonstrate how they "exhibit to us complemental aspects of the same reality" and "together tend towards perfect knowledge itself."[117] As the arbitrator in the borderland between the realms of nature and grace, Scottish philosophy could reestablish the harmony between science and theology. Shields had high aspirations for his efforts to reconcile faith and knowledge. As others labored to bring in the kingdom of God through social activism in the late nineteenth century, Shields believed that his "final philosophy" would create a *Scientia Scientiarum*. This was no esoteric endeavor to Shields. He believed that his final philosophy would help generate a millennial peace where "the reason of man shall stand forth coincident with the word of God."[118]

In response to the Newtonian revolution of the seventeenth century, Protestants had zealously embraced scientific developments and added new discoveries to the corpus of accepted knowledge. Yet their reconciliation of science and religion was superficial in that they failed to examine the speculative foundation upon which the scientific revolution rested. Instead of challenging science's first principles, they became science's chief defenders and, consequently, were confident that objective scientific investigation would only confirm Christian truth.[119] Amid the second scientific revolution of the nineteenth century, which prompted a crisis of faith for many Protestants, Shields defended the traditional arrangement. He championed the earlier view of science, the epistemological and metaphysical assumptions upon which it rested, and continued to pursue knowledge in both science and Scripture, as he put it, without determining "*a priori* their respective limits, contents, and prerogatives."[120] Any conflict, he asserted, was "not because of any actual disagreement between natural facts and revealed truths, not even because of any essential defects in our instruments of knowledge, but simply because of some wrong induction from nature or some false interpretation of Scripture." The scientist and religionist, he argued, looked at identical facts "as phenomena of nature" and "as manifestations of God," respectively. Their different viewpoints, nevertheless, were "not only equally true, but equally essential to make up the whole truth in regard to those facts."[121] During the second scientific revolution, this older view of science was crumbling under the pressures of scientific positivism. In the nineteenth century, science had become more speculative in its method at the same time that it restricted knowledge, based on the Kantian distinction, to that which could be empirically derived from the phenomenon alone. Science, by effectively cutting off access to the noumenon through nature, had thus subverted the arguments of natural theology. For many, this epistemological revolution meant that knowing anything about what or who was in the noumena was either "Unknowable" (Spencer) or a matter of agnosticism (Huxley).[122] In contrast, Shields, like Paley and Butler before him, offered students an array of teleological arguments gleaned from the older disciplines of astronomy and geology as well as from recent discoveries in such new fields as sociology.[123] While he criticized the epistemologies and metaphysics of Positivism and Absolutism, the traditional commitment to an allegedly objective science left Shields only able to complain that too many scientists, philosophers, and theologians were wrongly restricting science's purview.

In trying to push air back into the leaky balloon with various arguments from design, Shields made a special effort to convert evolution into an ally. While early historians, such as Draper and White, portrayed the conservative Protestant response to Darwinism as one of militant opposition, recent studies suggest that the reception within the Protestant intellectual community was actually more varied. Initially, both scientists and theologians were skeptical of the transmutation theory because it lacked sufficient empirical evidence. By 1875, however, some version of Darwin's theory had gained general acceptance in the scientific community.[124] Among theologians, however, the reception was more tepid. The most articulate repudiation of Darwinism came from Princeton. Charles Hodge answered the question posed by the title of his book, *What Is Darwinism?* (1874), with a resounding assertion that Darwinism was atheism because Darwin's concept of natural selection undermined the design or teleological purpose in nature.[125] Other Protestants attempted a reconciliation. Some advocated a Christian Darwinisticism by slightly modifying their Scottish philosophy and biblical interpretation in order to accommodate their theology to evolution. Others espoused a more radical Christian Darwinism in which they thoroughly revised their theology to conform with German idealism to make the peace between science and religion.[126] Of these two kinds of reconciliation, Shields taught students the former, a position which had been championed first within the Princeton community by President McCosh. Over the course of his career, McCosh elaborated this reconciliation by first distinguishing between evolution and Darwinism and then placing evolution within a theistic framework that identified natural selection with the secondary causes and God as the first cause of evolution. Evolution, he said, was "the method by which God works." Still capitalizing on the prestige of science, he then pointed to the process of evolution in nature as evidence of divine design to strengthen his teleological argument.[127] To foster this constructive attitude toward science in general and evolution in particular, the trustees even created an academic prize in 1874 for the best paper on an assigned topic involving science and religion. The year McCosh debated Eliot over religion in collegiate education, for example, the prize was awarded to the best senior essay on "Creation and Evolution."[128]

Other Princeton professors during McCosh's presidency recognized the danger that Darwin posed to the harmony between science and religion, though not all shared the same solution to reconcile potential conflicts between them. Mathematics professor John T. Duffield (1823–1901), arguing a position much like Charles Hodge's, held that the language of the Genesis account of creation was "utterly irreconcilable with Evolutionism."[129] By contrast, Princeton's distinguished Professor of Physical Geography and Geology, Arnold H. Guyot (1807–1884), attempted a reconciliation. In *Creation; or The Biblical Cosmogony in the Light of Modern Science* (1884), he claimed that the "outlines" of the order of creation unearthed by scientific research "were precisely those of the grand history of life given in the First Chapter of Genesis."[130] After McCosh came to Princeton in 1868, the college hired only scientists who advocated the harmonization of evolution and theism like Guyot. George Macloskie (1834–1920) was one such scientist. He had studied under McCosh in Ireland and joined Princeton's faculty in 1874 as Professor of Biology and Botany. Like Shields and McCosh, he advocated a theistic interpretation of evolution. He explained to students in a biology class that Christianity was not "unfriendly" to free scientific research and that the arguments of Darwin's *Origin*, if properly interpreted, "show that the argument from Design is as strong as it can possibly be." "Of all beings," said the doxological scientist, "a student of nature is inconsistent with himself if he is not a pious man."[131] Even Charles Hodge's successors at the seminary gradually embraced a view of evolution similar to that of Shields and McCosh.[132]

Despite the elevated role that he assigned his professorship, Shields was not above incorporating into his science and religion class certain elements of the older Evidences of Christianity course. He offered students apologetic arguments for belief in revealed religion from the sciences of astronomy, geology, and anthropology.[133] The Bible, he insisted, taught neither science nor anything that conflicted with science, and he rejected any limitation of the Bible's inerrancy to things spiritual. He blamed, moreover, the "unscientific" and hostile biblical interpretations of the "Rationalistic schools" on their abandonment of the inductive method. However, he approved of the more "Reverent" school that used "the Higher Criticism learnedly in defense of the traditional authority and historicity of the sacred records."[134] In the end, Shields attempted to defend the harmony of faith and knowledge in order to preserve the intellectual foundation of a sound and active Christian faith. By persuading students of the scholarly soundness of evangelical orthodoxy, Shields helped to cultivate the Christian character of the nation's future leaders and ultimately contributed to the promotion of evangelicalism in the national culture.

A critical appreciation for certain uses of higher criticism of the Bible within the college notwithstanding, Bible instruction under President McCosh was essentially a devotional exercise. By directing "the mind and the heart" of each student "toward the Savior and toward the truth," McCosh believed that his Bible class not only served as a ballast to the liberal arts curriculum but also provided the nation's future leaders with a proper set of spiritual values. In his first English Bible lecture in 1868, McCosh told the Princeton student body that he planned to use their Sabbath afternoon meetings to present papers "free from all narrow sectarianism" on "a biblical subject, fitted to give instruction in the meaning of the Word, to illustrate its history, its geography, and its doctrine; to furnish evidence of its genuineness and divine origin, and answer plausible objections to its truthfulness; and especially meant with the Spirit to quicken spiritual life in the soul." In four years, he expected to give students a "complete course of biblical instruction" covering the life of Christ, Old Testament "prefigurations of Christ," the "development of Christ in the Church," and "Christian doctrine." McCosh wanted the course to be a "spiritual exercise" complete with singing and prayers. No grades, he promised, would be given. In addition, he intended to meet with each class during the week to discuss his lecture.[135] Gradually, however, the weekday meeting took on a more academic character. In the fall of 1870, sophomore Bible classes were designated to give their recitations in the Greek New Testament, and all students received grades for the course. To encourage scholarship, moreover, an academic prize was awarded to the two top Bible students in each graduating class.[136]

With "excessive reluctance," McCosh asked the trustees in 1876 to reconsider "the manner" in which they offered Bible instruction. The increasing size of each entering class and his growing responsibilities outside the classroom made the five weekly meetings of Bible instruction an increasing burden for McCosh.[137] In the fall of 1876, the trustees reduced Bible instruction to one weekday recitation for each academic class with the president or a tutor, but by November, McCosh called the new plan inadequate and devised another scheme. In this plan, McCosh taught seniors the "Gospels and Life of Christ." James O. Murray (1827–1899), who had pastored the prestigious Brick Presbyterian Church in New York City before his election to the Holmes Professorship of Belles Lettres and English Language and Literature in 1875, lectured juniors on the Old Testament prophetic books and New Testament book of Acts. Greek Professor Reverend Samuel Stanhope Orris (1832–1905) taught the gospel of John, not surprisingly, in Greek to sophomores. Another Presbyterian minister, Theodore Whitefield Hunt (1844–1930), led the freshmen in a study of the Old Testament poetic literature and the "Parables of our Lord." Certain tutors, graduate students, and young professors assisted Hunt and Orris with their Bible classes. McCosh deemed the new scheme a success and the trustees agreed.[138] The program remained basically unchanged until the fall of 1882, when freshmen and sophomores in the School of Science were given separate biblical instruction by biology professor George Macloskie.[139] The next year McCosh turned the senior Bible class over to Murray, who in turn was succeeded by Alexander T. Ormond. Each Bible instructor was a Presbyterian minister, with the exception of Ormond, and their assistants, such as Andrew F. West, were trusted members of the college community.[140] Although none of these professors was a bona fide biblical scholar, several were genuine experts in their own fields. They provided students with examples that one could be both a scholar and a student, as McCosh put it, of the "living Word." McCosh proudly reported to the trustees in the fall of 1884 that Bible instruction was given by professors "whose hearts are in the work."[141] Conservative Presbyterians in the larger Princeton community appreciated McCosh's commitment to Bible instruction; the *Presbyterian* observed that Bible instruction "was systematized and widened" under McCosh.[142]

Along with Darwinism, the higher criticism of the Bible threatened to undermine the intellectual credibility of the broadly evangelical Protestant theology taught at Princeton. The same romantic historical consciousness that had eased the reception of Darwin's natural history had also sparked an interest in human history. Historicism, first articulated by Johann Gottfried Herder (1744–1803) and later developed by Leopold van Ranke (1795–1886), viewed every aspect of reality—society, institutions, morality, law, economics, religion—as part of one grand evolutionary stream. Any phenomenon could be understood by locating its historical origins and progress.[143] Just as Darwinism's developmental rather than divinely created and static conception of the origin of species disrupted the classical structures of traditional theology and natural theology, historicism's relativistic conception of history overturned the traditional view of the Bible. In nineteenth-century evangelical Protestant theology, the Bible's truthfulness, and therefore its authority, hinged upon its factuality. The Bible, it was believed, was comprised of both history and supernatural revelation. The Bible's factuality was perspicuous and immutable. Higher criticism, as opposed to textual criticism, sought to discover how the biblical text reached its present form by examining its authorship, authorial intent, dating, and theological substance. Higher criticism proposed a variety of disturbing conclusions about the Old Testament, such as that Isaiah had three authors and that Daniel dated from the Maccabean period. Most unsettling was the Graf-Wellhausen theory of the Hextateuch's composition, which asserted that the present text was the product of four different sources combined into one document by a variety of editors over the course of hundreds of years. The same Hegelian understanding of history also shaped higher criticism of the New Testament. The search for the "historical Jesus," begun with D. F. Strauss's *Das Leben Jesu* (1835), gave rise to a variety of critical theories about the identity of Jesus, as well as source-critical theories about the nature of the Synoptic Gospels.[144] The result was that higher criticism disputed the factuality of the Bible, a circumstance which in turn cast doubts on its authority.

In the antebellum period, higher criticism had made few inroads into American theological circles because conservative biblical scholars rejected its philosophical foundation and tamed its radical conclusions.[145] In the postbellum period, the crisis surrounding higher criticism, like Darwinism, escalated because of its initial association with Comtean positivism. Some of higher criticism's more aggressive proponents, such as Ernest Renan (1823–1892) through his *Vie de Jésus* (1863), were professing positivists who offered purely naturalist explanations of the origins of Christianity.[146] The controversy over higher criticism entered a new stage in the 1880s, when the faculties of Union and Princeton seminaries debated its virtues and vices, respectively, in the pages of their joint publication, the *Presbyterian Review*. Unlike Union's faculty, the Princeton theologians saw little value in the use of higher criticism and had no sympathy for the antisupernaturalism intrinsic to historicism. But the theological landscape had not yet divided into warring camps of conservatives and liberals, and the Princeton theologians noted this fact. Patton, for example, distinguished between the "evangelical criticism" made by scholars, like those at Union, who still "believe in the gospel" and those more radical critics who did not.[147]

While the value of higher criticism was being debated in higher academic circles, Princeton undergraduates studied the Bible in a manner that stood on the more traditional side of the controversial questions of the day. In their spring semester, for example, seniors heard McCosh's lectures on "Doctrine in the book of Romans," which not only offered broadly evangelical explanations of fundamental Christian beliefs, such as justification, repentance, and sanctification, but also made applications for students' personal lives from the text. One senior wrote in his classnotes, for example, that the message of Romans 5 was to "Confess thy transgressions to the Lord."[148] The faculty did not directly address pertinent questions raised by higher criticism. Instead, the professors dealt with issues raised by higher criticism indirectly by advocating traditional interpretations. McCosh, for example, taught the Mosaic authorship of the Pentateuch and dated the book of Daniel during the Babylonian captivity and the four Gospels and all the New Testament epistles before A.D. 70.[149] Diatribes against Protestant modernism were largely absent from McCosh's lectures despite his disdain for the theological tradition begun by Schleiermacher. Yet occasionally he would lapse into criticisms, as when he told students that Schleiermacher's basic conviction—the essence of religion was a feeling of dependence upon God—"would make religion too like the obedience which a dog renders to its master."[150] Henry Van Dyke Jr., whose academic gifts were held in high esteem, not least of all by himself, found McCosh's lectures less than intellectually challenging. "I wanted to learn something on the Doctrines this year," he wrote his father in the fall of 1870, "but as things look now there will be a great deal of wading for a very few intellectual shrimp."[151] McCosh's colleagues proselytized students with the same evangelical faith. James O. Murray portrayed evangelical Protestantism as the quintessential rational religion, explaining, for example, that St. Paul's discourse with the Athenians on the Areopagus appealed to natural revelation, natural theology, and the special revelation of Christ to demonstrate the reasonableness of the gospel.[152] Biologist George Macloskie used his lectures to the School of Science students to bolster faith in the concord of science and religion. Science, he asserted, was Christianity's strongest ally: "Modern criticism and scientific investigation are destroying every system of religion except that of the Bible, and are showing Infidelity itself to be inconsistent and unsatisfying; and are shutting the door against every other hope except that presented in the gospel."[153]

In addition to Bible classes, daily worship services helped to nurture the evangelical faith of students. If colleges abandoned compulsory chapel, McCosh asserted in his 1886 debate with Eliot, "the floating sentiments in the air will crystallize into the ice of Agnosticism with all its chilling and deadly influence; and the great body of the young men will settle down into the conviction that nothing can be known of God, of the world above or the world to come." The nation, McCosh explained, could ill-afford to have every college graduating a "a few hundred agnostics every year." They, McCosh reasoned, would first "chill the atmosphere around them" and then "oppose those grand philanthropic and missionary efforts which are one of the glories of our country."[154] Given such potentially damaging consequences to the Christian character of American civilization, McCosh yielded little ground on the importance of mandatory daily chapel and Sunday services.

As president, McCosh presided over the religious life of the college, and his Sabbath morning sermons set the moral tone for the week. His favorite college sermons were optimistically evangelical and decidedly evangelistic. In one sermon, for instance, McCosh urged students to imitate the apostle Peter, who, after denying Christ, was forgiven and devoted his life to Christian service. This life-changing experience of forgiveness, McCosh explained, "sends forth men . . . to become Sabbath-school teachers, to spread a hallowed influence in the social circle, to take part in prayer-meetings, to become ministers, to become missionaries."[155] Baccalaureate addresses provided McCosh with one final opportunity to press home this message. In his 1876 sermon to graduating seniors, McCosh noted that there were divisions "not only in society at large, but in the individual; not only in the house, but in the heart." Although the Kingdom of God was slowly prevailing, more "Christian soldiers" were needed. "For this work and warfare you have received a suitable training in this college."[156] Princeton, the president believed, had done its part in preparing the nation's leaders to serve the nation and the kingdom of God.

In the fall of 1877, and despite the protest of one trustee, McCosh began to share his preaching responsibilities on Sabbath mornings with the other clerics on the faculty.[157] They had a similar message for students. John T. Duffield preached more confrontational sermons, perhaps stemming from his more pessimistic premillennialist theology. In one sermon, Duffield said he saw three types of Princeton students: those who loved the Lord, those who did not, and those "who amid conflicting hopes and fears, know not what answer to give." He tried to persuade this "third class" to come to Christ with pleas and even threats. "If any man *love not the Lord Jesus Christ*," he concluded the sermon, "that man shall be anathema, anathema—accused when the Lord shall come."[158] George Macloskie took a less threatening tactic. "Your country has plenty of lawyers and statesmen," he observed in one sermon, "but it is in great want of true ones: overflooded with doctors, engineers, professors in colleges, editors of newspapers, competitors in merchandize, but is in great want of honest men in all professions. . . . Whatever is your plan of life harken to God's appeal: be courageous to study and to do His will.[159] In all their preaching, McCosh and his clerical colleagues tried to keep the "ice of Agnosticism" from settling upon the campus and consequently upon American society. Moreover, once institutions like Harvard began to abandon compulsory chapel, Princeton found that its mandatory chapel policy was a valuable asset for cultivating public relations with parents and conservatives in the institution's larger community of support, for it signaled the college's commitment to established religious values in an age of change.

Though the primary purpose of obligatory worship was to help set students' priorities for this life and the one to come, its subsidiary purpose was to help to fashion the college into a community. "No bond will connect students and Professors so closely," McCosh contended in his debate with Eliot, "as the religion of love."[160] In the nineteenth century, chapel was the only activity that gathered the entire college together on a regular basis. A bell summoned students to assigned seats at morning chapel before breakfast and to vesper services in which McCosh or another minister led a brief devotional service.[161] Sabbath services followed a Presbyterian form of worship, and the Lord's Supper was occasionally celebrated at the evening service.[162] As the college grew, seating everyone became a problem until, after a lengthy campaign, McCosh persuaded a wealthy industrialist, Henry G. Marquand, to construct a new building at a cost of $130,000 in 1882. To ensure that this sacred space held a prominent place on campus, McCosh wanted it to have a bell tower "as high as the tower of Babel."[163]

The evangelistic and community-building aspects of religious worship coalesced in one event every college year. Since the early nineteenth century, the Presbyterian church annually celebrated the Day of Prayer for Colleges on the final Thursday of January. During the typical Day of Prayer, Presbyterians from the town gathered at First Church for a service in which they heard reports on the religious work at Princeton and in other colleges. On campus, afternoon classes were cancelled, and students were required to attend chapel to hear a guest preacher, while seminary students concurrently met in Miller Chapel for the same purpose. In the evening, college students were invited, along with the entire Princeton community, to hear a second sermon by the guest preacher. This service was followed by class prayer meetings organized by the Philadelphian Society where professors like McCosh, Duffield, and Murray spoke.[164] To arouse student interest in divine things, McCosh brought Princeton Seminary professors and some of the day's evangelical superstars to campus for the Day of Prayer. At the 1886 service, held just days before McCosh's second debate with Eliot, A. T. Pierson, a popular Presbyterian evangelist from Philadelphia, addressed the religious "doubts and questionings" of students.[165] Some students eagerly anticipated the annual event. Henry Van Dyke Jr., himself converted at the Day of Prayer in 1869, asked his father to pray that many of his classmates would come to faith during Princeton's services in 1870. For others, cancelled classes meant nothing more than, as one student put it, a much needed "holiday."[166]

McCosh was passionately concerned with the state of religion on campus. At virtually every meeting of the Board of Trustees, he assessed the spiritual condition of the campus; sometimes he observed that students were content to use the ordinary means of grace, but other times he discerned a special "work of grace." At the June 1884 meeting, for example, he reported, "There were prayer meetings held nightly in nearly every entry of the college buildings, and these were greatly blessed." "A number were led to devote themselves to God, and Christians had their faith and love quickened. For all this we give God thanks."[167] There was also a pastoral side to McCosh's presidency, and the college was small enough to allow him and others to minister individually to students. When one student lay ill in his room, the Reverends McCosh and Murray visited and prayed with him.[168]

McCosh and his colleagues invested large sums of time and effort to make Christian men out of boys. The weight of this paternalism, not surprisingly, made many students rather unruly. Walter Lowrie (1868–1959), a member of the Class of 1890 and the son of an important Presbyterian minister, organized with classmates the "N.B.D. Quartette," the "Never Been Drunk Quartette." They flaunted their rebellion against the temperance beliefs of the day, but did so rather quietly by meeting in Lowrie's room on Sabbath afternoons to drink beer and zinfandel instead of attending the sacred music concerts held on campus.[169] Other students found the college's Presbyterian ethos stifling. Writing to his father, one student said that John T. Duffield, one of the more prominent Presbyterian clerics on the faculty, was "a little touched in matters of the College's interest by what may be called Presbyterian Jesuitism."[170] The daily grind of required chapel not only elicited private acts of rebellion and passive resistance but also provoked more public acts of rebellion than any other mandatory college practice. While the college authorities hoped that sacred time would frame students' entire day, morning and evening chapel were the scene of some of the most notorious acts of irreverence. Some disturbances were juvenile, such as locking the freshmen out of the chapel building; sometimes destructive, such as tarring the chapel benches; and sometimes creative, such as placing a cow in the pulpit before a morning service. Disruptive behavior typically led to faculty admonishment and parental notification, and not infrequently suspensions.[171] Yet not all students hated the chapel services. Students gave positive reviews of interesting sermons regularly in the *Princetonian*, the campus newspaper, and occasionally requested from professors permission to publish a particularly moving sermon.[172] When the Dartmouth student newspaper and Cornell University's president belittled Princeton's practice as anachronistic, students defended the value of compulsory chapel. Yet, while students universally neither enjoyed nor condemned mandatory chapel services, many felt that they had too much of it. The "frequency of the exercise," as one undergraduate delicately put it, was the primary cause of student "inattention." Students grew weary of being treated like boys. More freedom, student sentiment ran, would actually achieve the desired results.[173]

Students not only rebelled against established religious practices on campus but also organized a fellowship that allowed them to be responsible for their own activities. At Princeton, the most important student-led fellowship was the Philadelphian Society. Next to Clio and Whig Halls, the two student debating societies, it was the largest organization on campus. Students had founded the society in 1825, in the manner of a secret society or fraternity, to provide themselves with an extracurricular life independent from the college administration. Students in the society held weekly meetings, prayer groups, Bible studies, and other activities. By the time McCosh assumed Princeton's presidency, the organization enjoyed the informal support of the college administration. To obtain full membership in the society, a student had not only to make an evangelical profession of faith but also to win the unanimous approval of all members. These membership requirements were not perfunctory exercises. One student, for example, regularly attended meetings for two years before he was finally elected a full member as a junior. In 1879, the society raised money from alumni to construct Murray Hall next to the chapel to serve as a home for its activities.[174]

The Philadelphian Society helped students carve out a place for independent religious activities free from faculty oversight. The society also played an active role in the building of an evangelical empire at home and abroad in the late nineteenth century. Luther Wishard, Class of 1877, who was president of the society in his senior year, helped organize the Intercollegiate Young Men's Christian Association, and, in fact, the Philadelphian Society became the college's chapter of the Y.M.C.A. Furthermore, Princeton regularly sent large delegations to regional Y.M.C.A. meetings and to D. L. Moody's Northfield Bible Conferences for college students. The 1886 Moody conference generated new interest in foreign missions. Two Princeton students, John N. Forman, Class of 1884, and Robert P. Wilder, Class of 1886, helped to found the Student Volunteer Movement for world missions, an organization that helped to send hundreds of college graduates overseas as missionaries.[175]

While the Philadelphian Society at Princeton enjoyed widespread support on campus, it was not the only source of voluntary religious activity among the student body. Special lectures by popular ministers, professors, and temperance advocates held at the seminary or in one of the town's churches regularly attracted large numbers of students.[176] Episcopal students, moreover, organized their own fellowship group, the St. Paul's Society, in 1876.[177] In the early 1870s, students even organized a temperance society, which McCosh, a lifelong temperance advocate, heartily supported.[178] A review of a typical week in the life of one devout undergraduate reveals just how many religious opportunities students had available. On Sunday, he attended George Macloskie's Sunday School Class at Second Presbyterian Church and morning worship in the college chapel, discussed missionary work with friends and participated in the class prayer meeting in the afternoon, and worshipped at First Presbyterian Church in the evening. Besides Bible class and morning and vesper services, he attended class prayer meetings on Monday, Tuesday, and Wednesday evenings, and the Philadelphian Society meetings on Thursday and Saturday evenings.[179] At least in the life of this student, Princeton was something of an Ivy League Bible college.

The students' and the administration's commitment to promoting the evangelical faith on campus coalesced in religious revivals. Though not annual events, revivals had been frequent at Princeton since Green's presidency. Many students expected to see "an increase of religious interest" sometime during their college days. "No class," Henry Van Dyke Jr. wrote his father, "has left the college without witnessing a revival of religion."[180] McCosh recalled that Princeton experienced "seasons of deep religious earnestness" five times during his presidency. The most memorable revival came in the winter of 1876. Learning that D. L. Moody and Ira Sankey were conducting services in Philadelphia, after having gained international fame in Great Britain, members of the Philadelphian Society asked the administration to bring the evangelistic team to campus for the annual Day of Prayer. Though Moody and Sankey were unable to come for that day, President McCosh and Charles Hodge persuaded them to hold services at Princeton the second weekend in February. With McCosh and many professors present, Moody told students why the old-time religion was still relevant. In one address, "Why should I be interested in the Son of God," the charismatic and irenic evangelist made a "calculated" effort to explain to the "honest doubters" why God was the source of all wisdom. The services were apparently so successful that McCosh cancelled Monday classes to hold another meeting. The local press reported that "Many professors, clergymen, students, and townspeople" accompanied Moody and Sankey to the train depot and sang "Hold the Fort" as they departed.[181] After being examined by McCosh, Murray, and the session of First Presbyterian Church, more than 260 students participated in a special communion service. At the following Board of Trustees meeting, McCosh joyfully reported that one hundred students had been converted, seventy "backsliders" had been aroused, and another hundred got "some heat from the burning fire." McCosh also reported that his weekly Bible class had been "a great pleasure" that entire semester. After hearing McCosh's report, the board passed a resolution noting that these events were "an answer to the prayers of the pious founders of the Institution."[182]

The revival of 1876 also fulfilled the educational aspirations of the successors of Princeton's pious founders. Many students came to personal faith and embraced the evangelical religion that they were being taught in chapel services and in the Bible, natural theology, apologetics, and ethics classes. This evangelical faith, McCosh and his colleagues believed, not only helped to balance the secular side of the curriculum but also provided a unifying center to the entire educational endeavor. Together, the program of religious education and the traditional classical curriculum enabled Princeton, like other institutions, to fulfill its historic mission of serving both the church and the nation. Though detractors questioned the relevance of the old-time "discipline and piety" curriculum in the late nineteenth century, Princeton, like other institutions, remained committed, sometimes aggressively, to this traditional arrangement. If, as McCosh and others believed, the Christian character of the nation depended now more than ever on having intelligent and virtuous leaders, then the college could not forsake its mission. The hegemony of evangelical Protestantism over American culture further bolstered their confidence that Princeton was successfully fulfilling the religious side of the institution's mission. Yet larger pressures were mounting both inside and outside of Princeton that were beginning to threaten the established convictions and customs associated with this religious mission. Princeton, like other colleges in the postbellum period, attempted to advance its education program and thus expand its civic mission. New demands on Princeton's civic mission raised questions about traditional religious practices and commitments. Ironically, McCosh and his pious colleagues on the faculty and Board of Trustees were themselves chiefly responsible for cultivating these new aspirations.

Chapter 2

Religion and University Aspirations, 1868–1888

"I have hitherto discouraged all proposals to make Princeton College a university," President McCosh told the trustees in June of 1885. "I am of the opinion," he went on to announce, "that the time has now come for considering the question." Seizing the momentum from what many in Princeton considered a victorious debate with Harvard's Charles W. Eliot, McCosh launched a formal campaign to make the College of New Jersey a university. He promised that his forthcoming paper, "What an American University Should Be," would fully explain how and why the board should take this next logical "step" in the institution's development. Although this was the first time that he officially broached the subject with the trustees, McCosh had long been laying the groundwork to build what he considered would be the crowning achievement of his presidency. With regard to this ambition, the trustees' minutes preceding this announcement reveal a calculated plan by McCosh to convince the board that the college was making exceptional progress toward becoming a university. He would begin by winning the board's approval for a particular reform or a new program on the grounds that it was essential if the institution was to advance its civic mission like its rivals, Harvard and Yale. Then, within a year or two, he would proclaim the reform or program a remarkable educational success and a major benefit to American society. The reorganization of biblical instruction in 1876 illustrates this process.

Although McCosh had promised the Princeton community in his inaugural address that he harbored no plans to "revolutionize your American colleges or to reconstruct them after a European model," the College of New Jersey experienced a gradual evolution toward becoming a university under McCosh's leadership.[1] Spurring consistent improvements in the faculty, curricula, and campus, McCosh led the college out of its antebellum educational doldrums, and, by 1885, he was ready, like his peers at Harvard and Yale, to lead his college into the promised land of American universities. The answer to the question he posed to the trustees was quite clear to McCosh: "I think we can make Princeton College, at the stage to which we have now come, a high class university."[2] The trustees, however, gave another answer and left McCosh outside of the promised land.

McCosh and his colleagues sought to advance Princeton's civic mission during his twenty-year presidency without compromising its religious mission. McCosh, the trustees, and many on the faculty strove to transform the College of New Jersey into a genuine university that would rival the likes of Harvard and Johns Hopkins in terms of academic character and, at the same time, provide a bona fide evangelical Protestant alternative to them. Specifically, they raised the institution's educational mission through academic professionalization and specialization. During this period, McCosh and his colleagues also attempted to broaden the institution's influence over the nation by increasing the size of the student body. Finally, in order to finance the improvements to the academic program and the enlargement of the student body, they expanded the institution's community of support beyond Presbyterian circles. Despite efforts to preserve Princeton's traditional religious customs and convictions, the educational advancements produced by academic professionalization and specialization began to alter the established pattern of how the institution fulfilled its religious mission. The growth of the student body and the expansion of the institution's community of support presented other challenges to the traditional religious mission of Princeton. While the immediate impact of these challenges appeared minimal, over time, however, they produced unintended, indeed ironic, results. Although Princeton did not become a university during McCosh's tenure, the educational achievements made during his presidency nevertheless paved the way for the institution's future transformation into a university that came, at least in name, in 1896. The advancements made during McCosh's presidency established new commitments and priorities that, when combined with larger intellectual and social changes sweeping across America in the final decade of the nineteenth and first decade of the twentieth century, would later lead to a dramatic reorganization of the relationship between Princeton's religious and civic missions.

Religion and Professionalization of the Faculty

Throughout his administration, McCosh and his colleagues sought to advance Princeton's civic mission by improving the college's academic program through the professionalization of the faculty and specialization of the undergraduate and graduate curriculums. These efforts strengthened Princeton's service to the nation. A more professionalized faculty expanded the frontiers of human knowledge and provided American society with practical technological advancements. A professional faculty also served the nation's educational interests by better equipping students to meet society's most urgent needs. McCosh and others were vigilant in their efforts to improve Princeton's education program. They did not want Princeton to fall behind other institutions. Throughout the 1870s and 1880s, McCosh and other professors constantly compared Princeton's progress to other institutions, most notably Harvard, Yale, and other elite East Coast institutions. The willingness of McCosh and others to compare Princeton constantly and publicly to other institutions reveals the depth of the institution's commitment to keeping pace with the latest educational advancements in the land. This rivalry involved more than institutional pride because serving the public's educational interests stood at the heart of the institution's mission. It was also in the institution's self-interest that it kept pace with other colleges and universities. As a private and nondenominational institution, Princeton depended heavily upon its larger community of support for both students and donations. If that community became convinced that Princeton was a bad investment, the college would find itself in dire straights. As McCosh and others tried to advance Princeton's civic mission, they had no intention of compromising the institution's religious mission. The professionalization of the faculty, nevertheless, slowly began to alter important convictions and practices traditionally associated with Princeton's religious mission.

During McCosh's presidency, professional academic competence became as important to the administration, and as much a prerequisite for hiring, as theological orthodoxy. In the fall of 1876, McCosh asked the trustees to establish endowed chairs in order to attract first-class scholars. "Great pains must be taken, if this course is followed, to secure for the new chairs men of known intellectual ability and scholarship. Why should not Princeton," McCosh asked, "be able in this respect to match any institution in the country?" With this new priority in mind, McCosh began to see Princeton's policy of hiring only Presbyterians as a liability and used the threat of competition from rival institutions to persuade the board to break the informal but solid hold of Presbyterians on the faculty. "I think it proper to add that I found the College a professedly religious one, and I have labored to keep it so. I found it a Presbyterian College, and mean to leave it so. But I reckon it perfectly consistent with this, that we should take at times an instructor belonging to another evangelical denomination, provided he be very eminent in his department. This will not injure but rather strengthen our Presbyterianism."[3] McCosh did not want to subvert the institution's historic relationship with the Presbyterian community nor undermine its ability to stand with the nation's best colleges and universities. Rather, he sought to open up the faculty to additions from the larger evangelical Protestant community to ensure that the college could find enough competent scholars. Although many historians have suggested that professional expertise and sound religion were mutually exclusive in the late nineteenth century, McCosh and his colleagues considered them perfectly compatible.[4] By recruiting scholars who were theologically orthodox, he believed, Princeton could best serve the educational interests of Presbyterians in particular and of the nation in general, thus leaving Princeton's religious mission intact. The trustees' Committee on Curriculum went to work formalizing a hiring guideline and presented a four-point policy at the next board meeting that was designed to improve the quality of the faculty and to preserve the institution's nonsectarian, evangelical Protestant character. First, if several candidates' qualifications were equal, a "decided preference" was to be given to graduates of the college. Second, the board was committed to "look only for men of the highest abilities and aptness to teach." Third, the trustees remained dedicated to hiring "no man to fill the high position of a Professor in this College, so noted in the past for its religious tone, who is not known to be a decided Christian." Finally, they wanted to hire "not only those who are known to be Christians, but those, as far as practicable, who are members of the Presbyterian church, or of those denominations closely allied to it, as the Reformed Dutch, and the Congregational."

Immediately after ratifying, without hesitation, this formal policy, the board approved the addition of three new professors to the faculty. The comments entered into the trustees' minutes about each reflect the new policy. Concerning the scientist Charles A. Young, for example, the minutes read, "He is what is known in New England as an orthodox Congregationalist."[5] McCosh was not simply patronizing the religious concerns of the trustees when he highlighted the theological sympathies of the new faculty. While attempting to improve the quality of the faculty, the president as well as his colleagues sought out candidates whose theological views were sympathetic to the religious mission of Princeton. "We do not require candidates to belong to any particular denomination," McCosh prefaced one confidential inquiry into a candidate's background. "But as we are professedly a religious college," he added, "we should like our instructors to be persons showing respect to religion and attending on its public ordinances."[6] Such inquires were typical in the "old boys network" that continued to operate within the more elite circles of late-nineteenth-century American higher education. Besides scrutinizing the religious affiliations of candidates, McCosh frankly forewarned applicants that they were expected to be in sympathy with the college's religious orientation. "Princeton has the first claim upon you," McCosh wrote one of the college's brightest graduates, William Berryman Scott, who was completing his doctorate at the University of Heidelberg. McCosh made it clear to Scott that he had no intention of hiring an atheist to assist Arnold Guyot in teaching geology. "You are aware that the Trustees and all your friends here are resolved in keeping the College a religious one." McCosh then asked Scott about his experience in London, Cambridge, and Germany. "If a man has the will in him he will only be strengthened in the faith by such an experience. It will be profitable to me to find how you have stood all this." What makes McCosh's warning all the more telling is the fact that Scott was the grandson of Charles Hodge and had been raised in his grandfather's household since he was a child.[7] McCosh and the trustees had rejected other and more prominent scientists, including the biologist David Starr Jordan of Indiana University and later president of Stanford University and the paleontologist Edward Drinker Cope of the University of Pennsylvania, because of their theological liberalism or overly accommodationist positions toward Darwinism.[8] With the broader hiring guidelines, McCosh thus assembled a faculty that was still friendly to Princeton's religious orientation. "The great body of Professors and Tutors give to their instruction," the trustees' Committee on Curriculum approvingly reported in 1881, "a decided religious tendency."[9]

Two editorials in the student newspaper, the *Princetonian*, more fully illustrate the meaning of this nonsectarian hiring policy and its popularity. "Very frequently instructors are chosen, not because of any superior literal or scientific ability," an undergraduate observed in the fall of 1876, "but on account of their theological beliefs and tendencies." The student complained that Princeton was guilty of favoring Presbyterians for its faculty, a practice perpetuating a sectarianism which degraded the institution: "So long as the infinitesimal difference between High Church and Presbyterianism in Mathematics prevents us from enjoying the benefits of a valuable and needed instructor, we think there is just cause for complaint and criticism."[10] However, while hiring only Presbyterians was considered sectarian, hiring professors from within the larger family of evangelical Protestant denominations was viewed as nonsectarian. When an 1885 article in the New York *Nation* condemned Yale's unwillingness to hire scholars whose theological beliefs were out of accord with the majority of the faculty as the "death knell" of the institution's academic credibility, the *Princetonian* defended Yale's and Princeton's so-called sectarian hiring policy:

> In a word Princeton is orthodox in Faculty; and, in teaching, while the thought of all ages and beliefs is examined, nothing inconsistent with Christianity is called truth. . . . We certainly doubt the culture whose broadness has room for unbelief and whose depth is the shallowness of uncertainty. Princeton in her time has refused "men of genius and learning" admittance to her Faculty for their very "secret" convictions, and so far from sounding the death-knell to her culture, finds in pure orthodoxy the protection against decay.[11]

Students recognized the logic behind the prevailing commitment to hiring a theologically orthodox faculty. Brilliant but unorthodox professors, according to this argument, imperiled the intellectual foundations upon which the nation's virtue depended. In the course of professionalizing the faculty in the 1870s and 1880s, McCosh, the faculty, and the trustees committed Princeton to a hiring practice that was nonsectarian, but had clear limitations.

The persistent importance of theological orthodoxy should not obscure the professionalization of the faculty during McCosh's administration. In 1868, the full-time faculty numbered ten; none had earned a Ph.D. degree and seven were Presbyterian ministers. During the first eleven years of his presidency, the institution hired scholars largely from outside the Princeton community. McCosh hired eighteen individuals at the rank of professor who had no previous connection with the college. Of these eighteen professors, five had earned Doctor of Philosophy degrees, and another was a medical doctor. Only three were graduates of the seminary.[12] McCosh also wanted professors who could teach and not merely listen to student recitations as a perfunctory exercise to be endured before returning to the laboratory or library to resume their research. McCosh, for instance, told Johns Hopkins University President Daniel C. Gilman that he was well aware of a particular candidate's scholarship but was really "anxious to know whether he is *also a lively teacher*."[13]

While bringing in scholars from outside of Princeton, McCosh also began to train scholars from within the community. In his "library meetings," McCosh regularly gathered his best students and younger professors to hear papers in a German-styled seminar discussion.[14] He persuaded the trustees to establish academic prizes and post graduate fellowships for advanced study at Princeton or abroad in order to arouse the interests of undergraduates in academic careers.[15] Princeton sent many of its top students, or as the Scottish president called them "me bright young men," to Europe for graduate degrees with the hope that some would return to teach at the college. Students had to have their studies approved by the faculty before they went off to Europe, although some left without well-designed plans. William Berryman Scott's recollection of "the folly and muddleheadedness" of McCosh's and Guyot's advice reveals an almost comical lack of planning. "I was practically told," he recalled, "'Go to England and study something with somebody and when you have done that, go on to Germany and study something else with some other body' (in Dr. McCosh's phrase)." Thomas H. Huxley, "Darwin's Bulldog," surely must have smiled when Charles Hodge's grandson entered his laboratory at the Royal College of Sciences in London to seek permission to study with him.[16] McCosh kept constant vigil on the students' academic and spiritual progress while they were away. After advising Henry B. Fine on his preparation to join John T. Duffield in teaching mathematics, he warned, "There is less religion in Germany than in any country I was ever in. . . . You will feel the need of living near to God."[17] After four years at Princeton, however, some students found German idealism, *Bildung*, and beer rather refreshing. "The narrow views of old fogy theologians who have worked the seat of their dogmatic opinions through," one student wrote from Germany to a classmate back at Princeton, "though they warped and tortured my mind in its early perception of what, taken from their lips without question, was thought to be philosophic truth, cannot influence the opinions of a riper age or stem in me the current of Idealism."[18] Not surprisingly, this student, unlike Scott and Fine, did not join Princeton's faculty upon his return from Germany.

In addition to sending bright students to Europe for advanced degrees, Princeton also began to train its own faculty through its burgeoning graduate program. The first Ph.D. was awarded in 1879; during the first ten years of the doctoral program, six of its graduates eventually returned to serve on the Princeton faculty.[19] Of the nineteen individuals hired at the rank of professor in McCosh's final nine years, thirteen were alumni, eight had earned Doctor of Philosophy degrees, and two held Doctor of Science degrees. As with the first generation of professors hired under McCosh, few of the new faculty members were alumni of Princeton Seminary.[20] Compared to Harvard's faculty in 1884, where only 10 percent of the professors reportedly held the revered Ph.D. degree, Princeton's faculty was actually more professionalized in this regard since more than a quarter had earned either the D.Sc. or Ph.D. degree.[21]

By combining the traditional function of the faculty, teaching, with the new academic endeavor, research, Princeton made significant advances to its educational program. With a growing number of young scholars on the faculty, McCosh persuaded the trustees to arrange the schedules of these professors in order to accommodate their research interests alongside their teaching responsibilities: "There is a discussion in the present day as to whether the grand end of a university should be to give instruction in the highest branches to the rising generation, or to widen the boundaries of knowledge." Although he still believed that the "primary aim" of the college should be undergraduate education, the president told the board in 1880 that "Princeton is now in such a position that its instructors may engage in original research." At the June meeting of the following year, McCosh bragged that several young professors were publishing books and scholarly articles. In the teaching and research functions of the university, McCosh, Eliot at Harvard, White at Cornell, and other university builders of the day, found that "these two kinds of work aid each other."[22] Better teachers and scholars also promoted Princeton's civic mission.

In some of the nation's larger educational institutions, McCosh told the trustees in the winter of 1882, professors were satisfied to give lectures and did not pretend to take any interest in the character of their students. There was, he observed, "less of this spirit in Princeton than in any of the large colleges of the country" but, he added, "it would be to shut our eyes to what is very obvious not to notice that the spirit to which I have referred is creeping in among us." McCosh correctly diagnosed the source of the problem. The younger faculty members were "anxious to give the most advanced teaching," yet less than interested in overseeing the spiritual lives of students. Sustaining the *in loco parentis* policy proved problematic as the younger professors defined their vocational responsibilities more exclusively in academic terms. In the spring of 1882, the faculty passed a resolution that declared all professors responsible for student discipline and then created a faculty committee to deal with discipline problems. That same semester, the faculty abolished the mandatory weekday vesper services and streamlined the morning service for the following year. In explaining this reorganization to the trustees, McCosh recalled that when he came to Princeton the entire faculty attended all services religiously. By 1882, he said that less than two-thirds of the faculty had time for vespers and the "scientific men" were most frequently absent. "Every one who knows human nature," the Calvinist minister explained, "must be aware that if prayers are not attended to by the professors they cannot be long forced on the students." But the faculty, he reminded the trustees, had renewed their commitment to attend morning chapel.[23] Five years later, the faculty's interest had again waned, as certain tutors, instructors, and junior professors were assigned to proctor morning chapel. William Berryman Scott remembered how "utterly disgusted" he was to learn he had been assigned the "dirty work" of "spotting" in morning chapel.[24] The professionalization of the faculty impacted more than just chapel services. James O. Murray, whose very position as Dean of the Faculty was created in 1883 as a result of the professionalization, was often frustrated by all the mundane responsibilities that fell by default upon his shoulders. He threatened to resign in 1885 unless the faculty helped him with his overwhelming bureaucratic responsibilities.[25]

Professionalization weakened the faculty's interest in the *in loco parentis* policy and daily chapel. The younger scholars' absence from daily chapel not only undermined the sense of community within the college but also left students with fewer role models of pious scholars on campus. Yet the elimination of vesper services and streamlining of morning chapel were minor compromises of Princeton's traditional religious mission. Students still had to attend morning and Sunday services and take apologetics, Bible, and ethics classes. Moreover, many first-generation McCosh-era professors, such as Theodore Whitefield Hunt, George Macloskie, and James O. Murray, regularly led chapel services and actively participated in the extracurricular religious lives of students. McCosh continued to tout the faculty's oversight of students' lives as a major selling point of a Princeton education. And many parents still expected professors to take an interest in their sons' welfare.[26]

The concentrated efforts to improve the professional quality of the faculty not only altered traditional customs and convictions associated with how the institution fulfilled its religious mission but also obstructed the full professionalization of Bible instruction during McCosh's tenure. Although McCosh had improved the academic character of biblical instruction to a modest degree during his administration, the overall professional stature of the subject lagged behind the other disciplines. After McCosh decided that his new scheme for giving Bible instruction in the fall of 1876 was inadequate, the trustees' Committee on Curriculum had recommended that a full-time professor of biblical instruction be hired "who may give his whole time to that service."[27] This plan was contingent upon increasing the endowment of the Lenox Foundation, which had financed part of McCosh's salary as Lenox Professor of Biblical Instruction. In the meantime, the board approved McCosh's second revised plan that assigned several professors with seminary training responsibility for teaching these classes. Ironically, this scheme worked so well that it kept Bible instruction from being fully professionalized during McCosh's presidency.

Religion and Academic Specialization

Inseparably related to the advances Princeton's made to its public mission by improving its educational program through the professionalization of the faculty were the achievements accomplished through academic specialization. Academic specialization meant that Princeton professors were uncovering the past secrets of human and natural history in such new fields as paleontology, expanding the boundaries of human knowledge in such new disciplines as psychology, and creating practical knowledge that assisted American industry in such fields as mechanical engineering. In addition, students, having studied these new disciplines, especially in the sciences, were better able to serve as useful citizens in a rapidly changing American society. In short, academic specialization advanced Princeton's civic mission to American society. Academic specialization manifested itself in three aspects of Princeton's academic program: the growth of the curriculum and elective system, the creation of the School of Science, and the founding of the graduate program. As with the professionalization of the faculty, McCosh and his colleagues sought to improve Princeton's educational program through specialization without endangering the institution's religious mission. Nevertheless, during McCosh's presidency academic specialization, like professionalization, gradually began to alter the established strategies designed to fulfill the college's religious mission.

McCosh, in his inaugural address, "Academic Teaching in Europe," explained that "Realists" held that the grand aim of a university was to "impart knowledge" in order to "fit students for the professions," while "Idealists" maintained that it should be "to improve the faculties of the mind, to refine the taste, and to elevate the country by raising up an educated body of men, who draw up all who are under their influence to a higher level." McCosh, ever the mediating Scottish philosopher, proposed that the higher end of a university was "to educate" and this, he believed, embraced both extremes. To fulfill this aim McCosh was unequivocally committed to the traditional curriculum of Greek, Latin, mathematics, the physical, and, of course, the mental and moral sciences. Yet this was not enough. McCosh believed that the time-honored curriculum had to be tempered with newer, and sometimes more practical, disciplines such as French, German, the natural sciences, and the "social sciences," which he defined as political economy, international law, and history. McCosh, however, was no educational egalitarian. His commitment to expanding the college curriculum—giving students, as he put it, the opportunity to study "the new branches, without excluding the old"—was grounded in the elitist conception of the traditional liberal arts curriculum. In contrast to the land-grant universities, for instance, McCosh rejected any training of "artisans, or merchants, or manufacturers, or farmers, or shipbuilders" in collegiate education. Although not dishonorable vocations, these were trades best learned from "practical men in shops and fields." Even professional instruction, according to McCosh, formed a "lower" though not entirely "unworthy" end. He did believe that a liberal arts education was a form of professional education in that it prepared students for further study in theology, medicine, or law. The ideal university, he insisted, was a *studium generale* that incorporated not only undergraduate education but also advanced study. Princeton, McCosh hoped, would become an "intellectual metropolis" like ancient Athens whose encyclopedic curriculum would exert "a refining influence" that would eventually work its way "down to the provinces."[28] This flourish of elitist sentiment reflected how McCosh and others conceived of Princeton's civic mission. Through academic specialization, they believed, Princeton would only increase the refining influence that flowed down upon the struggling nation.

In 1869, the same year that Eliot, the architect of the elective system, was inaugurated as president of Harvard College, McCosh initiated a revised curriculum that included a number of elective courses for juniors and seniors. "Without lessening the pace of the old studies," McCosh reported to the Board at the close of the first term of his educational experiment, "we have added new ones and allowed selected studies which have induced young men who never studied hard before to enter heartily upon their work." After giving a ringing endorsement to McCosh's modifications, the trustees approved another recommendation to introduce "each new branch of study" to the curriculum as finances permitted.[29] Princeton's new curriculum remained conservative in that it preserved the traditional curriculum for the A.B. program, but it became progressive in adding new academic fields. Over the course of McCosh's administration, the institution's progressive conservativism fostered academic specialization by compressing a large portion of the classical curriculum into the first two years of study and, correspondingly, by expanding both the number of elective courses students were permitted to take and the total number of courses offered in the undergraduate curriculum. In the 1869–1870 academic year, for example, juniors chose two of five and seniors three of eight courses. Fourteen years later, juniors elected three of seven and seniors five of seventeen courses. The clearest evidence of the impact of specialization on Princeton's academic program is the radical growth of the undergraduate curriculum. In the 1869–1870 academic year, seventy-eight different courses were offered to students. From the fall of 1869 to the fall of 1873, the year the School of Science opened, undergraduate course offerings rose to 121. This growth continued unabated for the remainder of McCosh's presidency: from 179 in 1878–1879, to 212 in 1883–1884, to 227 in 1888–1889, the final year which McCosh helped to plan.[30] The rapid expansion of new courses led to the reorganization of the curriculum in 1884 into three departments for the A.B. program: philosophy, language and literature, and mathematics and natural science.[31] Given his dogmatic commitment to the traditional curriculum and his antagonism to Eliot's lax elective system, McCosh has often been portrayed as something of an educational paleoconservative.[32] In view of the 290 percent growth of Princeton's undergraduate curriculum, the introduction of a modest elective system, and the increasing professionalization of the faculty under McCosh's tenure, such a portrait appears more like a caricature. Academic specialization had a revolutionary impact on Princeton's traditional undergraduate curriculum just as it had at Harvard and other progressive educational institutions.

After laboring through two tedious years of recitations in required courses, students found the lectures and laboratory experiments of their elective courses, which were typically taught by the second generation of professors hired by McCosh, intellectually refreshing. Henry F. Osborn, who graduated from the college in 1877 and served on the faculty from 1880 to 1891, sarcastically recollected that classes in the freshman and sophomore years were "deliberately chosen to smother any love of learning. . . . Through this quiet vale of education somnolence we burst into the new thought and vision of our junior year under the inspiring lectures" of such professors as Cyrus F. Brackett in physics.[33] Princeton's curriculum, McCosh told the trustees in the fall before his first debate with Eliot, was "now approaching the ideal which I have all along set before me." Unlike those colleges that had made the "fundamental mistake" of adopting the elective system wholesale, Princeton, in McCosh's estimation, had not abandoned its traditional educational mission. Instead, through a judicious combination of the "rudimentary and fundamental" branches of learning and a number of elective courses, Princeton kept students from becoming "one-sided and prejudiced" while exposing them to new fields of study.[34]

Academic specialization not only improved the traditional liberal arts curriculum in the 1870s and 1880s but also precipitated dramatic advances in the sciences at Princeton. The Civil War had interrupted plans to establish a school of applied sciences in 1864. After reforming the Academic Department, McCosh revived the plan in 1871. "It is absolutely necessary," the president insisted, "to have such an addition if we are to keep up with the other great Colleges of the country."[35] While Harvard had already established the Lawrence Scientific School in 1847 and Yale the Sheffield Scientific School in 1854, in the postbellum revolution in higher education the sciences were fast becoming prominent programs not only in the land-grant universities, such as the University of Michigan, but also in newly created private universities, such as Clark University and Johns Hopkins University. These institutions were successfully meeting the educational needs of a nation whose expanding economy demanded more specialized knowledge, science, and technology. By doing so, they also appealed to the quintessential American values of democracy, individualism, and prosperity and forged a closer relationship between higher education and American society. In order to keep Princeton abreast with other leading colleges, John C. Green, a trustee of the college who had made millions through his trading, banking, and railroad ventures, supplied $200,000 for the establishment of the school in June 1872 and donated another $100,000 to create a department of civil engineering two years later.[36]

The John C. Green School of Science inaugurated a new era in the college's civic mission. Although Princeton had valued the sciences before the Civil War, (Joseph Henry [1797–1878], for instance, had made important contributions in the field of electromagnetism before he became director of the Smithsonian Institution in 1848), the new corps of professors hired after the Civil War included a remarkable number of scholars. In fact, the college invested as heavily, if not more heavily, in the sciences as it did in the humanities. Of the thirty-eight full professors hired during McCosh's presidency, sixteen were hired in the sciences, mathematics, and engineering. With more professionally trained scholars on the faculty, academic specialization in the School of Science's curriculum inevitably followed. The number of courses offered in the school, for instance, rose from 87 in 1878 to 134 ten years later, a 65 percent increase.[37] A more important consequence of specialization came in the form of scholarly contributions. William Berryman Scott (1858–1947), for instance, was a vertebrate paleontologist of international fame. The astronomer Charles A. Young (1834–1908) was an authority on the sun and a pioneer in spectrum analysis. The mathematician Henry B. Fine (1858–1928) produced widely used college textbooks in algebra and calculus. The physicist William F. Magie (1858–1943) developed invaluable applications of X-rays. The college's first engineering professor, Charles McMillan (1841–1927), frequently consulted state governments on sanitation and water problems and even planned the town of Princeton's first sewerage system. The physicist Cyrus F. Brackett (1833–1915) was a prominent authority on electricity and close associate of Thomas A. Edison.[38] With each new discovery, invention, and journal article, "learning and culture," as McCosh described it, flowed down from Princeton to improve the quality of life and raise the state of scholarship in America.

The School of Science attracted increasing numbers of students eager for a practical education. In 1876–1877, the school had 47 students, 10 percent of the entire student body; and in 1887–1888, ninety-five students, 18 percent of the student body. Compared to the modest growth of students enrolled in the B.A. program, the growth of the School of Science was nothing short of remarkable.[39] McCosh attributed the growing popularity of the School of Science to the lack of adequate high school preparation in Greek.[40] Undoubtedly, with more students, especially from public schools, attending college after the Civil War, the absence of a Greek entrance requirement made the School of Science a more accessible route to a Princeton degree. Still, the popularity of the School of Science also has to be attributed to the practicality of the degree and its potential profitability in a culture that increasingly valued useful knowledge. Although McCosh and others encouraged the growth of the sciences at the college, they never expected this part of Princeton's civic mission to be so popular.

They did hope, however, to make graduate education an important part of the college's educational mission. "The time must soon come," McCosh warned the trustees in June of 1875, "when we must devote our energies almost exclusively to the promotion of higher learning. It is this, and not any mere external accompaniments which will enable us to keep our place, and stand on the same level as the higher Colleges in the country. . . and to rival the Universities of Europe."[41] Although the founding of Johns Hopkins was still a year away, McCosh recognized that without a genuine graduate program, Princeton was slipping behind other elite institutions. Yale had already awarded the first American Ph.D. degree in 1861 and Harvard had organized its graduate department in 1872. Although the institution continued the practice of awarding gratuitous A.M. degrees to any alumnus who could pay a small fee and had stayed out of jail, postgraduate courses had been added to the curriculum when the School of Science opened. Princeton awarded its first "earned" master degree in 1877.[42] "If we go on as we are doing," McCosh told the trustees in June 1878, "we will soon be able to raise our College to the same level in respect to scholarship, as the Great European Universities." With McCosh's prodding, the board approved a trustee committee's report on "post-graduate courses and the higher degrees" for the next academic year.[43] In addition to the Master of Arts, Master of Science, Doctor of Philosophy, and Doctor of Science degrees, the college began to offer Doctor of Literature and Bachelor of Divinity degrees in the 1886–1887 academic year and a Doctor of Philosophy in Science the following year.[44] Along with the B.D. degree, students in the Ph.D. program in philosophy could concentrate their studies on evidences of religion, theism, and ethics.[45] By adding depth and breadth to an ever-growing academic program, McCosh and his colleagues sought to keep up with the leading universities in America.[46]

Despite McCosh's dogmatic pledges to preserve Princeton's religious mission, academic specialization altered the traditional curricular component of religious education. Charles W. Shields, Professor of the Harmony of Science and Revealed Religion, continued to teach the same number of hours over the course of McCosh's twenty-year tenure, but the continually growing curriculum pushed a certain number of his courses from the required into the elective part of the curriculum. In the fall of 1882, for example, part of Shields's required science and religion class was made elective in order to make room for other courses. By 1888, Shields was teaching two one-hour required courses to seniors and two two-hour elective courses to seniors.[47] The effect was just the opposite on the ethics course. In 1868–1869, seniors took one two-hour course in moral philosophy and political economy. Academic specialization, as noted in the previous chapter, divided this course in two. But the number of hours devoted to the study of ethics did not decrease as a result. In fact, it actually increased to three hours under McCosh.[48]

While the role of the science and religion and ethics courses continued to play a significant, albeit modified, role in the curriculum of the A.B. program, religious instruction in these two subjects was nonexistent in the School of Science program. When the school opened in 1873, ethics and science and religion courses were slated to be given in the final year, but by the time the first senior class matriculated, only the ethics course was offered and only as an elective.[49] This course was then eliminated the following year. The growth of the number of undergraduates in the School of Science meant that an increasing portion of students did not have obligatory instruction in ethics, natural theology, or apologetics—only in Bible. Yet the absence of instruction in these fields was never formally addressed by the trustees or faculty. This gap between the institution's public commitment to religious education and its actual practices may have stemmed from the primacy of the A.B. program over the B.S. program, despite the protests of McCosh and others to the contrary. The growing popularity of the B.S. program, moreover, made the absence of instruction in ethics and apologetics all the more visible. The lapse, however, was not lost upon the students. "Behold the glaring inconsistency!" observed one student editorial in the *Princetonian*: "The supremely moral and metaphysical Senior who has had the Greek Consciousness and a low grade in Physics is required to spend one hour a week in reconciling his religious views with what science he may have stumbled on in chemistry. But the Scientifs [*sic*], who has reduced base-ball, foot-ball and even Chapel cuts to a science, are not allowed the slightest opportunity for reconciliation."[50] By the end of McCosh's administration, almost one-fifth of the student body was being left "unreconciled." Though religious instruction remained a major part of a Princeton education, academic specialization had reduced its place in the curriculum. McCosh's public commitment to the religious education of students notwithstanding, academic specialization was altering Princeton's religious mission.

More important than its immediate impact on the curriculum, specialization fostered intellectual standards and an academic culture that further segregated faith and knowledge. Specialization, in short, helped to cultivate scholarship whose theological ramifications were simply not discussed. Many of the younger scientists appeared to have little interest in drawing out the theological implications of their research without consideration of whether or not it might bolster or undermine belief in the existence of God. William Berryman Scott provides an excellent case study. After reading his grandfather's book, *What Is Darwinism?* he became an "ardent anti-evolutionist."[51] But he later recalled that during his studies with Huxley,

"By degrees my anti-evolutionary beliefs seemed to drop away from me; it was so obviously the best and most probable explanation of the facts of nature, that before I was well aware of it, I had become a fully convinced evolutionist."[52] Scott, who remained a lifelong member of First Presbyterian Church in Princeton and even advised McCosh when he was writing *The Religious Aspects of Evolution* (1888), separated his professional work from his personal faith. Whereas older professors like Guyot and Macloskie not only contributed to their scholarly disciplines but also published the "doxological" implications of their scientific work, the theological implications of Scott's work, in his most productive years as an eminent palaeontologist, fell beyond his scholarly purview.[53] Neither Scott nor any of his associates were raving Comtean positivists, yet they were, in a sense, practicing ones. While this development had little immediate effect on the program of evangelical religious instruction and worship per se at the college, its long-term impact had tremendous consequences. In one way, this trend toward compartmentalization simply continued the old division of labor between science and religion.[54] By excluding questions of religion from their work, these scholars were simply employing the scholarly methods of the day and abiding by the emerging professional standards of their fields. What was new was that, in the quest for greater scientific objectivity, scholars stopped asking the doxological questions of their work; theological issues simply fell beyond the pale of their scholarly scrutiny. The segregation of faith and knowledge heightened the walls separating the realms of nature and grace. This development at Princeton and other colleges and universities in the late nineteenth century, moreover, increased the cultural authority of the professionally trained scientists. Since they were the only true scientific scholars, not ministers and theologians, they alone were the only ones competent to comment on scientific matters. Whereas McCosh and his older peers hoped Princeton would serve as a bulwark against secular science, especially the ever-menacing threat from Darwinism, Princeton's younger scientists, unlike their mentors, remained conspicuously silent on theological matters in the name of scholarly objectivity. Despite efforts to advance Princeton's educational mission through greater academic specialization without compromising its religious heritage, specialization was curbing the younger faculty's participation in a traditional activity associated with the institution's religious mission. This was happening, ironically, with McCosh's and his conservative colleagues' blessings.

The Changing Character of the Student Body

At the same time that the college was improving its educational mission through the professionalization of the faculty and academic specialization, Princeton was attempting to attract more students to the college in order to exert a greater influence over the affairs of the nation. The expansion of the economy in postbellum America and the increased value of a college degree brought a flood of students to America's colleges and universities. Princeton, like other colleges and universities after the Civil War, experienced dramatic growth. During

McCosh's presidency, the undergraduate enrollment rose an impressive 86 percent, from 281 to 523.[55] At the same time, ethnographic changes in the nature of American society in general and in college-age population in particular altered the character of American colleges and universities. Through its increasingly larger graduating classes, Princeton hoped to extend the college's religious and education missions to American society without compromising either. Like professionalization and specialization, however, changes in the denominational, social, and vocational composition of the student body slowly began to alter the character of Princeton.

In contrast to the research university model of higher education advocated by more innovative reformers such as Daniel C. Gilman and G. Stanley Hall, McCosh held that the undergraduate college, not the graduate program, stood at the heart of the university. For it was on the undergraduate level that McCosh believed the critical task of educating, both intellectually and morally, the nation's future generation of leaders took place. Yet Princeton could not expect to have a significant impact upon the growing nation with only sixty or seventy graduates a year. Consequently, McCosh employed a variety of tactics to attract more students to Princeton. Some state institutions, such as the University of Michigan, created certification programs for the state's secondary schools in order to raise the quality of secondary education and ensure themselves a supply of qualified students. Since Princeton was not a state institution, McCosh could only lobby the state government to improve the public school system.[56] Since the fruits of New Jersey's improving public school system were not immediately forthcoming, McCosh sought alternative means to increase Princeton's enrollment. In December 1872, the president complained that Princeton faced a "great deficiency of feeding schools" and suggested that the trustees consider erecting "Classical Academies in the States or in the cities in which they reside." At the subsequent board meeting, McCosh announced that Henry C. Marquand had offered $100,000 to establish "an Academy of the first class" at the college.[57] The Princeton Preparatory School opened the same year as the School of Science, with three instructors and thirty-eight students enrolled in its four-year program. Unlike preparatory departments at other and usually smaller colleges, the Princeton Preparatory School was not a remedial program but rather a full-fledged boarding school.[58] Although the school never flourished and closed in the spring of 1880, even with the program, McCosh continued to challenge the trustees to help him establish closer relations with "feeding schools, such as the New England Colleges have." From the day a student enters one of New England's boarding schools, McCosh told the trustees, "he hears of no other college but Harvard, of its professors, of its students, of its games and generally of its vast superiority over all other colleges. It would require more courage than can be expected of a boy to resist this influence, and in the nine cases out of ten the boy destined for Princeton goes to a New England college, where the religion of his father's household is entirely ignored."[59] Three trustees answered McCosh's challenge. John I. Blair (1802–1899) placed a private school, renamed Blair Presbyterian Academy, on solid financial footing in 1875.[60] Four years later, the two residuary legatees of the John C. Green Foundation, Caleb Smith Green Jr. (1819–1891) and Charles E. Green (1840–1897), purchased the Lawrenceville Classical and Commercial High School and created the Lawrenceville School at a cost of more than a million dollars. As Harvard and Yale enjoyed close relations with the St. Paul's School and Phillips Andover Academy, respectively, only Princeton's name was spoken at Lawrenceville.[61] In order to recruit students from outside the Middle Atlantic region, McCosh visited prominent graduates and the nascent alumni associations across the country and arranged to have entrance examinations given, beginning in 1877, in major cities such as Chicago, Louisville, and St. Louis.[62] McCosh also asked Presbyterian ministers to send their best students to Princeton, but to his chagrin, they were not too helpful. "I have further to say that the ministers of religion, even in the Presbyterian Church," he told the trustees, "do not seem to be so alive as they might to the importance of sustaining a college which is sound in the faith, which keeps up all the ordinances of religion, which defends the faith in the college lectures and in the public press, in an age when in so many of our public institutions religion is ignored, or is being invidiously undermined."[63]

The expansion of the student body presented Princeton with new problems in how it fulfilled its religious mission. With more students, the college struggled not only to house all its students on campus but also to oversee *in loco parentis* their spiritual lives. After a freshman shot and wounded a sophomore, McCosh explained to the trustees that fifteen of the seventeen students involved in the incident were renting rooms in town and suggested that more dormitories would alleviate such problems. In fact, he was constantly asking the trustees to build more dormitories.[64] In commemoration of the reunion of the Old and New School branches in the north in 1869, Presbyterians financed the construction of one of the four dormitories, appropriately named Reunion Hall, built during McCosh's administration and helped the college fulfill its *in loco parentis* duties.[65] The moderately priced rooms in the newly constructed Edwards Hall, McCosh told the trustees in 1880, "will be felt to be a great boon by the sons of ministers, farmers, storekeepers and tradesman all over the country, but specially in the Middle States." Still, McCosh was not content. Princeton, he insisted, still needed to forge closer relations with feeder schools in order to keep up with the "three most successful Colleges in the country": Harvard, Yale, and Michigan.[66]

The growth of the student body not only posed new obstacles in how the college supervised the student body *in loco parentis* but also began to alter the religious character of the college. Princeton, in short, was starting to become more religiously heterogeneous. Over the course of McCosh's tenure, the religious composition of the student body, like the faculty, began to lose its distinctly Presbyterian character. The broadening religious composition contrasts sharply with the narrowing geographical makeup of Princeton's student body. While the College of New Jersey attracted students from a broad geographical region during its first seventy-five years, the antebellum period saw a contraction in the institution's national appeal. At the beginning of McCosh's administration, Princeton had become the educational bastion of Scotch-Irish

Presbyterianism from the Middle Atlantic region.[67] During McCosh's tenure, the college continued to draw students primarily from New York, New Jersey, and Pennsylvania, but at the same time, the percentage of Presbyterians began to decline, though they never lost a statistical majority. In the Classes of 1872, 1875, and 1876, the first available years that the religious affiliations of the graduating class were surveyed in the senior yearbook, the *Nassau Herald*, the number of Presbyterians averaged 69 percent. In the final three classes to graduate under McCosh, that figure had dropped to 60 percent. The movement toward greater heterogeneity is also reflected in the rise of different denominational affiliations expressed by seniors. In the Classes of 1872, 1875, and 1876, students belonged to eleven different churches. That number rose to eighteen for the Classes of 1886, 1887, and 1888.

Episcopalians began to attend Princeton in greater numbers, to the point that, in McCosh's final seven years, the proportion of Episcopalians among seniors reached 20 percent or more in four different years. The trend troubled McCosh. "It is a circumstance worthy of being mentioned," McCosh told the trustees in November of 1879, "that one-third of the number of the present Freshman Class are Episcopalians. I merely state the fact; I do not draw any inference from it." Despite Princeton's nondenominational charter, McCosh clearly did not want Princeton to lose its ties to the Presbyterian community. "Only I may be permitted to remark," McCosh added, "that friendly Presbyterian ministers, both within and beyond the Board of Trustees," could be of service to the college by directing students its way. McCosh was so uneasy about the increased number of Episcopalians at Princeton that when the college was making plans for the public dedication of the new chapel building in 1882, he did not want to have any Episcopalians involved in the service in order to avoid giving Presbyterian supporters the impression that the college was becoming an Episcopalian institution.[68] Episcopal students, not surprisingly, elected to attend Trinity Episcopal Church in Princeton on Sunday mornings. This, incidentally, created another problem for a college administration committed to ensuring that students attended Sabbath morning worship services. Supervising the Episcopal students' attendance at Trinity's services became an annual problem. The faculty organized a committee to investigate the problem and assigned certain Episcopal professors, including Charles A. Young, or paid monitors to take attendance.[69]

While Princeton was starting to lose its Presbyterian ethos, the new diversity was still distinctly Protestant in coloration. In the twenty classes that graduated during McCosh's tenure, only nine graduating seniors identified themselves in the yearbook as Catholic and only one as Jewish.[70] While no precise data is available to gauge the ethnic and racial composition of the student body in this period, an informal examination of photographs from this period gives one the impression that the college was overwhelmingly composed of white, Anglo-Saxon, and, of course, male students. A few Native American and Asian students, ethnic groups among whom Presbyterians had strong home and foreign missionary works, graduated from the college, and McCosh reportedly defended the right of an African American Princeton Seminary student to cross-enroll in his psychology class in 1876.[71]

As Princeton started to become more religiously heterogeneous, albeit Protestant, in character, it also was becoming more socially exclusive. While furiously working to establish closer relations with the expanding network of private boarding schools, McCosh was more than irked to be told that Princeton was gaining the reputation of being a "rich man's school." "There is an opinion," McCosh told the trustees in June 1878, "that our college is not a place for indigent and struggling students." This is, McCosh added, "a fact that while, happily I think, the number of students belonging to the wealthier classes has greatly increased, the application on the part of poorer students has diminished."[72] Princeton indeed was becoming a favorite college for the sons of the nation's moneyed families. Several developments reflect this trend. A sample comparison of two different years reveals that student costs increased significantly. For the 1868–1869 academic year, student expenses (tuition, room, board, fuel, and other fees) cost $465. By 1887–1888, this figure had climbed nearly 36 percent to $723.50. Given the fact that during the length of McCosh's tenure the American economy experienced a period of sustained deflation in which the composite consumer price index in 1868 had declined by 33 percent by 1887, Princeton was offering increasingly more expensive accommodations that appealed to the social sensibilities of wealthier students. Despite his own misgivings, McCosh himself was largely responsible for making Princeton attractive to wealthier students by overseeing elaborate plans to beautify the campus.[73] At the same time, the trustees also made heroic efforts to keep the college affordable for poorer students, actually cutting the cost for students who opted for more impoverished living conditions. For the same two years, the lowest cost of a Princeton degree actually fell from $366 in 1868–1869 to $326.25, over 12 percent, in 1887–1888. At Harvard in 1887, by comparison, expenses averaged an estimated $446.[74] The rise in the proportion of undergraduates who came from exclusive boarding schools also indicates that the college was attracting the sons of America's wealthier families. Of the 118 students in the Class of 1876 whose secondary education could be determined from their alumni files, 6 percent came from boarding schools, growing to 13 percent in the Class of 1883 and to 29 percent in the Class of 1891.[75] At Harvard, by comparison, 2 percent of the freshmen entering in the Class of 1878 and 12 percent of Class of 1888 came from boarding schools.[76] While exact data is lacking, the growth in the percentage of Episcopal students appears to have coincided with the rise of students from elite boarding schools such as the Episcopalian St. Paul's School. Another barometer of the growing affluence of Princeton students was the fact that some had private servants, "the mark of somewhat higher social position" on campus, which Dean Murray feared would only exacerbate social distinctions among students. In an effort toward democratization, McCosh had banned fraternities and secret societies from campus early in his presidency, but they were replaced by eating clubs that eventually formed in large part because of the lack of adequate on-campus dining facilities. By the end of McCosh's tenure, such clubs had begun to construct lavish homes on Prospect Avenue.[77]

In a nation without an apprenticeship system or a landed gentry, the college diploma more and more became the means by which people obtained professional respectability and financial success.[78] Unlike the more vocationally oriented state universities, Princeton, during McCosh's administration, remained committed to the more elitist traditional curriculum. Yet an increasing number of Princeton graduates were entering new professions such as banking. No complaints were heard from McCosh or the trustees that students were entering new professions, since they hoped that through them the institution could extend its influence over the country and could eventually benefit from the financial prosperity of faithful alumni.

One aspect of this trend, however, troubled McCosh and the older members of the board and faculty and revealed that despite impressive efforts Princeton was not fully succeeding in its religious mission. "I am sorry to report," McCosh told the trustees in June 1877, "that only 13 of our graduating class [of 114] have as yet devoted themselves to the ministry." But McCosh quickly pointed out the positive side: "I am convinced that not a few of those devoting themselves to secular pursuits will show themselves excellent Christians."[79] Since its founding in 1746, one important way in which the college had sought to fulfill its religious mission was to prepare students to enter the ministry. For the first time since the presidency of Samuel Stanhope Smith in the early nineteenth century, the number of graduates entering the ministry was dropping precipitously. According to one survey, 26.7 percent of the graduates of Princeton's Academic Department between 1871 and 1875 entered the ministry. Over the next fifteen years, the number of future clerics dropped to 17.5 percent for the period 1876–1880, to 12.6 percent for 1881–1885, but slightly rose to 17.7 percent for 1886–1890. In growing numbers, students entered careers outside of the three traditional learned professions. Between 1871 and 1875, 70.8 percent of the B.A. students became ministers, lawyers, or physicians, but that figure dropped to 51.8 percent for the period 1886–1890. Business became an increasingly attractive profession; the percentages of students entering that field rose from 12.6 percent to 24.5 percent for the same two periods. Not only was the religious and social composition of Princeton's student body changing but so were the vocational aspirations of its graduates.

In response to McCosh's concern about the decline in preministerial candidates, the board created a special committee comprising McCosh, two trustees, Reverends Jonathan F. Stearns and C. K. Imbrie, and two professors, Reverends John T. Duffield and Lyman Atwater, to investigate the problem. The committee subsequently reported that this decline reflected a national trend. According to the same survey of thirty-six leading private and public colleges and universities, during the periods 1870–1875 and 1886–1890, respectively, 15.7 and 11.2 percent of the graduates of these institutions entered the ministry. Princeton was still doing better than its chief rivals: for the period 1886–1890, for instance, only 4.3 percent of Harvard's graduates, 6.6 percent of Yale's graduates, and 2.6 percent of Michigan's graduates entered the ministry.[80] To arrest this trend at Princeton, the newly formed committee proposed raising additional scholarship money for preministerial candidates.[81] Although the college received little formal support from the Presbyterian Church, U.S.A., the vast majority of the endowed scholarships were already designated for the education of preministerial candidates and the sons of Presbyterian ministers. In fact, the college had been giving the sons of Presbyterian pastors free tuition for decades, even when scholarship funds did not fully cover the cost of this practice, simply by remitting their tuition.[82] When the trustees had discussed altering this policy in 1881, Lyman Atwater told the board that he believed that the college would "suffer in numbers, order, moral, and religious tone, and even in its treasury, from the abandonment of this policy." The influential trustee Charles E. Green agreed and the practice remained unchanged.[83] While finding students interested in the ministry rather than new and more lucrative professions was a problem, financing their education would not be one so long as the president, influential professors, and trustees remained committed to the special interests of its older constituency regardless of the cost or the institution's nondenominational standing. While every effort was made to advance the ministry as a worthy vocation, the decline of preministerial students, as during the administration of Samuel Stanhope Smith, was a telltale sign that fundamental changes were taking place within American society at large and the institution. Although changes in the religious and social composition of the student body, as well as the vocational aspirations of students, did not directly challenge Princeton's religious mission during McCosh's presidency, they did alter the institution's character. Like the nation as a whole, the religious character of Princeton was changing in ways that could not be entirely foreseen or forestalled.

Religion and the Expansion of Princeton's Community of Support

As Princeton advanced its educational mission through professionalization, specialization, and growth of the student body, it also expanded its community of support beyond, though not to the exclusion of, the northern Presbyterian church. Although the immediate impact of the expansion of the institution's community of support was negligible, its long-term consequences for the future direction of the college were monumental. Besides becoming a new source of financial support for the college, the alumni became more directly involved in the affairs of the institution. As the social and vocational composition of the alumni changed, so did many of their aspirations for the college. For the first time since Samuel Stanhope Smith's presidency more than two generations earlier, a tension emerged between Princeton's religious and educational missions. This tension was a result of a growing conflict between the trustees, who considered Princeton a de facto Presbyterian college and were chiefly interested in seeing it uphold the religious values of the larger Protestant community, and the alumni, who valued Princeton's officially nondenominational standing and were concerned with its efforts to serve more national educational interests.

When McCosh became president in 1868, the college, like the nation, was still struggling to overcome the crippling effects of the Civil War. In the fall of 1860, enrollment had reached an all-time high of 314 students. It fell to 221 in the following year and dropped even further as students withdrew to take up arms. Some of the investments from the endowment had failed during the war, and by 1868 the entire endowment totaled slightly over $500,000. Perhaps most critical to the financial future of Princeton, there was, as one of McCosh's disciples aptly described it, an "absence of enthusiasm" for the college among the alumni.[84]

To finance his ambitious plans to revitalize the college, McCosh broadened the institution's larger community of support. After his inauguration, McCosh immediately turned to wealthy individuals already associated with the college and Princeton Seminary. John C. Green, who was a trustee at the seminary, donated $100,000 to the college at McCosh's inauguration, another $100,000 for a new library building, and financed, as noted above, the creation of the School of Science.[85] John A. Stewart (1822–1889), president of the United States Trust Company, and Robert Carter (1807–1889), a New York publisher, both gave generously to the college.[86] McCosh also reached out into the larger Scotch and Scotch-Irish Presbyterian community. Robert Bonner (1824–1899), an Irish immigrant and publisher of the New York *Ledger*, and Robert L. Stuart (1806–1882), principal stockholder in his family's candy and sugar business, were equally philanthropic.[87] Mary Stuart, Robert L. Stuart's spouse, deeded $100,000 to the college on the condition that the institution at no time would "be at variance with the principles of the Christian religion or antagonistic to the leading doctrines and general beliefs of the Presbyterian Church of the United States."[88] McCosh also encouraged the expansion of alumni associations whose identification with the college was not primarily based on the Presbyterian faith or Celtic race. As he told the trustees in 1884, McCosh traveled literally thousands of miles, "visiting Alumni Associations over the country with a view of keeping up an interest in the college in their districts."[89] Over the course of his presidency, McCosh enlarged the college's community of support beyond Princeton to include not only Presbyterians but also the alumni as a whole. Yet of the nearly $3 million McCosh raised for the college during his presidency, the greatest part came from people associated with the Presbyterian church.[90] With time that would change, as many alumni made fortunes.

Not until the very end of McCosh's presidency did the broader social, religious, and vocational composition of the alumni make inroads into the Board of Trustees. In contrast to Harvard, where it is said the president led, and Yale, where the alumni led, at Princeton the trustees dominated the college's affairs.[91] As with most other private nondenominational institutions, Princeton's board was self-perpetuating, and the trustees guarded this power as a sacred calling. Twelve of the twenty-five members, excluding the college president and state governor, an *ex-officio*, were required to be ministers by the charter. At Harvard, where Eliot described the ideal trustee as a "business or professional man" who was "public minded" and "successful in his own calling," no clerics served on the Corporation between 1884 and 1913, and among the alumni-elected Board of Overseers, the number of ministers dropped from six in 1875 to one in 1895.[92] Yet a religious requirement of some sort for board members was not an outdated practice in the late nineteenth century. When the University of Chicago opened in 1893, for example, its charter stipulated as "forever unalterable" that the president and two-thirds of the trustees had to be members of the Baptist church.[93] However, Princeton's near majority of clerics stood out as an exception even among private institutions. One survey of the boards of trustees of fifteen private colleges and universities revealed that in 1880–1881, 33.3 percent of the trustees were ministers.[94]

Throughout Princeton's history, Presbyterians, who had a strong interest in the affairs of Princeton Seminary, dominated the college's Board of Trustees. Between 1812 and 1868, thirty-six of the college's trustees were directors, trustees, or professors at the seminary.[95] Although not a formal requirement, it was practically a given that a trustee would be a member of the northern Presbyterian church. This pattern remained unchanged until nearly the end of McCosh's presidency. When McCosh was inaugurated, seventeen of the twenty-five trustees had connections with the seminary as alumni, professors, directors, or trustees. McCosh encouraged the close but informal relationship between the two institutions. Of the thirteen board members added during the first sixteen years of McCosh's tenure, eight had some association with the seminary.[96] At the other end of Dickinson Street, the college's presence at the seminary also remained strong. In addition to the individuals just mentioned, eleven other of the seminary's directors, seven of the trustees, and six of ten of the professors between 1868 and 1888 were alumni of the college. Three seminary professors also taught at the college some time during McCosh's administration.[97] Also telling of the close relationship between the leadership of the college and the seminary is the fact that two of the college's most influential professors, Lyman Atwater and Dean Murray, simultaneously served on the seminary's Board of Trustees for a total of forty-six years.[98] A brief review of some of the activities shared by the college and seminary further contextualizes the fraternal relations between the two institutions. The seminary faculty marched in the inaugural processions of McCosh and of his successor. In 1883, the college and seminary formed a joint committee to organize a celebration to honor the four hundredth anniversary of Martin Luther's birth. Also, the college invited the General Assembly of the Presbyterian Church, U.S.A., meeting in Philadelphia in 1888, to visit the campus.[99]

McCosh, often erroneously described as a liberal Presbyterian who freed the college from the tutelage of the seminary, did more than just encourage the close relationship between the college and the seminary. McCosh served on the seminary's Board of Directors from 1869 until his death in 1894.[100] McCosh had a strong affection for the theology propounded at the seminary. As a minister in the Church of Scotland, he fought against theological liberalism. He even joined the conservatives in forming the schismatic Free Church of Scotland, which sought to preserve the purity of the church from liberalism. His service at the seminary, therefore, was more than good politics. "There is a theology," McCosh told students

called the orthodox, sometimes known as the Princeton theology, defended
by good and great men some of them seeing the truth still more clearly in
the mansions above, but some of them still spared to us. It is in fact simply the Reformation theology. It is the theology of Paul and all his epistles.
If any of us have in any respect fallen beneath the spirit of Jesus and of the
Word, let us acknowledge our fault and amend; but we dare not meanwhile abandon the truth which has been held so firmly and defended so
ably among us.[101]

McCosh, like many of his colleagues on the board, had a strong personal
interest in the welfare of both the college and seminary, and thus he nurtured the
historic bonds between the two institutions.

Despite the conservative nature of many of their shared interests, McCosh
struggled to get the college's trustees to approve his progressively conservative
vision for Princeton. Although the minutes of the trustees are often too brief,
and the Victorian figures characteristically too polite, to reveal the exact nature
of their interaction, the private correspondence of one professor and the memoirs of several alumni, professors, and trustees suggest that McCosh often had
difficulties with the educational conservativism of the board. Shortly after
McCosh's inauguration, Charles W. Shields told his father that the new president faced a great task in "harmonizing"—Shields was always harmonizing—
"the conflicting parties" of "the older men," led by Professor Lyman Atwater,
and "the new rising party."[102] William Berryman Scott recalled that many of the
"hidebound conservatives" on the board were "a first class nuisance" who un-
ceasingly meddled in the administration of the college and adopted "an insuf-
ferably patronizing and condescending tone" toward the faculty.[103] McCosh
employed a variety of tactics to get what he wanted for "me college," at times
even pleading with the trustees. After reviewing the improvements achieved at
Harvard and Yale because of their trustees' work, for example, McCosh begged
Princeton's trustees to catch "a like spirit."[104] At other times he brazenly challenged them, as was the case with regard to the college's need for feeder schools.
And he was not above "table-thumping" and threatening the trustees, as exem-
plified in his resignation, in order to get a School of Philosophy.[105] Despite the
board's conservativism, McCosh successfully persuaded them to approve every
major reform he proposed, including the revision of the curriculum, the creation of the School of Science, and the professionalization of the faculty. Disagreements among board members notwithstanding, McCosh's reforms did not
grip the campus with dissension. Shields wrote his father that, to the contrary,
McCosh's reforms had created "a very good tone" among the students and a
"better feeling" within the faculty because he had left "few questions of controversy remain to trouble the authorities of the college."[106]

While the Board of Trustees did not always quickly approve McCosh's progressively conservative plans for the college, many alumni and professors who
had graduated during his presidency did certainly catch the "spirit." The broader
background and interests of the alumni embodied the spreading influence that

Princeton aspired to have on the nation, and yet their identification with Princeton was not always as narrowly religious, as was the case with many of the trustees. The first manifestation of tensions between the college's religious and civic missions surfaced when the alumni appealed to the trustees in 1882 for more direct representation, and therefore power, in the leadership of the college. The will of the alumni, who were more interested in promoting the institution's national educational interests, crossed that of the trustees, who were more interested in preserving the institution's religious commitments. Such demands from alumni were not unique to Princeton. At the same time in New Haven, for example, there was a "Young Yale" movement, where younger alumni, likewise representing the broadening social composition of the emerging professional culture, campaigned for greater representation on the Yale Corporation.[107] Twice Princeton alumni had failed to persuade the trustees to create an ancillary Alumni Advisory Council to the board, a move that would have been less threatening to the power of the trustees than direct alumni representation. In the fall of 1882, they raised the ante with an even bolder proposal: the Chicago alumni club sent a memorial to the trustees requesting that all new trustees be elected directly by the alumni, instead of by the board itself, until one-quarter of the board was filled with their representatives. John T. Nixon (1820–1889), a judge and John C. Green Foundation legatee, William C. Roberts (1832–1903), a Presbyterian minister, and Samuel Bayard Dod (1838–1907), the director of Stevens Institute of Technology, all alumni of the college and closely associated with the seminary, formed a committee to study the proposition. Their response, approved by the entire board, disclosed a tension between those interested in meeting the educational needs of the Presbyterian community and those who had more national objectives. The trustees rejected the proposal, claiming that it did not promote the "prosperity and best interests of the college." "The Presbyterians," they explained, "as a rule are a stable people. . . . They are not apt to favour new and untried methods so long as old and tried methods worked well." Noting that the alumni memorial had pointed out that both Harvard and Yale had given representation to their alumni, the board coolly and rhetorically asked, "To what good result?"[108] The alumni's reply was immediate: contributions dropped.[109]

After this setback, McCosh worked to get more like-minded, progressive trustees elected to the board. As a result, in the final three years of his administration, when the board elected seven new trustees, all seven were alumni and, except for one, served on the board through the turn of the century. Two were attorneys, John K. Cowen (1844–1904) and James W. Alexander Jr. (1839–1915), whose father and grandfather were legendary members of the seminary's faculty. Three others were Presbyterian ministers: David R. Frazer (1837–1916) graduated from the former New School Union Theological Seminary in New York; George B. Stewart (1854–1932), an alumnus of and professor at Auburn Theological Seminary; and Francis B. Hodge (1838–1906), scion of one of Princeton's most prominent families. Lastly, Moses Taylor Pyne (1855–1921), a wealthy businessman, may have best represented Princeton's version of Eliot's ideal "public spirited" trustees. As an Episcopalian, Pyne was also the first non-Presbyterian trustee for several generations.[110]

Together, these men mark the influx of a new breed of trustee who more fully shared McCosh's university aspirations for Princeton. Like many of the professors hired in McCosh's final nine years as president, fewer of the trustees had direct associations with Princeton Seminary. Although they came late to McCosh's administration, in subsequent years they would shape the course of the institution. Until then, the college would remain a de facto Presbyterian institution serving the nation's educational interests as the older, more conservative trustees defined these two missions.

The University Campaign

In light of the impending crisis in higher education which he saw coming, McCosh had told the trustees on the eve of his first debate with Charles Eliot, "It is well that we have our own house in order to meet it, as I believe we have in these new branches, which the generosity of our friends has enabled us to establish, and which enable us to compete with any other college in the country."[111] In the months before he launched his formal campaign to persuade the board to make the college a university and in order to remind them of the distance that Princeton had advanced in less than twenty years, McCosh paraded some of the institution's successes before the trustees, including the creation of the School of Science, the establishment of a graduate program, the construction of new dormitories, classroom buildings, and a museum, and the increase in the endowment. He noted at one of the board meetings in the fall of 1884 that besides the full program of biblical instruction, the "interesting and vital questions involved in the relation of religion and science, are expounded and illustrated."[112] McCosh may have accepted the invitation to debate Eliot as a God-given opportunity to defend Princeton's traditional curriculum on a national stage, but he hoped to use any political capital ensuing from the debate to convince the trustees that the best way to provide a competitive educational alternative to Harvard was to make the evangelical College of New Jersey into a university.

In the summer of 1885 and at the age of seventy-four, McCosh publicly launched the university campaign with his address "What An American University Should Be." "It now lies with the college authorities," McCosh insisted, "to determine whether they are prepared to make Princeton college a university." Repeating many of the same educational positions he had expressed in earlier speeches and in his debates with Eliot, McCosh presented a compelling argument for why some of the nation's better colleges in general, and Princeton in particular, should take the next step forward in their evolutionary development. The critical difference between a college and a university, in McCosh's estimation, was that the former was only "a teaching body" whereas the latter served larger and more national educational interests by promoting "higher learning." Since the B.A. program still held an "essential place in a university," a university would continue to fulfill its traditional civic mission by providing the nation with "a body of truly educated men in all our professions." In fact, many colleges, he observed, performed a useful purpose "so far as they teach thoroughly the fundamental and disciplinary branches of literature, science, and

philosophy, and also impart religious instruction to give a high tone of the mind."
Although not a biological Darwinist, he was something of an educational Darwinist. Many weaker colleges, he believed, "will give way, by the force of that
law of our world, 'the struggle for existence,' which demands that the weak die
while the strong survive." To McCosh, some of these survivors should evolve
into universities: "The grand aims of the university should be to promote all
kinds of high learning, in literature and science, in the liberal arts and in philosophy." In McCosh's estimation, the civic mission of a university did not
subvert but rather transcended that of a college.

McCosh offered a clear plan for transforming a college into a university.
First, a university did not need to built *de novo*, but should use the foundation
laid by the preexisting college. By adding new departments and faculty, the
college becomes a *studium generale* and "need only to mount one step higher
and to organize into a university." Finally, an American university did not need
to slavishly "mold itself upon any European model," but rather should shape its
organization according to its own unique circumstances. For this reason, a university, "so situated as not to be within reach of law courts or hospitals, would
not wish to have a law school or a medical school." In a postscript to the published version of the address, McCosh appealed directly to the alumni to support his quest to make their alma mater a university: "All the late advances in
this college have tended toward making it take a comprehensive character, such
as is implied in the name 'University.'"[113]

From his initial proposal in June 1885 until the board reached its final decision in
June 1887, McCosh presented the proposal in the most conservative terms. In February 1887, after first reviewing the virtues of the college's curriculum, McCosh
told the trustees, "I think every educated man will allow that in all this we have a
Studium Generale which is the essence of a university. . . . True, we have not Medicine, nor Law; but professional schools are not necessary to a university, which is a
place of learning, and not of the practical arts." McCosh was equally candid about
the institution's need to raise more endowed professorships and to expand further
the curriculum. Yet he did not ask for millions of dollars to construct an impressive
college to house the graduate program.[114] In McCosh's estimation, the college had
reached a critical juncture in the advancement of its educational mission: "Princeton
College is so situated that it must either go forward or back."[115] At four different
board meetings, McCosh challenged the trustees to make the college into a university in order to keep pace with other elite institutions. "All our rival colleges, Harvard,
Johns Hopkins, Pennsylvania, are called universities, and the step lately taken by
Yale will compel us," he reasoned, "if we are wise, to do the same, if we are to rank
with these institutions in public estimation."[116] By keeping up with other elite universities, McCosh was confident that the investment would bring rich dividends,
increasing Princeton's enrollment, which had stalled in the mid-1880s, and spurring
contributions, which had dropped off in comparison to earlier years. Becoming a
university, McCosh hoped, "may gain us a new period of prosperity."[117] The faculty, at least according to the depiction of William M. Sloane, a second-generation
McCosh-era professor, wholeheartedly supported the proposal. Nearly all the alumni

associations, McCosh reported, had passed resolutions in support of it as well. Moreover, students had wholeheartedly approved their president's aspirations.[118] McCosh assured the trustees that extending the civic mission of Princeton posed no threat to the religious mission of the institution: "It should always be understood that this proposal does not contemplate any change in the historical character of the College in respect of religion or the kind of learning and subjects taught."[119] It was probably no coincidence that McCosh at this crucial juncture challenged Harvard's president to a second debate over the role of religion in collegiate education.

In response to McCosh's university proposal, the Board of Trustees in November 1886 asked two trustees, Caleb S. Green and Charles E. Green, to join the Committee on Curriculum, comprising some of the board's most conservative members, to investigate the matter.[120] After more than six months of discussion, the committee made its recommendation to the entire board at graduation 1887. Before hearing the committee's report, McCosh made one final plea. He assured the board that the faculty would not demand a salary increase and that the alumni would increase their contributions if their alma mater was a university. "Everything," he concluded, "that is good in a college can be retained in a university, its good order, its discipline, *its religion.*" The committee report raised three questions related to making the institution a university: What "University courses" were being taught, what legal steps needed to be taken, and, most decisively, was it "expedient for the college to assume the name of a university?" In answer to the first two questions, the committee found that Princeton already offered thirty-two university courses, and Judge Green determined that the board would need to get legislative approval for any title change. When the answer to the final question was read into the minutes, surely McCosh's heart dropped: "We answer that in our judgement it is *inexpedient* at this time to do so."[121] However, the trustees had not repudiated the idea of becoming a university, but only resisted the move at this juncture. The reluctance of the board stemmed from its fiscal and, more important, educational conservatism. Although fear about surrendering traditional religious convictions and customs were not the central reason why the board resisted McCosh's university aspirations, they were inseparably intertwined with the trustees' conservatism. In a day when revolution was sweeping across American higher education, many universities, such as Harvard, as McCosh himself observed, were abandoning the classical curriculum and traditional religious education. The trustees were hesitant to make Princeton a university if such a move would eventually threaten the historic educational and religious commitments of the institution. Through the university campaign, tension between the institution's dual missions clearly emerged along the same lines as had the disagreement over alumni representation on the Board of Trustees. The alumni, who shared McCosh's university aspirations, represented the institution's more national educational interests. The older members of the trustees, who shared McCosh's conservative philosophy of higher education, represented the educational ideals of the college's Presbyterian community.

At the fall meeting of the trustees, three months later, McCosh announced his retirement, effective at graduation 1888. "I leave the College," he concluded, "in a healthy state intellectually, morally, and religiously."[122] "I have sought all along," the president told the trustees at the following board meeting, "to make our college rank with the higher colleges of the country, always retaining our *special religious character*." Through the professionalization of the faculty and academic specialization, McCosh had advanced the civic mission of Princeton without compromising the institution's religious mission in any immediate and obvious way. Enrollment, like the college's larger community of support, had also expanded over the past twenty years. Yet McCosh was not entirely satisfied with the institution's progress. He issued a stern challenge to the trustees: Princeton must either "vigorously march forward, or slide backward into the position of a second-rate college. If an impression gets abroad among our bright young men that there are these colleges in the country more advanced than Princeton, they will go to those instead of coming here."[123] Princeton, according to McCosh, could further advance its civic mission by becoming a university without jeopardizing its historic religious mission. In his autobiographical reflection of his administration, McCosh recalled the failed university campaign with heartfelt disappointment. "At one time I cherished a hope that I might be honored," he said, to see the college become a university. "I would," he promised, "have embraced in it all that is good in our college; in particular, I would have seen that it was pervaded with religion, as the college is." Yet, he added, "I have always been prepared to contend with the enemies of the college, but I am not ready to fight with its greatest benefactors." One day, he hoped, Princeton could achieve this broader public goal while preserving its religious heritage. "The college has been brought to the very borders," he concluded, "I leave it to another to carry it over into the land of promise."[124]

Chapter 3

The Travails of Becoming a University, 1888–1902

In bringing the College of New Jersey to the brink of university status, McCosh stood on the verge of the promised land. As the nineteenth century was coming to a close, alumni, professors, and trustees in Princeton, like those at many other American colleges and universities, were eager to see the institution position itself so that it would be better able to meet society's need for moral and thoughtful leaders, practical knowledge, and scientific expertise once the nation entered the twentieth century. With the future direction of the institution hanging in the balance, the choice of who should succeed McCosh divided the college community along the same lines as had emerged earlier over both the alumni's attempt to secure direct representation on the Board of Trustees and McCosh's failed attempt to make the college a university. Whereas McCosh harmoniously upheld the college's dual mission through the breadth of his scholarly interests, the warmth of his evangelical piety, and the force of his personality, the two candidates who vied for the presidency after his resignation possessed only a portion of McCosh's qualities and appealed to only one part of the Princeton community.

Francis L. Patton appealed to those primarily, though not exclusively, interested in preserving Princeton's heritage as an evangelical college. According to McCosh, the "older men" among the trustees, faculty, and alumni "want a minister," and on these grounds, the forty-five-year-old Patton seemed like a natural successor to McCosh. A native of Bermuda, Patton had graduated from University College of the University of Toronto; had attended Knox College, also of the University of Toronto; and had graduated from Princeton Theological Seminary in 1865. Ordained that same year in the Old School Presbyterian church, he served as pastor of a church in New York City. Cyrus H. McCormick (1809–1884), the farming machine magnate and patron of conservative Presbyterian causes, persuaded Patton to accept a position as the Professor of Didactic and Polemical Theology at the Presbyterian Seminary of the Northwest (later McCormick Theological Seminary) in Chicago in 1873. Patton had opposed the rising tide of Protestant modernism on American soil, just as McCosh had opposed the moderatism in the Church of Scotland and had helped organize the schismatic Free Church of Scotland a generation earlier. Patton lived up to his title as a polemical theologian when, in 1874, he challenged the orthodoxy of Chicago's most popular pulpit prince, David Swing. In the first—and one of the most colorful—trials of the reunited Old and New School northern Presbyterian church, Patton gained a reputation as a "heresy hunter" for driving Swing from the church. In 1881, A. A. Hodge offered Patton the opportunity to join the "ablest old-school theologians in the Church" at Princeton Seminary. Through a gift of one of the college's and seminary's greatest benefactors, Robert L. Stuart, Patton became the first Stuart Professor of the Relations of Philosophy and Science to the Christian Religion. Besides his work at the seminary, Patton began teaching ethics at the college in 1883 and became the Professor of Ethics the following year. In both faculty positions, Patton was committed to propagating McCosh's views on the harmony of science, religion, and morality.[1]

If Patton represented the evangelical side of McCosh's legacy, the second candidate, William M. Sloane, represented the educational side. Sloane appealed to those more interested in advancing the civic mission of Princeton, a group that wanted to transform the college into a national university. As a graduate from Columbia College in 1868, Sloane (1850–1928) served as the personal secretary for the noted historian George Bancroft in Berlin in 1872, and earned a Ph.D. at the University of Leipzig in 1876. Among the first group of bona fide scholars recruited by McCosh, Sloane taught Latin at Princeton from 1876 until he was appointed Professor of History eight years later. Sloane represented the "New Princeton," as a friend described him to Woodrow Wilson: "He believes in gentlemanly scholars who can be men of affairs; he is opposed to pietism as such . . . and is nothing of a prig."[2]

With the encouragement of the younger faculty members, a group of influential New York City alumni actively resisted the election of Patton. Some critics wanted an experienced administrator to bring efficiency to the growing business of the institution. Others complained about Patton's British citizenship. Students feared that they would be "admonished, sermonized, disciplined after John Knox fashion." Many felt his Chicago days were an embarrassment to the institution.[3] McCosh himself offered a plan that he hoped would pacify both sides. He recommended making Patton president and creating the position of vice-president for Sloane. "Either alone will be opposed," McCosh wrote a confidant. "Let both have a place and all parties will be reconciled."[4] Unwilling to bow to outside pressures, however, the older trustees rejected McCosh's advice and elected the Presbyterian minister. "I hope," McCosh wrote a former student after the decision, "Dr. Patton may turn out as a practical a man as he is a powerful dialectician."[5] Patton himself expressed no misgivings. Yet as powerful educational, social, and theological forces washed over the nation at large and the College of New Jersey in particular in the 1890s, Patton proved to be a rather paradoxical character, and Princeton during his presidency manifested a mixture of tensions and contradictions between its evangelical mission and its function as a public institution.

Speaking at the annual New York Alumni Club dinner as president-elect in March 1888, Patton employed his wit and charm to overcome the criticisms of his antagonists. Princeton professor William Berryman Scott recalled that Patton had temporarily converted "the opposition by a truly great speech, the greatest speech I ever heard from any man."[6] In reference to his lack of administrative experience, Patton drew laughter when he said that he "ought to be able to understand a balance-sheet as well as to grade an examination paper." Alluding to his predecessors, Witherspoon and McCosh, he quipped, "It is manifest that there is more joy among the Alumni over the one President who has been naturalized than over the ninety-and-nine that have needed no naturalization." He candidly addressed, however, the issue of how his faith would influence his administration: "I shall not shrink from saying further that we must keep Princeton a Christian College." No church, he believed, is "broader in her catholicity," or has "taken a deeper interest in the cause of higher education" than the Presbyterian church. "But," the Presbyterian minister quickly added, Princeton "is too big to be sectarian." Patton explained how this commitment to nonsectarian Christian education would be worked out at the officially nondenominational College of New Jersey: when an "Episcopalian comes to us and is under the supervision of his rector on Sunday, he shall not hear a philosophy taught to him on Monday that undermines his faith in God. We mean that he shall deal with its facts and problems of life under theistic conceptions; this is something more than daily prayers in chapel, though we shall have them, too."[7] By the end of his speech, Patton had his opponents standing on the tables, waving their napkins, and yelling in a frenzy of enthusiasm. "Such a personal triumph," Scott recalled, "I never witnessed before or since. He had converted his opponents and began his administration with the heartiest good wishes of all parties."[8]

At his inauguration, and perhaps to the surprise of many in the audience, Patton proclaimed that "Princeton is already a university, if there ever was a university in the world." He elaborated a model of higher education that distinguished three characteristics of a university, according to which Princeton had already achieved university status. First, Princeton was a *studium generale*, "a place of general resort," where students pursued liberal studies. Second, Princeton enjoyed academic freedom, within certain bounds, he quickly added; the trustees and professors were obliged to ensure that there would be no confusion in the academic disciplines over religion. A communist would not teach political economy, Patton reasoned, "nor is it part of university freedom to open the halls of science and philosophy to men who teach atheism or belittle the Christian faith." Finally, he argued, Princeton was "not bound by party politics or sectarian Theology." Although Patton supported a strict Old School Presbyterianism within the church, at the university he favored the broader evangelical nonsectarianism of his predecessor. He praised the mission of the nearby seminary, but believed that the college had a different organization and purpose. For this reason Princeton was autonomous from political partisanship and theological sectarianism. He promised to consider a change of title at the appropriate time.[9]

Patton pledged to meet the interests of all in the Princeton community by preserving the historic nonsectarian Christian character of the institution while making steady improvements to its undergraduate and graduate programs. Patton, like McCosh before him, professed his commitment to a vision of Princeton that better met the educational needs of the nation and helped to preserve the Christian character of American society. However, during Patton's tenure the once harmonious relationship between the institution's religious and civic missions became antagonistic as four controversies rocked the college: a crisis over the chaotic state of the undergraduate curriculum, a debate over whether a nonsectarian institution like Princeton should hire a professor who happened to be a Unitarian, a controversy with Presbyterian temperance advocates over student drinking, and, finally, a crisis over the absence of a genuine graduate school in the university. While not the subject of controversy inside of the university, evangelical Protestant theology and the traditional program of religious education designed to inculcate the nation's future leaders with faith slowly began to loose their place as the unifying center of the curriculum and the larger intellectual life of the university for both educational and intellectual reasons. Taken together, these controversies convinced many younger professors, trustees, and alumni that upholding nonsectarian evangelical Protestant ideals and meeting the nation's educational needs as a university were not compatible endeavors. As educational, intellectual, and social changes swept across the Princeton campus and the nation, a deep-seated incongruity between the institution's dual missions emerged. Patton himself embodied many of these contradictions. And to many of the more progressive members of the university community, Patton and his old-fashioned educational and theological commitments hindered, not advanced, Princeton's public mission. This chapter, in short, explores the travails of an institution whose evangelical heritage came into conflict with its expanding civic mission. The chapter will examine first the growing crisis centered on the chaotic state of the ever-expanding undergraduate curriculum and then the quiet collapse of support for the place of evangelical Protestantism inside the university. The remaining controversies that further widened the gap between the institution's civic and religious missions will then be explored.

Crisis One: Curricular Chaos and Religious Education

"I believe," Patton professed at his inauguration, "that the learning acquired at a university should be regarded as valuable for its own sake rather than for the sake of the use that is to be made of it." Patton's elitist conception of the educational mission did not preclude professional training, but, he insisted, "it will naturally take a subordinate place in our plans." Patton believed that Princeton's traditional curriculum of Latin, Greek, literature, history, political economy, philosophy and natural science, along with the "partly obligatory and partly optional" system, best educated students for public service.[10] As Patton told the trustees in June 1896, his guiding principle was that "it is the first and most imperative duty of the University to lay a sure foundation of *liberal culture* during the four years leading to the bachelor's degree."[11] While Patton professed commitment to the educational philosophy of McCosh, the first crisis of his presidency concerned the relevance of the old-time educational theory for an institution aspiring to be a major national university in the twentieth century. This crisis, which involved no divisive public manifestations, simmered slowly for years among the younger faculty and trustees, and gradually eroded Patton's credibility as an effective president.

"We can enlarge upon the *trivium* and *quadrivium* of medieval learning," Patton observed at his inauguration, "only as in the slow processes of evolution new sciences are born and new departments accepted as solid additions to knowledge."[12] The three forces that drove the enlargement of the curriculum in the past decades continued to accelerate it during Patton's presidency: first, the corps of young scholars recruited by McCosh wanted to offer courses and conduct research in new subspecialties. Latin professor Andrew F. West (1853–1943) proudly reported in the *Educational Review* in 1894, "Every important division of human knowledge" is being added to the curriculum so that Princeton will "realize her full university life, as well as a great development and organization of higher studies for university students."[13] The second force, symbiotically related to academic specialization, was the professionalization of the faculty, or the creation of, as William M. Sloane described it, "the aristocracy of scholars."[14] The growth of the undergraduate curriculum begun in the previous decades continued unabated in the final decade of the nineteenth century. In the first year of Patton's presidency, 227 different undergraduate courses were offered, and, by the fall of 1901, the curriculum had grown nearly 50 percent to 332 different classes.[15]

The culture of professionalism further encouraged the growth of the elective system. McCosh had earlier warned that if the college did not keep abreast of the latest intellectual developments, students would go elsewhere. Patton agreed, likening the university to a business in which the trustees were the partners, professors the salesmen, and students the customers.[16] Judging by the growth of enrollment, the college was doing a good job of selling a Princeton education: undergraduate enrollment more than doubled, from 574 in 1888–1889, to 963 in 1895–1896, and to 1233 in 1901–1902.[17] Princeton had not bowed to the "scientific cult," philosophy professor Alexander T. Ormond insisted, but remained adamantly committed to the "republican equality" of a curriculum where "pure science and pure literature" stood side by side.[18] But Princeton, as Patton had promised in 1889, deliberately made modifications so that a student would find the curriculum "more directly helpful in his life work," especially to those interested in attending law or medical school.[19] Furthermore, while Princeton graduates still entered the three traditional professions, more students went into business than ever before.[20] In response to the growing culture of professionalism, as well as to scholarly interests of the faculty, Princeton gradually compressed the traditional curriculum into the first two years and expanded the elective system in the final two years. In 1888–1889, 34 percent of the A.B. courses and 22 percent of the courses for the general science degree in the School of Science program were electives. These figures rose, respectively, to 47 percent and 23 percent in 1895–1896 and to 50 percent and 42 percent in 1901–1902.[21]

The final decade of the nineteenth century at Princeton was one of spectacular growth, both in the number of students and in the number of course offerings. This growth, which was characteristic of many universities in the late nineteenth century, had one major effect on the undergraduate program at Princeton: chaos reigned, or at least the undergraduate program seemed to lack any sense of coordination. After Patton's first round of curricular revisions, one senior complained to his mother that he found the new system "so complicated that it is difficult to get started."[22] In the first term of the 1888–1889 academic year for A.B. students, seniors chose three courses from a list of fourteen electives; by the fall of 1895, A.B. students chose six electives from a list of fifty-one courses, and in the fall of 1901, seven from seventy courses.[23] The increasingly diverse vocational aspirations of students and the growing intellectual interests of the faculty fueled the expansion of the curriculum. On the one hand, this growth indicates the institution's commitment to its civic mission. Princeton, at least in theory, encouraged its faculty to enlarge the frontiers of specialized knowledge, and, as important, offered its graduates a depth of learning appropriate for a society that more and more valued practical knowledge and professional expertise. On the other hand, the near absence of order in the curriculum subverted these advances as well as the foundation of "liberal culture" upon which they supposedly rested. While attempting to preserve the classical curriculum and provide students with the opportunity to concentrate in one or two disciplines, the cumulative effect of the curriculum's lack of balance contributed to what professor William Berryman Scott described as the intellectual "stagnation" that characterized much of Patton's presidency.[24]

Patton's indifference toward slothful students further compounded these problems. The discipline slowly slipped out of the old-time "discipline and piety" educational philosophy. While the burden of maintaining the *in loco parentis* policy had been shared by the president and the faculty in previous generations, the professionalization of the faculty in the 1890s left Patton chiefly responsible for ensuring that students attended to their studies. Yet Patton demonstrated little interest in the matter. Increasing numbers of students went to college merely to get their degree as a passport of sorts to professional success, and loopholes in the curriculum allowed such students to take the easiest courses. Another problem was the presence of a sizable group of "special students" who attended the college for up to four years but did not earn a degree. These students skipped class with impunity and lowered the overall academic character of undergraduate education. The future novelist Booth Tarkington (1869–1946), for example, transferred to Princeton as a junior special student and spent most of his time writing plays for the Triangle Club that he had helped to organize.[25] The proliferation of extracurricular activities, especially football, further distracted students from their studies. In the 1896–1897 academic year, for example, forty-one different clubs ranging from the Banjo Club to the St. Paul's School Club thrived on campus. In this decade, Princeton developed something like a cult of college life, described romantically in the short stories of the *Nassau Literary Magazine*.[26] Some of Princeton's younger faculty members, moreover, were not serious scholars, or at least not in the classroom. One student complained to his mother in 1900, for instance, that French professor Arnold Guyot Cameron (1864–1947), grandson of Princeton Professor of Geology Arnold

Guyot and son of Princeton Professor of Greek Henry C. Cameron, devoted many of his lectures to describing the best wines from different regions in France.[27] For many professors, Princeton as a university in the 1890s was doing a worse job of educating the nation's future leaders than it had done as a college twenty years earlier.

As it turned out, while Patton shared McCosh's philosophy of higher education, he placed it within an Oxford and Cambridge model of the undergraduate education. Perhaps drawing on his own undergraduate experience at the University of Toronto, which was modeled on the British system, Patton believed that the undergraduate population could sustain only a small group of serious and self-motivated intellectuals. The others would profit merely socially from their college experience. Only on future playing fields, such as the halls of the Senate or America's corporate board rooms, would the benefits of a student's Princeton days be fully realized. To Patton, efforts to enlarge the circle of earnest students by reform was an unrealistic dream. One faculty member recalled that Patton was unopposed to "the spectacle of the young barbarians all at play, and went so far as to believe that their friendship might in the future years be a source of benefit to the university." Another said that Patton openly stated in faculty meetings that he had "no belief in discipline and that it was good for a young man to come to college, even if he did no more than rub his shoulders against the buildings."[28]

Although Patton professed publicly that mandatory religious education was an essential part of a Princeton education, his indifference toward student behavior spilled over into his attitude toward chapel and Sunday worship services. While the faculty continued to mete out *pensums* and even expulsions, Patton did little to correct, and actually contributed to the perpetual problem.[29] After going to morning chapel in December 1897 and finding neither Patton nor a faculty member present to lead the service, an alumnus berated the president in a letter to the *Daily Princetonian*. Ironically, at a recent meeting of the trustees, the board had recommended that Patton pay closer attention to overseeing the chapel services.[30] Walter Lowrie (1868–1959), who lived with the Patton family in Prospect in 1900, recalled the president's "indolent" attitude toward leading morning chapel, and another Princeton alumnus called Patton the "ablest and laziest" preacher he had ever heard.[31]

According to McCosh's philosophy, chapel services not only nurtured students' faith but also drew students and professors into a community bound together by Christian love. During Patton's administration, two pressures, in addition to the president's own indifference, helped to undermine the latter purpose. By 1898, the college had grown so large that it was impossible to seat the entire student body and faculty in Marquand Chapel at one time. Only the daily absence of a large number of students made it possible to accommodate everyone who showed up for the service in the building. As a result, in the fall of 1898, the weekday service was divided in two; freshmen and sophomores worshipped at 8:00 a.m. and juniors and seniors at 8:45 a.m.[32] Further undermining the community-building purpose of the daily service was the fact that an increasing number of faculty members, preoccupied with their own professional pursuits, did not attend the services. One student exposed the inconsistency between Princeton's professed commitment to the *in loco parentis* policy in a survey published in the *Nassau Literary Magazine* and the fact revealed by this survey that on average only two professors attended the daily service.[33] The Day of Prayer provides another illustration of how educational and professional concerns impacted established evangelical practices. Because classroom time was becoming so precious to professors, the annual event was shifted from the last Thursday in January to a Sunday in February. Despite student petitions that voluntary attendance would make the services more of a genuine worship experience, the trustees still defended mandatory attendance on the old *in loco parentis* grounds and repeatedly urged the professors to attend chapel. Still, the trustees, having sensed that daily chapel had lost its vitality, searched for new ways to make the services more attractive. After much discussion, they devised a new plan to invigorate the services: they purchased new hymnals from the Presbyterian Board of Publication.[34]

The chaotic state of the curriculum and Patton's permissive attitude toward lazy students did not go unnoticed. Faculty dissatisfaction with the curriculum cast doubts on the appropriateness of the old-time educational philosophy for a major American university. After the college became a university at the sesquicentennial celebration in 1896, the minutes of the faculty and trustees read like a litany of dire needs for revising the undergraduate program. To address the curriculum crisis, as well as a number of other problems, the trustees organized a Committee on University Affairs. In June 1897, their report graciously commended Patton for being "fully acquainted" with the university's problems, but recommended "that discipline be administered with [a] firmer hand" and "that studies be better co-ordinated." Yet Patton took no concrete steps to resolve the problem. So the following year, the committee again complained about the "grave, perplexing, and intricate problems" surrounding the administration of discipline for more than eleven hundred students, and about the "incorrigibly indolent" students who "endeavor to secure their degree with the least possible outlay of effort." And again they castigated a curriculum that allowed students to "take the easiest courses available." Many younger professors, Arnold Guyot Cameron notwithstanding, were zealous evangelists for their particular disciplines and wanted to ensure that the students shared in their enthusiasm. "There is a feeling in our Faculty," Patton admitted to the trustees in December 1897, "that the intellectual activity of the undergraduates is very far from being what it should be."[35] The younger faculty envisioned that once Princeton took the title of university the undergraduate program would begin to flourish, not languish. They grew increasingly frustrated with Patton's inaction as the opportunities to shape American culture passed with each graduating class. So the faculty themselves took steps to advance the university's educational mission. In the fall of 1900, the faculty, led by Andrew F. West and William F. Magie, organized a committee to press for reform; other chief proponents of reform were among the alumni of the McCosh era. Professors, like Woodrow Wilson (1856–

1924) and Henry B. Fine, gave their support to any proposal that would help fulfill McCosh's dreams and their hopes of making Princeton an outstanding university. Instead, Patton had his own solution. He wanted Princeton to adopt a "pass-honor" system, like that at Cambridge University, in which the best students pursued an aggressive plan of study and the rest of the student body took their degrees in a more gentlemanly fashion.[36] Without the adoption of this solution, Patton deemed most of the curriculum problems as "incurable."[37] In fact, Patton's plan would have only institutionalized the problems of student laxity and curricular chaos. In a day when many colleges and universities were offering purely utilitarian education designed to increase personal profit and serve the most basic societal needs, such as agriculture, the very idea that Patton would be content to see Princeton give "gentlemen's degrees" railed against the values historically associated with a classical liberal arts education. This larger educational context makes Patton's proposal all the more preposterous and explains why the faculty never gave Patton's recommendation serious consideration. The final report of the faculty Committee on University Reform, which underwent five revisions, lamented that the "condition of scholarship among our students was one of demoralization." They proposed sweeping reforms so that the curriculum would be "co-ordinated in such a way as to provide a curriculum of *liberal culture* of the purely collegiate type."[38] Content to permit the indolent to have their Princeton degrees, Patton killed the report when he argued against it and urged that it be referred to committee. If the university performed an essential civic purpose by providing the nation's future leaders with a classical liberal arts education complemented by a judicious offering of elective courses in more practical and specialized areas of knowledge, then the confused state of the undergraduate curriculum, in the eyes of West, Wilson, and other younger professors and trustees, represented a betrayal of Princeton's public mission. The crisis over the undergraduate curriculum not only epitomized the subversion of Princeton's civic function in the opinion of many professors, trustees, and alumni but also gave credence to their doubts about Patton's ability to fulfill their vision of Princeton as a truly national university.

The Decline of Evangelical Protestant Hegemony

While Patton was indifferent to problems with the undergraduate curriculum, he was eager to defend the Christian purposes of that curriculum. "True culture," the president explained in his inaugural address, "culminates in religion." "The education therefore that is to prove a valuable element in civilization cannot be indifferent to the claims of divine truth." It was not enough, in Patton's estimation, for students to be skilled in mathematics, familiar with the great literature of the world, and aware of the latest developments in science.[39] According to Patton's educational philosophy, the liberal arts curriculum had to foster the faith of students. "Physics," Patton insisted in another address, should make a student "more truthful, Astronomy more reverent, Literature more genial, Social Science more benevolent, Philosophy more believing."[40] Besides this "indirect religious influence," Patton assigned a positive role for compulsory religious education, which played a key role in fulfilling the institution's religious mission. "I believe in the education," he observed at his inauguration, "that fits men not only for life but for eternal life." Since the intellectual and spiritual well-being of students, and ultimately the welfare of Christian civilization, depended heavily upon the university's religious education program, Patton insisted, like McCosh before him, that there could be no compromise in this area. "The best Christians," Patton believed, "are the best citizens."[41]

During Patton's presidency, traditional evangelical convictions and customs continued to enjoy a prominent public place within the life of the institution. Religious instruction and worship, philosophy professor Alexander T. Ormond told an audience at the National Education Association meeting in 1897, were "cardinal points" in a Princeton education because they balanced the liberal arts curriculum and provided "spiritual life and inspiration" for students.[42] Yet stirring only slightly beneath the surface of this conviction were important changes taking place that did not portend well for the traditional religious mission of Princeton. To be sure, public professions about the importance of evangelicalism's role within the university were not empty rhetoric. In fact, during Patton's tenure certain advancements made in religious instruction raised the academic character of the discipline and brought it more in line with the general professionalization of the rest of the curriculum. At the same time, many within Princeton, as in the Protestant church in general, found theological modernism to be an intellectually attractive alternative to the old-time religion. By the 1890s, ecclesiastical battles replaced theological debates between Old School Presbyterians and more liberal Presbyterians. While the university continued to promote a broad evangelicalism in its official program of religious education, the Presbyterian battles of the decade and the larger intellectual debates they represented began to undermined the evangelical theology's place as the unifying center of the college's intellectual and institutional life. The ecclesiastical battles of the decade fractured the theological consensus within the university. Despite the prominence of several university officials in the efforts to curb the spread of liberalism within the Presbyterian church, many within the university community sided against the Old School party and wanted to distance the university from the Presbyterian church in general and Princeton Seminary more particularly. Meanwhile in the classroom, Patton and others became increasingly defensive in their advocacy of traditional evangelical beliefs. At the same time, as faculty participation *in loco parentis* in the religious life of the student body decreased and the activity of the Philadelphian Society increased, the Y.M.C.A. became the university's de facto campus ministry in the 1890s. When compared to the absence of mandatory religious education at Harvard, Johns Hopkins, Cornell, and elsewhere in the 1890s, Princeton's conservative public stance toward matters religious easily masked the significant changes that were taking place in how the university sought to fulfill its religious mission. These changes raised doubts in the minds of many within the university about the allegedly intellectual character and nonsectarian nature of evangelicalism and its role within an institution devoted to serving national, not parochial, interests.

In postbellum America, theological controversies struck almost every Protestant denomination. Southern Methodists, for instance, forced Alexander Winchell out of his position at Vanderbilt University in 1878, and Southern Baptists did the same to Crawford H. Toy at Louisville Seminary the following year, both for their questionable views on Genesis. Yet the real debates over modernism took place north of the Mason-Dixon line. A number of factors combined to make the northern Presbyterian church particularly susceptible to theological controversy: a tradition of a learned clergy, an ascending series of church courts, a steadfast commitment to a seventeenth-century confession, and the fragile peace that had been struck at the reunion of the Old and New School factions in 1869. At Princeton, several prominent college professors and trustees played important roles in upholding Calvinism, inerrancy, and the Scottish commonsense views of truth—in short, defending the traditional faith by rejecting modernity. These events not only involved important Princeton figures but also influenced the status of evangelicalism on the campus and played an instrumental role in determining how conservatives would response to theological modernism in the future. In 1889, dozens of Presbyteries sent overtures to the General Assembly asking the denomination to consider a revision of the church's confession. Some wanted to write a new creed that was wider in scope and more progressive in orientation. Others simply hoped to tone down some of the harsher elements of the calvinistic Westminster Confession by modifying its teaching, for example, on infant damnation. While many conservative Presbyterians, including Princeton College graduate and Princeton Seminary professor John DeWitt, argued against revision, the leader of the campaign to stop revision was Francis L. Patton. By persuading the moderates that the radicals really sought to abandon Calvinism in order to create a broad church, Patton exploited the division between proponents of radical revision and proponents of modest revision.[43] As the proposed revisions slowly worked their way through the Presbyterian system over the following two years, support gradually dissipated for even the slightest revisions, a dissipation that can be attributed in large part to the heresy trial of Union Seminary (New York) professor Charles A. Briggs. In *Whither? A Theological Question for Our Times* (1889), Briggs (1841–1913) had argued that the true and historic orthodox Reformed Protestant tradition had been perverted by modern confessional "betrayers" who propagated a vile "orthodoxism." "Orthodoxism," according to Briggs, was "haughty and arrogant," assumed "the divine prerogatives of infallibility and inerrancy," refused "to accept the discoveries of science or the facts of history," and preferred "the traditions of man to the truth of God."[44] The leading "betrayers," in Briggs' opinion, taught at Princeton Seminary. Conservatives were irate. Even the theologically irenic James McCosh castigated "the living heresies" of Briggs with a satirical reply in *Whither? O Whither? Tell me Where* (1889).[45] Matters only got more heated when, in his inaugural address to the John T. Robinson chair of biblical theology, Briggs cast aspersions on the "bibliolatry" of conservatives who taught, for example, the doctrine of inspiration and inerrancy and the Mosaic authorship of the Pentateuch.

In a long process that would weave its way back and forth between the General Assembly and the Presbytery of New York, Princeton theologians played a decisive role in prosecuting (and critics would add persecuting) Briggs for heresy. At the 1891 General Assembly, Princeton Seminary professor and Princeton College trustee William H. Green won election as moderator. Green appointed President Patton chairman of the Committee on Theological Seminaries that initiated the process that led to Briggs's eventual dismissal. Another trustee, John J. McCook, a Harvard-educated lawyer, headed the conservative team that tried Briggs for heresy in the liberal Presbytery of New York. At the 1892 assembly, the denomination affirmed in the so-called Portland Deliverance that the doctrine of biblical inerrancy, as formulated by A. A. Hodge (1823–1886) and B. B. Warfield (1851–1921) eleven years earlier, was a fundamental teaching of the church. While the specific charges against Briggs focused on his denial of inerrancy and his apparent duplicity in professing to subscribe to the Westminster Standards, the real source of the controversy concerned the problem of history. In their article on inspiration, Hodge and Warfield argued that the Scriptures not only contained the word of God "but ARE THE WORD OF GOD, and hence that all their elements and all their affirmations are absolutely errorless, and binding the faith and obedience of men."[46] Predicated upon the Scottish commonsense philosophy, this view of the Bible held that truth was in essence a timeless and objective statement of fact that could be known by any unbiased observer who properly used the Baconian scientific method. Though careful not to deny that the Bible reflected the historical perspective of the individual biblical authors, Hodge and Warfield emphasized that divine guidance so thoroughly superintended their writing that the historical element was almost superficial.

By contrast, Briggs's positive theological statements as well as his criticisms of the Princeton position were shaped by the relativistic and evolutionary views of historicism. Although he was not as thoroughgoing a devotee of historicism as many of the second-generation higher critics—he affirmed, for example, the virgin birth of Christ—the polemical cast of his writings and their abrasive tone alienated even moderate Presbyterians. After exhausting the appeal process, Briggs was excommunicated. He entered the more tolerant Episcopal church, which in the 1890s was something of a haven for erstwhile Presbyterians. In the trial's aftermath, Union Seminary severed its ties with the Presbyterian church, while the conservatives successfully drove the more consistent modernists Arthur G. McGiffert and Henry Preserved Smith from the church.[47]

Yet in a day when many found agnosticism to be intellectually and morally compelling, the trials of pious scholars like Briggs, who were only trying to reconcile faith with modern thought, was seen as medieval. While Patton upheld a strict Old School confessionalism within the church, he taught a broadly evangelical Protestantism within the university. "Tho [*sic*] a Presbyterian by confession," one instructor said, "he is no sectarian in the faith he preaches."[48] Yet to many within the academy, even the broadly evangelical Protestantism espoused at Princeton University was deemed no less sectarian than the simon-pure Old School Presbyterianism taught at Princeton Seminary. In the name of nonsectarianism, president Andrew D. White, for instance, boasted that he kept all "sensational preaching" by evangelical revivalists out of Cornell University; guest preachers at Cornell, he insisted, "never advocated sectarianism, but have presented the great fundamental truths upon which *all religion* must be based." The Boston modernist Phillips Brooks was one such representative of broad religion whom White enjoyed bringing to Cornell to preach.[49] For many important educational leaders, the liberalism championed by people like Brooks was far more nonsectarian than even the broad evangelicalism of McCosh or D. L. Moody. To some, Princeton's allegedly nonsectarian character was tarnished because President Patton and trustees like Green and McCook had participated in the prosecution of Briggs and also because the college was often associated with the seminary in these theological matters. Their discomfort only increased when the secular media identified the college with the censure of Briggs and spoke in general terms of "The Princeton Element in the Presbyterian Church." A "false and misleading designation," explained an embarrassed undergraduate, "probably arises from a confusion, in the minds of many, of Princeton College with the Princeton Theological Seminary. Between the College and the Seminary there is no organic connection whatsoever." "With the Briggs case," he added, "Princeton College has nothing whatever to do."[50] Many alumni, likewise, attempted to separate the university from the seminary and the Presbyterian church. In a popular history of America's leading universities in 1898, Jesse Lynch Williams (1871–1929), who would become in 1900 the editor of the *Princeton Alumni Weekly* and later go on to win a Pulitzer Prize, became almost hysterical in his efforts to distance the university from the church. The university, he complained, had a "reputation for being a denominational College, which it is not proud to own; chiefly because it does not own it. It is not a Presbyterian institution. It never has been. There is no denominational creed taught in the University. There never was. There is no denominational discrimination of any kind. There could not be even if desired."[51]

Williams was correct in that the university was not a Presbyterian institution nor did it teach a distinctly Presbyterian theology. However, the broad evangelicalism advanced at the university rested upon the same supernatural beliefs as the Old School Presbyterianism taught at the seminary. Undoubtedly, in Princeton's 150-year history not everyone in the institution's larger community of support shared the prevalent view that the advancement of evangelicalism was an essential mission of the university. In 1898, however, the evangelical consensus within the university, as represented by the institution's historic association with the Presbyterian church and Princeton Seminary, had been broken.

Although the Presbyterian church controversies of the 1890s were a harbinger of things to come in the 1920s and 1930s, it would be historically anachronistic to characterize the differences between the conservatives and liberals in either the Presbyterian church or at Princeton University at this time as irreconcilable. Only the most extreme proponents of modernism were pushed out of the church. In comparison to Briggs, for example, Henry Van Dyke Jr.'s liberalism was more moderate and was framed in a distinctly amiable and nonpolemical fashion. His service on Princeton Seminary's Board of Directors in the 1890s illustrates the fact that serious theological disagreements had not turned into a complete rupture. The younger Van Dyke (1852–1933) was part of a group of young intellectuals in the progressive era who rejected the evangelical worldview of their parents but sought in newly created vocations to fashion an educated democracy that would establish laws that would, in turn, produce a moral democracy. Van Dyke's father, a prominent Presbyterian minister in Brooklyn, had recommended Patton to Cyrus H. McCormick for the Presbyterian seminary in Chicago in 1871 and later gave the charge at Patton's inauguration at Princeton Seminary in 1881.[52] At his father's insistence, young Henry matriculated at Princeton Seminary and sought, like other progressive-minded intellectuals, to pursue his work through the traditional vocation of the pastorate. Upon graduation, he studied at the University of Berlin, pastored a Congregational Church in Rhode Island, and eventually moved to the prestigious Brick Presbyterian Church in New York City in 1883, where he gained fame for his novel *The Other Wise Man* (1896) and other literary works. Like a few other prominent Princeton figures, such as the trustee George S. Black, Van Dyke had supported confessional revision, had defended Briggs, and, when Briggs's ouster was imminent, had pleaded for the subordination of theological differences to the unity of the church. Van Dyke was also offered a position at the modernist Andover Seminary, and Charles Eliot found his theology nonsectarian enough to earn him a semester at Harvard as the "Preacher to the University."[53] In 1899, Van Dyke joined Princeton University's faculty as a Professor of English.

Amid the intellectual crisis of the Gilded Age, Van Dyke represented an alternative between militant evangelicalism and avowed atheism that many found persuasive. Van Dyke presented this alternative to Princeton students at every opportunity. In a series of lectures first given at Yale and published with the fitting title, *The Gospel for an Age of Doubt*, Van Dyke articulated a liberal message that he shared with college students searching for a way to keep their Christian faith in a modern world. In Van Dyke's estimation, many people had doubts not just about particular doctrines, such as the inspiration of Scripture, but about "the deepest and most vital truths of religion," such as the existence of God or the reality of the soul. He blamed the increase in unbelief on science and the growth of human knowledge. Van Dyke expressed admiration for the "older dogmatic methods" of such great lights as John Calvin, Jonathan Edwards, and Charles Hodge, who defended the faith by constructing "a complete and consistent system of doctrine in regard to God and man, the present world and the future." Beyond admiration, though, he neither approved of nor criticized their works. He graciously dismissed them as passé. By "adopting itself to the changed conditions" of the present day, Van Dyke believed that a new method would produce "even mightier works" to vindicate the claims of theology. Since the early nineteenth century, science had been gradually restricting knowledge to the empirically observable. Positivists and agnostics, Van Dyke observed, held that nothing could be known about God who existed in the noumena, or that "it is impossible for God to reveal Himself to man." Because traditional theologians continued to apply scientific standards of certainty to theology, they faced the continual task of repudiating or harmonizing "scientific" conclusions, including those of higher criticism. Van Dyke shared the doubters' misgivings about the epistemological certainty of Christianity as it was formulated in the older orthodoxy.

Van Dyke's way out of this dilemma began with theology's starting point. He argued that theology had to begin with the "immediate and overwhelming reality and nearness of spiritual things." This "unseen power" was not only immanent in nature but culminated in the final revelation, the incarnation of Jesus Christ. While beyond empirical confirmation (or refutation), this experience of the unseen produced historical results—the history of Jesus Christ's life and resurrection and the history of belief in the church—that could be pointed to as evidence of the unseen's reality.[54] When compared to Patton's lectures on the importance of the dogma of the resurrection or to Professor Ormond's insistence on empirical knowledge as the foundation for faith, Van Dyke's theological exposition, though formed under Hodge, was nondoctrinal. His more metaphorical interpretation of the gospel reflected not only his literary predisposition but also his commitment to the liberal tradition, which had begun with Horace Bushnell, and its understanding of the nature of theology.[55] Van Dyke's more progressive theology appears to have influenced both his brother and his father. Paul Van Dyke's three-year appointment as a church historian at Princeton Seminary was not renewed because, as B. B. Warfield described it, "in the present theological unrest . . . he would not be in full harmony with our Princeton standpoint."[56] The senior Van Dyke, a long-time director at Princeton Seminary, accepted a professorship at Union Seminary in April 1891, but died before his installation.[57] More important than his influence over his family was Van Dyke's popularity as a lecturer within the university. Among students, he was a favorite. After one address, for instance, the secretary of the Philadelphian Society recorded in his minutes that some fifty students lingered to talk personally with Van Dyke.[58]

While the temperate modernism of liberals like Van Dyke enjoyed increasing favor in the Princeton community, the formal program of religious instruction remained in the hands of the unambiguous evangelicals. Yet for several reasons, the conservatives started to loose their grip on the religion courses in the 1890s. "[A]lthough the matter of giving Biblical instruction [is] only now beginning to excite the attention in some quarters," Patton smugly reported at his inauguration, "it has never been neglected here."[59] For the first three years of Patton's administration, the same collection of professors continued to give Bible instruction as under McCosh. But as new courses were introduced into the curriculum and as the professors who taught the Bible courses found this "extra demand" on their time "difficult to meet," the old plan proved unworkable, forcing a reduction in compulsory Bible instruction.[60] As a result, Patton assumed responsibility for giving compulsory biblical instruction to all four classes in the fall of 1891, a restructuring that was not perceived as a weakening of the institution's commitment to Bible instruction but simply as a "change in the manner" that was "sure to win the approbation of the college at large."[61] Only two years later, the required Bible courses for juniors and seniors became electives, but Patton continued to teach a required Bible course for freshmen and sophomores.[62] Just seven years earlier, McCosh was ready to go to the wall to preserve Bible instruction as a constitutive, and therefore compulsory, part of a Christian liberal arts education. Now Patton was dismantling Princeton's program of Christian education. The reduction in the Bible's "clear and unmistakable" place within the mandatory curriculum did not come as a result of liberal Protestant antagonism to evangelicalism or from aggressive atheists intent on secularizing the university. Instead, the reduction was the consequence of an attempt to rebalance Princeton's religious obligation with competing, and equally valued, commitments stemming from Princeton's civic mission. The growth of the student body, the professional interests of the faculty, and the goal of providing students with more opportunities to gain expertise in the most current scholarship combined—not conspired—to reorganize how Princeton gave students a religious education in the Bible. Still, Princeton students continued to receive more hours of Bible instruction than their peers at either Harvard or Yale. A 1898 survey, based on course enrollments and hours per course, reveals that 6 percent of every Princeton student's education was devoted to biblical instruction. By contrast, the average Yale and Harvard students devoted only 1.1 percent and 0.2 percent of their studies to the Bible, respectively.[63]

To help compensate for the reduction in mandatory Bible classes, the trustees established the T. H. P. Sailor Bible Instructorship. Patton recruited Robert E. Speer (1867–1947), valedictorian of the Class of 1889 and a football star who had attended Princeton Seminary for a year, to offer an elective Bible class in addition to his work as the secretary for the northern Presbyterian church's Board of Foreign Missions.[64] In response to a request by preministerial students, courses in Hebrew, taught by seminary professors, also joined the elective curriculum in 1889.[65] To the amazement of some within the Princeton community, in 1895 President Patton hired his son, George S. Patton (1869–1937), as an Assistant Professor of Biblical Instruction even though he had only attended Princeton Seminary.[66] Two years later, the younger Patton was sent off to Europe to pursue graduate work in biblical studies and ethics at the University of Berlin and Cambridge University. Upon his return in 1899, he was promoted to Assistant Professor of Moral Philosophy with the understanding that he would assume chief responsibility for biblical instruction.[67] Patton took a further step in the professionalization of biblical instruction when in 1895 the university created the Department of Biblical Literature, giving biblical instruction, at least in principle, an equal standing with the other academic disciplines.[68]

Princeton, President Patton told an audience of graduating seniors, has "aimed to educate you so that you may become scholars, and not pedants . . . theologians, and not textualists; religious men and not dealers in cant phrases or slaves of a *stupid literalism*."[69] Throughout the 1890s, the curriculum preserved Princeton's traditional array of Bible courses as offered in the previous decade.

The broadly evangelical theological orientation of these courses, which in the past had represented a centrist theological position, was becoming a decidedly conservative one in the 1890s, as higher criticism and Darwinism undermined the credibility of orthodoxy in the eyes of many intellectuals and Protestant modernism provided an alternative for others. While broadly evangelical, Patton wanted to avoid the sort of populist literalism associated with certain streams of late-nineteenth-century evangelical Protestantism, such as dispensationalism. The president was confident that he and his colleagues afforded students a more thoughtful familiarity with the Bible. George S. Patton's New Testament Introduction class, for example, was essentially a course in lower criticism, in which students not only learned the Bible's content but also engaged in a more critical discussion about the history of the Bible. The younger Patton outlined the Latin and Hebrew influences on the Koine Greek of the New Testament, the history of the Greek text and its various Latin and Syriac translations, the value of quotations from the early church fathers for resolving discrepancies among various manuscripts, and the history of Bible translations. Textual criticism, he taught, "seeks to ascertain and restore the exact words used by the Apostles," since copyist errors "have rendered the manuscripts we have by no means an infallible witness." Patton's course also illustrates how religious instruction, though more scholarly in character, was still a form of religious education.[70]

John G. Hibben (1861–1933), a trusted member of the Princeton community, replaced Speer as the third Bible instructor on the faculty. The son of an Old School Presbyterian minister, Hibben had graduated from Princeton College in 1882, studied in Germany on a graduate fellowship, attended Princeton Seminary, and with Professor John T. Duffield's and James McCosh's encouragement entered the Presbyterian ministry. But after a "grim experience" as a pastor in Chambersburg, Pennsylvania, he returned to Princeton to earn a Ph.D. in philosophy.[71] Hibben's courses were as conservative in theological orientation as those of the Pattons—Hibben assigned a pre-exilic date to the book of Joel and a sixth-century B.C. date to the book of Daniel. His classes proved to be among the more popular elective courses.[72] Hibben's courses also continued the emphasis on proselytism, his Old Testament history course, for instance, being essentially a series of character studies of Old Testament figures such as Abraham, Moses, and David.[73] Patton's and Hibben's courses implicitly addressed some of the pertinent issues raised by higher criticism, such as the authorship and dating, by teaching the more conservative positions. However, the more controversial issues raised by higher criticism, such as source theories for the Synoptic Gospels, went unaddressed because the classes were not seminary-level courses but a form of religious education. Bible classes maintained a "higher" purpose, as the president explained to one baccalaureate audience: "We have tried to show that the unchanging Word of God is not a fossil to be laid upon the shelf, but the directing principle of life, the inspiration of its movement, and the law of its variations."[74] While the Bible classes had this devotional purpose, they also ran the possible risk of leaving doubts in students' minds as to whether conservatives had substantive answers to the most burning questions of the day.

Amid all of the curricular revisions of the 1890s, President Patton's ethics course remained a staple of compulsory curriculum for students enrolled in the A.B. program. Yet as the School of Science's enrollment continued to grow, so did the gap between the institution's professed commitment to teaching all students their personal and republican duties and its failure to offer ethics courses to students in the B.S. program. Since Patton maintained that ethics was no less rigorous a science than those courses taught in the John C. Green School of Science, he added the ethics course to their required curriculum in the fall of 1894.[75] This correction marked another advancement of traditional religious interests in the university.

D. H. Meyer argues in his study of nineteenth-century moral philosophy that by the time James McCosh published *Our Moral Way* in 1892 darkness had long since fallen on the old-time academic moralists.[76] However, while the grand synthesizing course in moral philosophy had been broken down into its constitutive parts two decades earlier, the *fin de siècle* had not yet come for Scottish philosophy and ethical instruction at Princeton. Patton continued to guide America's future leaders to the solid ground of the Scottish metaphysics and intuitionism through an ever-increasing perilous array of late nineteenth-century moral theories ranging from the idealism of Thomas H. Green and Francis Bradley to the utilitarianism of John S. Mill to the "evolutionism" of Leslie Stephen and Herbert Spencer. Patton taught students the same fundamental truths, as outlined in the first chapter, concerning the universal laws of nature and morality and each individual's own moral nature and obligations. Insofar as he took into account other ethical systems, his work marks an advancement over the earlier academic moralists. In the 1890s, however, Patton grew increasingly defensive in his advocacy of the Scottish philosophy and ethics. He devoted more attention to criticizing alternative ethical theories, especially those flowing out of Britain. His defensiveness suggests that the tide in ethics was changing and, despite his best efforts, the president could not prevent its new course. "Men say we must study the facts in an historical spirit and gather our induction out of what we see," Patton complained. "The science of ethics becomes the science of what is, rather than of what ought to be, and if a doctrine of right survives at all, it is the doctrine that whatever is is right." This "worship of the *Zeitgeist*," Patton was sure, "is associated with the denial of all *a priori* ideas."[77] Upon his return from Cambridge, George S. Patton offered an upperclass elective course, not surprisingly, on British ethics in which he continued, like his father, to advocate the McCosh tradition and to keep utilitarian and idealist ethicists outside the walls of Nassau Hall.[78]

In the fall of 1889, a course in the Evidences of Christianity taught by President Patton replaced the Science and Religion class taught by Charles W. Shields as part of the compulsory curriculum for the A.B. program. Shields's course, meanwhile, was added to the growing list of elective courses.[79] This shift stemmed from longstanding criticisms Patton had with Shields's work. Patton, who could barely mask his contempt for some evangelicals' thoughtless biblical literalism, demonstrated little patience for Shields's cautious efforts to elaborate a defense of orthodox Christianity. For his part, Shields felt that he was "perpetually exposed to a cross-fire" from the Princeton theologians on one side and the college scientists on the other. When Shields published *The Final Philosophy* back in 1877, he won mixed reviews from Patton. Although Patton appreciated Shields's exhaustive survey of modern opinion (he cited the opinions of more than 700 scientists, philosophers, and theologians), his dogmatic faith, his belief in the supernatural inspiration of the Bible, his Scottish philosophy, and, most important, the overall objective of the work, two aspects of the work disturbed him deeply. To Patton, Shields not only exaggerated the conflict between science and religion but also fostered unwittingly a spirit of agnosticism because he merely proposed the possibility of a final philosophical solution without developing such a solution in any detail. Patton complained that students were consequently locked "in a dungeon of dreary nescience until some knight of philosophy sounds the note of deliverance."[80] The "scientific men" treat "theologians as we treat the Indians. If they mark out a 'reservation,' and tell them to stay there, back they come in a little while, telling them to move on."[81] According to Patton, Shields was only telling theologians that one day they would be able to leave the reservation. Patton also had doubts about the very legitimacy of Shields's professorship; he found the elevated role that Shields assigned to philosophy unnecessary and pretentious. Although both colleagues wanted to preserve the perspicuity and unity of truth, Patton objected to the fragmenting effect that the specialization of knowledge was having on the unity of truth in particular and on higher education in general. "A comprehensive philosophy must deal with truth as truth," Patton insisted, "and all that pretends to truth must submit to the proper tests of certitude." What the "great summative science" was called was "a matter of minor importance." Patton suggested it be called "philosophy" to manifest the spirit in which truth was sought or "science" to indicate that it is a systematic exhibition of what is known, but "its most appropriate title will be Theology" since theism was its subject.[82] In the face of mounting criticism from "secular science," Patton said in another address, "The true course is to give up, or make a stand."[83] Published in 1889, Shields's sequel to *The Final Philosophy* still lacked a constructive argument for the credibility of Christianity. The philistines were at the gates, and for Patton Shields was simply taking too long to return fire.

Consequently, Patton offered his own class in the Evidences of Christianity, in which the president presented students "the exceptional evidence" which demonstrates "that Christianity is and that anti-Christian systems are not capable of rational defense."[84] The intellectual state of affairs among Protestant apologetics frustrated Patton. "We cannot shut up our libraries," he insisted, "nor suppress investigation. . . . It is useless to veto thought or write an *Index expurgatorius*."[85] The president had the same impatience with the apologetics of many evangelicals as he did for Protestant modernists, for he felt that both groups propagated an insidious form of anti-intellectualism. The "world will not long continue to value a religion," he said, "which it believes to be irrational, no matter who it is that commends it to our consideration."[86] Patton re-

jected pietistic evangelical apologists who would allow the "debate to be settled
by the quiet operation of the Spirit of God." Patton also dismissed the appeals
of biblicists to the inspiration and infallibility of the Bible to settle all questions.
They mistakenly carried the method of apologetics, he believed, into dogmatic
theology, making the *minimum quid* of apologetics, the *maximum quid* of dogmatics: "'Because, this is all that is needed for the defense of a supernatural
theology, this, therefore, is all that is of value in belief. . . . And this is the evil
tendency of the hour."[87] Modernists, while more academically fashionable, were
equally anti-intellectual in Patton's estimation:

> And whether it be Tertullian or [Albrecht] Ritschl, [Wilhelm] Hermann
> or [Samuel Taylor] Coleridge, or Isaac Taylor or [A. J.] Balfour, or [Ben-
> jamin] Kidd or [William H.] Mallock, or the modern high-potency
> dilutionists of the Ritschlian School, who in this country are giving us an
> ethico-sentimental naturalism as the new Gospel for the twentieth cen-
> tury, I make bold to tell them all alike that Christianity will be denied a
> hearing in the court of feeling once she has been non-suited at the bar of
> reason.[88]

The need of the hour, Patton believed, was a "defense of the defenses." And
he was ready to provide it. By first establishing a "sound metaphysics" and "the
a priori elements of knowledge as absolutely true," Patton held that one can
then examine the evidence of science which in the final analysis favored the
rationality of Christianity.[89] Patton thus employed the traditional arguments of
natural theology to make his case for the probable existence of God. After dem-
onstrating the rationality of this proposition, he then constructed an argument
for the plausibility of supernatural revelation. He examined the Bible's trust-
worthiness as an historical document and the evidence of its divine authorship
and infallibility to establish the possibility that the Bible was a divine revelation. After laying this elaborate foundation, he then built an argument from the
traditional pieces of evidence, such as miracles and the divinity of Christ, to
prove the truthfulness of Christianity.[90] This course was dropped from the curriculum after the 1898–1899 academic year, another victim of the expansion of
the curriculum. Patton's elective apologetic course in Theism remained part of
the curriculum.[91]

With the reduction of mandatory religious education in the 1890s, the Philadelphian Society began to play a greater role in the university's efforts to fulfill
its religious mission. In the wake of the elimination of compulsory English
Bible courses for upperclass students, the society organized an impressive selection of extracurricular Bible classes for "the deepening and nourishing of the
spiritual life of the University." While the college courses had taken on a somewhat more academic character, these classes were designed to "inculcate the
habit of personal, daily, thorough and *devotional* Bible study."[92] In the spring of
1893, fourteen different classes attracted 228 students, while the following year,
the society arranged a "comprehensive course," which covered the life and teach-

ings of Christ and the work of the apostles. Interest in the Bible remained strong among students throughout the decade, as evidenced by the 201 students who enrolled in the program in 1901.[93]

The proliferation of these extracurricular Bible classes was just one component of the ministry of the Philadelphian Society in the 1890s. Like Y.M.C.A.s at other colleges and universities, Princeton's chapter flourished in this decade: only the combined membership of Clio and Whig Halls had more students.[94] The society, in addition to offering Bible classes, held weekly missions studies, class prayer meetings, and large group meetings, and all this work was supervised by student-led committees. In 1892, for example, students ran committees on religious meetings, Bible study, membership, missions, finance, intercollegiate relations, deputation, nominations, the library, the Northfield Conference, and town work.[95] Because of the society's sprawling endeavors, it hired a graduate secretary, typically a recent Princeton graduate, each year starting in the fall of 1892 to help oversee the organization's work. Five years later, the university's trustees took two additional steps to enhance the society's ministry further. They approved the creation of a Graduate Advisory Committee, comprising some of the university's more prominent religious leaders, to assist the society, and they also sanctioned making the graduate secretary position permanent in order to add continuity to the society's leadership. The advisors chose Lucius H. Miller, a pious member of the senior class and president of the society, as the first graduate secretary.[96] After a semester under the new arrangement, Patton told the trustees that the religious condition of the university "is showing a decided improvement as compared with previous years."[97] One advisory committee member, Cleveland H. Dodge, financed an addition onto Murray Hall in 1899 to provide more room for the society's expanded ministry. Murray–Dodge Hall, the *Princeton Alumni Weekly* gleefully reported, gave Princeton "the finest Y.M.C.A. building of any college in the country."[98]

Patton told one permanent secretary that the work of the society "supplemented" the faculty in tending to "the spiritual welfare and the moral tone of the university."[99] When American colleges had been small in number and many professors were ministers, Patton explained on another occasion, the need for the Y.M.C.A. was nominal. "Now, probably to the advantage of the university, a man is not put into a professorship because he is a minister, but because he knows his subjects; and that is a good thing." Educational success, however, had a price. People "cannot rely upon the faculty alone to furnish the religious teaching or religious life or religious example." Consequently, the need for the Y.M.C.A. "is growing more every year."[100] Despite the chaotic condition of the undergraduate curriculum, the expansion of the curriculum and further professionalization of the faculty in the 1890s represented a distinct advance in the university's civic mission. This advancement, however, took a toll on the established customs in how Princeton fulfilled its religious mission. The prosperity of the Philadelphian Society helped to counterbalance the loss. In a day when professors were more interested in teaching and scholarship than in overseeing the spiritual lives of students, the Philadelphian Society was turning into the de facto campus ministry.

From one perspective, the vitality of the Philadelphian Society during the 1890s reveals the growing self-government of Princeton's student body. The decade offered other similar signs of student independence. Despite Patton's Calvinistic misgivings, an honor code was adopted in 1893. Students also began to clamor for the administration's approval of an official student government organization.[101] Viewed from another angle, however, students in the Philadelphian Society lost a certain amount of independence. The creation of the Alumni Council to help oversee the work of the Philadelphian Society and the organization's closer cooperation with the president and trustees detracted from students' independence.

Episcopal students had their own organization. Like the Philadelphian Society, the St. Paul's Society had weekly meetings and ministries to the Princeton community, but in comparison to the former organization, it had a more social orientation. The group held smokers and, for example, sponsored lectures on Robert Browning's poetry and on the value of hobbies.[102] Yet the larger Philadelphian Society, which directly cooperated with the administration, held the more central role in the life of the university. In the late 1890s, the Philadelphian Society assumed a practical responsibility in the life of the institution by organizing the freshman orientation for the administration. With elaborate planning, members greeted new students and their parents when they arrived on campus, ran an information desk, distributed a college handbook that they had printed, and hosted a large reception.[103] "It was a most inspiring gathering and gives good promise of a warm religious atmosphere in old Princeton this year," reported one aged alumnus after speaking at a society meeting in the early fall of 1898.[104]

Also, in comparison to previous decades, the Philadelphian Society played a more important part in nurturing the faith of students. Besides the annual addresses by professors John T. Duffield, James O. Murray, and other older ministers on the faculty, a standard parade of popular evangelical leaders addressed the Philadelphian Society. J. Wilbur Chapman, A. T. Pierson, both evangelists, and H. Clay Trumbull, editor of the *Sunday School Times*, preached their pietistic, premillennialist message to students. D. L. Moody even returned to campus for the Day of Prayer in 1890. While modest in comparison to the events of 1876, the college enjoyed a notable revival in the winter of 1894.[105] The day of evangelical hegemony over the campus Y.M.C.A., however, had come to an end. Not surprisingly, given the fractured theological consensus within American Protestantism and the larger university community, some of liberal Protestantism's most popular advocates began to press their message on campus. Charles C. Hall, president of Union Seminary, and Henry Sloane Coffin, a Presbyterian pastor in New York City who was soon to join Union's faculty, for instance, offered students a way to avoid agnosticism as well as what they considered to be an outdated Protestantism.[106]

While Protestant modernism joined conservative evangelicalism in the life of the university's campus ministry, more traditional religious interests continued to express themselves in the last decade of the nineteenth century at Princeton.

This interest is most evident in the heightened involvement in foreign missions. Students organized a "missions band" to study the subject. Since Princeton alumni had played such a prominent role in founding the Student Volunteer Movement, the Philadelphian Society sent large delegations to S.V.M. conferences as well as to D. L. Moody's annual Northfield Student Conferences. Among others, the leading apostles of foreign missions, Robert E. Speer, John R. Mott, Henry Luce, and C. T. Studd, urged students to do their part in fulfilling the S.V.M.'s watchword, "the evangelization of the world in this generation."[107] The Philadelphian Society took up this challenge in 1889 by adopting as the university's missionary John N. Forman, an 1884 graduate of the college who had attended Princeton Seminary. The society campaigned yearly to raise money to finance Forman's work with the Presbyterian church in India. As students who knew Forman personally moved on after graduation, however, interest in his work slowly waned. In March 1898, the society organized a mass meeting of the student body to discuss the problem and eventually resolved, "We, the undergraduates of Princeton University, do hereby signify our intention of transferring our support from Mr. J. N. Forman '86 to another who shall serve in his stead as our representative on the foreign field." At a subsequent meeting, students selected Robert R. Gailey as "Princeton's representative in the Foreign Missionary field" and pledged to raise a thousand dollars in support. A graduate from Princeton Seminary, though not ordained, Gailey combined evangelistic work and education in teaching English to college students with the Y.M.C.A. in Tien-tsin, China. The work of the Y.M.C.A. in the late nineteenth century, like that of many other independent and denominational missions agencies, took a rather broad view of evangelization. This included not only converting the lost but also "civilizing" them. Gailey, in a sense, was not only Princeton's spiritual ambassador but also its imperialist representative, working to uplift China with western civilization. In addition to Gailey, dozens of Princeton alumni went overseas. When thirteen graduates who were missionaries in Syria established an alumni organization, the *Princeton Alumni Weekly* proudly observed, "From Syria to Hawaii, the sun never sets on the Princeton flag."[108]

The sun was beginning to set, however, on the harmonious relationship between Princeton's religious and civic missions. Notwithstanding the improvements made in biblical instruction, the advances achieved in the university's civic mission through professionalization and specialization weakened a key part of the university's religious mission—mandatory religious education. The vitality of the Philadelphian Society helped to offset the loss from these changes. Patton and his colleagues continued to defend a broadly evangelical orthodoxy against the criticisms of Darwinists, utilitarian and idealist ethicists, and other assailants. Meanwhile, Protestant modernists began to gain a hearing within the university community for a message that offered an alternative way to reconcile faith with modernity. As manifested in the crisis over the undergraduate curriculum, many within the university already had suspicions about the relevance of the old-time curriculum and the traditional educational philosophy that framed it. Evangelicalism was losing its place as the unifying center of the university.

Misgivings about the intellectual credibility of supernatural Protestantism further undermined the confidence of many in the university's ability to serve both national educational interests and traditional Protestant ones. Crises over the university's nonsectarian character and its nondenominational standing further damaged the relationship between Princeton's civic and religious mission.

Crisis Two: A Unitarian at a Nonsectarian University?

As Patton hoisted the university's flag before the western world's intellectual leaders at Princeton's sesquicentennial celebration, he dogmatically insisted, "It has been the aim of those who have governed this institution to make and keep it a Christian college."[109] In light of the college's "steady and marked progress along conservative and wise lines," the trustees had chosen the sesquicentennial celebration in October 1896 as the most expedient occasion to take the next step forward in the institution's development by taking the title of a university. The decision to keep pace "with the leading institutions of learning in the country" was as easy for the trustees to make in 1895 as it was difficult for them to refuse eight years earlier.[110] Patton had pledged from the beginning of his administration to make Princeton "a great American University."[111] In the years following his inauguration, the student body and faculty had both almost doubled, eight new buildings had been added to the campus, another impressive building, Blair Hall, was under construction, and over a million dollars had been raised for the endowment.

In his sesquicentennial address, "Religion and the University," Patton explained to representatives from Cambridge, Paris, Heidelberg, Harvard, Yale, and some of the world's other great universities what it meant for Princeton to be a Christian university. "The interests of the college," Patton said in homage to Princeton's founders, "have always been in the hands of religious men, and of men, I may say, belonging, as a rule to a particular branch of Protestant Christendom; but it has never been under ecclesiastical control." Like his predecessor, Patton considered Princeton a de facto Presbyterian but an officially nondenominational institution. As such, Christianity played several important roles within the university. What made the institution Christian, Patton explained, was that Christianity centered the entire educational endeavor: "Christianity underlies, informs, unifies, and is the unexpressed postulate of all instruction." In particular, Christianity's place in the university was to rationalize the truths of the faith free from "ecclesiastical leading strings." "*Credo quia impossibile* is not the basis of a sound apologetic; and whether it be Tertullian or Mr. Kidd who would have us think so, it can never be rational to believe in an irrational religion." Though the "rationalizing process may go wrong," Patton insisted, "that is no reason why men should stop thinking." The role of Christianity in the curriculum involved more than an elementary course in biblical instruction for underclassmen and upperclass Bible courses whose "scientific thoroughness" could "compare to any other department." "Secular themes," he said, had to be discussed "in a religious spirit and under Christian conceptions" and, conversely, "religious themes" should be discussed "in a scientific spirit and according to scientific principles." A truly Christian university, Patton believed, addressed the great questions of the day. In the past, the mandatory course in Christian evidences was sufficient for handling this task. But evolution changed the way people thought; now, everything was being examined from a historical point of view, giving fundamental religious questions a new prominence: "One man cannot study genetic psychology without facing the problem of a separate and enduring selfhood, and without asking whether the world is to be construed according to a theistic or a pantheistic metaphysics." In Patton's judgment, Princeton faced a choice: "We must be silent and hand over the discussion to the sceptic, or we must show ourselves worthy of the high place we have already won in the department of religious philosophy, and take a strong position on the side of historic Christianity." Patton hoped that the university, while standing "aloof from sectarian controversy," would defend those "fundamental truths in philosophy and in religion" in which "Christians of every name have a common interest." Finally, he believed that a Christian university helped to "shape the Christian character of the nation." "University men," Patton said, drawing upon the prevalent Whiggish conception of higher education, "are in an ever increasing degree to be the influential men in this nation." It was necessary, he insisted, that the nation's future leaders have their "moral and religious natures" trained "as well as their intellectual powers. . . . And if the graduates of our universities should turn their back upon the religion of their fathers, we might as well exclaim: 'If the light that is in thee be darkness, how great is that darkness!'"[112] Patton's ideas about what it meant for Princeton to be a Christian university were soon to be tested.

Another vision of Princeton's purpose emerged during the sesquicentennial celebration. In "Princeton in the Nation's Service," Professor Woodrow Wilson underscored, as the title suggests, the institution's civic mission over its Protestant heritage. Wilson, though no less committed a Christian than Patton, believed that Christianity was not so much something to be taught as something that provided the "pith to service." For Wilson, it was almost incidental that the college's founders were Presbyterian; "They acted," he insisted, "without ecclesiastical authority, as if under obligation to society rather than to the church." The difference between these two understandings of Princeton's guiding purpose was one of emphasis, and both had legitimate claims on McCosh's legacy for the university. Patton stressed his predecessor's religious interests for the college; Wilson emphasized his mentor's national aspirations. From as far back as the Revolutionary War and the constitutional convention, Wilson insisted, Princeton graduates were "citizens and the world's servants." A collegiate education ought, therefore, "to implant a sense of duty." To this end, the classical curriculum was useful not merely for fostering mental discipline but also for teaching "the truths which have lasted a thousand years." History, politics, and science, so long as they did not encourage the "contempt of the past" as so much of the scientific spirit had done, served the same purpose. In short, a university had to be a place "to learn the truth about the past and hold debate about the affairs of the present." "Who," Wilson concluded, "shall show us the way to this place?"[113]

In the early 1890s, the university continued to recruit faculty from its own alumni. Some professors, such as George S. Patton, Arnold Guyot Cameron, and Caspar Wistar Hodge Jr. (1870–1937), returned to Princeton through nepotism.[114] Others, like Woodrow Wilson and Henry Van Dyke Jr., joined the faculty the old-fashioned way: their friends endowed chairs for them.[115] Those professors who had no previous connection with Princeton were still part of the larger Protestant establishment that continued to dominate America's top colleges and universities. Bliss Perry (1860–1954), for example, came to Princeton from Williams College where he had taught English and his father was a professor of political economy.[116] Patton, like McCosh before him, used an informal theological hiring policy to safeguard the institution's evangelical mission. He warned prospective professors of the administration's interest in preserving the university's religious orientation: "My attention has been called to the fact that in your discussion of the origin of the State you minimise [*sic*] the supernatural, and make such unqualified application of the doctrine of naturalistic evolution and the genesis of the State," Patton told Wilson in 1890 when he informed him that he had been elected to replace the pious Alexander Johnston, "as to leave the reader of your pages in a state of uncertainty as to your own position and the place you give Divine Providence." The trustees, Patton cautioned Wilson, "mean to keep this College on the old ground of loyalty to the Christian religion" and "would not regard with favour such a conception of academic freedom or teachings as would leave in doubt the very direct bearing of historical Christianity as a revealed religion upon the great problems of civilization."[117]

While Patton had little difficulty in finding professors to agree with the institution's unofficial practices intended to preserve the college's evangelical Protestant character, some newer faculty members had rather different ideas about what it meant to pursue Christian scholarship. Some older professors, like the biologist George Macloskie, continued to draw out the apologetical and "doxological" implications of their work. However, younger scholars, following the same scientific standards, left matters of the faith to the theologians and pursued truth in the natural realm, unconcerned about the consequences for the theologians' work.[118] James Mark Baldwin (1861–1934) was one such professor. As a Princeton undergraduate, Baldwin had led his class prayer group, participated in the Philadelphian Society, and even walked miles on Sunday afternoons to teach Sunday School classes in Stony Brook. After graduation, he studied psychology under Wilhelm Wundt at Leipzig where, as he put it, he experienced "an apostolic call to the 'new psychology.'" He returned to Princeton to complete his Ph.D. dissertation on Spinoza under McCosh while teaching French at the college and taking Patton's classes in apologetics and theism at the seminary. Because Spinoza was one of his *bêtes noires*, McCosh refused to accept the dissertation until Baldwin reworked the study to "refute materialism." In 1887, he married William Henry Green's daughter, Helen, and went off to teach at Lake Forest University and then at the University of Toronto. In 1893, Baldwin returned to his alma mater. Patton welcomed him to the faculty with the warning that it was "a *sine qua non* that any one who teaches philosophy in Princeton College should be in full intellectual sympathy with evangelical Christianity as a miraculous revelation of God, and that he should not hold a philosophy that is incompatible with this position." Baldwin certainly enhanced Princeton's academic reputation. Having been elected vice-president of the International Congress of Psychology in London in 1892, Baldwin founded the *Psychological Review* in 1894, won a medal from the Royal Academy of Science and Letters in Denmark in 1896, and served as president of the American Psychological Association in 1897. He was also a faithful member of the First Presbyterian Church in Princeton. Before his appointment, Baldwin informed Patton that in a forthcoming publication on mental development he applied evolutionary theory to the mind as well as to the body. Patton told Baldwin that he had "nothing to fear" so long as he confined his work to psychology and did not encroach upon the fields of philosophy or biology. Baldwin later recalled that he saw "two Pattons—a Calvinist of the most thorough stripe in the pulpit, but a person of immense charity among the 'sinners' of the world the rest of the week."[119] In his work, Baldwin applied Darwinism to psychology by adopting the genetic method to his discipline. Baldwin's work signals that an important transition in American intellectual culture was taking place in the late nineteenth-century university. Just as the ethical concerns of Jonathan Edwards and the New England Theology continued to inform the pragmatism of John Dewey, his naturalism notwithstanding, McCosh's interests in the nature and source of human knowledge and its social ramifications still shaped the substance of Baldwin's academic interests even if Darwinism had undermined Baldwin's commitment to the older faculty psychology.[120] Despite Patton's claims to the contrary, "science and religion," as Baldwin explained, "were kept *strictly apart* from each other in Princeton." Like other younger faculty members, he pursued his scholarship with a fearless indifference to its theological implications.[121]

Early in his Princeton career, Woodrow Wilson, much like Baldwin, once described Patton as "a man of most liberal outlook . . . outside of church battles."[122] Patton, however, proved to be no latitudinarian within the university when Wilson recommended hiring an avowed Unitarian for a new professorship in American history. It was at this juncture in Patton's presidency, in a controversy surrounding this attempted appointment, that two visions of Princeton's mission came into direct conflict. Just two weeks after the sesquicentennial celebration, Wilson asked his friend, Frederick Jackson Turner (1861–1932), if he would be interested in the position. Teaching at the University of Wisconsin, Turner had gained national fame for his 1893 address, "The Significance of the Frontier in American History." In response to Turner's inquiry concerning doctrinal tests for the faculty, Wilson wrote, "I think I can say without qualification that no religious tests are applied here. The president and trustees are very anxious that every man they choose should be earnestly religious, but there are no doctrinal standards amongst us."[123] Wilson was wrong.

The possibility of adding a Unitarian to the faculty sparked a bitter but private controversy among the faculty and trustees. The disagreement highlighted a division within the institution between those who saw in Turner a premier scholar who appealed to their aspirations to make Princeton a first-class national university and others who found Turner's religious affiliations unacceptable given their commitment to upholding traditional Protestant ideals. Analysis of this division reveals a shifting definition of what it meant for the institution to be a nonsectarian university. To Patton, the university's nonsectarian character stopped at the borders of a traditional nineteenth-century Protestant worldview, whereas for Wilson the institution's nonsectarian standing meant something much broader. The battle over Turner also brought into the foreground two rather different understandings over what constituted a university. To Patton, a university was basically a larger College of New Jersey. It upheld, however tenuously, the traditional Protestant worldview and encouraged its professors to harmonize their scholarship in new fields of knowledge with that worldview. In contrast to many American colleges, Daniel C. Gilman said in his presidential address at the International Congress on Higher Education in 1893, American universities "are free from every form of intellectual despotism."[124] To Wilson, like Gilman, a university had to be free from even informal ecclesiastical control. Consequently, a university included a variety of intellectual viewpoints. Beneath Patton's feet Princeton was becoming, at least in this one respect, a modern university. Ironically, Turner's scholarship probably posed no more of a threat to the traditional Protestant worldview espoused by Patton than did Baldwin's physiological psychology to McCosh's faculty psychology and Patton's ethics or Scott's work in paleontology to the Shields-McCosh harmonization of theism and evolution. Symbolically, however, Turner's Unitarianism threatened Princeton's nonsectarian evangelical Protestant mission.

At first, Patton equivocated by delaying his decision, an act which only frustrated Wilson.[125] In the end, the president resolved the problem by rejecting the proposal for a new chair in history, later telling one of the more liberal trustees that he could not "conscientiously nominate Mr. Turner," despite the fact that he did recommend Turner's colleague, Charles R. Haskins, for a position in European history.[126] Turner's Unitarianism troubled more than just Patton, however. Wilson complained to his wife that Andrew F. West had "showed the most stubborn prejudice" against Turner. In a letter to Wilson, George S. Black, the president of Auburn Seminary and one of the more progressive trustees, raised several problems that the institution would face in hiring Turner. The threat of Turner's "religious influence within the college" was secondary to the danger he posed to the financial well-being of the university. For Black, the central issue was "the inexpediency of letting the orthodox Presbyterians," who donated so much money to the university, "see us appoint a Unitarian."[127] To Patton and the ruling majority, the university's nonsectarian character was limited to a broadly evangelical Protestantism. To Wilson and a minority, this commitment to evangelicalism was really a sectarianism that hindered the institution's growth as a genuine university and thus threatened its civic mission. In the aftermath of the rejection of Turner, John G. Hibben confided to a friend that the sesquicentennial celebration was a "great misfortune." It was fruitless to think "that Princeton under its present management could become a University.... [W]e can't hope to be anything but a respectable, *old-fashioned Presbyterian college*."[128] Left with the unpleasant task of informing his friend of Patton's decision, Wilson was equally despondent. He wrote Turner, "I am probably . . . the most chagrined and mortified fellow on this continent."[129] While the Turner crisis ended with a victory for those interested in preserving Princeton's evangelical mission, it only strengthened Wilson's and other younger faculty members' resolve to overcome the sectarianism that they had come to see as a handicap to their national university aspirations for Princeton and ultimately to the university's civic mission.

Crisis Three: Princeton's "Grogshop" and the Presbyterian Problem

"It was enough to cause tears in the Presbyterian corner of heaven," lamented the Committee on Temperance of the Synod of New York, "to know that the professors had given such a measure of sanction to the use of wine, beer, and whisky by their students."[130] Just weeks after the internal controversy over Turner came to an end, the university was embroiled in a rather public conflict with many Presbyterians over the institution's toleration and alleged encouragement of student intemperance. If during the Turner controversy Princeton seemed like an "old-fashioned Presbyterian college" in the eyes of professors with national educational aspirations, during the controversy over the Princeton Inn the university seemed like a thoroughly secular institution in the eyes of those with evangelical expectations. To temperance advocates within the Presbyterian church and the larger pan-Protestant community, the university was apparently faltering in its religious mission.

The controversy began innocently enough when the Princeton Inn's license expired. Moses Taylor Pyne, a trustee of the university, and several other alumni owned the hotel, located on the corner of Stockton Street and Bayard Avenue. A license was needed because the hotel had a grill room that served beer and wine (and possibly hard liquor). To renew the license, the management obtained the requisite twelve signatures from the property's neighbors, including former president Grover Cleveland, Mary Hodge Scott, and university professors Charles Greene Rockwood Jr., Allan Marquand, and Charles W. Shields. In July, the *New York Voice*, a mouthpiece of prohibitionist sentiment, alerted the teetotaling public that Princeton University, "born of high Presbyterian parentage," had "taken to the bottle in old age." The *Voice* followed this announcement with a series of sensational articles describing the "drunken orgies" of undergraduates and the plight of frightened homeowners who were driven to "guard their property with clubs and shot-guns." In the fall, the *Voice* published an eighteen-page special edition to throw gasoline on the fire.[131] The Women's Christian Temperance Union and, more important, prohibitionist champions in the Presbyterian church weighed into the controversy by condemning not only those Presbyterians who had signed the petition but also the students, the trustees, and even Patton.[132] Presbyteries and synods from New York to California protested the university's alleged complicity in running a tavern for students. Ironically, at the same meeting that the Synod of New Jersey admonished the university over the Princeton Inn, it was laying plans to honor the Presbyterian church's role in the founding of the College of New Jersey with a commemorative tablet to be placed on the main doorway into Nassau Hall.[133] Prohibition was one reform movement during the progressive era in which Protestant modernists, pietists, and revivalists, as well as liberal Catholics and secular reformers, agreed.

Prohibition, they hoped, would eradicate the source of such social evils as crime, poverty, and prostitution. Many of the Protestants involved in the movement, moreover, were driven by a desire to preserve the Christian character of America.[134] In 1871, the prohibitionist element in the northern Presbyterian church had persuaded the General Assembly to pass a resolution, offered in the form of pastoral advice, which condemned the manufacturing of alcohol and the "reprehensible complicity" of anyone who rented property used in its traffic.[135] Compared to earlier decades, support for temperance among the faculty had clearly waned; and Patton, unlike McCosh, was known to polish off a couple of bottles of French wine with friends during evenings of conversation.[136] In the face of growing professional responsibilities, the faculty's commitment to the *in loco parentis* policy was also shrinking; supervising the behavior of a couple of hundred students in McCosh's day had been an easier task than sitting guard over a thousand students during Patton's presidency. Notwithstanding the yellow journalism of the *Voice* and the anger of Presbyterians, intemperance among students was clearly a greater problem in the 1890s than in past decades when students even had their own temperance society. Throughout the decade, students were routinely disciplined for intoxication, including one undergraduate who, while drunk and riding a bicycle, ran down a professor.[137]

While the university was losing its small-college character and pro-temperance sentiments were dwindling, prohibitionist Presbyterians expected the Presbyterians on the faculty, especially the ministers, to champion temperance convictions. Although many were doused with condemnation, temperance advocates singled out professor Charles W. Shields, the sole Presbyterian minister who signed the petition, for special denunciation. In one article recounting the trouble that the Inn caused its neighbors, the *Voice* sarcastically mused that Shields was "too busy figuring out the harmony of science with revealed religion to be disturbed" by "the racket."[138] Patton was caught in a dilemma. On the one hand, he was a Presbyterian minister and president of an institution whose founding and growth largely depended upon generous Presbyterians committed to higher education. On the other, he not only served as president of a self-professing nondenominational institution but also personally shared the Old School Presbyterian commitment to Christian liberty in the use of alcohol. In the end, Patton defended the doctrine of Christian liberty, the faculty's right of private association, and the university's independence from the church.

Fed up with abuse from Presbyterians, Shields decided to withdraw from the church with, as he put it, "heartfelt reverence and affection for a church in which so long I had lived and in which I had hoped to die."[139] At a special November meeting of the Presbytery of New Brunswick called to address Shields's request, twelve Presbyterian ministers from both the university and seminary faculty, it was reported, "rallied around President Patton in a solid phalanx, and fought against all efforts to criticize the college saloon or Dr. Shields in any way whatever." Before a large audience of students and townspeople at First Presbyterian Church in Princeton, Patton and his colleagues fought a technical battle, over parliamentary procedure and the book of discipline, against prohibitionist ministers who wanted to bring Shields up on charges. After hours of wrangling, Shields was dismissed from the denomination, but the minority attached a resolution to the motion calling attention to the church's 1871 declaration. As an observer described the events: "The first resolution bowed Dr. Shields out of the Presbyterian Church; the second administered a sly kick as he reached the door."[140] Shields joined the Episcopal church and was ordained a deacon in 1898 and a priest the following year. On first impression, Shields's decision to become an Episcopalian seems curious, yet he had a life-long interest in liturgy, and may have found in the Episcopal church an aesthetic balance to his rational defense of traditional Protestantism. Ironically, Shields's withdrawal only further incensed the prohibitionists.[141]

Patton's frustration was palpable in a letter to one trustee, "I am more sorry than I can say that so many of our Presbyterian Synods have condemned us without a hearing and have done us damage so unjustly."[142] He called a special meeting of the faculty at which they decided that no new regulations were needed to deal with student intemperance, only the enforcement of existing ones. Some professors were apparently so incensed at the reaction of Presbyterians that they wanted to eliminate the scholarship of free tuition for the sons of Presbyterian ministers. Ironically, the trustees had just renewed their commitment to continue these scholarships after Professor John T. Duffield argued that these students had a "religious influence" that helped Princeton "maintain her character as an Institution under evangelical religion's influence."[143] The elimination of scholarships was never given any official consideration. After the December meeting of the trustees, Patton went on the offensive against the intemperance of both the student body and the prohibitionists. Patton and others continued to preach abstinence to the student body. Patton and Dean Murray sent a letter to students' parents informing them that the trustees had instructed the faculty to enforce "literally and strictly" the university's ban on student drinking on or off campus.[144] At the same time, the university also issued a press release exonerating Shields and the institution.[145] When students returned from Christmas vacation in January 1898, the president preached a sermon, as directed by the trustees, on "The Duty of Self-Control," which admonished the students that, while "absolute prohibition" was unbiblical, Christians were bound by St. Paul's ethical maxim: "'If meat make my brother to offend, I will eat no flesh while the world standeth.'" If not in detail, at least in principle, Patton and others within the university continued to believe that it was a critical function of the university to shape the Christian character of the nation through the moral education of its future leaders. Consequently, he challenged them to learn self-control while they were young because they needed "an unclouded mind, trained intellect, good manners, strict integrity, [and] high moral purpose" for their future careers in which they will have an immeasurable influence over the lives of other people.[146]

At the annual dinner of the Princeton Club of New York that same month, Patton vindicated the university's independence. Professor Shields joined Patton at the table of honor, and every time his name was mentioned the alumni reportedly "sprang to their feet and cheered him." When the "eating and drinking" were completed, Patton addressed the audience of some 300 alumni, including some of his harshest critics. "I am loyal to my church. I know the law and the constitution of my church and I know that much of what has lately been quoted as the law of that church is not law and has no binding authority. But whether it has or not, I cannot consent to have the law of that church as such imposed on Princeton University" [Tremendous applause]. While "I hold my place at the head of your *alma mater*," the Presbyterian minister added, "I will do what in me lies to keep the hand of ecclesiasticism from resting on Princeton University."[147]

Ironically, Patton, whose election was opposed by those who loathed his strict Presbyterian confessionalism, defended the university's nondenominational status. This irony testified to the fact that new social realities and changes in the religious values inside the university in particular and American society at large added to the tensions between Princeton's civic and religious missions. In other words, changes in the university's civic mission, as evidenced in the crisis over the undergraduate curriculum and the Turner controversy, were not the only sources of the breakdown of the once harmonious relationship between Princeton's civic and religious missions. The Turner controversy had proved to be a victory for those vigilant to preserve the nonsectarian evangelical Protestant ideals of Princeton's heritage. Yet it was a costly victory, not only in that Patton alienated part of the faculty but also because evangelical Protestant hegemony over the life of the university proved to be fairly tenuous. By contrast, the temperance controversy resulted in a victory for those more interested in building a national university because it helped to codify the institution's standing as an officially nondenominational university. It also alienated many of those with evangelical expectations of the university. Changing educational, theological, and social values inside Princeton and within the nation at large upset the once harmonious relationship between the university's evangelical mission and its civic duties. The tangled mixture of Princeton's nonsectarian evangelical commitments and its nondenominational standing left few within the community pleased about the university's direction.

Crisis Four: The Lack of a Graduate College

"Princeton," wrote Henry Fairfield Osborn in the early twentieth century, "must progress with the rest of the educational world. In the past fifteen years we have stood absolutely still so far as any radical reconstruction is concerned, and we now occupy a unique and isolated position among the larger universities of the world." Coming from one of McCosh's "bright young men," this was a searing indictment of Patton's presidency. What made it all the more poignant was that Osborn wrote this in a pamphlet he privately circulated among influential alumni. Osborn had long given up on Patton whom he later characterized as an educational "medievalist."[148] He had left Princeton in 1891 for the opportunity to teach graduate students at Columbia University and to head the Natural History Museum in New York City. Osborn's words indirectly point to the final crisis of Patton's presidency, which centered on the absence of a bona fide graduate school at Princeton and Patton's lack of leadership to rectify this deficiency. Without a first-class graduate program, Osborn and others in the university believed, Princeton was not merely failing to improve the university's educational mission but was actually abrogating its civic responsibilities.

Assuming the title university had become almost a religious quest for many associated with the college in the 1890s. Students, like the faculty, regularly measured Princeton's growth against Harvard, Yale, and German universities.[149] Students also held out the goal of becoming "Princeton University" as a motive for abolishing the practice of student hazing.[150] Some alumni and faculty pretentiously spoke of "Princeton University" well before 1896.[151] For the grand sesquicentennial celebration, the trustees and faculty approved, after hundreds of hours of discussion, many of the trappings commonly associated with a university, such as academic gowns and hoods.[152] Also, in a conscious effort to cultivate an academic ethos like that of the two great English universities, the institution adopted the Gothic architectural style for its new buildings. Even the town of Princeton was becoming more cosmopolitan, as rich alumni like Moses Taylor Pyne and other important figures like Grover Cleveland and the writer Laurence Hutton moved into palatial mansions in Princeton.[153] While the faculty likely reveled in these new institutional trappings, becoming a university did not inaugurate for them an educational millennium. For many on the faculty it was only a beginning of Princeton's expanded public mission. They envisioned a major graduate program befitting the new title.

"Which of these methods of graduate study shall we foster at Princeton University?" Patton asked the trustees on the eve of the sesquicentennial celebration. "Shall we aim at pure culture? or shall we establish professional schools?" According to the president, the faculty "prefer the establishment of a graduate college, having for its object the promotion of advanced study in philosophy, science and literature." Hoping to seize the momentum generated by the sesquicentennial, the faculty immediately petitioned Patton and the trustees to create a committee to establish a graduate college. In their memorial to the trustees, presented at the first meeting after the celebration, they insisted that without a graduate college, "Princeton will be placed in a position of great discredit in comparison with other American Universities." Princeton, they noted, was already losing students "to the non-professional schools of Harvard, Cornell, Columbia, Johns Hopkins, and Chicago." This was despite that on paper, Princeton matched up well against the nation's top universities. According to a 1898 report of the U.S. Commissioner of Education, Princeton ranked ninth in the number of students in its graduate program, ahead of Berkeley, Stanford, and Wisconsin. Yet a majority of the 130 graduate students were seminarians, or "seminoles," cross-enrolled in the university's A.M. program.[154] The trustees agreed, formed a Graduate College Committee, and resolved that a well-equipped graduate program "will be of the highest service to American university education."[155] Yet the committee toiled without success. At almost every subsequent board meeting, they reported that no progress had been made because of a lack of financial support. In the fall of 1898, the faculty repeated its conviction that the graduate college represented "the highest interests of the University" and demanded that steps be taken to secure its success, but in the board meeting the following spring, the committee said it would ask to be discharged if it would not discourage the faculty.[156]

The lack of progress can be attributed in part to Patton's model of graduate education. The president, faculty, and trustees agreed that Princeton did not need professional schools to be a genuine university, only a graduate program. They differed, however, on the exact nature of that program, a difference that brings into clearer focus the different understanding of the nature of a university that was at work in this crisis. Princeton's faculty grew tired of standing on the sideline while other universities, such as Chicago and Michigan, busily aided the advance of American society. They wanted an independent "graduate college" that offered both specialized research by scholars in various disciplines and advanced training for the next generation of scholars. By contrast, Patton spoke of a "graduate department" that simply extended undergraduate studies to a more elevated plane.[157] To Patton, a university was merely an evolutionary step above the college species, but to Wilson and others a university was an entirely new genus. When Patton insisted at his inauguration that Princeton was already a university, he assumed that a university was not very different from the College of New Jersey. Consequently, since Patton was satisfied with Princeton's modest progress in graduate education, he offered little or no help to the Graduate College Committee, going no further than writing a few letters to wealthy patrons and briefly mentioning, in his speech announcing the name change at the sesquicentennial celebration, the need to raise an endowment for graduate studies.[158]

Although the crisis surrounding the absence of a strong graduate college was in large part a conflict between two different models of graduate education, it came to symbolize Patton's lack of decisive leadership over the affairs of the university. Other university presidents managed their institutions with the efficiency of executives of major corporations. President William Rainey Harper, for example, directed the University of Chicago's success with the zealous enthusiasm of a biblical prophet intent on creating an American Zion of religion, education, and democracy. By contrast, Patton, in the most generous terms, ran Princeton like the pastor of a small country church. He opened important meetings with scripture, prayer, and sometimes even a sermon.[159] His reports to the Board of Trustees were so brief that sometimes he did not even present a written report. Eventually, the trustees ordered him to prepare a formal report for each meeting.[160] Patton's amateurish style of management is evident in other aspects of his administration. Patton did not have an official "office"; rather he had a "study." More important, he did not have a secretary, and he was thus saddled with the incredible task of carrying on his own correspondence. Always the gentleman, Patton responded to even the most ridiculous letter including one from a person asking if the twentieth century began in the year 1900.[161] However, Patton was often criticized for his negligence in responding to important letters. In 1897, the trustees said that one of the most urgent needs of the administration was to appoint a university secretary: the institution "can no longer proceed with the old fashion methods," reported the trustees' minutes, but it was not until 1901 that a secretary was actually hired.[162] One of Patton's few accommodations to modern methods came in his dress. At the beginning of his administration, Patton wore a Prince Albert coat with a stock and sported side whiskers distinctive of many ministers in his day. By the turn of the century, he had donned a jacket and tie and shaved off the sideburns. Patton's lack of leadership was in part a sin of omission in that he often failed to take advantage of opportunities to improve Princeton. Woodrow Wilson, for example, came to Princeton in 1890 with the promise that a law school would be built. With this promise in hand, Wilson wrote out elaborate plans for the school. In 1891, when Theodore Dwight retired from Columbia Law School, many alumni and friends urged Patton to seize Dwight and start a law school. Patton failed to press the matter and the opportunity passed. As late as 1902, Patton was still talking about starting a law school "in the near future."[163]

Besides committing educational heresy in the opinion of those devoted to advancing the university's civic mission, Patton's indolent leadership bred frustration among the faculty, many of whom were McCosh-era alumni. One professor recalled that a division emerged within the faculty in the late 1890s between the "young faculty," whose "floor leader" was Woodrow Wilson, and the "old guard." Some of the "Young Turks" tried to make the best of the bad situation. The "malcontents," as Hibben described himself and his friends, met regularly at Paul Van Dyke's house to smoke cigars and commiserate over the terrible state of affairs at the university. Others, like Henry Fairfield Osborn and William M. Sloane, gave up and left for other universities. Meanwhile, Wilson's disillusionment slowly turned into contempt for the "shrewd man of metaphysics," as he privately described Patton. Wilson even pondered leaving several times when various universities offers him their presidencies. But friends persuaded him to stay and underwrote salary increases to make life in Princeton more tolerable.[164]

Recent changes in the composition of the Board of Trustees did not bode well for Patton's indifference to the faculty's calls to improve the university's civic mission. In fact, these changes bolstered the younger faculty's unwillingness to give up its vision of bona fide graduate education at Princeton and eventually led to the establishment of a graduate college despite Patton's indifference. When Patton took office, the Board of Trustees was filled with many old conservatives whom McCosh called "dotards," but in the ensuing decades many of these older conservatives died. In 1898, for example, Patton memorialized the passing of Charles E. Green, one of the more conservative trustees, in most wistful terms: "He would have lost his right arm rather than do anything that would sacrifice or put in jeopardy her Christian name. . . . For should Princeton ever move from her old Christian anchorage, she would be faithless to the memory of the men who had dowered her with their wealth, labors and prayers." Cyrus H. McCormick Jr. (1859–1936) saw these changes in the board in another light. "Every one of the recent elections in the Board of Trustees is a hopeful sign," he wrote Wilson, "and augurs well for the broadest interests of Princeton University."[165] Between 1896 and 1901, sixteen new trustees were elected, with the greatest single change coming in 1901 when the alumni finally won five new chairs which they elected directly.[166] Although the charter still preserved twelve chairs for ministers among the trustees, many of these new and influential trustees were McCosh-era alumni, like McCormick and Pyne, who were known to have "valued success and thought in large terms."[167]

When the faculty could not establish a graduate school with Patton's support, they decided to do it without him. In June 1900, the faculty petitioned the board about the lack of a graduate college. Realizing the seriousness of this resolution, Patton offered to head another committee to investigate the need to establish a "graduate department," but thereby played right into Professor West's hands.[168] West, whose efforts to reform the undergraduate curriculum had already been foiled by the president, worked behind the scenes to get three sympathetic and powerful trustees, George B. Stewart, Simon John McPherson, and Charles B. Alexander, appointed to Patton's committee. West even wrote the committee's report and ensured that Princeton would have a graduate school and not a mere "graduate department." More important, the committee recommended that the dean of the graduate college become an *ex-officio* member of the standing committee on the graduate college and submit his report directly to the trustees, effectively by-passing President Patton. Indeed, as intended, a graduate college was established, along with a dean who did not stand under Patton's authority. The "overthrow" was completed when West himself was elected dean. It was reported that "Patton did little more than stand by and look on."[169]

By the turn of the century, the once harmonious relationship between Princeton's religious and civic missions had given way to confusion and conflict. To some Presbyterians, as manifested in the Princeton Inn controversy, Princeton had abandoned its evangelical mission. To others within the university, Princeton's evangelical mission bordered on a sectarianism that hindered its public mission. When added to the complaints about the chaotic state of the undergraduate program and the battle over hiring Frederick Jackson Turner, the crisis surrounding the lack of a first-class graduate program only amplified the misgivings over the university's failure to fulfill its civic duties. Despite Patton's indifference, a small circle of professors and trustees had taken decisive steps to fulfill their vision of the university's enlarged public mission and established a graduate college without the president's support. More steps, however, were needed to secure that the university would not falter in this new civic endeavor.

A "Remedy" for Princeton's Problem

In 1901, Professor R. T. H. Halsey of Yale, a Princeton graduate, invited a group of Princeton trustees to dinner at the Waldorf Hotel in New York City. He also invited friends from Columbia, Harvard, and Johns Hopkins. Halsey asked his friends from the other schools to describe Princeton's reputation in the academic community. The trustees "were told in no uncertain terms that Princeton was becoming the laughing stock of the academic world, that the President was neglecting his duty, the professors theirs, and the students neglecting theirs, that Princeton was going to pieces."[170]

In early 1902, a conspiracy emerged to "remedy" Princeton's problem. On March 12, 1902, three professors—Cyrus F. Brackett, Henry B. Fine, and Woodrow Wilson—met privately with two trustees, David B. Jones and Cyrus H. McCormick Jr., to discuss what Wilson had earlier described as "the sinister influence" at Princeton. McCormick suggested that an executive committee be formed, incidentally consisting of three professors and two trustees, to administer the affairs of the university for Patton. In this way, Jones wrote to another trustee, the president would effectively be reduced to a "figurehead." Insisting that the proposal be presented as if it "originated wholly with the trustees," Wilson authored the plans for the committee. The entire scheme, they determined, would be conducted in secrecy in order to preserve Patton's dignity and also to protect the university from public ridicule for forcing its president out of office.[171] Yet, if Patton opposed the idea, they would suggest that he resign. When Jones, one of the new alumni trustees, and McCormick, whose father had hired Patton nearly thirty years earlier for the Presbyterian seminary in Chicago, approached the president, he was not amenable to the idea and threatened to resign in protest. In the following weeks, Patton wavered between his options: fight, submit, or resign. He seemed to soften when he wrote one trustee that he was open to the idea of an executive committee so long as it was "in accordance with strictly academic ideals and precedents and in a way that would conserve the traditional spirit of Princeton University."[172] Patton's position was strengthened when one of the more progressive trustees, Moses Taylor Pyne, "ratted" out the conspirators, as Jones put it, by telling the president that the entire board did not know about the proposal and not all those who did supported it.[173]

Just before commencement exercises in 1902, the plot came to fruition. After meeting with Jones and McCormick in Chicago, Patton conceded, deciding it would be in the best interests of Princeton if he resigned.[174] He was promised financial compensation and a professorship of ethics. Before he officially tendered his resignation at the board meeting, Patton took care of one final piece of personal business. He endowed a chair in moral philosophy for his son with money donated to Princeton designated for use according to the president's discretion. Once he resigned, the trustees suspended the by-laws and immediately elected Wilson as president with Patton's blessing. After Patton formally introduced the president-elect to the trustees at a brief meeting following the graduation exercises, the group sang "Old Nassau" and dispersed for the summer.[175] The faculty minutes of June 14 recorded that Patton's resignation came "as a surprise" and that his administration was "both brilliant and successful." A trustee later wrote Wilson that his election was "the act of Providence," perhaps not realizing how fully Wilson's friends had given Providence plenty of help.[176]

Patton and his fourteen-year presidency at Princeton was characterized by contradictions and paradoxes. He fought for a strict adherence to Old School Presbyterian principles within the church but encouraged a broad Christianity within the university. He opposed theological modernism at every turn yet supported the scholarship and professional development of his faculty. He was a devoted Presbyterian minister, but he jealously guarded the independence of the university against the encroachments of intemperate Presbyterians clamoring for the closing of the Princeton Inn. As a person, the genteel Patton was beloved by many if not all in Princeton; as a leader, he was at best tolerated, but often loathed. He was a witty after-dinner speaker who delighted many Princeton audiences, but an "inefficient" leader with little vision who took few concrete steps to improve the university. He championed a progressive combination of the traditional curriculum and newer disciplines, yet was content to allow the nation's future leaders to enjoy fully their youth. Upon his retirement from the university, Patton assumed the newly created presidency of Princeton Seminary, where he served as little more than the senior faculty member with a lofty title. It was a job, and a place, which agreed well with Patton. Historians have largely dismissed Patton as a throwback to an earlier generation better suited to lead Princeton before the Civil War than into the twentieth century.[177] Yet this portrait misses the larger point revealed in Patton and his presidency. The contradictions and paradoxes that characterized Patton and his tenure at Princeton reveal that a deep incongruity in American higher education's evangelical mission and its expanded civic mission had emerged in the late nineteenth and early twentieth centuries.

Patton actively sought to safeguard one aspect of McCosh's legacy, a commitment to evangelical Protestant higher education, yet in terms of another aspect of McCosh's other legacy, a commitment to advancing Princeton's academic standing, Patton proved to be unsuccessful. Ironically, Patton presided over the demise of his own vision for Princeton despite certain efforts to avert the changes sweeping across higher education, the Protestant church, and American society in the late nineteenth century. During much of McCosh's presidency, the institution's official public purpose harmoniously coexisted with its evangelical Protestant mission. As a de facto Presbyterian college that propagated a broadly evangelical Protestant theology and worldview shared by most Presbyterians and the larger Protestant community, the college served the nation's educational interests. During Patton's presidency, fundamental tensions between these two commitments emerged as a result of changes in the educational, intellectual, and social realities of the day and the university's efforts to advance its civic mission. In keeping with the general trend of university education in America, Princeton expanded its public mission during the 1890s through academic specialization, the professionalization of its faculty, the enlargement of its student body, and, at least to a modest degree, its graduate program. Yet Patton's indifference to the chaotic state of the undergraduate program, lazy students, and the absence of a well-developed graduate program cast grave doubts upon the traditional old-time "discipline and piety" educational philosophy and Patton's limited vision of graduate education. At the same time, the supernaturalism of evangelical Protestant theology came under increasing attack and the intellectual appeal of liberal Protestantism grew more viable. The traditional strategies intended to sustain the institution's evangelical Protestant character, as evidenced in Patton's refusal to hire the Unitarian Frederick Jackson Turner, came to be seen by many in the community as a form of sectarianism incompatible with a national university. The sacred cause of higher education had become a matrix of conflicting and often contradicting commitments. While Patton's personal failures as a leader undoubtedly compounded Princeton's difficulties, the forces of change had so divided allegiances, reordered old commitments, and created new priorities inside the university that it seems unlikely that any person could have preserved the old arrangement between the institution's civic and religious missions. Upon Patton's resignation, it was Wilson who faced the grand challenge of making Princeton a university that would serve the nation's educational needs in the twentieth century and somehow conserve its Protestant mission to shape the Christian character of American society.

Chapter 4

Making the University Safe
for Democracy, 1902–1910

The service of institutions of learning is not private but public," Woodrow Wilson proclaimed at his inauguration as Princeton University's thirteenth president. "Princeton for the Nation's Service," the title of Wilson's 1902 inaugural address, captured his vision of Princeton's mission. The nation, Wilson believed, desperately needed the university. The nation and its affairs, he observed, continued to "grow more and more complex" as a result of industrialization and bureaucratization. Furthermore, as successive waves of non-Protestant and non-Anglo-Saxon immigrant groups—"the more sordid and hapless elements" of southern Europe, as he described them elsewhere—congregated in the nation's growing cities, Wilson, like other Protestant leaders of his day, feared that America's democratic society stood on the verge of chaos. The very fabric of American society seemed to be ripping apart under the weight of ethnic and religious diversity. Like other educators of the day, Wilson envisioned the modern university's playing a crucial role in ordering the nation's business and political affairs and shaping the aspirations and values of the American people. A university education, Wilson explained, was "not for the majority who carry forward the common labor of the world" but for those who would lead the nation and mold the "sound sense and equipment of the rank and file." The university's task was twofold: "the production of a great body of informed and thoughtful men and the production of a small body of trained scholars and investigators." The latter function gave the university a larger civic mission than a college. According to Wilson's vision, Princeton would not train "servants of a trade or skilled practitioners of a profession." By enlarging the minds of students and giving them a "catholic vision" of their social responsibilities, Princeton instead would cultivate "citizens" who would live under the "high law of duty." "Every American university," Wilson concluded, "must square its standards by that law or lack its *national* title."[1]

Wilson's inauguration appeared to confirm the New York *Sun*'s assessment of his election: "the *secularization* of our collegiate education grows steadily more complete." Conventional interpreters, likewise, viewed the election of laypersons as presidents of American universities as evidence of the secularization of higher education in the late nineteenth and early twentieth centuries.[2] Subsequent developments at Princeton concerning religion during Wilson's presidency,

127

moreover, appear to confirm this evaluation. The university abandoned a variety of strategies, such as mandatory Bible classes, previously used to fulfill the university evangelical mission.

The installation of the first layperson as Princeton's president seemed to point the school toward a mission more worldly than his long line of predecessors, all Presbyterian clergymen, would have countenanced. Yet to conservative Presbyterians, ever vigilant against threats to evangelicalism's role in the church and society, the election of Wilson did not represent a "decided rupture" with the past. A leading conservative denominational periodical reassured its readers "that Princeton, so long a fountain of Christian truth and training . . . will continue steadfastly true to its traditions and be loyal to the great facts and faith of Christianity."[3] Wilson himself and his vision of Princeton's role within the nation inspired this confidence.

Presbyterians in the university's larger community of support had good reason to think that Wilson would not forsake Princeton's religious mission. Wilson (1856–1924) had briefly attended Davidson College before enrolling in Princeton College, graduating with the celebrated Class of 1879. He attended law school at the University of Virginia for a year before practicing law in Georgia. Yet a desire for an academic career, fostered by McCosh, led him to enroll in Johns Hopkins University for graduate work in political science and history. As a professor at Bryn Mawr College, he published an important work, *Congressional Government* (1885), for which Johns Hopkins awarded him a Ph.D. in lieu of a dissertation. He also taught at Wesleyan College before returning to his alma mater in 1890. Wilson's Presbyterian genealogy was as impressive as his scholarly credentials. Born in Staunton, Virginia, he was the son of Joseph R. Wilson, a Princeton Seminary alumnus and prominent leader of the southern Presbyterian church, and Jesse Woodrow Wilson, the daughter of a Presbyterian minister. Wilson himself was an elder at the Second Presbyterian Church in Princeton and later at the more upscale First Presbyterian Church, both churches dominated by the theological interests of Princeton Seminary.[4] Wilson's background gave conservatives in the university community little reason to doubt that he would not uphold their evangelical expectations of the university.

More important than Wilson's Presbyterian lineage was the fact that he shared their Protestant vision of America. To be sure, Wilson did not hold all of the theological convictions or educational policies of his conservative predecessors, Patton and McCosh. These differences explain the significant departures that occurred during his administration from the evangelical strategies previously employed to advance the university's religious mission. Yet Wilson shared their most basic conviction that the university should endeavor to Christianize America. Instead of viewing Wilson's election as evidence of Princeton's secularization, conservative Presbyterians embraced Wilson, for he shared their fundamental hope that the university would help provide a unifying center to a nation increasingly divided by ethnic and religious diversity.

According to Wilson, religion and education were organically related. Education, he believed, was essentially spiritual in character. Faith, he explained at his inauguration, provided "moral efficiency" to a university education. History, he insisted, demonstrated that those "ages of strong and definite moral impulse have been the ages of achievement." And, he reasoned, "the moral impulses which have lifted highest have come from Christian people,—the moving history of our own nation were proof enough of that." Wilson's educational and religious speeches, as John M. Mulder observes, are virtually indistinguishable because he repeatedly focused on the same two themes: the spiritual of education and the gospel of service. To Wilson, religion was not a subject taught, but a spirit that infused the curriculum. Nor was religion a confessional standard to which the faculty conformed but rather a disposition that inspired the entire educational endeavor. "I do not see how any university" can cultivate a catholic vision, he confessed in his inauguration, "if its teachings be not informed with the spirit of religion, and that the religion of Christ, and with the energy of a positive faith."[5] Wilson often described universities as "the nurseries of the nation's ideals" and believed that a university education would recreate and transform students into enlightened citizens.[6] Education brings "emancipation from narrowness—from narrowness of sympathy, of perception, of motive, of purpose, and of hope. And the deep fountains of Christian teaching are its most refreshing springs." Wilson thus blended Protestantism and democracy into a civic religion. To Wilson, like his predecessors McCosh and Patton, the university was the key institution for cultivating Christian citizens who could unite a divided people and lead the triumph of Protestantism over the affairs of the nation.

Wilson's election represented not a repudiation but a reconfiguration of Princeton's dual mission. From Witherspoon to McCosh, Princeton had been devoted to serving the nation and to maintaining its broadly evangelical heritage. McCosh had envisioned Princeton as an evangelical university that would serve the nation's civic and religious interests harmoniously. The growing plurality of American society, as well as the tensions inherent to McCosh's vision, subverted many of the strategies designed to create a national evangelical university. When these civic and religious commitments became incompatible under Patton's administration and the president was forced to choose between them, Patton demonstrated a clear preference for the institution's evangelical heritage. By contrast, Wilson focused primarily upon Princeton's public mission. Yet he did not abandon the university's religious mission; rather, he conformed it to the institution's public standing. Given the growing doubts about evangelicalism's intellectual credibility and the increasing concerns about the progressively heterogeneous character of American society, the key strategies designed to fulfill the institution's religious mission, such as mandatory classes in Bible, or to safeguard its religious character, such as informal theology tests for prospective faculty, seemed like sectarian relics at odds with Princeton's aspirations to national leadership. Thus Wilson eliminated parochial practices or replaced them with ones more compatible with the institution's broader civic mission. Correspondingly, in liberal Protestantism Wilson found a religion compatible with the institution's new "liberal culture" educational philosophy and with modern science. While important differences concerning the nature and role of Protestantism in the university divided Wilson's presidency from that of his predecessors, the larger Protestant mission of the institution continued to inspire Wilson and his colleagues. This common goal provided an important but often overlooked source of continuity between the religious mission of the old-time college and that of the modern university.

This chapter will first examine Wilson's reforms of the university, involving both the revitalization and the transformation of old educational values. The chapter will then explore the impact that Wilson's reconfiguration of the institution's dual mission had on the established policies and practices previously intended to perpetuate and safeguard its evangelical character. Finally, the chapter will briefly review the battle over Wilson's proposed Quad Plan and graduate college to analyze how the social conservativism of the community limited his progressive vision of Princeton's civic mission.

The Educational Revolution of the "Augustan Age"

One-time Princeton professor Henry Fairfield Osborn wrote to Woodrow Wilson shortly after his election, "I feel confident that the Augustan age is opening for Princeton.... Your task will be an easy one because of the enthusiasm and united support of the alumni and I trust the general public."[7] Princeton's "Augustan age" opened with President Wilson instituting a series of reforms that brought order to the undergraduate program and improved the graduate college. Wilson reorganized the faculty, revised the chaotic curriculum, inaugurated the preceptorial system, and recruited several outstanding scholars for the struggling graduate program. According to professor William Berryman Scott, the opening of Wilson's presidency brought "a wonderful revivification and clearing of the air" in Princeton.[8]

The intellectual revitalization of Princeton under Wilson sprang in large part from the new "liberal culture" philosophy of higher education that he implemented through the reorganization of the curriculum. Wilson's undergraduate classmate and educational ally, Henry Fairfield Osborn, perhaps best summarized the ideas behind the liberal culture philosophy of education: "The college course must . . . stand distinctively for culture, not in the restricted medieval sense of book learning but in the broad sense of the cultivation of knowledge, of individual judgment and opinion, reasoning, observation of men and things, expression, and the firm establishment of those high ethical and aesthetic standards which lend to all further specialization the absolutely essential elements of truth, beauty and service."[9]

In the final two decades of the nineteenth and the first two of the twentieth century, the liberal culture educational philosophy gained popularity among a small number of educators at elite colleges and universities. Liberal culture provided an alternative not only to the utilitarianism evident at many state universities, such as the University of Wisconsin, and to the specialized research model of Johns Hopkins and Clark Universities, but also to the old-time discipline and piety educational philosophy that had dominated established institutions such as Yale and Princeton. As president of Princeton University, Wilson become one of the leading champions of the liberal educational philosophy.[10] "What is the principle object of a liberal education?" Wilson asked Princeton alumni at a dinner in Washington, D.C. "It is," he answered, "to liberate men from the dull round of one idea, to broaden their minds and their ability to conceive."[11] A truly liberal education, Wilson insisted, was "narrowed to no one point of view, to no one vocation or calling."[12]

To Wilson, a liberal culture education prepared Princeton's graduates for public service. The privilege of a college education, he asserted in his inaugural address, "is for the minority who plan, who conceive, who superintend, who mediate between group and group and must see the wide stage as a whole."[13] Arthur T. Hadley, Wilson's counterpart at Yale, insisted that a liberal education "is not liberal in the sense of being unrestricted; it is liberal in the sense of being a preparation for citizenship."[14] A liberal education at Princeton would give the nation's future leaders a depth of knowledge and a breadth of vision unmatched by either the specialized research or more utilitarian universities. "This higher sort of education," Wilson said in a 1903 speech, was "for the few—for the few chosen" who would "stand at the front" of American society "and offer themselves as guides."[15]

Princeton's liberal culture vision of higher education, Wilson believed, directly benefited national interests by preparing broad-minded leaders for public service. Wilson also believed that the university indirectly assisted American society by serving as a role model for other universities struggling to order their undergraduate programs in the twentieth century. Wilson, like other educational reformers of the day, wanted to strengthen the bond between his university and American society. Charles R. Van Hise's "Wisconsin idea," for example, tried to improve this union by having the university solve some of the state's technical and social problems and by enlarging the opportunity for a university education through extension courses. William Rainey Harper envisioned the University of Chicago as part of a broad system of education that would link specialized scholarship with undergraduate, professional, and graduate training, as well as with more popular forms of education such as correspondence courses and Sunday schools.[16] By contrast, Wilson's vision of Princeton's role in American society was more elitist than democratic. He hoped that through its new undergraduate program, as he told the trustees, Princeton would exert "leadership" among America's universities and in this way exert an enlightening influence upon American society.[17]

Wilson's new educational vision entailed both the revitalization of McCosh's discipline and piety educational philosophy and its transformation. In his inaugural address, Wilson, like McCosh before him, insisted that the traditional curriculum—Greek, Latin, mathematics, and English—held a prominent place in a liberal education, but the "circle of liberal studies" had expanded so much in the past generation that it was no longer "possible to make these few stand for all." Unfortunately, as the university widened the circle of knowledge in "our attempt to escape the pedantry and narrowness of the old fixed curriculum, we have gone so far as to be in danger of losing the old ideals." Although he appreciated that the traditional curriculum helped to discipline students' minds and to familiarize them with a body of knowledge considered important to be a well-educated gentleman, he believed that a modern liberal education would have to do more. "We seek in general education, not universal knowledge, but the opening up of the mind to a catholic appreciation of the best achievements of men and the best processes of thought since days of thought set in." The purpose of the liberal culture curriculum, therefore, transcended the older discipline and piety education. The liberal culture educational philosophy, moreover, transformed the works studied in the traditional curriculum into a canon containing the best aesthetic, moral, and social values of western civilization. These values, he believed, were essential for citizens to be leaders of American society.[18]

Wilson's dogmatic insistence that a liberal culture education preserved the unity of knowledge most clearly illustrates how his new educational philosophy both revitalized and transformed the older discipline and piety educational philosophy. Sounding very much like McCosh, Wilson lamented "that we have so spread and diversified the scheme of knowledge in our day that it has lost coherence." In his inaugural address, he declared that learning "is not divided. Its kingdom and government are centered, unitary, single." For McCosh, the unity of knowledge meant the harmonious coexistence of the truths derived from natural revelation and reason with those learned from divine revelation. During McCosh's administration, the traditional liberal arts curriculum contained the former, while the mandatory Bible classes and chapel services taught the latter, and the required courses in apologetics and natural theology reconciled any "apparent" conflicts between the two. By contrast, Wilson's insistence on the preservation of the unity of knowledge concentrated exclusively on natural revelation. In the aftermath of the curricular chaos of the Patton administration, Wilson revived the university's commitment to the preservation of the unity of truth, with the significant change that supernatural revelation was discarded in favor of a sole focus on the unity of human knowledge. This shift marks a decisive break with the previous educational philosophy and curriculum of Princeton. Theology no longer provided a unifying center to the undergraduate curriculum. Wilson had placed Princeton's conventional portrait of liberal education within an entirely new framework, a change that would have dramatic consequences for traditional religious education at Princeton.

Although Wilson removed the unifying theological center that had shaped collegiate education under McCosh, he still shared the covenantal theological heritage of McCosh and his other nineteenth-century predecessors. To be sure, the main thrust of Wilson's educational views, as John M. Mulder observes, was basically antitheoretical and had little interest in the more abstract questions of epistemology and metaphysics that preoccupied McCosh and Patton.[19] Yet Wilson's efforts to bring coherence to the university had their roots in his covenantal mode of thinking that had been nurtured by his upbringing in the southern Presbyterian church of James H. Thornwell. According to the covenant or "federal" theology of Thornwell and other Presbyterian theologians, God had established a covenant of grace, which involved God's offer of salvation, and a covenant of nature, which concerned God's moral law for nations. Covenant theology essentially offered, according to Mulder, a comprehensive view of "the individual, the church and society, each with its own function and place within the divine scheme of government of the world." While this "covenant of politics" provided a rational and predictable "government to every dimension of human life," a careful balance between the individual and the group was necessary for peace to prevail. Consequently, in the face of the rampant disorder which he had inherited from Patton's presidency, Wilson stressed the organic, or community, side of the balance in order to restore harmony to the university community.[20]

This covenantal mode of thinking, moreover, provided Wilson with a rationale for removing theology as the unifying center of Princeton's undergraduate curriculum. Because the curriculum, according to Wilson's covenantal mode of thinking, should embody those truths relevant to the covenant of nature, not the covenant of grace, the new liberal arts curriculum that he implemented did not have a parochial character. Wilson's professional work as a scholar also illustrates the important effect that the distinction between the covenant of grace and the covenant of nature had on his educational philosophy. This distinction enabled Wilson as a professor of political science, like his predecessor Alexander Johnston, to keep his Christian faith in God's immutable commands for the individual divorced from his study of the natural forces that shape the development of government. Although he drew out broadly moral concerns in his study of the development of constitutional government and the evolution of civil law, he did not appeal—to Patton's chagrin—to Scripture or divine Providence to explain their origins. In this way, he avoided violating the professional standards of the day.[21] Since all educational issues, such as the curriculum and scholarly methods, were ultimately grounded in the covenant of nature, Wilson's nontheological educational philosophy transcended the sectarian interests that had plagued Princeton during Patton's administration. Instead, Wilson established an educational platform that could appeal to a national audience.

In order to prepare Princeton's students to serve the nation, Wilson believed that the undergraduate curriculum had to nurture "the intimate and sensitive appreciation of moral, intellectual, and aesthetic values" characteristic of a liberal culture education.[22] Yet the curriculum, as it stood at the end of Patton's tenure, was hardly the incarnation of these values. At his first meeting of the Board of Trustees, Wilson said that after thirty years of "miscellaneous enlargement" the curriculum needed "a thorough-going readjustment." Reorganizing the curriculum was not incidental but critical to Princeton's civic mission. After completing the revisions, Wilson told the alumni in 1904, "we are engaged in nothing less than in determining what the next generation shall be."[23]

Wilson began his revision of the curriculum by bringing efficiency to the administration. Throughout the late nineteenth and early twentieth centuries, universities experienced the same sort of bureaucratic transformation that was reorganizing American businesses, churches, and government.[24] Along with his covenantal theology, this revolution of organizational efficiency was another source prompting Wilson's restructuring of the university. He first merged the Academic Department and the John C. Green School of Science into one faculty, an action that removed the second-class status of the latter program. He simultaneously reorganized the faculty into eleven departments: philosophy, history and politics, art and archaeology, classics, English, modern languages, mathematics, astronomy, physics, chemistry, and the natural sciences. Together these new departments represented the key components of Princeton's new ideal curriculum. Wilson made other changes as well, replacing Samuel R. Winans, one of Patton's old cronies, as Dean of the Faculty with the "Young Turk," Henry B. Fine, and placing like-minded colleagues at the head of each department. Wilson brought organizational efficiency not only to the academic departments but also to the university's bureaucratic operations. The university furthermore hired dozens of minor administrators and secretaries to take over many of the responsibilities previously handled by professors. In addition, Wilson hired a personal secretary.[25]

Upon this foundation, Wilson worked carefully with a faculty committee to renovate the undergraduate curriculum.[26] The new curriculum, approved by the trustees in June 1904, possessed three distinctive features. First, the university created a new degree, Bachelor of Letters, for those students who, as the president explained, wanted a "humanistic" education but did not have the knowledge of Greek prerequisite for admission to the A.B. degree.[27] In the "battle of the classics" of the late nineteenth century, the study of Greek had suffered major casualties, if not mortal wounds. Harvard made Greek an optional entrance requirement for its B.A. degree in 1886. Yale did the same in 1903. Yet Wilson refused to capitulate to this trend and declared, "When Princeton drops Greek, she will be ready to open her doors to the 'co-eds.'"[28] Wilson defended the Greek requirement for its humanistic value, on the basis that it helped to train students in the "intellectual movements of the modern world," not because it was necessary to prepare candidates for the ministry as McCosh and Patton had argued. Correspondingly, the faculty made the entrance requirements for the B.S. and B.Litt. degrees almost the same as those for A.B. degree. "You understand, gentlemen," Wilson told the alumni when he unveiled his new curriculum, "we are for liberal culture, and that we also stand by preference for classical culture."[29]

A second distinction of the new curriculum was that it required a broad selection of traditional courses for all three degrees. All freshman studied English, Latin, mathematics, and French or German. Sophomores took physics, logic, psychology, and Latin and electives from a limited number of offerings. All classes were made a uniform three hours in credit, and each student took five courses a semester. In this new scheme, the total number of undergraduate courses actually dropped. In the final year of Patton's presidency, the university offered 332 different courses, but by 1904–1905 that figure had dropped to 211.

The pressures of academic specialization, however, gradually reversed the trend so that by 1910, Wilson's final year as president, the university offered 276 different courses.[30]

The most significant feature of Princeton's new curriculum was the major-grouping system. The major-grouping system required juniors and seniors to concentrate a majority of their electives in one of the university's eleven departments, thereby avoiding, according to Wilson, both "narrow specialization" and a "miscellany of subjects."[31] The new curricular requirements rectified the chaos that had slowly emerged in the elective system while Patton was president and put Princeton in the vanguard of the movement to harness the elective system. Rumblings against the now aging free-elective system had even been heard at Harvard, when Abbott Lawrence Lowell began to criticize the system in 1903. As president in 1909, Lowell actually revised Harvard's elective system after a pattern similar to Princeton's curriculum. Princeton "declares that all her bachelor degrees," English professor George M. Harper wrote in the *Educational Review*, "shall stand for liberal culture, as opposed to practical training." The university's new curriculum, he added, "is for Princeton merely the reaffirmation of principles to which she has always been faithful."[32] Despite professed commitments to tradition, the new major-grouping system revealed that Princeton's liberal culture curriculum, contrary to conventional interpretations, had multiple purposes. The major-grouping system not only provided students with a solid foundation in the liberal arts but also allowed them to explore specialized fields of knowledge, and it prepared some students for a vocation, such as engineering, immediately upon graduation.[33]

The first major revision of the curriculum in Princeton's 157-year history won nearly unanimous praise. Writing in the conservative *Presbyterian*, one alumnus applauded the new scheme and expressed the hope "to see the standards raised to the highest ideals and productive for the best practical results."[34] An editorial in the *New York Times* observed that, amid all the educational disorder in American universities created by the free elective, Princeton's new curriculum "enters as a comprehensive attempt to reduce chaos to order."[35] Students were taken aback, not unfavorably, by Wilson's bold plan; as one wrote in the *Nassau Literary Magazine*, "The traditional conservative spirit of Princeton— the spirit that frowns on every change—has received a profound shock."[36] Wilson himself was probably the most impressed admirer of the new curriculum. After reporting about its successes at the end of the fall semester in 1904, he told the trustees, "The baccalaureate degree is *again* made to stand for a definite, ascertainable body of training."[37]

In light of the university's growing student body and the lax standards of Patton's administration, Wilson proposed to the trustees in the fall of 1902 that Princeton adapt the tutorial system of Oxford University by hiring no less than fifty preceptors. The idea of adapting Oxford's tutorial system as a way of reinvigorating the undergraduate program had first been considered during the lazy days of Patton's administration. Wilson and West, among other Princeton professors, were noted anglophiles who turned not to Germany but to England for solutions to the university's problems.[38] In the summer of 1902, West had even been dispatched to study England's entire educational system. The preceptorial system, Wilson told the alumni, would be employed in those disciplines that formed the "gist" of a liberal education—the humanities and natural sciences. The preceptor would hold the rank of an assistant professor, would have faculty voting privileges, and would serve as a "guide, philosopher, and friend" to the students.[39] For many courses students had two class lectures and one preceptorial weekly. Laboratory work replaced the preceptorial meeting in the science courses. Princeton's adaptation of the Oxford system, incidentally, did not include the pass-honor distinction that Patton had recommended a decade earlier.

To Wilson, the preceptorial system directly advanced Princeton's civic mission: "Princeton must supply this country with thoughtful men, who will stand behind the statesman, for the life of a nation depends upon the thought and principle of its people." The preceptorial system would ensure that Princeton graduates were such "thoughtful men."[40] As he had done in his inaugural address, Wilson looked to Princeton's past for inspiration in planning for the university's future with the preceptorial system. "We are forming plans for a new Princeton . . . like the old Princeton," the president told Andrew Carnegie in a request for money for the preceptorial system. In his appeal to Princeton's history, however, Wilson did not go back to the college's founding in 1746 but to Witherspoon's presidency during the Revolutionary War, when the college's direct service to the nation was more obvious. "Witherspoon," he wrote Carnegie, "made Princeton an instrument of patriotic public service; we mean, if we can, to make her the same again."[41] Wilson, moreover, believed that the preceptorial system would not only allow Princeton to serve the nation more efficiently but would also provide inspiration for other American universities. When the trustees approved the adoption of the preceptorial system in June 1905, Wilson predicted that it and the major-grouping system "are likely to prove a reformation to University education in this country."[42]

In the fall of 1905, Princeton introduced the preceptorial system of undergraduate instruction. Together with the modern liberal culture curriculum, the preceptorial system breathed new life into the undergraduate program. The preceptorial system was Wilson's most radical innovation and his most enduring contribution to undergraduate education at Princeton, and to American collegiate education in general, insofar as other institutions, such as Harvard, Yale, Swarthmore, and Reed, adopted Princeton's program. While Wilson is usually credited with the innovation, he could not have achieved it without the cooperation of the faculty, the approval of the trustees, and the financial support of the alumni.[43] Whereas the undergraduate program at research-oriented universities was ancillary to the graduate program, such as at Johns Hopkins, or was one among many schools, such as at Cornell, at Princeton the undergraduate program found a secure place at the very heart of the university.

The preceptorial system reflected Wilson's revitalization and transformation of another key element in McCosh's educational program. As Wilson explained to the alumni, the plan combined the best aspect of the small colleges—personal contact between the teacher and student—with the best elements of the modern university—the wide selection of courses and the presence of "original and inspiring men of science and letters."[44] Wilson and his colleagues hoped to recreate for their students their own undergraduate experience during the halcyon days of McCosh's presidency.[45] Nineteen years earlier, McCosh had argued in his debate with Charles W. Eliot that "the religion of love" bonded students and professors into a community. The preceptorial system, however, shifted the bond between students and faculty from religious to educational grounds. The object of Princeton's preceptorial system, Wilson wrote in *Harper's Magazine*, was "to prevent the disintegration of the university, its disintegration in that essential feature of all vital teaching, the intimate acquaintance and contact of pupil and teacher."[46]

Wilson's prediction about the success of the major-grouping and the preceptorial systems came to fruition. An editorial in the students' *Nassau Literary Magazine* declared the preceptorial plan "universally popular with the undergraduate body." Most of the faculty hailed the system a grand success.[47] Professor John G. Hibben told a group of alumni that the reform had created a new feeling of academic responsibility among the students, and William Berryman Scott, upon returning from a sabbatical in Europe, claimed that "a revolution had taken place in the life of Princeton."[48]

Liberal culture received expression in more than just the new curriculum and the preceptorial system at Princeton. Even the collegiate Gothic architecture, which the university adopted during the flurry of building construction surrounding the sesquicentennial celebration, embodied the values that the university was seeking to nurture. Although Princeton was founded on the model of the Scottish dissenting academies, the administration, ironically, turned to Oxford and Cambridge for inspiration as it made plans for the twentieth century. By adopting collegiate Gothic, Wilson said, "we have added a thousand years to the history of Princeton by merely putting those lines in our architecture which point every man's imagination to the historic traditions of learning in the English-speaking race."[49] The university's architect, Ralph Adams Cram, also linked a liberal education with Gothic architecture, as he told a group of alumni that the style "is absolutely expressive of the civilization we hold in common with England and of the ideals of a liberal education now firmly fixed at Princeton."[50] Gothic architecture, T. J. Jackson Lears observes, promoted a sense of continuity with aristocratic traditions of the past and eased the tradition to a more secular and specialized mode of cultural authority.[51] The adoption of collegiate Gothic in many ways embodied the transition from McCosh's theological to Wilson's liberal culture educational philosophy.

While Gothic architecture may have helped to create a more academic ethos, the revised curriculum and preceptorial system corrected the lax academic standards that had emerged under Patton's presidency. The revised undergraduate program went hand in hand with another initiative begun at the outset of Wilson's presidency: Wilson and his colleagues agreed to "purge" the undesirable element from the student body through tougher standards. Even before the implementation of the new curriculum and the preceptorial system, the faculty expelled record numbers of students for academic failure. The trend continued throughout Wilson's presidency despite the alarm of alumni who worried about their sons' flunking out.[52] Undergraduate enrollment even dropped briefly.[53] "Princeton is no country club," one student wrote his father in December 1904. Instead of the "robust gentlemen" of the Class of 1906, the same student complained in another letter, if Wilson had his way by 1910 Princeton would be populated by the "four-eyed greaser," "dilapidated cripple," and the "narrow minded and colossal ass."[54] "Student life is hell," another student recorded in his diary in January 1907. The student flunked out at the end of the year.[55]

"Dr. McCosh founded the modern Princeton," Andrew F. West told a meeting of alumni. Completely ignoring Patton's presidency, West went on to explain that McCosh's "pupil and successor has taken what he found, has developed it, and carried it along, and the ideas he represents are the full expression of what Princeton ought to be."[56] To many within the community, Wilson was carrying on to completion McCosh's legacy, or at least one part of it. A 1906 review in the *Princeton Alumni Weekly* of the university's progress since the sesquicentennial celebration gave West and many other people plenty of good reasons to have faith in Wilson's vision of Princeton as an institution that lived up to its university title. Since the fall of 1896, the faculty had more than doubled, growing from 82 to 166, the endowment had increased from $1.677 million to $3.284 million, the library's holdings had doubled, the number of eating club houses had increased from four to thirteen, the number of buildings on campus had doubled, and even the campus itself had grown through land acquisitions from 225 to 538 acres.[57] After visiting Wilson at Princeton as part of his tour of leading American universities, a correspondent from the Glasgow *Herald* wrote that the American university president "must be a business man, prepared to lead a life of Rooseveltian energy."[58] For Wilson, succeeding Patton who was more like George B. McClellan than the "Rough Rider," this was high praise.

In his first four years as president, Wilson had proved to be a visionary leader who worked with the faculty and trustees to fulfill their shared ambition to make Princeton a national university dedicated to public service. Wilson's efforts to advance Princeton's civic mission entailed the revitalization and the alteration of many educational values associated with the nineteenth-century college. The new liberal culture curriculum drew inspiration from the humanistic values and the courses associated with the old-time curriculum, yet theology no longer framed and unified the undergraduate curriculum. The preceptorial system, not religious worship, sought to create a close community between students and faculty in which enlightened citizens could be trained. Although evangelical convictions and practices no longer molded the shape of the curriculum, traditional Protestant concerns regarding the religious education of students and the larger Protestant mission of higher education resurfaced in other parts of the curriculum and life of the university. In a nation divided by ethnic and religious diversity and faced with new social problems created by industrialization and urbanization, Wilson believed that Princeton had a civic responsibility. He asserted, "No man in these troublesome times can distinguish the right course of action unless he has a broad and intellectual mind." The new curriculum and preceptorial system, Wilson and his colleagues were confident, provided the nation's future leaders with the liberal perspective necessary to guide the nation.

Making the University Safe for Religion

During the presidency of Patton, the once-harmonious relationship between Princeton's dual heritage—upholding broadly evangelical Protestant ideals and meeting the nation's educational needs—had broken down into competing and sometimes conflicting sets of interests. On one side, many conservative Presbyterians castigated Patton and the university for allegedly forsaking its Christian mission by failing to champion evangelical mores regarding temperance. On the other, Wilson and a coterie of progressive professors and trustees loathed Patton's unwillingness to hire the renowned, but Unitarian, scholar Frederick Jackson Turner. These conflicting sets of interests had seemingly stalled the institution's progress in the eyes of Wilson and his allies. Wilson resolved these conflicts by giving priority to the university's public mission. He was not shy about telling Presbyterians about the change; "Public service is our word, public welfare our ideal," Wilson told a meeting of the Presbyterian Union in Newark, New Jersey, in April 1905.[59] Wilson dropped conventions and customs that appeared to foster sectarianism and conflicted with the institution's nondenominational, public standing and its national aspirations. The impact of the university's new civic priority was most evident in a key strategy previously designed to secure Princeton's evangelical orientation: faculty hiring policies. The university's new public mission, moreover, affected the university's historic relationship with the northern Presbyterian church and Princeton Seminary. Important changes on the board of trustees and the expansion of the university's community of support beyond the Presbyterian church, moreover, promoted the institution's new civic orientation.

In the late nineteenth century, McCosh had raised professional competence to the level of important as theological orthodoxy when hiring new faculty. He recruited professors not only from the Presbyterian communion but also from the larger Protestant community and warned them of his expectation that their academic work should remain compatible with an orthodox faith. Patton attempted to preserve the institution's religious character through this policy. But as the controversy over Frederick Jackson Turner dramatically illustrated, Wilson and many of his colleagues found the line between the institution's Christian heritage and its professedly nonsectarian public standing too tightly drawn at the borders of evangelical Protestantism. Consequently, Wilson and his colleagues initiated new hiring practices based primarily on the scholarship, not the theology, of a prospective professor. If evangelical orthodoxy conflicted with Princeton's principal purpose and inhibited its recruitment of renowned scholars, as Wilson and professors like John G. Hibben believed during the Turner controversy, then removing such informal theology requirements positioned the institution to gather an excellent faculty. The new criteria met the goal of making Princeton a top-flight university and conformed with what Wilson and his colleagues considered to be the institution's principal purpose.

Besides breathing new life into the undergraduate program, the preceptorial system also brought a massive infusion of new blood into the faculty. The recruitment of the bright young corps of preceptors clearly illustrates the new grounds for hiring faculty, primarily in that Wilson did not give the religious commitments or affiliations of prospective preceptors the same consideration as his predecessors. In hiring preceptors, Wilson was essentially interested in finding capable intellectuals who could relate to students. Wilson asked Frederick Jackson Turner, for example, about a candidate's scholarship and "his personality and antecedents."[60] The president did not merely want competent scholars but preceptors who, as he explained to the students, "were *clubable*" and could easily fit into the university's social milieu.[61] Wilson worked with each department in selecting the preceptors, and he even met personally with each candidate before he was hired. In the process, Wilson did not fail to leave an indelible impression: "I had never before talked face to face with so compelling a person," remembered Robert K. Root. "Had Woodrow Wilson asked me to go with him and work under him while he inaugurated a new university in Kamchatka or Senegambia I would have said 'yes' without further question." Wilson, by taking part in hiring each preceptor, ensured that they would be loyal to him. After receiving a job offer from Wilson, William Starr Myers wrote in his diary, "Thank God for this . . . should mean a future career for me."[62] By the fall of 1905, Wilson had found forty-seven "clubable" scholars who shared his vision.

The sudden converge of these young scholars upon the university in the fall of 1905 brought a diversity of backgrounds, educational experiences, and scholarly interests unknown to Princeton when it was a college. Of the original forty-seven preceptors, only nine had done their undergraduate work at Princeton. Thirty-four had earned a Ph.D. degree, including six at Harvard, five at Johns Hopkins, four at Chicago, and three each at Yale, Columbia, and Princeton. None had graduated from Princeton Seminary. Just as Daniel C. Gilman had pillaged many of the elite institutions when he was organizing Johns Hopkins's first faculty in 1876, Wilson recruited preceptors away from teaching positions at Princeton's chief rivals, including Harvard, Columbia, Yale, and Chicago.[63]

To transform Princeton into a national university with a first-class faculty, Wilson was willing to hire professors whose scholarship or church affiliations were unsympathetic to Princeton traditions. Wilson assured the philosopher Frank Thilly (1865–1934), a popular teacher at the University of Missouri and a rising figure in the academic world, that his lack of church membership would not be an "embarrassment" to the university and that his conviction that philosophy was not a branch of revealed religion was compatible with Princeton's educational ideals.[64] In 1904, Wilson hired the first Jewish member of Princeton's faculty, Horace Meyer Kallen, and the first Catholic, David A. McCabe, in 1909. While the faculty, like the student body, remained overwhelming Protestant in composition, the presence of Catholic, Jewish, and atheist scholars foreshadowed the theological diversity that would eventually characterize the modern university.[65]

Just as Wilson made scholarly competence, not religious affiliation, the central criterion for hiring new faculty members, he used professional qualifications to guide his firing policy as well, sometimes with apparently ruthless results. Wilson even fired one incompetent professor whose family connections with the university antedated the Civil War, an act that contrasts sharply with McCosh's reputed toleration of incompetent professors on his faculty. At the beginning of his presidency, the trustees had given Wilson the unusual authority "to create such vacancies in such force as he may deem for the best interests of the University."[66] The eccentricities of the French professor Arnold Guyot Cameron, whose name was almost synonymous with Presbyterian Princeton, quickly wore thin on the new president. Despite the fact that the Class of 1904 had chosen him their favorite professor, or perhaps because of it, Wilson informed Cameron in the spring of that year that his contract would not be renewed after the following academic year. At a meeting with the president at Prospect, Cameron became so enraged that Wilson withdrew the offer of an additional year and ordered him out of the house. Cameron described Wilson as the "Devil" and his colleagues as "villainous knaves," and reportedly never again set foot on campus though he lived in Princeton for the rest of his life.[67]

Wilson more than made up for the loss of Cameron by hiring several renowned scholars such as Frank Frost Abbot and Edward Capps in classics and Harry A. Garfield in politics. Despite Wilson's allegedly anti-science views, he also hired several outstanding scientists including James Hopwood Jeans in mathematics, Edwin G. Conklin in biology, and Owen Willans Richardson in physics.[68] Like many of the preceptors, a number of these scholars came to Princeton because of Wilson. When Capps asked Conklin why he came to Princeton, Conklin answered, "Woodrow Wilson, and what brought you here?" "The same," was Capps' reply.[69]

Between 1902 and 1909, Princeton's faculty grew from 98 to 162, an increase of 65 percent. By 1909, 57 percent of faculty professors held a Ph.D. degree or its equivalent, and a surprising 75 percent of the preceptors had doctorates. In all, 60 percent of the faculty, including those at the rank of instructor, held Ph.D. degrees. Even more spectacular was the turnover in the faculty. By the fall of 1909, 57 percent of the professors and preceptors on the staff had come to Princeton since Wilson's inauguration, while in all three ranks—professor, preceptor, and instructor—the figure is an even more astonishing 68 percent.[70] In short, Wilson had gathered a faculty that was more scholarly, more diverse, and, perhaps most important for the long-term character of the university, unfamiliar with McCosh, Patton, or Princeton when conservative Protestant orthodoxy prevailed in the recruitment of the faculty.

Wilson's reconfiguration of Princeton's dual mission not only put an end to the hiring practices that had been used to safeguard Princeton's evangelical character but also led to a distancing of the university from the Presbyterian church.

"Sectarianism," Harvard President Charles W. Eliot believed, would "impair the public confidence in the impartiality and freedom of the university."[71] The northern Presbyterian church, which in the late nineteenth and early twentieth centuries was controlled by conservatives, represented the kind of sectarianism incompatible with a university's public standing and national aspirations. Consequently, Wilson and others attempted to free the university from any kind of informal control that the Presbyterian church might exert over the institution. In his confrontation with Patton before the Presbyterian Union in 1902, for instance, Wilson took umbrage at his predecessor's casual reference to Princeton as a Presbyterian institution. As he had stated in his sesquicentennial address, Wilson believed that the connection between Princeton and the Presbyterian church was largely incidental. "It is a Presbyterian college," Wilson told Patton, "only because the Presbyterians of New Jersey were wise and progressive enough to found it.... The college is based on nonsectarianism."[72] Wilson's revisionist history found its way into a number of publications, including the 1902–1903 edition of the university catalogue. In a section on the history of the college's founding, the catalogue noted that, after the 1741 schism between Old and New Side Presbyterians, several Presbyterians who were associated with the New Side's Presbytery of New York and who were dissatisfied with the academic quality of the Log College decided to organize a genuine liberal arts college. "Convinced of the futility of awaiting united synodical action, and of the evils which would arise from the supervision of a church judicatory, they determined upon independent though concerted action." They wanted to establish a college in New Jersey, "without assistance from either synod, which they 'probably neither sought nor desired.'"[73] This last clause was particularly galling to many Presbyterians. William H. Roberts, Stated Clerk of the General Assembly of the northern Presbyterian church, challenged Wilson in a letter in February 1907 to produce historical evidence to support the claim that the ministers involved in Princeton's founding believed that evil would arise from the supervision of a church judicatory and that they did not want support from the Synod of New York. Roberts claimed that historical evidence in the church's records proved the opposite.[74] In the following year's catalogue, the section on Princeton's founding was abridged and the controversial passage dropped, most likely because Wilson did not want to risk a controversy with a still sizable portion of the institution's constituency while he tried to reform the university.[75]

Wilson and the trustees more than talked about Princeton's independence from the Presbyterian church. In order to qualify for retirement funds offered by the Carnegie Foundation for the Advancement of Teaching, Wilson persuaded the trustees to declare Princeton an officially nondenominational institution in 1906.[76] The Carnegie Foundation, building upon various attempts to improve the quality of American higher education, had offered to finance the pensions of professors at private colleges and universities. According to the Carnegie Foundation, the chief culprit for the often backward conditions at many American colleges was their denominational ties. Consequently, the foundation offered money to only nonsectarian private institutions. Woodrow Wilson, Nicholas

Murray Butler of Columbia, David Starr Jordan of Stanford, Arthur T. Hadley of Yale, and McCosh's old nemesis, Charles W. Eliot, served on the original board and formulated the qualifications for pension funds. Henry Smith Pritchett, president of the Carnegie Foundation, defended their decision to exclude denominational schools before a group of hostile Southern Methodist educators in 1906. He argued that denominational schools limited academic freedom by teaching distinctly denominational beliefs, diluted the limited amount of available church funds among a plethora of weak schools, and inefficiently managed their affairs. To clinch his argument, Pritchett contended, as Eliot had done in his 1886 debate with McCosh, that denominational schools did not serve the general public's interests but only those of one small parochial community.[77] Only fifty-one institutions qualified for Carnegie funds; more than two hundred did not. To dine at Carnegie's table, more than a dozen institutions, including Brown and Rutgers, immediately dropped their church affiliations, and others, such as Vanderbilt and Swarthmore, did the same shortly thereafter. The Carnegie Foundation, along with John D. Rockefeller's General Education Board, may have caused some unintended results as many schools, like Centre College in Kentucky, actually drew closer to their denominations.[78] While Princeton's declaration of independence was a mere formality since the institution had always been nondenominational, it symbolized the new direction of the university. Less than a generation earlier, McCosh had welcomed the friendly patronage of the Presbyterian church and looked to Presbyterians for financial support and students. Now Princeton's administration sought to distance the university from the church because denominational affiliations, however informal, contradicted the national orientation that American universities sought to cultivate. Princeton's historic connection with the Presbyterian church, in short, conflicted with the university's enlarged civic mission.

Furthermore, the tradition of giving free tuition to the sons of Presbyterian minister and to preministerial candidates fell victim to Wilson's efforts to advance the university's civic mission. Pritchett had identified tuition scholarships for preministerial candidates as an important indicator of the sectarianism of the denominational college. With no professor like Lyman Atwater or John T. Duffield forceful enough to advocate for this special privilege, which had been established to meet the needs of the Presbyterian church, and with no trustee like Charles Ewing Green influential enough to protect it, the trustees agreed to merge all scholarships into one grand fund. These "university scholarships" were then assigned on the basis of financial need or academic ability.[79] Although many needy ministers' sons and preministerial candidates likely received these scholarships, they did so on the basis of new criteria, and the university thus had ended another practice deemed incompatible with the its standing as a public university.

A more important result of the university's expanded civic mission was the decline in the relationship between the university and Princeton Seminary. To be sure, official relations between the seminary and the university were not hostile. At Wilson's inauguration, for instance, Patton expressed the traditional understanding of the complementary relationship between the university and the seminary. "What promotes the prosperity of the one," he believed, "promotes the prosperity of the other."[80] A trivial though telling sign of the relationship between the two institutions is the fact that the seminary's faculty marched in the academic procession at Wilson's inauguration and the university's faculty at Patton's inauguration as the seminary's president.[81] Seminary students, moreover, could still cross-enroll in the M.A. program at the university, and actually constituted a majority of the university's graduate student body until the fall of 1908.[82]

Still, the university and the seminary were on separate paths leading in different, if not opposite, directions in the early twentieth century. The academic interests of the university's faculty simply eclipsed those of the seminary's faculty. The correspondence between Harris Kirk and Theodore Whitefield Hunt, one of the old guard conservatives in the university, provide insight into the decline in the relationship between the university and the seminary. As pastor of the prominent Franklin Street Presbyterian Church in Baltimore, where Woodrow Wilson had worshipped as a graduate student at Johns Hopkins, Kirk (1872–1953) was a pulpit prince whose winsome personality, thoughtful sermons, and cosmopolitan conservativism won praise from Presbyterians across the theological spectrum. He was in essence a younger, Southern, and more theologically conservative version of Henry Van Dyke Jr. When Princeton Seminary offered him a position as a professor of homiletics in 1909, more than a dozen seminary professors and trustees encouraged, even pleaded, with him to join their faculty. Since Kirk had preached several times at the university, he wrote friends there for advice. In response to Harris Kirk's inquiry regarding the possibility of bringing about a "better feeling" between the seminary and university if he accepted the position at the seminary, Theodore Whitefield Hunt wrote, "There is no friction between them that is at all serious." "Of course," he explained, "among our 160 faculty members, only five or six of whom are clergymen, and many of whom have no very specific church relations, there cannot be expected to exist any great interest in a theological seminary. It simply lies outside of their thought and life."[83] Within the past few years, a majority of the faculty who had been associated with the seminary, such as George Macloskie, Samuel Stanhope Orris, John T. Duffield, and James O. Murray, had either retired or passed away. Not only did the institution have new and broader purposes than previously had been the case, but also, as Hunt pointed out, the seminary faculty's academic interests simply stood beyond those of the university's faculty.

Not only did the university's faculty share few interests with the seminary's theologians but the university community had fewer contacts with the seminary community. When compared to previous decades, the seminary attracted fewer Princeton University graduates in the first decade of the twentieth century. Between 1870 and 1879, for instance, 31.8 percent of the seminary's student body had graduated from the College of New Jersey. Between 1900 and 1909, that figure had dropped to 10.5 percent.[84] University students not only had fewer friends at the seminary but many undergraduates also looked down upon the proletariat lifestyle of those at the seminary. One undergraduate from the class of 1905, for instance, recalled that the university students had a "low opinion" of seminarians: from "our more lofty collegiate heights," he explained, they "often dressed poorly," were "uncouth and ungroomed," and "seemed closed in mind."[85]

More important than the decline in common academic interests and in social contracts between the university and the seminary, a discernable amount of intellectual hostility emerged between the institutions in the early twentieth century. Among the university faculty, President Wilson wrote Harris Kirk in 1909, "There is at present a considerable lack of sympathy" for the theologians at the seminary. "We have a great admiration for many of the men in the Seminary faculty," he explained, "but there can be no doubt that the Seminary does in some large degree deserve the reputation which it has for resisting in an unreasonable degree the liberalizing tendencies of the time." Not only had the university's mission changed, but so had, at least according to Wilson, the seminary's purpose. In the continuous debate over theological modernism and confessional revision, the seminary had taken an increasingly strident position, prompting Wilson to tell Kirk that, while he had no quarrel with those who maintain "very stoutly the orthodox tenets of the older church," he admitted that he despised people, like some at the seminary, who did so in an "illiberal" manner.[86] The day after receiving Wilson's letter, Kirk declined the seminary's offer.

Wilson, to be sure, did not want to distance the university because he was an atheist. "My life," he told a friend, "would not be worth living if it were not for the driving power of religion, for *faith*, pure and simple. I have seen all my life the arguments against it without ever having been moved by them."[87] Two other aspects of Wilson's personal faith are also clear. First, he never experienced anything like a crisis of personal faith as had troubled so many Victorian intellectuals. Professor of economics Winthrop M. Daniels, remembered once asking Wilson if he thought it possible to maintain the traditional view of the inspiration of the Scriptures in light of higher criticism. "He said frankly that it was impossible," Daniels recalled, "but the admission he made did not seem either to interest or to disturb him overmuch."[88] Furthermore, Wilson had little affection for the theological dogmatism of his predecessor and the seminary. Shortly after his inauguration, both Wilson and his predecessor addressed the Presbyterian Union in New York City: "Believe me," Wilson told Patton, "you engender the spirit of doubt by stating a thing dogmatically. Between the ages of eighteen and twenty-two you create doubt by ramming dogma down the throat."[89] Wilson's personal theological views not only played a critical role in determining the role of religion within the university but also helps to explain why he sought to distance the university from the influence of the Presbyterian church and Princeton Seminary. Wilson loathed conservative Presbyterians. He abhorred, for instance, the southern Presbyterians who had attacked his uncle, James Woodrow, for attempting to harmonize evolution and theism. When the conservative southern Presbyters successfully drove his uncle from his position at Columbia Seminary in 1885, Wilson wrote his wife, "our dear church... has indeed fallen upon evil times of ignorance and folly!"[90] Theodore Whitefield Hunt offered an insightful description of Wilson's faith. Hunt wrote that the president had never stopped to formulate his faith "in anything like a dogmatic deliverance of doctrine as embodied in a definite creed or confession." "His faith was so incorporated in the sum and substance of his innermost self and such an integral part of his moral constitution," Hunt observed, "that doctrine and duty, thought and life, creed and character were consolidated and fused into the everyday expressions of his experience."[91]

While Wilson, unlike Henry Van Dyke Jr., was not an outspoken advocate of theological modernism, he, like Van Dyke and others at the university, had no sympathy for the conservative supernatural Protestantism taught at the seminary. Well before the fundamentalist-modernist controversies of the 1920s, the strict confessionalism of the seminary attracted few disciples from the university. Many Princetonians regretted the often widespread popular association of the university with the seminary. For instance, in an article on Princeton in *Leslie's Weekly*, James W. Alexander Jr., a trustee of the university whose father and grandfather had taught at the seminary, complained about the "unnatural error" many people made in linking the two institutions. The university, he emphatically asserted, was a "nonsectarian" institution, "without the restrictions of ecclesiastical tenet," standing entirely separate from the seminary.[92] By the end of Wilson's presidency, fraternal relations had clearly become frigid. As a reporter for the *Independent* in 1909, Edwin E. Slosson visited Princeton and the thirteen other founding universities in the Association of American Universities, and concluded that "The Theological Seminary in the same town is somewhat *ostentatiously* kept at a distance. It is not so nearly allied with the University as Union Theological Seminary is with Columbia."[93]

Wilson's efforts to transform Princeton into a major university dedicated to public service, along with the attendant changes this goal entailed for the institution's past policies and relationships, enjoyed the support of both the trustees and many in the university's larger community. That more progressive members of the board had a like-minded leader in Wilson derived in part from Wilson's efforts to broaden not only the university's purpose but also the composition of the Board of Trustees. Although this expansion had begun during Patton's presidency, it accelerated appreciably during Wilson's tenure. The turnover in the board provides the clearest evidence of change: in Wilson's final year as president, 1909, only fifteen of the trustees had been on the board when he was inaugurated. In a sense, the change in the composition of the trustees was both a cause and an effect of the university's new-found public orientation: a cause in that Wilson plotted to get like-minded individuals on the board, and an effect in that they supported the president's reforms in at least the first four years of his tenure. The expansion of the university's mission and, consequently, the broadening of the composition of the Board of Trustees is also evident in the precipitous drop in the overlap between the seminary's and the university's boards. In the fall of 1902, ten of twenty-seven trustees had graduated from the seminary or were serving on its faculty or its boards. By the fall of 1909, that figure had dropped to six and included one seminary alumnus, Melancthon W. Jacobus, who was a professor at Hartford Seminary, and another alumnus, Simon

J. McPherson, who was a trustee at McCormick Seminary. Two other trustees served as professors at liberal rivals of Princeton Seminary: George B. Stewart at Auburn and David R. Frazer at Union in New York. Another indicator of the declining relationship between the university and the Presbyterian church was the fact that of the thirteen trustees who joined the board between the fall of 1902 and the fall of 1909, only one was a minister, John DeWitt, who taught at Princeton Seminary.[94] One reason for the decline in the number of new clerical trustees was that few of the continuing members of that class died while Wilson was president. Another and more significant reason was that the trustees altered the charter in 1906 and reduced the number of seats on the board reserved for clerics from twelve to eight.[95] The drop in the number of ministers on Princeton's board paralleled similar trends at other institutions; according to one survey of the boards of fifteen colleges and universities, 23 percent of the trustees in 1900–1901 were clerics and 16.5 percent in 1910–1911.[96]

During Wilson's tenure, the board also lost several of its more conservative trustees. In 1905, Robert Garrett (1875–1961), an 1897 alumnus who had won two gold medals and one silver at the first modern Olympic Games and was principal owner of his family's successful investment firm, replaced the Reverend Francis B. Hodge. In 1908, Thomas D. Jones (1851–1917), whose brother David had helped oust Patton from office, succeeded the Reverend Elijah R. Craven, who had been on the board since 1859. Wilson forced John J. McCook, probably the most outspoken conservative trustee, and Charles B. Alexander to resign in March 1906 over the protests of certain other trustees when an insurance company whose board McCook and Alexander served on was involved in a financial scandal.[97] All but two of the new trustees had graduated from the university. However, while less conservative than previous generations, the board was not entirely progressive in every educational and religious matter, as Wilson and his successor eventually learned.[98]

If the revitalized Board of Trustees supported Wilson's national aspirations for Princeton, the alumni financed them. The shift within the university's community of support that had begun under McCosh came to completion during Wilson's administration. The alumni, whose identification with the university was often based on nonreligious grounds, replaced Presbyterians as Princeton's main source of financial aid. Still, many Presbyterians looked upon Princeton as a de facto Presbyterian institution and continued to give their money to the university. In 1904, for example, one woman gave a large sum to the university because of what President Patton had done, as she put it, "in the defense of the Bible, evangelical truth and sound doctrine throughout the church."[99] Wilson, however, turned to the alumni, not to Presbyterians, to finance his reforms. When, at the Chicago Alumni Association meeting in November 1902, Wilson announced his plans to reorganize the undergraduate program, he asked the alumni to help him raise a breathtaking 12.5 million dollars to make Princeton a truly national university.[100] The alumni responded by digging deeply into their pockets. To keep the university's needs constantly before its graduates, Wilson had annual financial reports published in the *Princeton Alumni Weekly* and regularly spoke to alumni clubs. As a group, the alumni became more directly involved in managing the affairs of the university, as witnessed by the increased number of alumni chairs on the Board of Trustees. In order to finance the preceptorial system, the trustees approved in 1905 the creation of the Committee of Fifty, which immediately opened an office on Wall Street. The following year the committee became a permanent ad hoc organization. In 1909, it became the Graduate Council, with committees on finance, class records, publicity, preparatory schools, alumni associations, and undergraduate activities. At the same time, Alumni Trustee A. K. Imbrie was appointed secretary of the Board of Trustees and charged with reorganizing the financial management of the institution.[101]

Another significant change can be seen in the rapid growth of the student body, providing the university with more alumni to whom they could appeal for money. More students graduated from the university between 1896 and 1906 than had graduated from Princeton in its first 150 years combined. By 1906, there were thirty-nine alumni associations, including clubs in Hawaii, Los Angeles, Paris, and Toledo, Ohio.[102] In addition, more students were entering lucrative professions: in the classes that graduated between 1891 and 1895, 15.2 percent of the A.B. students entered the ministry and 22.4 percent went into business, while in the classes of 1901 to 1905, only 3.9 percent went into the ministry and 36.2 percent into business. This trend was paralleled at other elite universities.[103] As evidenced in the implementation of the new curriculum and the preceptorial system, Wilson had capitalized, literally, on the enthusiastic support of the alumni to help transform Princeton into a major American university.

Like the trustees, many alumni shared Wilson's vision of Princeton as a national university. Wilson had distanced the university from the Presbyterian church and Princeton Seminary. More important to the long-term direction of the university, he had altered hiring practices considered sectarian and contrary to the institution's broadened civic mission. The university Wilson envisioned served not a small community but the entire nation.

Making Religion Safe for Democracy

Alongside the gradual modifications of those policies and practices that had been previously used to guard Princeton's evangelical character and ethos, Wilson conformed the university's program of religious education to its expanded civic mission. Henry Smith Pritchett, president of the Carnegie Foundation, identified mandatory religious instruction as an important indicator of the sectarianism of denominational colleges.[104] Not only were mandatory Bible courses considered a sectarian educational practice but the evangelical theology, which had once represented a centrist position within American Protestantism, as noted above, had come to be seen by Wilson, Pritchett, and others within academia as a form of intellectual sectarianism. Religion, Wilson believed, "cannot be handled like learning. It is a matter of individual conviction and its source is the heart."[105] Henry Van Dyke Jr.

put it a little more baldly: "You cannot put Christianity into the curriculum, but you can keep it in the daily life and spirit of the university."[106] Through his father's nepotism, George S. Patton had secured an endowed professorship in moral philosophy with responsibilities for overseeing biblical instruction. But as soon as Wilson became president in the fall of 1902, he took the drastic step of eliminating both the compulsory and elective Bible courses that the younger Patton taught. When Wilson reorganized the faculty two years later, he simply abolished the Department of Biblical Literature. These were just the first two of several decisive steps that Wilson took to conform Princeton's program of religious education to its standing as a public institution.

Despite the demise of mandatory Bible instruction in the evangelical faith, Wilson and other leaders in the university continued to insist that Princeton was a Christian institution. In his introduction to *The Handbook of Princeton*, published in 1905 as a tool to recruit students for the university, Wilson wrote that "a strong and manly religion" dominated Princeton. "Sound and liberal learning," he explained, "and equally sound and *liberal religion* lie together at the foundation of all that her sons most admire in the University."[107] Likewise, Professor Andrew F. West told a group of alumni in 1908, "By its charter Princeton is non-sectarian, by its history it is profoundly Christian."[108] Wilson and his colleagues did not abandon Princeton's religious mission, but rather modified it to conform to the university's broadened civic mission. Wilson and others in Princeton continued to champion Princeton's religious mission—to nurture the Christian character of American society through the religious education of its leaders—but did so in new ways and in new places. The university's enlarged civic mission impacted dramatically the courses in Bible, ethics, apologetics and natural theology, the mandatory chapel services, and the extra-curricular activities of the Philadelphian Society during Wilson's presidency. Although Princeton's program of religious education underwent a dramatic transformation in the early twentieth century, Protestant interests continued to play a crucial role in the modern university.

Measured against McCosh's dogmatic commitment to evangelical Bible instruction, the elimination of Patton's Bible classes and the Department of Biblical Literature marked a major step in the marginalization of religion in undergraduate education. Wilson had removed the "sun" from McCosh's educational solar system. In the old-time college, Andrew F. West explained, every aspect of collegiate education was devoted "to serving the cause of Christ." "Yet perhaps," he wistfully observed, "the ideal was too high ever to be realized generally by men as men were and still are." He blamed the demise of theology as the unifying center of undergraduate education on academic specialization, "sectarian warfare," the influx of wealthy students whose only purpose in college was "self-indulgence," and American society's insatiable need for professional training.[109]

But for other Princeton professors the old ideal was still viable; to them the elimination of Bible classes did not necessarily represent the secularization of the curriculum. To Wilson and others, religion was a matter more of life than of doctrine. For these advocates of liberal culture the curriculum—the natural revelation side of McCosh's educational equation—possessed the most catholic human values, including religious values, of western civilization. The humanities, as James Turner observes, met their need for spiritual enlightenment and offered its own form of coherence in place of the passé supernatural universe. Philosophy, literature, and the fine arts provided the "spiritual" face of a liberal education.[110]

Protestant champions of liberal culture sacralized, not secularized, the modern university curriculum. The sacralization of the liberal arts curriculum rested upon Protestant modernism's understanding of the immanence of God in creation. As the supernatural ramparts of evangelical Protestantism were collapsing under the weight of scientific positivism and historicism, so did the intellectual credibility of the epistemological and psychological foundations of the old-time discipline and piety educational philosophy. By rejecting the traditional distinction between the supernatural and the natural, modernism overcame the threat of science to Christianity by arguing that God was present in and revealed through the development of human history and the evolution of culture. Consequently, liberals affirmed biological evolution, without the trappings of the awkward argument for theistic evolution, and interpreted it to be the means God used to create the world. In the same way, they understood the humanities to be a product of the workings of God in and through culture and also a record of the supermundane reality of the existence of God. Just as modernists found reasons—not empirical and rational evidence—in nature and biblical history to nurture the self-evidencing or intuitive experience of the reality of God, so did some advocates of a liberal education, such as Wilson and Van Dyke, find inspiration in the study of the humanities for both their faith in the presence of God in human history and their hope for society's progress toward greater enlightenment. "I do not see how the spirit of learning," Wilson insisted, "can be separated or divorced from the spirit of religion. At its heart lies that which is ideal, which elevates and ennobles, while it quickens the pulse and fills the lungs with a new and vivifying breath,—the love of truth, the desire to see with the eyes of the mind, to see the things which are invisible and which stand fast through all generations."[111] Although the abolition of mandatory evangelical Bible instruction marked a decided departure from established practices designed to fulfill Princeton's religious mission, Protestant interests had reappeared in the sacralization of the liberal arts curriculum. Wilson and others at Princeton, like their predecessors a generation earlier, sought to mold the Christian character of students and ultimately American society through the curriculum. According to Wilson's covenant theology, the liberal arts curriculum stemmed from the covenant of nature, not the covenant of grace. For this reason, its subject matter was nonsectarian. But by viewing this curriculum from a spiritual perspective they found a way to nurture the Protestant faith of the nation's future leaders in an ostensibly nonsectarian manner.

Ironically, the elimination of the Bible courses and Department of Biblical Literature left Princeton in even worse shape than Harvard since Harvard undergraduates in the fall of 1902 could at least take elective Bible courses. A 1905 survey of 271 American colleges and universities revealed that 209 of them, including Stanford, Michigan, Wisconsin, and Yale, offered some form of Bible instruction as part of their regular curriculum.[112] Yet the first decade of the twentieth century saw little consensus among educators as to whether biblical instruction truly belonged in the formal curriculum. Some educators, such as Wallace N. Stearns of the University of Illinois, opposed biblical instruction on the grounds that it fostered a sectarianism incompatible with public education. M. H. Buckham, president of the University of Vermont, similarly insisted that universities could not teach the "dogmatics and denominationalism" associated with the older evangelicalism that had once dominated much of American higher education.[113] Other educators, typically those at private institutions, resisted biblical instruction on religious grounds. William DeWitt Hyde, president of Bowdoin College, for example, argued that since religion is essentially "an attitude of heart and will toward God," the Bible per se could not be taught like other subjects, although it could be incorporated into philosophy, literature, and history courses.[114] Those favoring biblical instruction, such as University of Chicago President William Rainey Harper and Professor Ernest DeWitt Burton, contended that the Bible should be part of a college curriculum so long as it was taught in a scientific manner. If there were no Bible courses, they believed, students would consider the subject unimportant. To promote Bible study, Harper and like-minded educators at Chicago and other colleges, universities, and seminaries organized the Religious Education Association in 1903. They hoped that through the scientific study of religion, higher criticism, and the burgeoning fields of the psychology and sociology of religion, every American, from Sunday School to university students, could better learn the Bible.[115] Therefore, by abolishing biblical instruction in 1902, Princeton stood out as an exception among most American colleges and universities, an exception that conservative Presbyterians clearly noticed. Writing in the *Princeton Theological Review* in 1903, one such orthodox Presbyterian argued, "To hold that a liberal education involves a good acquaintance with English literature, but not the Bible is an *absurdity*."[116]

Wilson's solution for Princeton's lack of biblical instruction was even more stunning than his elimination of the Bible courses. At the same time that Wilson launched the preceptorial system in 1905, he reintroduced Bible instruction into the curriculum, but instead of assigning the courses to the conservative George S. Patton, he hired a liberal Protestant, Lucius H. Miller, who had recently graduated from Union Theological Seminary in New York. Wilson had been planning this step for some time, and his rationale is fairly clear: although he believed that biblical instruction was not essential to a liberal education, it was not incompatible with it so long as it avoided the sectarian dogmatism of Patton's conservative evangelicalism.

Miller was the perfect person for Wilson to hire. His evangelical background pleased conservatives in the larger community. As a Princeton undergraduate, Miller (1876–1949) had served as president of the Philadelphian Society, and after graduating in 1897 he became its first Permanent Secretary. He also met, literally, Wilson's "clubable" criteria; he was a member of the Cap and Gown, one of the more exclusive eating clubs on campus. In 1899, Miller had gone to the Middle East as a missionary, teaching Bible and English at the Syrian Protestant College in Beruit. Like many in his day who had been raised in the evangelical faith, Miller found the orthodoxy of his youth increasingly difficult to affirm. In 1902, he enrolled in Union Seminary, where he, like others, sought to reconcile his Christian faith with modernity. His time at Union, as Miller himself described it, "put me on my feet" intellectually. He decided to forego ordination in the Episcopal church in order to pursue a scholarly career as a layperson. When he came to Princeton three years later, Miller was far more liberal in his theology than he had been in his undergraduate days and passionately hoped to rescue students from unbelief.

"I believe in missions and I believe in the Bible," Miller wrote his classmates in their reunion yearbook ten years after graduating, "because I believe in Christianity." But, he said, he would not condemn those who did not believe. In a veiled reference to the conservative theology that had dominated Princeton in their college days, Miller explained why he could not damn unbelievers: too often, he said, "Christianity has been so grossly misrepresented and misinterpreted by its own supporters." In keeping with the scientific methods of the age, Miller hoped to save students' faith by using higher criticism for a scientific examination of the Bible. "My chief aim in the classroom," he wrote, was to present the literature of the Bible so that students would gain "an independently favorable attitude toward it," find "a secure foundation for their religious faith," and yet keep "a perfect openness toward those changes of thought which are bound to come." In a report to President Wilson after his first year of teaching, Miller added a second reason: he wanted to awaken a better feeling of "what the Bible has to give" in order to lead more students into the ministry. Since fundamentalism had not yet emerged as a distinct movement, it would be anachronistic to say that Wilson had removed the aura of fundamentalism from Princeton by replacing Patton with Miller. Still, Miller's irenic liberalism was more compatible, both intellectually and educationally, with the values of a liberal education—certitude, progress, and unprejudiced truth—than the supernaturalism of his predecessor.[117]

In his Old and New Testament courses, which he offered in alternating years, Miller tried to nurture the faith of students through "those intellectual explanations of the Old Faith that are necessitated by the changes in our modern life & thought."[118] Not much of an original thinker, Miller was a popularizer of the best of modernist theology in a genteel, perhaps "clubable," manner. His first foray into scholarship, "Modern Views of the Bible and of Religion," an article published in the *South Atlantic Quarterly* in 1908, nicely summarizes the new views of the Bible and Christianity he taught to students.

"We are living in a different world from that inhabited by our grandfathers," Miller explained. Evolution has raised "the questions of the ultimate whence and whither." The new astronomy and biology have made the universe "so big that man has trembled for his age-long importance." The new physics and chemistry "have made him fear for his very existence." Miller pointed to the scientific method as the crucial source behind this "new universe": "The new scientific method, based on the uniformity and the universality of natural law," made people "wonder who and when God and religion come in." Modernity, in short, had changed every intellectual endeavor.

Previously, Miller observed, philosophers and theologians, such as McCosh and Patton "jumped out of their skin," as German philosophers put it, in their journeys into the noumena. But since Kant, human knowledge had been limited to what could be known exclusively by experience. Because of this, agnostics "feel that truth is too much for human limitation." They say people can know nothing with certainty and particularly that nothing can be known about God. Meanwhile, the conservatives think that all the changes brought on by modern science since Kant have no consequences for their faith; they "put God into their pocket with their printed creed." The three classical arguments of natural theology for the existence of God still carried weight with these people, he said, only because they are ignorant of the great changes that have taken place around them. For example, the teleological argument and Paley's famous "eye illustration" became "nonsense" in light of Darwin's theory of adaptation to environment. Darwin had demonstrated that the intricate arrangements of the eye "had developed in all its powers by that environment itself" and had not been designed beforehand by God for the purpose of seeing. The uniformity and universality of the laws of nature even rendered the quintessential argument of Christian apologetics obsolete. The miracles of Christ, he contended, could not be understood as "'violations of nature,' for nature cannot be violated."[119]

Miller insisted, as Andrew D. White had argued in his *History of the Warfare of Science with Theology in Christendom* (1896), that the real conflict was between science and dogmatic theology, not between science and Christianity. In a move characteristic of liberal Protestantism, Miller resolved the alleged conflict by abolishing the distinction between the sacred and the secular. By doing so, Miller repudiated the arguments that James McCosh and Charles W. Shields had taught a generation of Princeton students in favor of a Christian Darwinism. He reinterpreted the classical arguments of natural theology according to this new paradigm. For example, the old cosmological argument failed, he argued, because people could no longer reason from an effect to an invisible cause "outside of and before the world." But if God was immanent in nature, one sees the "power which rules the world is not material." "The modern religious man may find in this, not the old cosmological proof of God, but certainly a most solid scientific basis for his belief in the supremacy of mind in the universe."[120]

Miller rejected the supernatural evangelical theology, indeed the entire nineteenth-century Protestant worldview, taught to Princeton students under McCosh and Patton. However, Miller continued to attempt to nurture a Christian, more specifically a Protestant, faith in students like his predecessors. The Protestantism Miller advocated in the classroom was liberal instead of evangelical in character. Like William Rainey Harper and other scholars attempting to preserve the Protestant faith by adjusting it to modernity, Miller reasoned that higher criticism could establish an intellectual foundation for belief that was scientific and, therefore, inclusively nonsectarian in character. According to Miller, higher criticism was simply the application of the scientific method to the past and in the case of the Bible to biblical history. Higher criticism, Miller, Harper, and other contended, was an objective science, free from dogma. By arguing for a scientific study of the Bible through higher criticism, Miller was also claiming as his ideal the natural sciences that had been transforming America and American universities since the nineteenth century.[121] Higher criticism, in short, resonated well within the walls of Princeton because it could furnish the foundation for a faith that was nonsectarian, compatible with modern science, and, therefore, harmonious with the national mission of the institution.

The aim of historical criticism, Miller taught, was twofold. The first goal was to set forth Jesus, both "as the individual in his relation to God and to his fellow man" and "as the founder of a great community of brotherly-minded individuals." Higher criticism of the Old Testament revealed that the Hebrews' conception of God had gradually developed over time. In the same way, historical criticism of the synoptic gospels discerned what was factual from what was merely possible, probable, and improbable (e.g., "legends" and "mistakes") in order to give a more accurate picture of the founder of Christianity. The second goal of biblical criticism was to help create a more social gospel. Miller argued that Jesus' teaching regarding the Kingdom of God united all as "children of the Father" and "brothers to their fellows" and avoided the individualistic concern with one's own salvation and personal duties to God (as Francis L. Patton was teaching at this time in his ethics courses). In the extension of the Kingdom of God, Miller asserted, "lies the hope of our modern life." Those who still clung to "the outworn individualism" of early Protestantism only needed to observe the social needs about them in order to see how it failed society. "No individualistic gospel will meet those needs, and if the real gospel is not something more, it must go."[122] While the social gospel that Miller advocated to students reversed nineteenth-century Protestant priorities by making Christianity a means to the end of Christianizing American civilization, as Robert T. Handy observes, in its own way the social gospel perpetuated an old Protestant triumphalism: "in its unreflective clinging to the idea of the triumph of Protestant civilization," the social gospel "exhibited real continuity with the earlier nineteenth century."[123] Although Miller's message differed dramatically from the revivalistic gospel propagated in the previous century, Princeton's Bible professor still aspired to shape the Christian character of American society.

Before Miller submitted his first article to the *South Atlantic Quarterly* for publication, he had sought out Wilson's approval lest he arouse the wrath of conservatives within the university community or the ire of the president. Wilson, who appreciated Miller's loyalty "toward Princeton," shared Miller's conviction that higher criticism made his work scientific and therefore irrefutably nonsectarian in character. He assured Miller that he "did not see how any reasonable person could object" to the article, since it dealt with its subject *"from the point of view of modern times,* with moderation and good sense."[124]

Grumbling's about Miller's liberalism from conservative Presbyterians, however, began to trickle slowly into the president's office. One father of a prospective student told Wilson that he was wary of sending his son to Princeton because he had heard the Bible instructor taught "destructive criticism" and the "most liberal views regarding the person of Christ, the Trinity, and the atonement."[125] Before answering the charge, Wilson sent the letter to Miller, who in turn provided the president with a response that he incorporated *in toto* in his reply. Miller retreated behind the scientific character of higher criticism to defend his work and then to argue that historical criticism actually strengthened, not subverted, genuine faith. The course, Miller wrote, emphasized the positive conclusions of the "sane, constructive, historical method" and this enabled students to see "the real depth and beauty and power" of the Bible. In reference to his teaching about Christ, Miller assured the father that he upheld Christ as "the real savior of mankind" and did so with "profound conviction." In his part of the letter, Wilson said that if biblical instruction was to have the same academic character as other parts of the curriculum, it could only be taught as a "great body of literature." Still, Wilson believed, like Miller, that academic science and practical piety went together. Because of "the extraordinary character of the books," Wilson explained to the annoyed father, students saw "their inevitably divine character as a revelation of God to man."[126] Not everyone objected to Miller's work. One student told Miller that before he took his course he "was very critical if not completely sceptical" about Christianity. After Miller's "broad and comprehensive" course, he found his faith and joined the church. Miller forwarded the letter to Wilson who found it "most interesting and encouraging."[127]

While not threatened by conservative Presbyterians in the university community, Wilson clearly wanted to avoid antagonizing them. When Miller and the president made plans to hire a preceptor to assist Miller in the spring of 1909, Wilson said he wanted to be careful about whom he hired because some parents were "so sensitive" about theological matters it would be "unfavorable" if they thought that the university were "taking advantage" of their sons.[128] Miller found a like-minded assistant in Frank L. Janeway, a Presbyterian minister. As a Princeton undergraduate, Janeway, like Miller, had been a member of both the Philadelphian Society and the Cap and Gown eating club. After graduating in 1901, he served as the Permanent Secretary of the Philadelphian Society. He also attended Union Seminary and, just before coming to Princeton, was the pastor of the Dartmouth College Church. In addition to assisting Miller, he helped oversee the work of the Philadelphian Society as the Graduate Advisory Committee's on-campus consultant.[129] That same year, Miller began to offer both his Old and New Testament courses each semester.[130]

When compared to McCosh's broad evangelicalism, Miller's liberalism marked another decided departure from established religious convictions. This break should not obscure, however, the continuity in the Protestant mission of the modern university in the early twentieth century. In Miller's liberal Protestantism, Wilson found a way, on the one hand, to avoid the sectarian dogmatism associated with the older evangelicalism and, on the other, to help fulfill the religious mission of Princeton in the early twentieth century. As had the Bible courses taught by McCosh and Patton in the previous century, Miller's Bible courses continued to attempt to nurture the Protestant faith of Princeton students and ultimately to shape the Christian character of American culture.

The cumulative effect of Wilson's reconfiguration of Princeton's civic and religious mission was as momentous on the other established parts of Princeton's traditional program of religious education—the ethics, apologetics, and harmony of science and religion classes—as it was for Bible instruction. Since the early nineteenth century, ethics had been a constitutive part of a Princeton education, but with the implementation of Wilson's liberal culture curriculum in the sweeping revision of 1904, Francis L. Patton's ethics course moved off center stage. However, while it was not essential to a liberal education, like English or psychology classes, the study of ethics was not believed to be incompatible with it. Accordingly, the ethics course became an elective, co-taught by the former president and his son. Yet at least one student found the Pattons' arguments for the Scottish commonsense realism less than persuasive. John S. Burgess, a member of the Class of 1905, recalled that Francis L. Patton gave Herbert Spencer "short shift," Henry Sidgewick "was considered to have only fragments of truth," while the "difficult but metaphysical" T. H. Green was "given a higher rating." In Burgess's opinion, Patton swept "aside all factual or empirical approaches to ethics" for his own "historically inexplicable sense of obligation to do right" based on "certain metaphysical hypotheses as to the nature of God and man."[131] In many ways, Patton personified the clear-eyed confidence in the Scottish philosophy that had earned both the college and the seminary their well-deserved reputation as a bastions of commonsense realism in the nineteenth century. By the turn of the century, as this one undergraduate's experience suggests, students often viewed the Princeton theologians' philosophical certainty as baseless arrogance.

Despite the presence of the Pattons on the faculty, a quiet revolution was taking place in the teaching of philosophy at the university. Besides teaching undergraduate courses, George S. Patton taught four graduate courses in ethics. Like his father and McCosh before him, the younger Patton tried to forge a *via media* between idealists, utilitarians, and empiricists.[132] Yet the philosophical alternatives to Scottish realism were no longer outsiders to Princeton, approaches that students only studied in their textbooks and lectures, as had been the case when Princeton was a college. Frank Thilly, whom Wilson hired in 1904, was a philosophical idealist and had written an introductory textbook on ethics.[133] Ironically, George S. Patton had reviewed the work three years earlier, agreeing with Thilly that ethics could not be based upon the "pleasure principle," as utilitarians contended, but rather had to be grounded upon the intuitive categorical imperative of "oughtness." Patton, however, took issue with what he considered to be Thilly's insufficient explanation of the source and nature of this "'feeling of obligation within us.'" Simply to assert the existence of a sense of moral duty and to describe its development were inadequate justifications for the reality of moral duty. To Patton, Thilly simply missed the central truth that the categorical imperative rested upon certain metaphysical realities. Moral obligation, the "what ought to be," Patton insisted, was revealed in both the universe and human nature, and ultimately "in the divine Thinker, whose thought is progressively revealed in the whole sphere of phenomenal existence."[134]

Although Thilly left Princeton in 1906 for a position at Cornell, his successor, Norman Kemp Smith (1872–1958), was a noted exponent of Kantian-Hegalian philosophy. In addition to hiring Smith, there was decided shift among the university's philosophers away from Scottish commonsense realism toward idealism.[135] Even John G. Hibben and Alexander T. Ormond, who had been trained at Princeton by McCosh, demonstrated a new appreciation of idealism after the turn of the century.[136] Theologically, the drift toward idealism made good sense; the old Scottish philosophy of McCosh, Shields, and the Pattons had tethered itself between German idealism, with its emphasis on the intuitive character of knowledge, and Comtean positivism, with its empiricist interests. In the face of the never-ending threat of scientific positivism and the seemingly overwhelming evidence against supernatural Christianity, the idealism of Friedrich Schleiermacher and Immanuel Kant, as subsequently refined by Albrecht Ritschl and his heirs, provided an intellectual foundation for a theology that stood upon the experience of the individual believer and the shared values of the Christian community, not the supernatural acts of God. To many Protestants, this position was far more tenable than evangelicalism since it was impervious to the criticisms of science that had undermined the older orthodoxy and the Scottish realism upon which it rested.[137]

The university was no longer the bastion of Scottish philosophy that McCosh had aspired for Princeton. In Wilson's educational revolution, the university's intellectual horizons expanded as he hired scholars from outside the closely knit Princeton community. Although Princeton's Philosophy Department hardly matched Harvard's triumvirate of William James, Hugo Münsterberg, and Josiah Royce, a new diversity of intellectual viewpoints, characteristic of the modern university, was clearly emerging. In Princeton's revolutionary development into a university, the institution no longer propounded a single worldview but now offered its students a variety of worldviews, represented by the diverse interests of such scholars as the Pattons, Thilly, and Smith. The emergence of Princeton University from the College of New Jersey signaled more than just a paradigm shift from one intellectual solar system to another; the university now presented the traditional nineteenth-century worldview as just one intellectual solar system amid a galaxy of alternatives. Intellectually, the university was becoming something other than just the larger college that Patton had envisioned.

Whereas Bible classes in the curriculum of a liberal education could be defended on the basis of their literary value, despite Miller's avowed evangelistic motives, the apologetic and natural theology courses were tainted with distinctly sectarian evangelical interests and with a premodern supernaturalism. For thirty-seven years, Charles W. Shields held (or sat in, as Francis L. Patton thought) the first endowed chair in any American university specifically devoted to the harmony of science and religion. When Shields retired in 1903, Wilson and the faculty also retired the course in the harmony of science and religion. In the major curriculum revision of 1904, Francis L. Patton's elective apologetic course also dropped out of the curriculum. Yet the elimination of these courses did not mean an interest in the harmony of science and religion had disappeared among the faculty, as Miller's work demonstrates. There were no Robespierres on the faculty who wanted to turn Marquand Chapel into a temple dedicated to the worship of the Supreme Being, Reason. There was still, as one student described it, "the polite and formal touching the hat to religion in the college classroom."[138]

Despite the reverence still accorded religion, the university saw enormous changes in religious worship during this period, changes that were even more dramatic than those in religious instruction. McCosh and his colleagues had required students' attendance at daily and Sunday chapel services, where a broadly evangelical faith was propagated. This commitment was predicated not only upon the evangelical Protestant hegemony over American culture but also upon the educational conviction that these such exercises helped to balance the secular side of the curriculum. More than fifteen years after the debate between McCosh and Eliot, there was still little consensus in higher education about the value of mandatory chapel services. Some educators, especially in state universities, argued for a completely voluntary scheme on the basis that compulsory chapel failed to obtain, as one educator put it, "any appreciable favorable results" in the average eighteen-year-old student. Andrew D. White of Cornell took a different approach, hoping through voluntary services "to attract young men to chapel, and not to drive them into it."[139] Most denominational colleges held fast to McCosh's position: mandatory chapel.[140] At many other nondenominational private colleges and universities, the line between the institution's public orientation and its past religious affiliation was more ambiguous.[141] Wilson chose a mediating path for Princeton's chapel policy by requiring students to attend a certain number of chapel services each week. The university thereby avoided the kind of parochialism associated with denominational colleges, while preserving a certain amount of continuity with traditional *in loco parentis* responsibilities.

At the same time, and over the protests of arch-conservative trustee John J. McCook, Wilson recommended at his first meeting of the Board of Trustees in 1902 the abolition of the Sunday evening worship services.[142] Two years later, daily chapel was reduced from twenty to fifteen minutes. As professional interests eclipsed religious ones, the faculty's presence at daily chapel decreased, as students were never slow to mention. One student complained sarcastically in the *Daily Princetonian*, "Usually the only member of the Faculty present is the one conducting the service."[143] The most important change in the chapel program came in the fall of 1905. Despite McCook's objection, the faculty recommended and the trustees approved the reduction of daily chapel services to ten minutes. More significantly, students were required to attend only two of the daily services each week.[144]

In McCosh's day, obligatory attendance at daily and two Sunday chapel services overwhelmed many students. In response, they argued that more freedom would achieve more genuine worship services. Now that the McCosh generation of students had come of age within the leadership of the university, they made the changes for which they had lobbied as students. As a result, the undergraduates no longer regarded chapel as a "burden" or "limitation of their liberties," Professor John G. Hibben explained. "Consequently, the chapel service is no longer regarded as a merely perfunctory exercise, but has become more truly a form of *real worship,*" the brevity of the services notwithstanding.[145] Hibben's argument for the change was in essence the same one that Charles W. Eliot had made twenty years earlier in his debate with McCosh. While students predictably deemed the new arrangement "very fair and very acceptable," not all of the alumni were pleased. "Why not," one sarcastically asked in the alumni magazine, "abolish compulsory chapel altogether?"[146] Likewise, not all of Wilson's faculty supported the new chapel system. The president had to ask at least one professor to make sure that he ended his early morning class in time to allow students to get to chapel.[147] Since the new format for daily chapel had proved to be a grand success, according to a majority of the faculty and students, the following year the trustees approved a similar scheme for Sunday services. Students were required to attend at least half of the services each academic year.[148] Incidentally, the faculty's obsession with ensuring that the Episcopal students actually attended Sunday morning services at Trinity Episcopal Church had long disappeared.

According to the university's charter, the president was responsible to oversee the institution's religious services. Though a layman, Wilson often led the services and frequently preached himself, his sober piety, one student recalled, bringing a spirit of "reverence and sincerity" into the often raucous services.[149] In all his work in overseeing the preceptorial system and the university's fundraising activities, supervising Sunday chapel services proved to be too great a burden for the president. In order to give the president a needed day of rest, the trustees passed the president's responsibility for directing Sunday services onto Paul Van Dyke. They also approved a plan to create a formal University Preachers series, much like the one Harvard had instituted in 1886.[150] During Patton's presidency, evangelicals had dominated the roster of guest Sunday preachers. Under Wilson, liberal Protestantism became the established religion of Sunday chapel. Harry Emerson Fosdick, Lyman Abbott, and other celebrated liberals of the day preached modernism as the only logical alternative to both premodern evangelicalism and atheism. However, if faced with a choice between the latter two, it is clear that some modernists would not opt for the old-time religion. "But even atheism, it seems to me, is better than the dead and dry religion which exists without praise, without good works, without personal prayer," Henry Van Dyke Jr. advised students going off to college.[151] The only notable conservative to preach regularly to undergraduates was Patton himself.[152]

The new chapel requirements and the attraction of some of liberal Protestantism's superstars did not eliminate student disturbances. The faculty expelled students not only for disrupting chapel but also for not attending them. Wilson wrote one father, for example, that the university could not afford too many "embarrassing" Sunday absences.[153] After three years in the new scheme, students began to press Hibben's argument to its logical conclusion. The most effective way to eliminate chapel disturbances and foster genuine reverence, one student argued, was to restore chapel "to its true position of dignity as a place of *voluntary* worship." For those who attend chapel to worship, the student added, compulsory chapel "must seem like a form of blasphemy."[154]

The intellectual, educational, and institutional rationales notwithstanding, the vitality of the Philadelphian Society helped to soften the impact of the dramatic changes in religious instruction and worship. The campus Y.M.C.A. helped to relieve tensions between serving the nation's educational interests and preserving the university's traditional commitment to the religious education of the nation's future leaders. At colleges and universities that had eliminated compulsory chapel and Bible and Evidences for Christianity classes, educators often pointed to the extracurricular sphere of collegiate life as the most appropriate place for the university to nurture the faith of students. Voluntary religious organizations, especially at some of the nation's elite private and large state universities, avoided the problems associated with foisting religious beliefs—no matter how broadly construed—upon students at institutions chartered to serve only public interests. After studying the activities of voluntary religious organizations at several large midwestern state universities, University of Wisconsin professor William A. Scott declared, "The atmosphere of our state universities is pre-eminently Christian." Pointing to voluntary chapel services, the plurality of denominations represented on the faculty and Board of Trustees, and especially the work of the Y.M.C.A., even Andrew D. White insisted that Cornell "is a Christian Institution."[155] At Princeton, the Philadelphian Society came to serve as the university's de facto campus ministry. The administration came to depend heavily upon the Y.M.C.A. to help fulfill the university's religious mission. Moreover, the society's Graduate Advisory Committee, which in many ways paralleled the workings of the Graduate Alumni Council, ensured that the university would not neglect the religious needs of students.

Religious education in the voluntary sphere of undergraduate life made good sense on other grounds. In McCosh's day, many professors had been deeply interested in the spiritual welfare of the students, and with a student body that numbered four or five hundred, maintaining the religious component of the *in loco parentis* policy was not too difficult. By the turn of the century, three forces undermined these traditional practices. The professionalization of the faculty eroded professors' personal interest in pastoral ministry to the students. At the same time, students grew increasingly resentful of the paternalism of the *in loco parentis* policy, and consequently clamored for more independence, which the administration slowly began to give them. Evidence of this development is the formal organization of the student government in June 1905. In short, the administration began to treat students more like adults than like boys. Finally, the simple fact that the student body grew to over thirteen hundred by the end of Wilson's tenure made these older customs impractical. A strong Y.M.C.A. program resolved problems between Princeton's religious and civic missions and helped to meet the spiritual needs of students in a more nonsectarian fashion.

With its various ministries, such as Bible study groups, missions work, and freshman orientation, Princeton's Philadelphian Society was the model Y.M.C.A.

program for the nation. In 1900–1901, 501 students belonged to the society. By the fall of 1910, membership jumped to 815 members.[156] Like his predecessor, Wilson spoke regularly at the society's weekly meetings, though his addresses—"Laws of the Lord" and "The College Man and Public Life"—were far more moralistic than theological in orientation.[157] Theological modernists also addressed the society in greater numbers than in the previous decade. Henry Van Dyke Jr. told students that the key to Christ's power over people was his "personal magnetism," and he encouraged students to cultivate similar traits. Justification by faith, Harry Emerson Fosdick explained to students, is not "an enemy of science" and "requires us to believe only the great truths of religion." Still, conservatives continued to speak to the students with some frequency; Albert Clay, an archaeology professor at the University of Pennsylvania, assured his audience that archaeology "has now proved beyond a doubt that the Old Testament was founded on fact and not upon the inventions of later Hebrew writers."[158] Sometimes liberal and conservative speakers directly contradicted one another. One of the regular conservative speakers, Francis L. Patton, told students that some modern conceptions of Christianity dismiss doctrine or "drift toward the social side of Christianity." Instead, he insisted, Christianity "is a supernatural revelation of the way to salvation by the atonement of Christ." A little more than a year later, Union Seminary theologian George W. Knox told students that the essence of religion was life, not doctrine, and it had "its foundations deep within a man's being."[159] Since liberals and conservatives had not yet divided into two irreconcilable camps, the two streams of American Protestantism occasionally appeared on the same stage. In March 1908, for instance, Princeton Seminary Professor Charles R. Erdman arranged for university students to hear the evangelist G. Campbell Morgan in Alexander Hall. He was introduced to the student body by none other than Princeton's most prominent modernist, Henry Van Dyke Jr.[160]

The mixing of liberal interests with more traditional evangelical ones was evident in other aspects of the work of the Philadelphian Society. With the elimination of mandatory Bible instruction, the organization's Bible studies saw an impressive increase in enrollment, especially among the underclassmen to whom Miller's elective classes were not available. Total enrollment grew from 362 in 1903–1904 to 669 in 1909–1910.[161] Besides students' interest in Bible study, two other factors help to account for the growth of the Bible groups. One was that the Philadelphian Society and the St. Paul's Society joined efforts in 1903–1904 to offer Bible classes; but perhaps the most important factor was Lucius H. Miller. As a past president and paid staff worker for the society, Miller got involved in training Bible study group leaders and superintending the entire program.[162] In the fall of 1908, Miller also persuaded several professors and local pastors to lead Bible groups. The same eclectic union of conservative and liberal interests is evident in the subjects studied as well as the leadership of these groups. Frederick N. Willson, who had taught mandatory Bible classes under McCosh twenty years earlier, led a group studying "Science and the Scientific Method in Relation to Faith." By contrast, Miller taught a course on "The Social and Political Significance of the Teaching of Jesus" and R. B. Pomeroy, a Union Seminary graduate and curate at Trinity Church, led a study on "Some Fundamental Relations to Life."[163] Moreover, graduate students also participated in Bible groups during this decade. One year, William P. Armstrong, a New Testament professor at the seminary, led the group; another year a graduate student, Raymond B. Fosdick, younger brother of the popular preacher, taught the class.[164]

In the first decade of the twentieth century, a growing interest in the social gospel surfaced in the Philadelphian Society. Miller helped to broaden the Bible study program's orientation beyond personal piety by linking the Bible groups with settlement work in Trenton, in New York, and in several rural communities around Princeton. By 1910, social action, Miller reported, was a "fixed feature" of the Bible study program.[165] Although not all modernists advocated the social gospel, many social gospellers found modernism's views on the nature of religious experience and its optimism about society's progress far more congenial than revivalist Protestantism. At this time, the "Great Reversal" was just beginning to take place, a time when evangelicals abandoned their social concerns because the social gospel was becoming exclusively identified with liberal Protestantism.[166] During Wilson's presidency, evangelical students were still interested in social Christianity, and they regularly invited social gospellers to speak about urban missions.[167] In 1908, the society founded the Princeton Summer Camp on Barneget Bay on the New Jersey shore for "poor boys of New York City and Philadelphia."[168] The following year, Miller persuaded President Wilson to help him organize a conference on campus in order to promote social action, and Josiah Strong, noted author of *Our Country* (1896), spoke on "The Religious Significance of Social Service" at this event.[169]

The university's campus ministry not only attempted to evangelize America but also labored to Christianize the world. Throughout the first decade of the twentieth century, Robert Gailey, "the University's missionary in China," represented traditional interests in evangelism and education. In 1905–1906, the Philadelphian Society agreed to a plan of the International Committee of the Y.M.C.A. to move its work from Tientsin to Peking. In 1906, Dwight W. Edwards, Class of 1904, was the first of several Princeton graduates to join Gailey; and, with an initial anonymous gift of $30,000, plans were laid to construct a home for "Princeton-in-Peking" as the work came to be known.[170] Professor Miller, chairman of the executive committee of Princeton-in-Peking, recruited John S. Burgess, Class of 1905, to join Gailey and Edwards in 1909. Burgess embodied the growing liberal side of the Philadelphian Society. Raised in an orthodox Presbyterian home, Burgess grew disenchanted with the old faith as an undergraduate. After studying with the noted liberals Henry Churchill King at Oberlin and Arthur C. McGiffert at Union Seminary, he became a thoroughgoing modernist. As one of the university's missionaries in China, he "represented," as he described himself, "the social idealistic faith of the liberal American Christianity."[171]

Evangelicals and liberals worked well together because everyone wanted to fill China with "western and Christian ideas," aid China's "renaissance," and do his part "toward saving China."[172] In other words, they not only held a commitment to "civilize" China but also shared common assumptions about western intellectual and cultural superiority. Given the nondenominational and eclectic character of their work, the different religious interests of the evangelicals and liberals could be subsumed easily under their shared educational and social goals. At the first "Peking Day" rally held to raise support for the work in 1910, John R. Mott, dean of American missions, praised the university for meeting the needs of "the minds and bodies" of the Chinese people. "But," he added, "you have not overlooked the religious work."[173]

While the Philadelphian Society thrived throughout Wilson's presidency, the society began to lose some of its evangelical fervor. Part of this decline can be attributed to other extracurricular activities that attracted students' interests, most notably football and the eating clubs. Another factor was the growing uneasiness among some students, even the most devout ones, with the older forms of evangelism and piety. Burgess described some of the Philadelphian Society's more evangelistic-minded students as "gospel sharks," and those interested in missions, typically the sons of ministers and missionaries, as "too pious" for his liking.

Yet membership in the Philadelphian Society was not unpopular; if anything, being a Christian on the Princeton campus in the early twentieth century was fashionable. The leaders of the society were consistently among the university's most popular students. In 1909, for example, one of the two newly elected permanent secretaries was president of his junior class, captain of the basketball team, a member of the Triangle Club, and voted most popular man in his class. The other secretary was president of the Mount Hermon School Club, secretary of his junior class, and voted the most respected man in his class. An article in the *Princeton Alumni Weekly* boasted that in the past few years the secretary's position in the Philadelphian Society had been filled by a varsity football player, editor of the *Princetonian*, and other "well known men" who "commanded the respect of the whole college."[174] The society, like the eating clubs, even held its own "smokers."[175] Many of the most cosmopolitan eating club members, Burgess recalled, occasionally attended class prayer meetings in Murray-Dodge Hall. "They gave 'standing' to that institution and inevitably a man of this approved type would be made graduate secreaty [*sic*] of Murray-Dodge."[176]

In the early twentieth century, the university's intellectual horizons had multiplied and theology no longer provided a unifying center to the new liberal culture curriculum. Despite the dramatic departures from the established evangelical convictions and practices of the nineteenth century, however, Princeton's religious mission remained firmly intact in the early twentieth century. While conventional interpreters correctly observe important departures from established evangelical practices in the early twentieth century, they often ignore the important lines of continuity, as evidenced at Princeton, in universities' programs of religious education. Miller's Bible courses advanced a liberal Protestant faith more compatible with the educational and intellectual values of the modern university. The Bible classes, along with the other courses in Princeton's old program of religious education, were offered as electives, a circumstance that also fit the nonsectarian ideals of the day. Mandatory attendance at chapel services had been reduced for the same reason. Standard treatments, moreover, have neglected the critical role that the Y.M.C.A. had in the daily lives of students and the importance that this organization played in many modern colleges' and universities' efforts to perpetuate their historic Protestant mission. While the Philadelphian Society was officially a voluntary organization, the Y.M.C.A. at Princeton, like elsewhere, served as the administration's de facto campus ministry. In one important respect, the early twentieth century saw an expansion, not a contraction, of the university's religion mission. Through the Y.M.C.A., the university not only sought to Protestantize American culture but now more than ever before was actively engaged in trying to Protestantize the entire world.

A Country Club in the Nation's Service

In four short years, Wilson had taken several dramatic steps toward fulfilling his and other McCosh-era alumni's vision of Princeton as a major national university. He also conformed the university's program of religious education to its enlarged civic mission. With these advancements, Wilson and his colleagues hoped, Princeton would equip students to find a place and keep their faith in the modern age. The *New York Evening Post* went so far as to report that, in his first four years as president, Wilson had "ruined what was universally admitted to be the most agreeable and aristocratic country club in America by transforming it into an institution of learning."[177] While the *Evening Post* correctly observed that Wilson had transformed Princeton into a center of learning, the university was still a country club, however.

In the spring of 1906, President Wilson suffered a stroke. After a period of recuperation in England, he returned to Princeton in the fall with a commitment to reform Princeton even further.[178] Early in his presidency, Wilson touted Princeton's "democracy" and considered "the absence of social distinctions [and] the treatment of every man according to his merits" one of the university's most cherished characteristics.[179] Yet over his tenure, Wilson grew dissatisfied with the socially exclusive character of a institution expressly committed to serving the public's interests. After reviewing "the slow . . . and yet increasingly certain decline of the old democratic spirit" of Princeton and the concurrent "multiplications of social divisions" within the university, an emboldened Wilson made a radical proposal to the trustees in December 1906. He recommended merging the eating clubs, or the "aristocracy of the stomach" as one alumnus described them, with residential colleges that he hoped to construct.[180] In these residential colleges, like those at Oxford and Cambridge, students and unmarried professors would live and eat in community.[181] The Quad Plan would give visible, institutional expression to the educational reforms already achieved. With it Wilson hoped to renew the democratic spirit in Princeton and integrate social and intellectual life among undergraduates. "When we introduced the preceptorial system we made the greatest strategic move," Wilson told the trustees in June 1907, toward reviving undergraduate education "that has been made in the *whole history* of the American university." The Quad Plan, he believed, would not only remedy many problems at Princeton but also provide a worthy role model for other universities facing similar problems.[182]

During the late nineteenth century, Princeton had become, as Wilson contended, socially exclusive, drawing its students almost solely from the elite ranks of the Protestant establishment. McCosh had begun this trend with his efforts to beautify the campus, to attract the sons of affluent Americans, and to provide the university with a constant supply of students from boarding schools. The increase in student expenses and the rise of the number of students from elite boarding and preparatory schools provide the clearest evidence of the university's socially exclusive character. While Princeton kept the lowest estimated range of expenses down during Patton's presidency, the university raised it continuously during Wilson's presidency. In 1887–1888, the lowest estimated expenses stood at $326.25. In 1902–1903, this figure remained the same, $326. By 1909–1910, the figure had risen to $369.60, a 13 percent increase. By comparison, the university attempted to keep the highest range of expenses fairly constant during Patton's and Wilson's presidencies. In 1887–1888, the highest estimated expenses stood at $723.50. In 1909–1910, that figure stood at $714.60, a 1 percent decrease. Since the consumer price index dropped approximately 4 percent, when comparing 1887 to 1909, the administration made it more difficult for poorer students to attend Princeton at the same time it tried to restrain costs for wealthier students.[183] Since membership in one of the eating clubs was more expensive than boarding in one of the university's dining halls, the highest range of expenses was actually greater than that published. A better indicator of the university's increasingly elite social milieu is the dramatic rise in the number of students who attended private schools. In 1909, for instance, 78 percent of the student body had attended one of the elite secondary schools, such as Andover, Exeter, and Lawrenceville. When compared to 65 percent of Yale students, 47 percent of Harvard students, and 9 percent of Michigan students who had the advantage of such a private secondary education, Princeton clearly attracted more sons of the nation's wealthiest families than three of its chief competitors.[184] Although the university had built enough dormitories to house all of the upperclassmen and one-third of the freshmen on campus, not all of the rich students found the new dormitories sufficiently luxurious. While one student in the Class of 1908, for example, purchased a $4,600 limousine, hired a chauffeur, and lived in a five-room suite in the First National Bank building, other students lived in Edwards Hall, the lowest-priced dormitory on campus, commonly known as the home of the "untouchables."[185] Princeton was, as one student aptly described it, a place where the "American gentry" was educated.[186]

Within the exclusive milieu of the university, the eating clubs further divided undergraduate life into social cliques. The clubs, which had begun out of necessity during McCosh's presidency, gradually evolved into an elaborate social hierarchy with Ivy Club, comprising the wealthiest students, standing, or perhaps lounging, at the top. Sophomores created their own clubs, which served as feeders into the upperclass clubs. Members of the sophomore clubs wore different colored ties and bands on their felt or straw hats to distinguished one club from another. The freshmen, too, formed their own clubs, which then served as feeders or "followings" into the sophomore clubs. As one alumnus recalled, there was "cut-throat competition and intrigue" among students to get into a club. "[W]e were always afraid of our actions" as underclassmen, a junior wrote his father, "lest we be queered for upper class club."[187] Failure to get elected to a club left many students heartbroken and ashamed.[188]

The socially exclusive character of the university was inseparably related to the religious homogeneity of the student body. Half of the students who entered Princeton in the fall of 1902 were Presbyterian. In the fall of 1909, 38 percent of the students were Presbyterian. Although the percentage of incoming Presbyterian students dropped below a statistical majority in 1904, this change did not correspond with a dramatic increase in non-Protestant students. Between the fall of 1902 and the fall of 1910, an average of 16 Catholic and 5.5 Jewish students matriculated at Princeton each year.[189] Instead, Episcopal students made up for the drop in Presbyterian students, rising from 20 percent of the freshman class in 1902 to 30 percent in 1909.[190] It was the slight increase in enrollment of non-Protestants that drew the attention of the administration, however. Whereas McCosh had worried about the rising numbers of Episcopalians attending Princeton, Dean Fine, for example, told the trustees that he found it "interesting" that fourteen Catholics had enrolled in the class of 1907.[191]

The experience of Jewish students with the eating clubs illustrates how indivisible the university's ethno-religious homogeneity was from its social elitism. It appears that Jewish students were excluded from the clubs out of hand. "I was rudely awakened," one Jewish student wrote Wilson, "by discovering all my classmates landed in clubs, while I wandered hopeless on the outskirts, an Ishmaelite and outcast. True I wore no yellow cap, the badge of disgrace imposed by the simple, brutal mediaeval customs on my forefathers; but the absence of a cap or insignia of any sort branded me as an outsider."[192] One outside observer, a newspaper reporter who visited Princeton in 1909, saw a link between the university's Protestant character and its social elitism: "The Christian tradition of Princeton, the exclusiveness of the upper-class clubs, and the prejudices of the students keep away many Jews, although not all—there are eleven in the Freshman class. Anti-Semitic feeling seemed to me more dominant at Princeton than at any of the other universities I visited." "'If the Jews once got in,'" the reporter was allegedly told, "'they would ruin Princeton as they have Columbia and Pennsylvania.'"[193]

Although Wilson's attack on the club system was not motivated by a contemporary concern for gender and racial inclusivity, the exclusive character of Princeton is further illustrated by the university's attitude toward the education of women and African Americans. The Evelyn College for Women was located in Princeton and had some very informal associations with the university through certain university professors who served on its Board of Trustees. When the struggling college collapsed in 1897, the university made no effort to provide for the town's young women as Harvard and Radcliffe or Columbia and Barnard had done.[194] African American students earned Princeton degrees, but they came down Dickinson Street from the seminary and cross-enrolled in the university's M.A. program. When an African American wrote Wilson with questions about gaining admission into the undergraduate program, the president told his secretary to inform him that "it is altogether inadvisable for a colored man to enter Princeton."[195] Ironically, as a university that professed, and at times even celebrated, its newfound devotion to serving national educational interests, Princeton stood out as an exception among the fourteen founding members of the Association of American Universities in its exclusion of African Americans and, along with Yale, in its neglect of the education of women.[196]

In proposing the Quad Plan, a new note sounded in Wilson's thinking about social problems. Wilson, who was raised a conservative southern Democrat, was becoming politically progressive in his thinking. Unrestricted industrialization and urbanization, as many social gospellers and progressive reformers of the day had pointed out, had increasingly stratified American society. Like many liberal Protestants and reformers, Wilson was convinced that moneyed interests were subverting many of the nation's ideals about democracy. His attitude toward the education of African Americans and women notwithstanding, Wilson hoped the Quad Plan would overcome some of the divisive results created by the social conservativism of the university's elite Protestant community. By reforming Princeton, Wilson aspired to influence the rest of American higher education. "Undoubtedly, if we would give Princeton the highest distinction and the academic leadership in the country," Wilson told the trustees in proposing the Quad Plan, "we must . . . lift her intellectual life and achievements out of mediocrity" and "make her . . . a conspicuous model and example."[197] Wilson's Protestant vision of the university and ultimately the nation suffused his desire to reform the club system. He hoped to construct a model Christian community whose graduates would exert a similar enlightening influence upon a divided nation. However, the social conservativism of the Protestant establishment thwarted Wilson's more progressive vision for Princeton and American culture.[198]

Temporarily converted by Wilson's impassioned plea to restore democracy to undergraduate life, the trustees unanimously approved the Quad Plan in June 1907. But over the summer, opposition to the Quad Plan blossomed into a campaign to defeat it. Many students resisted the plan because it threatened the "sanctity" of their clubs. Andrew F. West, Jesse Lynch Williams, editor of the *Princeton Alumni Weekly*, Henry Van Dyke Jr., and Paul Van Dyke led the opposition campaign from within the university itself. Many of the older faculty members also took umbrage at Wilson's dictatorial tactics in proposing the plan without consulting them, as he had with his earlier reforms. When the faculty debated and voted on the plan in the early fall, the preceptors, almost to a man, sided with the president who had personally hired them, while most of the older professors, including one of Wilson's closest friends, John G. Hibben, and the theological conservatives, Francis and George S. Patton, opposed it.[199] Younger alumni, especially those in the influential alumni clubs on the East Coast, rabidly resisted the plan. While Wilson regarded his plan as "a scheme of salvation" and "a fight for the restoration of Princeton," many others saw it as the damnation of their cherished clubs and a unjustified attack on wealth.[200] It soon became painfully clear to the trustees that the alumni were not going to under-write the Quad Plan's two-million-dollar price tag as they had done Wilson's earlier reforms. After much debate, the trustees forced a disappointed but defi-ant Wilson to withdraw the plan at their October meeting.[201]

At the same time that Wilson launched his Quad Plan campaign, Dean West and his supporters among the trustees had begun to pressure the president to construct a graduate college on campus. In the subsequently battle over where to build the graduate college, Wilson once again ran into problems arising from the social conservativism of the Protestant establishment. After four years of patiently supporting Wilson's reforms of the undergraduate program, West ex-pected the administration to turn its attention to another important element of Princeton's expanded civic mission; a graduate college, West had emphatically told the trustees a year earlier, "is not only necessary to our reputation as a true university," but it "will also give Princeton unique distinction among the uni-versities of America and will make her justly eminent in the eyes of the univer-sities of the Old World as a home of the noblest standards of liberal education." Two recent developments further strengthened West's cause: in the spring of 1906, Josephine Thomson Swann's estate had left the university $275,000 for the construction of a graduate college, and that fall Wilson and the trustees had persuaded West to decline the presidency of Massachusetts Institute of Tech-nology in order to remain at Princeton to oversee the development of the gradu-ate program.[202]

Wilson, West, and the trustees agreed that Princeton's rural setting precluded the creation of a medical school and probably even a law school. Princeton's future standing as a major university, they believed, lay in graduate education in the humanities and sciences. Both Wilson and West hoped to build a residen-tial graduate college modeled after those at Oxford and Cambridge. Despite the vast areas of agreement between the president and the dean, there was one sig-nificant point of disagreement: in his inaugural address, Wilson said he wanted to build the graduate college at the "geographic heart" of the university so that its windows "open straight upon the walks and quadrangles and lecture halls of the *studium generale*."[203] Dean West, by contrast, envisioned a gathering of graduate students living and learning in a secluded community.[204] West's luxu-rious plans for the graduate college further complicated the disagreement over location. West was the son of a controversial Presbyterian minister and leader of the premillennialist movement, an important source of early-twentieth-cen-tury fundamentalism. Although he had distinctly middle-class roots, through marriage West had become something of a bon vivant, thriving in the growing, cosmopolitan town of Princeton.[205] Merwick, the temporary home of graduate students on Bayard Lane, had earned West's plans for the graduate college a well-deserved elitist reputation. On Wednesday evenings, for example, the dean hosted extravagant dinners at which students wore evening clothes beneath their academic gowns.[206] At least one trustee worried that West's "luxurious" views of graduate education "will result in simply making the Graduate School a great big upper class Club."[207] Several of the university's more prominent professors, as well as many lower paid preceptors and assistant professors, were troubled by West's pretentious plans. After receiving the Swann gift, the alumni, faculty, and trustees split into opposing camps supporting either West or Wilson, and the ensuing controversy divided Princeton more deeply than any disagreement in the previous fifty years. Almost all of the Presbyterian ministers on the faculty and the trustees, liberals and conservatives alike, opposed Wilson's plan. Although the controversy was fought over great educational principles, the personalities and personal animosities between the principal protagonists infused the entire affair. After two years of debate, the trustees finally agreed in April 1908 to build the college, as Wilson proposed, at the center of the campus.

In the spring of 1909, however, Wilson's plans were sullied by a gift from William Cooper Procter, a rich soap manufacturer. Procter, an alumnus of Princeton and close friend of West, promised $500,000 on two conditions: that the university match the gift and build the college on a site other than Prospect. That fall the trustees changed their minds, accepted the Procter gift, and agreed to West's preferred location for the college, on the golf course almost a mile from the heart of the campus.[208] Wilson faced a dilemma: he could accept the Procter gift and compromise one of his sacred goals or reject it because of his principles and incur the wrath of the alumni in the process. Foreshadowing his future decision as president of the United States regarding the League of Nations and its eventual outcome, Wilson chose the latter course and went on the offensive to defend his position. In a *Scribner's Magazine* article entitled, "What is a College For?" Wilson complained that the "side shows" have "swallowed up the circus" at many American universities like Princeton. To Wilson, the problem was caused by the influx of "the sons of very rich men" who expected to inherit wealth and could not be motivated to take their studies seriously. The solution, as he had earlier proposed in the Quad Plan, was to abolish "heterogeneous congeries of petty organizations" and create "a single university family" in which teachers and students would live "as intimate members."[209] In February 1910, Procter withdrew his gift just as West and Moses Taylor Pyne had secretly planned.[210] The alumni, predictably, were livid. Wilson stated his position bluntly before the hostile Princeton Club of New York: "When the country is looking to us as men who prefer ideas even to money, are we going to withdraw and say, 'After all, we find we were mistaken: we prefer money to ideas'?" "The business of every university is a spiritual, an intellectual thing," he insisted, and to forsake this purpose would be "not only un-American but utterly *unserviceable* to the country."[211]

Having failed to persuade the alumni that moneyed interests were subverting the university's civic mission, Wilson directly assailed the social conservativism of the Protestant establishment. In an address before the alumni club of Pittsburgh in April 1910, the president leveled a brutal attack on the influence of wealth on the university and on mainstream Protestantism. American universities, he insisted, were "looking to the support of wealth rather than to the people."

Perhaps annoyed by the criticisms of the clerics on the faculty and among the trustees and seeing an opportunity to create some political capital, Wilson turned his guns in a populist attack on the social exclusiveness of the Protestant church. He fired,

> I hope that the last thing I will ever be capable of will be casting a shadow on the church, and yet the churches—the Protestant churches, at least— have dissociated themselves from the people. . . . They serve certain strata, certain visible uplifted strata, and ignore the men whose need is dire. The churches have more regard to their pew-rents than to the soul and in proportion as they look to the respectability of their congregations to lift them in esteem, they are lowering themselves in the whole level of Christian endeavor.

Wilson, as John M. Mulder observes, had previously praised college-educated Americans as a kind of intellectual aristocracy. Wilson also enjoyed the largesse of generous Princeton alumni. This same person was suddenly rejecting the intellectual and social leaders of the nation, as well as the people who helped put him in office and financed his reforms. Now Wilson saw the true American spirit, as he put it, in the great mass of "unknown and unrecognized men" whose powers were slowly being developed and "will emerge with opinions which will rule."[212] "A more unsparing denunciation of the churches of the country," the *Pittsburgh Dispatch* reported, "could scarcely have come from the lips of the most radical Socialist leader." The audience, the newspaper added, "seemed to sit as though stupefied with surprise."[213] Wilson's opponents regarded his rhetoric about democracy as merely a political ploy to gain popular support. He had, however, little support inside the university. In fact, administering the affairs of the university during the controversy had become extremely difficult for Wilson. Cyrus H. McCormick, one of the trustees who had helped put Wilson into office, quietly floated the idea of creating a committee of three trustees and two professors to manage the institution's affairs, much like the one that had been proposed during the last days of Patton's presidency.[214]

The controversy came to an abrupt and surprising conclusion. On May 18, Isaac C. Wyman, a wealthy alumnus whom Dean West had befriended, died and left his entire estate to Princeton to construct a graduate college and appointed his lawyer and West as the executors of his will. When Wilson got word that the gift would probably mean "at least two million" dollars, he told his spouse, "We've beaten the living, but we can't fight the dead—the game is up."[215] Procter offered his gift again, and the trustees finally settled on West's golf course location.[216] Wilson saw the handwriting on the walls of Nassau Hall: he had not only lost the battle over the graduate college but also his ability to lead the university. In the summer of 1910, he took up an offer from the Democratic party in New Jersey to run for the governorship and formally resigned the university's presidency after his election that November.[217] "With a deep sense of our loss in Dr. Wilson's resignation," read the faculty's memorial, "it is yet with feelings of pride that we *spare* him to the wider service of the state, to which he has been called. Princeton has ever been the mother of statesmen and of men who have responded to the call of *public service*, and she takes pride in this opportunity of affording a notable proof that the spirit of older Princeton still lives in her sons."[218] The loss of Wilson was one which many in Princeton suffered gladly in service to the nation.

The popularity and numerous successes of Woodrow Wilson's first four years as president of Princeton University contrasted sharply with the difficulties and failures of his final four years. Wilson's vision of more fully integrating academic and social life and undergraduate and graduate education faltered upon the rocks of the university's social conservativism and at the hands of a politician, Dean Andrew F. West, the likes of whom Wilson would not face again until he crossed paths with Senator Henry Cabot Lodge in the battle over the League of Nations. Wilson's presidency, which had begun with so much hope and with enthusiastic support from all quarters of the university community, ended with disappointment and division. Ironically, the hostility and intrigue generated by these controversies were unmatched by any of the Presbyterian ecclesiastical conflicts that were so abhorred by the liberal Protestants in the university.

Despite the troubles surrounding the university after 1906, Wilson had done nothing less than refashion the college into a modern university dedicated to public service. He accomplished this by replacing the old-time "discipline and piety" philosophy of higher education with a liberal culture philosophy, by revising the curriculum and inaugurating the major-grouping system, by establishing the preceptorial system, and by hiring a faculty on the basis of scholarship and teaching ability. These educational advancements had repercussions well beyond Princeton. The influence of Wilson's model was also evident in the growing popularity of the major-grouping system, adapted even at Harvard under President Lowell; in the inauguration of some variant of the preceptorial system at other colleges and universities; and in the establishment of residential colleges at many universities including Harvard, Yale, and eventually Princeton. As a result, Wilson went far toward fulfilling the McCosh-era alumni's vision of Princeton as a major national university. Moreover, Wilson had firmly established the basic pattern of educational commitments and interests that would guide Princeton throughout the twentieth century. This was an important legacy Wilson left at Princeton.

In the reconfiguration of Princeton's dual heritage, religion was not lost. Rather, the traditional interest in nurturing the faith of students was modified to conform with the university's newfound commitment to its public mission. Wilson and his allies, in effect, widened the Whiggish conception of higher education. The nature and role of religious education within the university shifted from an evangelical Protestant to a more liberal Protestant orientation. From an ideological perspective, the old nineteenth-century Protestant worldview, emphasizing the harmonious coexistence of the natural and supernatural, no longer provided the framework for a liberal education. Scientific naturalism and competing philosophical perspectives had undermined the credibility of the Scottish realism that had supported the older Protestant worldview and framed the older discipline and piety educational philosophy. By contrast, the liberal Protestant theology espoused in the classrooms and pulpits of Princeton in the early twentieth century was more congenial to modernity. Less compulsory forms of religious education—elective Bible classes, more voluntary chapel services, and the Philadelphian Society—helped the university resolve tensions between its civic and religious missions. As Wilson told students upon the eve of his resignation, Princeton "has always stood for the spirit of manhood, for patriotism, for sound learning and true religion and highest of all, the fear of God."[219] Yet the new configuration provoked a great deal of controversy during the presidency of Wilson's successor and threatened to subvert the unity of the community and ultimately the university's mission to advance the Christian character of American society.

Chapter 5

Religion and the Modern
American University, 1910–1928

Princeton, read a trustees' report in January 1927, "has always recognized a *dual obligation* to its undergraduates." One side of this commitment involved providing "a curriculum which will meet the needs of a modern university" and the other involved creating within students "those spiritual values which make for the building of character."[1] Wilson had reshaped Princeton into a modern university and had left as his legacy an unyielding commitment to serving national interests. Undergraduate education, graduate training, and a variety of impressive specialized research programs enabled the university to help meet the nation's need for liberal, civic-minded leaders and the demand for science and practical technology. Wilson and his successors in early-twentieth-century Princeton continued to insist, like their nineteenth-century predecessors, that Protestantism was indispensable to the public good and that civic institutions, such as Princeton, served public interests when they sought to inculcate students with a nonsectarian Protestant faith. In this way, the university, they believed, helped mainline Protestantism play a unifying and integrative role in a nation of increasing cultural and religious diversity. By doing so, they reasoned, Princeton, like other private colleges and universities, would maintain its historic religious mission to advance the Christian character of American society.

During the presidency of Wilson's successor, John G. Hibben, controversies challenged the new configuration of Princeton's Protestant and civic missions. These controversies, however, helped to strengthen the new ways in which the university attempted to fulfill its religious mission in the twentieth century. In liberal Protestantism, the university found a religion that was compatible with modern science and the public mission of the university. Those traditional evangelical convictions and practices that had survived Wilson's presidency were disestablished during Hibben's tenure. Fundamentalists' criticisms of the university hastened this process in two ways. Sometimes fundamentalist attacks upon the university convinced the administration to adopt policies that guaranteed the displacement of traditional evangelical convictions and practices. This was the case, for example, when fundamentalists' condemnations of the theological liberalism of the university's Bible professor accelerated the administration's approval of a policy of academic freedom. Yet fundamentalists, contrary to conventional interpretations, often supported efforts to marginalize or secularize the undergraduate program. This was evident, for instance, in the fundamentalists' efforts to eliminate mandatory religious instruction and worship. At the same time, some of the university's more secular-minded cultural modernists, such as F. Scott Fitzgerald, criticized the Protestant hegemony over the university. Their criticisms, like those of the fundamentalists, fell upon deaf ears. Student opposition to mandatory chapel and, more important, to the alleged cultic activities taking place inside the Philadelphian Society in the mid-1920s precipitated a major reevaluation and reorganization of the university's program of religious education in 1927–1928. These controversies also helped to lay the groundwork for the creation of a department of religion where religion would be studied more as an academic discipline than as a subject of overt proselytism.

Despite the "second disestablishment" of Protestant cultural hegemony in the 1920s, mainline Protestants remained firmly entrenched in many of the nation's most important cultural institutions. The religious controversies of the 1910s and 1920s at Princeton reveal the mainline Protestant response to cultural diversity and questions of assimilation. They also indicate how mainline Protestantism continued to dominate Princeton, like many other private colleges and universities, for a large part of the twentieth century. In response to the religious controversies, the administration attempted to homogenize diversity and dissent through the bureaucratic centralization of the university's program of religious education in its new chapel and its newly created office of the Dean of the Chapel. The internal division created by these controversies notwithstanding, the university still aspired to shape the Christian character of students and ultimately the nation. As at other colleges and universities during the tumultuous 1920s, the events at Princeton helped to preserve the Protestant mission of American higher education for more than another generation.

Electing a Peacemaker

Wilson's departure for the New Jersey statehouse did not itself signal an end to the divisions that had plagued the university. The new president, the trustees determined, would have to be an alumnus, able "to unite, not disintegrate, the university faculty," who had the "force, character and Christian bearing" to lead the institution. After laboring fifteen months, the trustees elected the fifty-year-old John G. Hibben as Princeton's fourteenth president; yet conflict surrounded even this decision. "When I heard of this election, I was greatly disappointed and cast down," recalled Professor William Berryman Scott, "for I feared that it signified the triumph of Mr. Wilson's bitterest enemies." Several trustees shared this sentiment. Although the board had not always agreed on whom they wanted to elect, as was the case with Patton, they had presented a united public front by making the inevitable decision of the majority unanimous. At Hibben's election, however, nine trustees had their negative votes recorded against him.[2] Hibben immediately went to work at healing old wounds. "I represent no group or set of men, no party, no faction, no past allegiance or affiliations—but one united Princeton!" Hibben exclaimed in his first speech before the alumni.[3] And at his first faculty meeting, one professor recorded in his diary, the new president made "a good, dignified, conservative & conciliatory opening speech." Professor Scott later amended his initial impression: "Dr. Hibben's genial and kindly nature rapidly healed the breach which the violent controversies had made."[4]

Although Wilson had "other engagements" that prevented him from attending his successor's inauguration, personal differences did not keep Hibben from expressing a deep loyalty to his predecessor's vision of the civic and Protestant missions of the university. Education, Hibben asserted, is both conservative and progressive. Education preserves "those great human forces" that cultivate "the advancement of knowledge and the civilization of the world." At the same time, he reasoned, education was progressive in that it fosters freedom. Hibben's "ideal university education" then consisted of "liberal studies" that "free the mind from the natural and artificial obstacles to its progressive development." Through the first two years of required courses in the humanities, a student acquired not only a deep appreciation of the present world but also "something of the form and spirit of its classical languages and literature" and "something of its history, its art, customs, manners, morals and institutions." Like Wilson, Hibben believed that the world of knowledge was not an assortment of "shifting and variable elements" but "a body of universal truths, independent of age and of race, which vitally concern the ultimate values of life and which determine the possibilities of human development." Despite the overt commitment to the liberal arts, Princeton's curriculum, like those at other universities, served several functions. The university's new curriculum and major-grouping system, Hibben reasoned, allowed students to cultivate their special abilities and vocational interests by concentrating in one department "in a broad-minded spirit which transcends the utilitarian demands of any particular profession or technical pursuit." Hibben, like Wilson and his other predecessors, asserted that the grand purpose of a Princeton education was to influence the nation's culture through the training of its leaders. Those who enjoyed "the privileges of an education," he said, form the "aristocracy" who would "rule and influence" their communities. The university expected "every man who bears the Princeton mark and who is true to the Princeton traditions to serve his day and generation with fidelity, and to bear upon his soul the burden of humanity."[5]

To fulfill its civic mission, Hibben counseled, the university would draw upon the "Christian faith and hope" deeply embedded in its heritage. In this way, Princeton, like other private colleges and universities in the early twentieth century, would fulfill its religious mission. "Our hope and our prayer," Hibben concluded his inaugural address, was that the sons of Princeton "may keep the faith with the past while moving forward to possess the new lands of promise and of plenty." Although Hibben did not share all of Wilson's progressive vision of Princeton and American culture, he was confident, like Wilson, that the university would assist Protestantism's triumph over America.[6]

"The Devil in the Cap and Gown"

"You are a light in a dark place," Union Seminary's Henry Sloane Coffin wrote Lucius H. Miller in December 1913, "and we do not want the candlestick removed." "I have put all fear of heresy hunters behind my back," Princeton's Bible professor said in his reply. "I have for some time been of the conviction that there is nothing to do but to speak and write with absolute frankness."[7] Earlier in his career at Princeton, Miller had demonstrated a great deal of caution in his work; his views were mildly liberal in theological orientation, and he had even asked the president for permission to publish them. Although Miller subsequently remained committed to Ritschlian theology, a sabbatical year of study at the University of Berlin and at the University of Heidelberg with Ernst Troeltsch in 1911–1912 had inspired him. In a lengthy synopsis of the thought of the father of the *Religionsgeschichliche Schule* published in the *Harvard Theological Review*, he wrote, "While such men as Ernst Troeltsch live and work in Germany, religion will not die out, and just so long will seekers after truth from other lands be drawn thither, to return, not merely with a clearer vision, but with a warmer heart and *stronger purpose*."[8]

Miller soon demonstrated a "stronger purpose" of his own. He became more aggressive in his proclamations of modernist thought and made elaborate plans to establish a "Department on the History and Literature of Religion." In 1913–1914, he contributed a four-article series on the life, teaching, and divinity of Jesus to *Biblical World*, a popular liberal Protestant monthly published by the University of Chicago Divinity School; the four articles were republished as a book, *Our Knowledge of Christ*, in the fall of 1914. Although he expressed a sincere respect for the "spiritual power" of his conservative upbringing, Miller felt that "the old has become increasingly unsatisfying" for many in his generation. As a result, he and others "have been obliged to readjust our views for the very sake of that Christian faith we long for and need." By making such an adjustment with the aid of scientific higher criticism, Miller hoped to show many of his peers that their "desertion" of the church "is unnecessary, harmful, and wrong." One such accommodation to modern thought, for example, concerned the incarnation of Christ: "If human nature is recognized as potentially divine, the divinity of Christ will be thought of as such an impartation of divine life, in the realms of the ethical and the religious, as will infallibly draw men to God." Thus, he concluded, people could still affirm the divinity of Christ by its "continued revivification through the adoption of its statement to advancing knowledge."[9] Although Miller's intention was to cultivate a Protestant faith in the nation's future leaders by harmonizing Christianity with modern thought, some in the university community thought he was pouring the acids of modernity upon the true faith. Miller's efforts precipitated a controversy over the propagation of Protestant modernism within the university, a debate over the place of biblical instruction within the curriculum, and a crisis over academic freedom.

"Under the regime of Drs. McCosh and Patton," the *Presbyterian* observed, "Princeton sent out men who carried a stalwart evangelical message. . . . But the message which to-day goes out from her department of Bible Studies is stoutly antagonistic to the Protestant Evangelical faith."[10] Miller's liberalism disturbed conservative Presbyterians, many of whom were university alumni from the McCosh and Patton eras. And the *Presbyterian*, published in Philadelphia, a stronghold of both Princeton alumni and conservative Presbyterians, did much to inflame their opposition to Miller. David S. Kennedy, one of the magazine's editors, assured Miller privately that their complaints were not personal but "simply a defense of what we hold to be sacred and true." Yet many of the conservative Presbyterians' fulminations were so malicious that, in the genteel climate of Princeton, where politeness was a cardinal virtue, Miller's critics appeared to have nothing but a personal vendetta against him. While some conservatives published their criticisms, others spoke privately with President Hibben. John W. Nicely, a Presbyterian minister from Chicago, a university alumnus, and father of two prospective students, told the president that he regretted to see such liberal views propagated by "a Professor of Princeton University." "The only logical place for us, if his statements be true," he concluded, "is in a Unitarian Church."[11]

Not everyone, however, found Miller's liberalism threatening to the religious mission of Princeton. Shailer Mathews, editor of the *Biblical World* and a leading New Testament higher critic at the University of Chicago, reassured a nervous Miller that his work was "anything but radical." "I cannot imagine how the University should be in any way exercised over the matter. If liberty of teaching means anything it certainly means such temperate writing as your articles." As he had done previously, Miller forwarded Mathews's supportive letter, as well as similar ones from younger alumni, to Hibben as evidence that he was upholding academic science and the university's religious mission. Miller may have also wanted to remind the president that as a professor in a university he should have the liberty to teach what he wanted in his Bible classes.[12]

At the same time that the conservative Presbyterians attacked Miller for his theological modernism, the Bible professor made an impassioned plea to the president and trustees to establish a Religion Department and to hire two instructors to help him teach the wide array of courses, such as Relations of Christianity to Social Problems, that he wanted to offer students. Miller argued that a familiarity with the literature of the Bible and with church history should be part of a "liberal arts degree from Princeton." Miller's efforts to secure a stronger place for religious instruction was part of a larger movement in the early twentieth century to promote the academic study of religion in American colleges and universities. Led by Charles Foster Kent at Yale and those associated with the growing Religious Education Association, Bible professors at many institutions were arguing that full-fledged Bible departments should be included in a liberal education in order to educate the future religious leaders of American and to advance the scientific study of religion.[13] Furthermore, Miller believed that the academic study of religion helped to advance the religious mission of the university. "Princeton," Miller explained, "should never adopt the necessary attitude of the State Universities—no religious responsibility for the students. If she did, she would forfeit her charter, the respect of most of her sons and friends, and also a great opportunity in a day of great religious need." With a department, he concluded, "we may properly maintain the Christian traditions of the university." To clinch his argument, Miller appealed to institutional pride: "Finally, we are in danger of being left behind other universities, even the State Universities, many of which are recognizing increasingly the place of such studies in any scheme of general education." Miller had a point. In a survey of fifty-four private and public colleges and universities in 1916, the Religious Education Association reported that fifty-two offered elective Bible classes and eighteen, typically denominational colleges, still had required Bible instruction. All of the private, nondenominational universities in the survey, including Columbia, Pennsylvania, and Yale, offered more courses in religion than Princeton.[14] Ironically, Miller failed to mention that Princeton once had a Department of Biblical Literature and that the President Hibben himself had taught English Bible.[15] At their spring meeting in 1914, the trustees agreed to hire an assistant for Miller but tabled discussion on the proposed department.[16] After "a full and thorough-going discussion of the situation *in all its phases*," as the trustees' minutes cryptically report at their subsequent June meeting, they decided again to postpone any decision on a department. They did agree, however, to establish an annual lecture series on "the nature of Christianity or on the history and literature of the Bible."[17] As students and faculty prepared to return to the university in the fall, a raging tempest broke in Princeton that made the earlier controversy look like a gentle spring rain.

"The Devil, squirming and wriggling in 'cap and gown,' has been permitted and allowed, by some inconceivable miscalculation—or inscrutable lack of vigilance—on the part of those in authority to undulate himself into the chair of 'Biblical Instruction' in one of our great universities." The alleged "devil in cap and gown" was none other than Professor Miller. In a thirty-page pamphlet by the same title, Ford C. Ottman belittled Miller and condemned his modernist theology. Ottman was a Presbyterian minister from Stamford, Connecticut, and had been a classmate of Hibben's at Princeton Seminary in the early 1880s. He distributed his polemic at the Bible Conference of the Stony Brook (Long Island) Association of Presbyterian Clergymen the last week of August.[18] The news media picked up quickly on the story and stoked the flames of controversy with their sensationalistic articles on the pamphlet.[19] The conservative *Presbyterian* also leaped into the fray. "Princeton University," one article insisted, "has long been cherished as a Presbyterian stronghold," with presidents like McCosh and Patton of "international reputation" at the helm. "The new regime evidently contemplates alliance with 'liberalism,' which means scouting the authority of the Scriptures as a guide to faith and a record of historical truth." While Miller believed that his work demonstrated the university's enduring commitment to its Christian heritage, many conservatives believed that his presence marked a defection from it. Princeton, the conservatives insisted, had to teach "*the fundamentals* of the Christian faith," and they threatened to boycott the university."[20]

The theological landscape of American Protestantism, which in previous decades had been characterized by significant differences, not irreconcilable divisions, had turned into warring camps of conservatives and liberals in the 1910s. For several years conservative Presbyterians had been trying to stop the rising tide of liberalism in the church, especially as graduates from Union Seminary in New York sought ordination. They persuaded the General Assembly in 1910 to adopt a five-point declaration that defined the "essential and necessary" doctrines—the inerrancy of Scripture, the virgin birth, substitutionary atonement, bodily resurrection, and the miraculous powers of Christ—that all candidates for ordination were expected to affirm. Among those Union graduates whose ordination was held up by judicial action was Tertius Van Dyke, son of Professor Henry Van Dyke Jr.[21] Conservative Presbyterians found Miller's work at Princeton as dangerous as the presence of liberal preachers in the church. Union Seminary, they believed, threatened the orthodoxy of both the Presbyterian church and Princeton University. "Prof. Miller is one of the brood produced by Union Seminary," the *Presbyterian* remarked, "who have been permitted to stealthily creep into the church and Christian institutions, and in the name of 'advanced views' introduce their detestable and vicious teachings."[22] The rift between theological conservatives and liberals in the Princeton community, however, does not fully explain the crisis created by Miller's work at the university.

With the outbreak of war in Europe—among the world's most "civilized" nations—conservative Presbyterians, like other Americans, were beginning to sense a growing crisis in American society. Although many had been "cheerfully laying dynamite" in the hidden cracks of nineteenth-century culture long before 1914, as Henry F. May has remarked, it took military confrontation to detonate the explosives that collapsed the walls of Victorian America.[23] The growing anxiety about the moral condition of the republic intensified the conservative Presbyterians' frustration with the spread of modernism. The *Presbyterian* identified theological liberalism as "the real cause of the European war" and suggested that "bad instruction in American universities will end in some similar break-out in our own land. . . . With [the] repetition of Union Seminaryism at Princeton, evangelical Christians will have to take a choice of the trilemma: either send their boys elsewhere, forbid them to take the Bible course at Princeton, or yield them up to the baldest infidelity, both with regard to the Bible and Christ." These larger fears about the collapse of Christian America fed many conservative Presbyterians' frustration with the university. While the university was "not required to become sectarian," the *Presbyterian* insisted, to be "true to her history and traditions . . . she ought not to supplant the teachings of such men as McCosh, McClain [*sic*], Duffield, and Patton with bald Unitarianism."[24] In a day when many feared that American society was teetering on the verge of chaos, many conservative Presbyterians were convinced that the nation's future leaders, like the nation itself, now needed more than ever to be grounded firmly in the evangelical faith.

While fundamentalism as a distinct movement would not emerge in American culture until after the First World War, when it did surface many Presbyterians, especially those associated with Princeton Seminary, would play a key part in the movement. The Miller controversy reveals, however, that many conservative Presbyterians were already manifesting fundamentalism's defining characteristic, a militant opposition to both modernism in theology and the cultural changes that modernism endorsed.[25] The first fundamentalist-modernist controversy in Princeton, therefore, did not take place in the 1920s at Princeton Seminary with New Testament Professor J. Gresham Machen's opposition to theological liberalism in the church, but rather occurred in 1914 at the university in the dispute over Miller's orthodoxy and his position at the university. The conservatives' opposition to Miller's liberalism also foreshadows one of the eventual outcomes of the fundamentalist-modernist controversies of the 1920s and 1930s. So relentless were the conservatives in their criticisms of Miller's liberalism that they eventually alienated the majority of people within the community who were willing to tolerate a certain degree of theological diversity in order to preserve religious unity in the university and ultimately its religious mission to American society.

Friends, some colleagues, and perhaps the university's administration advised Miller to remain silent in the face of the fundamentalists' attacks in order to avoid giving them any more ammunition for their criticisms.[26] To be sure, Miller was no passive victim of the conservatives' criticism. As expressed in his letters and writings, Miller had become more militant in his advocacy of liberal Christianity. He also shared many common concerns with the conservatives. He too was anxious to safeguard the Protestant faith of students at a time when Victorian culture seemed to be collapsing. Miller was also ready to match the conservatives' fire with his own in a battle over the soul of the university. He told John McDowell, a member of the Graduate Advisory Board of the Philadelphian Society, that he suspected the two sons of David S. Kennedy, one of the editors of the *Presbyterian*, were acting as "spies" for their father. One son was an undergraduate and the other a recent alumnus who was studying at the seminary. Miller also had the vague notion that Princeton Seminary was somehow behind the controversy. He wanted to expose the Kennedy boys in an article in the *Daily Princetonian* or exclude them from Murray-Dodge Hall, and he sarcastically mused that the latter option might mean he would have to employ "some 'muscular Christianity.'" McDowell counseled against any action, especially barring the alleged spies from the Murray-Dodge Hall. He also told Miller not to drag the seminary into the controversy unless he had "proof that the Seminary is officially backing it."[27] Although the university trustees publicly denied that they had discussed the controversy at their fall meeting in 1914, they did create an informal committee to explore their options.[28]

The recent furor over academic freedom at Lafayette College probably gave the trustees plenty to consider as they waited to reconvene. In the spring of 1913, the president of Lafayette College, Ethelbert Warfield, had forced a philosophy professor, John Mecklin, to resign because of his alleged theological unorthodoxy. Many in Princeton knew personally both Lafayette's president and controversial philosophy professor. Warfield was a university alumnus, the brother of Princeton theologian B. B. Warfield, and the president of the seminary's Board of Trustees. Mecklin, like Warfield, was a Presbyterian minister and a Princeton Seminary graduate. After the Civil War, an increasing number of educators, most with unorthodox religious or political views, were caught up in controversies over academic freedom. Despite the fact that many professors lost their jobs, support for academic freedom, especially from within professional societies, grew steadily in the late nineteenth century. The German concept of *Lehrfreiheit*, which in America came to mean the freedom for professors to pursue their teaching and scholarship independent of political or religious restraint, helped to fuel the growth of academic freedom. Perhaps John Dewey best expressed the goal of academic freedom in 1902, when he delineated two types of American institutions: any "ecclesiastical, political, or even economic corporation holding certain tenets," he argued, had a right "to maintain and propagate its creed." These "teaching bodies, called by whatever name," were not to be confused with "the university proper." The "aim and object of the university," by contrast, was to investigate, verify, interpret, and communicate truth, "untrammeled by external fear or favor." Along the same lines, Columbia University President Nicholas Murray Butler said, "A true university is conceivable in no other atmosphere than that of freedom."[29] Mecklin appealed his dismissal to two professional societies, the American Philosophical Association and the American Psychological Association. These organizations formed a joint committee, headed by Johns Hopkins Professor Arthur O. Lovejoy, to investigate the firing. Although Warfield resisted their inquiry as unjust and intrusive, Lafayette's trustees eventually forced Warfield to resign but did not reinstate Mecklin.[30]

The events at Lafayette and the Miller controversy at Princeton not only coincided with the creation of the American Association of University Professors (A.A.U.P.) on January 1 and 2, 1915, and the canonization of academic freedom as an essential feature of the American university but also accelerated Princeton's adoption of a policy of academic freedom. Three Princeton University Professors—Edward Capps, Edward M. Kemmerer, and Howard C. Warren—joined Lovejoy on the A.A.U.P.'s organizational committee. Professor Warren helped write the A.A.U.P.'s policy on academic freedom, which expressed a position much like the one advanced by John Dewey, the organization's first president.[31] Warren was interested both personally and professionally in guaranteeing that fundamentalists would not subvert the advancements achieved in the university's public mission during Wilson's presidency. Like many professors in the early twentieth century, Warren became a thoroughgoing cultural modernist during his career at Princeton. As a young psychologist and assistant to Professor James Mark Baldwin in the 1890s, Warren had been attending meetings of the Society for Ethical Culture in New York City. Warren's involvement in this association of freethinkers made President Patton leery of giving him a regular position on the university's faculty. When Patton questioned him about his theological orthodoxy, Warren, as he put it, was able to "satisfy Dr. Patton's modest demands without stultifying myself in my own eyes."[32] Two decades later, Warren led the effort to convince the trustees to adopt the A.A.U.P.'s policy on academic freedom. No longer would Princeton's faculty, like those at other institutions, have to conform their scholarship to religious orthodoxy or commit intellectual duplicity in order to secure a position in the university. Not everyone, however, supported these new gains in the university's civic mission. In response to an article that Warren had written on academic freedom in the *Atlantic Monthly*, one fundamentalist alumnus castigated him for helping to create an environment in which Professor Miller was "free" to espouse his "Unitarian" theology.[33] While some conservatives opposed Warren, others, ironically, aided him in his quest for academic freedom for the university's faculty.

The Miller controversy placed Hibben and the trustees in a dilemma. On the one hand, they already had a controversy with fundamentalists over the institution's departure from the evangelical convictions and practices previously employed to fulfill the university's Protestant mission. On the other hand, if they ousted Miller, they would face another controversy with a faculty that favored the public-service side of the university's mission. Pragmatic concerns further complicated the administration's dilemma over its religious mission and its civic responsibilities. The university was about to launch an endowment campaign in the spring of 1915, and a controversy over academic freedom would have jeopardized those plans. "We are in the midst of a progressive development of our affairs in which a united Faculty, a united body of undergraduates and alumni," a trustees committee counseled, "all must co-operate with singleness of purpose to attain the one desired end of Princeton's growth and well being." Unlike urban and state universities, which had regional orientations, Princeton, as one article on the campaign observed, was of "a different type with a strong national purpose and tradition."[34] A controversy over academic freedom would also have subverted this national aspiration. Conservatives offered Hibben and the administration an unexpected way out of this dilemma.

Just days after the creation of the A.A.U.P., the trustees met to hear from the informal committee, headed by President Hibben, that had been created to investigate their options. The first option was direct and simple: they could fire Miller. This option was unacceptable, the committee counseled, because it "would at once precipitate a violent and protracted discussion as to the privileges of academic freedom." The second option was to "remove Professor Miller" by abolishing all courses in biblical instruction from the curriculum. Fundamentalists on the university's Board of Trustees, surprisingly, favored this option. John DeWitt (1842–1924), one of the more conservative trustees and a professor at Princeton Seminary, for instance, insisted that Princeton's interests would best be served if the university simply eliminated all Bible instruction. He wrote Hibben, "I am thoroughly persuaded that the interests of the University will be promoted by the abolition of all theological courses, like the one taught by Mr. Miller. . . . I think also that the sooner the university abolishes them, and confines itself to teaching courses in the Humanities, Philosophy, and Sciences, the sooner it will relieve itself of the difficulties and criticisms for which Mr. Miller's conduct is largely responsible."[35] After consulting several influential professors, the committee dismissed this option because they were sure that it would be interpreted by the faculty and the rest of the academic world "as an indirect and not a wholly ingenuous method of removing Professor Miller."[36] A generation earlier McCosh had defended the value of Bible classes in the curriculum as an important way to safeguard the Christian purposes of collegiate education. When judged by McCosh's definition of the role of Bible classes in the curriculum, McCosh's theological heirs inside the university, ironically, were advocating the secularization of the Princeton's curriculum.

This was not the first time conservatives had advocated the abandonment of established religious practices at Princeton. Conservatives had likewise encouraged the administration to eliminate another major piece of Princeton's traditional program of religious education: mandatory attendance at chapel services. Students' dissatisfaction with having to attend the 8:15 a.m. chapel twice a week and half the Sunday services each year had been growing in recent years. Their frustration culminated with the notorious "chapel revolt" of March 10, 1914. "It began by sounds of coughing in several parts of the building which in a few seconds became an epidemic," the front-page article in the *New York Times* reported. "Nearly every student in the chapel took it up, and their combined efforts were so successful that the preacher was compelled to stop abruptly before the end of the sermon."[37] Since the spring of 1911, a majority of the faculty had repeatedly recommended to the trustees, without success, that all services be made voluntary.[38] The occasional chapel disturbance, the lack of faculty participation, and the simple fact that the entire student body could not be seated at one time helped to undermine the community-building function that McCosh had earlier envisioned for the services. Many students and faculty also believed that mandatory attendance turned the services into a blasphemous parody. "No doubt our ancestors, more deeply instilled than we with the great truths of a stout Presbyterianism," wrote one undergraduate, were able to "reconcile" the opposing ideals of mandatory attendance and a worship service. But students today, he asserted, simply could not. To many, chapel had only one purpose. An article in the *Daily Princetonian* captured the dominant sentiment with the question, "Shall religion be used to fill the function of the alarm clock?"[39] After the chapel strike of 1914, the faculty again took up the cause of making chapel services voluntary.[40] Like the conservative trustee John DeWitt's argument for the abolition of Bible classes, some fundamentalist Princeton supporters, angered by the constant parade of modernists into the pulpit of Marquand Chapel, reversed their position on mandatory chapel. So long as Princeton "held to her historical and traditional announcement," one argued, the university "was right, and she was supported in her compulsory chapel. . . . But to compel our youth, ranging from seventeen to twenty-four years of age, to attend chapel, and then pump them full of Unitarianism and other unbelief, is unjust and outrageous."[41] No mandatory chapel or liberal Bible instruction, conservatives were now arguing, was a better policy than subjecting the nation's future leaders to the "infidelity" of liberalism.

Hibben and the entire Board of Trustees rejected the fundamentalists' plea to abolish Miller's Bible classes and mandatory chapel attendance. At their January 1915 meeting, the board determined not to take action against Miller nor to eliminate his classes. In the fall of 1915, the trustees left the mandatory Sunday chapel attendance policy intact but did agree to make the weekday services entirely voluntary. At the end of the fall semester, Hibben declared the new policy a grand success. The change, he insisted, "is in no sense an abandonment of the daily morning worship which has been conducted in this institution continuously for 169 years. On the contrary, it is earnestly hoped and confidently expected that this voluntary service will tend to revive the true spirit of religion in the University."[42]

The trustees' decision to keep Miller was a victory for those favoring the public mission of Princeton. While Patton had once refused to hire the Unitarian Frederick Jackson Turner to teach history because he threatened the evangelical character of the institution, now, according to the fundamentalists, Princeton had a Unitarian teaching Bible. Because the university's primary guiding purpose was to serve national educational interests, and since academic freedom had become a defining characteristic of such public institutions, Hibben and the trustees preferred academic freedom over its past commitment to evangelical Protestantism. The decision outraged some fundamentalist Presbyterians. One, writing in the *Presbyterian*, lamented the board's decision to keep on the faculty "another smiler with his knife under his cloak" whose teaching threatened to ruin students in this life and for eternity. Others in the community, especially the faculty, were pleased. Howard C. Warren, who had little sympathy for Miller's theology, told him that many of his colleagues were "deeply interested in your *official* welfare on account of the scurrilous attacks ... and organized efforts by non-professional men to have you removed from the Princeton Faculty."[43] The adoption of a formal policy of academic freedom in the spring of 1915, moreover, guaranteed that Protestantism, evangelical or liberal, would no longer provide a unifying center for undergraduate education at Princeton. So long as professors abided by professional standards in meeting their academic responsibilities, they had the freedom to subvert, or for that matter to champion, Protestant values. Nevertheless, religion would no longer provide an intellectual criterion to which all professors had to conform. Given academic freedom's growing prevalence in American higher education, it is likely that the university would have adopted the policy if there had been no controversy over Miller's Bible classes. The Miller controversy, however, hastened their decision to do so.

The battle over Miller was not only a victory for those intent on safeguarding Princeton's civic mission but also a triumph for those devoted to preserving the university's traditional Protestant mission. While academic freedom could prevent liberal Protestantism from officially providing a unifying center to the undergraduate program, it did not mean that the university could not continue to advocate religious faith through more informal means, such as elective Bible courses. Fundamentalists in the community saw the problem that religious pluralism created for the institution's commitment to its Protestant mission. Until this point in the twentieth century, conservatives had insisted that the university uphold nineteenth-century evangelical convictions and practices, and they had hoped to assimilate diversity by converting outsiders. The institution must respect, McCosh insisted throughout his presidency, students whose religious scruples kept them from joining this community. But in the face of the more informal liberal Protestant hegemony over the religious affairs of the university, many influential fundamentalists, though certainly not all, reversed their position on the role of religion in the life of the institution. Now they wanted Princeton to adopt a more Jeffersonian solution for the place of religion in a public institution. They preferred the near total disestablishment of religious instruction in collegiate education—voluntary chapel and no Bible classes—to the university's liberal Protestant program of religious education. However, while that program was far more informal than it had been in the nineteenth century, Protestantism remained the established religion of the university. Like McCosh and his generation, Hibben and his colleagues hoped to assimilate religious diversity through a program of religious education. They resisted, therefore, the fundamentalists' efforts to surrender the university's religious mission. To be sure, the trustees' decision to adopt a policy of academic freedom and to avoid a second major controversy that would have undermined the capital campaign informed their decision not to fire Miller. Yet the commitment to academic freedom and the pragmatic concern to avoid alienating donors should not obscure the persistence of the Protestant mission at Princeton. While the administration, like other mainline Protestant institutions, was willing to tolerate a certain degree of theological diversity in order to maintain the unity of the university, liberal Protestants like Hibben refused to abandon religious education—mandatory chapel and elective Bible instruction—because they remained committed to the Protestant mission of Princeton. In fact, they proved to be the true conservatives. The university, they believed, had a responsibility to mold the Christian character of students and ultimately to shape the Christian character of American culture.

Quieter Revolutions during the Age of Innocence:
Religion in the Ethics Classroom and on the Campus

The controversy over Miller's Bible classes revealed the fact that a radical transformation in biblical instruction had taken place at Princeton. Equally dramatic, though much more quiet, revolutions were taking place in the teaching of ethics and in the extracurricular religious life of the student body in the second decade of the twentieth century. Although developments in each area, much like those in Bible instruction, marked major departures from established evangelical practices, these changes did not signal the end of Princeton's Protestant mission but rather its adjustment to the modern concerns of the university.

When George S. Patton resigned as professor of moral philosophy in the spring of 1914 to move to Bermuda in order to join his father, who had retired a year earlier as president of the seminary and as Stuart Professor of Ethics at the university, the curtain had finally come down on the moral philosophy taught at Princeton for nearly a hundred and fifty years. Gone also were McCosh's dreams of making the institution a bastion of the Scottish philosophy.[44] In the spring of 1915, the university recruited the neo-Hegelian idealist, George Herbert Palmer (1842–1933), who had recently retired from Harvard, to commute from Cambridge to teach the senior elective course in ethics for the year.[45] The following year Princeton hired as Patton's successor the idealist Warner Fite (1867–1955), who had earned a Ph.D. at Pennsylvania, done further graduate work at Berlin and Munich, and taught at Williams, Chicago, Texas, Indiana, and Stanford. The revolutionary developments in the teaching of ethics, which had begun in the previous decade, added another facet to the university's growing intellectual diversity while maintaining the institution's commitment to shaping the moral values of the nation's future leaders.

Like many other developments at Princeton after the turn of the century, the revolution in the teaching of ethics was a rather conservative one. Although not a disciple of McCosh, Fite was part of the larger genteel tradition—European training, Victorian morality—that still dominated many elite colleges and universities.[46] Fite provided students with a broad introduction to ethics, ancient and modern, and attempted to bridge the gap between the theoretical and the practical. Fite was something of an eclectic idealist, combining certain elements of utilitarianism, which he consistently referred to as "heathenism," with his idealism. The strength of idealism, according to Fite, lay in its more satisfactory account of a "higher morality," which taught that people were "rational beings," as opposed to "mechanical objects," who should consciously direct their thoughts and actions toward the "full realization" of their capacities. This realization awakened in people certain "appreciations of truth and reality" and provided them with a "moral motive and guide." In Fite's estimation, utilitarianism's strengths were its clarity and concrete nature, the very traits that idealism lacked. Its chief fault, he believed, was that it neglected what people considered to be of the "highest value." "Between a too narrow and ignoble estimate of our moral capacity and a too highly strung effort to transcend our capacity, there is a certain constant adjustment of responsibility and capacity most favorable for a maximum of sustained growth." "The man," Fite contended, "who arrives at this adjustment most nearly and maintains it most constantly is he who best fulfills the demands of a genuine moral life."[47] In comparison to the Pattons' Scottish commonsense philosophy, Fite's work indicated that another decisive break with established convictions had taken place. But when compared, for instance, to John Dewey's utilitarianism, Fite continued to teach students that there were transcendent moral values. In this way, Fite's teaching marked another important line of continuity in how the university sought to shape the Christian character of American society.

With the reduction of mandatory chapel attendance and the elimination of required Bible, ethics, and apologetics classes in the first decade of the twentieth century, the Philadelphian Society took on an even greater role in helping the university fulfill its religious mission. Originally founded as an independent expression of students' religious interests in the early nineteenth century, the society had slowly become an arm of the administration and a key agent in its efforts to foster the religious life of students. The society, the general secretary reported in 1916, "simply desires to be an efficient servant of the President and Trustees of the University as they plan for the religious welfare of Princeton."[48] Because of the voluntary nature of the organization, the society offered the university a way to nurture the faith of students while avoiding the taint of sectarianism associated with mandatory religious practices in the early twentieth century.

During the second decade of the twentieth century, the campus Y.M.C.A., like the other parts of the university's program of religious education, took on a more liberal theological orientation. At the beginning of the decade, guest speakers came from both sides of the theological divide. William Jennings Bryan and C. I. Scofield, for instance, lectured at meetings, and J. Gresham Machen regularly spoke to the McCosh Club, a group of preministerial students who belonged to the society. The society also heard from some of liberal Protestantism's most prominent figures, including Henry Churchill King, Norman Thomas, Harry Emerson Fosdick, and Henry Sloane Coffin.[49] By the middle of the decade, liberal speakers dominated the society's weekly meetings. The society's social gospel activities—summer camp for boys, settlement work, and Princeton Boys Club—prospered. By contrast, more traditional activities, such as Bible study groups, did not fare as well in this decade. In 1910–1911, enrollment stood at 488 with an average attendance of 388. By the fall of 1915, enrollment had dropped to 272 with an average attendance of 158.[50] However, the university's mission work, Princeton-in-Peking, thrived. Lucius H. Miller, one of the directors of the mission, reported in 1914 that more than $95,000 had been raised to construct a large building and two homes for the five staff members and their families. In all, more than 750 alumni gave money to the work.[51] To inspire Princeton students toward a life of piety, Cleveland H. Dodge, a trustee and patron of Protestant causes, financed the sculpturing of a life-size bronze statue of a student dressed in football gear, holding books in one arm, with an academic gown draped over a shoulder, and looking bravely into the future. The statue, entitled "The Christian Student," was dedicated in May 1913 during a meeting of the World's Christian Student Federation at the seminary and was installed beside Pyne Library across from Murray-Dodge Hall to remind students daily of their spiritual responsibilities.[52]

The quiet revolution toward liberalism was most evident in the society's revised membership requirements and statement of purpose. To obtain membership in the society in the nineteenth century, a student had to give testimony to a conversion experience and gain the unanimous consent of the members. In 1914, students determined that this practice was too sectarian and changed the requirement to "membership in Princeton University and in the Christian Church." All students who belonged to a church were now *ipso facto* members of the society unless they requested otherwise. Those not associated with a church could become full members by signing "a statement of personal faith in Christianity and of allegiance to Christ," or associate members by signing a statement of "sympathy with the ethical aims of Christianity." More than 64 percent of the student body belonged to the organization in 1914–1915. While the new membership requirements indicate that the society had jettisoned many of its past evangelical convictions, the society remained firmly committed to the triumph of Protestantism at home and abroad. The goal of the society, the revised statement of purpose read, was to develop students' Christian character, to train them for work in the church, and "to further the advance of the *Kingdom of God* in Princeton University, the United States of America, and throughout the world."[53]

"Clubable" Christianity and Controversy

Just weeks after the trustees decided not to dismiss Lucius H. Miller, Princeton was embroiled in another religious controversy. Charles R. Erdman, a professor of practical theology at Princeton Seminary, wanted to bring the evangelist Billy Sunday, who was preaching in Philadelphia, to campus to hold a revival service. While in Philadelphia, Sunday (1862–1935) had been invited by Provost Egar Fahs Smith to preach to the student body at the University of Pennsylvania. After some 3000 Penn students attended the revival service, Erdman hoped Sunday would have the same success at his alma mater. Previously, Erdman had worked with university's administration to bring the evangelist G. Campbell Morgan to Princeton. But such moments of cooperation between conservatives and liberals gave way to hostility during the cultural crisis of the mid-1910s. After traveling to Philadelphia to hear the controversial evangelist for himself, Hibben refused Erdman's request to hold the revival on campus and explained that "the university authorities feel that the place to hear him is a religious edifice rather than a college building and withhold their official auspices."[54] After two lengthy meetings, the seminary faculty voted unanimously to sponsor the revival themselves. Arrangements were made to hold two services, one for seminarians and another for undergraduates, at First Presbyterian Church, which was conveniently adjacent to the campus.[55]

After giving the seminarians some advice on evangelistic preaching, Sunday preached his well-known sermon "Dr. Jekyll and Mr. Hyde" to a packed house of undergraduates. All, he argued, were Mr. Hydes who suppressed their Dr. Jekylls because of their love for sin. Despite human wickedness, Sunday promised his young audience, God "is the friend of sinners but the enemy of sin." But instead of a traditional altar call at the end of his sermon, perhaps in an accommodation to Princeton's highbrow atmosphere, Sunday asked students to come forward and shake his hand as "a pledge that they mean to live Christian lives." After some six hundred students went forward, some reporters declared the revival a grand success while others observed that students went up merely to shake the hand of someone famous.[56] The administration's rebuff of Sunday and the opposition of other universities to revivalist preachers, according to conventional interpretations, exemplify of the general secularization of American higher education in the early twentieth century.[57]

A week after Sunday visited Princeton, President Hibben and the Philadelphian Society launched the university's first Religious Emphasis Week. The contrast between the revivalist Sunday and the week's featured speaker and their respective messages could hardly have been greater. In contrast to the evangelist from the cornfields of Iowa, the university hosted Albert Parker Fitch (1877–1944), a graduate of Harvard University and Union Theological Seminary in New York. Instead of Sunday's diatribe against sin, the youthful and polished president of Andover Theological Seminary gave four evening "addresses." Whereas Sunday was forced to hold his services off campus, Fitch held his lectures in Alexander Hall on campus. Even the name, a Religious Emphasis Week, had a more sophisticated ring to it than a revival service. Employing the romantic experiential definition of Christianity and the German idealism upon which it rested, Fitch presented students with a religion that was compatible with modern science. Religion, Fitch told students in his first address, is "the sense of the supermundane of reality—the perception that the significance and power of the universe" lay behind and are hidden within "its visible and temporal expressions." The authority of this religion rests—not on the supernatural revelation of the Bible—but on this "veritable and undeniable" experience. Fitch's subsequent lectures attempted to draw out the intellectual relevance of modernism for his audience, which averaged nine hundred students at each lecture. Fitch's message was not only Protestantism expressed in a modern idiom but also a faith that would make students "clubable." Fitch concluded his final address with an altar call befitting Princeton students' social sensibilities. With assurances that they would not be forced to make a "mechanical" sign of commitment, Fitch outlined the four immediate consequences that a religious life should have for students: they should study "more scrupulously," avoid profanity, devote themselves to "unselfish and sacrificial service," and earnestly commit themselves to "the keeping of the eternal."[58] In sharp contrast to Sunday's fundamentalism, Fitch offered students a religion that would make them both modern and gentlemen. Fitch's liberalism was a faith that Princeton's administration deemed appropriate for one of the nation's most influential civic institutions to advocate.

Fundamentalists within the university community, however, had a rather different opinion of the university's efforts to hold a modern revival. Even before Fitch lectured, the *Presbyterian*, lamented that the university kept Billy Sunday, a Presbyterian minister, off campus, but planned to host a liberal like Fitch, who "shred[s] the Bible to pieces."[59] To be sure, the alliance between the revivalist Sunday and the scholarly conservatives at Princeton Seminary had to be one of the oddest of the burgeoning fundamentalist movement. The cultural crisis of the decade often united conservatives with different backgrounds and interests. This is evident, for example, in the publication of *The Fundamentals* (1910–1915), the twelve-volume collection of essays by conservative laypeople, preachers, and scholars. The marriage of convenience between Sunday and the seminary faculty suggests that the coalition of populist and scholarly conservatives had not come to an end with the publication of *The Fundamentals*.[60] Instead, Sunday's revival at Princeton indicates that the alliance was in a healthy state, and the success of this particular operation, moreover, boded well for future cooperation. Despite his pugnaciousness and vaudevillian antics, Sunday preached—at least in the eyes of many Princeton fundamentalists—the same message that evangelicals had preached for generations on American college campuses. Amid the cultural turmoil of the day, Sunday had a message that they wanted the nation's future leaders to hear. Publicly, this was why Erdman had invited him and a major reason why conservatives at the seminary supported Sunday. J. Gresham Machen, for instance, had a more intellectual conception of religious knowledge than Sunday and other popular fundamentalists leaders.[61] Yet Machen wrote his mother during the controversy that while Sunday's "methods are as different as could possibly be imagined from ours . . . we support him to a man simply because, in an age of general defection, he is preaching *the gospel.*"[62]

The shock that Princeton fundamentalists felt at Hibben's snub of Sunday turned to anger after Fitch's lectures. To describe Fitch's teaching as Trinitarian, one critic contended, "is no more honest than to tag a sack of sawdust as rolled oats."[63] To many of the fundamentalists, the exclusion of Sunday and presence of Miller were further evidence that the university had abandoned its religious mission. One older alumnus recalled his days as a Princeton student when D. L. Moody, with McCosh's approval, preached the "old-time religion" to students; sadly, he observed, "now Princeton shuns the 'Holy Ghost.'"[64] "The fact that the ruling authorities of the University" openly "antagonize the Christian traditions of the institution" by refusing to sponsor Billy Sunday while welcoming "an opponent of the evangelical faith" left another critic to conclude that the university had strayed from its founding purpose.[65]

While they were largely silent during the Miller controversy, critics of fundamentalism within the university community responded to this latest attack. Dean Andrew F. West, who had rejected the uncouth pietism of his youth, presented a litany of off-color quotes from Sunday to support the university's refusal to sponsor the evangelist.[66] Yet Sunday upset more than the social sensibilities of some within the university. Although not as large or maybe as vocal as the fundamentalists, many students and younger alumni defended the administration's decision. Just as the attempt to hold an old-fashioned revival at Princeton united a populist fundamentalist with the more scholarly ones at the seminary, the opponents of Sunday also formed a coalition comprising liberal Protestants and more secular-minded modernists in the community. To the cultural modernists, Sunday epitomized the antiprogressivism of conservative Protestantism that had no place, in their opinion, in an elite center of American culture like Princeton.[67] One such alumnus, the writer Struthers Burt, commended Hibben for withholding the university's imprimatur from a fundamentalist preacher who was "so rash as to say that revivalism is the right path to God" while another complained about Sunday's "Fifteenth Century ideas."[68] The antifundamentalist opposition to Sunday also stemmed from these cultural modernists' understanding of the purpose of the university, which stood in sharp contrast to that of Sunday's supporters. To Sunday's critics, fundamentalism was too dogmatic to answer students' intellectual questions. "We may be worked up into brief and benighting pseudo-religious ecstasies by any muddle-headed evangelist who chooses to excite us abnormally by what he calls prayer," asserted Edmund Wilson Jr., a member of the senior class and aspiring social critic, "but we are not, it seems, to be allowed to hear the most serious of all questions considered in a serious way."[69] These cultural modernists, however, had little else to say in support of the university's sponsorship of the liberal Protestant Fitch's lecture series.

Others in the Princeton community defended the decision to ban Sunday by drawing upon the university's religious mission. These were liberal Protestants who opposed Sunday on educational and theological grounds. The university, the editors of the *Princeton Alumni Weekly* warned, "must be careful to respect the faith of all faiths and creeds, and as students and investigators, however closely allied we personally may be to any one sect or doctrine, leave a free field to all, lest, in the words of the poet, one good custom should corrupt the world." Since a "university's business is with truth only," the editorial unapologetically asserted, Princeton could not propagate religious views that would meet the approval of "the *sectarians*."[70] For Hibben, Fitch's message met the nonsectarian criteria of the kind of religion a public—not parochial—institution should advocate. Hibben, who had graduated from Princeton Seminary, earned a Ph.D. in philosophy at the university, and taught students a conservative evangelical theology as a Bible instructor during Patton's administration, had slowly become a theological liberal in the early twentieth century. This evolution, first evident in Hibben's philosophical reversal from Scottish commonsense realism to idealism, was now complete. Although the president had remained publicly silent during the Miller controversy, Hibben made a brief but decisive response to the fundamentalists' attack on Fitch's theology as non-Christian: "I wish it to be clearly understood that I, both as a minister of the Presbyterian Church and as President of Princeton University, stand ready to defend" Fitch's lectures as "essential elements of Christian belief."[71] According to Hibben and contrary to the charge of fundamentalists as well as the evaluations of many conventional interpreters, Princeton, like many other private colleges and universities, had not abandoned its religious mission in the early twentieth century.

After the Sunday-Fitch controversy, several events temporarily mollified fundamentalist Princetonians. In April, ex-president Francis L. Patton delivered five addresses on the "Fundamentals of Christianity" for the lecture series that the trustees had established a year earlier. As the *Presbyterian* put it, conservatives found "some encouragement" in the fact that the trustees had invited Patton, "a man in fullest sympathy with the historical and evangelical position of Princeton," to speak on campus.[72] In the fall of 1915, John N. Sayre resigned as general secretary of the Philadelphian Society to become rector of an Episcopal church in New York. Instead of hiring another recent graduate to replace Sayre, the society's advisory committee wanted someone more experienced in campus ministry; consequently, they hired Thomas S. Evans, who had graduated from Princeton in 1897 and had directed successfully the Y.M.C.A. work at the University of Pennsylvania for fifteen years. Students believed that Evans meant "large success for the future of Princeton's religious work."[73] "We recognize that Princeton University is not a denominational institution," the *Presbyterian* observed, "but there is no reason why it should not be definitely and positively Christian, or why its religious development should not be in harmony with its historic position." They interpreted Evans' arrival as a sign of "good hope toward maintaining Princeton in her historical position of a strong, definite and catholic evangelicalism."[74] First Presbyterian Church of Princeton also hired an assistant minister to serve as its campus pastor. Since both the Episcopalian rector and the Presbyterian minister were associate staff members of the Philadelphian Society, the university now had two denominational chaplains on campus.[75] Despite criticisms from the fundamentalists, the university's 1915 Religious Emphasis Week revealed that the institution was still interested in cultivating the religious interests of student. What had changed was only the type of Protestantism the university would advocate to the nation's future leaders.

The Pyrrhic Victory for Fundamentalists

"My position here," Miller wrote Woodrow Wilson in the fall of 1916, "has been made intolerable for me by the forces of conservativism and indifferentism whose representatives are in control." As if he needed to, Miller added, "the methods and tendencies of these men you know better than anyone else." Miller had decided to resign and had asked the president of the United States to help him find a position that would bring him "into more direct touch with the big problems now confronting our country."[76] The conservatives in the university community at large and some, like John DeWitt, who sat on the Board of Trustees, loathed Miller's theology. While they had been unable to fire Miller, force his dismissal by eliminating Bible instruction, or revert to a time when evangelicalism dominated the institution's program of religious education, they had successfully created a climate so antagonistic that the Bible professor found it insufferable. John S. Burgess, a student and friend of Miller's who had worked with Princeton-in-Peking, later recalled that "many of the influential alumni who 'had an interest in the religious life of the undergraduates' and who were themselves traditionalists looked with apprehension at having a 'Unitarian' on the faculty. They were not concerned with scientists and philosophers who had no appreciation of religion whatsoever, but if Luke was to teach religion, he must give out the right brand!"[77] In addition to the endless stream of criticism, fundamentalists repeatedly threatened to send their sons elsewhere. In the fall of 1915, for instance, the *Presbyterian of the South* reported that freshman enrollment had dropped at Princeton because of Miller: "This apparent trend toward Unitarianism can not be acceptable to some of the most substantial and evangelical patrons of Princeton University, and we suspect they have sent their sons elsewhere for that reason." In actuality, freshmen enrollment had risen, albeit by just one student.[78]

Although President Hibben shared Miller's modernism and believed, as evidenced in his defense of Fitch's theology and its place within the university, that it was the type of Christian faith that a nonsectarian university should advocate, he never defended publicly Miller's theology or his academic freedom. Given his stated desire for peace and the trustees' decision to respect Miller's academic freedom, it is likely that Hibben did not want to antagonize the fundamentalists any further by defending the Bible professor. Hibben was probably grateful to receive Miller's resignation since it freed the university from the criticisms of fundamentalists. And since Miller's resignation was voluntary, the faculty, or at least the majority who favored the public service side of the university's mission, had little formal ground to condemn his departure as a violation of academic freedom. For his part, Miller never raised the issue.

The faculty, organized by Howard C. Warren, did send a letter, signed by fifty-five of the university's sixty-eight full professors, to the trustees regarding Miller's resignation. Rather than defend Miller's academic freedom or his theology, the faculty protested the criticisms of the scientific methods employed by the professional experts in the university. They praised Miller's Christian character and asked the trustees "to find a way to retain" him or to replace him with someone else with his "scientific attainment and sympathy with the modern methods of investigation that prevail in Princeton University." By criticizing Miller's scholarship, the fundamentalists were attacking the scientific model that had been transforming American higher education, indeed America, for nearly two generations. On these grounds, the fundamentalists threatened the very civic mission of the university and, not surprisingly, professors like William Berryman Scott signed the protest letter. Not all of the faculty, however, feared this assault on the larger civic mission of the university. Howard McClenahan, Dean of the College, refused to sign the letter simply because, as he told Miller, he did not believe that Bible instruction, modernist or otherwise, was essential to a liberal education at "an undergraduate college such as Princeton." Another professor, Frederick N. Willson, declined to sign the statement for an entirely different reason. Willson, who had taught English Bible to students in the School of Science during McCosh's presidency and served as an elder at the conservative First Presbyterian Church, believed in, as he told Professor Warren, "the tenability and impregnability of the old 'evangelical' doctrines." This holdover from the *ancien régime* still considered it a principal function of Princeton to propagate a broad evangelicalism.[79]

The faculty's defense of the scientific expertise and professional competence of Miller also highlighted the reversal of fortunes of the nineteenth-century Protestant enlightenment synthesis of faith and reason. To McCosh and many other educators of his generation, natural science was an objectively valid source of truth that could demonstrate the truthfulness of the Bible. According to their Scottish philosophy, truth, whether in the realm of nature or supernaturally revealed in the Bible, was a fixed entity that the unbiased mind could inductively discover. With the scientific revolution begun by Darwinism, scientific positivism and historicism, predicated upon post-Kantian epistemology and metaphysics, limited knowledge to only that which people could have access to scientifically, the realm of the phenonema. As a result, the allegedly neutral scientific method, instead of supporting orthodox theology, was now assaulting it by providing alternative and purely naturalistic explanations of the development of nature and of religion itself. This change was evident, for instance, in Darwinism and biblical criticism. By advancing academic specialization and the professionalization of the faculty, McCosh and others helped to foster the segregation of science and theology. Now their support for the Baconian-Newtonian scientific assumptions and method had come full circle to subvert the intellectual credibility of the faith of their early twentieth-century successors. Consequently, fundamentalists' criticisms of Miller not only threatened the civic mission of the university but also assaulted science and reason.

Furthermore, the fundamentalists' attack on the university was an attack on the faculty's social status. American university professors in the early twentieth century enjoyed, when compared to the antebellum period, greater social prestige than clerics. Unlike the fundamentalists, they had the scientific expertise, as evidenced in their Ph.D. degrees, to speak with competence on scientific matters. Also, unlike the fundamentalists, their scholarship aided society's progress in a variety of practical ways. Princeton's faculty refused to concede any cultural capital to an obscurantist like Billy Sunday and his allies, even if they did have Princeton degrees. By attacking the scientific methods employed inside the university, fundamentalists posed a menace to the civic mission of the modern university, science and reason, and the professional status of faculty. Such criticisms constituted a cause of fundamentalism's marginalization from the American university. For this reason, the resignation of Miller was a pyrrhic victory for the fundamentalists.

The controversy over Miller also exemplifies the fundamentalists' and liberal Protestants' responses to religious diversity and the question of assimilation. Fundamentalists in 1916 constituted a minority in the university community. They resisted the homogenizing efforts of the administration in either one of two ways. Sometimes they argued that Princeton should continue to promote an orthodox Protestantism, as demonstrated during the Sunday-Fitch controversy. At other times, however, they advocated the complete elimination of Bible instruction and mandatory chapel attendance, as evidenced in DeWitt's rationale for ousting Miller and other fundamentalists' advocacy of the abandonment of Princeton's traditional chapel policy. The first option was unacceptable to liberal Protestants like Hibben because it meant advocating a premodern theology that conflicted with modern science, reason, and the university's civic mission. The second option was equally unacceptable because it was tantamount to abandoning the university's religious mission. While McCosh had deemed biblical instruction essential to the welfare of students and ultimately the nation, fundamentalists were willing to adopt a basically Jeffersonian position toward religious education in the curriculum—secularization—rather than allow their sons to be inculcated with liberal Protestantism. Not only did the administration reintroduce Bible education to the curriculum in the 1920s, albeit in a rather ad hoc fashion, but, more important, they refused to give up the university's religious mission. As noted earlier, liberal Protestants at Princeton in the twentieth century, like their conservative predecessors in the nineteenth century, attempted to assimilate religious diversity. They widened, in short, the old Whiggish conception of higher education and offered a new sacred canopy made up of a new enlightenment synthesis of Protestant liberalism, modern science, and democracy, under which to unite the student body and ultimately the nation. In this way, the university attempted to maintain its religious mission to preserve the Christian character of American society.

When fundamentalists, like the trustee John DeWitt, advocated the complete abandonment of traditional religious practices, they further alienated themselves from the American university. At times they acted as "insiders" to the mainstream Protestant establishment. They shared with liberal Protestants the common goal of building something like a "Christian America" and only differed with liberals over what type of Protestantism should predominate. At other times, however, they appear to have given up their hope of achieving this ideal. Therefore, besides liberal Protestants' active role in driving fundamentalists to the institutional and intellectual margins of the university, fundamentalists themselves were moving in that direction. And as conservative trustees and professors, like DeWitt and Willson who retired in 1920 and 1923, respectively, left the board and faculty, fundamentalism's influence declined even further as Hibben and the board replaced them with others who shared their vision of Princeton's religious mission.

As for Miller, he fared better than his courses. Although he failed to persuade President Wilson to help him find a job in public service, James Imbrie, a grandson of one of the arch-conservative ministers who had served as a trustee during McCosh's presidency, helped secure the unemployed professor a position. Miller went into banking.[80]

Making the World Safe for Democracy

While the university may have avoided further controversy by Miller's retirement, the Princeton community was more than ready to involve itself in another conflict. When President Wilson asked Congress to declare war on Germany on Good Friday, April 2, 1917, many students, professors, and trustees stood ready to make good on the university's commitment to public service. Between 1917 and 1919, the university offered moral support and direct military assistance to the Allies' cause. These efforts had a wide-ranging impact on the institution, for they turned the university into a military base for training and research, tested the limits of academic freedom, and curtailed the campus activities of the Philadelphian Society. The long-term effects of the war on Princeton were equally monumental. After the university demilitarized, Hibben, the faculty, and the trustees revised the undergraduate and graduate programs to meet the nation's peacetime needs more effectively. The war altered more than just Princeton's educational programs; the war caused many students, like many Americans, to grow disillusioned with the Victorian idealism that had given meaning to many activities in the Progressive era, including the war itself. Yet amid all the dramatic educational, intellectual, and social upheavals inside the university and in American culture in general, Hibben and his administration labored to preserve Princeton's religious mission.

Given the high moral purpose of the war, which was only an extension of the high moral purpose of the university, the Princeton community supported eagerly Wilson's efforts to make the world safe for democracy. After the declaration of war, the trustees sent the nation's commander-in-chief a message endorsing "his efforts to place the country in her rightful position upon the side of Justice and Civilization in the war against frightfulness and barbarianism."[81] They also expunged from their records the honorary degree that the university had given to Count Johann van Bernstroff, Ambassador of the Imperial German Government, in 1914.[82] Many students likewise welcomed the opportunity to fight, as one student in the *Daily Princetonian* put it, for the "fundamental principles of humanity and justice."[83] President Hibben was a particularly outspoken propreparationist and, once war was declared, an enthusiastic patriot. Although not all theological liberals were eager militarists, Hibben's modernism provided him with a rationale to support the military venture. In his baccalaureate address of June 1917, Hibben linked the "war against war" with the gradual realization of the Kingdom of God: the allies' cause was justified, he believed, not only because democracy was at stake but also because the principles of righteousness, justice, and honor guiding the war effort were "indissolubly associated" with "the eternal forces of the world which have their source in God," who "shall finally determine the victory of every cause consonant with his law and love." Hibben told a baccalaureate audience two years later that, despite the terrible human cost, the war revealed that "a vision of the kingdom of God" was still being "progressively realized on earth."[84]

The ardent support of the Allied war efforts created a climate within the university intolerant of pacifism. When a group of university and seminary students and one university instructor organized a chapter of the Anti-War League in March 1917, President Hibben refused to allow them to use Alexander Hall to hold a meeting at which Stanford University President David Starr Jordan was scheduled to speak. Once again the banned meeting was held at First Presbyterian Church. The *New York Times*, in a front-page story, reported that students and several faculty members hissed and interrupted Jordan when he ventured a criticism of Wilson's foreign policy. When the instructor complained that Hibben's ban and the audience's behavior were tantamount to an attack on academic freedom, students and professors responded with more hissing. History professor Henry Jones Ford dismissed the pacifists as "manifestly absurd" for thinking they had a right to speak on private property just because they were part of the university.[85] The general sentiment of the university community toward the war may have been best summarized by a faculty resolution the trustees approved in June 1918: "No student shall be admitted into the University for instruction and education and no person shall be appointed to any place or office in the University who does not sympathize with our Government's purpose in the prosecution of the war."[86]

"Upon our entry into the war," President Hibben later recalled, "every resource of the University was placed at the government's disposal."[87] The president may have actually understated the case. Before 1917, the faculty had gone so far as to organize military science courses and a summer military training program for students. Some faculty members, especially those who were British citizens, such as the philosopher Norman Kemp Smith, left for Europe, and many students volunteered for the Esadrille Lafayette and Red Cross ambulance units. Given the high moral purpose of the war, alumni, students, and faculty members enlisted in impressive numbers after April 1917. In the fall of that year, enrollment stood at 40 percent below the previous year, and by the fall of 1918 more than half of the teaching staff were on leave. In all, 6170 Princetonians served in the military or in civilian capacities related directly to the war effort. The army established a Students' Army Training Corps on campus; the navy also had a training unit, complete with twelve cutters and two whale boats patrolling Lake Carnegie. The faculty, moreover, brought its scientific expertise to bear directly on the Allies' war effort. Palmer Laboratory helped to develop equipment for the Sound Ranging Service of the Army, and Chemical and 1877 Laboratories preformed research on gas warfare. Perhaps the most dramatic development in the university's effort to serve the national interest came in the curriculum. The faculty abandoned its once-sacred commitment to the four-year undergraduate curriculum by creating three-year A.B., B.Litt., and B.S. degree programs.[88]

The war also affected dramatically the Philadelphian Society. In an address before a packed audience in Alexander Hall in March 1917, John R. Mott challenged Princeton to supply the British Army Y.M.C.A. with twenty workers. As with other dimensions of the university's life, the Philadelphian Society responded zealously to the wartime need. By December, more than eighty undergraduates and alumni were overseas. Like the U.S. Army, the National War Work Council of the Y.M.C.A. established a headquarters on the campus and trained more than a thousand secretaries for work in France.[89] The society had so reduced its work on campus that the *Daily Princetonian* complained in the spring of 1918 that the influence of the organization was "stronger abroad than at home."[90]

"The end which we have in view at Princeton," President Hibben told a group of alumni shortly after the Armistice, "is that our University may play the some [*sic*] role in our national life in the coming days of peace as in the period of war."[91] The university's success in assisting the nation's triumph over Germany hastened the administration's efforts to expand its civic mission during peacetime. Even before peace was officially reached, Princeton renewed its campaign to raise $14 million for the university's endowment. The 1919 Campaign, as it was called, was just one element of the university's efforts to enlarge its role in the nation's life. "If we are to deserve the name of a *national University*," the president told the trustees in the fall of 1919, "we must give evidence to the world that we possess a national consciousness, that is the sense that the highly individualized lives of the present day belong to the larger life of the nation as a whole, and the feeling of responsibility that everyone, as a patriotic duty, must make himself fit to play his part in it." In order "to advance the interests, influence and usefulness of Princeton as a National University," that same year the trustees approved the creation of the National Alumni Association of Princeton to serve as an umbrella organization over the various alumni clubs.[92] Two years earlier, the trustees had enlarged the board by the addition of three members known as Regional Trustees. In 1922, the Regional and Alumni Trustees were combined so that eight different parts of the country were represented by each Regional Trustee. The university also established "regional scholarships" to attract students from across the country.[93]

At the same time that the university took steps to strengthen its national appeal, the trustees in 1922 limited undergraduate enrollment to approximately 2000 students, a decision that came in a decade in which college enrollment across the nation would double. Admission, Hibben told the alumni, was now based on the "two simple principles of scholarship and good character."[94] Nervous that their sons would not get into the university, Hibben assured alumni that Princeton would give their sons special consideration. Under, or perhaps because of, the new policy, Princeton remained almost exclusively Protestant. The freshmen class that entered the university in the fall of 1922 included 227 Episcopalians, 190 Presbyterians, 38 Congregationalists, 26 Methodists, 32 Catholics, and 25 Jews.[95]

The faculty also revised the undergraduate curriculum in 1923 in order to prepare students better for service to the nation. As a result, upperclassmen took four, not five, courses each semester, concentrated their work in one department, enrolled in directed reading courses, and took comprehensive examinations at the end of each year. The faculty hoped that the modified curriculum would equip graduates with "a broad field of knowledge," mastery of "the fundamentals in some particular field," and "a habit of independent work."[96] The new curriculum more fully combined Wilson's ideas about liberal education with elements from both the vocational and specialized research models that had been introduced into higher education a generation earlier. In this way, Princeton's undergraduate program paralleled similar developments at other colleges and universities, such as Dartmouth, Yale, and Michigan in this decade. Yet of the twenty-three members of the Association of American Universities in 1919, only Princeton and the Catholic University of America required Greek for admission into their A.B. programs. That year Princeton's faculty voted to drop this vestige of the traditional nineteenth-century curriculum. Even Dean West supported this decision.[97] Although Wilson had predicted that when Princeton dropped Greek it would open the doors to coeds, it would take fifty years before the university admitted women to the undergraduate program. While the elimination of Greek made Princeton theoretically more accessible to students from public high schools, the university continued to draw students almost exclusively from private boarding and preparatory schools. As late as the fall of 1928, for instance, only 14 percent of the entering freshmen had been educated exclusively at public schools.[98]

When Princeton took the title of university in 1896, President Hibben recalled more than thirty years later, the institution assumed that one of its "essential functions" was to "conserve and enlarge the field of human knowledge." Since the sesquicentennial, graduate training and specialized research had become more than just side ventures that young faculty members pursued alongside their undergraduate teaching. Advanced education and scholarship had taken on lives of their own, and their role within the university was far larger than anything that McCosh or anyone in his generation could have foreseen. At Princeton and other major research universities, the graduate and research programs helped to connect the university with American society in ways that could never have been envisioned when the institution was understood to be a place primarily where the nation's future leaders were trained in the liberal arts tradition. Through specialized research, the university provided the American economy and society with practical applications of knowledge, especially in the hard and political sciences. This was most evident at Princeton in the period under consideration when, for example, the university established endowed research professorships in the sciences in the 1920s, a School of Architecture in 1919, the Industrial Relations Section in 1922, and a School of Public and International Affairs in 1930 (later the Woodrow Wilson School), as well as encouraged the founding of the independent Institute for Advanced Study in 1930. By 1930, Princeton ranked among the top twenty recipients of research grants from government and industry.[99] The expanded civic mission of the university in the twentieth century, in short, entailed a multitude of functions—undergraduate education, advanced training, and specialized scholarship—that helped to meet the nation's insatiable thirst for trained experts and practical knowledge.

By contrast, Princeton's administration strained to preserve the university's religious mission during the 1920s. This struggle was related inseparably to the plight of mainline Protestantism during this decade. Protestantism, as the de facto national religion, many historians have observed, experienced a "second disestablishment" in the 1920s.[100] The informal hegemony that mainstream Protestantism had long enjoyed over American cultural and religious life because of its numerical pluralities and the strength of its institutions and organizations collapsed during this decade. Divisions within mainline Protestant denominations coupled with changing patterns of migration and immigration and the growth of industry and cities helped to subvert Protestant cultural hegemony. To be sure, most Protestants remained confident that America was a Christian nation. And Protestants, as evidenced in their united successful opposition to the Catholic Al Smith's presidential campaign, still enjoyed moments of hegemony. But the expansion of the government's role in the nation's economic and social life and the increased cultural plurality of the nation eventually resulted in a stricter neutrality when state courts and, most important, the Supreme Court addressed questions involving church and state. The grand cultural changes of the 1920s set the groundwork for raising the wall separating church and state in the 1940s through the revision of laws that had previously supported the informal Protestant establishment.[101] Developments at Princeton in the 1920s illustrate the mainline Protestant response to cultural diversity and explain how and why mainline Protestantism remained firmly entrenched in many of the nation's leading colleges and universities for more than another generation.

The "Lost Generation" and Campus Religion in the 1920s

"Princeton," Thomas S. Evans, general secretary of the Philadelphian Society, explained to the Y.M.C.A.'s financial contributors, "cannot be looked upon as the religious center that it was a generation ago. In the midst of the beauty of its surroundings there is a conspicuous absence of religious fervor, and an ethical rather than an evangelical Christian atmosphere." He blamed the predominance of theological liberalism within the university for his failure to carry out a "comprehensive plan for the development of the religious interests of Princeton." Like other conservatives, Evans gave up on the university and resigned in the summer of 1918. Militant Presbyterians, displaying the type of paranoia that gave the epithet fundamentalist its pejorative connotation, interpreted Evans's departure as evidence that a "secret" power, "operating through German philosophy and its kindred theology," was attempting "to shift the University from its foundation on historical evangelical Christianity."[102]

After a rather unproductive year in the Philadelphian Society, President Hibben recruited Samuel M. Shoemaker (1893–1963), who graduated from the university in 1916, to return to Princeton in the fall of 1919 as the general secretary.[103] Under Shoemaker's leadership and with the aid of several associate secretaries, including Henry P. Van Dusen, the future president of Union Seminary in New York, the Philadelphian Society enjoyed a resurgence of activities. While many fundamentalists deemed private and state universities beyond repair, many educators at these institutions continued to describe them as Christian, and pointed to the activities of the campus Y.M.C.A.s as evidence.[104] With the elimination of Bible courses and weekday mandatory chapels, Hibben likewise relied upon the society to help give Princeton its Christian character, and judging from his reports of the society's activities, the campus Y flourished. After describing the work of the Philadelphian Society to the trustees in 1920, Hibben insisted, "It is safe to say that at no time in recent years has there been on the Princeton campus as much interest in religious matters."[105] Hibben's evaluation was less than accurate.

During the Roaring Twenties, indifference and irreligion, alongside the pious activities of the Philadelphian Society, thrived on the Princeton campus as at many other colleges and universities. Although the faculty disciplined students routinely for all sorts of "unchristian" behavior, intoxication in particular, many students flaunted publicly their rebellion against Victorian mores.[106] The unpublished autobiography of one member of the Class of 1924 chronicled four years of hard drinking and club hopping in New York City.[107] According to another student, the football coach, troubled by low attendance at his games, complained that the undergraduates were becoming "effeminate" and were too preoccupied with fashionable clothes and weekend trips to New York. The same student, a theologically conservative Episcopalian, wrote his father in 1924, that "the majority" of his classmates "do not *even know when Easter comes*."[108] Perhaps most telling of the presence of unbelief on campus is a 1927 *Daily Princetonian* survey of student religious beliefs. When given a choice between theism or atheism, belief won by a vote of 973 to 101; but when faced with a choice between theism and agnosticism, the latter won by a 573 to 525 margin.[109] "In the old times," a student wrote, "our fathers had answered the Sphinx, and went about their business, being that they had freed the City of Man for all time. But the monster has come back, and we cannot give it the answers our fathers gave." The student, however, was not too troubled by what he described as the *"mal de siècle"*: "Luckily for our sanity and peace of mind, this eternal mocking Sphinx that no man answers is often hidden by the white clouds of a Spring day, or fades altogether in the strong sunlight, or is forgotten in the midst of laughter."[110]

The unbelief and irreligion evident on the university campus were part of the larger postwar rebellion of the "lost generation" against American Victorianism. The experience of many American youths in the trenches of France both raised and confirmed doubts about American idealism. While dormitories and other monuments built on the Princeton campus were intended to commemorate the ultimate sacrifice that many students had made in the war, for some students and young alumni they served as permanent reminders of the failures of the Wilson generation. After the war, many intellectuals voiced distrust for Victorian values and authority.[111] American writers, such as Ernest Hemingway, eschewed the small-town values represented in the sentimental works of such popular writers as Henry Van Dyke Jr. Many lived as expatriates in Europe and wrote with a grim realism, if not cynicism, about businesses, churches, higher education, and other institutions associated with the American dream.[112]

No one better expressed the rebellion against the Victorianism of American higher education than Princeton's own F. Scott Fitzgerald in *This Side of Paradise*. Set in Princeton before the war, when Fitzgerald himself was a student at the university, the novel's protagonist, Amory Blane, indulged in four years of drinking, necking, and social climbing while at the same time holding Victorian Princeton in contempt. When the novel was published in 1920, President Hibben told Fitzgerald in a letter that he was deeply distressed by his portrayal of Princeton as a place where "young men are merrily living for four years in a country club and spending their lives wholly in a spirit of calculation and snobbishness.... It would be an overwhelming grief to me ... should I feel that we have nothing to offer but the outgrown symbols and shells of a past whose reality has long since disappeared."[113] However, whereas a previous generation of students had romanticized "college life," the expatriate Fitzgerald living in Paris had a cult following at his alma mater. The stories of many of these campus bohemians in the *Nassau Lit* and other student publications expressed cynicism like that articulated by Fitzgerald.[114]

The more secular-minded modernists in the university community, like

Fitzgerald, detested liberal Protestantism as much as they loathed fundamentalism. When Hibben refused to sponsor the Billy Sunday revival in 1915, he had won the support of the more secular-minded modernists in the university community. But when Hibben promised that the 1919 Campaign would to give a portion of its funds to further the campus ministry of the Philadelphian Society, the same young rebels resisted his efforts to propagate Victorian Protestantism among the undergraduates. In 1920, Edmund Wilson Jr. and F. Scott Fitzgerald, for example, complained bitterly in the alumni weekly about Hibben's plan to give more financial support to the Y.M.C.A.[115] The coalition of liberal Protestants and cultural modernists proved to be as fluid as the alliance between populist and scholarly fundamentalists. The venue and issue at stake determined whether and on what terms these different groups would unite.

The rebellion of college students against the triumphal Protestantism of Victorian America was symptomatic of what one historian has called "the American religious depression" of the 1920s and early 1930s. A sudden decline in foreign missions, church attendance, and church donations and a precipitous rise in scientism, behaviorism, and humanism provided other manifestations of the spiritual malaise infecting Protestantism during this period. The "second disestablishment" of mainline Protestant cultural hegemony, combined with the failures of Protestant triumphalism, nourished popular suspicions about the identification, if not amalgamation, of Christianity and American culture that had shaped Protestant attitudes for the past generation.[116] The rapid decline of the war spirit, mainline Protestant theologian Walter M. Horton remarked in 1930, led "to a wave of spiritual depression and religious skepticism, widespread and devastating."[117]

Two other factors unique to American higher education also contributed to the rise of irreligion and indifference on university campuses. First, in the 1920s, American colleges became centers of rebellion against the paternalism of the ruling generation. For example, 87.7 percent of the Princeton students surveyed in a 1926 poll favored a repeal of Prohibition. When Hibben banned autos from campus the following year, the senior council protested this infringement upon student freedom by resigning en masse.[118] Second, Princeton, like other institutions during the 1920s, attracted students interested more in getting a college degree as their passport to success than in getting a liberal education. "In this last decade," a 1928 guidebook to American colleges proclaimed, "higher education has become . . . a fetich [*sic*] in America. . . . [A] college degree is a stamp of social superiority, its lack, a social stigma. Each one believes that it is a magic key to happiness, success, and riches."[119] Princeton, moreover, attracted the idle rich committed to having an uproariously good time before embarking on the road to success.

In the fall of 1923, the campus bohemians clashed with the pious members of the Philadelphian Society over the teachings of Frank Buchman. Buchman (1878–1961) was a Lutheran minister who had worked as the general secretary of the Y.M.C.A. at Penn State and as a part-time extension lecturer in Personal Evangelism at Hartford Theological Seminary. He had befriended Shoemaker when the two worked in China during the war. After the war, the charismatic

Buchman created his own organization, the First Century Christian Fellowship, which later became Moral Re-Armament, or the Oxford Movement, and would eventually gain notoriety for its sympathetic overtures to Nazi Germany in the late 1930s. Buchman had a strong following among the leaders of the Philadelphian Society as well as among students at Harvard, Yale, Oxford, and other prominent universities. In comparison to Billy Sunday's revivalistic meetings, moreover, Buchman concentrated on evangelizing individuals and small groups. In *Soul Surgery* (1919), Howard A. Walter, a Princeton alumnus, summarized Buchman's unique five-point evangelistic plan of confidence, confession, conviction, conversion, and continuance. First, one needed to gain the confidence of the person with whom one was going to work by being honest about one's own spiritual life. Such honesty, one hoped, would lead the person to confess his or her sins, particularly sexual sins or "impurity," as Buchman obliquely referred to them. The third step was to bring the person to a sense of conviction that he or she needed an absolute freedom from sin. Those convicted then needed to experience a conversion whereby they would surrender freely their will to God. This conversion was followed by a detailed plan to help new believers continue a life of victorious Christian living. Buchman's message was an amorphous combination of pietism, Keswick holiness teaching, and Christian moralism. Theologically, Buchman cannot be classified as a fundamentalist or modernist. By design, he was distinctly a-theological and for this reason he attracted students from different church backgrounds.[120]

In Shoemaker's first year at Princeton, Buchman spoke regularly to the Philadelphian Society, conducted "interviews" on campus, and held weekend "house parties" in Princeton or New York City, at which he and his disciples evangelized students according to his methods. In the spring of 1920, Shoemaker credited Buchman with rejuvenating the Y.M.C.A.'s fortunes. Buchman, he told the society's directors, "has been the inspiration and guide of nearly all the spiritual experiences we have through this year, as individuals and as groups." "Unlikely men" have been brought into "the Kingdom," "defeated" Christians "awakened to new power," non-Christians "roused to unprecedented interest," and "the group at the center bound together in a bond of common experience and a joy of conquest that has not been known here in years."[121] In a day when many felt Victorian Protestantism lacked meaning and value, Buchman attracted many students with his presentation of the Christian life as an exhilarating experience of constant communion with God.

Despite Buchman's popularity among the Philadelphian Society, his message and methods put off many students, especially the campus bohemians. Some began to complain to Hibben about "Buchmanism" and, as one critic described it, the "holier-than-thou attitude of those who did good works or 'met the challenge.'" Students' criticism reached a climax in the fall of 1923 when Edward Steese, a member of the senior class, threatened to publish in a student newspaper, aptly titled *The Cannonade*, an alternative publication to the *Daily Princetonian*, a sarcastic attack on Buchman and his obsession with students' sexual "impurities." President Hibben, who could not afford to see the society lose the confidence of the student body, attempted to reconcile the parties by holding an informal meeting at Prospect. After both sides vented their anger, the dispute subsided temporarily. Hibben later reported that he had banned Buchman from campus at this meeting; he also said that Buchman had told him privately that he believed that 80 percent of the students were homosexuals. Buchman's disciples, however, later denied both points.[122] In the summer of 1924, after a disagreement with the student leaders of the organization over Buchman's influence, Shoemaker resigned as general secretary of the Philadelphian Society and went on to become the rector of an Episcopal church in New York City. Other disciples of Buchman, most importantly Shoemaker's successor, Ray Purdy, remained on campus, as did student critics of "Buchmanism."

Attempting to Return to Religious Normalcy

Like the American people, who, according to President Warren G. Harding, wanted a "return to normalcy" after the World War, Hibben's efforts to broker a peace between the Philadelphian Society and the campus bohemians was part of a larger attempt to return the university's program of religious education to a state of harmony. In a day when mandatory chapel epitomized the heavy hand of paternalism of the ruling generation, Hibben and his colleagues, like administrators at other colleges and universities, struggled to arouse students' spirituality through the services. They also tried to introduce to the undergraduate curriculum a more academic approach to the study of religion. In both areas, however, the administration struggled to return normalcy to the religious life of the university.

On the evening of May 14, 1920, Marquand Chapel burned to the ground. Many students and their dates left dances at the eating clubs to watch the blaze. The superstitious considered the fire a good omen for the athletic contests scheduled for the next day. "The Tiger," the *Daily Princetonian* wryly observed, "indeed celebrated coming victories over Yale and Harvard with a unique bonfire."[123] The trustees decided to rebuild the chapel, revealing that they still considered it a critical responsibility of the university to oversee the spiritual lives of students. "We could take the position," explained trustee Edward D. Duffield, president of the Prudential Insurance Company and son of one of the university's most theologically conservative professors in the nineteenth century, "that after all we are an educational institution, and all of our duties consisted in providing classrooms and teachers, and that as far as the moral and spiritual life went, we assumed no responsibility whatever. That would have been a theoretically tenable position, but it has never been Princeton's position." "Princeton *still* exists as a *Christian institution*" he dogmatically insisted, and has an "obligation" to oversee "the moral life of the undergraduates." Princeton's responsibility to nurture the moral lives of students impinged directly upon the university's mission to American society. Like McCosh a generation earlier, Duffield reasoned that the welfare of the nation depended immediately upon the religious education of its leaders. "[I]f we are to continue to do the work that Princeton was dedicated to, sending boys out from that institution imbued with the idea of service... to make this a better nation and a better world," Duffield believed, then the construction of a new chapel was "essential."[124]

Although the decision to rebuild was immediate, funds for the project were not as forthcoming. With the 1919 Endowment Campaign already underway, the trustees had pledged not to solicit money from the alumni for any other project until the campaign was completed. During the interlude, the community fought over the plans for the new building. In November 1921, Hibben and Ralph Adams Cram, the university's architect, unveiled those plans. They decided to build the new chapel where the old one had stood. Its very location at the center of campus, Hibben asserted, was "a symbol of the place of religion in the great task of preparing man adequately for his life and work in the world" and stood "as the University's protest against the materialistic philosophy and drift of our age."[125] Cram planned to construct a massive fourteenth-century Gothic chapel. With a width of 58 feet, an interior length of 270 feet, a 76-foot height from the pavement to the crown of the vault, and seating for two thousand, the new chapel was second in size only to the college chapel at King's College, Cambridge. Cram believed that the Gothic architecture embodied the transcendent religious values that the university aspired to uphold in an age of doubt. The Gothic chapel, he asserted, "would work silently and subconsciously toward bringing back once more into undergraduate life, those supra-material, super-intellectual forces which, to say the least, add so immeasurably to the joy and fullness of life." Furthermore, he believed that the Gothic chapel would "unite itself with all the great traditions of Christian architecture and yet adapt itself to the changed conditions of the world."[126] Not everyone, however, was pleased with the decision to build a medieval chapel at a college founded by Presbyterians. A wave of letters in the *Princeton Alumni Weekly* condemned the building even before construction began. "The whole environment of Princeton," one old alumnus argued, "should be suggestive (as always heretofore) of the spirit of evangelical Christianity . . . rather than worldly pomp and exaltation."[127] The Gothic chapel even unnerved the Presbyterian sensibilities of some theological modernists in the community. Henry Van Dyke Jr. privately told the president that Cram was "permanently afflicted with the delusion" that preaching was "defunct" and that worship in the future would consist of purely liturgical services. Van Dyke wanted Princeton to be "true to type" and construct a chapel that would foster "a spirit of reasonable and united reverence" and "even" possibly attract "the most hardened and obstreperous professor."[128] Amused by the debate, one young bohemian among the alumni suggested that the university go back to an earlier period in church history and construct catacombs. "Lest any of our more patriotic alumni think that this would show us as too greatly influenced by foreign ideals," he added, "the cave could be tastily draped in red, white, and blue bunting."[129]

While the destruction of Marquand Chapel may have been a good omen for the baseball team, it did not bode well for the future of the mandatory Sunday chapel services. Holding the services in Alexander Hall only compounded students' dissatisfaction. One student complained in a letter to his mother that many of his classmates talked during the service while others read newspapers.[130] In the winter of 1922–1923, students mounted another campaign for voluntary services. "There is," one wrote in the *Daily Princetonian*, "a certain analogy between Princeton's compulsory religion and British colonization (with a Bible in one hand and a whiskey bottle in the other); the expected good is often outweighed by the resultant evil." The "psychological effect" of "ram-rod" religion subverted the "spiritual attitude" needed for genuine worship. A decade earlier many students believed that the sole purpose of compulsory daily chapel was to get them out of bed early in the morning. In the 1920s, many felt that Sunday chapel's only function was to keep them in Princeton over weekends.[131]

Although the trustees refused to change the chapel policy, they took the student unrest as a sign that the university was not adequately fulfilling its responsibilities of overseeing the religious life of the student body. Student indifference and rebellion against mandatory chapel demanded action. At the board meeting in the spring of 1923, the Committee on Undergraduate Life reported that they had met and given "the religious situation" "earnest consideration." They recommended that the university procure the funds necessary to begin construction of the new chapel and suggested the possibility of establishing a position, "under some appropriate title," for someone to be charged with "the general supervision of the religious welfare of the University." They also asked the board to consider creating "a course or courses on the Literature of the Bible." Because the Philadelphian Society played "an important role in the religious life of the University," but had difficulty raising sufficient funds through its annual canvass in recent times, the committee also urged the trustees to grant direct financial aid to the organization.[132] Despite the opposition over constructing a Gothic chapel, Hibben and the trustees believed that the building would play an important role in how the university fulfilled its religious mission in the twentieth century. Thus, in June, they broke ground for the new chapel. The above-described dispute over Frank Buchman the following winter and another dramatic student revolt against mandatory Sunday chapel in the spring of 1925, which included a protest signed by more than a thousand students, only added urgency to the trustees' search to find a way to meet its religious responsibilities more effectively.[133]

Although most students despised mandatory chapel, many students expressed an interest in a more academic study of Christianity. In the early 1920s, Princeton, ironically, stood out as one of the few schools that offered no Bible courses. Denominational colleges still required a full slate of Bible courses; for example, Grove City College, a Presbyterian institution, made all students take six such courses. But even the prestigious, private universities—Princeton's chief rivals—offered elective English Bible courses; Columbia and Harvard, for example, offered such courses.[134] In 1920, students had even petitioned the trustees for courses on the ethics, history, and literature of the Bible, arguing, as one wrote in the *Daily Princetonian*, that such courses should be part of "a broad and liberal education."[135]

As it had done in previous decades, the Philadelphian Society attempted to meet students' desires for religious instruction. Beginning in the fall of 1922, for instance, several faculty members participated in an annual Sunday evening lecture series on Christianity sponsored by the Philadelphian Society. That fall, for example, Princeton Seminary Old Testament Professor John D. Davis (1854–1926), astronomer Henry Norris Russell (1877–1957), biologist Edwin G. Conklin (1863–1952), and paleontologist William Berryman Scott each gave four lectures on the Evidences of Christianity. Crowds were so large that the lectures had to be moved from Murray-Dodge to Alexander Hall.[136]

As a result of student interest and the Committee on Undergraduate Life's recommendation, the trustees agreed in the fall of 1923 to add a course on the history of Christianity. In the nineteenth century, religious instruction was, what historians would later describe as, Christian education, whose primary goal was to nurture the Protestant faith of students. The courses that, under McCosh and Patton, had a broadly evangelical orientation had taken a decidedly liberal slant under Miller in the early twentieth century. In the 1920s, Princeton, like many other institutions, was coming slowly to the position that the Bible could be studied as literature or history and thus have a legitimate place within a liberal arts education. To be sure, twentieth-century advocates of religious instruction desired to arouse, like their nineteenth-century predecessors, the Protestant faith of students indirectly through the academic study of religion. But given the scientific character of the methods employed in the academic study of religion, they were adamant that their scholarship avoid proselytism and transcend the dogmatic assumptions upon which Christian education in the nineteenth century had rested. A trustees' report on the new course in the history of Christianity revealed the emergence of this new understanding of the potential academic character of religious instruction. According to the report, the trustees expected the new course to address primarily the historical facts concerning the origins of Christianity and the historical conditions that produced the New Testament writings.[137]

Melanchthon W. Jacobus, chair of the trustees' curriculum committee, recruited Harris E. Kirk, the southern Presbyterian minister who had turned down a position at Princeton Seminary in 1909, to teach the senior elective each spring semester for five years beginning in 1925. Kirk (1872–1953) traveled from Baltimore to Princeton to lecture on Monday afternoons and Tuesday mornings. Kirk's lectures were so popular with students that at the conclusion of his first semester, they petitioned to have the course offered both semesters; pastoral responsibilities, however, made this impossible. The essence of Christianity, as Kirk expressed in his most popular work, *The Religion of Power* (1916), was its historicity. The Bible contained a historical record of God's supernatural actions to redeem humanity. The Old Testament pointed forward to the first advent of Christ, and the New Testament was an historical record of Christ's life, death, and bodily resurrection, as well as a testimony of the early church's faith in that supernatural event and in a future second advent.[138] Kirk was no historicist but taught students a rather traditional Protestant understanding of the historical character of Christianity. On this count, he shared more with the fundamentalists and the theologians at the seminary than he did, for example, with President Hibben.

Yet Kirk's work does not mark the return of fundamentalism to the classrooms of Princeton. Kirk, to be sure, espoused orthodox beliefs, but he was no fundamentalist. He had refused the opportunity to align with the conservative wing of the northern church when he turned down the opportunity to teach at the seminary. In fact, fundamentalists were marginalized increasingly in the university during the 1920s. While the university still attracted students from fundamentalist backgrounds and some fundamentalists occasionally addressed the Y.M.C.A., many Presbyterian fundamentalists, like Evans, the Y.M.C.A. general secretary, abandoned their interest in Princeton during this decade. In the nineteenth century, conservative Presbyterians had considered Princeton a Christian institution. In the 1920s, they depicted the choice in higher education as one between irreligious, secular universities and Christian, denominational colleges.[139]

The growing intellectual obscurantism of populist fundamentalists during the 1920s also accounts for their marginalization from the university in this decade. At the Scopes "monkey trial" in Tennessee in 1925, press coverage depicted the great Populist William Jennings Bryan as an ignorant opponent of evolution and defender of biblical literalism and his allies as redneck dimwits. As a result, in the trial by public opinion and the press, George M. Marsden observes, it was clear that the twentieth century, the cities, and the universities had won a resounding victory, and that the country, the South, and the fundamentalists were guilty as charged.[140] The anti-intellectualism of some fundamentalists in the Princeton community in the 1920s only confirmed what had happened at the Scopes trial. President Hibben and professors Conklin, Russell, and Scott, for instance, affirmed the existence of God and the harmony of science and religion, though on grounds more similar to the Christian Darwinism advocated by Lucius H. Miller than to the Christian Darwinisticism espoused by McCosh or Charles W. Shields. These professors also criticized William Jennings Bryan's campaign against the teaching of evolution in public schools.[141] Some fundamentalists denounced them as unqualified to speak on matters of religion. Others, perhaps forgetting the work of McCosh and Shields, raised doubts about the very possibility of harmonizing evolution and theism. The *Presbyterian* even turned to George McCready Price, a Seventh-Day Adventist and the progenitor of "creation science," to repudiate the university faculty's harmonization of Christianity and evolution. According to Price's "scientific creationism," God created all species by divine fiat in six twenty-four-hour days without the aid of evolution and the earth was only a few thousand years old. Ironically, even the rockribbed conservatives at the seminary were more hospitable to the harmonization of evolution and theism than were these fundamentalists.[142]

Yet even the more scholarly fundamentalism espoused at the seminary was marginalized in the university community in the 1920s. Moderate evangelical and liberal Presbyterians were willing to tolerate a certain degree of theological latitude in order to preserve the church's role as the custodian of American culture. To them, the strict confessionalism of fundamentalists like J. Gresham

Machen threatened the unity of the church and ultimately endangered the Christian character of American society. Consequently, the scholarly fundamentalists enjoyed little support from the university community. Writing Charles W. Eliot in 1924 to correct his misapprehension that Princeton University and Princeton Seminary were part of one institution, President Hibben confided, "Personally, I am not in sympathy with the ultra-conservative theological position of the Seminary." In fact, Hibben had already made his opposition to the seminary well known. He denounced the fundamentalists in his 1923 baccalaureate address, for instance, for removing the liberal Harry Emerson Fosdick from the pulpit of a Presbyterian church in New York City. In 1924, Hibben, Henry Van Dyke Jr. and several others at the university signed the Auburn Affirmation, which called for the toleration of liberalism within the northern Presbyterian church.[143] While some within the university actively opposed the fundamentalist menace to the Presbyterian church, most simply dismissed the confessional orthodoxy of the seminary as passé. "The Seminary represents, to all intents and purposes," an editorial in the *Daily Princetonian* remarked in 1925, "a spirit within the Presbyterian Church which is not in accord with the general tendency of the times. It is in very fact a creed-bolstered institution."[144] While Kirk's lectures on the history of Christianity may have presented students with a rather traditional view of the origins and development of Christianity, his presence at the university did not represent the presence of fundamentalism in the classrooms of Princeton. The anti-intellectual and sectarian tendencies of the fundamentalists in this decade left them with little influence inside the university. Their dwindling influence at the university paralleled similar declines in the affairs of the seminary, the Presbyterian church, and American culture at large in the 1920s.

In addition to Kirk's lectures on the history of Christianity, the academic study of religion surfaced in other courses offered at the university in the 1920s. Robert W. Rogers's senior elective class in Ancient Oriental Literature served as a partial course in Old Testament studies. Rogers (1864–1930) taught full time at Drew Theological Seminary and was also the Visiting Professor of Ancient Literature on the Paton Foundation from 1919 to 1929. He was a distinguished scholar of Assyriology, Hebrew, and the Old Testament whose *A History of Babylonia and Assyria* (1901) stood out as one of the most competent works in the burgeoning field of ancient Near Eastern studies. Unlike Kirk, he fully accepted the modern critical views of the Old Testament, but, as a biographer noted, he possessed "such tact and consideration for the normal growth of his students" that he escaped the ecclesiastical censure of the Methodist church. In his lectures on the literature of Egypt, Babylonia, and Assyria, Rogers addressed the Hebrew religion on historical and literary, not theological, grounds. In the fall of 1927, the university organized a Department of Oriental Languages and Literature, and hired Philip K. Hitti (1886–1978), who taught the Ancient Oriental Literature course in place of Rogers.[145] In addition to Warner Fite's ethics course, A. A. Bowman (1883–1936), a Professor of Logic at the university from 1912 to 1926, offered an upperclass elective on the Ethics of Christianity in four different semesters in the 1920s. Bowman was an idealist. His principal scholarly concern was the epistemology of religious knowledge. Like many theological liberals of his day, Bowman believed that the essence of Christianity was ethics, an "interpretation of life." In his undergraduate class, Bowman outlined the philosophical foundation for this understanding of Christianity and the New Testament ethical principles that gave it meaning. The philosophical justification for Christianity was not based on scientific "evidences of the supernatural power in the natural world," as, for instance, Shields had taught a generation earlier, but upon the subjective experience of God. This experience stood "impervious" to the criticisms of positivistic science because it was not based on "natural knowledge." Faith, he argued, produced a "feeling" of a personal relationship with God and consequently "the self-authentication of the spirit." Ethics was essential to Christianity because the experience of the spirit's "self-authentication" came from "holy living."[146]

Although he did not teach undergraduate courses in the period under consideration, Paul Elmer More's presence at the university in the 1920s deserves mention because it signifies the growing intellectual diversity of the faculty and, more important, reflects the administration's effort to find scholarly teachers of religion. More (1864–1937), who had been literary editor at the *New York Evening Post* (1903–1909) and the *Nation* (1909–1914), retired to the town of Princeton in 1914. Four years later President Hibben persuaded him to teach a graduate seminar once a year in Greek philosophy. More and his lifelong friend and fellow New Humanist Irving Babbitt of Harvard University were stern critics of both the individualism and the sentimentalism of the romantic tradition, as well as the naturalism and relativism associated with Darwinism and pragmatism. These New Humanists were cultural traditionalists, defensive of classical principles in the arts, skeptical about the goodness of human nature, and neo-Burkean in their political and social views.[147] In such works as *The Christ of the New Testament* (1924) and *Christ the Word* (1927), More criticized the "pathetic" efforts of liberal Protestantism to preserve Christianity while "depriving" it of any supernatural basis. More, however, was not a fundamentalist. He espoused a Platonic Christianity that called for a restoration of the doctrine of the supernatural incarnation to Christian thinking.[148] Although he had journeyed back to a Christian faith after his youthful rejection of his Calvinist upbringing and a brief dalliance with Hinduism, he still could never bring himself to join a church.

The trustees' curriculum committee reported in January 1924 that the courses taught by Bowman, Kirk, and Rogers involved "the *presentation* of Christianity" as "a basic element in the education," "not as a religious *propaganda*," which was "not the function of an educational institution." The "failure to draw this line of demarcation," the report added, had left many students "largely ignorant of Christianity" and "indifferent to religion." Princeton, they concluded, "can succeed in making its students intellectually aware of Christianity, as a philosophy, a literature, and a history." This new rationale for the academic study of religion, it was hoped, would indirectly "remove" students' "indifference to religion." Although not a constitutive part of a liberal education—these courses, for instance, stood on the margins of the curriculum, being listed as an addendum in the catalogue, and, moreover, Kirk and Rogers were adjunct professors who had the reputation of teaching "snap" courses—the academic study of religion was beginning to gain entrance into the university curriculum.[149] Two years later, the Committee on University Life again asked the trustees to increase the number of religion courses. The study of religion, the trustees insisted, constituted "an *obligation* of Princeton to its *historic past*," "a glorious opportunity for its future," and "a lasting service to our day and generation." But the committee made it clear that they wanted religion taught on "the same *intellectual plane* as other subjects" in the curriculum.[150] Nearly a decade after fundamentalists had argued for the complete secularization of the undergraduate curriculum, Hibben cited occasionally the subordinate purpose of these courses as evidence of the university's continued commitment to its Protestant mission. The president, for instance, told the alumni in 1923 that Rogers's and Bowman's courses demonstrated that the "theory of the Princeton education is that modern life is fundamentally religious and that Princeton must teach the fundamentals of Christianity." Although these courses still had a decidedly Protestant orientation and the unambiguous, if subordinate, goal to cultivate the Protestant faith of students, not to mention that later scholars would question the epistemological neutrality guiding the assumptions about the scientific character of the academic study of religion, they did not constitute—at least to Hibben, the trustees, and faculty—a return to the dogmatic Christian education of the previous generation.[151]

The Buchman Controversy

"For the past four years," President Hibben insisted in October 1926, "it has been my firm conviction that there is no place in Princeton for 'Buchmanism.'"[152] The president's conviction notwithstanding, "Buchmanism" had persisted on the university campus. In May 1926, Ray Purdy, general secretary of the Philadelphian Society, had asked several students to Murray-Dodge Hall, where Frank Buchman was waiting to invite them to a weekend house party in Princeton. Although Purdy later denied that he had known that Buchman had been banned from campus, a week after this incident he did go to Hibben to "confess" his indiscretion. Before classes began in the fall, a group of Philadelphian Society members, led by Purdy, joined students from Harvard and Yale in an evangelistic campaign organized by the local ministerial association in Waterbury, Connecticut. The *Churchman*, an Episcopalian weekly, ran a series of articles on the campaign, criticizing "the Frank Buchman–Samuel Shoemaker cult" that dominated the ten-day event. The *Churchman* called "Buchmanism" a "new sect" and described it as "vividly anti-rationalistic," preoccupied with the confession or "washing out" of auto-erotic sins, and promoting an almost gnostic understanding of the Christian life. *Time* magazine picked up the story and further underscored the close connection between Buchmanism and Princeton's Philadelphian Society.[153]

In the fall of 1926, Buchmanism became a *casus belli* at Princeton University. Since part of the funds collected in the yearly Community Chest Campaign went to the Philadelphian Society, many students were slightly more than reluctant to donate money to support a "cult" on campus. Buchman's meddlesome tactics and preoccupation with sex grated against the social sensibilities of many students. More important, the Philadelphian Society's hyper-spirituality and sectarian devotion to Buchman's teachings made the organization more exclusive than any eating club on campus. The senior council organized an open forum at the end of October to discuss the situation. When asked at the end of the meeting whether "an undesirable 'Buchmanism'" was practiced by the Philadelphian Society or by any of its graduate secretaries, 253 students answered yes and only 65 said no. Students also approved a resolution to support an investigation into the Philadelphian Society.[154]

Hibben was more than ready to oblige the students since Buchmanism threatened the religious mission of the university by undermining the credibility of Princeton's de facto campus ministry. In particular, Hibben opposed Buchman because, as he later wrote Yale University President James R. Angell, he placed an "undue emphasis upon sex as the source of all sin," exacted public confession as part of his "program," disturbed students who had a highly sensitive and introspective nature, and exhibited "a total lack of tolerance of other forms of Christian experience or belief." The president appointed a committee, comprising trustees, professors, administrators, and students, to investigate the Philadelphian Society. This committee held four hearings and invited twenty students who reportedly had been left distraught by Buchman's teaching and the society's activities. When none appeared, they held private interviews with each. Only two students made negative comments about Buchman, and these were based on innuendo and gossip heard from other students.[155] Members of the society, by contrast, said only positive things about Buchman and Purdy. "In so far as we have been able to see the influence of Frank Buchman in the life of Ray Purdy," insisted the student cabinet, "it has been valuable and good, and has not been of the obnoxious character so generally ascribed to it."[156]

The committee's report, presented to the Board of Trustees in January 1927, attempted to resolve the controversy without further undermining the standing of the Philadelphian Society in the eyes of the university community. The report reprimanded a contrite Purdy for violating Hibben's ban and, in one of its more grand understatements, noted that the present "misunderstanding" kept many students from affiliating with the society. But with "no evidence" to "substantiate or justify" the charges that the society had engaged in "personal work" that "invaded" the privacy of students' lives and made the "confession" of "sexual immorality" a "condition of the Christian life," the report fully exonerated the society. In addition to a number of organizational changes in the society, the committee recommended three ways in which the trustees could immediately improve the religious life of the university. They asked the trustees to increase the number of "religious courses" offered and to address "the question of the establishment at an early date of a *Department of Religion.*" They also recommended that voluntary daily chapel services be improved. Finally, they urged that a *"University Chaplain"* be hired to assist the president in overseeing "the religious life of the University."[157]

Despite Hibben's efforts to elicit an amicable solution to the controversy, few on campus were satisfied with the report. Hibben gave Purdy and the other secretaries the spring semester to gain the confidence of the student body and told them to have nothing more to do with Buchman. The *Daily Princetonian*, Buchman's chief critic, soon threatened to renew its attack on the society.[158] Purdy, ready neither to denounce his mentor nor to compromise his convictions, published an open letter in the *Daily Princetonian* professing his personal allegiance to Frank Buchman and Buchman's teachings as the essence of Christianity. The *Daily Princetonian* responded by calling for the "abandonment of rigorous personal evangelism and religious propaganda."[159] Fed up with the controversy, Hibben told Purdy and the other secretaries that their contracts would not be renewed at the end of the semester. In righteous indignation, Purdy and the others announced their immediate resignation. The student cabinet likewise resigned.[160] Noting that the "Philadelphian Society has recently passed through an ordeal of fire," the *Daily Princetonian* declared an end to the controversy. "In our humble opinion," the editorial declared with notable glee, the Philadelphian Society "has had enough."[161]

Settling on a Solution

Disputes over religion and what role it should play within the university plagued Princeton throughout Hibben's presidency. Because the Buchman controversy had eroded most students' interest in the Philadelphian Society, the administration could no longer rely upon the organization to help it fulfill the university's religious mission. While Hibben and his colleagues could have left the responsibility for the religious lives of the undergraduates in the hands of the Episcopalian and Presbyterian campus ministries, the administration still considered it an institutional responsibility to instruct students in a nonsectarian religion and in a manner compatible with its public purpose.

Mainline Protestants believed that Christianity, through its conversion of individuals or its virtuous influence upon public institutions, was essential to the public good. To be sure, they could tolerate a certain degree of religious diversity, but the need for social order and stability required cultural uniformity. The Buchman controversy jeopardized the religious unity of the university and ultimately threatened its religious mission. This was unacceptable to the administration. Consequently, the administration attempted to assimilate diversity and dissent by centralizing the university's program of religious education in a new bureaucratic structure. Thus, they created a new office, Dean of the Chapel, to govern the religious life of the institution, and they consolidated religious activities under his auspices in the new chapel building. Mainline Protestants in other important cultural institutions responded to the menace of fundamentalism in the same way. In the northern Presbyterian church, for instance, moderate and liberal Presbyterians were willing to tolerate some religious heterogeneity in order to preserve the efficiency of the church's witness to American society. In the face of fundamentalists' divisive insistence on strict adherence to the church's confessional standards, they turned to the bureaucratic centralization of diversity to resolve discord, maintain the unity of the church, and sustain its influence upon American society. This was evident, for example, in the reorganization of Princeton Seminary's Board of Directors and Board of Trustees in 1929 and decision to consolidate of the church's missionary efforts in 1934.[162] In the subsequent generation, new pressures would produce another reevaluation, but for Hibben and many of his colleagues the university had found a way through the Dean of the Chapel and the new chapel program to mold the Protestant character of the student body and thereby to shape the national culture. Although Princeton's bureaucratic solution to the place of religion in collegiate education stood closer to Eliot's perspective than to McCosh's in their 1886 debate, Hibben and his allies, like their nineteenth-century predecessors, continued to attempt to advance the Christian character of American culture. In fact, because of its reorganization of religious instruction and worship in the late 1920s, Princeton stood among the early leaders of a movement to safeguard a place for religion in American higher education.

The centerpiece of the university's solution to the place of religion in collegiate education was the university chaplain. In the spring of 1927, Hibben asked the trustees to hire a Dean of the Chapel who would be given the "general supervision of the religious interests of the students."[163] With the professionalization of the faculty, professors' involvement in the religious lives of students had declined precipitously since the late nineteenth century. In one sense, the decision to hire a chaplain marked the demise of another established custom: professors were no longer responsible for the oversight of the religious lives of students. But by hiring a chaplain, the trustees adjusted the university's *in loco parentis* policy to new educational realities: they delegated them to the Dean of the Chapel. Other institutions, including Colby in 1922, Yale in 1927, and the University of Pennsylvania in 1932, like Princeton, created official chaplaincies to help them resolve difficulties surrounding the place of religion on campus.[164] In the wake of the Buchman controversy, Hibben and the trustees wanted to find, according to Melanchthon W. Jacobus, "a man of mind, as well as of spirit" who would "commend himself as absolutely sincere."[165] In February of the following year, they found those qualities in Robert R. Wicks. Wicks (1882–1963), a graduate of Hamilton College and Union Theological Seminary, was pastor of Second Congregational Church of Holyoke, Massachusetts, and chaplain at Mount Holyoke College.[166] The trustees assigned Wicks three responsibilities: to oversee the extracurricular religious activities on campus, to "do such teaching in the field of Religion as, in consultation with the President and the Dean of the Faculty, may seem to him desirable," and to supervise all chapel services.[167] H. Alexander Smith, Secretary of the University, wrote Jacobus that Wicks was "going to solve this Princeton problem if anybody can." Even the typically cynical *Daily Princetonian* greeted the news of Wicks' hiring with unbridled enthusiasm.[168]

While the university had a "problem" with religion in the 1920s, this problem was not entirely unique to Princeton. Throughout this decade, many institutions struggled with the question of religion's role in undergraduate education. At the tenth annual meeting of the Association of American Colleges in 1924, for example, the three keynote speakers addressed this very question. Mainline Protestant organizations, such as the Religious Education Association, and its journal, *Religious Education*, helped to keep the question before many educators.[169]

In February 1928, Princeton confronted this problem directly by hosting a conference on religion in college life. In their efforts to safeguard the Protestant mission of undergraduate education at Princeton, Hibben and some of his colleagues hoped to resolve the issue for the rest of American higher education. Attending the meeting were fifty-eight presidents, thirty deans, sixty-eight professors, and thirty-two headmasters, representing eighty-one different denominational, private, and state colleges and universities and eighteen boarding schools. This was not the first time that Princeton had hoped to remedy a problem facing a large part of American higher education. Woodrow Wilson, for instance, had introduced the preceptorial system in 1905 with the expressed intent to solve one of Princeton's problems and to influence other institutions of higher learning. At Hibben's meeting, however, because of the diversity of institutions represented, no definitive position was reached concerning the three central topics of discussion: chapel, religion courses, and extracurricular activities. Yet a certain amount of consensus appeared in the meetings' proceedings. Extracurricular religious organizations, "whether official or voluntary," such as the Y.M.C.A. and university chaplains, had the "enthusiastic support" of all the institutions present. Educators also agreed that religion courses should have "an academic dignity equal" to other courses, but differed over whether they should be offered on an elective or required basis. Although most were adverse to flagrant evangelism, the consensus held that religion courses "must be more than the objective and scientific presentations of bodies of historical materials"; they must challenge the student "to venturesome and heroically constructive living in his own situation." By contrast, discussions over chapel exercises turned into a "barren controversy." Among denominational schools and public universities, there was little debate; the former had required services and the latter an entirely voluntary program. Private institutions, which were trying to balance their religious heritage and public mission, divided on the question. By requiring students to attend at least half the Sunday services each academic year, Princeton was not out of step with a large part of higher education, however. A 1926 National Student Federation poll, for instance, revealed some 176 college and university presidents favored mandatory Sunday attendance and 136 opposed it. While these representatives of America's colleges and universities disagreed on specifics, all were committed to helping the nation's future leaders be, as President Hibben put it, "benefactors of mankind" and contributors to "the 'coming of the Kingdom of God upon earth.'"[170]

The new chapel was the second key element in Princeton's solution to the place of religion in undergraduate education. Other colleges and universities, including Chicago, Syracuse, and Duke, also built new chapels in this period to help them revitalize their programs of religious education.[171] Princeton's Gothic chapel, dedicated appropriately on Memorial Day 1928 with a spectacular medieval ceremony, gave architectural expression to the type of nonsectarian Christianity that the administration believed civic institutions should advance. "In building this Chapel," the president said at the dedication, "the University has consciously striven to enter into what we regard as the true artistic heritage of Christendom as a whole, without respect to sectional divisions or partial or petty emphasis."[172]

While the new chapel enjoyed a prominent part in the religious life of the institution, the Philadelphian Society had fallen on hard times after the Buchman controversy. In his first year as chaplain, Wicks had little to do with the organization. This was part of Hibben's plan to bring, as he outlined in a letter to the new dean, the society under the chaplain's guidance in order to "better coordinate all religious activities of the college."[173] In the spring of 1927, the society had reorganized its Board of Directors by giving alumni, faculty, students, and trustees equal representation. The graduate secretaries now served as mere "advisors" to the student cabinet so that the Y.M.C.A. became, as the *Daily Princetonian* described the change, "a purely student organization."[174] The society also changed the terms of membership: no longer were all students who belonged to Protestant churches *ipso facto* members; students had to join voluntarily. The society also abandoned its historic interest in evangelism. Members decided to do this, as Eugene Carson Blake, president of the society in 1927–1928 and future general-secretary of the World Council of Churches, explained, because they wanted to adopt a policy of "an all-inclusive nature," tolerant of a wide divergence of religious opinions, in order "to give expression to the deepest religious convictions and desires of the Princeton student body."[175] With the arrival of Wicks the following year, the society concentrated on "social service work," such as the summer camp for boys and Princeton-in-Peking, which had become an educational enterprise exclusively. In the previous two years, the student cabinet reported in 1928, "there has been a minimum of evangelical and Christian education work done."[176] Despite the society's efforts to broaden its appeal by dropping the society's traditional interest in evangelism, few students wanted to be involved. The cabinet cancelled the annual three-day lecture series in January 1928 as well as the upperclass discussion groups because of "student apathy." These were difficult days for the Philadelphian Society, perhaps best symbolized by the toppling of the Christian Student statue by drunk students during graduation in 1929.[177]

In the spring of 1929, Wicks met with the student cabinet to discuss the possibility of centralizing all religious activities in the chapel. "There are many of us coming to think," Wicks suggested, "that the solution of this problem lies in centering the religious life of the University in the Chapel, rather than in a separate organization."[178] The following spring, he convinced the society to suspend its work for one year in order to "shake it free from the traditional difficulties." In its place, he proposed the creation of a Student-Faculty Association, which would have representatives from the faculty and student council as well as the Episcopalian and Presbyterian campus ministries. Together with the dean, this association would oversee the religious activities of the campus.[179] This plan, once it was adopted, brought an end to the Philadelphian Society; interest in reviving the society the following year never materialized. The chapel—its dean, the Student-Faculty Association, and their activities—had effectively forged religious unity in the university by assimilating diversity and dissent in one bureaucratic structure under the administration's authority. Ironically, the centralization of religious activities in the new chapel also meant that students no longer had their own religious organization. Although Wicks did not want to segregate the religious life of the student body from the corporate life of the university, he created a separate organization, located in just one building, albeit a rather impressive one, on campus.

Fundamentalist Presbyterians lamented the demise of the Philadelphian Society. "In our estimation," one wrote in the *Presbyterian*, "this is all a result of pure 'funk' on the part of those in charge."[180] Fundamentalists, however, were not the only ones who had misgivings about the exclusion of evangelism and other traditional evangelical interests in the creation of the Student-Faculty Association. H. Alexander Smith, who left Princeton in 1930 and eventually became a U.S. senator, also expressed doubts about the liberal and social-service orientation of the chaplain's new program. In the spring of 1929, he told Frank L. Janeway, Lucius H. Miller's one-time assistant, that he was "convinced" that Hibben had made "a mistake" in how he had restructured the religious life of the university since it had resulted in "killing for the present at least of any movement towards what we might call the evangelical side of religious work here."[181]

Although Wicks had successfully centralized the extracurricular religious activities of the university, he failed to take on a significant role in teaching religion in the undergraduate curriculum. Some trustees, as Melanchthon W. Jacobus described it, hoped to "put Christianity into the curriculum," by building a Religion Department around the chaplain.[182] The faculty, however, opposed efforts to give Wicks teaching responsibilities. After giving Wicks the "fool title" of Dean of Religion, one professor complained in the spring of 1928, "he is insisting on giving a Freshmen course, a religious academic course designed to provide the Freshmen with religious conviction." "There is unanimous opposition to this," he added, "but pressure properly directed by one or two trustees may put that fool program across."[183] At least in the eyes of some professors, Wicks had little interest or ability to teach the ethics, history, or literature of Christianity as an academic discipline. If any pressure was directed to secure Wicks teaching responsibilities, it failed. Wicks's title was changed to Dean of the Chapel before he assumed his responsibilities officially. While the reorganization of the religious life of the university in 1928 did not lead directly to the establishment of a religion department, it helped lay the groundwork for one.

With the new chapel, the university had effectively centered the religious life of the university under the administration's authority. "I believe that there is universal recognition," Hibben said at the end of the first semester in the new building, "that the Chapel has already become a new center of the spiritual life" of the university.[184] Just before the new chapel opened in the spring of 1928, the senior council told the administration that they had an unparalleled opportunity to make "a complete and permanent change in the campus attitude toward chapel attendance" by making all chapel services voluntary. Yale, Princeton's closest peer, for instance, had adopted an entirely voluntary chapel policy two years earlier, and Princeton students drew inspiration continuously from their rival's example. Several influential figures within the university, including the astronomer Henry Norris Russell and the trustee Robert Garrett, privately urged the administration to adopt this policy.[185] When the trustees agreed to hire a chaplain, they also decided to postpone any policy change until the new dean had assessed the situation.[186] After a year on campus, Wicks agreed with student and faculty sentiment. In a brilliant stroke of campus politics, he proposed the "abolition" of mandatory Sunday chapel services. In its place, he recommended that students be required to attend either half the Sunday morning services each year, which was the established policy, or Sunday evening lectures. This policy, Wicks argued, removed the "mental hazard" that many students felt the mandatory policy had erected against genuine worship on Sunday mornings, not to mention how it hampered weekend trips to New York.[187] The plan was progressive enough to satisfy temporarily students' desire for independence and conservative enough to preserve a Princeton tradition.

In the twentieth century, Princeton's civic mission had expanded in ways that James McCosh did not, could not, have envisioned in 1868. The university's devotion to undergraduate education, which prepared students for the modern age by combining elements of liberal culture, specialization, and vocational training models of higher education, the Graduate College, and the various schools, institutes, and specialized programs extended Princeton's service to the nation in numerous ways. Despite controversies and criticisms from Princeton fundamentalists on the right and, though fewer in number, cultural modernists on the left, the university preserved its religious mission in the early twentieth century. To be sure, nineteenth-century evangelical customs and convictions no longer provided the unifying focus to the intellectual life of the university in the twentieth century. In the early twentieth century, fundamentalism conflicted with the educational values and scientific standards of the modern age. As Dean Wicks put it, the "unreality" of such "conventional religion can never be made at home among thinking people, and therefore cannot be made part of the religious life of a university, where students are trained to be impatient with unreality." Yet the expansion of the university's civic mission did not lead to the abandonment of the institution's religious heritage. In other words, the displacement of nineteenth-century evangelical interests and practices, at Princeton as well as at other colleges and universities, did not lead to the secularization or marginalization of Protestantism in the university in the twentieth century. Rather the university had adjusted its religious mission to modern educational realities and the nation's growing cultural pluralism. Liberal Protestantism not only safeguarded the sanctity of modern science but also directed the nation's future leaders to look beyond the material to transcendent, unseen realities for inspiration to help usher in the Kingdom of God in America. In the face of religious diversity and controversy dividing the university in particular and the nation in general, the administration attempted to assimilate plurality and forge unity by centralizing Princeton's program of religious education in the new chapel. Echoing a conviction that had dominated Princeton for generations, Wicks insisted in 1928 that the university's program of religious education was "free from all denominational narrowness and sectarian propaganda."[188] Consequently, Hibben refused to abandon the nation's future leaders to the despair and atheism rampant in American culture. Despite the "second disestablishment" of old-stock Protestant hegemony over the national culture in the 1920s, mainstream Protestantism remained firmly entrenched at Princeton, as at other elite colleges and universities. By adjusting the university's program of religious education to its expanded civic mission and to the nation's growing cultural pluralism, Hibben and his colleagues at Princeton sought to preserve Protestantism's role in a civic institution and ultimately to shape the Christian character of American society.

Epilogue

It has been the major thesis of this study to demonstrate that religion's nature and role at Princeton University in the nineteenth century was not abandoned but accommodated to the prevailing intellectual standards and educational values in order to conform to the expanded civic mission of the university in the early twentieth century. Although many of the particular events surrounding this transformation were unique to Princeton, the general pattern of educational, religious, and social developments represents changes that took place in private colleges and universities throughout the nation. To be sure, evangelicalism no longer provided the unifying center to the intellectual life of the university. The established convictions and customs designed to support and to transmit the evangelical faith also met their demise in the early twentieth century. The challenges created by powerful intellectual and social forces sweeping across higher education and American culture, as well as conflicts intrinsic to the earlier vision of evangelical higher education, precipitated these changes. In an attempt to resolve these tensions, the university found in liberal Protestantism a faith that was more compatible with modernity, complementary to the liberal culture curriculum, and tolerant of diversity than fundamentalism in the early twentieth century. Although the university abandoned many evangelical values and practices in the early twentieth century, traditional Protestant concerns about the religious education of college students resurfaced in new areas. The Y.M.C.A., for example, became the university's de facto campus ministry and Bible courses in the early twentieth century took on a more scientific character. Although a degree of religious diversity was tolerable, as evidenced, for example in the various perspectives represented in the Philadelphian Society in the 1920s and in the ad hoc religion courses in the 1920s, the need for stability made too much diversity and too many religious controversies a threat to the unity of the institution, its religious mission, and, finally, the Christian character of American society. Consequently, the university, like other mainline Protestant organizations threatened by disorder, assimilated diversity and resolved dissent by centralizing the program of religious education in a bureaucratic structure. In this way, Hibben and his colleagues, like their nineteenth-century predecessors, envisioned Princeton, like many other private institutions, playing an important role in helping to forge a national Christian culture despite the "second disestablishment" of the 1920s.

This new fusion of civic and religious purposes, however, proved hard to maintain in the mid-twentieth century as the nation grew increasingly more religiously pluralistic and the university attracted students and professors with more divergent religious beliefs and practices or none at all. A brief examination of the role of religion at Princeton and at other private colleges and universities after World War II reveals the persistence of the Protestant mission of American higher education in the mid-twentieth century. The difficulty that Princeton faced in attempting to preserve its Protestant mission is most evident in a religious controversy involving the university's Catholic chaplain in the mid-1950s. The final collapse of Protestant hegemony over American culture and the concurrent intellectual and social unrest of the 1960s brought an end to the Protestant establishment at Princeton and at other private colleges and universities. The study will conclude with brief examination of this 1950s religious controversy and a short review of the subsequent developments in American higher education to determine the contemporary role that religion plays at most private colleges and universities.

Although the United States and its allies were fighting communism in Korea and waging a cold war with the Soviet Union in the early 1950s, many Protestant educators believed that secularism posed a greater threat to the Christian faith and ultimately to democracy than did communism. "Secularism," according to Princeton University's professor of religion George F. Thomas, rested upon a philosophy of scientific naturalism and bred a lethal "indifference" toward religion.[1] Many academics feared that universities nourished secularism as well as anti-Christian prejudices and ethical relativism. In 1948, Sir Walter Moberly, a distinguished Oxford philosopher, made this very point in his widely read work, *The Crisis in the University.* "In the assumptions governing syllabus and academic method," he insisted, "the universities of to-day are, implicitly, if unintentionally, hostile to the Christian faith."[2] That same year, a large-scale survey of the treatment of religion in college textbooks, funded by the Edward W. Hazen Foundation and the American Council on Education, likewise concluded that Christianity faced indifference at best and hostility at worst.[3]

While many educators complained about the destructive effects of secularism, Christianity's role in American higher education was on the rise after World War II. The renewed interest in Christianity, in Protestantism in particular, was part of a larger revival sweeping across mainline Protestant churches in the late 1940s and 1950s. The neo-orthodox theological renaissance, which sought to avoid the optimism of liberalism and the dogmatism of fundamentalism, helped to fuel this revival in higher education and mainline churches.[4] Merrimon Cuninggim, in his 1947 assessment of the spiritual state of American higher education, concluded that "the time of profound interest in religion has arrived," and that "prospects for the achievement of a vitally religious atmosphere in higher education were *never brighter.*" After reorganizing its program of religious education in 1928, Cuninggim observed, Princeton was in the vanguard of a movement to strengthen the place of Protestantism in American higher education in the twentieth century.[5]

At Princeton and other American universities, extracurricular religious activities flourished after World War II. While Princeton still required freshman and sophomores, much to their chagrin, to attend Sunday morning worship services in the university chapel for at least half the academic year, voluntary religious activities had rebounded since the collapse of the Philadelphian Society in the late 1920s. The Student Christian Association (S.C.A.), which succeeded the Student-Faculty Association, orchestrated, among other activities, annual conferences, the Princeton Summer Camp, and "home precepts," where students and professors gathered weekly to deepen their "knowledge about the Christian faith."[6] Denominational campus ministries also thrived. The prosperity of the S.C.A. and denominational ministries at Princeton mirrored the vitality of similar ministries at other colleges and universities. For instance, the United Student Christian Council (U.S.C.C.), an interdenominational organization established in 1944, coordinated campus ministries throughout the nation. In 1959, the U.S.C.C. joined the Student Volunteer Movement and Interseminary Committee of the Y.M.C.A. and Y.W.C.A. to form the National Student Christian Federation (N.S.C.F.).[7]

In addition to a growing religious interest among students, the academic study of religion rose dramatically after World War II. According to one survey of 167 church-related and private institutions, undergraduate enrollment in religion courses had risen 47 percent between 1954 and 1964. Nearly two-thirds of the Ph.D. programs in religion in the United States and Canada in 1970 had been established after the Second World War.[8] Princeton University, moreover, led the movement to make the academic study of religion a part of a liberal arts education. In 1935, a Special Committee of the Faculty on Religious Education had distinguished between the practice of religion and the formal teaching of religion and concluded that the latter should be considered an important part of a genuinely liberal education. Consequently, the committee recommended that the university hire a religion professor.[9] In 1940, George F. Thomas (1899–1977) joined the faculty as a professor of religion. In 1945, the university organized an undergraduate religion department and ten years later inaugurated a graduate program.[10] While the faculty distinguished between the practice of religion and the study of religion, many saw these two objectives as complementary parts of the university's larger program of religious education. Although the religion department had "no formal connection" with the work of the Dean of the Chapel or the S.C.A., Professor Thomas explained to a colleague at Dartmouth College in 1951, "we try to cooperate in every possible way." Many religion professors across the nation echoed this sentiment.[11]

At Princeton and elsewhere in the 1950s, many educators attempted to make Protestantism the unifying center of the intellectual life of the university. "If the moral breakdown and spiritual crisis of our time are not to destroy our Western civilization, if the secularism which has dominated our education is not to rob our American democracy of its higher meaning and to stunt and dehumanize the lives of our children and their children," insisted Thomas, "we must renew our religious faith and make it the basis of all our teaching."[12] The Faculty Christian Fellowship (F.C.F.), organized in 1952, attempted to nurture a Christian faith among scholars in the same way the U.S.C.C. worked among students. The following year, the F.C.F. established an academic journal, the *Christian*

Scholar, devoted to nurturing "a full exploration of Christian faith and thought" in relation "to the whole task of higher education."[13] Thomas and other Princeton professors served in the national leadership of the F.C.F. and published regularly in its journal. To counter the perceived apathy and even animosity toward religion in higher education, the Hazen Foundation sponsored a series of studies to demonstrate how the Christian faith could be related constructively to the humanities and the social and natural sciences. Several influential Princeton professors, including Thomas and E. Harris Harbison (1907–1964), Professor of History, participated in this as well as in other ventures to make Protestantism the new center of university education.[14] Pointing to the various campus ministries, the work of the Dean of the Chapel, and the religion department, one university official in 1958 concluded that Princeton "gladly recognizes the place of the Christian faith in its long tradition and its importance for its ongoing life."[15]

The revival of interest in Protestantism in the 1950s fulfilled many of the aspirations of Princeton's early twentieth-century leaders for the university. The university enriched the Christian character of American society by nurturing the faith of students and strengthening the intellectual standing of Protestantism among scholars. Since freedom was an essential characteristic of mainstream Protestant theology, mainstream Protestantism, many educators believed, did not threaten academic freedom or the larger civic mission of the university. Although Professor Thomas, for instance, wanted to strengthen the role of Protestantism in the American university, he insisted that this change would not constitute "a return to the 'Christian university' of the Middle Ages or . . . seventeenth-century Puritanism" and bring about the end to "intellectual liberty" and lead to the imposition of "religious uniformity upon its faculty and its curriculum."[16] "While Catholicism may regard secular culture as inimical to the highest values of Christianity," the neo-orthodox theologian Reinhold Niebuhr argued, "Protestantism at its best cannot make such an estimate of our liberal-democratic culture. Protestantism believes that faith must be achieved in freedom."[17] So in the university classroom, Professor Thomas argued, for instance, that the Christian professor did not force his religious beliefs upon anyone but rather attempted "to draw out *a deeper dimension*" and to provide "*a more ultimate and inclusive interpretation*" of the subject matter.[18] Protestantism, in short, infused education with moral meaning. In more general terms, neo-orthodoxy conceived of its service to democracy as one of providing a realistic critique of liberal culture itself and common beliefs, such as the innate goodness of humanity. Because religion was considered essential to the well-being of democracy, this arrangement worked well in civic institutions, such as Princeton University, where the majority of people considered mainstream Protestantism a nonsectarian religion. As Hibben and others had earlier envisioned, Princeton, like other private colleges and universities in the 1950s, continued its attempt to shape the Christian character of American culture. Not everyone in the Princeton community, however, considered the university nonsectarian or even Christian.

"It is at least tenable," asserted Hugh Halton, O.P., "that Princeton has been trying, like Lear, to have it both ways: to reject its classical and rational Christian tradition in practice and yet at the same time to retain it in theory." Halton queried, "Are we not saying that Christianity is very sensible 'apart from its Christianity?'" From his vantage point as an outsider to both the university and the mainline Protestant establishment, Father Halton (1913–1979), the Catholic chaplain at Princeton University in the mid-1950s, saw a major incongruity between Princeton's standing as a nonsectarian Christian university and what he perceived as the "dogmatic secularism" and "abusive liberalism" prevalent in the university. According to Halton, mainstream Protestantism was serving as the established religion of the university while it was subverting the faith of students, both Catholic and Protestant, who held more traditional Christian beliefs.[19]

Halton was not the first Catholic to question the professed Christian character of one of the nation's leading private colleges or universities in the mid-twentieth century. As more Catholics made their way into the elite academic centers of American culture, many were less than satisfied with the religious character of what they found. At Harvard in the late 1940s, Leonard Feeney, a Jesuit chaplain at the St. Benedict Center, promulgated the doctrine that there is no salvation outside the church (*extra ecclesiam nulla salus*), denounced the university's curriculum as a cesspool of secularism, and encouraged students to drop out of the institution before Archbishop Richard J. Cushing was able to silence him. At Yale in 1952, William F. Buckley Jr., in his book, *God and Man at Yale*, chastised his alma mater for not being sufficiently Christian.[20] While Halton's later histrionics about communist subversives infiltrating Princeton and other elite universities eventually got him banned from the Princeton campus in the fall of 1957, his criticisms of the secularism and the Protestant establishment and the controversy they generated in 1955–1956 illustrate the difficulty that Princeton, like other universities, faced in trying to maintain the fusion of civic and religious purposes in a nation progressively more diverse in its religious and ethnic composition and more socially pluralistic in its aspirations. Once the Protestant consensus in the university was broken, mainstream Protestantism could be seen as a menace to the institution's civic mission as fundamentalism had been in the early twentieth century. Although the final demise of the mainstream Protestant establishment and the collapse of the neo-orthodox renaissance in the 1960s played decisive roles in reconfiguring the nature and role of religion at Princeton and other private colleges and universities, change was already taking place in the 1950s. The Halton controversy not only prefigured the religious diversity that would reshape the university in the 1960s but also anticipated contemporary discussions about the role of religion in higher education.

Halton began his campaign against the university in the spring of 1955 by denouncing the atheism and "metaphysical mumbo" of one of the university's more distinguished philosophy professors, Walter T. Stace (1886–1967). Before the spring semester ended, Halton launched another series of sermons criticizing the university for allowing its curriculum to fragment under the weight of academic specialization.[21] Halton was not alone in lamenting the shattering effects that the dominant empirical and pragmatic philosophies of modern higher education were having on human knowledge. Robert Maynard Hutchins, Chancellor of the University of Chicago, and his colleague, the philosopher Mortimer J. Adler, hoped to make metaphysics the integrative element in undergraduate education and consequently to provide American democracy with a common set of values. In the mid-twentieth century Catholic renaissance, Catholic educators, led by the Etienne Gilson, Christopher Dawson, and Jacques Maritain, who taught at Princeton in the early 1950s, likewise sought to overcome the same problem through the integration of neo-Thomistic philosophy and knowledge.[22] In the fall of 1955, Halton charged that the university discriminated against Catholics. He discouraged Catholic students from attending the S.C.A.'s fall conference because Catholics were excluded from addressing the gathering. Halton also complained about the absence of Catholics on the faculty of the religion department. He did not doubt "the desire" of religion department "to be objective" in their teachings about Catholicism, but since an estimated 45 percent of the courses dealt with Catholicism and 12 percent of the undergraduates were Catholic, he contended, it only seemed "to be fair" to have a Catholic with "scientific training" teaching these courses.[23]

Both Halton and the leaders of the Protestant revival in the university shared establishmentarian tendencies. Both wanted to see the university bolster the faith of students and shape the Christian character of American society. Yet Halton's religion threatened the Protestant mission of the university in two important ways. Halton's Catholicism not only conflicted with the conception of knowledge that dominated Princeton and a large part of American higher education but also threatened to undermine the university's civic purpose. The dominant conception of knowledge limited knowing and knowable reality to that which was discernable by science and discursive, empirical reason. In light of the widespread acceptance of scientific naturalism and its purely quantitative, mechanistic, and instrumental way of knowing, the supernatural Christianity that Halton espoused was distinctly antimodern. By contrast, Professor Thomas, for instance, advanced a view of religion that subscribed to the prevailing two-realm theory of truth. In the *Christian Scholar*, Thomas wrote that the "modern view" sees truth as "a product of the scientific way of thinking." "The Christian conception of truth," by contrast, "insists upon other methods to attain truth than that of the scientific method." The Christian conception, he argued, "not only employed reason and sense perception, but also intuition, imagination, and feeling... in the discovery of truth." Religious truths, Thomas insisted, "can never be demonstrated by historical, scientific, or philosophical arguments."[24] Consequently, the religious beliefs of Thomas and other Protestants in the university faced no threat from scientific criticism and, more important, posed no threat to modern science, beyond modest efforts to contain its scope and humanize its effects. Halton's supernatural theology, however, enjoyed no such luxury.

Not only did Halton's premodern theology contradict the dominant conception of knowledge in the mid-twentieth century, but it also conflicted with the prevailing conception of intellectual freedom advocated by a liberal university. Professor Harbison, in his response to Halton's criticisms of the religion department, held out the possibility that one day the university might hire a Catholic. Any such appointment, however, would come with three conditions. The person, Harbison insisted, must "ignore the compulsion to represent" Catholicism "officially," "put scholarship before controversy," and "be free enough from ecclesiastical discipline to devote himself whole-heartedly to the community of scholars and teachers that is Princeton University."[25] While many academics in the 1950s feared secularism more than communism, others viewed Catholicism as the greatest threat to academic freedom and ultimately to democracy. In the years before the Second Vatican Council, many civil libertarians and mainline Protestants, as evidenced for example in Paul Blanshard's work, *American Freedom and Catholic Power* (1949), believed that Catholicism would infiltrate educational institutions as the first step toward tyrannizing American society.[26] While communism posed a serious danger, explained Harbison in an article on academic freedom in the *Christian Scholar*, the "more immediate threat to intellectual liberty is better described as fascist."[27] To Harbison and others in the university, Halton's Catholicism represented a fascism. Although Halton said he only wanted to see one Catholic teacher in the religion department, many in the university saw Halton's plea as a disingenuous attack, as Harbison wrote in the *Daily Princetonian*, upon the "liberal ideal," under "the banner of liberalism itself."[28] According to Harbison, Halton's Catholicism represented a fascist threat not only to intellectual freedom, and thus the civic mission of the American university, but also to democracy. Halton took Harbison's criticism as an opportunity to point out the parameters of the university's commitment to pluralism. In response, Halton asked Harbison, "Are we 'liberal' or aren't we? If we can embrace committed atheists—as we have—how in the name of liberalism can we exclude 'a monk'?"[29] To mainstream Protestants, a certain amount of diversity might be acceptable but the need for order made cultural uniformity imperative. After Willard Thorp, a professor of English, asked the priest in an open letter in the *Daily Princetonian* if he had chosen the "proper" way of speaking in a university where free speech was "desirable and necessary," Halton asked Thorp if he was "suggesting that I give up the right to say the Creed and defend its doctrines in my chapel?" The university, as Halton pointed out, could tolerate Catholicism so long as it resembled the prevailing mainline Protestantism of the day.[30]

In January 1956, Halton launched a new campaign in which he attacked the "straightforward communism" of Princeton, Harvard, and Columbia and other universities. After suffering through more than a year of Halton's unbridled attacks, the trustees decided to withdraw the "courtesies and privileges" it extended to the Catholic chaplain. While Halton's "latterday McCartheyism," as one student described it, gained him brief national fame, his red-baiting innuendos obscured his initial criticisms of the Protestant establishment of Princeton.[31] Moreover, his latter criticisms did little to dissuade his critics of their suspicions about the priest's authoritarian and right-wing leanings. In fact, they made it easy for those inside the university to dismiss his initial criticism.

Nevertheless, the early phase of the Halton controversy reveals the mainline

Protestant character of the university and Protestantism's intimate connection with the university's public mission. To be sure, Protestants were no longer the only ones in this picture. An increase in the number of Catholics and Jews on the faculty and in the student body, and non-Protestant campus ministries, such as the Aquinas Institute and the Hillel Foundation, founded after World War II, reveal that Princeton, at least demographically, was not quite as exclusively Protestant as it had been in the early twentieth century. In this respect, the religious heterogeneity of Princeton in the 1950s foreshadowed the diversity that would help to reshape the role of religion in the university in the 1960s.

Yet Protestants still predominated. One non-Catholic student, the editor of the *Daily Princetonian*, made this observation during the Halton controversy. After reviewing the denominational affiliations of the religion professors, the theological orientation of the chapel program, and the activities of the S.C.A., he concluded that the evidence suggested that "Princeton is strongly promoting Protestantism over all other major religions."[32] This impertinent undergraduate had a point. The Dean of the Chapel and his assistant were Protestants. The S.C.A. was dominated by Protestants and their interests. Beside the work of scholars like Thomas and Harbison, the undergraduate and graduate programs in religion looked strikingly similar to that of a mainline Protestant seminary's curriculum.[33] The social exclusivity and ethnic homogeneity of the student body in the 1950s, moreover, supported the Protestant hegemony over the university as they had in the early twentieth century.[34] And when some within the university, like George W. Elderkin, Professor Emeritus of Art and Archeology, responded to Halton's initial criticisms of Princeton with vicious nativist attacks upon Catholicism, Princeton's reputation as an exclusively Protestant institution was only further strengthened.[35] Despite the declarations of the university's "nonsectarianism" and the growing diversity evident in the university, Protestantism remained the established religion of Princeton, like many other private colleges and universities, in the 1950s.

A 1970 *Princeton Alumni Weekly* article entitled, "Is God Alive?" described Father Halton as "a noisy chaplain in a quiet time." The chaplains at Princeton in the 1960s, the author suggested, were quiet in a noisy time. When Halton hounded Princeton, Ernest Gordon, Dean of the Chapel, explained, "'The WASP tradition was still strong here.'" According to Gordon, the "'WASPy club capitalism'" of Princeton had fallen prey to the diversification of the student body and the emergence of the civil rights movement in the 1960s.[36] Gordon correctly identified two forces that had helped to undermine the waning influence of the Protestant establishment over American society and the elite, culture-shaping centers of American higher education, like Princeton, that were closely associated with it. Religious pluralism, which had been a reality since the first Puritans arrived on the American shores in the seventeenth century, had become a more recognized cultural reality after World War II. At the same time, the internal restructuring of American religion accelerated the declining importance of Protestantism in American culture. The proliferation of socially conservative and liberal special purpose groups, which cut across previously hardened denominational lines, weakened mainstream Protestant churches in the late 1950s and 1960s.[37] Membership in the United Presbyterian Church in the U.S.A. between 1965 and 1982, for example, dropped almost 29 percent.[38] If the united Protestant opposition to Al Smith in 1928 signaled mainstream Protestantism's continued vitality in the 1920s despite the "second disestablishment," the election of John F. Kennedy as president symbolized its final demise in American public life.

While mainline Protestants, or at least their leaders, and ecumenical organizations, such as the National Council of Churches, joined the African American-led civil rights movement in the 1950s, many college students in the late 1950s and early 1960s saw the Protestant establishment as part of the nation's problem with prejudice, not part of its solution. Peter Berger, in a 1961 study commissioned by the N.S.C.F., for instance, harshly criticized the Protestant establishment for abandoning its prophetic mission to seek justice in a day of unprecedented social upheaval in order to enjoy the largesse of its accumulated social prestige and economic wealth.[39] The war in Vietnam and increased domestic conflicts over racial discrimination in the mid- and late 1960s only increased students' hostility toward the Protestant establishment.

At the same time that religious pluralism and the social upheavals of the 1960s were undermining the waning cultural hegemony of the mainline Protestant establishment at large, the collapse of the neo-orthodox theological movement at the hands of the self-styled secular theologians marked the end of mainline Protestants' influence within the intellectual life of the nation's leading private colleges and universities. The neo-orthodox theologians had failed to challenge the dominant scientific conception of knowledge and had continued to uphold the strict separation of the realm of faith and the realm of knowledge. Consequently, theology remained firmly grounded in the epiphenomena, or as Paul Tillich put it, "the God above God."[40] By contrast, the secular theologians adopted the prevailing positivist conception of knowledge, identified it as the only realm of truth, and thus obliterated any distinction between faith and knowledge, religion and science, or the church and the world. Harvey Cox, in his best-selling work *The Secular City* (1965), which, ironically, was written originally for the N.S.C.F., said it a "mistake" for Christians to combat the allegedly secular character of the university with a leavening influence of Protestantism. The real problem with the university, he contended, was the Protestant church. The church stood at odds with the university, "the focal point of social change," because it was still acting as an "'established' church," which had "at least as much of a vested interest in the present structure of the American economy and society as the medieval church had in feudalism." Rather than opposing the secularization of the university, Cox encouraged Christians to promote it in order to help break down the barriers of divisiveness in American society. Although neo-orthodoxy remained popular in some church-related colleges and seminaries, secular theology's brief rage in academic circles had a devastating impact on Protestant efforts to influence the intellectual life of the nation's elite academic institution.[41]

The final demise of the Protestant establishment in American culture and the intellectual collapse of neo-orthodoxy disestablished Protestantism in the nation's private colleges and universities in the 1960s. The most obvious result produced by the confluence of these grand social and intellectual developments was an admission policy that better reflected the civic mission of these institutions. Princeton, Yale, Williams, and other institutions were no longer the exclusive training grounds for white, male Protestants. The growth in diversity at these leading educational institutions coincided with and was aided by the mass educational movement begun after World War II. During this period of dramatic growth, many of the nation's leading private colleges and universities dismantled the formal and informal barriers that had excluded all but white males with Protestant backgrounds to enroll at their institutions. Nowhere were these changes more evident than at Princeton. Although the university began to admit African American students under the V-12 program during World War II, less than a dozen enrolled between 1950 and 1961. In the early 1960s, however, Princeton began to recruit African American students in the same way it sought to attract students from private boarding schools. The university also began to admit women into its undergraduate program in the fall of 1969. The demise of the Protestant establishment also brought an end to the ethno-religious homogeneity of Princeton and other elite institutions. A 1970 survey of the religious backgrounds of freshmen, for example, reveals that Episcopalians, typically one-third of the students between 1920 and 1950, had dropped to 10 percent. Presbyterians likewise fell to 9.6 percent. By contrast, Catholics had leaped to 18 percent and Jews grew to 13.5 percent of the entering class. Students with no religious affiliation, 28 percent, constituted the single largest group. These changes in the composition of the student body led to a dramatic decline in membership in the elite eating clubs and, consequently, the clubs' dominance over social life. Princeton also took steps to accommodate the religious convictions of non-Christians. In 1971, Princeton opened a kosher kitchen in Stevenson Hall, located on Prospect Street along with the other eating clubs.[42]

In light of the declining influence of mainstream Protestantism over the affairs of the nation, the flaccidity of neo-orthodoxy in intellectual circles, and the growing religious diversity inside American universities, the remaining symbols of Protestant hegemony came tumbling down. With fewer Protestants on campus, many sacrosanct policies and more informal customs appeared to privilege Protestantism at the expense of non-Protestants and to conflict with the public purposes of the educational institution. In the spring of 1958 at Harvard, for example, many faculty and students complained about the policy that permitted only Christians to use Memorial Chapel for worship services. When confronted with the charge of religious discrimination, the Harvard Corporation abolished the policy. The most enduring and prominent symbol of the Protestant establishment in the nation's leading private institutions, mandatory chapel, met its end in the 1960s. Princeton, for instance, abolished obligatory attendance at Sunday morning worship services for sophomores in 1960 and, finally, for freshmen in 1964.[43]

The demise of Protestant hegemony had an equally momentous impact on the religion departments at the nation's colleges and universities. Because of the "confused state of theology" following the demise of the neo-orthodox revival and the absence of "a tough-minded and aggressive" theological alternative that could "transform (or be intended to transform) cultural attitudes and social institutions" in America, observed Princeton University's John F. Wilson in 1968, the academic study of religion entered a period of instability in the 1960s.[44] Religion departments often labored under the suspicion that they were engaged in a form of proselytism because of their largely Protestant orientation. At its establishment in 1965, the National Endowment for the Humanities, for instance, did not designate religion as one of the disciplines it would fund.[45]

Two developments in the 1960s helped to reverse the academic study of religion's low standing in American higher education. When the U.S. Supreme Court's 1963 decision *Abington School District v. Schempp* outlawed the mandatory practice of religion in public schools, which in this particular case concerned state-sponsored devotional Bible readings, it also cleared the path for the academic study of religion in public educational institutions, especially state universities. At the same time, a methodological revolution was taking place within the field itself, a revolution which did not come without controversy. Richard Schlatter, in a forward to Clyde A. Holbrook's *Religion, A Humanistic Field* (1963), which was sponsored by Princeton University's Council of the Humanities and the Ford Foundation, noted, "A considerable body of American scholars are of the opinion that religious studies are no part of the humanities, no part of the liberal arts, not an objective scholarly discipline."[46] Princeton's John F. Wilson took issue not with Schlatter's criticism but with Holbrook's conventional justification for incorporating the academic study of religion in the university. Rather than contending, as religion professors at Princeton and elsewhere had argued throughout the 1950s, that religion provided a "liberalizing" influence in a liberal arts education, Wilson recommended that scholars adopt a "phenomenological approach" to the study of religion. This approach would allow the field to share the "empirical mood" of American scholarship, and more important, would place the discipline on a scientific foundation.[47] Although scholars debated the merits of traditional methods and the allegedly theologically neutral character of the social scientific approach, the newer methods quickly eclipsed the older one in university circles. Signs of this change were already apparent in the 1960s. In 1964 the National Association of Biblical Instructors, founded in 1909 to improve religious instruction in church and academic institutions, was reorganized as the American Academy of Religion (A.A.R.) in order to advance the organization's professional stature and to reflect the growing popularity of the social scientific study of the discipline.[48] Meanwhile, neo-orthodox efforts to relate the Protestant faith to scholarship faded, as evidenced in the collapse of the F.C.F.'s *Christian Scholar* in 1967. Although traditional concerns continued to dominate many mainline seminaries, Protestant hegemony over the religion departments in most of the nation's colleges and universities met its end in the 1960s.

By contrast, Protestant campus ministries at many of the nation's leading private colleges and universities survived the tumultuous 1960s—barely. The Presbyterian campus ministry at Princeton, for example, involved more than a hundred students in 1955. Fifteen years later, that number dropped to twenty.[49] The decline of campus ministries was in part a result of campuses' growing religious pluralism; there were simply fewer Protestants on campus to join these groups. A more important reason was the fact that many students considered them accomplices of the conservative social forces aiding and abetting imperialism at home and abroad. As political radicalism and the counterculture movements swept through universities in the forms of the Free Speech movement, drug culture, and sexual revolutions, denominational ministries and ecumenical organizations, such as United Christian Movement (U.C.M.), which had been reorganized from the N.S.C.F. in 1966, turned toward political action. If they maintained the traditional perspectives and practices of their predecessors, many campus ministers found themselves risking social isolation, or, even worse, identification with the source of the nation's problems. In retrospect, many campus ministers seemed to do little more than follow the protesting waves of students across campus. "There's a revival going on," said the Assistant Dean of the Chapel at Princeton University in 1970. "The task of the campus minister is to find out where it's happening and to help it along."[50] The demise of the U.C.M. in 1969 illustrated the irrelevance of mainline campus ministries. Ecumenical organizations at local campuses met similar fates. The S.C.A. at Princeton, for instance, disbanded in 1967 after a year of debate over whether an organization devoted to "social service" but straddled with "titular Christianity" could be "filled with people of other faiths." Consequently, the S.C.A. "withered away," as Dean Gordon described it, in order "to offer more inviting forms of participation to those not classified as being within the 'C' of the S.C.A."[51] While evangelical para-church organizations, such as Inter-Varsity Christian Fellowship and Campus Crusade for Christ, began to grow on many campuses, denominational ministries lost contact with most students. In the opinion of the campus ministers at the University of Wisconsin, a report by two sociologists concluded in 1969, "the traditional notion of a student religious group is as archaic as it is ineffectual."[52] While Protestant ministries survived the turbulent 1960s, they found themselves competing with evangelical and other religious groups for students.[53]

Mainline Protestant and many Catholic church-related institutions of higher education more or less followed the same path as private colleges and universities in the 1960s.[54] By contrast, at other Catholic colleges, and at many fundamentalist and evangelical institutions, as well as at colleges founded by ethnic Protestant traditions, religion continues to attempt to provide, albeit in various ways and to varying degrees, a unifying center to the intellectual and social life of the community.[55] Today, however, many of these institutions struggle to define and promote their civic mission in a meaningful way. They also face a dizzying array of challenges, including a culture of mediocrity that undermines excellence in teaching and scholarship, an inability to make the institutions' professed theological commitments relevant to modern and postmodern thought or a growing estrangement from those commitments, an ethnocentrism and a nepotism that subverts creativity and vision, a dwindling membership in their founding denominations and a corresponding decline in denominational commitments to support higher education, an elevation of technique over liberal learning, and external and internal economic forces and social pressures that reduce an undergraduate education to a commodity.

The triumph of the civic mission at private colleges and universities, such as Princeton in the 1960s, did not result in the complete secularization of higher education as many Protestant educators in the late nineteenth century predicted (and as many conventional historians describe and social critics depict). During the turbulent 1960s, the Whiggish conception of religion's role in higher education gave way, more by default than by design, to the Jeffersonian model, which encouraged the practice of religion as an extracurricular activity. At private colleges and universities and state institutions, the Jeffersonian model provided a workable solution; it preserved a place for religion in an educational institution devoted to serving a civic mission and a national audience. While religion, Protestant or otherwise, no longer provides the unifying center to undergraduate education or, more broadly, the intellectual life of the university, voluntary religious activities and organizations, have thrived in open-market competition for students' attention since the 1960s. Evangelical para-church ministries have done especially well in this new situation. At Princeton in the fall of 1995, for instance, twenty-one different religious organizations, such as the Presbyterian Westminster Foundation, Campus Crusade for Christ, Muslim Students Association, Baha'i Club, and the Center for Jewish Life, hold weekly meditation, prayer, or worship services and sponsor a variety of other formal and informal activities.[56] The religious diversity of the modern university reflects the cultural and intellectual plurality of American culture.

It is tempting to conclude historical examinations by resolving all historical conflicts and tensions, but questions about the role of religion in American higher education persist. In the early twentieth century, the American university became, what Clark Kerr would later call, a "multiversity," serving a variety of educational functions and social purposes.[57] The structural diversity of private and state institutions, as well as the nation's growing religious diversity, portend against seeing any religious tradition providing a unifying center to the entire educational endeavor.[58] Given the reality of the nation's religious pluralism and the civic mission of the university, some educators have suggested that, in addition to its role in the private lives of students and faculty, religion might enrich the academic programs and scholarship of the university in new ways. Some scholars, typically evangelicals in the reformed tradition, mainline Protestants, and Catholics, have joined postmodernists in raising doubts about the epistemological neutrality of modernity and the scientific models of scholarship that typically prevail in the American university. More important, scholars in these different religious traditions have offered a variety of ways in which religion might make a more substantial contribution to the diverse intellectual life of the university and play a more constructive role in higher education's civic mission to American democracy.[59] If the history of Protestantism in American higher education in the late nineteenth and early twentieth centuries can offer any wisdom to these contemporary discussions, they ought to seek working, not definite, solutions that, on the one hand, do not exclude religion from the intellectual tasks of the academy and, on the other, do not seek hegemony but genuinely respect religious pluralism.

Notes

References in the notes employ the following abbreviations:

BRPR	*Biblical Repertory and Princeton Review*
BW	*Biblical World*
DP	*Daily Princetonian*
ER	*Educational Review*
NLM	*Nassau Literary Magazine*
NPR	*New Princeton Review*
NYT	*New York Times*
PAW	*Princeton Alumni Weekly*
Pres	*Presbyterian*
PB	*Presbyterian Banner*
PresRev	*Presbyterian Review*
PRR	*Presbyterian and Reformed Review*
PP	*Princeton Press*
Pr	*Princetonian*
PRev	*Princeton Review*
PTR	*Princeton Theological Review*
RE	*Religious Education*

Introduction

1. "Correspondence: New York," *Pr*, 13 Feb. 1886, 6; "Religion in Colleges," *NYT*, 4 Feb. 1886, 2; "Religion in College," *New-York Daily Tribune*, 4 Feb. 1886, 7.

2. James McCosh, *Religion in a College: What Place It Should Have. Being an Examination of President Eliot's Paper, Read Before the Nineteenth Century Club, in New York, Feb., 3, 1886* (New York: A.C. Armstrong and Son, 1886), 5, 18; idem, "The Place of Religion in College," in *Minutes and Proceedings of the Third General Council of the Alliance of the Reformed Churches Holding the Presbyterian System* (Belfast: Alliance of Reformed Churches, 1884), 469, emphasis added; *Catalogue of the College of New Jersey, Year 1885–86* (Princeton: Princeton Press, 1885), 75–85, 151–52.

3. Charles W. Eliot, "What Place Should Religion Have in a College?" 2, 9, emphasis added, 1886, Charles W. Eliot Papers, UA I 5.150, Box 334, Folder 36. Courtesy of the Harvard University Archives.

4. "An Alumnus," "The Princeton Problem," *Pres*, 8 Apr. 1915, 9, emphasis added.

5. Princeton University, Minutes of the Trustees of Princeton University (hereafter TM), 12 Feb. 1885, Seeley G. Mudd Manuscript Library, Princeton University. Published with

permission of Princeton University Library; Richard Hofstadter, "The Revolution in Higher Education," in *Paths of American Thought*, ed. Arthur M. Schlesinger Jr. and Morton White (Boston: Houghton Mifflin, 1963), 269–90; United States Bureau of the Census, *Historical Statistics of the United States: Colonial Times to 1957* (Washington, D.C.: Bureau of the Census, 1960), 7, 210–12; *Reports on the Course of Instruction in Yale College; By a Committee of the Corporation, and the Academic Faculty* (New Haven: Printed by Hezekiah Howe, 1828); John Higham, "The Matrix of Specialization," in *The Organization of Knowledge in America, 1860–1920*, ed. Alexandra Oleson and John Voss (Baltimore: Johns Hopkins University Press, 1979), 3–18, quote on 10.

In Richard Hofstadter's evaluation of antebellum collegiate education, the Yale Report best exemplifies the low state of education in the antebellum period. Richard Hofstadter and Walter P. Metzger, *The Development of Academic Freedom in the United States* (New York: Columbia University Press, 1955), 279. For similar and derivative evaluations of the Yale Report and antebellum collegiate education, see Frederick Rudolph, *The American College and University: A History* (New York: Vintage, 1962), 110–35; idem, *Curriculum: A History of the American Undergraduate Course of Study since 1636* (San Francisco: Jossey-Bass, 1977), 54–98. Recent scholarship has revised Hofstadter's appraisal of both the Yale Report and antebellum higher education. See James McLachlan, "The American College in the Nineteenth Century: Toward a Reappraisal," *Teachers College Record* 80 (1978): 304–305; Natalie A. Naylor, "The Ante-Bellum College Movement: A Reappraisal of Tewksbury's Founding of American Colleges and Universities," *History of Education Quarterly* 13 (1973): 261–62; David B. Potts, "American Colleges in the Nineteenth Century: From Localism to Denominationalism," *History of Education Quarterly* 11 (1971): 366; Douglas Sloan, "Harmony, Chaos, and Consensus: The American College Curriculum," *Teachers College Record* 73 (1971): 224–26; Wilson Smith, "Apologia pro Alma Matre: The College as Community in Ante-Bellum America," in *The Hofstadter Aegis: A Memorial*, ed. Stanley Elkins and Eric McKitrick (New York: Knopf, 1974), 125–53; Melvin I. Urofsky, "Reform and Response: The Yale Report of 1828," *History of Education Quarterly* 5 (1965): 53–67.

On the rise of academic specialization and professionalization and their impact on postbellum higher education, see Laurence R. Veysey, *The Emergence of the American University* (Chicago: University of Chicago Press, 1965), 1–10; idem, "Higher Education as a Profession: Changes and Continuities," and Daniel Kevles, "American Science," in *The Professions in American History*, ed. Nathan O. Hatch (Notre Dame: University of Notre Dame Press, 1988), 15–32, 107–125; Burton J. Bledstein, *The Culture of Professionalism: The Middle Class and the Development of Higher Education in America* (New York: Norton, 1976), 80–128, 132, 240; Conrad Cherry, "Boundaries and Frontiers for the Study of Religion: The Heritage of the Age of the University," *Journal of the American Academy of Religion* 57 (1990): 807–27; idem, "The Study of Religion and the Rise of the American University," in *Religious Studies, Theological Studies and the University-Divinity School*, ed. Joseph Mitsuo Kitagawa (Atlanta: Scholars Press, 1992), 115–35; idem, *Hurrying Toward Zion: Universities, Divinity Schools, and American Protestantism* (Bloomington: Indiana University Press, 1995); Robert L. Church, "Economists as Experts: The Rise of an Academic Profession in the United States, 1870–1920," in *The University in Society*, ed. Lawrence Stone, 2 vols. (Princeton: Princeton University Press, 1972), 2:571–609; Mary O. Furner, *Advocacy and Objectivity: A Crisis in the Professionalization of American Social Science, 1865–1905* (Lexington: University Press of Kentucky, 1975); Dorothy Ross, "The Development of the Social Sciences," Daniel Kevles, "The Physics, Mathematics, and Chemistry Communities: A Comparative Analysis," and Hugh Hawkins, "University Identity: The Teaching and Research Functions," in *Organization of Knowledge*, 107–38, 139–72, 285–308.

6. Fritz K. Ringer, "The German Academic Community," in *Organization of Knowledge*, 409–29; Hofstadter and Metzger, *Development of Academic Freedom*, 369–412; Veysey, *Emergence of University*, 57–179, 385–418; idem, "Higher Education as a Profession," 21–27; idem, "Stability and Experiment in the American Undergraduate Curriculum," in *Content and Context: Essays on College Education*, ed. Carl Kaysen (New York: McGraw-Hill, 1973), 5–6; Rudolph, *College and University*, 241–308, 329–72, 392–439; idem, *Curriculum*, 99–244. An estimated 9,000 Americans studied in Germany between 1820 and 1920. Jungen Herbst, *The German Historical School in American Scholarship: A Study in the Transfer of Culture* (Port Washington, N.Y.: Kennikat, 1965), 1, n.1.

7. Hofstadter, "Revolution in Higher Education," 269–76, 279–90; Hofstadter and Metzger, *Development of Academic Freedom*, 277–319, 367–412; Veysey, *Emergence of the American University*, esp. 11, 15–16, 21–56, 80, 112, 203–204, 280–81, 311, 327–77; Rudolph, *College and University*, esp. 297–99, 432–33, 419–20; idem, *Curriculum*, esp. 106–109, 156–57, 174, 177, 203–204, 222–23; Earl H. Brill, "Religion and the Rise of the University: A Study of the Secularization of American Higher Education, 1870–1910," (Ph.D. diss., American University, 1969); Mark A. Noll, "Christian Colleges, Christian Worldviews, and an Invitation to Research," introduction to *The Christian College: A History of Protestant Higher Education in America*, by William C. Ringenberg (Grand Rapids: Christian University Press and Eerdmans, 1984), 24–32; Ringenberg, *Christian College*, 97–106; George M. Marsden, "The Soul of the American University: A Historical Overview," in *The Secularization of the Academy*, ed. George M. Marsden and Bradley J. Longfield (New York: Oxford University Press, 1992), 13–21; idem, *The Soul of the American University: From Protestant Establishment to Established Nonbelief* (New York: Oxford University Press, 1994), 101–12, 134–49; Warren A. Nord, *Religion and American Education: Rethinking a National Dilemma* (Chapel Hill: University of North Carolina Press, 1995), 63–86, 96–97.

8. John Dewey, "From Absolutism to Experimentalism," in *Contemporary American Philosophy*, ed. George P. Adams and William P. Montague, 2 vols. (New York: Macmillan, 1930), 2:19, quoted in Martin E. Marty, *Modern American Religion*, Vol. 1, *The Irony of It All, 1893–1919* (Chicago: University of Chicago Press, 1986), 87.

9. James Leuba, *The Belief in God and Immorality: A Psychological, Anthropological and Statistical Study* (Chicago, 1921 [1916]), 252–53, as cited in Marsden, *Soul of the University*, 293.

On the spiritual crisis in the Gilded Age, see Paul Carter, *The Spiritual Crisis of the Gilded Age* (Dekalb: Northern Illinois University Press, 1971); D. H. Meyer, "American Intellectuals and the Victorian Crisis of Faith," *American Quarterly* 27 (1975): 585–603; Arthur M. Schlesinger Sr., "A Critical Period in American Religion, 1875–1900," *Proceedings of the Massachusetts Historical Society* 64 (1932): 523–47; James Turner, *Without God, Without Creed: The Origins of Unbelief in America* (Baltimore: Johns Hopkins University Press, 1985).

On the critical intellectual developments that fostered this crisis in the late nineteenth and early twentieth centuries, see Charles W. Cashdollar, *The Transformation of Theology, 1830–1890: Positivism and Protestant Thought in Britain and America* (Princeton: Princeton University Press, 1989); Stanley Coben, *Rebellion against Victorianism: The Impetus for Cultural Change in 1920s America* (New York: Oxford University Press, 1991); William R. Hutchison, *The Modernist Impulse in American Protestantism* (Cambridge: Harvard University Press, 1976; rprt., New York: Oxford

University Press, 1982); T. J. Jackson Lears, *No Place of Grace: Antimodernism and the Transformation of American Culture, 1880–1920* (Chicago: University of Chicago Press, 1983); Bradley J. Longfield, *The Presbyterian Controversy: Fundamentalists, Modernists, and Moderates* (New York: Oxford University Press, 1991); George M. Marsden, "The Collapse of American Evangelical Academia," in *Faith and Rationality: Reason and Belief in God,* ed. Alvin Plantinga and Nicholas Wolterstorff (Notre Dame: University of Notre Dame Press, 1983), 219–64; idem, *Fundamentalism and American Culture: The Shaping of Twentieth-Century Evangelicalism, 1870–1925* (New York: Oxford University Press, 1980); Henry F. May, *The End of American Innocence: A Study of the First Years of Our Own Time, 1912–1917* (New York: Knopf, 1959; rprt., Chicago: Quadrangle Books, 1964); James R. Moore, *Post-Darwinian Controversies: A Study of the Protestant Struggle to Come to Terms with Darwin in Great Britain and America, 1870–1900* (Cambridge: Cambridge University Press, 1979); Lewis Perry, *Intellectual Life in America: A History* (New York: Franklin Watts, 1984); Jon H. Roberts, *Darwinism and the Divine in America: Protestant Intellectuals and Organic Evolution, 1859–1900* (Madison: University of Wisconsin Press, 1988); Gary Scott Smith, *The Seeds of Secularization: Calvinism, Culture, and Pluralism in America, 1870–1915* (Grand Rapids: Christian University Press, 1985).

10. Noll, introduction to *Christian College,* 29. See also ibid., 24–32; Hofstadter, "Revolution in Higher Education," 27–79; Hofstadter and Metzger, *Development of Academic Freedom,* 320–66; Veysey, *Emergence of the American University,* 40–50, 128, 137–38, 203–204; Rudolph, *College and University,* 410–20, 345–48; idem, *Curriculum,* 139, 156–57, 174, 177; Brill, "Religion and the Rise of the University"; Ringenberg, *Christian College,* 114–40; Marsden, "Soul of the American University," 21–25; idem, *Soul of the University,* 113–33, 150–256, 267–356; Nord, *Religion and American Education,* 63–86, 96–97.

11. TM, 13 Jan. 1927; "Philadelphian Society, with Revised Secretarial Force, Announces Vigorous Plans for Year of Varied Activity," *DP,* 29 Sept., 1924, 1, 3–4; Princeton University, *Report of the President for the Year Ending July 31, 1925* (Princeton: Princeton University Press, 1925), 50–52; Edwin G. Conklin, *The Direction of Human Evolution* (New York: Scribner, 1921); idem, "Biology and Religion: Must We Continue the Age-Old Conflict?" *PAW,* 18 Mar. 1925, 548–49, 556.

12. James Bryce, *The American Commonwealth,* 3 vols. (London: Macmillan, 1888), 3:474. The terms Jeffersonian and Whig are used in a typological as opposed to a strictly historical sense. Historically, the Jeffersonians were Democratic-Republicans in the late eighteenth and early nineteenth centuries whose political opponents were the Federalists. In the subsequent generation of American politics the Democratic-Republican party became the Democratic party and opposed the Whig party. In the mid-nineteenth century, Whiggery was not only a political party but also a larger cultural tradition with distinctive political and social ideas. Robert Kelley, *The Cultural Pattern in American Politics: The First Century* (New York: Knopf, 1979); Daniel Walker Howe, *The Political Culture of the American Whigs* (Chicago: University of Chicago Press, 1979); idem, "The Evangelical Movement and Political Culture in the North during the Second Party System," *Journal of American History* 77 (1991): 1216–39.

On the Whiggish conception of higher education and the moral philosophy courses, see Henry F. May, *The Enlightenment in America* (New York: Oxford University Press, 1976), 307–62; D. G. Hart, "American Learning and the Problem of Religious Studies," in *Secularization of the Academy,* 198–200; Daniel Walker Howe, *The Unitarian Conscience: Harvard Moral Philosophy, 1805–1861* (Cambridge: Harvard University Press,

1970; rprt., Middletown, Conn.: Wesleyan University Press, 1988); D. H. Meyer, *The Instructed Conscience: The Shaping of the American National Ethic* (Philadelphia: University of Pennsylvania Press, 1972); George P. Schmidt, *The Old Time College President* (New York: Columbia University Press, 1930; rprt., New York: AMS Press, 1970), 108–45; Douglas Sloan, "The Teaching of Ethics in American Undergraduate Curriculum, 1876–1976," in *Ethics Teaching in Higher Education*, ed. Sissela Bok and Daniel Callahan (New York: Plenum, 1980), 1–9; Wilson Smith, *Professors and Public Ethics: Studies of Northern Moral Philosophers before the Civil War* (Ithaca: Cornell University Press, 1956); Louise L. Stevenson, *Scholarly Means to Evangelical Ends: The New Haven Scholars and the Transformation of Higher Learning in America, 1830–1890* (Baltimore: Johns Hopkins University Press, 1986), 5–6, 114–16; Marsden, *Soul of the University*, 79–100; idem, "Soul of the American University," 25–26.

Standard treatments overlook not only the critical role that Bible and evidences of Christianity courses, mandatory chapel services, and voluntary religious activities played within nineteenth-century higher education but also the theological framework in which the curriculum rested. The secular disciplines taught students those truths derived from natural revelation and learned by human reason while the Bible and other components of the religious education program taught those truths provided by special revelation. In fact, the old-time "discipline and piety" philosophy of higher education might be better described as a theology of higher education.

13. On the "second disestablishment," see Robert T. Handy, *Undermined Establishment: Church-State Relations in America, 1880–1920* (Princeton: Princeton University Press, 1991); idem, *A Christian America: Protestant Hopes and Historical Realities*, rev. ed. (New York: Oxford University Press, 1984), 24–56; Martin E. Marty, *Modern American Religion*, Vol. 2, *The Noise of Conflict, 1919–1941* (Chicago: University of Chicago Press, 1991). The term "mainstream" and its synonyms are used in a descriptive, not normative, sense. For a discussion of the descriptive use of this term, see William R. Hutchison, "Preface: From Protestant to Pluralist America," *Between the Times: The Travail of the Protestant Establishment in America, 1900–1960*, ed. William R. Hutchison (Cambridge: Cambridge University Press, 1989), x–xi.

14. On cultural pluralism and also the "disestablishment" of mainstream Protestantism in higher education, see Dorothy C. Bass, "Ministry on the Margin: Protestants and Education," in *Between the Times*, 48–71; Bradley J. Longfield, "'For God, for Country, and for Yale,': Yale, Religion, and Higher Education," and Robert Wood Lynn, "'The Survival of Recognizably Protestant College': Reflections on Old-Line Protestantism, 1950–1990," in *Secularization of the Academy*, 146–69, 170–94; Marsden, *Soul of the University*, 117–35, 252, 256–58, 357–428; Douglas Sloan, *Faith and Knowledge: Mainstream Protestantism and American Higher Education* (Louisville: Westminster John Knox Press, 1994).

15. Alexander Leitch, *A Princeton Companion* (Princeton: Princeton University Press, 1978), 222–23, 262–66, 436, 458; Princeton University, *General Catalogue, 1746–1906* (Princeton: Published by the Graduate Council, 1930). The Congregationalists, Disciples of Christ, Episcopalians, Presbyterians, United Lutherans, and the white divisions of the Baptists and Methodists, which according to Hutchison dominated the Federal Council of Churches, comprised the mainline Protestant establishment. William R. Hutchison, "Protestantism as Establishment," in *Between the Times*, 6–11.

16. The most comprehensive institutional history ends its survey at the sesquicentennial celebration of 1896. Thomas Jefferson Wertenbaker, *Princeton, 1746–1896* (Princeton: Princeton University Press, 1946). See also Varnum Lansing Collins, *Princeton* (New York:

Oxford University Press, 1914); Charles G. Osgood, *Lights in Nassau Hall* (Princeton: Princeton University Press, 1951); Willard Thorp, Minor Myers Jr., and Jeremiah Stanton Finch, *The Princeton Graduate School: A History* (Princeton: Princeton University Press, 1978). Several other studies examine Princeton in part of the period under consideration. See L. Bruce Leslie, *Gentleman and Scholars: College and Community in the "Age of the University," 1865–1917* (State College: Penn State University Press, 1992); Marcia Graham Synnott, *The Half-Opened Door: Discrimination and Admissions at Harvard, Yale, and Princeton, 1900–1970* (Westport, Conn.: Greenwood Press, 1979); Howard B. Maxwell, "The Formative Years of the University Alumni Movement as Illustrated by Studies of the University of Michigan, Columbia, Princeton, and Yale Universities, 1854–1918," (Ph.D. diss., University of Michigan, 1965).

James McCosh and Woodrow Wilson have been the subject of two outstanding biographies, J. David Hoeveler Jr., *James McCosh and the Scottish Intellectual Tradition: From Glasgow to Princeton* (Princeton: Princeton University Press, 1981), and John M. Mulder, *Woodrow Wilson: The Years of Preparation* (Princeton: Princeton University Press, 1978). On Wilson, see also Henry W. Bragdon, *Woodrow Wilson: The Academic Years* (Cambridge: Belknap Press of Harvard University Press, 1967); August Heckscher, *Woodrow Wilson: A Biography* (New York: Scribner, 1991); Arthur S. Link, *Wilson: The Road to the White House* (Princeton: Princeton University Press, 1947).

Chapter 1

1. James McCosh, "The Place of Religion in College," in *Minutes and Proceedings of the Third General Council of the Alliance of the Reformed Churches Holding the Presbyterian System, Belfast, 1884* (Belfast: Alliance of Reformed Churches, 1884), 468–70.

2. Jonathan Dickinson to Theophilus Howell, 30 Jan. 1746/7, General Manuscripts (Miscellaneous), Box DI-DN, Manuscript Division, Rare Books and Special Collections, Princeton University Library. Published with permission of Princeton University Library.

3. Charles W. Eliot, "What Place Should Religion Have in a College?" 1, 3–4, Eliot Papers.

4. Ibid., 5–8.

5. Ibid., 9–10, 11, 13–14. Concerning ethics courses, Eliot said, "Nobody has as yet shown how to teach morality effectively without religion. There is as yet no such thing as a science of ethics. What the future may have in store in the way of systematic ethical teaching we do not know; but at present moral theories cannot be separated in practice from religious doctrines, and cannot be effectively used as guides, safeguards, and incentives without appeal to religious motives and affections." Ibid., 14.

6. James McCosh, *Religion in a College: What Place It Should Have. Being an Examination of President Eliot's Paper, Read Before the Nineteenth Century Club, in New York, Feb., 3, 1886* (New York: A.C. Armstrong and Son, 1886), 5. McCosh wanted to have their addresses published together but Eliot declined. Ibid., preface.

7. Ibid., 18, 9.

8. Ibid., 10–12.

9. Ibid., 14–17, 19–20.

10. Ibid., 19–22.

11. "Religion in College," *NYT*, 4 Feb. 1886, 2.

12. George McLean Harper, "Misunderstanding at Harvard: How Dr. McCosh Left the 250th Anniversary in What He Thought Was Righteous Indignation," *PAW*, 16 Feb. 1940, 437.

13. William R. Hutchison, *The Modernist Impulse in American Protestantism* (Cambridge: Harvard University Press, 1976; rprt., New York: Oxford University Press, 1982), 2. According to Hugh Hawkins, critics characterized Eliot's religious views, with some justification, as "Unitarianism raised to the nth power." *Between Harvard and America: The Educational Leadership of Charles W. Eliot* (New York: Oxford University Press, 1972), 138. See also George M. Marsden, *The Soul of the American University: From Protestant Establishment to Established Nonbelief* (New York: Oxford University Press, 1994), 181–95.

14. Eliot, "What Place Should Religion Have in a College?" 14–15. In his longest theological discussion, presented in 1909, Eliot reveals an even clearer affinity toward modernism. "The Religion of the Future," *Harvard Theological Review* 2 (1909): 389–407.

15. McCosh, *Religion in a College*, 22, 7–8.

16. McCosh, "Place of Religion in College," 468.

17. Hutchison, *Modernist Impulse*, 41–110; Lefferts A. Loetscher, *The Broadening Church: A Study of Theological Issues in the Presbyterian Church since 1869* (Philadelphia: University of Pennsylvania Press, 1954), 9–39; Mark S. Massa, *Charles Augustus Briggs and the Crisis of Historical Criticism* (Philadelphia: Fortress Press, 1990), 53–68; Mark A. Noll, *Between Faith and Criticism: Evangelicals, Scholarship, and the Bible in America* (San Francisco: Harper and Row, 1982), 15–27.

18. See, for example, Richard Hofstadter, "The Revolution in Higher Education," in *Paths of American Thought*, ed. Arthur M. Schlesinger Jr. and Morton White (Boston: Houghton Mifflin, 1963), 269–90; Richard Hofstadter and Walter P. Metzger, *The Development of Academic Freedom in the United States* (New York: Columbia University Press, 1955), 277–412; Frederick Rudolph, *The American College and University: A History* (New York: Vintage, 1962), 264–86, 329–54; idem, *Curriculum: A History of the American Undergraduate Course of Study since 1636* (San Francisco: Jossey-Bass, 1977), 107–109, 203; Lewis Perry, *Intellectual Life in America: A History* (New York: Franklin Watts, 1984), 281–91; William C. Ringenberg, *The Christian College: A History of Protestant Higher Education in America*, with an Introduction by Mark A. Noll (Grand Rapids: Christian University Press and Eerdmans, 1984), 224–46.

19. D. G. Hart, "Faith and Learning in the Age of the University: The Academic Ministry of Daniel Coit Gilman," in *The Secularization of the Academy*, ed. George M. Marsden and Bradley J. Longfield (New York: Oxford University Press, 1992), 107–45; Daniel C. Gilman, *An Address before the Phi Beta Kappa Society of Harvard University July 1, 1886* (Baltimore, 1886), 21, as quoted in Laurence R. Veysey, *The Emergence of the American University* (Chicago: University of Chicago Press, 1965), 162.

20. Thomas E. Frank, *Theological, Ethics, and the Nineteenth-Century American College Ideal: Conserving a Rational World* (San Francisco: Mellen Research University Press, 1993); James P. Wind, *The Bible and the University: The Messianic Vision of William Rainey Harper* (Atlanta: Scholars Press, 1987); Bradley J. Longfield, "From Evangelicalism to Liberalism: Public Midwestern Universities in Nineteenth-Century America," in *Secularization of the Academy*, 46–73; Marsden, *Soul of the University*, 134–49, 167–80.

21. Louise L. Stevenson, *Scholarly Means to Evangelical Ends: The New Haven Scholars and the Transformation of Higher Learning in America, 1830–1890* (Balti-

more: Johns Hopkins University Press, 1986); Marsden, *Soul of the University*, 22–27, 123–33; Robert S. Shepard, *God's People in the Ivory Tower: Religion in the Early American University* (Brooklyn: Carlson, 1991).

22. James McCosh, *The Life of James McCosh: A Record Chiefly Autobiographical*, ed. William M. Sloane (New York: Scribner, 1896), 262–63; idem, "Place of Religion in College," 465–70; idem, "A Presbyterian College in America," *Catholic Presbyterian* 4 (1880): 81–87; *Report of Proceedings of the First General Presbyterian Council Convened at Edinburgh, July 1877*, ed. J. Thomson (Edinburgh: Thomas and Archibald Constable, 1877), 97–98.

23. Eliot, "What Place Should Religion Have in a College?" 1–2, 8–9, 10–11, 13, emphasis added. Eliot observed, "In the great majority of American colleges—which are of course Evangelical Protestant without prescribed ritual—no Roman Catholic, Episcopalian, Friend, Unitarian, Swedenborgian, Universalist, or Jew can get a permanent appointment, except perhaps in the, till lately, despised department of modern languages." Ibid., 6.

24. McCosh, *Religion in a College*, 21.

25. McCosh, "Presbyterian College in America," 85; idem, *Religion in a College*, 8–9.

26. Of the five students, one was Catholic and four gave no religious affiliation. The latter four may have been masking their association with an unpopular religion. *Nassau Herald, 1886*, 68–69.

27. McCosh, *Religion in a College*, 5. See also idem, "Place of Religion in College," 468–69.

28. McCosh, "Presbyterian College in America," 84–85.

29. McCosh, *Religion in a College*, 7–8. From his inauguration to his farewell address, McCosh insisted that Princeton respected the consciences of students. Idem, *Inauguration of Rev. Jas. M'Cosh, D.D., LL.D., as President of Princeton College, October 27, 1868* (Princeton: Printed at the Standard Office, 1869), 32; idem, "Place of Religion in College," 468; idem, *Twenty Years of Princeton College: Being a Farewell Address Delivered June 20th, 1888 by James McCosh, D.D., LL.D., Litt.D.* (New York: Scribner, 1888), 59.

30. John F. Wilson, *Public Religion in American Culture* (Philadelphia: Temple University Press, 1980), 9; Winthrop S. Hudson, *The Great Tradition of the American Churches* (New York, 1953), 108, as quoted in Robert T. Handy, *A Christian America: Protestant Hopes and Historical Realities*, rev. ed. (New York: Oxford University Press, 1984), 56. For similar interpretations, see Sydney E. Ahlstrom, *A Religious History of the American People* (New Haven: Yale University Press, 1972), 385–509; Handy, *Christian America*, 24–56; Winthrop Hudson and John Corrigan, *Religion in America*, 5th ed. (New York: Macmillan, 1992), 107–202; Mark A. Noll, *A History of Christianity in the United States and Canada* (Grand Rapids: Eerdmans, 1992), 218–44; Martin E. Marty, *The Righteous Empire: The Protestant Experience in America* (New York: Dial, 1970), 14–130.

31. Robert T. Handy, *Undermined Establishment: Church-State Relations in America, 1880–1920* (Princeton: Princeton University Press, 1991; idem, *Christian America*, 159–84. Fourteen million people immigrated to America between 1861 and 1900 and another fourteen million between 1901 and 1920. All statistics are drawn from United States Bureau of the Census, *Historical Statistics of the United States: Colonial Times to 1957* (Washington, D.C.: Bureau of the Census, 1960), 7, 56–57; Roger Finke and Rodney Stark, *The Churching of America 1776–1990: Winners and Losers in Our Religious Economy* (New Brunswick: Rutgers University Press, 1992), 110–14; Shlomith

Yahalom, "American Judaism and the Question of Separation Between Church and State," (Ph.D. diss., Hebrew University of Jerusalem, 1981), 32, as cited in Handy, *Undermined Establishment*, 146.

32. *Church of the Holy Trinity v. United States*, 143 U.S. 457 (1892) at 471, as quoted in Handy, *Undermined Establishment*, 13.

33. Charles Hodge, "Parochial Schools," *BRPR* 18 (1846): 433–41.

34. Handy, *Undermined Establishment*, 30–48; Gary Scott Smith, *The Seeds of Secularization: Calvinism, Culture, and Pluralism in America, 1870–1915* (Grand Rapids: Christian University Press, 1985), 74–89.

35. A. A. Hodge, "Religion in the Public Schools," *BRPR* 3 (1887): 47. For similar expressions of "Christian America" by members of Princeton's faculty, see Lyman Atwater, "Religion and Politics," *Report of Proceedings of the Second General Council of the Presbyterian Alliance, Convened at Philadelphia, September, 1880*, ed. John B. Dales and R. M. Patterson (Philadelphia: Presbyterian Journal Co., 1880), 323–29; William M. Sloane, "The Renascence of Education," *PresRev* 6 (1885): 465.

36. Handy, *Undermined Establishment*, 189.

37. Robert Kelley, *The Cultural Pattern in American Politics: The First Century* (New York: Knopf, 1979); Daniel Walker Howe, *The Political Culture of the American Whigs* (Chicago: University of Chicago Press, 1979).

38. D. H. Meyer, *The Instructed Conscience: The Shaping of the American National Ethic* (Philadelphia: University of Pennsylvania, 1972), viii–ix. See also Daniel Walker Howe, *The Unitarian Conscience: Harvard Moral Philosophy, 1805–1861* (Cambridge: Harvard University Press, 1970; rprt., Middletown, Conn.: Wesleyan University Press, 1988), 205–35; George P. Schmidt, *The Old Time College President* (New York: Columbia University Press, 1930; rprt., New York: AMS Press, 1970), 108–45; Wilson Smith, *Professors and Public Ethics: Studies of Northern Moral Philosophers before the Civil War* (Ithaca: Cornell University Press, 1956), 77–80.

39. Daniel Walker Howe, "The Evangelical Movement and Political Culture in the North during the Second Party System," *Journal of American History* 77 (1991): 1216–39; Marsden, *Soul of the University*, 79–100; idem, "The Soul of the American University: An Historical Overview," in *Secularization of the Academy*, 25–26; Douglas Sloan, "The Teaching of Ethics in the American Undergraduate Curriculum, 1876–1976," in *Ethics Teaching in Higher Education*, ed. Sissela Bok and Daniel Callahan (New York: Plenum, 1980), 2–3; Stevenson, *Evangelical Means*, 5–6, 114–16.

40. "Charters of the College of New Jersey, October 22, 1746 and September 14, 1748," in Thomas Jefferson Wertenbaker, *Princeton, 1746–1896* (Princeton: Princeton University Press, 1946), 396–97.

41. [Samuel Blair], *An Account of the College of New Jersey: in which are described the methods of government, modes of instruction, manners and expences of living in the same* (Woodbridge, N.J.: Printed by James Parker, 1764), 45–46, Rare Books and Special Collections, Princeton University Library. Published with permission of Princeton University Library. For similar statements, see the correspondence between the trustees and Governor Belcher after the second charter was approved and a pamphlet Gilbert Tennent and Samuel Davies distributed in Great Britain while trying to raise money for the college. TM, 13 Oct. 1748, 1:12–13; College of New Jersey, *A General Account of the Rise and State of the College* (London, 1754), 4–5, Rare Books and Special Collections, Princeton University Library. Published with permission of Princeton University Library.

42. Jonathan Dickinson to undesignated correspondent, 3 Mar. 1746/7, Box DI-DN, General Manuscripts (Miscellaneous).

43. Histories of Princeton College, Presbyterian higher education, and the Presbyterian church written within the past generation by scholars with no official affiliation with the institution have recognized the identification of religious and larger educational interests at the founding of the college. Francis I. Broderick, "Pulpit, Physics, and Politics: The Curriculum of the College of New Jersey, 1746–1794," *William and Mary Quarterly* 6 (1949): 43–57; David C. Humphrey, "The Struggle for Sectarian Control of Princeton, 1745–1760," *New Jersey History* 91 (1973): 77–90; Alison B. Olson, "The Founding of Princeton University: Religion and Politics in Eighteenth-Century New Jersey," *New Jersey History* 87 (1969): 133–50; Mark A. Noll, *Princeton and the Republic: The Search for a Christian Enlightenment in the Era of Samuel Stanhope Smith* (Princeton: Princeton University Press, 1989), 16–22; J. David Hoeveler Jr., *James McCosh and the Scottish Intellectual Tradition: From Glasgow to Princeton* (Princeton: Princeton University Press, 1981), 215–19; Douglas Sloan, *The Scottish Enlightenment and the American College Ideal* (New York: Teachers College Press, 1971), 58–60; Howard Miller, *The Revolutionary College: American Presbyterian Higher Education, 1707–1837* (New York: New York University Press, 1976), 1–102; Leonard J. Trinterud, *The Forming of an American Tradition: A Re-examination of Colonial Presbyterianism* (Philadelphia: Westminster, 1949; rprt., New York: Books for Libraries Press, 1970), 71–165; Randall Balmer and John R. Fitzmier, *The Presbyterians* (Westport, Conn.: Greenwood Press, 1993), 31–35. Institutional histories published before McCosh's inauguration take the same perspective. Archibald Alexander, *Biographical Sketches of the Founder, and Princeton Alumni of the Log College* (Princeton: J. T. Robinson, 1845), 125; College of New Jersey, *The First Centennial Anniversary of the College of New Jersey. Celebrated June, 1847* (Princeton: J. T. Robinson, 1848), 11–34; College of New Jersey, *An Historical Sketch of the College of New Jersey* (Philadelphia: Joseph M. Wilson, 1859), 16; [William Armstrong Dod], *History of the College of New Jersey, From Its Commencement, A.D., 1746 to 1783. [Prepared Originally for The Princeton Whig, Feb. 1844]* (Princeton: J. T. Robinson, 1844). Institutional histories written by individuals associated with the college and published during McCosh's administration, likewise, underscored the close relationship between religious and educational interests and sometimes accentuated the school's special interest in preparing candidates for the ministry. Samuel Davies Alexander, *Princeton College during the Eighteenth Century* (New York: A. D. F. Randolph, 1872), vii, xv; idem, "Princeton College," *Scribner's Magazine*, May 1877, 626–27; John Maclean, *History of the College of New Jersey, from its Origin in 1746 to the Commencement of 1854*, 2 vols. (Philadelphia: Lippincott, 1877), 1:61–69, 2:411–22; John F. Hageman, *History of Princeton and Its Institutions*, 2 vols. (Philadelphia: Lippincott, 1879), 2:231, 297, 320.

44. Between 1748 and 1768, only 53 percent of Princeton's students came from the middle colony states of New York, New Jersey, and Pennsylvania; 25 percent came from New England; and 11 percent from the South. In the first twenty classes, more graduates entered the ministry than any other profession: 158 students, 47 percent, became ministers; 49 students, 15 percent, became lawyers; and 44 students, 13 percent, became physicians. James McLachlan, *Princetonians, 1748–1768* (Princeton: Princeton University Press, 1976), xx–xxii.

45. Noll, *Princeton and the Republic*, 6, 16–243.

46. "Proposal to General Assembly," (1811), as quoted in Wertenbaker, *Princeton*, 147–48. Presbyterian Church, U.S.A., *Minutes of the General Assembly of the Presbyterian Church in the United States of America from its Organization, A.D. 1789 to A.D. 1820* (Philadelphia: Presbyterian Board of Publication, [1847]), 499–501; Lefferts A.

Loetscher, *Facing the Enlightenment and Pietism: Archibald Alexander and the Founding of Princeton Theological Seminary* (Westport, Conn.: Greenwood Press, 1983); Noll, *Princeton and the Republic*, 244–71. When Henry Kollock, the college's professor of theology, resigned in 1806, he told the trustees that he found the number of students interested in theology "so small as to render my labours of little consequence." TM, 25 Sept. 1806, quoted in ibid., 178.

47. Ibid., 214–15.

48. Ashbel Green, *Discourses, Delivered in the College of New Jersey; Addressed for the First Degree in the Arts; with Notes and Illustrations, including a Historical Sketch of the College, from its Origin to the Accession of President Witherspoon* (Philadelphia: Littell, 1822), 286. This entire work underscores this point.

49. According to Thomas Jefferson Wertenbaker, Princeton entered an educational "nadir" between 1812 and 1868 in which the college actually became the "step-child of the church." *Princeton*, 118–152. Wertenbaker's description of Princeton between 1822 and 1868 anticipates in many ways the dismal view of the antebellum collegiate education later popularized by Richard Hofstadter. Noll tempers Wertenbaker's analysis by suggesting that in the antebellum period the college "never abandoned a firm commitment to science, reason, and philosophy" but began "to look more fervently to piety, faith, and revelation as the foundation of their efforts to sustain the church and revive the republic." *Princeton and the Republic*, 256. Sloan offers the most sweeping revision of Wertenbaker's interpretation of Princeton in this period. *Scottish Enlightenment*.

50. McCosh, *Inauguration of M'Cosh*, 5–6, 11–12, 14, 32, emphasis added.

51. McCosh, "Presbyterian College in America," 85. See also idem, "Place of Religion in College," 465–66.

52. William C. Roberts, "Higher Education in the West," *PresRev* 9 (1888): 219. For similar statements, see idem, "The American College," *Minutes and Proceedings of the Third General Council*, 472–76; Lyman Atwater, "A Plea for Higher Education and Presbyterian College," *BRPR* 34 (1862): 656–58.

53. TM, 8 Nov. 1877, 5:654.

54. Maclean, *History of the College of New Jersey*, 1:63, 69. Lyman Atwater presumes a similar perspective in "Plea for Higher Education," 635–68.

55. F.T.B., "Princeton College Catalogue," *Pres*, 6 Feb. 1886, 7. Histories of the Presbyterian church published during McCosh's tenure also acknowledged the historic connection between the college and the church. Charles A. Briggs, *American Presbyterianism: Its Origin and Early History* (New York: Scribner, 1885), 404–10; Robert P. Kerr, *The People's History of Presbyterianism in all Ages* (Richmond: Presbyterian Committee of Publication, 1888), 186; *Encyclopedia of the Presbyterian Church in the United States of America*, ed. Alfred Nevin (Philadelphia: Presbyterian Encyclopedia Publishing Co., 1884), s.v. "Princeton College." Church histories written before McCosh's presidency make the same point. Robert Baird, *Religion in the United States of America* (Glasgow and Edinburgh: Blackie, 1844; rprt., New York: Arno Press, 1969), 338, 543–45; Charles Hodge, *The Constitutional History of the Presbyterian Church in the United States of America: Part II, 1741–1788* (Philadelphia: Presbyterian Board of Publication, 1851), 241–44; Richard Webster, *A History of the Presbyterian Church* (Philadelphia: Joseph M. Wilson, 1857), 258. The fullest institutional history correctly credits McCosh with setting in motion those forces that led to the institution's transformation into a university but incorrectly suggests he intentionally attempted to reduce the influence of the Presbyterian church and Princeton Seminary in order to achieve this goal. Wertenbaker, *Princeton*, 290–343. L. Bruce Leslie largely overlooks McCosh's

university building activities but does credit him with reducing the influence of the seminary on the college. *Gentlemen and Scholars: College and Community in the "Age of the University," 1865–1917* (State College: Penn State University Press, 1992), 8, 28, 118.

56. Jonathan F. Stearns, *Liberal Education a Necessity of the Church* (New York: John F. Trow, 1860), 22. For similar statements by Princeton professors on the "christianizing" influence of religiously trained graduates, see Atwater, "Pleas for Higher Education and Presbyterian College," 655–58; idem, review of *Three Discourses upon the Religious History of Bowdoin College*, by Egbert C. Smith, *BRPR* 31 (1859): 37; James C. Moffat, review of *The Historically Received Conception of the University*, by Edward Kirkpatrick, *BRPR* 35 (1863): 587–88.

57. Andrew F. West, "What is Academic Freedom?" *North American Review* 140 (1885): 444. For similar statements, see Francis Lieber, "The Necessity of Religious Instruction in Colleges," *Presbyterian Quarterly and Princeton Review* 2 (1873): 651–56; Lyman Atwater, "Proposed Reforms in Collegiate Education," *PRev* 5 (1882): 112–17.

58. "Religion in College," *Pres*, 13 Feb. 1886, 11, emphasis added. For similar comments, see "Library Meeting," *Pr*, 22 Feb. 1886, 1; "Correspondence. New York," *Pres*, 13 Feb. 1886, 6; "Correspondence. New York," *Pres*, 6 Mar. 1886, 6.

59. Atwater, "Proposed Reforms in Collegiate Education," 112–13, 115–17.

60. "Education Bills before Congress," *NPR* 2 (1886): 132–33.

61. TM, 12 Feb. 1885, 6:597–98.

62. Alexander Oleson and John Voss, "Introduction," in *The Organization of Knowledge in America*, ed. Alexander Oleson and John Voss (Baltimore: Johns Hopkins University Press, 1979), x.

63. TM, 12 Feb. 1885, 6:598.

64. Charles W. Eliot, "Liberty in Education," in *Educational Reform: Essays and Addresses* (New York: Century, 1898), 126–27, 137–39, 142. Hawkins offers a useful summary of Eliot's work with the elective system in *Between Harvard and America*, 80–119. Yale College President Noah Porter had been invited to participate in the debate but declined. McCosh, *Life of McCosh*, 199–200.

65. Eliot, "Liberty in Education," 143–44, 145–48.

66. James McCosh, *The New Departure in College Education: Being a Reply to President Eliot's Defense of it in New York, Feb. 24, 1885* (New York: Scribner, 1885), 4, 7, 10–13. McCosh reviewed his debate with Eliot and offered a scathing summary of the disadvantages of the elective system and the virtues of Princeton's curriculum in his autobiography, *Life of McCosh*, 198–205.

67. McCosh, *New Departure in College Education*, 15–18.

68. Ibid., 19. Discipline, McCosh told the trustees, was not only "a means for punishing crime," but also a way "to prevent evil by kindness, by fatherly care, [and] by religion." TM, 18 June 1882, 6:347.

69. Veysey, *Emergence of University*, 22–28, 35, 39, 41–43, 48–50. Institutional histories of Princeton overlook McCosh's commitment to the "piety and discipline" educational philosophy in their portrayals of McCosh's university building activities. James W. Alexander Jr., *Princeton—Old and New* (New York: Scribner, 1899), 61–66; Varnum Lansing Collins, *Princeton* (New York: Oxford University Press, 1914), 221–50; Edwin M. Norris, *The Story of Princeton* (Boston: Little, Brown, and Co., 1917), 199–223; Wertenbaker, *Princeton*, 290–343; John Rogers Williams, *The Handbook of Princeton*, with an introduction by Woodrow Wilson (New York: Grafton, 1905), 23–24. J. David Hoeveler's biography stands out as an exception in this regard. *McCosh*, 248–60.

70. McCosh, *New Departure in College Education*, 16.

71. McCosh, *Religion in a College*, 11.

72. McCosh, *New Departure in College Education*, 10–11, 18, 21–23.

73. "Correspondence. New York," *Pres*, 7 Mar. 1885, 6. Austin Phelps of Andover Theological Seminary congratulated McCosh for unmasking the "agnostic decline" of Harvard under Eliot who had also "let down" the institution's academic standards. Austin Phelps to James McCosh, 20 Mar. 1885, James McCosh Papers, Seeley G. Mudd Manuscript Library, Princeton University. Published with permission of Princeton University Library. Newspaper editorials on the debate were divided over whose plan was superior. The *New York Times* endorsed Eliot's plan over the "old cast iron plan" of McCosh whereas the *New-York Daily Tribune* favored McCosh's curriculum. "Elective Studies," *NYT*, 26 Feb. 1885, 4; "Liberty of Choice in Colleges," *New-York Daily Tribune*, 26 Feb. 1885, 4.

74. Editorial, *Pr*, 6 Mar. 1885, 1.

75. West, "What is Academic Freedom?" 433, 443–44. West went so far as to charge that it was an "academic misrepresentation" for Harvard to call its degree a Bachelor of Arts. "President Eliot's Report," *Independent*, 13 May 1886, 5. For similar criticisms of Harvard, see idem, "President Eliot's Report," *Independent*, 6 May 1886, 4–5; "Mr. Lowell on Education," *NPR* 3 (1887): 131–33; Francis L. Patton, "Dr. McCosh on the New Departure in College Education," *PresRev* 6 (1885): 346; "Electives in College Studies," *NPR* 2 (1886): 284–85.

76. McCosh, *Twenty Years of Princeton College*, 51–52.

77. Henry F. May, *The Enlightenment in America*, (New York: Oxford University Press, 1976), 348.

78. *New York Observer*, 4 June 1868, quoted in Hoeveler, *McCosh*, 228–29.

79. James McCosh to D. Maclagen, 10 July 1879, McCosh Papers.

80. Hoeveler, *McCosh*, 111–46. McCosh summarizes this middle path in, *The Scottish Philosophy, Biographical, Expository, Critical, From Hutcheson to Hamilton* (New York: Robert Carter, 1875), 7–11, 459–60, and idem, *Twenty Years of Princeton College*, 29–30.

81. Sydney E. Ahlstrom, "The Scottish Philosophy and American Theology," *Church History* 24 (1955): 257–72; Theodore Dwight Bozeman, *Protestants in an Age of Science: The Baconian Ideal and Antebellum American Religious Thought* (Chapel Hill: University of North Carolina Press, 1977), 3–31, 80–85, 101–59; Elizabeth Flowers and Murray G. Murphey, *A History of Philosophy in America*, (New York: Putnam, 1977), 1:203–73, 312–29, 2:517–28; Frank, *American College Ideal*, 35–68; S. A. Grave, *The Scottish Philosophy of Common Sense* (Oxford: Clarendon Press, 1960), 1–150; E. Brooks Holifield, *The Gentlemen Theologians: American Theology in Southern Culture, 1795–1860* (Durham: Duke University Press, 1978), 77–100, 110–18, 127–54; Herbert Hovenkamp, *Science and Religion in America, 1800–1860* (Philadelphia: University of Pennsylvania Press, 1978), 3–117; Howe, *Unitarian Conscience*, 27–44; Bruce Kuklick, *Churchmen and Philosophers: From Jonathan Edwards to John Dewey* (New Haven: Yale University Press, 1985), 15–19, 66–75, 78, 141–45; George M. Marsden, "The Collapse of American Evangelical Academia," in *Faith and Rationality: Reason and Belief in God*, ed. Alvin Plantinga and Nicholas Wolterstorff (Notre Dame: University of Notre Dame Press, 1983), 219–64; idem, "Evangelicals and the Scientific Culture: An Overview," in *Religion & Twentieth Century American Intellectual Life*, ed. Michael J. Lacey (New York: Woodrow Wilson International Center for Scholars and Cambridge University Press, 1989), 26–33; idem, "Everyone One's Own Interpreter?

The Bible, Science, and Authority in Mid-Nineteenth-Century America," in *The Bible in America: Essays in Cultural History*, ed. Nathan O. Hatch and Mark A. Noll (New York: Oxford University Press, 1982), 79–100; idem, *Fundamentalism and American Culture: The Shaping of Twentieth-Century Evangelicalism, 1870–1925* (New York: Oxford University Press, 1980), 55–62; May, *Enlightenment in America*, xvi, 337–50 passim; Meyer, *Instructed Conscience*, 3–120; Sloan, *Scottish Enlightenment*, 103–257; idem, "The Teaching of Ethics," 2–9; Smith, *Professors and Public Ethics*, 3–73; John W. Stewart, "The Tethered Theology: Biblical Criticism, Common Sense Philosophy, and the Princeton Theologians, 1812–1860," (Ph.D. diss., University of Michigan, 1990), 139–91; James Turner, *Without God, Without Creed: The Origins of Unbelief in America* (Baltimore: Johns Hopkins University Press, 1985), 49–63, 73–113.

82. George Santayana, "The Intellectual Temper of the Age," *Winds of Doctrine: Studies in Contemporary Opinion* (New York: Scribner, 1913), 1, quoted in Handy, *Undermined Establishment*, 126.

83. Paul Carter, *The Spiritual Crisis of the Gilded Age* (Dekalb: Northern Illinois University Press, 1971), 3–10, 17–42; D. H. Meyer, "American Intellectuals and the Victorian Crisis of Faith," *American Quarterly* 27 (1975): 585–603; Arthur M. Schlesinger Sr., "A Critical Period in American Religion, 1875–1900," *Proceedings of the Massachusetts Historical Society* 64 (1932): 523–47; Turner, *Without God, Without Creed*, 171–225.

84. James McCosh to John DeWitt, 31 May 1886, McCosh Papers.

85. *Catalogue, 1869–70*, 26.

86. TM, 8 Feb. 1883, 6:422; 18 June 1883, 6:459; Princeton University, *General Catalogue of Princeton University, 1746–1906* (Princeton: Published by the University), 36, 60, 250. The moral philosophy class was renamed ethics in the 1876–1877 academic year.

87. William Henry Green, a professor at the seminary and a trustee of the college, told Henry Van Dyke Sr. that Patton's joint appointment benefited both institutions. The college, he said, profited because Patton was a good teacher and the seminary because he attracted more of the college's graduates to the seminary. William Henry Green to Henry Van Dyke Sr., 27 Nov. 1886, Box 16, Henry Van Dyke Family Papers, Manuscript Division, Rare Books and Special Collections, Princeton University Library. Published with permission of Princeton University Library. Lyman Atwater, *Ethics and Political Economy from Notes Taken in the Lecture Room of Lyman Atwater* (Trenton: Sharp, 1878).

88. Francis L. Patton, *Syllabus of President Patton's Lectures on Ethics* (n.p., 1892), 2, emphasis added, Seeley G. Mudd Manuscript Library, Princeton University. The 1892 syllabus is used as the primary source because it follows the same outline as the earliest available printed syllabus but with a little more detail. It also follows the same outline as classnotes available from the fall of 1888. Robert E. Speer, Ethics Class Notebook, Robert E. Speer Papers, Archives, Princeton Seminary Libraries. The textbook for Patton's classes was the Edinburgh moral philosopher Henry Calderwood's *Handbook of Moral Philosophy*, 14th ed. (London: Macmillan, 1888).

89. Patton, *Syllabus on Ethics*, 7–9.

90. Patton, *Syllabus on Ethics*, 9–10. Final examination questions in Patton's courses reveal his interest not only in teaching students about different ethical systems but also in convincing them of the superiority of his own. On a final examination in 1884, for example, Patton asked: "The Materialist asserts that motives are simply impulses and that choice is the function of the strongest impulse. Is this an adept account of man's

motivity? If defective, how so?" College of New Jersey, Examination in Ethics, 14 Jan. 1884, in Smith Ordway Diary, Box 1, Smith Ordway Diaries, Manuscript Division, Rare Books and Special Collections, Princeton University Library. Published with permission of Princeton University Library.

91. Patton, *Syllabus on Ethics*, 9–18 quotes on 14, 17, 18. See also idem, "The Meaning of Oughtness," *PresRev* 7 (1886): 127–50. Patton outlines the "triangular" argument between positivists, idealists, and Scottish realists in "Contemporary English Ethics," *NPR* 1 (1886): 177–99.

92. Patton, *Syllabus on Ethics*, 25–26.

93. Speer, Ethics College Notebook, n.p. On teleological and deontological ethical theories in the early nineteenth-century moral philosophy, see Meyer, *Instructed Conscience*, 157–62.

94. Patton, *Syllabus on Ethics*, 26–31.

95. Speer, Ethics Class Notebook, n.p.

96. Patton, *Syllabus on Ethics*, 33–36, quote on 36. This notion of self-development was another feature of earlier moral philosophers. Meyer, *Instructed Conscience*, 64–66.

97. Patton, *Syllabus on Ethics*, 3.

98. *History of American Politics* went through nine printings in its first ten years and was reprinted as late as 1910. Richard P. McCormick, "Alexander Johnston: An Appreciation," *Journal of the Rutgers University Libraries* 46 (1985): 14–15, 20–21; *Dictionary of American Biography*, ed. Allen Johnson et al. (New York: Scribner, 1928–37), 15:36–37 [hereinafter cited as *D.A.B.*].

99. McCormick, "Alexander Johnston," 18, 22.

100. Robert E. Speer, Jurisprudence and Political Economy Notebook, 11, 13–15, 16–52, Speer Papers. Alexander Johnston, *Syllabus in Jurisprudence* (Princeton: Princeton Press, n.d.); idem, *Syllabus in Jurisprudence and Political Economy* (Princeton: Princeton Press, 1886); idem, *Lectures on Political Economy* (Trenton: Edwin Fitzgeorge, 1884).

101. "Alexander Johnston," *PP*, 27 July 1890; Alexander Johnston, Faculty File, Seeley G. Mudd Manuscript Library, Princeton University. Published with permission of Princeton University Library.

102. Charles W. Shields, *The Final Philosophy, or System of Perfectible Knowledge Issuing from the Harmony of Science and Religion* (New York: Scribner, 1877), 21.

103. *D.A.B.*, 17:104–105; Charles W. Shields, *Philosophia Ultima* (Philadelphia: Lippincott, 1861). Review of *Philosophia Ultima*, by Charles W. Shields, *BRPR* 33 (1861): 576.

104. Friends guaranteed $1200 of his $1800 yearly salary for five years if the college supplied the balance. Charles W. Shields to James R. Shields, 15 May 1865; Charles W. Shields to James R. Shields, 23 June 1865; Charles W. Shields to the People of the Second Presbyterian Church, 24 Sept. 1865; Charles W. Shields to James R. Shields, 25 Oct. 1866; Box 3, Charles W. Shields Papers, Manuscript Division, Rare Books and Special Collections, Princeton University Library. Published with permission of Princeton University Library.

105. In 1861, Charles Hodge had approached Shields with a position as professor of church history. With a position at the seminary, Shields wrote his father, "I would be free from many of the solicitous of a pastoral charge [*sic*], and that it would enable me to at length to make valuable contributions to *theology*." In spite of the unanimous recommendation of the seminary's directors, the General Assembly elected Samuel Moffat. Charles Hodge to Charles W. Shields, 27 Apr. 1861; Charles W. Shields to James R. Shields, 11 June 1861, Box 3, Shields Papers, emphasis added. Shields wrote Maclean

that his goal "was to present in my instruction, as far as I should be able, a systematic illustration of the harmony of biblical and scientific truth, involving an argument for the Divine authority of the Holy Scriptures and the Christian Religion." Charles W. Shields to John Maclean, 25 June 1865, Box 4, Shields Papers. Shields's interest in teaching at the seminary and his description of his position at the college suggest that Charles W. Cashdollar's assertion that Shields wanted a position at the college in order to "escape the pressures of orthodoxy" is mistaken. *The Transformation of Theology, 1830–1890: Positivism and Protestant Thought in Britain and America* (Princeton: Princeton University Press, 1989), 119–20.

106. Charles W. Shields, *Introductory Lecture on the Relations of Science and Religion* (Philadelphia: Henry B. Ashmead, 1866), 15–16. In the first term of the junior year in 1868, which lasted until Christmas break, students took "Natural Theology," which studied Paley's *Natural Theology*. In the second and third terms, January to June, they studied Butler's *Analogy of Religion, Natural and Revealed* in a course by the same title. It was renamed "Christian Evidences" in 1869. Seniors completed Butler's *Analogy* in their first term and took Shields's science and religion course in the final two terms. These courses, as shall be outlined in the next chapter, changed over the course of McCosh's administration. *Catalogue, 1868–69*, 22–23; *Catalogue, 1869–70*, 24.

107. William Paley, *Natural Theology*, ed. Francis Young (London: Ward, Lock, and Co., n.d.), 17–20, 53, 263, 267.

108. Joseph Butler, *The Analogy of Religion, Natural and Revealed*, ed. Joseph Cummings (New York: Phillips and Hunt, 1884), 33–36, 69–83, 355.

109. Shields appeared to demand little from students in these classes. On exams, for example, Shields asks such straightforward questions out of the textbook as "Examine Paley's illustration as applied to the development of plants and animals." According to Lee, students cheated with impunity. Professor Shields' Science and Religion Examination, Dec. 1878, Box 413, Blair and Lee Family Papers; Blair Lee to Samuel Phillips Lee, 16 Oct. 1878; Blair Lee to Samuel Phillips Lee, 6 June 1879, Box 274, Blair and Lee Family Papers; Blair Lee to Elizabeth Blair Lee, 7 June 1879, Box 270, Blair and Lee Family Papers, Manuscript Division, Rare Books and Special Collections, Princeton University Library. Published with permission of Princeton University Library. Another student expressed similar impressions four years later. Ordway Diary, 16 Mar. 1883, Box 1, Ordway Diaries.

110. In an assessment of Comte's thought in 1858, Shields said that it contained "a little leaven of truth" and "a formidable mass of error." "The Positive Philosophy of Auguste Comte," *BRPR* 30 (1858): 2. Early in his career, Shields also expressed an interest in finding a common ground for uniting the Protestant church through worship. *Directory for Public Worship and the Book of Common Prayer Considered with Reference to the Question of a Presbyterian Liturgy* (Philadelphia: Martien, 1867).

111. Cashdollar, *Transformation of Theology*, 119–20, 334–38. Shields slowly published the lectures from his "Science and Religion" course in three volumes over the course of his career. In 1877, he published *Final Philosophy*. This work was republished twelve years later with a sequel volume. Idem, *Philosophia Ultima or Science of the Sciences Vol. I. An Historical and Critical Introduction to the Final Philosophy as Issuing from the Harmony of Science and Religion*, rev. ed. (New York: Scribner, 1888); idem, *Philosophia Ultima or Science of the Sciences Vol. II. The History of the Sciences and the Logic of the Sciences* (New York: Scribner, 1889). In 1900, he published *The Scientific Evidences of Revealed Religion* (New York: Scribner, 1900). This work was posthumously revised by William M. Sloane and published as a third volume to his

earlier works, *Philosophia Ultima or the Science of the Sciences Vol. III. The Scientific Problems of Religion and the Christian Evidences of the Physical and Psychical Sciences,* with a Biographical Sketch by William M. Sloane (New York: Scribner, 1905). Shields's lecture notes roughly follow the same argument outlined in these works with a concentration on the material presented in the first volume. Lecture Notes on Science and Religion, Box 1, Shields Papers. One student wrote his mother that Shields simply read from his book in his lectures. Blair Lee to Elizabeth Blair Lee, 30 Oct. 1879, Box 270, Blair and Lee Family Papers.

112. Shields, *Final Philosophy,* 3, 6, 20–21.

113. Ibid., 474.

114. John Draper, *History of the Conflict between Religion and Science* (London: Henry S. King, 1874); Andrew D. White, *A History of the Warfare of Science with Theology in Christendom,* 2 vols. (New York: Appleton, 1896). For a similar portrayal of the hostile reception of Darwinism during the revolution in higher education, see Hofstadter and Metzger, *Development of Academic Freedom,* 320–63. Changes in the historiography of the reception of Darwinism are outlined in James R. Moore, *Post-Darwinian Controversies: A Study of the Protestant Struggle to Come to Terms with Darwin in Great Britain and America, 1870–1900* (Cambridge: Cambridge University Press, 1979), 19–102; John Durant, "Darwinism and Divinity: A Century of Debate," in *Darwinism and Divinity: Essays on Evolution and Religious Beliefs,* ed. John Durant (Oxford: Basil Blackwell, 1985), 9–39.

115. Turner, *Without God, Without Creed,* 182, 184. Some historians have recently argued that evidence in Darwin's papers suggests that he may not have rejected natural theology *in toto.* John H. Brooke, "The Relations Between Darwin's Science and His Religion," in *Darwinism and Divinity,* 40–75.

116. Shields, *Final Philosophy,* 52–431, quotes on 53, 67, 406.

117. Ibid., 435–561, quotes on 474, 551. Shields outlined the epistemology, metaphysics, and conception of revelation of his "final philosophy" in *Philosophia Ultima,* 2:296–410. Cashdollar observes: "Shields's grand scheme was less than convincing; the polarities of positivism versus revealed religion and Comte versus Hegel were parallel on one side only (positivism and Comte matched, but revealed religion and Hegel did not), and it is not entirely clear that Shields realized this." *Transformation of Theology,* 337. Evaluations of the persuasiveness of Shields's argument aside, it should be noted that Shields did not match revealed religion with Hegel, but rather tried to preserve the *via media* of Scottish philosophy between the philosophical antipodes of Hegel and Comte in order to uphold revealed religion.

118. Shields, *Final Philosophy,* 14, 16–17, 20, 551; Moore, *Post-Darwinian Controversies,* 45. James R. Moore observes a parallel between Shields and Herbert Spencer, who also devoted a large part of his life to constructing a unification of all knowledge based on a reconciliation of science and religion. Ibid., 358–59, n.79. Shields, not surprisingly, had little affection for Spencer's philosophy. *Final Philosophy,* 220, 297.

119. James Ward Smith, "Religion and Science in American Philosophy," *The Shaping of American Religion,* ed. James Ward Smith and A. Leland Jamison (Princeton: Princeton University Press, 1961), 413–20; Marsden, "American Evangelical Academia," 223–24; Turner, *Without God, Without Creed,* 96–104.

120. Shields, *Philosophia Ultima,* 2:440. He defined science as exact, verified, organized knowledge. Ibid., 2:42–43.

121. Idem, *Final Philosophy,* 10, 16. See also idem, *Philosophia Ultima,* 2:33–41.

122. Marsden, "American Evangelical Academia," 245–47; Smith, "Religion and

Science," 420–25; Turner, *Without God, Without Creed*, 157–60, 179–82.

123. Shields, *Philosophia Ultima*, 2:420–28. Shields's explanation of miracles from the scientific point of view, however, tended to stress, in a concession to positivism, a more strictly naturalistic interpretation when compared to the scientific explanations of theologians. Shields, for example, observed that the miraculous appearance of the Star of the Nativity at Jesus' birth is no more incredible than the scientific discoveries of unknown stars. Idem, *Scientific Evidences*, 71–73. Cashdollar makes a similar point in *Transformation of Theology*, 357. For a less naturalistic view of the scientific explanations of miracles from a contemporary, see for example, Charles Hodge, *Systematic Theology*, 3 vols. (rprt., Grand Rapids: Eerdmans, 1986), 1:617–36.

124. Jon H. Roberts, *Darwinism and the Divine in America: Protestant Intellectuals and Organic Evolution, 1859–1900* (Madison: University of Wisconsin Press, 1988), 3–87; Moore, *Post-Darwinian Controversies*, 125–90; Ronald L. Numbers, *The Creationists: The Evolution of Scientific Creationism* (Berkeley: University of California Press, 1992), 3–7.

125. Charles Hodge, *What Is Darwinism?* (New York: Scribner, 1874), 48, 52, 176–77. The Protestant rejection of Darwinism is outlined in Moore, *Post-Darwinian Controversies*, 193–216; Roberts, *Darwinism and the Divine*, 91–116; Mark A. Noll and David N. Livingstone, introduction to *What Is Darwinism? And Other Writings on Science and Religion*, by Charles Hodge (Grand Rapids: Baker, 1994), 11–35; Jonathan Wells in *Charles Hodge's Critique of Darwinism: An Historical-Critical Analysis of Concepts Basic to the 19th Century Debate* (Lewiston, N.Y.: Edwin Mellen Press, 1988). The Catholic Church likewise resisted Darwinism. Harry W. Paul, "Religion and Darwinism: Varieties of Catholic Reaction," in *Comparative Reception of Darwinism*, ed. Thomas F. Glick (Chicago: University of Chicago Press, 1988), 403–36.

126. Moore, *Post-Darwinian Controversies*, 217–345; Roberts, *Darwinism and the Divine*, 117–73; Numbers, *Creationists*, 7–19.

127. James McCosh, *The Religious Aspect of Evolution* (New York: Putnam, 1888), 1–8, 58–68, quote on 58. For similar comments, see idem, *Life of McCosh*, 234; idem, *Christianity and Positivism: A Series of Lectures to the Times on Natural Theology and Christian Apologetics* (New York: Robert Carter, 1871), 78–88. For the most useful surveys of McCosh on evolution and Darwinism, see Hoeveler, *McCosh*, 202–11; Roberts, *Darwinism and the Divine*, 19–20, 120, 125–26; Moore, *Post-Darwinian Controversies*, 245–51. Shields espouses theistic harmonization with evolution throughout his works. See, for example, *Philosophia Ultima*, 2:339–43; idem, *Scientific Evidences*, 79–106. Shields cited Charles Hodge on Darwin as illustrative of the "indifferentists" who considered evolution incompatible with theism. *Final Philosophy*, 176.

128. *Catalogue, 1885–86*, 137.

129. John T. Duffield, "Evolutionism Respecting Man, and the Bible," *PR* 1 (1878): 155.

130. Arnold H. Guyot, *Creations; or The Biblical Cosmogony in the Light of Modern Science* (New York: Scribner, 1884), vii. See also ibid., 1–28.

131. George Macloskie, Biological Problems Lecture Notes, Box 2, George Macloskie Papers, Manuscript Division, Rare Books and Special Collections, Princeton University Library. Published with permission of Princeton University Library. See also idem, "Scientific Speculation," *PresRev* 8 (1887): 617–25; idem, "Concessions to Science," *PresRev* 10 (1889): 220–28. In a personal notebook, Macloskie took copious notes on and made criticisms of Hodge's *What Is Darwinism?* Commonplace Book B, Box 4, Macloskie Papers.

132. While historians have recognized the significant divergence of opinion between McCosh and Hodge, most have overlooked the vast areas of agreement between the two. Hodge distinguished between evolution and Darwinism and acknowledged very tentatively that certain theories of evolution could be harmonized with theism. McCosh, moreover, agreed with Hodge insofar as he acknowledged that certain theories of evolution have "been turned to atheistic purposes." Hodge, *What Is Darwinism?*, 50–51, 106; McCosh, *Religious Aspect of Evolution*, 58. The theologians at the seminary gradually adopted, with certain theological reservations notwithstanding, a theistic interpretation like that of McCosh. A. A. Hodge, in the first edition of his *Outlines of Theology*, agreed with his father's position. The younger Hodge subsequently revised his position and agreed with McCosh that the natural theologian could be "friendly" toward any evolutionary theory that did not deny divine immanence and providence. *Outlines of Theology* (New York: Robert Carter, 1860), 25–26; idem, *Outlines of Theology* rev. ed. (New York: Robert Carter, 1879), 38–41. See also idem, review of *Natural Science and Religion*, by Asa Gray, *PresRev* 1 (1880): 586–89. B. B. Warfield, who entered Princeton in the first year of McCosh's presidency, took a position much more sympathetic toward evolution than either of his predecessors at the seminary. Warfield said that he could "raise no question as to the compatibility of the Darwinian hypothesis of evolution with Christianity." The liberalizing influence of McCosh was evident in Warfield's willingness to stress naturalistic causation over divine providence in his use of evolution in a teleological argument. "Teleology," he said, "is in no way inconsistent with— is rather necessary involved in—a complete system of natural causation. Every teleological system implies a complete 'causo-mechanical' explanation as its instrument." He also had no trouble reinterpreting Genesis 1–2 in order to harmonize it with theistic evolution. *The Present-Day Conception of Evolution* (Emporia, Kans.: College Printing Office, n.d.), 7; idem, "Charles Darwin's Religious Life: A Sketch in Spiritual Biography," *PresRev* 9 (1888): 575–602; idem, "Creation versus Evolution," *Bible Student* 4 (1901): 1–8; idem, review of *Darwinism Today*, by Vernon L. Kellogg, *PTR* 6 (1908): 649; idem, "Calvin's Doctrine of Creation," *PTR* 13 (1915): 196, 209–10. Francis L. Patton, like Warfield, agreed that evolution could be given a teleological interpretation but he seemed content to wait for more conclusive proof to confirm evolution before he would make any major revision of his apologetical system. He did, however, admire McCosh's efforts to show that as "a theory explanatory of the origin of species it was a mistake to regard it as atheistic or in irreconcilable hostility to the Bible." Francis L. Patton, "Evolution and Apologetics," *PresRev* 6 (1885): 138–44; idem, "James McCosh: A Baccalaureate Sermon," *PRR* 6 (1895): 658. These developments are overlooked, for example, by Roberts, *Darwinism and the Divine*, 100. Institutional histories of Princeton likewise recognize only the divergence of opinion between Hodge and McCosh on evolution. However, they anachronistically read McCosh's harmonization of evolution and theism as a post–Scopes Trial sympathy for Darwinism and imply that this entailed an antifundamentalist hostility toward orthodox Protestant theology. Wertenbaker, *Princeton*, 311–12; Leslie, *Gentlemen and Scholars*, 88–89, 92. The response of the Princeton theologians to evolution is outlined in David N. Livingstone, *Darwin's Forgotten Defenders: The Encounter Between Evangelical Theology and Evolutionary Thought* (Grand Rapids: Eerdmans, 1987), 11–14, 92–94, 100–22, 132–33; Gary Scott Smith, "Calvinists and Evolution, 1870–1920," *Journal of Presbyterian History* 61 (1983): 335–52.

133. Shields, *Scientific Evidences*, 51–187, 217–59; idem, *Philosophia Ultima*, 2:428–37.

134. Shields, *Scientific Evidences*, 1–50, 188–216, quote on 40. When Shields finally published his natural theology and apologetics, he won high praise from the Princeton theologians. Henry C. Minton of San Francisco Presbyterian Seminary applauded his defense of

inerrancy but took exception to his minimizing of the miraculous. Warfield was even more effusive in his appreciation of the 1900 volume: "The work as it now stands completed is a storehouse of information, an inspiring example of serious argumentation, and a powerful defense of the fundamental elements of the Christian religion against now fashionable assailants." Henry C. Minton, review of *The Scientific Evidences of Revealed Religion*, by Charles W. Shields, *PRR* 12 (1901): 453–54; B. B. Warfield, review of *Philosophia Ultima Vol. III*, by Charles W. Shields, *PTR* 6 (1906): 542.

135. James McCosh, "A Method of Teaching Religion in a College," *BRPR* 41 (1869): 72–75. McCosh's official title was "President and Robert Lenox Professor of Biblical Instruction." McCosh followed the same schedule as that of his predecessor with the exception that under Maclean freshmen had studied biblical history and geography and sophomores Charles Hodge's *Way of Life*. McCosh outlined his plan for the trustees and advertised it in the college catalogue beginning in 1869. *Catalogue, 1867–68*, 18–19; TM, 12 Dec. 1868, 5:28; *Catalogue, 1869–70*, 23, 26.

136. According to the *Catalogue, 1868–69*, 23, certain weekday recitations used the Greek New Testament. In the *Catalogue, 1870–71*, 42, freshmen, sophomores, and seniors had their recitations in the Greek New Testament. Report Cards, 1871–1873, Box 20, Allan Marquand Papers, Manuscript Division, Rare Books and Special Collections, Princeton University Library. Published with permission of Princeton University Library. The George Potts Bible Prize, established in 1867, awarded copies of Matthew Henry's Bible commentary, *Catalogue, 1885–86*, 137.

137. TM, 26 June 1876, 5:486.

138. *Catalogue, 1876–77*, 32; TM, 9 Nov. 1876, 5:518–19, 540. The trustees also passed a resolution noting that they "warmly" approved of the new program. TM, 18 June 1877, 5:581; 19 June 1877, 5:629. Leslie wrongly claims that Bible instruction came to an end in 1876 because of student misbehavior at the Sabbath afternoon lectures. *Gentlemen and Scholars*, 97.

139. Beginning in 1878–1879, McCosh taught seniors the Pentateuch and "Christian Doctrines in Romans." *Catalogue, 1878–79*, 42; *Catalogue, 1882–83*, 122.

140. Hunt was assisted by Latin professor Andrew F. West from 1883–1884 through 1887–1888, John H. Westcott, a Latin tutor and Ph.D. candidate in 1886–1887; and George Black Roddy, a Latin tutor in the 1887–1888. Besides Orris, Greek Professor Samuel R. Winans lectured sophomores on the Gospel of Luke in the 1884–1885 and 1886–1887 academic years. In 1884–1885, Professor of Political Economy and Jurisprudence Alexander Johnston assisted Ormond with the junior class. *Catalogue, 1883–84*, 130; *Catalogue, 1884–85*, 145; *Catalogue, 1885–86*, 151; *Catalogue, 1886–87*, 159; *Catalogue, 1887–88*, 159. *General Catalogue*, 241–42, 251, 279.

141. TM, 13 Nov. 1884, 6:570–71; 26 June 1876, 5:486. For similar statements, see ibid., 26 June 1871, 5:168; 13 Nov. 1879, 6:109.

142. "The Death of a Noted Divine," *Pres*, 21 Nov. 1894, 4.

143. Georg G. Iggers, *The German Conception of History* (Middletown, Conn.: Wesleyan University Press, 1968), 6; "Historicism," *Dictionary of the History of Ideas*, ed. Philip P. Wiener (New York: Scribner, 1973), 2:456–462; Massa, *Briggs*, 4–6; Turner, *Without God, Without Creed*, 136–37, 150–57.

144. Ahlstrom, *Religious History*, 771–74; Jerry W. Brown, *The Rise of Biblical Criticism in America, 1800–1870: The New England Scholars* (Middleton, Conn.: Wesleyan University Press, 1969); Ira W. Brown, "The Higher Criticism Comes to America," *Journal of Presbyterian History* 38 (1960): 193–212; Robert W. Funk, "The Watershed of the American Biblical Tradition: The Chicago School, First Phase, 1892–

1920," *Journal of Biblical Literature* 95 (1976): 4–22; W. Neil, "The Criticism and Theological Use of the Bible, 1700–1950," in *Cambridge History of the Bible: The West from the Reformation to the Present Day*, ed. S. L. Greenslade (Cambridge: Cambridge University Press, 1963), 3:238–93; Alan Richardson, "The Rise of Modern Biblical Scholarship and Recent Discussion of the Bible," in *Cambridge History of the Bible*, 3:294–318; Marsden, "Everyone One's Own Interpreter?" 79–100; Massa, *Briggs*, 3–13; Noll, *Between Faith and Criticism*, 11–31; Thomas H. Olbricht, "Intellectual Ferment and Instruction in the Scripture," in *The Bible in American Education: From Source Book to Text Book*, ed. David L. Barr and Nicholas Piediscalzi (Philadelphia: Fortress, 1982), 97–119; J. C. O'Neill, "History of Biblical Criticism," *Anchor Bible Dictionary*, ed. David Noel Freedman (New York: Doubleday, 1992), 1:726–729; Stewart, "Tethered Theology," 29–99: Ferenc M. Szasz, *The Divided Mind of Protestant America, 1880–1930* (University, Ala.: University of Alabama Press, 1982), 15–41.

145. Brown, *Rise of Biblical Criticism*, 180; Stewart, "Tethered Theology," 290–91.

146. Cashdollar, *Transformation of Theology*, 182–205.

147. Francis L. Patton, "The Dogmatic Aspect of Pentateuchal Criticism," *PresRev* 4 (1883): 361. A. A. Hodge and B. B. Warfield likewise distinguished between "the more strict and the more lax views of Inspiration maintained by believing scholars." "Inspiration," *PresRev* 2 (1881): 236.

148. Blair Lee, Bible Course Notebook, Box 249, Blair and Lee Family Papers.

149. Blair Lee, Chemistry Course Notebook, 1879, Box 249, Blair and Lee Family Papers; Old Testament History Chart, Box 413, Blair and Lee Family Papers; St. Paul's Travels—Dr. McCosh. Freshman Year, Class of '77, McCosh Papers; McCosh, "Method of Teaching Religion," 74–75.

150. James McCosh, *The Propriety of Acknowledging the Lord in All our Ways: The Baccalaureate Sermon Preached before the College of New Jersey, June 16, 1878* (New York: Robert Carter, 1878), 16.

151. Henry Van Dyke Jr. to Henry Van Dyke Sr., 27 Sept. 1870, Box 133, Van Dyke Papers.

152. Lee, Bible Course Notebook, Murray's Lectures on Acts, 1879, Box 249, Blair and Lee Family Papers.

153. George Macloskie, Bible Lessons, Old Testament, Fall 1885, School of Science, 7, Box 1, Macloskie Papers.

154. McCosh, *Religion in a College*, 13.

155. McCosh, "The Sifting of Peter," *Gospel Sermons*, 198.

156. McCosh, *The World a Scene of Contest: The Baccalaureate Sermon Preached before the College of New Jersey, June 25, 1876* (New York: Robert Carter, 1876), 25–26.

157. Elijah R. Craven protested the move because, as he wrote, it altered "an immemorial custom of this Institution." TM, 8 Nov. 1877, 5:676.

158. According to the notations on the cover of this sermon manuscript, Duffield preached it at least five times in the college chapel. John T. Duffield, Sermon I Cor. 16:22 Manuscript, Box 1, Duffield Family Papers, Manuscript Division, Rare Books and Special Collections, Princeton University Library. Published with permission of Princeton University Library.

159. George Macloskie, "Be Strong and of Good Courage," Sermon Manuscript, Notes on New Testament, Box 1, Macloskie Papers.

160. McCosh, *Religion in College*, 21.

161. Princeton University, Minutes of the Faculty of Princeton University (hereafter FM), 12 Sept. 1870, 300, Seeley G. Mudd Manuscript Library, Princeton University.

Published with permission of Princeton University Library; Blair Lee to Elizabeth Blair Lee, 12 Dec. 1877, Box 269, Blair and Lee Family Papers.

162. *Catalogue, 1870–71*, 41; Ordway Diary, 30 Sept. 1884; 11 May 1885, Box 1, Ordway Diaries.

163. TM, 17 Dec. 1873, 5:333; 22 June 1874, 5:347; 18 June 18 1877, 5:585; "College Chapels," *Pr*, 28 May 1886, 1; Allan Marquand to Henry G. Marquand, 25 Nov. 1879, Box 15, Marquand Papers.

164. "Day of Prayer for Colleges," *PP*, 31 Jan. 1885; "Correspondence. New York," *Pres*, 6 Feb. 1886, 6; FM, 25 Jan. 1884, 250; Ordway Diary, 25 Jan. 1883; 12 Jan. to 31 Jan. 1884, Box 1, Ordway Diaries.

165. "The Services of Yesterday," *Pr*, 29 Jan. 1886, 1. McCosh wrote Allan Marquand that he felt Pierson's visit was "a good work of grace in our College." James McCosh to Allan Marquand, 4 Feb. 1886, Box 16, Marquand Papers.

166. Henry Van Dyke Jr. to Henry Van Dyke Sr., 22 Jan. 1870, Box 133, Van Dyke Papers; Blair Lee to Elizabeth Blair Lee, 29 Feb. 1879, Box 270, Blair and Lee Family Papers.

167. TM, 16 June 1884, 6:537. For similar reports, see ibid., 22 Dec. 1869, 5:91–92; 26 June 1871, 5:114; 18 June 1872, 5:249; 23 June 1873, 5:298–99; 24 June 1874, 5:346–47; 16 Dec. 1874, 5:381; 28 June 1875, 5:399; 17 June 1878, 6:24; 14 Nov. 1878, 6:43; 13 Feb. 1879, 6:59; 12 Feb. 1880, 6:134; 22 June 1880, 6:153; 20 June 1881, 6:248; 10 Nov. 1881, 6:293; 8 Feb. 1883, 6:423; 19 June 1882, 6:370; 8 Feb. 1883, 6:423; 14 Feb. 1884, 6:512; 16 June 1884, 6:537; 12 Feb. 1885, 6:597; 15 June 1885, 6:617; 11 Feb. 1886, 6:701; 11 Nov. 1886, 6:756; 10 Feb. 1887, 7:3–4; 10 Nov. 1887, 7:84–85. While McCosh was likely playing to the interests of the trustees in these reports, the spiritual welfare of the campus appears to have been a genuine concern of his. He made similar reports to individuals whose favor he did not need to curry. James McCosh to William Berryman Scott, 15 Dec. 1879; James McCosh to Theodore Monroe McNair, 19 Apr. 1888, McCosh Papers.

168. Ordway Diary, 24 Feb. 1882; 29 Apr. 1884, Box 1, Ordway Diaries.

169. Walter Lowrie, Autobiographical Vol. 1:31–32, Box 1, Walter Lowrie Papers, Manuscript Division, Rare Books and Special Collections, Princeton University Library. Published with permission of Princeton University Library.

170. Blair Lee to Samuel Phillips Lee, 3 Feb. 1879, Box 274, Blair and Lee Family Papers.

171. Ordway Diary, 27 Sept. 1880, Box 1, Ordway Diaries; John D. Davis to Allan Marquand, 13 Nov. 1872, Box 12, Marquand Papers; Alexander Leitch, *A Princeton Companion* (Princeton: Princeton University Press, 1978), 86; FM, 19 May 1875, 475; 28 Oct. 1881, 92.

172. *Pr* 21 Oct. 1881, 75; Charles W. Shields to Allan Marquand, 24 Feb. 1873, Box 18, Marquand Papers; John T. Duffield, *A Sermon Delivered in the Chapel of the College of New Jersey, Dec. 19th, 1876* (Princeton: Press Printing Establishment, 1877).

173. "The Editor's Table," *Pr*, 21 Oct. 1881, 86; "Should Chapel be Abolished?" *Pr*, 12 Mar. 1885, 295; editorial, *Pr*, 23 Sept. 1881, 53–54. See also *Pr*, 19 Oct. 1876, 5–6; *Pr*, 2 Nov. 1876, 1–2.

174. Ordway Diary, 7 Oct. 1882; 1 Oct. 1883; Box 1, Ordway Diaries; Matthew M. Coburn, "The Philadelphian Society: An investigation into the demise of an evangelical student Christian organization at Princeton University in the 1920s," (Senior Thesis, Princeton University, 1991), 4–15.

175. Ibid., 12–28; Philadelphian Society, *One Hundred Years, 1825–1925: The Phila-*

delphian Society of Princeton University Commemorates the 100th Anniversary of Its Founding (n.p., [1925]), 7–12; William K. Selden, *The Princeton Summer Camp, 1908–1975* (Princeton: Printed by Princeton University Press, [1987]), 1–13; Clarence P. Shedd, *Two Centuries of Student Christian Movements: Their Origin and Intercollegiate Life* (New York: Association Press, 1934) 137–52; Robert P. Wilder, *The Student Volunteer Movement* (New York: SVM, 1935), 7–13, 36–63 passim; Daniel Sack, "'Refreshed in the Company of My Brethren': The Campus Religious Establishment and Student Agency at the College of New Jersey," *American Presbyterians* 73 (1995): 219–28.

176. In one month alone, Paul Martin, Class of 1882, recorded in his diary hearing a lecture by Henry Calderwood and sermons by Scottish, French, and Indian Presbyterian ministers. Paul Martin Diary, 4 Oct. 1880; 13 Oct. 1880; 22 Oct. 1880; 31 Oct. 1880; Box 1, Paul Martin Papers, Manuscript Division, Rare Books and Special Collections, Princeton University Library. Published with permission of Princeton University Library.

177. Leitch, *Princeton Companion*, 87.

178. Students held a rally in the fall of 1873 and passed several resolutions condemning intemperance "on the grounds of propriety, morality and religion." TM, 17 Dec. 1874, 5:329. Temperance was a consistent topic of discussion among the faculty and trustees. See FM, 17 Mar. 1871, 313–14; 20 Feb. 1874, 410–11; 19 Dec. 1877, 575; 23 Jan. 1885, 323; 23 Sept. 1887, 541; TM, 28 June 1869, 5:56; 27 June 1870, 5:114; 24 June 1874, 5:347; 25 June 1875, 5:399; Charles W. Shields to James R. Shields, 17 Mar. 1874, Box 3, Shields Papers; McCosh, *Life of McCosh*, 17–18, 35. McCosh campaigned for stricter state antiliquor laws and persuaded some professors to run in local elections on a temperance platform. Hoeveler, *McCosh*, 80–81, 254.

179. Ordway Diary, Jan. 15 to 21 Jan. 1882, Box 1, Ordway Diaries.

180. Henry Van Dyke Jr. to Henry Van Dyke Sr., 22 Jan. 1870, Box 133, Van Dyke Papers.

181. "Messrs. Moody and Sankey in Princeton," *PP*, 12 Feb. 1876; McCosh, *Twenty Years of Princeton College*, 54–55; Minutes of the Philadelphian Society, 1875–1880, 26 Mar. 1876, Box 2, Student Christian Association Records, Seeley G. Mudd Manuscript Library, Princeton University. Published with permission of Princeton University Library; "Correspondence," *Pres*, 22 Jan. 1876, 3; "The Princeton Revival," *Pres*, 12 Feb. 1876, 8; "The Movement in Princeton," *Pres*, 4 Mar. 1876, 4; E. J. Goodspeed, *A Full History of the Wonderful Career of Moody and Sankey, in Great Britain and America* (New York: Goodspeed, 1876), 407–15.

182. TM, 26 June 1876, 5:483–84. McCosh also reported that Episcopal students did not participate in the communion service for matters of conscience.

Chapter 2

1. James McCosh, *Inauguration of Rev. Jas. M'Cosh, D.D., LL.D., as President of Princeton College, October 27, 1868* (Princeton: Printed at the Standard Office, 1868), 15.

2. TM, 15 June 1885, 6:618.

3. TM, 9 Nov. 1876, 5:516.

4. Richard Hofstadter, "The Revolution in Higher Education," in *Paths of American Thought*, ed. Arthur M. Schlesinger Jr. and Morton White (Boston: Houghton Mifflin, 1963), 276–77; Richard Hofstadter and Walter P. Metzger, *The Development of Aca-*

demic Freedom in the United States (New York: Columbia University Press, 1955), 230–32, 297–98, 352; Frederick Rudolph, *The American College and University: A History* (New York: Vintage, 1962), 394–416 passim; Laurence R. Veysey, *The Emergence of the American University* (Chicago: University of Chicago Press, 1965), 45.

5. TM, 8 Feb. 1877, 5:557.

6. James McCosh to [?] Coffree, 18 June 1875, McCosh Papers. For similar inquiries, see Asa Gray to James McCosh, 11 Apr. 1874, McCosh Papers; Daniel C. Gilman to Arnold Guyot, 11 Nov. 1870, Box 62, Cameron Family Papers, Manuscript Division, Rare Books and Special Collections, Princeton University Library. Published with Permission of Princeton University Library; Ethelbert B. Warfield to Henry C. Cameron, 12 July 1888, Box 22, Cameron Family Papers.

7. James McCosh to William Berryman Scott, 15 Dec. 1879, McCosh Papers; William Berryman Scott, *Some Memories of a Palaeontologist* (Princeton: Princeton University Press, 1939), 1–9.

8. David Starr Jordan, *The Days of a Man*, 2 vols. (Yonkers-on-Hudson, N.Y.: World, 1922), 1:150–51; E. D. Cope to A. Cope, 16 Mar. 1873, in Nathan Reingold, ed., *Science in the Nineteenth-Century: A Documentary History* (New York: Hill and Wang, 1964), 245. James R. Moore notes that the geologist Joseph LeConte of the University of California was likely rejected as Guyot's successor because of his growing theological liberalism, *Post-Darwinian Controversies: A Study of the Protestant Struggle to Come to Terms with Darwin in Great Britain and America, 1870–1900* (Cambridge: Cambridge University Press, 1979), 385, n. 81.

9. TM, 21 June 1881, 6:281.

10. "Sectarianism in Princeton," *Pr*, 22 Sept. 1876, 7.

11. Editorial, *Pr*, 13 Nov. 1885, 2. W. Bruce Leslie misinterprets the board's action in 1876 in three ways. He anachronistically reads the modern definition of nonsectarianism (a respectful indifference to the religious affiliation of faculty applicants) into McCosh's 1876 plea to hire more non-Presbyterians, assumes that ordination is an indicator of sectarianism, and ignores the larger commitment to hiring from only within the evangelical Protestant community. *Gentlemen and Scholars: College and Community in the "Age of the University," 1865–1917* (State College: Pennsylvania State University Press, 1992), 65–66. Leslie quotes out of context the 1876 article in the *Princetonian* as evidence of the popular commitment to a modern nonsectarianism. He also overlooks the second article. Ibid., 96.

12. During the first part of McCosh's tenure, Princeton hired only five professors who were alumni of the college. The three Princeton Seminary graduates were among these five college alumni. Princeton University, *General Catalogue of Princeton University, 1746–1906* (Princeton: Published by the University), 33–35.

13. James McCosh to Daniel C. Gilman, 11 Dec. 1876, quoted in Leslie, *Gentlemen and Scholars*, 67.

14. James McCosh, *The Life of James McCosh: A Record Chiefly Autobiographical*, ed. William M. Sloane (New York: Scribner, 1896), 180. Two alumni who became professors at Princeton under McCosh recall that these meetings played a major role in cultivating their interests in an academic vocation. Henry Fairfield Osborn, *Creative Education in School, College, University, and Museum: Personal Observation and Experience of the Half Century 1877–1927* (New York: Scribner, 1927), 114; Scott, *Some Memories*, 50.

15. TM, 22 Dec. 1869, 5:105; 27 June 1870, 5:131–32; 24 June 1872, 5:217.

16. William Berryman Scott, Notebook on Some Memories of a Paleontologist,

10:206, Box 6, William Berryman Scott Papers, Manuscript Division, Rare Books and Special Collections, Princeton University Library. Published with permission of Princeton University Library. In his published biography, Scott's description of McCosh and Guyot's counsel is carefully edited out. *Some Memories*, 85. Scott describes his experience with Huxley in ibid., 84–96.

17. James McCosh to Henry B. Fine, 16 Feb. 1885, McCosh Papers. For a similar warning, see James McCosh to James Mark Baldwin, 2 Dec. 1884, in James Mark Baldwin, *Between Two Wars 1861–1921: Being Memories, Opinions, Letters Received*, 2 vols. (Boston: Stratford, 1926), 2:199–200.

18. J. P. Kennedy Bryan to Allan Marquand, 16 Jan. 1874, Box 11, Marquand Papers.

19. Willard Thorp, Minor Myers Jr., and Jeremiah Stanton Finch, *The Princeton Graduate School: A History* (Princeton: Princeton University Press, 1978), 42.

20. Two Ph.D. and both D.Sc. degrees were earned at Princeton. Of the remaining five doctorates on the faculty, two were earned at Leipzig, and one each at Jena, Heidelberg, Berlin, and Johns Hopkins. Three had also attended or graduated from Princeton Seminary. Princeton Theological Seminary, *Biographical Catalogue of the Princeton Theological Seminary, 1815–1932*, comp. Edward H. Roberts (Princeton: Published by the Trustees of The Theological Seminary of the Presbyterian Church, Princeton, New Jersey, 1933), 35–37.

21. The figures for Harvard's faculty comes from Burton J. Bledstein, *The Culture of Professionalism: The Middle Class and the Development of Higher Education in America* (New York: Norton, 1976), 267; *Catalogue, 1884–85*, 8–9. Of the thirty faculty members at Princeton in 1884 with the rank of professor, six had Ph.D. and two D.Sc. degrees. Two others had earned M.D. degrees. Several of those who had honorary degrees (including honorary Ph.D. degrees), such as Samuel Stanhope Orris and Andrew F. West, had studied in Europe. *General Catalogue*, 33–36.

22. TM, 11 Nov. 1880, 6:191; 20 June 1881, 6:249; Edward Shils, "The Order of Learning in the United States: The Ascendancy of the University," in *The Organization of Knowledge in Modern America, 1860–1920*, ed. Alexandra Oleson and John Voss (Baltimore: Johns Hopkins University Press, 1979), 28–29.

23. TM, 9 Feb. 1882, 6:329; 19 June 1882, 6:348; FM, 15 May 1882, 119–23; 5 June 1882, 129.

24. FM, 16 Sept. 1887, 531; Scott, *Some Memories*, 136.

25. TM, 20 Nov. 1885, 377.

26. TM, 14 June 1884, 6:537; James McCosh, "Oversight of Students in Princeton College," *New-York Evangelist*, 17 Apr. 1884, 8. One despondent mother, for instance, pleaded in a twelve-page letter to art professor Allan Marquand in the fall of 1881 for his aid in rescuing her son who had lost "his childhood's faith." This happened, she explained, the year before he enrolled at Princeton when as a plebe at West Point he shared a tent with "a declared atheist" during "Beast Barracks." The young man, best remembered by his classmates for sporting a beard and a blasé attitude, dropped out at Christmas. Mildred Carlisle to Allan Marquand, 19 Oct. [1881], Box 12, Marquand Papers; Jonathan Sturges, *History of the Class of '85, of Princeton College* (Princeton: MacCrellish and Quigley, 1885), 6.

27. TM, 9 Nov. 1876, 5:548.

28. McCosh, *Inauguration of M'Cosh*, 16, 18–25.

29. Students chose electives both from traditional subjects such as mathematics, Greek, and Latin, and from certain newer ones like astronomy, French, and German. *Catalogue, 1869–70*, 27; TM, 22 Dec. 1869, 5:87, 104–105.

30. *Catalogue, 1869–70*, 21–23; *Catalogue, 1873–74*, 18–20, 32, 43–44; *Catalogue, 1878–79*, 22–25, 42, 61–67; *Catalogue, 1883–84*, 42–43; 68–72, 87–89, 98–101, 130; *Catalogue, 1888–89*, 52–55, 87–89, 93–95, 129. A trivial, though telling, sign of the impact of specialization is the expansion of the college catalogue. In 1868–1869, the catalogue was 32 pages and in 1887–1888 176 pages.

31. TM, 18 June 1883, 6:447–57; 15 June 1884, 6:535.

32. Veysey, *Emergence of the University*, 11 n. 26, 51–52; Frederick Rudolph, *Curriculum: A History of the American Undergraduate Course of Study Since 1636* (San Francisco: Jossey-Bass, 1977), 23, 194–95; idem, *College and University*, 298; Hugh Hawkins, *Between Harvard and America: The Educational Leadership of Charles W. Eliot* (New York: Oxford University Press, 1972), 97, 124–25, 129, 240. For an alternative perspective, see J. David Hoeveler Jr., *James McCosh and the Scottish Intellectual Tradition: From Glasgow to Princeton* (Princeton: Princeton University Press, 1981), 216–311; Thomas Jefferson Wertenbaker, *Princeton, 1746–1896* (Princeton: Princeton University Press, 1946), 190–343. Institutional histories of Princeton written in the period under consideration likewise credit McCosh with transforming the college into a university. James W. Alexander Jr., *Princeton—Old and New* (New York: Scribner, 1899), 61–66; Varnum Lansing Collins, *Princeton* (New York: Oxford University Press, 1914), 221–50; John DeWitt, "Princeton College,"in *Universities and Their Sons: History, Influence and Characteristics of American Universities*, ed. Joshua L. Chamberlain, vol. 1 (Boston: Herndon, 1898), 521–26; Edwin M. Norris, *The Story of Princeton* (Boston: Little, Brown, 1917), 199–223; Thorp, Myers, and Finch, *Princeton Graduate School*, 14–43; John Rogers Williams, *The Handbook of Princeton*, with an introduction by Woodrow Wilson (New York: Grafton, 1905), 23–24.

33. Osborn, *Creative Education*, 112. Osborn's experience was not unique. William Berryman Scott found that the junior year brought about "a complete change in atmosphere." *Some Memories*, 43.

34. TM, 13 Nov. 1884, 6:565. In the Spring of 1885 McCosh repudiated, in a letter to the *New York Tribune*, Andrew D. White's allegation that Princeton forced all students to take the same courses "without a quiver." The letter is reprinted in "Elective Studies at Princeton," *Pr*, 4 May 1885, 1.

35. TM, 20 Dec. 1871, 5:201; Thorp, Myers, and Finch, *Princeton Graduate School*, 21.

36. William K. Selden, *The Legacy of John Cleve Green* (Princeton: Printed by Office of Printing Services Princeton University [1987]), 6–13, 27–29.

37. *General Catalogue*, 33–37; *Catalogue, 1878–79*, 64–67; *Catalogue, 1888–89*, 85–88, 93–95.

38. Alexander Leitch, *A Princeton Companion* (Princeton: Princeton University Press, 1978), 32, 64–65, 162, 177–78, 246–48, 307, 311–12, 432–33, 534–35.

39. The School of Science program expanded from three years to four years in the fall of 1876. In the fifteen years between the opening of the School of Science in 1873 and 1888, the rate of growth for students enrolled in the A.B. program averaged less than 1 percent per year. By contrast, the School of Science enjoyed an 18 percent annual growth rate between 1876, when four full classes were enrolled, and 1888. After reaching a high of 430 students in the 1875–1876 academic year, enrollment in the Academic Department actually dropped several times and only recovered in McCosh's final year, when 428 students enrolled.

40. TM, 9 Nov. 1882, 6:386–87; *Catalogue, 1873–74*, 21–22, 43.

41. TM, 28 June 1875, as quoted in Thorp, Myers, and Finch, *Princeton Graduate School*, 26.

42. *General Catalogue*, 373; Thorp, Myers, and Finch, *Princeton Graduate School*, 21–22.

43. TM, 17 June 1878, as quoted in ibid., 28. Until the 1882–1883 academic year, the provisions for graduate degrees were placed in the catalogue almost as an addendum. In that year, information on all advanced degrees were collected under the title "Graduate Courses in the Academic and Scientific Departments." In 1887–1888, the title of the graduate program was changed to "University Courses in the Academic and Scientific Departments." Ibid., 29.

44. No one earned any of these three degrees. The B.D., according to the trustees' minutes, was to be awarded to Princeton Seminary graduates who pursued a course of study prescribed by the seminary faculty and were examined after one or two years of residency, Princeton Seminary graduates who pursued supervised study for three years without residency, or graduates from any college or seminary who pursued a supervised course of study. The faculty appointed Princeton Seminary professors William Henry Green, Charles A. Aiken, and B. B. Warfield to give examinations for the B.D. degree. TM, 21 June 1886, 6:735; FM, 23 Sept. 1887, 532.

45. TM, 10 Feb. 1887, 7:25.

46. Thorp, Myers, and Finch, *Princeton Graduate School*, 29–30. Between 1877 and 1888, Princeton awarded five Ph.D. degrees, seven D.Sc. degrees, six M.S. degrees, and fifty-four A.M. degrees, of which thirty-six (66 percent) went to seminarians cross-enrolled at the college. *General Catalogue*, 373–75.

47. TM, 9 Nov. 1882, 6:409. In the 1868–1869 academic year, there were only two terms for the senior year. Thus, Shields technically taught only five courses for five hours that year. In the next academic year, the senior year was divided into three terms, hence dividing his courses into six terms and six hours. *Catalogue, 1868–69*, 22–23; *Catalogue, 1869–70*, 24–25; *Catalogue, 1887–88*, 83–85.

48. Between 1882–1883 and 1886–1887, the three hours of ethics instruction was given over to two terms in the senior year. In 1887–1888, the course was compressed into one three-hour course. *Catalogue, 1887–88*, 87.

49. *Catalogue, 1873–74*, 44; *Catalogue, 1876–77*, 47.

50. Editorial, *Pr*, 7 Oct. 1881, 65.

51. Scott, *Some Memories*, 49.

52. Scott, Notebook on Some Memories of a Paleontologist, 4:230, Box 1, Scott Papers. This recollection did not appear in his published autobiography.

53. James McCosh, *The Religious Aspects of Evolution* (New York: G.P. Putnam's Sons, 1888), xii, n.1. Outside of one presentation at one of McCosh's library meetings, where Scott espoused his theistic evolutionist position and repudiated the special creation of the species, Scott apparently had little to say on the harmony of science and religion during McCosh's tenure. "Library Meeting," *Pr*, 29 Nov. 1887, 1. Membership File, First Presbyterian Church of Princeton, Archives, Princeton Seminary Libraries. Cyrus F. Brackett, who was called to a new chair in physics and helped found the department of electrical engineering, displayed a similar disinterest. Brackett's home and that of his neighbor, astronomy professor Charles A. Young, a student recalled, "was for some time jokingly known as the 'Atheists' Corner.'" Fred B. Rogers, "Cyrus Fogg Brackett: Physicist and Physician," *Journal of the Medical Society of New Jersey* 52 (1955): 453. Hoeveler cites this article as evidence that McCosh "was willing to bring professors of professional accomplishment to Princeton even when they had no commitment to religion." *McCosh*, 244. Leslie uses the latter part of Rogers's quotation as evidence to support his view that "McCosh even tolerated a few skeptics and hired two

talented young scientists who had little pretension of theism" and was willing "to expose students to agnostic scientists." *Gentlemen and Scholars*, 33, 66. Rogers provides evidence that clearly contradicts Hoeveler's and Leslie's contention that Brackett was a skeptic if not an avowed atheist. Brackett, Rogers recalled, was "a lifelong student of the Bible as well as a forceful orator and proved popular as a speaker at daily college chapel services." Seven years after he moved to Princeton, Brackett joined First Presbyterian Church and remained an active member until his death. But like Scott, his scholarly research did not include questions concerning the religious ramifications of his work. Rogers, "Brackett," 455. Young, who was hired in part because he was an "Orthodox Congregationalist," had studied for a year at Andover Theological Seminary and was a member of Trinity Episcopal Church in Princeton throughout his career. In 1894, Young published a teleological argument for the existence of God from recent discoveries in astronomy. Membership File, First Presbyterian Church of Princeton; Joshua L. Chamberlain, ed., *Universities and Their Sons: History, Influence and Characteristics of American Universities with Biographical Sketches and Portraits of Alumni and Recipients of Honorary Degrees*, vol. 2 (Boston: Herndon, 1899), 240–41; FM, 5 Dec. 1884, 301; C. A. Young, *God's Glory in the Heavens* (Cranbury, N.J.: George W. Burroughs, 1894).

54. On the separation of theological concerns and methodological interests, see George M. Marsden, *Soul of the American University: From Protestant Establishment to Established Nonbelief* (New York: Oxford University Press, 1994), 156–59; idem, "The Soul of the American University," in *The Secularization of the Academy*, ed. George M. Marsden and Bradley J. Longfield (New York: Oxford University Press, 1992), 15–16, 21–22; Larry Shiner, "The Meaning of Secularization," in *Secularization and the Protestant Prospect*, ed. James F. Childress and David B. Harned (Philadelphia: Westminster, 1970), 30–42.

55. The total enrollment was 604 in 1887–1888, a 215 percent increase. *Catalogue, 1868–69*, 19; *Catalogue, 1887–88*, 39.

56. Rudolph, *Curriculum*, 161–62; Bledstein, *Culture of Professionalism*, 279; Hoeveler, *McCosh*, 302.

57. TM, 18 Dec. 1872, 5:246; 27 Mar. 1873, 5:289.

58. *Catalogue, 1873–74*, 46–47.

59. TM, 13 Nov. 1879, 6:110; 12 Feb. 1880, 6:135–36. See also ibid., 23 June 1873, 5:295–96; 17 Dec. 1873, 5:334; 16 Dec. 1874, 5:378.

60. Blair also endowed a chair of geology, gave money to increase faculty salaries, and constructed a building bearing his name at the college. Leitch, *Princeton Companion*, 59–60; Hoeveler, *McCosh*, 304.

61. The school opened with 122 students in 1883 and had over two hundred by 1888. The school was something of a junior Princeton College. The Board was controlled by Princetonians and, judging by Charles Ewing Green's correspondence to the headmaster, evangelical Protestantism dominated the religious life of the campus. The original board comprised John C. Green's son, Caleb Smith Green Jr. and his nephew Charles Ewing Green, John T. Nixon, all college trustees, the former headmaster Rev. Samuel Harrill, Princeton Seminary professor Charles A. Aiken, Princeton College Professor William M. Sloane, and Parker Gummere, a Trenton attorney. McCosh chose James Cameron Mackenzie, a Scottish immigrant, to serve as the new headmaster. Charles Ewing Green to J. C. Mackenzie, 10 Nov. 1884; Charles Ewing Green to J. C. Mackenzie, 25 Apr. 1885; J. C. Mackenzie Papers, John Dixon Library, Archives, Lawrenceville School, Lawrenceville, New Jersey. Roland J. Mulford, *History of the Lawrenceville*

School, 1810–1935 (Princeton: Princeton University Press, 1935), 87–90, 97; James McLachlan, *American Boarding Schools: A Historical Study* (New York: Scribner, 1970), 197–205; Hoeveler, *McCosh*, 304–305.

62. Hoeveler, *McCosh*, 305.

63. TM, 8 Nov. 1883, 6:478. See also ibid., 13 Nov. 1879, 6:109.

64. TM, 17 June 1878, 6:22–23; 12 Dec. 1869, 5:90; 16 June 1879, 6:81; 12 Feb. 1880, 6:135.

65. TM, 28 June 1869, 5:60. McCosh reported to the trustees in 1869 that only 200 of the 325 students, or 61 percent, lived on campus. By McCosh's final year, I estimate from students' room locations listed in college catalogue that 81 percent of the 523 students lived in dormitories or with their families in town. TM, 12 Dec. 1869, 5:90; *Catalogue, 1887–88*, 21–39.

66. TM, 12 Feb. 1880, 6:135–36.

67. Leslie, *Gentlemen and Scholars*, 14–15; Wertenbaker, *Princeton*, 113.

68. TM, 13 Nov. 1879, 6:109; Henry G. Marquand to Allan Marquand, 2 Feb., [1882], Box 15, Marquand Papers.

69. FM, 5 Dec. 1884, 301; 12 Dec. 1884, 303; 23 Oct. 1885, 368–69; 24 Sept. 1886, 445; 20 Jan. 1888, 562; 20 Jan. 1888, 563.

70. All statistical information regarding the religious composition of the student body is drawn from the senior yearbook. Unfortunately, the yearbook is not an exact indicator of religious composition because it excludes those students who did not graduate. On average, six students, or 7 percent, of each class gave "none" as their religious preference, a term that may have masked an unpopular religious affiliation. Students who gave no response to the question of religious affiliation for the Classes of 1872, 1875, 1877 were listed under "heathen" or "infidels." The percentage of graduating seniors from New Jersey, New York, and Pennsylvania fluctuated during McCosh's tenure but remained rather high: in the Class of 1872, 68 percent of the seniors came from these three states, 70 percent in the Class of 1880, and 77 percent in the Class of 1888. *Nassau Herald, 1872*, 39; *Nassau Herald, 1875*, 54; *Nassau Herald, 1876*, 56; *Nassau Herald, 1877*, 66; *Nassau Herald, 1878*, 55; *Nassau Herald, 1879*, 54–55; *Nassau Herald, 1880*, 47–48; *Nassau Herald, 1881*, 49–50, *Nassau Herald, 1882*, 53, 55; *Nassau Herald, 1883*, 57, 59; *Nassau Herald, 1884*, 57, 59; *Nassau Herald, 1885*, 68, 70; *Nassau Herald, 1886*, 68–69; *Nassau Herald, 1887*, 64, 67; *Nassau Herald, 1888*, 71–73, 76.

71. Marcia Graham Synnott, *The Half-Opened Door: Discrimination and Admissions at Harvard, Yale, and Princeton, 1900–1970* (Westport, Conn.: Greenwood Press, 1979), 174–76.

72. TM, 17 June 1878, 6:23. See also ibid., 14 Feb. 1884, 6:511.

73. McCosh outlined his beautification of the campus in, *Twenty Years of Princeton College: Being a Farewell Address Delivered June 20th, 1888 by James McCosh, D.D., LL.D., Litt.D.* (New York: Scribner, 1888), 9–15.

74. All figures are estimates. *Catalogue, 1868–69*, 28; *Catalogue, 1887–88*, 157; George Herbert Palmer, *Expenses at Harvard: An Address by Professor George Herbert Palmer Before Harvard Graduates, Commencement Day, 1887* (Cambridge: John Wilson, 1887), 9; John J. McCusker, *How Much Is That in Real Money? A Historical Price Index for Use as a Deflator of Money Values in the Economy of the United States* (Worcester: American Antiquarian Society, 1992), 328–29.

75. All figures are estimates based on an analysis of the alumni records. Alumni Files, Classes of 1876, 1883, and 1891, Seeley G. Mudd Manuscript Library, Princeton University. Published with permission of Princeton University Library. The Lawrenceville

School became the greatest source of boarding school students during McCosh's tenure. In the fall of 1886, for example, McCosh reported to the trustees that the Lawrenceville School supplied twenty students to the freshmen class. TM, 11 Nov. 1886, 6:753.

76. McLachlan, *American Boarding Schools*, 205.

77. In 1887, Ivy Hall became the first eating club to build a house. Frederic C. Rich, *The First Hundred Years of the Ivy Club, 1879–1979: A Centennial History* (Princeton: The Ivy Club, 1979), 34; Leitch, *Princeton Companion*, 146. Murray made his comments in TM, 12 Feb. 1885, 6:601–602. See also ibid., 11 Nov. 1880, 6:217.

78. Bledstein, *Culture of Professionalism*, 33; Veysey, *Emergence of the University*, 265–66; Rudolph, *College and University*, 289; idem, *Curriculum*, 152.

79. TM, 18 June 1877, 5:581. See also ibid., 14 Feb. 1878, 5:680.

80. Bailey B. Burritt, *Professional Distribution of College and University Graduates* (Washington, D.C.: Government Printing Office, 1912), 20, 84, 101, 105, 143. These percentages are only for graduates of the B.A. programs. The figures for Princeton, which were included in Burritt's original table, were subtracted to calculate this percentage. It should also be noted that the law profession was increasingly related to that of business in the late nineteenth century.

81. TM, 8 Nov. 1877, 5:647–75.

82. TM, 24 June 1872, 5:220. Besides these scholarships, three of four charitable funds were specified for preministerial students and other worthy students. *Catalogue, 1885–86*, 152–65. Leslie correctly observes that the official Presbyterian support for the college was minimal. He specifically notes that the New Brunswick Presbytery annually donated several prizes and scholarships for five to eight preministerial students, but overlooks the other forms of financial aid given to Presbyterians. *Gentlemen and Scholars*, 35.

83. TM, 10 Nov. 1881, 6:313–14. According to the trustees' minutes, 144 of 416 students in the Academic Department received free tuition, but there were only 62 scholarships to cover the cost. Ibid., 6:311. McCosh reported in 1888 that 170 students were receiving some sort of financial assistance. *Twenty-Years of Princeton College*, 33.

84. Collins, *Princeton*, 161–62, 410; McCosh, *Life of McCosh*, ed. Sloane, 182.

85. TM, 26 June 1871, 5:167; John F. Hageman, *History of Princeton and its Institutions*, 2 vols. (Philadelphia: Lippincott, 1879), 2:291. Green was a trustee of Princeton Seminary from 1853 to 1876. *Biographical Catalogue*, xvii.

86. Stewart, one of the few nonalumni trustees of the college, served on the board from 1868 to 1899. Carter was also a director at the Seminary from 1856 till his death. *General Catalogue*, 22; *Biographical Catalogue*, xi; Princeton Theological Seminary, *Necrological Reports*, (Princeton: J. T. Robinson, 1899), 2:10; *D.A.B.*, 3:542–43; 18:10–11.

87. Stuart also created the endowed chair in the Relations of Philosophy and Science to the Christian Religion for Francis L. Patton at Princeton Seminary in 1881. *D.A.B.*, 18:176–77; 2:437–48.

88. TM, 11 Nov. 1880, quoted in Hoeveler, *McCosh*, 283.

89. TM, 9 Nov. 1882, 6:414. At the end of his presidency, McCosh listed the establishment of eighteen alumni associations among his major achievements. McCosh, *Twenty-Years of Princeton College*, 31. Less than 20 percent of the leadership of the alumni associations in 1885 were ministers, whereas attorneys, doctors, and business leaders constituted roughly 60 percent. *Catalogue, 1885–86*, 124–29.

90. McCosh, *Twenty Years at Princeton College*, 32.

91. Hoeveler, *McCosh*, 295.

92. Veysey, *Emergence of the University*, 350–51; Hawkins, *Between Harvard and America*, 121–22.

93. There were no religious stipulations for any other position in the university. James P. Wind, *The Bible and the University: The Messianic Vision of William Rainey Harper* (Atlanta: Scholars Press, 1987), 112–13. By contrast, when Johns Hopkins University opened in 1876, its board included seven businessmen, four lawyers, one doctor, but no ministers. Rudolph, *College and University*, 174.

94. The fifteen institutions were Williams, Lafayette, Amherst, Wesleyan, Hamilton, Lawrence, Carleton, Beloit, Wabash, Knox, Yale, Pennsylvania, Cornell, Dartmouth, and Princeton. For five state universities (Nebraska, Missouri, Minnesota, Iowa, and Michigan), 4.3 percent of the trustees were clerics for the same year. Earl McGrath, "The Control of Higher Education in America," *Educational Record* 17 (1936): 264–65.

95. Wertenbaker, *Princeton*, 150.

96. In 1868, three of the college's trustees were professors at the seminary, three were trustees, seven were directors, and ten were alumni. Of the new college trustees added to the board between 1868 and 1884, one was a professor, two were trustees, two were directors, and three were alumni of the seminary. *General Catalogue*, 21–23; *Biographical Catalogue*, xi–xii, xvii–xviii.

97. Two of the college's greatest benefactors, John C. Green and Robert L. Stewart, also served on the seminary's board of trustees. The three seminary professors who also taught at the college were James C. Moffatt (1811–1890), a lecturer in Greek literature between 1861 and 1877; Charles A. Aiken (1827–1892), a Professor of Language and Literature between 1866 and 1869; and Francis L. Patton who taught ethics and other courses between 1883 and 1913. Ibid.; *General Catalogue*, 33, 36, 58.

98. *Biographical Catalogue*, xvii–xviii.

99. *Inauguration of M'Cosh*, 4; Francis L. Patton, *The Inauguration of the Rev. Francis Landey Patton. D.D., LL.D., as President of Princeton College* (New York: Gray Brothers, 1888), preface; FM, 5 Oct. 1883, 226; 27 Apr. 1888, 576–77, 581.

100. *Biographical Catalogue*, xi.

101. James McCosh, "The Royal Law of Love," *Gospel Sermons* (New York: Robert Carter, 1888), 216. For characterizations of McCosh as a liberal Presbyterian who liberated the college from the seminary, see August Heckscher, *Woodrow Wilson: A Biography* (New York: Scribner, 1991), 27–28; Hoeveler, *McCosh*, 238–39, 273–79; Leslie, *Gentlemen and Scholars*, 32, 35; Wertenbaker, *Princeton*, 311–12, 331–32.

102. Charles W. Shields to James R. Shields, 5 Nov. 1868, Box 3, Shields Papers.

103. William Berryman Scott, Notebook on Some Memoirs of a Palaeonotologist, 7:389, Box 6, Scott Papers. This recollection is also excluded from Scott's published biography. Moses Taylor Pyne, another McCosh-era alumnus and trustee, recalled that many of the trustees "spent most of their time fighting Dr. McCosh." Henry Fairfield Osborn, ed., *Fifty Years of Princeton '77: A Fifty-Four Year Record of Princeton College and University* (Princeton: Printed at the Princeton University Press, 1927), 26, 237.

104. TM, 16 Dec. 1874, 5:379.

105. Scott, *Some Memories*, 75.

106. Charles W. Shields to James R. Shields, 11 Jan. 1873, Box 3, Shields Papers.

107. Louise L. Stevenson, *Scholarly Means to Evangelical Ends: The New Haven Scholars and the Transformation of Higher Learning in America, 1830–1890* (Baltimore: Johns Hopkins University Press, 1986), 63–66. On the rise of the alumni association during McCosh's presidency, see Hoeveler, *McCosh*, 297–300, 345–46; Howard B. Maxwell, "The Formative Years of the University Alumni Movement as Illustrated by Studies of the University of Michigan and Columbia, Princeton, and Yale Universities,

1854–1918," (Ph.D. diss, University of Michigan, 1965), 167–77.

108. TM, 9 Nov. 1882, 6:413–15. Nixon was a director from 1883 to 1889; Roberts graduated from the seminary in 1858 and served as a Presbyterian pastor and corresponding secretary of the Board of Home Mission; Dod, the son of Princeton College mathematics professor Albert B. Dod, graduated from the seminary in 1861. John T. Nixon, William C. Roberts, and Samuel Bayard Dod, Alumni Files.

109. Hoeveler, *McCosh*, 300.

110. John K. Cowen, James W. Alexander Jr., Moses Taylor Pyne, David R. Frazer, George B. Stewart, Francis B. Hodge, Alumni Files.

111. TM, 12 Feb. 1885, 6:597.

112. TM, 13 Nov. 1884, 5:565, 569.

113. McCosh presented this paper at the Fourth of July celebration in Woodstock, Connecticut in 1885. It was published and distributed to all the alumni, McCosh told the trustees, by two unnamed younger members of the board. James McCosh, *What An American University Should Be* (New York: J. K. Lees, 1885), 4, 5, 6–7, 9–10, 11, 15; TM, 11 Feb. 1886, 6:700.

114. TM, 10 Feb. 1887, 7:6. See also ibid., 11 Nov. 1886, 6:755; 20 June 1887, 7:34–36.

115. TM, 11 Nov. 1886, 6:755.

116. TM, 10 Feb. 1887, 7:6. For similar comments see ibid., 11 Feb. 1886, 6:700; 11 Nov. 1886, 6:756; 10 Feb. 1887, 7:6; 20 June 1887, 7:33.

117. TM, 11 Feb. 1887, 6:700. McCosh told the trustees that he was convinced that the alumni would provide more money if Princeton were a university. Ibid., 20 June 1887, 7:35.

118. Sloane admiringly wrote that McCosh had built a *Studium Generale* at Princeton embracing the ideal that "all the liberal arts was the core of a true university." McCosh, *Life of McCosh*, 244–45, quote on 244. On the alumni, see TM, 11 Feb. 1886, 6:700; 10 Feb. 1887, 7:6. For student sentiment, see "American Universities," *Pr*, 28 Sept. 1885, 1; "Proceedings of the Board of Trustees," *Pr*, 17 Nov. 1886, 1; "Trustees' Meeting," *Pr*, 11 Feb. 1887, 1; Editorial, *Pr*, 11 Feb. 1887, 2.

119. TM, 11 Nov. 1886, 6:755, emphasis added.

120. William C. Roberts (1832–1903), Samuel H. Pennington (1806–1900), E. R. Craven (1824–1908), Jonathan F. Stearns (1808–1889), William Henry Green (1825–1900), Thomas N. McCarter (1824–1901), James Addison Henry (1835–1906), and McCosh. Of these ten members, excluding McCosh, five were Presbyterian ministers, three were lawyers, one was a physician, seven were graduates of the college and four of the seminary, and seven had some association during their lifetime with the seminary as a professor, director, or trustee. Ibid.; *Biographical Catalogue*, xi–xii, xvii–xviii, xx–xxi.

121. TM, 20 June 1887, 7:35, 54–55, emphasis added.

122. TM, 10 Nov. 1887, 7:87.

123. TM, 9 Feb. 1888, 7:111–12, emphasis added.

124. McCosh, *Twenty Years of Princeton College*, 34–35.

Chapter 3

1. *Encyclopedia of the Presbyterian Church in the United States of America*, ed. Alfred Nevin (Philadelphia: Presbyterian Encyclopedia Publishing Co., 1884), s.v. "Francis L. Patton"; A. A. Hodge to Francis L. Patton, 8 Sept. 1880, A. A. Hodge Papers, Archives, Princeton Seminary Libraries. On Patton's involvement in the Swing trial and its significance in the history of Protestant modernism, see William R. Hutchison, *The Modernist Impulse in American Protestantism* (Cambridge: Harvard University Press, 1976; rprt., New York: Oxford University Press, 1982), 58–75. Patton outlines his commitment to McCosh's views on education, philosophy, and theology in "James McCosh: A Baccalaureate Sermon," *PRR* 6 (1895): 642–62.

2. William M. Sloane, Faculty File. The description of Sloane comes from Robert Bridge to Woodrow Wilson, 30 July 1889, *The Papers of Woodrow Wilson* [hereafter *PWW*], ed. Arthur S. Link, John Wells Davidson, David W. Hirst, John E. Little et al., 69 vols. (Princeton: Princeton University Press, 1966–94), 6:360.

3. Henry C. Cameron to Mina Cameron, 9 Mar. 1888, Box 10, Cameron Family Papers; Alfred Dennis, "President Patton," *PAW*, 25 Apr. 1930, 745; Alexander Leitch, *A Princeton Companion* (Princeton: Princeton University Press, 1978), 355.

4. James McCosh to J. Bayard Henry, 11 Jan. 1888, McCosh Papers.

5. James McCosh to James M. Baldwin, 15 Nov. 1889, in *Between Two Wars 1861–1921: Being Memories, Opinion, and Letters Received*, 2 vols. (Boston: Stratford, 1926), 2:203. While several studies have observed the widespread opposition to Patton's election, they overlook the important philosophical, theological, and, in many respects, educational positions that Patton shared with McCosh. J. David Hoeveler Jr., *James McCosh and the Scottish Intellectual Tradition: From Glasgow to Princeton* (Princeton: Princeton University Press, 1981), 332, 338–40; Willard Thorp, Minor Myers Jr., and Jeremiah Stanton Finch, *The Princeton Graduate School: A History* (Princeton University Press, 1978), 44; L. Bruce Leslie, *Gentlemen and Scholars: College and Community in the "Age of the University," 1865–1917* (State College: Penn State University Press, 1992), 117–18; Laurence R. Veysey, *The Emergence of the American University* (Chicago: University of Chicago Press, 1965), 52.

6. William Berryman Scott, *Some Memories of a Palaeontologist* (Princeton: Princeton University Press, 1939), 203.

7. Francis L. Patton, *Speech of Prof. Francis L. Patton, D.D., LL.D., President-Elect of Princeton College at the Annual Dinner of the Princeton Club of New York. March 15, 1888* (n.p., [1888]), 3–5.

8. Scott, *Some Memories*, 203.

9. Francis L. Patton, *Inauguration of the Rev. Francis Landey Patton, D.D., LL.D., as President of Princeton College* (New York: Gray Brothers, 1888), 26, 28–29, 39.

10. Ibid., 30–38, quotes on 30.

11. TM, 8 June 1896, 8:294, emphasis added. For similar comments, see Francis L. Patton, "The President's Address at the Opening of the College," *Princeton College Bulletin* 1 (1889): 6–8; ibid., "College or University? The Advantages of the Great University," *Saturday Evening Post*, 1 July 1899, 5.

12. Patton, *Inauguration*, 18.

13. Andrew F. West, "The Spirit and Ideas of Princeton," *ER* 8 (1894): 321.

14. William M. Sloane, "Princeton University," *Harper's New Monthly Magazine*, Nov. 1889, 893.

15. Graduate courses grew from 29 courses in 1888–1889 to 78 in 1901–1902. Un-

dergraduate courses that were open to graduate students were counted as undergraduate courses in this estimate. *Catalogue, 1888–89*, 25–51, 73–103; *Catalogue, 1901–02*, 81–121, 163–76.

16. Patton, *Inauguration*, 29.

17. *Catalogue, 1888–89*, 163; *Catalogue, 1965–96*, 199; *Catalogue, 1901–02*, 342.

18. Alexander T. Ormond, "University Ideals at Princeton," *National Educational Association. Journal of Proceedings and Addresses of the Thirty-Sixth Annual Meeting Held at Milwaukee, Wis., July 6–9, 1897* (Chicago: University of Chicago Press, 1897), 350. Patton and many of his colleagues also dismissed suggestions to make the bachelor's degree a three-year program. See, for example, Andrew F. West, "The American College," *PAW*, 21 Apr. 1900, 37.

19. "Princeton's Alumni in Brooklyn," *Pres*, 2 Mar. 1889, 9. After completing a comparative study with Harvard, Yale, Columbia, and the University of Pennsylvania, one trustee contended that it was imperative to add elective courses to prepare students to study law and medicine. "Otherwise," John J. McCook argued, "Princeton must honestly admit to its students, its alumni, and patrons, that it can no longer pretend to offer equal advantages with other institutions of corresponding rank but that it is inferior." Such courses were subsequently added to the curriculum. John J. McCook, Memorandum for Curriculum Committee, 8 Nov. 1894, Papers of the Trustees of Princeton University, Seeley G. Mudd Manuscript Library, Princeton University. Published with permission of Princeton University Library; FM, 30 May 1894, 567; TM, 8 June 1896, 8:295–96.

20. According to Bailey B. Burritt's survey, between 1891 and 1895, 15.2 percent of the A.B. graduates entered the ministry, 24.6 percent entered law, 10.9 percent entered medicine, and 22.4 percent entered business. *Professional Distribution of College and University Graduates* (Washington, D.C.: Government Printing Office, 1912), 105.

21. The expansion of the elective system is evidenced in the percentage of elective courses in the 1901–1902 academic year. In the academic program, freshmen had 13 percent, sophomores 27 percent, juniors 67 percent, and seniors 100 percent elective courses. For the degree in General Science, freshmen had no electives, sophomores and juniors 37 percent each year, and seniors 100 percent electives. All figures are estimates based on the minimum number of elective hours. *Catalogue, 1888–89*, 55–57, 85–88; *Catalogue, 1965–96*, 61–68, 97–99; *Catalogue, 1901–02*, 122–27, 177–80. The curriculum shifted from a three-term to a two-semester scheme in 1890–1891. Throughout the 1890s, the curriculum was constantly modified.

22. Walter Lowrie to Elizabeth Dickson Lowrie, 26 Sept. 1889, Box 10, Lowrie Papers.

23. The only apparent constraint in what courses a student could take was time conflicts between courses. *Catalogue, 1888–89*, 57; *Catalogue, 1965–96*, 64–68; *Catalogue, 1901–02*, 125–27.

24. Scott, *Some Memories*, 355.

25. Tarkington reportedly said that he imbibed some education at Princeton, "though it seems to me that I *tried* to avoid *that* as much as possible." Robert C. Holliday, *Booth Tarkington* (Garden City, N.Y.: Doubleday, 1918), 15. In 1888–1889, for example, there were 60 special students and in 1895–1896 110 such students. *Catalogue, 1888–89*, 158, 163; *Catalogue, 1895–96*, 187, 199.

26. *Bric-A-Brac (Princeton: Junior Class) 1897*, 181–259. See, for example, James Westervelt, "Princeton in the Past," *NLM* 47 (1891): 92–97; Jesse Lynch Williams, "One of the Freshman," *NLM* 47 (1891): 173–81; Booth Tarkington, "At the Inn," 59 *NLM* (1893): 676–87; John H. Thacher, "A College Cabal," *NLM* 50 (1894): 148–55; W. F. G.

Thacher, "The Lady, or the Tiger?" *NLM* 50 (1900): 509–19. One graduate, Jesse Lynch Williams, made a literary career out of glorifying college life at Princeton. See, for example, *Princeton Stories* (New York: Scribner, 1895).

27. John V. A. McMurray to Henrietta V. A. McMurray, 3 Nov. 1900, Box 25, John V. A. McMurray Papers, Manuscript Division, Department of Rare Books and Special Collections, Princeton University Library. Published with permission of Princeton University Library.

28. Hardin Craig, *Woodrow Wilson at Princeton* (Norman: University of Oklahoma Press, 1960), 71. Professor William Berryman Scott wrote in an unpublished section of his memoirs that "Dr. Patton's head was full of Oxford and failed to comprehend the great differences of conditions wh. [*sic*] made methods inapplicable here, save with important adaptations to the American environment." Notebook on Some Memories of a Palaeontologist, 10:598, Box 6, Scott Papers.

29 A *pensum* amounted to a fine of $1.00 per missed service. In 1901, the faculty expressed "embarrassment" at the large number of students who missed chapel because of illness, and resolved that students needed a medical certificate to be excused. TM, 11 June 1894, 8:12; FM, 18 Feb. 1898, 292; 9 Feb. 1900, 471–72; 5 June 1901, 562.

30. "Alumnus," letter to the editor, *DP*, 4 Dec. 1897, 2; TM, 14 June 1897, 8:511–12.

31. Lowrie, Autobiographical Vol. 2:174–75, Box 1, Lowrie Papers; Scott, Notebooks on Some Memories of a Paleontologist, 10:575, Box 6, Scott Papers.

32. TM, 21 Oct. 1898, 8:728. One service was held on Sundays only because enough students went home for weekends. TM, 20 Oct. 1899, 9:132.

33. In one week just nine of a hundred professors attended one or more of the week-day services. John V. A. McMurray, "Gossip: Of Matutinal Devotional Exercises," *NLM* 57 (1902): 339–41.

34. TM, 13 June 1892, 7:544–45; 9 Feb. 1893, 7:647–48; 23 Dec. 1898, 8:576, 584–85; 11 June 1900, 9:282–84; 10 June 1901, 10:17, 40. On student sentiment toward chapel, Editorial, *Pr*, 4 Mar. 1891, 2; "W," letter to the editor, *DP*, 14 Apr. 1893, 1; Editorial, *DP*, 22 Jan. 1898, 2.

35. TM, 14 June 1897, 8:509; 13 June 1898, 8:697–98; 23 Dec. 1897, 8:576–77.

36. Patton casually suggested the idea several times. Patton, *Speech*, 7; idem, "President's Address," 6; TM, 8 June 1896, 8:294; 23 Dec. 1897, 8:576–77; 13 June 1898, 8:697–700. On the blasé attitudes to academics bred by the "pass-honor" system at Cambridge, see Sheldon Rothblatt, *The Revolution of the Dons: Cambridge and Society in Victorian England* (London: Faber and Faber, 1968), 181–90. Several studies correctly assess Patton's modifications of the classical curriculum, the faculty's dissatisfaction with the state of the undergraduate program, and Patton's indifference to student indolence, but overlook the role that Patton's English model of undergraduate education played within the controversy. Earl H. Brill, "Religion and the Rise of the University: A Study of the Secularization of American Higher Education, 1870–1910," (Ph.D. diss., American University, 1969), 301; Leslie, *Gentlemen and Scholars*, 117, 183–86; Veysey, *Emergence of the University*, 28, 32, 52. Veysey, however, incorrectly attributes the changes in the curriculum to Patton's "surrender to the anticlerical element" in the faculty. Ibid., 52. Patricia A. Graham, likewise, incorrectly argues that Patton modified the curriculum because of "his disdain for rigorous intellectual discipline." *Community and Class in American Education, 1865–1918* (New York: John Wiley, 1974), 193–94.

37. TM, 13 Dec. 1900, 9:371. In the eyes of his critics, a satirical limerick, "Tis better to have gone and loafed / Than never to have gone," characterized Patton's atti-

tude. McCready Sykes, "Gentlemen—The 'Nineties,'" *PAW*, 6 Feb. 1931, 421.

38. FM, 16 Apr. 1902, 598–600, quote on 599, emphasis added. The committee on university affairs met more than twenty times to discuss reforms to the curriculum. In the spring of 1902 alone, they met five times to work out their proposals. FM, 26 Mar. 1902, 596; 9 Apr. 1902, 596; 11 Apr. 1902, 596–97; 14 Apr. 1902, 597–98; 16 Apr. 1902, 598–606; Hoeveler, *McCosh*, 346; Editorial Note, *PWW*, 12:292.

39. Patton, *Inauguration*, 42–43.

40. Patton, "Religion in College," *Princeton Sermons* (New York: Revell, 1893), 151.

41. Patton, *Inauguration*, 41–42.

42. Ormond, "University Ideals at Princeton," 355.

43. Francis L. Patton, *The Revision of the Confession of Faith. Read Before the Presbyterian Social Union, N.Y., Dec. 2, 1889* (n.p., n.d.); Francis L. Patton to Henry Van Dyke Sr., 13 May 1890, Box 25, Van Dyke Papers. On DeWitt's argument against revision, see, for example, his articles in *Ought the Confession of Faith to Be Revised?* (New York: n.p., 1890).

44. Charles H. Briggs, *Whither? A Theological Question for the Times* (New York: Scribner, 1889), 7–8, as quoted in Mark S. Massa, *Charles Augustus Briggs and the Crisis of Historical Criticism* (Philadelphia: Fortress Press, 1990), 78–79.

45. Hoeveler incorrectly cites this work as evidence of McCosh's opposition to Calvinism and "his remoteness from the seminary position." *McCosh*, 334. Just the opposite was the case. In this brief work, McCosh not only repudiated Briggs's use of higher critical methods and the Graf-Wellhausen theory in particular but also rejected his views on confessional revision. McCosh, moreover, demonstrated a keen interest in defending the Princeton Theology of Charles and A. A. Hodge. *Whither? O Whither? Tell me Where* (New York: Scribner, 1889). See also Talbot W. Chambers, "The Inaugural Address of Professor Briggs," *PRR* 2 (1891): 480–94; B. B. Warfield, "The One Hundred and Third General Assembly," *PRR* 2 (1891): 495–99.

46. A. A. Hodge and B. B. Warfield, "Inspiration," *PresRev* 2 (1881): 237.

47. Robert T. Handy, *A History of Union Theological Seminary in New York* (New York: Columbia University Press, 1987), 69–93; Lefferts A. Loetscher, *The Broadening Church: A Study of Theological Issues in the Presbyterian Church since 1869* (Philadelphia: University of Pennsylvania Press, 1954), 39–73; Massa, *Charles Briggs*, 78–109, 9–56; George M. Marsden, *Fundamentalism and American Culture: The Shaping of Twentieth-Century Evangelicalism, 1870–1925* (New York: Oxford University Press, 1980), 109–118; Gary Scott Smith, *The Seeds of Secularization: Calvinism, Culture, and Pluralism in America, 1870–1915* (Grand Rapids: Christian University Press, 1985), 23–35.

48. L. Burton Crane, "The Presidency of Princeton University," *Independent* 19 June 1902, 1483.

49. Andrew D. White, *Autobiography of Andrew Dickson White*, 2 vols. (New York: Century, 1905), 1:404–405.

50. "Princeton College and the General Assembly," *NLM* 49 (1893): 137–38.

51. Jesse Lynch Williams, "Princeton University," *The University and Their Sons: History, Influence and Characteristics of American Universities*, ed. Joshua L. Chamberlain, vol. 1 (Boston: Herndon, 1898), 552.

52. Robert M. Crunden, *Ministers of Reform: The Progressives' Achievement in American Civilization, 1889–1920* (New York: Basic Books, 1982), 15; William T. Hutchison, *Cyrus Hall McCormick: Harvest, 1856–1884* (New York: Appleston- Century, 1935), 250; Henry Van Dyke Sr., "The Charge," *Addresses at the Inauguration of the Rev.*

Francis L. Patton, D.D., LL.D., as Stuart Professor of the Relations of Philosophy and Science to the Christian Religion, in the Theological Seminary at Princeton, N.J., October 27, 1881 (Philadelphia: Sherman, 1881), 2–20.

53. Tertius Van Dyke, *Henry Van Dyke: A Biography* (New York: Harper, 1935), 3–204; Loetscher, *Broadening Church*, 58–59; Henry Van Dyke Jr., *A Plea for Peace and Work* (n.p., 1893). The younger Van Dyke debated B. B. Warfield as well as John DeWitt over revision. See, for example, the collection of their articles in *Ought the Confession of Faith to be Revised?*.

54. Henry Van Dyke Jr., *The Gospel for an Age of Doubt* (New York: Macmillan, 1897), 7–8, 9–15, 49–50, 51, 114, 69, 116–19. Further evidence of Van Dyke's mediating personality and temperate modernism is the fact that he won praise from both conservatives and modernists. John DeWitt, with whom he had longstanding theological disagreements, praised Van Dyke for his excellent preaching and pastoral ministry at Brick Church. Van Dyke was the University Preacher at Harvard in the spring of 1891. President Eliot of Harvard, in one of his more effusive expressions of praise, complimented Van Dyke after hearing him preach: "That sermon," he said, "could do no harm." George A. Gordon, a prominent Boston modernist, admired *The Gospel in an Age of Doubt* in a letter. A review of the book by a disciple of the Princeton theology praised Van Dyke's elegant style but disapproved of his undogmatic theology. Van Dyke served on the seminary's Board of Directors from 1884 to 1898. John DeWitt to Henry Van Dyke Jr., 16 Jan. 1899, Box 92, Van Dyke Papers; John DeWitt to Henry Van Dyke Jr., 28 Jan. 1908, Box 92, Van Dyke Papers; Van Dyke, *Van Dyke*, 179; George A. Gordon to Henry Van Dyke Jr., 2 Nov. 1896, Box 98, Van Dyke Papers. Timothy G. Darling, review of *The Gospel for an Age of Doubt*, by Henry Van Dyke Jr., *PRR* 8 (1897): 348–55.

55. D. G. Hart, "Poems, Propositions, and Dogma: The Controversy over Religious Language and the Demise of Theology in American Learning," *Church History* 57 (1987): 310–21; Hutchison, *Modernist Impulse*, 76–110; Bruce Kuklick, *Churchmen and Philosophers: From Jonathan Edwards to John Dewey* (New Haven: Yale University Press, 1985), 161–70.

56. In 1889, Paul Van Dyke was appointed as a professor of church history at the seminary for a three-year period. The faculty did not recommend him for a permanent position in the spring of 1892 because he was too sympathetic toward his brother's moderate liberalism and did not, according to B. B. Warfield, "stand cordially on the Princeton Seminary platform." Warfield recruited John DeWitt to replace him. Walter Lowrie, a senior at the seminary whose father was a prominent exponent of the Princeton theology and a director at the seminary, organized a demonstration to protest his dismissal. Paul Van Dyke to William Henry Green, 3 Mar. 1892; B. B. Warfield to William Henry Green, 8 Mar. 1892; B. B. Warfield to John DeWitt, 28 Mar. 1892; B. B. Warfield Papers, Archives, Princeton Seminary Libraries; Walter Lowrie to Elizabeth Dickson Lowrie, 24 Apr. 1892, Box 10, Lowrie Papers; Lowrie, Autobiographical Vol. 2:62–63, Box 1, Lowrie Papers; Princeton Theological Seminary, Minutes of the Faculty of Princeton Theological Seminary, 2 May 1892, Archives, Princeton Seminary Libraries.

57. The senior Van Dyke served on Princeton Seminary's Board of Directors from 1873–1891. James H. Moorhead, "Henry Van Dyke Sr.: Conservative Apostle of a Broad Church," *Journal of Presbyterian History* 50 (1972): 19–38; *Biographical Catalogue*, xii.

58. Minutes of the Philadelphian Society, 4 Feb. 1902, Box 2, Student Christian Association Records.

59. Patton, *Inauguration of the Rev. Francis Landey Patton*, 41.

60. "Proposed Change in Bible Instruction," *Pr*, 2 Feb. 1891, 1.

61. Editorial, *Pr*, 2 Feb. 1891, 2.

62. *Catalogue, 1895–96*, 61–66.

63. "Elective System," *DP*, 17 Mar. 1898, 1.

64. TM, 13 Nov. 1890, 7:392; Editorial, *Pr*, 17 Nov. 1890, 2.

65. Students petitioned for a Hebrew course in 1888. In the spring of 1889, Princeton College art professor Arthur L. Frothingham taught the course. In 1892, Princeton Seminary professor Chalmers Martin assumed responsibility for the class. In 1897, he expanded his offerings to include graduate-level courses in advanced Hebrew and Syriac. In 1900, Robert Dick Wilson, another seminary professor, succeeded Martin. Editorial, *Pr*, 21 Nov. 1888, 2; TM, 14 Feb. 1889, 192; 10 June 1901 10:43 *Catalogue, 1892–93*, 46; *Catalogue, 1897–98*, 57; FM, 24 Nov. 1900, 511.

66. TM, 14 Feb. 1895, 8:164–65; Princeton Theological Seminary, *Biographical Catalogue of the Princeton Theological Seminary, 1815–1932*, comp. Edward H. Roberts (Princeton: Published by the Trustees of The Theological Seminary of the Presbyterian Church Princeton, New Jersey, 1933), 447. George S. Patton's appointment was the subject of gossip at Princeton. Ellen Axson Wilson wrote her husband, "I was surprised to learn from todays [*sic*] 'Times' that George Patton was some time ago appointed assistant professor— in 'Biblical Instruction.' Did you know that. I didn't even know he taught. It seems a rapid rise. Truly it is a good and pleasant thing for a young scholar to have a fond father in the president's chair!" Ellen Axson Wilson to Woodrow Wilson, 18 Feb. 1895, *PWW*, 9:206.

67. TM, 22 Nov. 1899, 9:131–32. In another act of nepotism, Patton increased his son's salary with money donated to the university for use by his discretion. TM, 9 Nov. 1900, 9:312–13.

68. TM, 10 June 1895, 8:164–65.

69. Francis L. Patton, "The Letter and the Spirit," *Princeton Sermons* (New York: Revell, 1893), 169, emphasis added.

70. *Freshman Syllabus in Bible*, 1–23, quotes on 14, Seeley G. Mudd Manuscript Library, Princeton University . See also George S. Patton, "A Fruitful Method of Bible Study," *Bible Student* (1900), 209–12. In addition to such questions as, "Account for the loss of the original autographs of the New Testament, and show how it is owing to this loss that the need of N.T. Textual Criticism arises," Patton explicitly asked about the apologetic value of textual criticism with such topics as "Show the apologetic bearing of the lectures." Examination in Bible, Academic Freshmen, 8 Feb. 1897, Examination File, Seeley G. Mudd Manuscript Library, Princeton University. Published with permission of Princeton University Library.

71. *Biographical Catalogue*, 367. "May I express any strong desire and earnest hope," McCosh wrote Hibben before he went to Germany, "that you will still keep the ministry in view." James McCosh to John G. Hibben, 14 Aug. 1882, John G. Hibben Papers, Records of the Office of the President, Seeley G. Mudd Manuscript Library, Princeton University. Published with permission of Princeton University Library. John T. Duffield preached Hibben's ordination sermon. "Charge at the Ordination of John G. Hibben, May 19th, 1887," Box 2, Duffield Papers. The description of Hibben's pastoral experience comes from Walter Lowrie, a student and friend of Hibben. Lowrie, Autobiographical Vol. 1:37, Box 1, Lowrie Papers.

72. With thirty-five students enrolled, Hibben's class was the seventh most popular elective course of twenty-four electives in the fall of 1894. In the spring of 1898, his senior Bible class had eighty-nine students enrolled and was the second most popular of forty-nine courses. "Academic Electives for the First Term," *DP*, 3 Oct. 1894, 1; "Electives," *DP*, 25 Feb. 1898, 1.

73. *Syllabus on Junior-Senior Bible*; *Notes on Junior-Senior Bible*, Seeley G. Mudd Manuscript Library, Princeton University. On exams, for example, Hibben asked such questions as "State some incidents which reveal the character of Jonathan" and "Mention several incidents which illustrate Abraham's faith." Examination in Bible, Junior-Senior Elective, 30 Jan. 1899, William Penn Vail Examination Papers, Seeley G. Mudd Manuscript Library, Princeton University. Published with permission of Princeton University Library.

74. Patton, "Letter and the Spirit," 189–90.

75. Patton's ethics class was required of students enrolled in the B.S. in General Science and the B.S. in Chemistry but not of Civil Engineering Students. FM, 22 May 1894, 564; *Catalogue, 1894–95*, 98–101.

76. D. H. Meyer, *The Instructed Conscience: The Shaping of the American National Ethic* (Philadelphia: University of Pennsylvania Press, 1972), 131.

77. Patton, "Letter and the Spirit," 178–79; Meyer, *Instructed Conscience*, xiii. According to Douglas Sloan, the classic texts of America's nineteenth-century moral philosophers had almost been totally abandoned by 1900 and replaced by a diverse and sometimes confusing collection of texts primarily written by leading British ethicists. "The Teaching of Ethics in American Undergraduate Curriculum, 1876–1976," in *Ethics Teaching in Higher Education*, ed. Sissela Bok and Daniel Callahan (New York: Plenum, 1980), 22. Patton continued to use Henry Calderwood's *Handbook of Moral Philosophy* until 1900 when it was replaced with James Seth, *A Study of Ethical Principles* (New York: Scribner, 1898), and John S. Mackenzie *Manual of Ethics*, 4th ed. (London: University Tutorial Press, 1900). Both works continued to espouse the older ethical teachings. Leslie H. Cooke, Ethics Class Notes, Spring Semester 1901, Cooke Family Papers, MG 1031, New Jersey Historical Society; Francis L. Patton, *Syllabus on Ethics* [1903], Seeley G. Mudd Manuscript Library, Princeton University; Examination in Ethics, Senior Class, 25 Jan., 1986, Examination File; *Catalogue, 1900–01*, 52. Booth Tarkington wrote his parents that Patton's ethics class "looks innocent enough in the catalogue, but when one realizes that it means exhaustive examination, study criticism and attempted refutation of the Ethical Theories of Schaupenhauer [*sic*], Hegel, Kant and Herbert Spencer, involving complete study of those authors' works with Dr. Calderwood as a text, one begins to feel the serious nature of a senior study." After doing poorly on an exam, he wrote his mother, "Some men study all day and all night. There are better things to do for me." Booth Tarkington to John S. and Elizabeth Tarkington, 24 Oct. 1891; Booth Tarkington to John S. and Elizabeth Tarkington, 21 Apr. 1892, Box 186, Booth Tarkington Papers, Manuscript Division, Rare Books and Special Collections, Princeton University. Published with permission of Princeton University Library.

78. FM, 28 Feb. 1900, 481; TM, 8 Mar. 1900, 9:218; *Catalogue, 1900–01*, 53.

79. In 1890, Patton's class was added to the required curriculum of the School of Science, correcting another oversight which emerged during his predecessor's tenure. *Catalogue, 1889–90*, 28; *Catalogue, 1890–91*, 87.

80. Francis L. Patton, "The Final Philosophy," *PRev* 54 (1879): 559, 561, 566–68, 572. Shields's description of his position at Princeton comes from a letter to his father. Charles Woodruff Shields to James R. Shields, 25 Nov. 1871, Box 3, Shields Papers.

81. Francis L. Patton, *Pastors, Theology and the Age* (Philadelphia: Presbyterian Board of Publication, 1879), 5. In this work, Patton again chastised Shields for failing to offer a positive solution. Ibid., 7.

82. Patton, "Final Philosophy," 570–72, quote on 577.

83. Patton, *Addresses at the Induction of Rev. Francis L. Patton into "The Cyrus H. McCormick Professorship of Didactic and Polemic Theology,"* in the *Presbyterian Theo-*

logical Seminary of the North-West (Chicago: Printed by order of the Board of Directors of the Seminary, [1872]), 25.

84. *Catalogue, 1889–90,* 28. Because of the absence of Patton's lectures, student classnotes, or printed syllabi, what follows is a composite portrait of what Patton most likely taught in this course based on a review of the questions Patton asked on a final exam and what he published about these topics in works on philosophy, theology, and science. Evidences of Christianity, [1895], Examination File.

85. Francis L. Patton, "The Place of Philosophy in the Theological Curriculum," *PRev* (1882): 106.

86. Francis L. Patton, "Theological Encyclopedia," *PTR* 2 (1904): 126–28.

87. Patton, "Place of Philosophy," 108, 112.

88. Patton, "Theological Encyclopedia," 128.

89. Ibid., 106, 116, 118.

90. Francis L. Patton, *A Summary of Christian Doctrine* (Presbyterian Board of Publication, 1875; repr., Philadelphia: Westminster Press, 1928), 25–28.

91. The trustees' minutes simply read that the Evidences of Christianity course had been "omitted" from the curriculum. TM, 9 Mar. 1899, 9:51. Patton's two-semester "Theism" course was offered to undergraduates as an elective and to seminary students as a required course. It became a one-semester course in the fall of 1898. Patton was listed as a "Lecturer on Theism" in the seminary catalogue. TM, 12 June 1893, 7:705; FM, 22 May 1893, 564; Francis L. Patton, *Syllabus of Prof. Patton's Lectures on Theism* (Princeton: Princeton Press, 1886); idem, *Syllabus of Prof. Patton's Lectures on the Anti- Theistic Theories* (n.p., n.d.); *Catalogue, 1898–99,* 40, 82–83; *Princeton Theological Seminary Catalogue, 1898–99,* 5, 26, 38–39.

92. Bible Study Committee of the Philadelphian Society. General Secretary's Book, Lucius H. Miller, 1897–98, Box 5, Student Christian Association Records.

93. "Report of the Philadelphian Society," *Pr,* 1 Mar. 1893, 1; "Course in Bible Study," *DP,* 5 Oct. 1894, 1; "Philadelphian Society," *DP,* 12 June 1901, 2.

94. This conclusion is based on a comparison of membership statistics in the senior class yearbook for the 1890s. *Nassau Herald, 1889,* 78; *Nassau Herald, 1890,* 72; *Nassau Herald, 1891,* 70; *Nassau Herald, 1892,* 76; *Nassau Herald, 1893,* 84; *Nassau Herald, 1894,* 105; *Nassau Herald, 1895,* 95; *Nassau Herald, 1896,* 111; *Nassau Herald, 1897,* 197; *Nassau Herald, 1899,* 166; *Nassau Herald, 1900,* 134.

95. "Philadelphian Committees," *Pr,* 13 Dec. 1892, 1.

96. Cleveland H. Dodge, Luther D. Wishard, John J. McCook, Robert E. Speer, and T. H. P. Sailor constituted the first Advisory Committee. TM, 11 Mar. 1897, 8:442; 14 June 1897, 8:491–92.

97. TM, 23 Dec. 1897, 8:576.

98. "Dodge Hall," *PAW,* 6 Oct. 1900, 207.

99. Frank L. Janeway reports this in his paper, "What We Should Be Doing and Must Do," Minutes of the Philadelphian Society, 10 Jan. 1903, Box 3, Student Christian Association Records.

100. Francis L. Patton, "The Religious Life of the University," *Intercollegian* 22 (1899): 30–31.

101. FM, 18 Jan. 1893, 403; Leslie, *Gentlemen and Scholars,* 199–200.

102. In 1901, the Philadelphian Society had nearly 600 members and the St. Paul's Society almost 100. "Religion on the Campus," *PAW,* 23 Feb. 1901, 522; "St. Paul's Society Smoker," *DP,* 19 Dec. 1901, 1; "Address by Professor Axson," *DP,* 18 Mar. 1902, 1; "St. Paul's Society Address," *DP,* 14 Jan. 1902, 1.

103. New Students' Committee of the Princeton Philadelphian Society, General Secretary's Book, Lucius H. Miller, 1897–98; Students Handbook, Princeton University, 1900–1901, Box 10, Student Christian Association Records; "Philadelphian Society Reception to Freshmen this Evening," *DP*, 21 Sept. 1901, 1.

104. Theodore L. Cuyler, "Princeton, Old and New," *Evangelist*, 20 Oct. 1898, 4. In 1899, the Philadelphian Society broadened the terms of membership in the society. No longer did a full member have to be a member of an evangelical church but just had to sign an evangelical profession of faith. The "covenant" read: "It is my purpose as a Princeton man in God's strength, taking Jesus Christ as Savior and Lord, to live a consistent Christian life as I understand it to be set forth in the Bible. It shall always be my desire to promote the unity and welfare of the Philadelphian Society." An editorial in the student newspaper applauded the move away from the older "narrow-minded policy." "Meeting of the Philadelphian Society Cabinet," *DP*, 20 Nov. 1899, 1; Editorial, *DP*, 8 Dec. 1899, 2. While Leslie correctly observes that Princeton was religiously homogeneous during this period, he incorrectly claims that the new membership agreement opened the Philadelphian Society to non-Presbyterians. Any member of an evangelical church could belong to the society before this change. *Gentlemen and Scholars*, 109–10.

105. "Saturday Evening Meeting, Murray Hall," *Pr*, 23 Jan. 1891, 1; "Dr. Pierson's Address," *DP*, 26 Mar. 1897, 1; "Philadelphian Meeting," *DP*, 8 Dec. 1893, 1. The revival was organized by students and held in the town churches and college chapel. B. Fay Mills, an itinerant interdenominational evangelist, preached. "Religious Services," *DP*, 10 Jan. 1894, 1; "The Mills Meetings," *PP*, 27 Jan 1894, 2.

106. "Religious Services," *DP*, 6 Mar. 1897, 1; "Address in Murray Hall," *DP*, 1 Nov. 1901, 1.

107. Albert Reid, Report of the President, 182–83, Box 3, Student Christian Association Records; "Mission Band," *Philadelphian Bulletin*, Mar. 1892, 1; "Editorial," *Pr*, 6 June 1888, 2; "Editorial," *Pr*, 13 Apr. 1892, 2; "Northfield Conference," *DP*, 16 Apr. 1896, 1; "Murray Hall," *DP*, 8 Mar. 1898, 1; "Northfield Student Conference," *DP*, 25 Mar. 1902, 1; "Mr. John R. Mott," *DP*, 18 Apr. 1902, 1; "Philadelphia Meeting," *DP*, 19 Feb. 1894, 1; "Murray Hall," *DP*, 9 Apr. 1897, 1.

108. Reid, Report of the President, 183; "Philadelphian Business Meeting," *Pr*, 21 Feb. 1893, 1; "Resolutions Endorsed by the Philadelphian Society," *DP*, 9 Mar. 1898, 1; Editorial, *DP*, 11 Mar. 1898, 2; "The Sun Never Sets on the Princeton Flag," *PAW*, 15 Feb. 1902, 318. On the mixture of evangelizing and "civilizing" efforts of American Protestant missions in the late nineteenth century, see William R. Hutchison, *Errand to the World: American Protestant Thought and Foreign Missions* (Chicago: University of Chicago Press, 1987), 91–124.

109. Francis L. Patton, "Religion and the University," *Memorial Book of the Sesquicentennial Celebration of the Founding of the College of New Jersey and of the Ceremonies Inaugurating Princeton University* (New York: Scribner, 1898), 30–31.

110. TM, 10 June 1895, 8:181; 13 Feb. 1896, 8:257. Since 1892, a sesquicentennial committee had been making elaborate plans for the celebration. TM, 10 Nov. 1892, 7:539–41; 8 Nov. 1894, 8:68–77; 14 Feb. 1895, 8:21; 10 Mar. 1895, 8:134–36; 13 Feb. 1896, 8:252.

111. "The Annual Banquet of the Princeton Club of New York," *Pr*, 29 Mar. 1889, 1. For similar statements, see Patton, "Inaugural Address," 16; Editorial, *Pr*, 6 June 1888, 2.

112. Patton, "Religion and the University," 28–29, 37, 38, 41, 42, 45, 52, 52–53.

113. Woodrow Wilson, "Princeton in the Nation's Service," *Memorial Book*, 115, 103, 109–14, 116, 122, 127, 131. On the negative effects of modern science, Wilson

said, "This is the disservice scientific study has done us: it has given us agnosticism in the realm of philosophy, scientific anarchism in the field of politics. It has made the legislator confident that he can create and the philosopher sure that God cannot." Ibid., 128. William Berryman Scott recalled that "[m]any of the delegates, especially General Walker, then President of the Massachusetts Institute of Technology, were outraged by what they took to be an attack upon science, when the speaker was merely protesting against the application of methods drawn from the chemical laboratory to the problems of history." Scott, *Some Memories*, 128. Wilson's new vision of university was largely canonized in institutional histories written by Princetonians after 1896. The memorial volume published after the sesquicentennial celebration included a lengthy essay by John DeWitt that accented Princeton's de facto Presbyterian origins and nonsectarian evangelical Christian orientation. Charles W. Shields, in a supplementary essay to the volume, gives an alternative interpretation of the institution's founding that emphasized the college's nondenominational charter and public service orientation. John DeWitt, "Historical Sketch of Princeton University," *Memorial Book*, 317–453; Charles W. Shields, "Historical Note on the Origin of Princeton University," *Memorial Book*, 455–60. The clearest evidence of these two interpretations of the founding purpose and orientation of the university from this period comes in a massive 1898 volume on the histories of America's great universities. Alongside the above essay by John DeWitt, republished for the section on the College of New Jersey, stood one by Jesse Lynch Williams, a recent Princeton graduate, on Princeton University. Williams presents the Wilsonian vision, which accents the public service purpose and orientation of the university. John DeWitt, "Princeton College," *University and Their Sons*, 1:448–61; Williams, "Princeton University," *University and Their Sons*, 1:550–53. Although this historiographical shift began to take place after 1896, many older alumni and conservative Presbyterians continued to maintain the older perspective. See, for example, the reports of Presbyterian weeklies on the sesquicentennial celebration. "Princeton Correspondence," *Pres*, 16 Sept. 1896, 8–9; L.W.M. "Princeton University," *Pres*, 21 Oct. 1896, 9–10; "Princeton's Sesqui-Centennial," *Evangelist*, 22 Oct. 1896, 7.

114. For several years, Cameron plotted with his father to secure a position at Princeton. Hodge, before he succeeded his father at the seminary, was appointed a professor of philosophy in 1896 to the dismay of Wilson. Arnold Guyot Cameron to Henry C. Cameron, 31 Jan. 1891; Arnold Guyot Cameron to Henry C. Cameron, 27 Feb. 1892; Arnold Guyot Cameron to Henry C. Cameron, 24 May 1891; Box 40, Cameron Family Papers; Woodrow Wilson to Ellen Axson Wilson, 8 Feb. 1895, *PWW*, 9:180; TM, 14 Nov. 1895, 8:242; 14 June 1897, 8:489–90.

115. Robert Bridges led a group of friends to endow a chair for Wilson. Friends associated with the New York Alumni Club raised $100,000 to endow the Murray Professorship of English Literature for Van Dyke. Robert Bridges to Woodrow Wilson, 15 July 1889, *PWW*, 6:330; Robert Bridges to Woodrow Wilson, 7 Nov. 1889, *PWW*, 6:414; Robert Bridges to Woodrow Wilson, 19 Nov. 1889, *PWW*, 6:428; Robert Bridges to Woodrow Wilson, 24 Jan. 1890, *PWW*, 6:480; TM, 13 Feb. 1890, 7:311; 9 Mar. 1891, 8:51.

116. Bliss Perry, *And Gladly Teach: Reminiscences* (Boston: Houghton Mifflin, 1935), 114–25.

117. Francis L. Patton to Woodrow Wilson, 18 Feb. 1890, *PWW*, 6:527. Robert Bridge told Wilson that some within Princeton's administration "whisper behind their hands" that Wilson was "a little heterodox (shades of Calvin and Witherspoon protect us)." In 1898, Patton told a trustee that he "took pains to overcome the reluctant attitude of a strong minority in the Board of Trustees" to get Wilson elected. Robert Bridges to

Woodrow Wilson, 5 Nov. 1888, *PWW*, 6:411; Francis L. Patton to Cyrus Hall McCormick Jr., 4 Apr. 1898, *PWW*, 10:496.

118. Macloskie, for example, continued to argue for the harmony of science and religion in publications, classroom lectures, and before the Philadelphian Society. George Macloskie "The Testimony of Nature," *PRR* 1 (1890): 587–97; idem, "Common Errors as to the Relations of Science and Faith," *PRR* 7 (1895): 98–105; idem, "Theistic Evolution," *PRR* 9 (1898): 1–22; idem, "The Religious Outcome of Darwinism," Lectures on Elementary Botany [1892], Box 4, Macloskie Papers; idem, "Preliminary Talks on Science and Faith [1892]," Box 3, Macloskie Papers.

119. Baldwin's undergraduate activities are mentioned in Smith Ordway's undergraduate diary. Ordway Diary, 29 Oct. 1882; 1 Jan. 1883; Saturday Evening Murray Hall Meeting of Philadelphian Society 1883–1884 Academic Year; Box 1, Ordway Diaries. James Mark Baldwin, "James Mark Baldwin," *History of Psychology in Autobiography*, 2; idem, *Between Two Wars*, 2:19–20, 2:229, 1:56, 1:341; Membership Files, Papers of First Presbyterian Church of Princeton.

120. Baldwin, "Baldwin," 3, 6–7, 9; idem, *Between Two Wars*, 1:54–101 passim; Vahan D. Sewny, *The Social Theology of James Mark Baldwin* (New York: King's Crown Press, 1945), 1–12. Baldwin worked out his application of Darwinism to psychology in *Mental Development in the Child and the Race* (New York: Macmillan, 1894), *Social and Ethical Interpretations in Mental Development* (New York: Macmillan, 1897), and *Development and Evolution* (New York: Macmillan, 1902). On influence of Edwards and the New England Theology on Dewey, see Kuklick, *Churchmen and Philosophers*, 241–53.

121. Baldwin, *Between Two Wars*, 1:21, emphasis added. Wilson's work provides another illustration. After Wilson read a paper on "Sovereignty" in government to a group of Princeton intellectuals, Dr. McCosh grunted: "'Umph! I have always held that sovereignty rests with God.' 'So it does, Dr. McCosh,' responded Wilson, 'but I did not go quite so far back in my discussion.'" Ray Stannard Baker, *Woodrow Wilson: Life and Letters: Princeton 1890–1910* (Garden City, N.Y.: Doubleday, 1927), 2:18–19.

122. Woodrow Wilson to Albert Shaw, 3 Nov. 1890, *PWW*, 7:62.

123. Woodrow Wilson to Frederick Jackson Turner, 5 Nov. 1896, *PWW*, 10:40–41; Frederick Jackson Turner to Woodrow Wilson, 8 Nov. 1896, *PWW*, 10:42–45; Woodrow Wilson to Frederick Jackson Turner, 15 Nov. 1896, *PWW*, 10:50–54.

124. Daniel C. Gilman, "Higher Education in the United States," *University Problems in the United States* (New York: Century, 1898), 292.

125. Woodrow Wilson to Frederick Jackson Turner, 15 Dec. 1896, *PWW*, 10:78.

126. Francis L. Patton to Cyrus H. McCormick Jr., 4 Apr. 1898, *PWW*, 10:498.

127. Woodrow Wilson Diary, 20 Jan. 1897, *PWW*, 10:120; Woodrow Wilson to Ellen Axson Wilson, 16 Feb. 1897, *PWW*, 10:163–64.

128. Ellen Axson Wilson reported Hibben's comments in a letter to Woodrow Wilson, 31 Jan. 1897, *PWW*, 10:134–35, emphasis added.

129. Woodrow Wilson to Frederick Jackson Turner, 31 Mar. 1897, *PWW*, 10:201. After Haskins declined the position in European history, Princeton hired Paul Van Dyke, about whom Patton told a trustee, he "will give very general satisfaction to the Faculty and the Alumni." Francis L. Patton to Cyrus H. McCormick Jr., 4 Apr. 1898, *PWW*, 10:497. For similar assessments of the Turner controversy, see Hoeveler, *McCosh*, 341; John M. Mulder, *Woodrow Wilson: The Years of Preparation* (Princeton: Princeton University Press, 1978), 135.

130. *The Voice Extra*, Nov. 1897, 2.

131. The above quotations are taken from this compilation of articles. *The Voice Extra*, Nov. 1897, 2, 1, 3, 5.

132. "The National W.C.T.U. Protests," *New York Voice*, 18 Nov. 1897, 2; *The Voice Extra*, passim; "Princeton Inn Again," *PB*, 3 Nov. 1897, 1; J. F. Hill, "The Princeton Imbroglio," *PB*, 17 Nov. 1897, 2; "Princeton's Shame," *PB*, 8 Dec. 1897, 2. By contrast, Old School Philadelphia Presbyterians almost apologetically excused the actions of the professors by noting that the professors must have signed the petition "in a thoughtless, accommodating way." *Pres*, 3 Nov. 1897, 6. Patton received dozens of angry letters, and was still answering them the following year. See, for example, Francis L. Patton to J. F. Hick, 2 Mar. 1898, Patton Letterpress Books (hereafter PLB), 12:195, Records of the Office of the President, Seeley G. Mudd Manuscript Library, Princeton University. Published with permission of Princeton University Library; Francis L. Patton to Mrs. Thaw, 12 Apr. 1898, PLB, 12:369–75.

133. Synod of New Jersey, "Report of the Permanent Committee on Temperance," "Special Supplementary Report of the Committee on Historical Materials," *Minutes of the Seventy-Fifth Annual Session of the Synod of New Jersey* (Trenton: MacCrellish and Quigley, 1897), 81, 99–103. See *The Voice Extra*, 8–10, for a list of resolutions from different synods and presbyteries which condemn the university.

134. Norman H. Clark, *Deliver Us From Evil: An Interpretation of American Prohibition* (New York: Norton, 1976), 68–117; Robert T. Handy, *Undermined Establishment: Church-State Relations in America, 1880–1920* (Princeton: Princeton University Press, 1991), 134–35; Marsden, *Fundamentalism and American Culture*, 13; Smith, *Seeds of Secularization*, 150–52; Ferenc M. Szasz, *The Divided Mind of Protestant America, 1880–1930* (University, Ala.: University of Alabama Press, 1982), 64–65; James H. Timberlake, *Prohibition and the Progressive Movement 1900–1920* (Cambridge: Harvard University Press, 1963), 4–38.

135. Presbyterian Church, U.S.A., *Minutes of the General Assembly of the Presbyterian Church in the U.S.A.* (New York: Presbyterian Board of Publication, 1871), 590.

136. Walter Lowrie reported that he, the president, and his sons drank in one winter nearly a hundred bottles of ninety-eight-year-old wine that the president had given by one of Princeton's benefactors. Lowrie, Autobiographical Vol. 2.174–75, Box 1, Lowrie Papers. One exception among the faculty was George Macloskie, who gave a temperance address before the Christian Endeavor Society of the Second Presbyterian Church during the controversy. "Professor Macloskie on Temperance," *PP*, 18 Dec. 1897, 2.

137. TM, 9 June 1890, 7:321; 13 Nov. 1980, 7:368–70; 12 Feb. 1891, 7:404; 12 Nov. 1891, 7:483; 13 June 1892, 7:546; 10 June 1895, 8:147–48; 11 June 1895, 8:187–88; 14 June 1895, 8:217–18; FM, 27 Mar. 1895, 23.

138. *The Voice Extra*, Nov. 1897, 5.

139. "Dr. Shields' Withdrawal," *PP*, 13 Nov. 1897, 2.

140. *Voice*, 18 Nov. 1897, 1. Horace G. Hinsdale to Henry C. Cameron, 2 Dec. 1897, Box 16, Cameron Family Papers. The Presbyterian ministers from the university who sided with Patton were Henry C. Cameron, J. H. DeVrees, John T. Duffield, James O. Murray, Samuel Stanhope Orris, and, from the seminary, John D. Davis, John DeWitt, Joseph H. Dulles, William H. Green, George T. Purves, Geerhardus Vos, and B. B. Warfield. No one from either the university or the seminary opposed Shields.

141. See, for example, "Presbytery of New Brunswick and Professor Shields," *PB* 17 Nov. 1897, 1; "The Case of Dr. Shields," *PB*, 17 Nov. 1897, 6; "New Brunswick Presbytery," *Pres*, 17 Nov. 1897, 20–21; "Princeton Inn Creates a Presbyterian Controversy," *New York Journal*, 12 Nov. 1897, E-File, Archives, Princeton Seminary Librar-

ies. Shields denounced his critics by arguing that they undermined true temperance and Christian liberty and injured "the cause of pure religion." Charles W. Shields, "The False Temperance Agitation," *Outlook*, 8 Oct. 1898, 377–79.

142. Francis L. Patton to John A. Stewart, 3 Nov. 1897, PLB, 11:681.

143. *New York Sun*, 31 Oct. 1897, quoted in *The Voice Extra*, Nov. 1897, 15. In the fall of 1897, 73 of the 220 scholarships went to minister's sons. Incidentally, 70 other scholarships went to preministerial candidates and 70 others to those unable to pay tuition. The remaining eight were assigned by their donors. TM, 13 Feb. 1896, 270–76.

144. "University News," *PP*, 8 Jan. 1898, 3.

145. A copy of the release is in Charles W. Shields, Faculty File. TM, 23 Dec. 1897, 8:582–83.

146. Francis L. Patton, *The Duty of Self-Control: An Address to the Students of Princeton University, in Marquand Chapel, Sunday Afternoon, January 30, 1898* (Princeton: Princeton University Press, [1898]), 7–8, 13–14. On the Old School Presbyterian position on Christian liberty in reference to alcohol, see Charles Hodge, "Temperance Question," *BRPR* 15 (1843): 461–69; A. A. Hodge "Church Action on Temperance," *BRPR* 48 (1871): 595–632.

147. "The New York Dinner," *Alumni Princetonian*, 27 Jan. 1898, 2. The entire address was reprinted in this alumni weekly. The description of the dinner comes from "President Patton Defends the Inn," *New York Herald*, 21 Jan. 1898, 4. Patton's address left Old School Philadelphia Presbyterians nonplussed. "President Patton's Position," *Pres*, 26 Jan. 1898, 28.

148. Osborn's pamphlet, *The Medieval and True Modern Spirit in Education*, is reprinted in his biography, *Creative Education in School, College, University, and Museum: Personal Observation and Experience of the Half-Century 1877–1927* (New York: Scribner, 1927), 117, 115.

149. See, for example, "Harvard University Statistics," *DP*, 25 Oct. 1893, 1; "President Dwight's Annual Report," *DP*, 15 Apr. 1896, 1; M. M. Minnassian, "The German University," *NLM* 45 (1890): 617–19; H. W. Hathaway, "Princeton's Growth," *NLM* 45 (1890): 483–85; M'Cready Sykes, "Original Research in American Colleges," *NLM* 49 (1894): 441–45.

150. Editorial, *Pr*, 12 Oct. 1893, 2.

151. See, for example, "Princeton in Western Pennsylvania," *Pr*, 29 Apr. 1890, 1; Sloane, "Princeton University," 886–900; West, "Spirit and Ideals of Princeton," 313–26.

152. TM, 11 June 1894, 8:38–41; 10 June 1895, 8:171–78.

153. For first-hand accounts of these changes, see Scott, *Some Memories*, 229; Perry, *And Gladly Teach*, 135, 143–45.

154. "Statistics of Higher Education," *ER* 16 (1898): 402–404. An informal survey of where graduate students lived reveals that at least half were seminarians. *Catalogue, 1898–99*, 195–200.

155. TM, 8 June 1896, 8:296; 10 Dec. 1896, 8:425.

156. TM, 11 Mar. 1897, 8:459; 14 June 1897, 8:494; 23 Dec. 1897, 8:590; 10 Mar. 1898, 8:626; 13 June 1898, 8:680; 21 Oct. 1898, 8:771; 8 Dec. 1898, 9:40; 9 Mar. 1899, 9:71.

157. TM, 8 June 1896, 8:292–93.

158. *Memorial Book*, 20, 27; Francis L. Patton to Samuel T. Thompson, 20 Aug. 1898, PLB, 12:524–28; Francis L. Patton to Samuel T. Thompson, 31 Aug. 1898, PLB, 12:604–10; Francis L. Patton to [?], 13 Feb. 1900, PLB, 14:261–62.

159. See, for example, FM, 21 Sept. 1898, in *PWW*, 11:30.

160. TM, 14 June 1897, 8:511.

161. Francis L. Patton to W. D. Gamble, 30 Nov. 1897, PLB, 12:16. I estimate that over 8,000 of the 10,989 pages in Patton's presidential correspondence were written by Patton himself.

162. TM, 14 June 1897, 8:511.

163. Woodrow Wilson to Robert Bridge, 23 July 1889, *PWW*, 6:356; Editorial Note, *PWW*, 7:63–68; Thomas Jefferson Wertenbaker, *Princeton, 1746–1896* (Princeton: Princeton University Press, 1946), 377–78; Francis L. Patton to Francis L. Patton Jr., 18 Feb. 1902, PLB, 15:136.

164. Bliss, *And Gladly Teach*, 129–30; Woodrow Wilson to John G. Hibben, 15 Sept. 1899, *PWW*, 11:240–41; John G. Hibben to Woodrow Wilson, *PWW*, 20 July 1899, 11:180–81; Scott, *Some Memories*, 229–30; C. C. Cuyler to Woodrow Wilson, 16 May 1898, *PWW*, 10:529–30.

165. Hoeveler, *McCosh*, 295; "Obituary for Charles E. Green." *Princeton University Bulletin* 9 (1898): 71–72; Cyrus Hall McCormick Jr. to Woodrow Wilson, 2 Apr. 1898, *PWW*, 10:495.

166. TM, 19 Oct. 1900, 9:357–63; 10 June 1901, 10:45–46; Howard B. Maxwell, "The Formative Years of the University Alumni Movement as Illustrated by Studies of the University of Michigan and Columbia, Princeton, and Yale Universities, 1854–1918," (Ph.D. diss., University of Michigan, 1965), 190–201.

167. Editorial Note, *PWW*, 12:292. McCormick, for example, managed his father's machinery business, and Pyne held a law degree from Columbia and was president of the National City Bank of New York and the principal stockholder in the Delaware, Lackawanna and Western Railroad. Leitch, *Princeton Companion*, 300, 399.

168. TM, 6 June 1900, 9:250–51.

169. TM, 19 Oct. 1900, 9:364; 13 Dec. 1900, 9:383–86, 389; John G. Hibben to Woodrow Wilson, 25 Nov. 1900, *PWW*, 12:35–36; Scott, *Some Memories*, 233–34. Studies have correctly recognized the widespread dissatisfaction with Patton's lack of leadership among the more progressive members of the faculty, trustees, and alumni and West's role in the founding of the Graduate College; but they overlook the role that Patton's different understanding of the nature of graduate education played within the controversy. Henry W. Bragdon, *Woodrow Wilson: The Academic Years* (Cambridge: Belknap Press of Harvard University Press, 1967), 269–86; Brill, "Religion and the University," 305–306; Hoeveler, *McCosh*, 340–45; Mulder, *Wilson*, 133–34; Edwin M. Norris, *The Story of Princeton* (Boston: Little, Brown, and Co., 1917), 231–32; Charles G. Osgood, *Lights in Nassau Hall* (Princeton: Princeton University Press, 1951), 30–33; Willard Thorp, "The Founding of the Princeton Graduate School: An Academic Agon," *Princeton University Library Chronicle* 32 (1970): 1–30; Thorp, Myers, and Finch, *Princeton Graduate School*, 66–102; Editorial Note, *PWW*, 12:200–202.

170. Bragdon, *Wilson*, 275. This quote comes from an interview with Halsey.

171. Woodrow Wilson to David B. Jones, 19 Mar. 1902, *PWW*, 12:299; David B. Jones to Simon J. McPherson, 17 Mar. 1902, Simon J. McPherson Papers, John Dixon Library, Archives, Lawrenceville School; David B. Jones to Woodrow Wilson, 17 Mar. 1902, *PWW*, 12:294–96. Patton was oblivious to Wilson's criticisms. McCormick wrote Jones, "[C. C.] Cuyler reported that Dr. Patton believes that most of the criticisms against him come from Professor West. He expressed himself as thoroughly satisfied with the high position taken on all these questions by Woodrow Wilson." Cyrus H. McCormick Jr. to David B. Jones, 16 Apr. 1902, *PWW*, 12:342–43. For Wilson's comment about Patton, see Woodrow Wilson to Jenny Davidson Hibben, 26 June 1899, *PWW*, 11:136.

172. Francis L. Patton to James W. Alexander Jr., 5 Apr. 1902, PLB, 16:306.

173. Jones was disgusted with "Pyne's poltroonery" and said that Pyne and the other reluctant trustees "acted as if they were trustees of Patton's feelings and position, and not trustees of Princeton University." He added that he would rather pay Patton's settlement himself than "Jew Patton down." David B. Jones to Cyrus H. McCormick Jr., 31 May 1902, *PWW*, 12:384–85. Another trustee told McCormick that he "could not support such a revolutionary measure." James W. Alexander Jr. to Cyrus H. McCormick Jr., 7 Apr. 1902, *PWW*, 12:321.

174. Francis L. Patton to David B. Jones, 31 May 1902, PLB, 16:487–89; Cyrus H. McCormick Jr. to Moses Taylor Pyne, 3 June 1902, *PWW*, 12:295–96.

175. Mary Dod Brown Papers, Seeley G. Mudd Manuscript Library, Princeton University. Published with permission of Princeton University Library; TM, 9 June 1902, 10:149–50, 168; 11 June 1902, 10:182. The professors and trustees who worked to oust Patton had also laid plans to ensure that Wilson, not Henry Van Dyke, would succeed Patton. In May, they thought that Patton favored Henry Van Dyke because he was a minister. Professor Fine wrote Jones that "To anyone who knows Van Dyke the very possibility of his election seems absurd. . . . It would not be amiss if the Liberals could agree on their man right away. . . . I will venture to say without being asked that neither we nor anyone else in the Princeton faculty want Henry Van Dyke, barring Henry himself and Paul and the Pattons." Henry B. Fine to David B. Jones, 19 May 1902, *PWW*, 12:373–74. For similar assessments of Patton's ouster, see Bragdon, *Wilson*, 269–79; Brill, "Religion and the University," 331–34; Hoeveler, *McCosh*, 345–47; Mulder, *Wilson*, 156–57.

176. FM, 3 Dec. 1902, 7; Bragdon, *Wilson*, 277.

177. See, for example, Veysey, *Emergence of the University*, 41–42, 52.

Chapter 4

1. Woodrow Wilson, "Princeton for the Nation's Service," 25 Oct. 1902, *PWW*, 14:170, 177, 183–84, emphasis added; idem, *A History of the American People*, 5 vols. (New York: Harper and Brothers, 1902), 5:212.

2. New York *Sun*, 11 June 1902, 6, emphasis added, as quoted in Earl H. Brill, "Religion and the Rise of the University: A Study of the Secularization of American Higher Education, 1870–1910," (Ph.D. diss., American University, 1969), 275. For historians who interpret the election of laymen as university presidents in this period as a telltale sign of the secularization of higher education, see ibid., 360; William C. Ringenberg, *The Christian College: A History of Protestant Higher Education in America*, with an introduction by Mark A. Noll (Grand Rapids: Christian University Press and Eerdmans, 1984), 127; Frederick Rudolph, *The American College and University: A History* (New York: Vintage, 1962), 419; Laurence R. Veysey, *The Emergence of the American University* (Chicago: University of Chicago Press, 1965), 236.

3. L. Burton Crane, "The Presidency of Princeton University," *Independent*, 19 June 1902, 1484; "President Woodrow Wilson's Inaugural at Princeton," *PB*, 6 Nov. 1902, 5. For similar assessments, see "The Inauguration of Princeton's New President," *Pres*, 29 Oct. 1902, 20; Edward H. Rudd, "Woodrow Wilson, Princeton's New President," *Congregationalist*, 2 Aug. 1902, 154.

4. John M. Mulder, *Woodrow Wilson: The Years of Preparation* (Princeton: Princeton

University Press, 1978), 112–13.

5. Wilson, "Princeton for the Nation's Service," 14:184.

6. Wilson, "Notes for a Talk," *PWW*, 1 Nov. 1906, 16:479, quoted in Mulder, *Wilson*, 175.

7. Henry Fairfield Osborn to Woodrow Wilson, 2 Aug. 1902, *PWW*, 14:54.

8. William Berryman Scott, *Some Memories of a Palaeontologist* (Princeton: Princeton University Press, 1939), 256.

9. Henry Fairfield Osborn, *Creative Education in School, College, University, and Museum: Personal Observation and Experience of the Half-Century, 1877–1927* (New York: Scribner, 1927), 126–27.

10. Veysey, *Emergence of the University*, 180–251; idem, "The Academic Mind of Woodrow Wilson," *Mississippi Valley Historical Review* 49 (1963): 613–34; idem, "Higher Education as a Profession: Changes and Continuities," in *The Professions in American History*, ed. Nathan O. Hatch (Notre Dame: University of Notre Dame Press, 1988), 27–28; idem, "Stability and Experiment in the American Undergraduate Curriculum," in *Content and Context: Essays on College Education*, ed. Carl Kaysen (New York: McGraw-Hill, 1973), 6–8.

11. "Washington Alumni Receive a Message from Alma Mater," *Washington Post*, 28 Mar. 1903, *PWW*, 14:402.

12. Woodrow Wilson, "What is a College For?" *Scribner's Magazine*, Nov. 1909, *PWW*, 19:339. For a fuller expression of Wilson's view on the relationship between a liberal culture education and professional training, see his address before the Commercial Club of Chicago, *The Relation of University Education to Commerce* (Chicago, 1902), *PWW*, 14:228–45.

13. Wilson, "Princeton for the Nation's Service," 14:176.

14. Arthur T. Hadley, "The Purpose in Education," *Independent*, 4 Aug. 1904, 257, quoted in Brill, "Religion and the Rise of the University," 383.

15. Woodrow Wilson, "The Statesmanship of Letters," *The Eighth Celebration of Founder's Day at the Carnegie Institute Pittsburgh Thursday, November 5, 1903* (Pittsburgh, n.d.), *PWW*, 15:35.

16. Veysey, *Emergence of the University*, 105–109; Rudolph, *College and University*, 363–65; Conrad Cherry, *Hurrying Toward Zion: Universities, Divinity Schools, and American Protestantism* (Bloomington: Indiana University Press, 1995), 29–53.

17. TM, 21 Oct. 1902, 10:190.

18. Wilson, "Princeton for the Nation's Service," 14:177, 183, 178. Written shortly after the conclusion of Wilson's administration, Edwin M. Norris's institutional history says that Wilson's educational philosophy simply "reaffirmed Princeton's traditional position." *The Story of Princeton* (Boston: Little, Brown, and Co., 1917), 237. See also Charles G. Osgood, *Lights in Nassau Hall* (Princeton: Princeton University Press, 1951), 34, 36.

19. Mulder, *Wilson*, 188, n. 3.

20. Ibid., 7–8, 34–37, 165, quote on 8.

21. Ibid., 106–108; George M. Marsden, *The Soul of the American University: From Protestant Establishment to Established Nonbelief* (New York: Oxford University Press, 1994), 225.

22. Woodrow Wilson, Letter to the Editor, *Nation*, 28 Apr. 1910, 428, quoted in Veysey, "Academic Mind of Wilson," 633.

23. TM, 21 Oct. 1902, 10:187; *PAW*, 26 Nov. 1904, *PWW*, 15:534.

24. On the organizational transformation of American churches, businesses, and government, see Samuel Haber, *Efficiency and Uplift: Scientific Management in the Progressive Era, 1890–1920* (Chicago: University of Chicago Press, 1964); Ben Primer,

Protestants and American Business Methods (Ann Arbor: UMI Research Press, 1979); Louis Weeks, "The Incorporation of American Religion: The Case of the Presbyterians," *Religion and American Culture* 1 (1991): 101–18; Robert H. Wiebe, *The Search for Order, 1877–1920* (New York: Hill and Wang, 1967).

25. FM, 2 Dec. 1903, 30–31; TM, 8 June 1903, 10:307; 10 Dec. 1903, 10:375.

26. TM, 10 Dec. 1903, 10:373–75; FM, 19 Apr. 1904, 41; 21 Apr. 1904, 41; 22 Apr. 1904, 42; 25 Apr. 1904, 35–50.

27. "Revision of the Courses of Study," *PAW*, 18 June 1904, *PWW*, 15:380. This summary is based on TM, 10:439–59. For a detailed explanation of the new curriculum, see Editorial Note, *PWW*, 15:277–92. See also Henry W. Bragdon, *Woodrow Wilson: The Academic Years* (Cambridge: Harvard University Press, 1967), 293–94; Mulder, *Wilson*, 169; Brill, "Religion and the University," 396–402.

28. *New York Sun*, 15 Mar. 1905, quoted in Brill, "Religion and the University," 400. On the "battle of the classics," see Frederick Rudolph, *Curriculum: A History of the American Undergraduate Course of Study Since 1636* (San Francisco: Jossey-Bass, 1977), 180–88; Veysey, *Emergence of the University*, 94, 107, 118, 234.

29. "Revision of the Courses of Study," *PAW*, 18 June 1904, *PWW*, 15:380, 379.

30. All figures are estimates; the 1904–1905 and 1909–1910 figures include those graduate-level courses open to undergraduates. *Catalogue, 1902–03*, 81–121, 163–76; *Catalogue, 1904–05*, 108–69; *Catalogue, 1909–10*, 127–200.

31. Woodrow Wilson, Report to the Board of Trustees, 8 Dec. 1904, *PWW*, 15:561.

32. George M. Harper, "The New Program of Studies at Princeton," *ER* 29 (1905): 143–44. For similar interpretations of Wilson's revision of the curriculum, see Varnum Lansing Collins, *Princeton* (New York: Oxford University Press, 1914), 271–72; Norris, *Story of Princeton*, 238.

33. Veysey, *Emergence of the University*, 241–51; Rudolph, *Curriculum*, 227–29, 234–35.

34. Editorial, "Princeton University Commencement," *Pres*, 22 June 1904, 26.

35. Editorial, *NYT*, 23 Oct. 1904, *PAW*, 5 Nov. 1904, 94. See also "Princeton's New Curriculum," *New York Evening Post*, n.d., *PAW*, 22 Oct. 1904, 62–64.

36. Howard A. Walter, "The New Curriculum," *NLM* 60 (1904): 120.

37. Woodrow Wilson, Report to the Board of Trustees," 8 Dec. 1904, *PWW*, 15:563, emphasis added.

38. TM, 21 Oct. 1902, 10:187–88; "The Preceptors," *DP*, 28 Apr. 1905, *PWW*, 16:84–85. On the background of Princeton's adaptation of Oxford's tutorial system, see Andrew F. West, "The Tutorial System in College," *Short Papers on American Liberal Education* (New York: Scribner, 1907), 1–24. On Wilson's anglophile tendencies and the preceptorial system, see Mulder, *Wilson*, 45, 51, 78, 126–27, 129, 136, 151, 170–72, 191; Bragdon, *Wilson*, 9–10, 136, 33–34, 304–308; Brill, "Religion and the University," 402–12; Collins, *Princeton*, 274.

39. Woodrow Wilson, Report to the Board of Trustees, 14 Dec. 1905, *PWW*, 16:260.

40. *DP*, 14 June 1905, *PWW*, 16:141.

41. Woodrow Wilson to Andrew Carnegie, 17 Apr. 1903, *PWW*, 14:411–12.

42. TM, 12 June 1905, 10:565.

43. Rudolph, *Curriculum*, 234–35; Veysey, *Emergence of the University*, 212, 241.

44. "President Wilson's Address," *DP*, 14 June 1905, *PWW*, 16:139.

45. Woodrow Wilson, "The Personal Factor in Education," *Youth's Companion*, 12 Sept. 1907, *PWW*, 17:330; John G. Hibben, "The Preceptorial System at Princeton University," *Journal of Pedagogy* 18 (1906): 249–56.

46. Woodrow Wilson, "New Plans for Princeton," *Harper's Weekly*, 24 June 1905, 904, *PWW*, 16:146.

47. D.C. Vaughan, Editorial, *NLM* 61 (1905): 217. See also "The Preceptorial System," *DP*, 27 Feb. 1906, 2. Henry Van Dyke Jr., according to Herbert S. Murch, an English professor, was a constant critic of the preceptorial system because he preferred the accolades of students for his lectures more than small group discussions. Herbert S. Murch to Mrs. Murch, 3 Oct. 1909, Box 1, Herbert Spencer Murch Papers, Manuscript Division, Rare Books and Special Collections, Princeton University Library. Published with permission of Princeton University Library.

48. "Professor John Grier Hibben '82 on the Preceptorial System," *PAW*, 3 Feb. 1906, 313–15; Scott, *Some Memories*, 277.

49. Woodrow Wilson, *Speech of Princeton Woodrow Wilson of Princeton University at the Princeton Dinner Given at the Waldorf-Astoria December 9, 1902* (New York, n.d.), *PWW*, 14:269.

50. "The Architectural Development of the University," *PAW*, 9 Dec. 1908, 171.

51. T. J. Jackson Lears, *No Place of Grace: Antimodernism and the Transformation of American Culture, 1880–1920* (Chicago: University of Chicago Press, 1983), 188–89, 203–209.

52. In March 1904, for example, the faculty dropped 75 students. In March 1906, the faculty flunked out 71 students. TM, 10 Mar. 1904, 10:417; 8 Mar. 1906, 10:647.

53. *Catalogue, 1902–03*, 354; *Catalogue, 1907–08*, 406; *Catalogue, 1909–10*, 438.

54. Samuel J. Reid to Mr. Reid, 4 Dec. 1904; Samuel J. Reid to Mrs. Reid, 22 Sept. 1905; Samuel J. Reid Papers, Manuscript Division, Rare Books and Special Collection, Princeton University Library. Published with permission of Princeton University Library.

55. Melvin Hall Diary, 25 Jan., [1907], Box 2, Melvin Hall Papers, Seeley G. Mudd Manuscript Library, Princeton University. Published with permission of Princeton University Library.

56. Quoted in Robert E. Annis, "The First Annual Dinner of the Orange Alumni Association," *PAW*, 26 Nov. 1904, 144.

57. "The First Decade of Princeton University: A Review of Princeton's Remarkable Growth since the Sesquicentennial Celebration," *PAW*, 26 Oct. 1906, 87–92.

58. "A Scotch Writer on American Universities," *PAW*, 4 Mar. 1908, 356.

59. Quoted in "The University and the Nation," *Newark Evening News*, 11 Apr. 1905, *PWW*, 16:49.

60. Woodrow Wilson to Frederick Jackson Turner, 15 Apr. 1905, *PWW*, 16:58. For similar inquiries from Wilson, advisors, and prospective preceptors, see Wilson's correspondence from the spring of 1905, *PWW*, vol. 15.

61. "Press Club Banquet," *DP*, 17 Apr. 1905, *PWW*, 16:63.

62. Robert K. Root, "Wilson and the Preceptors," *Woodrow Wilson: Some Princeton Memories*, ed. William Starr Myers (Princeton: Princeton University Press, 1946), 15; William Starr Myers Diary, 6 May 1906, Box 22, William Starr Myers Papers, Seeley G. Mudd Manuscript Library, Princeton University. Published with permission of Princeton University Library. For similar comments, see Charles G. Osgood, "Woodrow Wilson," n.d., Box 2, Charles G. Osgood Papers, Manuscript Division, Rare Books and Special Collections, Princeton University. Published with permission of Princeton University Library; Thomas Jefferson Wertenbaker, "Woodrow Wilson and His Program at Princeton," *Woodrow Wilson in Retrospect*, ed. Raymond F. Pisney (Verona, Va.: McClure Press, 1978), 76–77.

63. This information is drawn from Wilson's review of each preceptor's educational

background in his Report to the Board of Trustees, 14 Dec. 1905, *PWW*, 16:253–59.

64. Woodrow Wilson to Frank Thilly, 1 Feb. 1904, *PWW*, 15:152–53; Frank Thilly to Woodrow Wilson, 4 Feb. 1904, *PWW*, 15:156–57.

65. Mulder, *Wilson*, 177. Mulder notes that Kallen, who later gained prominence as a leading Zionist and founder of the New School for Social Research, taught at Princeton for a year but was fired for some unknown reason. His obituary in the *New York Times* implied that he was dismissed from Princeton because he was a non-Christian. Mulder, however, contends that there is no evidence in Wilson's papers that he participated in the decision to dismiss Kallen or that Kallen was dismissed on religious grounds. Ibid., 177, n. 85.

66. TM, 21 Oct. 1902, 10:194.

67. Arnold Guyot Cameron to Henry C. Cameron, 7 Oct. 1905, Box 41, Cameron Family Papers. "Elected Most Popular Prof." *New Sunday News*, 1 May 1904, n.p.; Milton Halsey Thomas, "Minute On the Death of Dr. Arnold Guyot Cameron, Read to the Historical Society of Princeton, 17 Nov. 1947." Arnold Guyot Cameron, Faculty File. For a detailed description of the Cameron affair, see Editorial Note, *PWW*, 15:52–54.

68. Mulder, *Wilson*, 172.

69. Edwin G. Conklin, "As a Scientist Saw Him," *Woodrow Wilson: Some Princeton Memories*, 59.

70. All figures are estimates based on a comparison of university catalogues and exclude professors emeriti. *Catalogue, 1902–03*, 18–25; *Catalogue, 1909–10*, 20–35.

71. "Statement of President Eliot," in *An Appeal In Behalf of the Further Endowment of the Divinity School of Harvard University* (Cambridge: John Wilson and Son, 1879), 24, quoted in Cherry, *Hurrying Toward Zion*, 61.

72. "Wilson and Patton Differ," *New York Tribune*, 2 Dec. 1902, 4. For similar comments, see "Presbyterian Banquet," *Sun*, 5 Dec. 1902, *PWW*, 14:260–61.

73. *Catalogue, 1902–03*, 41. In the institutional histories written in the generation after Wilson's famed sesquicentennial address, a historiographical shift began to take place that canonizes the Wilsonian vision of Princeton. See, for example, James W. Alexander Jr., *Princeton—Old and New* (New York: Scribner, 1899), 53–57; John Rogers Williams, *The Handbook of Princeton*, with an introduction by Woodrow Wilson (New York: Grafton, 1905), 1–30; Collins, *Princeton*, 1–30, 247–48, 356–57; Norris, *Story of Princeton*, passim. See also, "The First History of Princeton," *PAW*, 11 Mar. 1905, 369–71.

74. William H. Roberts to Woodrow Wilson, 4 Feb. 1907, *PWW*, 17:28–29. Many older alumni and conservative Presbyterians during Wilson's presidency maintained the older interpretation of the founding purposes of Princeton. For example, the General Assembly of the northern Presbyterian church visited the university in June 1902 for the dedication of the memorial tablet to the church's role in the founding of Princeton. John DeWitt, a professor at the seminary, told the audience that while the charter placed the college under no ecclesiastical jurisdiction, Princeton was "the great mother of Presbyterian Colleges." "There have existed between this University and this Church," he concluded, "for a century and a half, an intimate friendship. Of this friendship I am sure that both the friends will say; *Esto perpetua.*" "Princeton University and the Presbyterian Church," *PP*, 14 June 1902, 6. For similar interpretations on the founding of Princeton, see Elijah R. Craven, "The Log College of Neshaminy and Princeton University," *Presbyterian Historical Society* 1 (1902): 308–14; "The Old Log College," *Pres*, 2 May 1906, 9; B. M. Gemmill, "Educational History of the Synod of Pennsylvania," *Pres*, 24 Dec. 1906, 7–9.

75. *Catalogue, 1907–08*, 45–46.

76. TM, 20 Oct. 1906, 10:732.

77. Henry S. Pritchett, "The Policy of the Carnegie Foundation for the Advancement of Teaching," *ER* 32 (1906): 83–99. See also idem, "The Relations of Christian Denominations to Colleges," *ER* 36 (1908): 217–41.

78. Andrew Carnegie to Woodrow Wilson, 14 Apr. 1905, *PWW*, 16:55; Woodrow Wilson to Andrew Carnegie, 18 Apr. 1905, *PWW*, 16:67; Henry Smith Pritchett to Woodrow Wilson, 9 June 1906, 16:419; *PAW*, 28 Apr. 1906, 550–51; Dorothy C. Bass, "Ministry on the Margin: Protestants and Education," in *Between the Times: The Travail of the Protestant Establishment in America, 1900–1960*, ed. William R. Hutchison (New York: Cambridge University Press, 1989), 51–56; Richard Hofstadter and Walter P. Metzger, *The Development of Academic Freedom in the United States* (New York: Columbia University Press, 1955), 361–62; L. Bruce Leslie, *Gentlemen and Scholars: College and Community in the "Age of the University," 1865–1917* (State College: Penn State University Press, 1992), 142, 165; David B. Potts, "American Colleges in the Nineteenth Century: From Localism to Denominationalism," *History of Education Quarterly* 11 (1971): 375; Marsden, *Soul of the University*, 281–87; Rudolph, *College and University*, 431–34.

79. TM, 8 Dec. 1904, 10:527; "Trustees Meeting," *DP*, 10 Dec. 1904, 3. Pritchett, "Relations of Christian Denominations to Colleges," 221.

80. "Dr. Patton's Address," 10.

81. TM, 25 Oct. 1902, 10:245; "Inaugural Exercises," *DP*, 14 Oct. 1903, 1.

82. In 1902–1903, 72 percent, 90 of the 124, graduate students were seminarians. That figure only dropped below 50 percent in 1908–09, when 43 of 91 students were seminarians. In the fall of 1903, the university began to charge a small fee to seminarians. The majority of seminarians were studying in the philosophy or the English departments. TM, 23 Oct. 1903, 10:365–66; 10 Dec. 1903, 10:394; 14 Jan. 1909, 11:129–30.

83. Theodore Whitefield Hunt to Harris Kirk, 9 June 1909, quoted in Donald G. Miller, *The Scent of Eternity: A Life of Harris Elliott Kirk of Baltimore* (Macon, Ga.: Mercer University Press, 1989), 407.

84. These figures were kindly supplied by Peter Wallace and Mark A. Noll. For an examination of the changing demographics of the seminary's student body, see their article, "The Students of Princeton Seminary, 1812–1929: A Research Note," *American Presbyterians* 72 (1994): 203–15.

85. John S. Burgess, Unpublished Autobiography, 139, Box 1, John and Stella Burgess Papers, Manuscript Division, Rare Books and Special Collections, Princeton University. Published with permission of Princeton University Library.

86. Woodrow Wilson to Harris Kirk, 10 June 1909, quoted in Miller, *Scent of Eternity*, 407. The only ministers on the faculty in 1909 were Francis L. Patton, Paul Van Dyke, Henry Van Dyke Jr., John G. Hibben, and Hunt. Ibid., 409–10.

87. Mrs. Crawford H. Toy, "Second Visit to the White House," diary entry dated 3 Jan. 1915, quoted in Arthur S. Link, "Woodrow Wilson: Presbyterian in Government," in *Calvinism and the Political Order*, ed. by George L. Hunt (Philadelphia: Westminster, 1965), 158. Characterizations of Wilson's theological views range from liberal Protestant to nonsectarian Christian to traditional Presbyterian to moralistic Christian. On the liberal view, see August Heckscher, *Woodrow Wilson: A Biography* (New York: Scribner, 1991), 42. On the traditional Presbyterian view, see Marsden, *Soul of the University*, 225, 229. On the nonsectarian Christian view, see Link, "Woodrow Wilson," 160–63; Bragdon, *Wilson*, 299. On the moralistic position, see Mulder, *Wilson*, 121–23, 127–29; Veysey, "Academic Mind of Wilson," 627–28.

88. Winthrop M. Daniels, *Recollections of Woodrow Wilson* (New Haven: Privately printed, 1944), 39.

89. "Wilson and Patton Differ," 4.

90. Woodrow Wilson to Ellen Axson Wilson, 11 Jan. 1885, *PWW*, 3:598. At times, Wilson's religious views pleased conservative Presbyterians in the university's constituency. This is evident in their response to his inaugural address. At other times, his religious views appealed to Unitarians and other Protestants noted for their nonsectarian theology. For instance, at a 1905 meeting of the Inter-Church Conference on Federation, a precursor to the Federal (and later Nation) Council of Churches, Wilson reportedly supported the exclusion of Unitarians from the convention. Yet Wilson assured a Unitarian minister who complained about his apparent sectarianism that newspaper reporters had been "utterly mistaken" about what he actually said and that his views on personal self-development and religious service were substantially the same as that of Unitarianism. "Dr. Wilson Hits at Excluded Faith," *NYT*, 20 Nov. 1905, *PWW*, 16:228–29; Woodrow Wilson to Minot Judson Savage, 22 Nov. 1905, *PWW*, 16:230–31.

91. Theodore Whitefield Hunt, "Woodrow Wilson's Attitude Toward Religion," [1924], n.p., Archives, Princeton Seminary Libraries.

92. James W. Alexander Jr., "'Princeton Spirit' and Its Justification," *Leslie's Weekly*, 23 June 190[?], 584; James W. Alexander Jr., Alumni File. See also Williams, *Handbook of Princeton*, 131–32; Collins, *Princeton*, 123; Norris, *Story of Princeton*, 125.

93. Slosson's articles were republished in his book, *Great American Universities* (New York: Macmillan, 1910), 100, emphasis added.

94. Princeton University, *General Catalogue of Princeton University, 1746–1906* (Princeton: Published by the University, 1908), 21–25; *Catalogue, 1909–10*, 17–18; Princeton Theological Seminary, *Biographical Catalogue of the Princeton Theological Seminary, 1815–1932*, comp. by Edward H. Roberts (Princeton: Published by the Trustees of the Theological Seminary of the Presbyterian Church, Princeton, New Jersey, 1933), xxi–xiii, xviii, xxi, 294, 297, 327, 337.

95. TM, 20 Oct. 1906, 10:731.

96. At five large state universities surveyed for the same two periods, the figure dropped from 6.3 percent to 0. Princeton is included in the figures for private institutions. Earl McGrath, "The Control of Higher Education in America," *Educational Record* 17 (1936): 264–65.

97. TM, 12 June 1905, 10:555–56; 9 Jan. 1908, 10:847; 8 Mar. 1906. 10:651; Woodrow Wilson, Grover Cleveland and William J. Magie to John J. McCook and Charles B. Alexander [ca. 29 Dec. 1905], *PWW*, 16:276; Bayard Henry to Moses Taylor Pyne, 2 Jan. 1906, *PWW*, 16:227–78; Moses Taylor Pyne to Woodrow Wilson, 5 Jan. 1906, *PWW*, 16:278–79.

98. These two nonalumni trustees were Archibald D. Russell (1853–1919) and Stephen S. Palmer (1853–1913). Russell was a New York real estate broker and a trustee of several banks and railroad companies; Palmer was the president of several mining, water, steel, and railroad companies. Archibald D. Russell and Stephen S. Palmer, Trustees Files, Seeley G. Mudd Manuscript Library, Princeton University. Published with permission of Princeton University Library.

99. The gift included $1000 for George S. Patton's annual salary, and $35,000 toward the endowment of his professorship. TM, 9 Mar. 1904, 10:537.

100. "President Wilson's Address," *PAW*, 13 Dec. 1902, 199–204.

101. TM, 12 June 1905, 10:579–80; 20 Oct. 1906, 10:727–31; 9 Apr. 1909, 11:171–74; Andrew K. Imbrie, Alumni File.

102. "First Decade of Princeton University," 87; *Catalogue, 1906–07,* 351–56. On the shift in Princeton's community of support from a Presbyterian identity to a purely alumni one, see Howard B. Maxwell, "The Formative Years of the University Alumni Movement as Illustrated by Studies of the University of Michigan and Columbia, Princeton, and Yale Universities, 1854–1918" (Ph.D. diss., University of Michigan, 1965), 201–31, and especially, Leslie, *Gentlemen and Scholars,* 117, 123, 144–45.

103. Bailey B. Burritt, *Professional Distribution of College and University Graduates* (Washington, D.C.: Government Princeton Office, 1912), 105. Burritt reported in 1912 that about one-third of the graduates of Harvard, Yale, Columbia, Pennsylvania, and Princeton were entering business. Ibid., 73.

104. Pritchett, "Relations of Christian Denominations to Colleges," 221.

105. Wilson, introduction to *Handbook of Princeton,* xii.

106. Statement made at 160th anniversary celebration of Princeton, quoted in Tertius Van Dyke, *Henry Van Dyke: A Biography* (New York: Harper and Row, 1935), 225.

107. Wilson, introduction to *Handbook of Princeton,* xii–xiii, emphasis added.

108. "Discipline, Religion, Democracy," *PAW,* 11 Nov. 1908, 107.

109. Andrew F. West, "The Changing Conception of 'The Faculty' in American Universities," *ER* 32 (1906): 2–3.

110. James Turner, "Secularization and Sacralization: Speculations on Some Religious Origins of the Secular Humanities Curriculum, 1850–1900," in *The Secularization of the Academy,* ed. George M. Marsden and Bradley J. Longfield (New York: Oxford University Press, 1992), 74–106, esp. 80–81.

111. Woodrow Wilson, "Baccalaureate Address," 11 June 1905, *PWW,* 16:126.

112. "The Bible in American Colleges," *BW* 26 (1905): 214–23.

113. Wallace N. Stearns, "Religious Education and State Universities," *BW* 27 (1906): 442–52; M. H. Buckham, "The Place of Religion in a Liberal Education," *RE* 2 (1907): 217. See also William H. Matlock, "Instruction in Religion in State Universities," *ER* 40 (1910): 256–65.

114. William DeWitt Hyde, "The Place of Religion in a Liberal Education," *Homiletic Review* 58 (1909): 286–87. Conservative Presbyterians rejected Hyde's argument and contended that religious instruction needed a definite place within a liberal education. "Religion and Liberal Education," *Pres* 20 Oct. 1909, 4. See also "Ignorance of the Bible," *Pres* 15 Jan. 1908, 3–4; Dwight M. Pratt, "Religious Life in our Colleges," *Homiletic Review* 58 (1909): 13–20.

115. [William Rainey Harper], "The University and Religious Education," *BW* 24 (1904): 323–29; [Ernest DeWitt Burton], "The Opportunity of the Colleges," *BW* 32 (1908): 3–6. For similar arguments, see William Rainey Harper, "What Can Universities and Colleges Do for the Religious Life of their Students?" *The Aims of Religious Education: The Proceedings of the Third Annual Convention of the Religious Education Association, Boston, February 12–16, 1905.* (Chicago: Executive Office of the Association, 1905), 110–13; [Ernest DeWitt Burton], "Religious Education in the Colleges," *BW* 36 (1910): 219–22; Edwin Starbuck, "Religion in General Education," *ER* 27 (1904): 53–59; Benjamin W. Bacon, "Courses Bearing on the Bible in Practical and Biblical Life," *The Religious Education Association. Proceedings of the Second Annual Convention, Chicago, March 2–4, 1904* (Chicago: Executive Office of the Association, 1904), 131–35. On the founding of the Religious Education Association, see Stephen A. Schmidt, *A History of the Religious Education Association* (Birmingham, Ala.: Religious Education Association, 1983), 11–55; Cherry, *Hurrying Toward Zion,* 40–44.

116. D. W. Fisher, "Christianity in the College," *PTR* 1 (1903): 262.

117. TM, 12 June 1905, 10:565, 570; Woodrow Wilson, Report of the President, 14 Dec. 1905, *PWW*, 16:248; Johyn H. Keener, ed., *Triennial Record of the Class of 1897 Princeton University* (New York: Grafton, 1900), 143–45; P. R. Colwell, ed., *Duodecennial Record of the Class of Eighteen Hundred and Ninety-Seven Princeton University* (Princeton: Princeton University Press, 1907), 138–39; Lucius H. Miller, Alumni File; Mulder, *Wilson*, 177. The first evidence that Wilson planned to hire another Bible instructor comes from two letters to Miller. Woodrow Wilson to Lucius H. Miller, 18 Mar. 1903; Woodrow Wilson to Lucius H. Miller, 26 Mar. 1903; Lucius H. Miller Papers, Manuscript Division, Rare Books and Special Collections, Princeton University. Published with permission of Princeton University Library.

118. Lucius H. Miller to Woodrow Wilson, 19 May 1906, *PWW*, 10:401.

119. Lucius H. Miller, "Modern Views of the Bible and of Religion," *South Atlantic Quarterly* 7 (1908): 309–15.

120. Ibid., 317, 312–14, quotes on 312.

121. Cherry, *Hurrying Toward Zion*, 91–102.

122. Miller, "Modern Views of the Bible and of Religion," 311, 316–19, quotes come from 318–19. For other expressions of Miller's modernism made during Wilson's presidency, see "The Authority of the Bible," *South Atlantic Quarterly* 9 (1910): 239–50; "Vigorous Talk," *DP*, 9 Oct. 1908, 1.

123. Robert T. Handy, *A Christian America: Protestant Hopes and Historical Realities*, rev. ed. (New York: Oxford University Press, 1984), 134–47, quote on 147. On the social gospel and the early-twentieth-century university, see Cherry, *Hurrying Toward Zion*, 187–95.

124. Woodrow Wilson to Lucius H. Miller, 17 Apr. 1908, Miller Papers, emphasis added.

125. George B. Logan to Woodrow Wilson, 29 Jan. 1909, *PWW* 18:17.

126. Woodrow Wilson to George B. Logan, 29 Jan. 1909, *PWW*, 19:24–25. Miller's draft of his reply is labeled "President Wilson's Reply to Letters about Biblical Teaching." Miller Papers.

127. Carson Sewall to Lucius H. Miller, 29 Mar. 1909; Woodrow Wilson to Lucius H. Miller, 30 Apr. 1909, Miller Papers.

128. Woodrow Wilson to Lucius H. Miller, 31 Mar. 1909, Miller Papers.

129. TM, 9 Apr. 1909, 11:158; Frank L. Janeway, Alumni File.

130. FM, 4 Apr. 1909, 259; TM, 14 Apr. 1909, 11:310.

131. Burgess, Unpublished Autobiography, 131–32, Box 1, Burgess Papers.

132. Patton taught History of English Ethics, Problems in Contemporary Ethics, Self-Realization and the Ethics of Idealism, and Hedonism and the Ethics of Naturalism. *Catalogue, 1907–08*, 124–25. Patton's continued commitment to Scottish realism is evidenced in several articles and critical reviews. See George S. Patton, review of *A Study of Ethical Principles*, by James Seth, *PRR* 6 (1895): 578–81; idem, review of *Moral Evolution*, by George Harris, *PRR* 8 (1897): 531–41; idem, review of *Ethics Descriptive and Explanatory*, by S. E. Mezes, *Psychological Review* 9 (1902): 418–30; idem, review of *A History of the Problems of Philosophy*, by Paul Janet and Gabriel Séailles, *Psychological Bulletin* 1 (1904): 166–69; idem, review of *La philosophie pratique de Kant*, by Victor Delbos, *Philosophical Review* 15 (1906): 536–42; idem, review of *Der Kampf un die Sittliche Welt*, by D. Wilh. Schmidt, *PTR* 5 (1907): 648–51; idem, "Beyond Good and Evil," *PTR* 6 (1908): 392–436; idem, review of *Les fonctions mentales dans les sociétés inferieures*, L. Lévy–Bruhl, *Philosophical Review* 21 (1912): 455–62.

133. Friedrich Paulsen, *A System of Ethics*, ed. and trans. Frank Thilly (New York: Scribner, 1899); Alfred Weber, *History of Philosophy*, trans. by Frank Thilly (New York:

Scribner, 1907). Thilly taught advanced courses in psychology, metaphysics, and epistemology. *Catalogue, 1905–06*, 121, 124; *D.A.B.*, 21:682–84.

134. George S. Patton, "Recent Works on Ethics," *Psychological Review* 8 (1901): 71–76, quote on 75. Patton made similar criticisms of Thilly's teacher, Friedrich Paulsen, in his review of the latter's *A System of Ethics* in *PRR* 11 (1900): 326–31.

135. A. J. D. Porteous, "Biographical Sketch: Norman Kemp Smith (1872–1958)," *The Credibility of Divine Existence: The Collected Papers of Norman Kemp Smith*, ed. A. J. D. Porteous, R. D. Maclennan, and G. E. Davie (New York: St. Martin's Press, 1967), 3–22; Norman Kemp Smith, *A Commentary to Kant's Critique of Pure Reason* (London: Macmillan, 1918); Alexander Leitch, *A Princeton Companion* (Princeton: Princeton University Press, 1978), 361–62.

136. See, for example, John G. Hibben, *The Philosophy of the Enlightenment* (New York: Scribner, 1910), in comparison to *The Problems of Philosophy* (New York: Scribner, 1898), 98–117. Hibben's shifting commitments are evident in his 1909 presidential address to the American Philosophical Association in which he left the door open to an intuitively derived source of knowledge, as he put it, behind the vitalist—as opposed to mechanical—conception of the evolution of the universe. "The Philosophical Aspects of Evolution," *Philosophical Review* 19 (1910): 113–36. This shift is also evident in Hibben's interest in deductive logic, which was indispensable to idealism, as opposed to inductive logic, which was vital to the Scottish philosophy. Idem, *Logic: Deductive and Inductive* (New York: Scribner, 1905), and compare with his earlier *Inductive Logic* (New York: Scribner, 1896). On Alexander T. Ormond's turned toward idealism, see, for example, his *Foundations of Knowledge* (New York: Macmillan, 1900), and *The Concepts of Philosophy* (New York: Macmillan, 1906).

137. William R. Hutchison, *The Modernist Impulse in American Protestantism* (Cambridge: Harvard University Press, 1976; rprt., New York: Oxford University Press, 1982), 122–32; Sydney E. Ahlstrom, ed., *Theology in America: The Major Protestant Voices from Puritanism to Neo-Orthodoxy* (Indianapolis: Bobbs-Merrill, 1967), 64–77; William E. Hordern, *A Layman's Guide to Protestant Theology*, rev. ed. (New York: Macmillan, 1968), 73–110; H. Shelton Smith, Robert T. Handy, and Lefferts A. Loetscher, eds., *American Christianity: An Historical Interpretation with Representative Documents*, 2 vols. (New York: Scribner, 1960–63), 1:255–308.

138. Burgess, Unpublished Autobiography, 149, Box 1, Burgess Papers.

139. James H. Canfield, "Religion and Public Education," *ER* 3 (1906): 455; Glenn C. Altschuler, *Andrew D. White: Educator, Historian, Diplomat* (Ithaca: Cornell University Press, 1979), 81. See also Wallace N. Stearns, "Moral and Religious Education in the Universities and Colleges," *The Materials of Religious Education. Being the Principal Papers Presented at, and the Proceedings of the Fourth General Convention of the Religious Education Association, Rochester, New York, February 5–7, 1907* (Chicago: Executive Office of the Association, 1907), 55–56.

140. See, for example, "Day of Prayer for Colleges," *Pres* 9 Feb. 1909, 5–6; "College Religion," *Pres*, 2 Feb. 1910, 4.

141. See, for example, George Harris, "The Required Religious Services of a College," *BW* 28 (1906): 240–50; Henry T. Claus, "The Problem of College Chapel," *ER* 46 (1913): 177–87. On chapel services in the early twentieth century, see Merrimon Cuninggim, *The College Seeks Religion* (New Haven: Yale University Press, 1947), 133–41; Bradley J. Longfield, "From Evangelicalism to Liberalism: Public Midwestern Universities in Nineteenth-Century America," *Secularization of the Academy*, 50–53; Ringenberg, *Christian College*, 125–26; George P. Schmidt, *The Liberal Arts College*

(New Brunswick: Rutgers University Press, 1957), 191–92; Clarence P. Shedd, *The College Follows Its Students* (New Haven: Yale University Press, 1938), 6–28; Veysey, *Emergence of the University*, 80, 204.

142. McCook's protests recorded in the trustees' minutes. TM, 21 Oct. 1903, 10:227; "Trustees Meeting," *DP* 22 Oct. 1902, 1.

143. Editorial, "Chapel," *DP*, 19 Oct. 1903, 2; "Chapel Services," *DP*, 26 Sept. 1904, 1.

144. Students had four excused absences per quarter. FM, 14 Oct. 1905, 96–97; TM, 21 Oct. 1905, 10:614–16; *Catalogue, 1905–06*, 246. Each student had a small card with his name on it which he turned in at the door to have his presence at chapel recorded. K. Sawyer Goodman Scrapbook 1905–06, Seeley G. Mudd Manuscript Library, Princeton University. Published with permission of Princeton University Library.

145. Harris, "Required Religious Services of a College," 248, emphasis added. Anson Phelps Stokes Jr., secretary of the Yale Corporation, said that the chapel service "is a factor of social importance in making the college feel its unity by bringing together all its students daily, and of moral importance in requiring that men must be up and dressed at an early hour, a serious deterrent to dissipation." Anson Phelps Stokes, "The Present Condition of Religious Life at Yale," in *Two Centuries of Christian Activities*, ed. James B. Reynolds, Samuel H. Fisher, and Henry B. Wright (New Haven: G. P. Putnam's Sons, 1901), 119, quoted in Brill, "Religion and the Rise of the University," 436.

146. Editorial, *DP*, 23 Oct. 1905, 2; *PAW*, 28 Oct. 1905, 68.

147. Woodrow Wilson to Charles W. McClure, 16 Nov. 1905, Box 4, Charles W. McClure Papers, Manuscript Division, Rare Books and Special Collections, Princeton University. Published with permission of Princeton University Library. Wilson had sent out a letter to each professor describing the new chapel arrangement and asked the faculty to help him oversee its implementation. Woodrow Wilson, "Notice to Members of the University Faculty in Regard to Seats in the Chapel," 6 Nov. 1906, Box 20, Myers Papers.

148. FM, 21 May 1906, 114; 5 Nov. 1906, 136; TM, 13 Dec. 1906, 10:745–46; *Catalogue, 1906–07*, 255.

149. Raymond B. Fosdick, *Chronicler of a Generation* (New York: Harper, 1958), 43. For similar observations, see Robert C. Clothier, "Woodrow Wilson as Educator and Administrator: A Student's Perspective," in *Woodrow Wilson in Retrospect*, 91; Bliss, *And Gladly Teach*, 155.

150. TM, 12 June 1907, 10:808.

151. Henry Van Dyke Jr., "To a Young Friend Going Away from Home to Get an Education," *ER* 26 (1903): 220–21.

152. *PAW*, 11 Feb. 1905, 300; "University Preachers Announced," *DP*, 1 Oct. 1910, 1. Anson Phelps Stokes Jr. of Yale suggested a list of university preachers to Wilson that included Lyman Abbott, George A. Gordon, Henry Churchill King, John R. Mott, and Robert E. Speer. Speer, Stokes noted, was not quite "broad" enough for Yale. Anson Phelps Stokes Jr. to Woodrow Wilson, *PWW*, 17:127–28. Dean Fine reported each change in chapel as a success to the trustees. TM, 11 Dec. 1902, 10:257; 21 Oct. 1903, 10:362; 14 Dec. 1905, 10:532; 11 June 1906, 10:676; 14 Mar. 1907, 10:764; 21 Oct. 1909, 11:243.

153. Woodrow Wilson to J. A. Medina 17 Oct. 1906, in Harold R. Medina Scrapbooks, Box 12, Harold R. Medina Papers, Seeley G. Mudd Manuscript Library, Princeton University. Published with permission of Princeton University Library. On student disturbances and punishment for skipping chapel, see Editorial, "Behavior in Chapel," *DP* 5 Nov. 1906, 2; FM, 18 Mar. 1907, 145; 6 May 1907, 146; 3 June 1907, 152; 28 Oct. 1907, 173; TM, 14 Apr. 1910, 11:314–15.

154. "Senior," Letter to the Editor, *DP*, 8 Oct. 1909, 1, emphasis added.

155. William A. Scott, "The Religious Situation in State Universities," *BW* 26 (1905): 28; Altschuler, *Andrew D. White*, 81. For similar arguments, Stearns, "Moral and Religious Education in Universities and Colleges," 53–57; idem, "Religious Education in State Universities," 442–52; Canfield, "Religion and Public Education," 459–60; Francis W. Kelsey, "The Problem of Religious Instruction in State Universities," *Education and National Character* (Chicago: Religious Education Association, 1908), 128–49.

156. Students Handbook, Princeton University, 1900–1901, 19, Box 14, Student Christian Association Records; "The Latest Attack on College Life," *PAW*, 27 Sept. 1911, 7.

157. "President Wilson's Address," *DP*, 27 Mar. 1903, *PWW*, 14:399; "Murray Hall Meeting Addressed by President Wilson," *DP*, 10 May 1907, *PWW* 17:140.

158. "Address by Dr. Van Dyke," *DP*, 24 Oct. 1902, 1; "Dynamic Faith," *DP*, 8 Feb. 1907, 1; "Murray Hall Address," *DP*, 20 Jan. 1905, 1.

159. "President Patton's Address," *DP*, 4 Dec. 1903, 1; "Dr. George W. Knox," *DP*, 11 May 1906, 1.

160. "Dr. Campbell Morgan at Princeton," *Pres*, 23 Mar. 1908, 20.

161. "Report of the General Secretary for the Year Ending June 15, 1904," *Philadelphian* 3 (1904): 8–9; "Report on Bible Work," *DP*, 13 May 1910, 1.

162. "Report of Bible Study Committee," *DP*, 13 Jan. 1906, 1; "Report of Bible Study Committee of Philadelphian Society," *DP*, 19 May 1901, 1; "Report on Bible Groups," *DP*, 14 Apr. 1910, 3.

163. "Bible Study Courses," *DP*, 19 Oct. 1908, 1; "Bible Classes Started," *DP*, 8 Oct. 1909, 1.

164. "Graduate Bible Student Course," *DP*, 7 Feb. 1903, 1; "Report of the Bible Study Committee," *DP*, 13 Jan. 1906, 1.

165. "Report on Bible Groups," *DP*, 14 Apr. 1910, 3.

166. Hutchison, *Modernist Impulse*, 164–72; George M. Marsden, *Fundamentalism and American Culture: The Shaping of Twentieth-Century Evangelicalism, 1870–1925* (New York: Oxford University Press, 1980), 81, 84, 90–93; Ronald C. White Jr. and C. Howard Hopkins, *The Social Gospel: Religion and Reform in Changing America* (Philadelphia: Temple University Press, 1976), 202–13.

167. "Murray Hall Address," *DP*, 8 May 1903, 1; "Mr. Samuel H. Hadley," *DP*, 9 Nov. 1905, 1; "Interesting Murray Hall Speaker," *DP*, 25 Oct. 1906, 1; "Murray Hall Address," *DP*, 1 Mar. 1907, 1; "Murray Hall Address," *DP*, 12 Nov. 1909, 1.

168. "Summer Camp," *DP*, 1 May 1908, 1; William K. Selden, *The Princeton Summer Camp, 1908–1975* (Princeton: Printed at Office of University Printing Services, [1987]), 19–26.

169. Lucius H. Miller to Woodrow Wilson, 26 Feb. 1909, *PWW*, 19:71–72.

170. "Mass Meeting," *DP*, 4 Oct. 1906, 1; *PAW*, 7 Apr. 1906, 491.

171. Burgess, Unpublished Autobiography, 32, 93, 229, 323, Box 1, Burgess Papers.

172. "Address by Mr. F. S. Brockman," *DP*, 17 Feb. 1905, 1; "The Real Situation in China," *PAW*, 14 Apr. 1906, 512–14; "Off for China!" *DP*, 15 Oct. 1909, 1.

173. "Peking Day," *PAW*, 14 Dec. 1910, 186.

174. "Two New Secretaries," *DP*, 5 June 1909, 1; "Religious Conditions in the University," *PAW*, 23 Nov. 1910, 137.

175. "Dean A. F. West to be Present at this Afternoon's Informal Gathering in Dodge Hall," *DP*, 28 Feb. 1908, 1.

176. Burgess, Unpublished Autobiography, 119–20, Box 1, Burgess Papers.

177. Quoted in Ellen Axson Wilson to Anna Harris, 12 Feb. 1907, *PWW*, 17:35.

178. Mulder, *Wilson*, 185–88.

179. Wilson, introduction to *Handbook of Princeton*, xvi. For similar descriptions, see George S. Patton, "At Princeton College," *Little Chap* 1 (1896): 50–51; "Discipline, Religion, Democracy," *PAW*, 11 Nov. 1908, 107; "Princeton Day in Cincinnati," *PAW*, 10 May 1911, 488–93.

180. Nelson Burr Gaskill to Woodrow Wilson, 26 June 1907, *PWW*, 17:230.

181. Woodrow Wilson, "A Supplementary Report to the Board of Trustees of Princeton University," 13 Dec. 1906, *PWW*, 16:519–25, quote on 523.

182. TM, 10 June 1907, 10:796, 797, emphasis added.

183. All figures are estimates. *Catalogue, 1887–88*, 157; *Catalogue, 1902–03*, 280; *Catalogue, 1809–10*, 332; John J. McCusker, *How Much Is That in Real Money? A Historical Price Index for Use as a Deflator of Money Values in the Economy of the United States* (Worcester: American Antiquarian Society, 1992), 328–29.

184. *Fourth Annual Report of the Carnegie Foundation for the Advancement of Teaching . . . October, 1909* (New York, 1910), 148, as cited in James McLachlan, *American Boarding Schools: A Historical Study* (New York: Scribner, 1970), 206. A 1911 survey of the secondary schools represented in Princeton revealed that only five of the twenty-eight schools were public. Of the top ten schools represented at Princeton, none were public schools. The university's primary feeder school was the Lawrenceville School with 143 students. The recently reestablished Princeton Preparatory School was second with 60 students, followed by the St. Paul's School with 54, Hill School with 51, and Mercersburg Academy with 43. "Report of the School Committee of the Graduate Council," *PAW*, 26 Apr. 1911, 459. In the fall of 1910, the curriculum committee reported to the trustees that 20 percent of the entering class came from public high schools. TM, 20 Oct. 1910, 11:400.

185. Gerald B. Lambert, *All Out of Step: A Personal Chronicle* (New York: Doubleday, 1956), 46–48; Fosdick, *Chronicler of a Generation*, 54. The figure on the dormitories comes from Bragdon, *Wilson*, 257.

186. Paxton Pattison Hibben, "University Education," *NLM* 58 (1903): 313.

187. Burgess, Unpublished Autobiography, 108, Box 1, Burgess Papers; Samuel J. Reid to Mr. Reid, 2 Oct. 1904, Reid Papers; Norris, *Story of Princeton*, 241–43.

188. A letter from a student to his mother illustrates the social pressures that the clubs created for many students. He had been asked to attend a reception at the Colonial Club but felt uneasy about going because he was not sent a written invitation. Already feeling out of place, he spoke to the wife of the author Laurence Hutton. "After awhile, she asked me, so that most of the people in the room could hear, 'Is this your club?' I regretted that it was not. 'What club do you belong to?' I had some further regrets, but hoped it would end there. Not a bit, 'Why don't you belong to any of the clubs? Don't you care for that sort of thing?' I explained that it was not a matter of my choice. At last Mrs. Hutton saw that the conversation was rather embarrassing, and I tried to smooth it over by saying that I probably had had too much to do, and so had been unable to do the sort of work necessary to a club election." John V. A. McMurray to Henrietta V. A. McMurray, 2 Feb. 1902, Box 27, McMurray Papers. For similar accounts about the social situation created by the club systems, see Paxton Pattison Hibben, "The Upper Class Club Problem," *NLM* 53 (1902): 68–76; Burgess, Unpublished Autobiography, 107–108, Box 1, Burgess Papers; Samuel J. Reid to Mr. Reid, 6 Mar. 1903; Samuel J. Reid to Mr. Reid, May 1904, Reid Papers.

189. TM, 21 Oct. 1904, 10:504; Marcia Graham Synnott, *The Half-Opened Door:*

Discrimination and Admissions at Harvard, Yale, and Princeton, 1900–1970 (Westport, Conn.: Greenwood Press, 1979), 179, 181. According to matriculation records, no Jewish students enrolled in the classes of 1903 and 1904. Ibid., 182, n. b.

190. TM, 21 Oct. 1902, 10:232–33; 21 Oct. 1909, 11:241.

191. TM, 21 Oct. 1903, 10:363. The dean of the College began reporting the denominational affiliation of incoming students to the trustees in the fall of 1902.

192. Leon Michel Levy to Woodrow Wilson, 25 June 1907, *PWW*, 17:223. Levy transferred to the University of Pennsylvania after his sophomore year. Ibid., 17:224, n. 1. See also Harold Zeiss to Woodrow Wilson, 27 June 1907, *PWW*, 17:233–34.

193. Slosson, *Great American Universities*, 105.

194. Francis Patricia Healy, "A History of Evelyn College for Women, Princeton, New Jersey 1887–1897," (Ph.D. diss., Ohio State University, 1967), 126–35.

195. A Draft of a Letter to G. McArthur Sullivan, 3 Dec. 1909, *PWW*, 19:550; Charles W. McAlpin to G. McArthur Sullivan, 6 Dec. 1909, *PWW*, 19:557–58. See also Woodrow Wilson to John Rogers Williams, 2 Sept. 1904, *PWW*, 15:462.

196. Slosson, *Great American Universities*, 104–105.

197. TM, 10 June 1907, 10:796, 797.

198. Mulder, *Wilson*, 191–92; Marsden, *Soul of the University*, 227–29.

199. FM, 26 Sept. 1907, 167–68; 30 Sept. 1907, 168–69; Andrew F. West, "Abstract of President Wilson's Speech to the Faculty," *PWW*, 17:422–24; Myers Diary, 26 Sept., 30 Sept., 7 Oct. 1907, Box 22, Myers Papers.

200. Woodrow Wilson to Cleveland H. Dodge, 1 July 1907, *PWW*, 17:240–41.

201. TM, 17 Oct. 1907, 10:819, 839; 9 Jan. 1908, 10:863. For the best accounts of the battle over the Quad Plan, see Mulder, *Wilson*, 187–203; Bragdon, *Wilson*, 312–36, 349–52; Leslie, *Gentleman and Scholars*, 117–25; Veysey, "Academic Mind of Wilson," 622–63. See also Collins, *Princeton*, 279–81; Graham, *Community and Class*, 200–202; Arthur S. Link, *Wilson: The Road to the White House* (Princeton: Princeton University Press, 1947), 45–57; Marsden, *Soul of the University*, 227–32; Norris, *Story of Princeton*, 248–50; Veysey, *Emergence of the University*, 246.

202. TM, 9 Mar. 1905, 10:548; 11 June 1906, 10:679; 20 Oct. 1906, 10:723–24.

203. Wilson, "Princeton for the Nation's Service," 14:183.

204. Andrew F. West, *The Proposed Graduate College of Princeton University* (Princeton: Princeton University Press, 1903).

205. After graduating from Princeton in 1874, West taught school for several years because he was unable to afford further education. In 1883, West returned to Princeton to teach Latin. That same year the college awarded West an honorary Ph.D. degree. His father, Nathaniel West (1826–1906), was one of the founders of the Niagara Bible Conference and author of *The Thousand Years in Both Testaments* (1889). The controversy surrounding the senior West stemmed as much from his personal problems as his premillenarian theology. When his second marriage failed in 1875, his wife accused him in both a lawsuit and newspapers of spouse and child abuse. This "treachery" was intended, the elder West told his friend Henry J. Van Dyke Sr. to cover her plans to steal his estate through a divorce. His stepson added insult to injury by selling some of his theology books to "buy beer and play billiards." In 1889, West unsuccessfully appealed the church's decision to dismiss him to the Presbytery, synod, General Assembly, and even state supreme court. Nathaniel West to Henry J. Van Dyke Sr., 21 Sept. 1875; Nathaniel West to Henry J. Van Dyke Sr., 29 June 1889; Nathaniel West to Henry J. Van Dyke Sr., June 1889, Box 41, Van Dyke Papers; *General Catalogue*, 241–42; Mulder, *Wilson*, 204; Bragdon, *Wilson*, 271–82.

206. Maxwell Struthers Burt, "Life at Merwick," *PAW*, 8 May 1907, 513–14. For another firsthand account, see Willard Thorp, "When Merwick was the University's 'Graduate House,' 1905–1913," *Princeton History* 1 (1971): 51–71.

207. Melancthon W. Jacobus to Woodrow Wilson, 20 Mar. 1909, *PWW*, 19:114.

208. TM, 9 Apr. 1909, 11:26–28; 14 June 1909, 11:192–93; 21 Oct. 1909, 11:244–48.

209. Wilson, "What is a College For?" 19:344, 337–38, 346.

210. TM, 13 Jan. 1910, 11:249–81; 10 Feb. 1910, 11:283–93.

211. Woodrow Wilson, "An Address to the Princeton Club of New York," *PAW*, 13 Apr. 1910, *PWW*, 20:346, 347, 348, emphasis added. On the alumni outrage after Proctor withdrew his gift, see the letters to the editor in *PAW*, 23 Mar. 1910, 388–94; 4 Apr. 1910, 428–34; 20 Apr. 1910, 464–67.

212. "Seymour Given Big Ovation," *Gazette Times*, 17 Apr. 1910, *PWW*, 20:364; Mulder, *Wilson*, 222.

213. "Disaster Forecast by Wilson," *Pittsburgh Dispatch*, 17 Apr. 1910, *PWW*, 20:366.

214. Cyrus H. McCormick Jr. to Edward W. Sheldon, 4 Mar. 1910, *PWW*, 20:213. For alumni criticisms of Wilson's populist appeal, see Alfred Pearce Dennis, *Gods and Little Fishes* (Indianapolis: Bobbs-Merrill, 1924), 102–106; Van Dyke, *Henry Van Dyke*, 228; Untitled Typed Manuscript Regarding Graduate College Battle, 20, n.d., Box 2, Wilson Farrand Papers, Manuscript Division, Rare Books and Special Collections, Princeton University. Published with permission of Princeton University Library.

215. Eleanor Wilson McAdoo, *The Woodrow Wilsons* (New York, 1937), 101, quoted in Mulder, *Wilson*, 223.

216. "The Will of Isaac C. Wyman '48," *PAW*, 25 May 1910, 548–50; TM, 9 June 1910, 11:320–31. Ironically, the Wyman estate "only" brought the university $623,000. John Marshall Raymond and Andrew F. West to Woodrow Wilson, 22 May 1910, *PWW*, 464, n. 3.

217. TM, 20 Oct. 1910, 11:393; 3 Nov. 1910, 11:409.

218. FM, 21 Nov. 1910, 292, emphasis added. This summary of the graduate college controversy closely follows several fuller accounts. Bragdon, *Wilson*, 271–82, 353–83; Leslie, *Gentleman and Scholars*, 151–52; Marsden, *Soul of the University*, 227–33; Mulder, *Wilson*, 203–28; Scott, *Some Memories*, 281–82; Willard Thorp, Minor Myers Jr., and Jeremiah Stanton Finch, *The Princeton Graduate School: A History* (Princeton: Princeton University Press, 1978), 103–51. See also Collins, *Princeton*, 283–84; Graham, *Community and Class*, 201–202; Link, *Wilson*, 59–91; Norris, *Story of Princeton*, 250–55; Veysey, *Emergence of the University*, 244–45.

219. "Princeton's 164th Year," *True American*, 23 Sept. 1910, *PWW*, 21:151.

Chapter 5

1. TM, 13 Jan. 1927, emphasis added.

2. The trustees made John A. Stewart, the senior member of the board, president pro tempore while they searched for Wilson's successor. TM, 20 Oct. 1910, 11:395; 3 Nov. 1910, 11:417; 12 Jan. 1912, 11:603.

3. "President Hibben's First Address to the Alumni," *PAW*, 24 Jan. 1912, 252.

4. William Starr Myers Diary, 15 Jan. 1912, Box 23, Myers Papers; William Berryman

Scott, *Some Memories of a Palaeontologist* (Princeton: Princeton University Press, 1939), 297.

5. John G. Hibben, "The Essentials of Liberal Education," *PAW*, 15 May 1912, 515–19. For similar expressions of Hibben's views of liberal education, see "Our Intellectual Tradition," *PAW*, 11 Oct. 1916, 39–40; "The Aim of Princeton," *PAW*, 16 Feb. 1921, 402–404. Hibben, according to the university archivist, destroyed most of his personal papers after his retirement. Because of the increased involvement of the alumni in the affairs of the university, the *PAW* published most of his addresses and also described many of the activities on campus. They serve as an excellent source on Princeton during Hibben's presidency.

6. Hibben, "Essentials of Liberal Education," 519.

7. Henry Sloane Coffin to Lucius H. Miller, 3 Dec. 1913; Lucius H. Miller to Henry Sloane Coffin, 6 Dec. 1913, Miller Papers.

8. Lucius H. Miller, "The Teaching of Ernst Troeltsch of Heidelberg," *Harvard Theological Review* 6 (1913): 450, emphasis added.

9. Lucius H. Miller, *Our Knowledge of Christ: An Historical Approach* (New York: Henry Holt, 1914), vi, viii, 156–57.

10. "The Princeton Work in Peking," *Pres*, 1 Apr. 1914, 7.

11. David S. Kennedy to Lucius H. Miller, 20 Mar. 1914; John W. Nicely to John G. Hibben, 2 Mar. 1914, Miller Papers.

12. Shailer Mathews to Lucius H. Miller, 14 Feb. 1914; Lucius H. Miller to John G. Hibben, 9 Mar. 1914; M. Willard Lampe to Lucius H. Miller, 26 Jan. 1914; G. Ellsworth Harris Jr. to Lucius H. Miller, 28 June 1914, Miller Papers.

13. See, for example, Charles Foster Kent, "Order and Content of Biblical Courses in College Curriculum," *RE* 7 (1912): 42–49; idem, "The Bible and the College Curriculum," *RE* 8 (1913): 453–58; Henry F. Cope, "Ten Years Progress in Religious Education," *RE* 8 (1913): 137–43. On the growth of the academic study of religion and the work of Kent and the Religious Education Association, see Stephen A. Schmidt, *A History of the Religious Education Association* (Birmingham, Ala.: Religious Education Association, 1983), 11–55; Conrad Cherry, *Hurrying Toward Zion: Universities, Divinity Schools, and American Protestantism* (Bloomington: University of Indiana Press, 1995), 91–102.

14. "Standardization of Biblical Courses," *RE* 11 (1916): 323.

15. Lucius H. Miller to John G. Hibben, Jan. 1914, Miller Papers.

16. The trustees agreed to hire John Nevin Sayre, general secretary of the Philadelphian Society, as biblical instructor for the 1914–1915 academic year and Ralph B. Pomeroy, rector of Trinity Episcopal Church in Princeton, as a lecturer without salary for the 1915–1916 academic year. TM, 9 Apr. 1914, 12:100, 119.

17. TM, 15 June 1914, 12:138, emphasis added.

18. Ford C. Ottman, *The Devil in Cap and Gown* (New York: Arno C. Gaebelein, 1914), 1.

19. See, for example, "Starts War Upon Princeton Teacher: Dr. Ottman Says Miller 'Lures Boys Into the Muculent Ooze of Free Thinking,'" *NYT*, 30 Aug. 1914, 15; "Find 'Devil in Cap and Gown' in Princeton University: 'No Crime More Dastardly Can Be Imagined,' Says Minister," *World*, 30 Aug. 1914, 7.

20. "Skeptical Teaching in Colleges," *Pres*, 16 Sept. 1914, 14. The publication of *Our Knowledge of Christ* in the fall of 1914 furthered the controversy, as more temperate reviews by liberals praised Miller's modernism and conservatives challenged it. See, for example, Herbert A. Youtz's review in *Harvard Theological Review* 10 (1917):

105; an anonymous review in *BW* 46 (1915): 127; William H. Johnson's review in *PTR* 13 (1915): 477–82; A. T. Robinson's review in *Review and Expositor* 12 (1915): 610.

21. T. S. Childs, "Dr. Van Dyke's Ordination Sermon," *Pres*, 11 June 1913, 8–9; Lefferts A. Loetscher, *The Broadening Church: A Study of Theological Issues in the Presbyterian Church since 1869* (Philadelphia: University of Pennsylvania Press, 1954), 97–99; Bradley J. Longfield, *The Presbyterian Controversy: Fundamentalists, Modernists, and Moderates* (New York: Oxford University Press, 1991), 24–25. The five points espoused by premillennialists substituted the premillenial return of Christ for the fifth point in the Presbyterian declaration. Ernest R. Sandeen, *The Roots of Fundamentalism: British and American Millenarianism, 1800–1930* (Chicago: University of Chicago Press, 1970; repr., Grand Rapids: Baker, 1978), xiv–xv.

22. "The Devil in Cap and Gown," *Pres*, 9 Sept. 1914, 5.

23. Henry F. May, *The End of American Innocence: A Study of the First Years of Our Own Time, 1912–1917* (New York: Knopf, 1959; repr., Chicago: Quadrangle Books, 1964), ix.

24. "Religious Instruction at Princeton," *Pres*, 14 Oct. 1914, 4; "Prof. Lucius Miller Denies Christian Resurrection," *Pres*, 25 Feb. 1915, 6.

25. George M. Marsden, *Fundamentalism and American Culture: The Shaping of Twentieth-Century Evangelicalism, 1870–1925* (New York: Oxford University Press, 1980), 141–42. According to Marsden's definition, fundamentalism was "a 'movement' in the sense of a tendency or development in Christian thought that gradually took on its own identity as a patchwork coalition of representatives of other movements." It was a loose coalition of co-belligerents from related traditions such as evangelicalism, revivalism, pietism, the holiness movements, millenarianism, Reformed confessionalism (such as Old School Presbyterianism), and other denominational traditionalists. Ibid., 4.

26. William K. Pentice to Lucius H. Miller, 1 Sept. 1914; William Starr Myers to Lucius H. Miller, 13 Sept. 1914; Mary B. Dale to Lucius H. Miller, 9 Nov. 1914; Varnum Lansing Collins to Lucius H. Miller, 20 Dec. 1914, Miller Papers.

27. Lucius H. Miller to John McDowell, 24 Oct. 1914; John McDowell to Lucius H. Miller, 27 Oct. 1914, Miller Papers.

28. Melanchthon W. Jacobus, one of the older members of the board, congratulated Charles W. McAlpin, secretary of the university, for "not allowing to get to press anything more regarding the Miller discussion." "It is evident," he added, "that we were right in our conviction that the press was expecting religious trouble in our meeting, and to my mind, anything we do in this matter until the outside discussion has died out will be interpreted by outsiders as a campaign in heresy-hunting on the part of the University." In the *DP*, the trustees denied discussing Miller. The trustees' minutes, moreover, record no discussion of the controversy. Melanchthon W. Jacobus to Charles W. McAlpin, 27 Oct. 1914, Box 28, Records of the Secretary, Seeley G. Mudd Manuscript Library, Princeton University. Published with permission of Princeton University Library. "Chapel Undiscussed in Fall Trustee Meeting," *DP*, 23 Oct. 1914, 1.

29. John Dewey, "Academic Freedom," *ER* 23 (1902): 1, 3; Nicholas Murray Butler, "Academic Freedom," *ER* 47 (1914): 291.

30. Richard Hofstadter and Walter P. Metzger, *The Development of Academic Freedom in the United States* (New York: Columbia University Press, 1955), 468–90; George M. Marsden, *The Soul of the American University: From Protestant Establishment to Established Nonbelief* (New York: Oxford University Press, 1994), 296–316; Frederick Rudolph, *The American College and University: A History* (New York: Vintage, 1962), 409–16; Laurence R. Veysey, *The Emergence of the American University* (Chicago:

University of Chicago Press, 1965), 384–418. In Germany, the concept of *Lehrfreiheit* meant the freedom for professors to teach what they wanted without administrative interference and to research and publish without restraint. What made the German concept of *Lehrfreiheit* unique was that the state, which controlled the university, guaranteed it and guarded professors from outside interests. Hofstadter and Metzger, *Development of Academic Freedom*, 367–412.

31. American Association of University Professors, *Report of the Committee on Academic Freedom and Tenure* (n.p., 1915), 6–29, in *American Higher Education: A Documentary History*, ed. Richard Hofstadter and Wilson Smith, 2 vols. (Chicago: University of Chicago Press, 1961), 2:680–78.

32. Howard C. Warren, "Howard C. Warren," *History of Psychology in Autobiography*, ed. Carl Murchison (Worcester: Clark University Press, 1930), 456.

33. Letter to the Editor, *Pres*, 18 Dec. 1914, 27. Howard C. Warren, "Academic Freedom," *Atlantic Monthly*, Nov. 1914, 689–99.

34. TM, 14 Jan. 1915, 12:14; "The Needs of Princeton University," *PAW*, 28 Mar. 1917, 564.

35. John DeWitt to John G. Hibben, 5 Oct. 1915, Hibben Papers.

36. TM, 14 Jan. 1915, 12:213.

37. "Princeton Chapel Revolt," *NYT*, 11 Mar. 1911, 1.

38. FM, 7 June 1911, 11:316; 21 Sept. 1911, 11:325; 20 Nov. 1911, 11:334–35; 4 Dec. 1911, 11:336; 15 Jan. 1915, 11:338; TM, 12 June 1911, 11:532; 12 Jan. 1912, 10:605.

39. Editorial, *DP*, 13 Dec. 1913, 2; "Chapel, An Alarm-Clock or Religious Stimulus?" *DP*, 21 Mar. 1921, 1. See also Editorial, "Compulsory Chapel," *DP*, 20 Jan. 1911, 2; Editorial, *DP*, 29 Sept. 1913, 2; Editorial, "Compulsory Chapel," *DP*, 16 Sept. 1914, 2; Editorial, "Religion by Compulsion," *DP*, 20 Mar. 1914, 2.

40. FM, 16 Mar. 1914, 11:445; 20 Apr. 1914, 11:448. Over the summer of 1914, trustees surveyed students' and recent graduates' opinions about making services voluntary and found that 40 percent thought they would attend voluntary weekday services and 81 percent the Sunday services. In the fall, at the height of the controversy over Miller, the *Daily Princetonian* conducted its own poll and found that students opposed compulsory weekday chapel 960 to 199 and compulsory Sunday services 578 to 572. The statistics for the trustees' survey come from a "Survey of Attitudes toward Chapel," dated 2 May 1915 found in the Records of the Secretary, Box 5; "Compulsory Daily Chapel Opposed by Big Majority," *DP*, 4 Nov. 1914, 1.

41. "Professor Lucius H. Miller's Book," *Pres*, 28 Jan. 1915, 7.

42. TM, 14 Jan. 1915, 214; 14 June 1915, 13:344–45; Princeton University, *Report of the President for the Year Ending December 31, 1915* (hereafter the president's report cited as *Report. . . [Year]*) (Princeton: Princeton University Press, 1915), 48–49.

43. "Professor Lucius H. Miller's Book," 6; Howard C. Warren to Lucius H. Miller, 16 Feb. 1915, Miller Papers.

44. TM, 15 Apr. 1914, 12:100; 9 June 1913, 11:843.

45. *Catalogue, 1914–15*, 32, 121; *D.A.B.*, 14:180–82; Bruce Kuklick, *The Rise of American Philosophy* (New Haven: Yale University Press, 1977), 215–27. Palmer's ethical system is outlined in *The Field of Ethics* (Boston: Houghton Mifflin, 1901).

46. Warner Fite, Faculty File; [Warner Fite], *A Complete Outline of Professor Fite's Lectures in Ethics* (Princeton: Printed by the Princeton Syllabi Co., [1917]); Douglas Sloan, "The Teaching of Ethics in the American Undergraduate Curriculum, 1876–1976," in *Ethics Teaching in Higher Education*, ed. Sissela Bok and Daniel Callahan (New York: Plenum, 1980), 22–25; *D.A.B.*, supp. 5:224.

47. Warner Fite, *An Introductory Study of Ethics* (London: Longmans, 1903), 261–62, 372–74. Ironically, George S. Patton reviewed this work and criticized Fite for caricaturing the views of utilitarianism with his confusing and "loose exposition." Review of *An Introductory Study of Ethics*, by Warner Fite, *Philosophical Review* 13 (1904): 379–81. For Fite's views on Dewey, see, for example, *Moral Philosophy: The Critical View of Life* (New York: Dial, 1925), 103–18.

48. Thomas S. Evans, "Report of the General Secretary of the Philadelphian Society," 13 Apr. 1916, Box 3, Student Christian Association Records. Another sign that the Philadelphian Society had become an arm of the administration is the fact that after 1911 the annual report of the secretary of the society was read at the spring meeting of the university's trustees and entered into the minutes. TM, 13 Apr. 1911, 11:494.

49. "William Jennings Bryan Talks on Religious Topic," *DP*, 13 Mar. 1911, 1–3; "Mr. C. I. Scofield Speaks in Murray Hall To-Night," *DP*, 30 Mar. 1911, 1; "Prof. J. Gresham Machen Will Address Students Again," *DP*, 3 May 1913, 3; "Dr. King Discusses Nature of Religion," *DP*, 2 Mar. 1912, 1; "Immigrant Situation a Challenge to America," *DP*, 27 Mar. 1914, 1; "Address Last Night, By Rev. H. E. Fosdick," *DP*, 19 Apr. 1912, 1; "Christianity A Protest, A Program, A Promise," *DP*, 23 Oct. 1914, 1.

50. "Bible Study Courses to be Under New Direction," *DP*, 27 Sept. 1911, 1; "Freshmen Bible Class Average Comes to 160," *DP*, 15 Nov. 1915, 1.

51. TM, 11 Apr. 1912, 11:651; 10 Apr. 1913, 11:823; "Scope and Work of Philadelphian Society," *DP*, 20 Oct. 1911, 4; "Religious Activities of Very Broad Scope," *DP*, 20 Apr. 1912, 4; Lucius H. Miller, "The Princeton Work in Peking," *PAW*, 22 Feb. 1914, 377–87.

52. "May To Be Active Month at Princeton Seminary," *DP*, 22 Apr. 1913, 1.

53. William K. Selden, *The Princeton Summer Camp, 1908–1975*, (Princeton: Printed at Princeton University Press, [1987]), 29; Evans, "Report of the General Secretary," 13 Apr. 1916. In the spring of 1915, the society reported that it had 858 church members, 86 members who signed the statement of faith, and 86 associate members. TM, 8 Apr. 1915.

54. "U. of P. Crowd Gym for Sunday's Message," n.p.; "Billy Sunday Preaching his Doctrine of Repentance to 3000 Students," *The Press* [Philadelphia], 9 Jan. 1915, 1, Scrapbook 6, Box 18, Reel 22, Collection 61, William and Helen Sunday Papers, Archives of the Billy Graham Center, Wheaton College; "Theological Seminary Invites Evangelist Sunday," *PP*, 27 Feb. 1915, 1–2.

55. Minutes of the Faculty of Princeton Theological Seminary, 20 Feb. 1915, 298; 1 Mar. 1915, 298; 2 Mar. 1915, 299.

56. "Sermon of the Rev. Wm. A. Sunday, 'Dr. Jekyll and Mr. Hyde,'" 17–18, Scrapbook 8, Reel 11, Collection 61, Sunday Papers; "H. W. Myers Jr., "Billy Sunday at Princeton," *Continent*, 18 Mar. 1915, n.p., Scrapbook 6, Box 18, Reel 22, Collection 61, Sunday Papers; "Evangelist Sunday at Princeton," *Pres*, 18 Mar. 1915, 6.

57. William C. Ringenberg, *The Christian College: A History of Protestant Higher Education in America*, with an introduction by Mark A. Noll (Grand Rapids: Christian University Press and Eerdmans, 1994), 122; Veysey, *Emergence of the University*, 280; Rudolph, *College and University*, 84–85.

58. Rolfe Cobleigh, "Billy Sunday, The Man and His Work," *PB*, 11 Mar. 1915, 10; Albert Parker Fitch, *Religion and the Undergraduate: Four Addresses Delivered at Princeton University, March 1915*, with an introduction by John G. Hibben (Princeton: Published under the auspices of the "Daily Princetonian," 1915); "Fitch, Albert Parker," *Who's Who in the Clergy*, ed. J. C. Schwarz (New York, 1936), 374.

59. "The Princeton Spectacle," *Pres*, 18 Feb. 1915, 4. See also "Princeton University and Billy Sunday," *Herald and Presbyter*, 17 Mar. 1915, 7; "Princeton's Exclusion of

Mr. Sunday," *PB*, 18 Mar. 1915, 6; "Princeton Alumnus," Letter to the Editor, *Pres*, 11 Mar. 1915, 11.

60. Sandeen, *Roots of Fundamentalism*, 162–207; William R. Hutchison, *The Modernist Impulse in American Protestantism* (Cambridge: Harvard University Press, 1976; repr., New York: Oxford University Press, 1982), 198, n. 24; Marsden, *Fundamentalism and American Culture*, 262, n. 31.

61. D. G. Hart, *Defending the Faith: J. Gresham Machen and the Crisis of Conservative Protestantism in Modern America* (Baltimore: Johns Hopkins University Press, 1994); Paul A. Carter, "The Fundamentalist Defense of the Faith," in *Change and Continuity in Twentieth-Century America: The 1920s*, ed. John Braeman, Robert Bremmer, and David Brody (Columbus: Ohio State University Press, 1968), 179–214; C. Allyn Russell, *Voices of American Fundamentalism: Seven Biographical Studies* (Philadelphia: Westminster, 1976).

62. J. Gresham Machen to Mary Gresham Machen, 28 Feb. 1915, J. Gresham Machen Papers, Montgomery Memorial Library, Westminster Theological Seminary.

63. "Dr. Fitch's Teachings at Princeton," *Pres*, 29 Apr. 1915, 3. See also "Baal's Priest in Alexander Hall," *Pres*, 25 Mar. 1915, 6–7.

64. "Princeton 1876 vs. Princeton 1915," *Pres*, 18 Mar. 1915, 11. See also William H. Johnson '88, Letter to the Editor, *PAW*, 10 Mar. 1915, 527; "An Alumnus," "The Princeton Problem," *Pres*, 8 Apr. 1915, 8–9.

65. "Dr. Fitch at Princeton," *Pres*, 25 Mar. 1915, 6.

66. Andrew F. West, "Mr. Sunday's Utterances," *PP*, 27 Feb. 1915, 2; idem, "Mr. Sunday and Princeton," *Pres*, 15 Apr. 1915, 9–10.

67. May, *End of American Innocence*, 126–27; T. J. Jackson Lears, *No Place for Grace: Antimodernism and the Transformation of American Culture, 1880–1920* (New York: Pantheon, 1981), 3–58, 261–97; Stanley Coben, *Rebellion against Victorianism: The Impetus for Cultural Change in 1920s America* (New York: Oxford University Press, 1991), 136–56; idem, "The Assault on Victorianism in the Twentieth Century," in *Victorian America*, ed. Daniel Walker Howe (Philadelphia: University of Pennsylvania Press, 1976), 160–81.

68. Maxwell Struthers Burt, Letter to the Editor, *PAW*, 24 Feb. 1915, 481; A. G. Young to Lucius H. Miller, 20 Mar. 1915, Miller Papers.

69. Edmund Wilson Jr., "The Fettered College," *NLM* 70 (1915): 518.

70. Editorial, *PAW*, 24 Feb. 1915, 475. See also "Theological Seminary Invites Evangelist Sunday," *PP*, 27 Feb. 1915, 1–2; "Concerning Mr. Sunday," *DP*, 8 Mar. 1915, 2.

71. John G. Hibben, Letter to the Editor, *Pres*, 22 Apr. 1915, 11. The letter was reprinted for the alumni in the *PAW*, 21 Apr. 1915, 674–75.

72. "Dr. Patton at Princeton," *Pres*, 6 May 1915, 4. See also "Raymond Robins at Princeton," *Pres*, 16 Dec. 1915, 5.

73. Weir Stewart, "The Unification of Princeton's Religious Work," *PAW*, 1 Dec. 1915, 227.

74. "Good News from Princeton University," *Pres*, 11 Nov. 1915, 4–5; "Princeton University and Christian Progress," *Pres*, 23 Dec. 1915, 4.

75. *PAW*, 11 Oct. 1916, 38; Weir, "Unification of Princeton's Religious Work," 226.

76. Lucius H. Miller to Woodrow Wilson, 30 Nov. 1916, Miller Papers.

77. Burgess, Unpublished Autobiography, 330, Box 1, Burgess Papers.

78. Editorial, *Presbyterian of the South*, 8 Dec. 1915, 1; *Catalogue, 1914–15*, 472; *Catalogue, 1915–16*, 508.

79. Letter to the Curriculum Committee of the Board of Trustees, Princeton Univer-

sity, 19 Jan. 1917; Howard McClenahan to Lucius H. Miller, 2 Feb. 1917; Frederick N. Willson to Howard C. Warren, 27 Jan. 1917, Miller Papers.

80. Lucius H. Miller to James Imbrie, 26 Dec. 1926, Miller Papers.

81. TM, 12 Apr. 1917, 15:189.

82. Princeton University, *Princeton in the World War* (Princeton: Princeton University Press, 1932), xiii; TM, 25 Oct. 1917, 16:7.

83. Editorial, "No Longer 'Too Proud to Fight,'" *DP*, 3 Apr. 1917, 2.

84. John G. Hibben, "The Baccalaureate Address," *PAW*, 20 June 1917, 868; idem, "The Baccalaureate Address," *PAW*, 18 June 1919, 751. For Hibben's propreparationism and prowar positions, see, for example, his "Preparedness Against War," *PAW*, 15 Dec. 1915, 282–84; idem, *The Higher Patriotism* (New York: Scribner, 1915). For the faculty's support for preparation and the war, see [Princeton University], *The World Peril: America's Interest in the War, by members of the faculty of Princeton University* (Princeton: Princeton University Press, 1917). Ray H. Abrams portrays the Protestant church's position toward the war as one of excessive militarism and cites Hibben's propreparationism and his work on behalf of the American Rights League as evidence of such extremism. *Preachers Present Arms* (New York: Round Table Press, 1933; repr., Scottdale, PA: Herald Press, 1969), 26, 34, 229, 256. Several more recent studies have revised Abrams's work by recovering a variety of more mediating and critical positions taken toward the war by both Protestants and Catholics. Hibben is not mentioned in these studies. See Hutchison, *Modernist Impulse*, 226–56; Marsden, *Fundamentalism and American Culture*, 141–53; and especially John F. Piper Jr., *The American Churches in World War I* (Athens: Ohio University Press, 1985).

85. "Dr. Jordan Hissed by Princeton Men," *NYT*, 27 Mar. 1917, 11; Evans Clark, Letter to the Editor, *DP*, 2 Apr. 1917, 2; Henry Jones Ford, "Free Speech," *DP*, 5 Apr. 1917, 3. See also Three Members of the Princeton Battalion, Letter to the Editor, *DP*, 28 Mar. 1917, 2; William L. Dempsey, Letter to the Editor, *DP*, 30 Mar. 1917, 2; William Marshall Brown, Letter to the Editor, *DP*, 31 Mar. 1917, 2.

86. TM, 15 June 1918, 16:262.

87. John G. Hibben, "Twenty Years of Progress," *PAW*, 15 Jan. 1932, 329.

88. Ibid.; "President Hibben's Annual Report," *PAW*, 16 Jan. 1918, 317–19; *Princeton in the World War*, xi–xxxvii, 603; *Catalogue, 1916–17*, 513–14; *Catalogue, 1917–18*, 509–10; *Catalogue, 1918–29*, 109–17; FM, 25 Apr. 1918, 12:177; 18 June 1918, 12:200.

89. "John R. Mott Makes Appeal for Workers," *DP*, 5 Mar. 1917, 1; *Princeton in the World War*, xxvii–xxviii.

90. Editorial, "A New Regime," *DP*, 1 May 1918, 2.

91. "President Hibben's Alumni Day Address," *PAW*, 26 Feb. 1919, 399.

92. TM, 23 Oct. 1919, emphasis added.

93. TM, 12 Apr. 1917, 15:312–13; *Report . . . 1922*, 14–15. In the fall of 1922, for example, every state in the union had at least one undergraduate at Princeton, and students from New York, New Jersey, and Pennsylvania constituted only 63 percent of the undergraduate body. *Catalogue, 1922–23*, 225–31, 429–31.

94. *PAW*, 25 Jan. 1922, 331; United States Bureau of the Census, *Historical Statistics of the United States, Colonial Times to 1957* (Washington D.C.: Government Printing Office, 1960), 210–11.

95. "President Hibben's Address," *PAW*, 8 Nov. 1922, 125; *Report . . . 1922*, 2–3. There is some evidence that Princeton may have had a quota limiting the number of Jewish students admitted each year. In Hibben's papers, there is a letter from Robert M. Hutchins to Steven Buenning, 17 Dec. 1970, in which Hutchins writes: "I had lunch

with Mr. and Mrs. Hibben sometime between 1930 and 1932. I asked Mr. Hibben how many negroes there were in Princeton. He said there weren't any. I asked why. He said, 'I don't know. They just don't seem to want to come.' I asked how many Jews there were in Princeton. Mr. Hibben said, 'About two hundred.' I said, 'How many were there last year?' He said, 'About two hundred.' I asked how many were there the year before that. He said, 'About two hundred.' I said that was very odd and asked how it happened. He said he didn't know; it just happened. Mrs. Hibben was outraged and said, 'Jack Hibben, I don't see how you can sit there and lie to this young man. You know very well that you and Dean Eisenhart get together every year and fix the quota.'" For a fuller discussion on the admissions policy at Princeton and religious and racial discrimination, see Marcia Graham Synnott, *The Half-Opened Door: Discrimination and Admissions at Harvard, Yale, and Princeton, 1900–1970* (Westport, Conn.: Greenwood Press, 1979), 188–92.

96. "The New Method of Study for Upper Classmen," *PAW*, 18 Apr. 1923, 580–81.

97. FM, 17 Mar. 1919, 12:208–209; Andrew F. West, "The Classics and Educational Reconstruction," *PAW*, 26 Feb. 1919, 401.

98. *Report . . . 1928*, 29.

99. Hibben, "Twenty Years," 318–20; Willard Thorp, Minor Myers Jr., and Jeremiah Stanton Finch, *The Princeton Graduate School* (Princeton: Princeton University Press, 1978), 152–86; Roger L. Geiger, *To Advance Knowledge: The Growth of American Research Universities, 1900–1940* (New York: Oxford University Press, 1986), 140–73.

100. Robert T. Handy, *Undermined Establishment: Church-State Relations in America, 1880–1920* (Princeton: Princeton University Press, 1991), 126–29, 189–91; idem, *A Christian America: Protestant Hopes and Historical Realities*, rev. ed. (New York: Oxford University Press, 1984), 159–84; William R. Hutchison, "Protestantism as Establishment," in *Between the Times: The Travail of the Protestant Establishment in America, 1900–1960*, ed. William R. Hutchison (New York: Cambridge University Press, 1989), 3–18. The exact dating of the transition, as William R. Hutchison describes it, from "Protestant to pluralistic America," hinges upon what particular feature of American culture one focuses. John F. Wilson argues that the demise of Protestant hegemony as the public religion can be dated anywhere between 1908, when America was declared by the Catholic Church no longer to be a missions field, and 1958, when the Catholic John F. Kennedy began his campaign for the presidency. Besides Handy, Martin Marty places the disestablishment of this de facto public religion in the 1930s, but argues that it was not fully realized until the intellectual, religious, and social upheavals of the 1960s. By contrast, Mark A. Noll argues that American culture entered the present context of religious pluralism in the 1920s, while Sydney E. Ahlstrom and Winthrop Hudson place it in the 1960s. William R. Hutchison, "Preface: From Protestant to Pluralist America," in *Between the Times*, vii–xv; John F. Wilson, *Public Religion in American Culture* (Philadelphia: Temple University Press, 1979), 14; Martin E. Marty, *Modern American Religion, Volume 2: The Noise of Conflict, 1919–1941* (Chicago: University of Chicago Press, 1991), 9–11, 392–95; Mark A. Noll, *A History of Christianity in the United States and Canada* (Grand Rapids: Eerdmans, 1992), 335–89; Sydney E. Ahlstrom, *A Religious History of the American People* (New Haven: Yale University Press, 1972), 1079–96; Winthrop Hudson and John Corrigan, *Religion in America*, 5th ed. (New York: Macmillan, 1992), 405–34.

101. Handy cites the two landmark Supreme Court Cases that incorporated the religious clauses of the First Amendment into the Fourteenth and made them applicable to the states (and by extension to all areas of government) as evidence of these develop-

ments. *Cantwell v. Connecticut*, 310 U.S. 296 (1940); *Everson v. Board of Education*, 330 U.S. 1 (1940); *Undermined Establishment*, 191.

102. "The Religious Crisis at Princeton University," *Pres*, 25 July 1918, 6–7.

103. "Shoemaker Returns to Princeton," *DP*, 25 Sept. 1919, 1, 4.

104. See, for example, David E. Thomas, "Progress at State Universities," *RE* 18 (1923): 237–40; R. R. Fleet, "The Religious Possibilities of the College," *RE* 72 (1926): 392–96.

105. *Report . . . 1920*, 57–58. See also *Report . . . 1923*, 51–53.

106. FM, 25 Sept. 1923, 12:383; 23 Mar. 1924, 12:439; 16 Nov. 1925, 12:462.

107. Edward Steese, "All in One Decade," 1975, Part 2, Box 1, Edward Steese Papers, Manuscript Division, Rare Books and Special Collections, Princeton University. Published with permission of Princeton University Library.

108. Nelson Burr to Mrs. H. R. Burr, 26 Sept. 1924, Box 2, Nelson R. Burr Papers, Manuscript Division, Rare Books and Special Collections, Princeton University. Published with permission of Princeton University Library. Nelson R. Burr to Harris R. Burr, 5 Mar. 1924, Box 1, Burr Papers.

109. "Students Feeling Divided on Problem of Personal Deity," *DP*, 3 Mar. 1927, 1.

110. Editorial, *NLM* 77 (1922): 336.

111. May, *End of American Innocence*; Lears, *No Place for Grace*; Coben, *Rebellion against Victorianism*; idem, "Assault on Victorianism in the Twentieth Century."

112. Frederick J. Hoffman, *The Twenties: American Writing in the Postwar Decade* (New York: Viking Press, 1955), 2–119.

113. John G. Hibben to F. Scott Fitzgerald, 27 May 1920, Hibben Papers. On Fitzgerald's life at Princeton and the anti-Victorian sentiment expressed in *This Side of Paradise* (New York: Scribner, 1920), see Arthur Mizener, *The Far Side of Paradise: A Biography of F. Scott Fitzgerald*, 2d ed. (Boston: Houghton Mifflin, 1965), 30–104. In his diatribe against American higher education, *The Goose-Step* (1923), Upton Sinclair, who had lived in Princeton in the early 1920s, was also particularly brutal toward the university. Princeton, he wrote, was "the most perfect school of snobbery in America . . . meant for gentlemen's sons . . . no Negroes, few Jews or Catholics . . . . The society clubs run, not merely the campus, but the faculty, and the endowment is presided over by the pettiest bunch of plutocrats yet assembled in our empire of education." Upton Sinclair, *The Goose-Step: A Study of American Education* (Pasadena: Published by the Author, [1923]), 111–21, quote on 112.

114. See, for example, "Editor's Table," *NLM* 76 (1920): 37–38, 161; Edward H. Coffey "Sacrifice," *NLM* 76 (1920): 82–95; T. S. Matthews, "Our Scotty," *NLM* 76 (1921): 320–22; Louis E. Laflin Jr., "Whose Hootch?" *NLM* 77 (1921): 65–72; "Editor's Table," *NLM* 78 (1923): 214–15; Parker Lloyd-Smith, "Where God Walks on the Campus," *NLM* 79 (1923): 35–40; Day Edgar, *In Princeton Town* (New York: Scribner, 1929).

115. Edmund Wilson Jr., Letter to the Editor, *PAW*, 25 Feb. 1920, 460; F. Scott Fitzgerald, Letter to the Editor, *PAW*, 10 Mar. 1920, 514.

116. Robert T. Handy, "The American Religious Depression, 1925–1935," *Church History* 29 (1960): 3–16.

117. Walter M. Horton, *Theism and the Modern Mood* (New York: Harper, 1930), as quoted in ibid., 6.

118. "Trustees Ban Student-Owned Automobiles," *PAW*, 4 Mar. 1927, 639; "Prohibition Decisively Condemned by Two Majorities, Emphatic for Repeal," *DP*, 7 May 1926, 1.

119. Rita S. Halle, *Which College?* (New York: Macmillan, 1928), 3, as quoted in David O. Levine, *The American College and the Culture of Aspiration, 1915–1940* (Ithaca: Cornell University Press, 1986), 113. On the growth of indifference and irreligion

at American colleges in the 1920s, see Paula S. Fass, *The Damned and the Beautiful: American Youth in the 1920s* (New York: Oxford University Press, 1977), 13–52; Helen Lefkowitz Horowitz, *Campus Life: Undergraduate Cultures from the End of the Eighteenth Century to the Present* (Chicago: Knopf, 1987), 118–41, 151–61; Marsden, *Soul of the University*, 332–56.

120. Howard A. Walter, *Soul Surgery* (New York: Association Press, 1919), 49–147. On Buchman's background and teaching, see the accounts written by Buchman's disciple Garth Lean, *Frank Buchman: A Life* (Longdon: Constable, 1985), 1–123. See also Walter H. Clark, *The Oxford Group: Its History and Significance* (New York: Bookman Associates, 1951), 25–66.

121. Samuel M. Shoemaker, Report of the General Secretary to the Board of Directors, 9–10, 25 Feb. 1920, Box 3, Student Christian Association Records.

122. Steese's account of Buchman and the Prospect meeting is found in his unpublished autobiography, "All in One Decade," Part 4, 2–6, Box 1, Steese Papers, and the Buchmanite perspective in Lean, *Buchman*, 102–105.

123. "Estimate Fire Damage Officially at $400,000," *DP*, 17 May 1920, 1, 6.

124. Edward D. Duffield, "Why Trustees?" *PAW*, 2 Apr. 1924, 530–31, emphasis added.

125. John G. Hibben, "The Proposed New Chapel," *PAW*, 23 Nov. 1921, 179.

126. Ralph Adams Cram, "Some Architectural and Spiritual Aspects of the Chapel," *PAW*, 25 May 1928, 987, as quoted in Sara Bush, "The Princeton Chapels," (unpublished paper, April 1994, Princeton University), 35; Ralph Adams Cram and Frank Ferguson, "The Architects' Description of the Chapel Designs," *PAW*, 23 Nov. 1921, 179, as quoted in ibid., 33–34. I am indebted to Bush's description of the architectural significance expressed in the Gothic chapel.

127. Henry C. Briggs, '96, Sem. '99, Letter to the Editor, *PAW*, 8 Mar. 1922, 467. See also Charles L. Candee '95, Letter to the Editor, *PAW*, 18 Jan. 1922, 311–12; R. H. Hepburn '71, Letter to the Editor, *PAW*, 13 Feb. 1922, 394–95; J. N. Dodd '93, Letter to the Editor, *PAW*, 8 Mar. 1922, 466–67.

128. Henry Van Dyke Jr. to John G. Hibben, 6 Nov. 1922, Box 121, Van Dyke Papers.

129. "1914," Letter to the Editor, *PAW*, 29 Mar. 1922, 527.

130. Nelson R. Burr to Harris R. Burr, 5 Mar. 1924, Box 2, Burr Papers.

131. Editorial, "Religion and the Ram-Rod," *DP*, 5 Mar. 1923, 2. See also Editorial, "Compulsory Chapel, Pro and Con," *DP*, 8 Nov. 1922, 2; Warren D. Brewster '23, Letter to the Editor, *DP*, 8 Nov. 1922, 2, 6; Alfred S. Dashiell, "The Undergraduate Week," *PAW*, 14 Mar. 1923, 470–71.

132. TM, 14 Apr. 1923.

133. "Philadelphian Cabinet Takes Stand on Chapel," *DP*, 1 Apr. 1925, 3–4; Lewis Mack, "The Undergraduate Week," *PAW*, 8 Apr. 1925, 629.

134. Willard E. Uphaus and M. Teague Hipps, *Undergraduate Courses in Religion at Denominational and Independent Colleges of America* (Ithaca: National Council on Religion in Higher Education, [1924]), 44, 56, 75.

135. Editorial, "Bible Course," *DP*, 28 Apr. 1920, 2.

136. *Report . . . 1922*, 48.

137. FM, 5 Nov. 1923; TM, 25 Oct. 1923; 10 Jan. 1924; *Report . . . 1923*, 54.

138. Harris E. Kirk, *The Power of Religion* (New York: Doran, 1916), see esp. 177–205. On Kirk's view of history and his lectures at Princeton, see Donald G. Miller, *The Scent of Eternity: A Life of Harris Elliott Kirk of Baltimore* (Macon: Mercer University Press, 1989), 302–307; 471–72. According to Donald G. Miller, Kirk often lectured

extemporaneously or used material from sermons or other addresses. When Kirk offered a similar course at Goucher College after 1928, he used *The Power of Religion* as an unofficial textbook. Donald G. Miller, letter to author, 17 Nov. 1994. Preceptors for Kirk's course were Professors Paul Van Dyke and Robert Scoon in 1925–1926, and S. Harrison Thomson, a graduate student at the university in 1926–1929. TM, 10 Jan. 1924; 28 Oct. 1926; 27 Oct. 1927; *Report . . . 1928*, Table III.

139. See, for example, Hugh T. Kerr, "Religious Education in America," *Presbyterian Advance*, 12 Feb. 1925, 8–9; Alford Kelley, "Denominational Colleges vs. State Universities," *Pres*, 11 June 1925, 8–9; "The Educational Question," *Pres*, 23 July 1925, 4–5; Harold McAfee Robinson, "Taking It For Granted," *Pres*, 23 July 1925, 6–7; E. Van Dusen, "Christian Education," *Pres*, 16 June 1927, 9–10.

140. Cherry, *Hurrying toward Zion*, 168; Marsden, *Fundamentalism and American Culture*, 186.

141. John G. Hibben, "Life's Higher Level," *PAW*, 17 June 1925, 902–903; Edwin G. Conklin, "Biology and Religion: Must We Continue the Age-Old Conflict?" *PAW*, 18 Mar. 1925, 548–49, 556; "Mr. Bryan is Misled by False Convictions," *DP*, 18 Jan. 1923, 1, 6; "Bryan Unfitted to Speak on Evolution Says Scott," *DP*, 16 Jan. 1923, 1, 6.

142. "Christianity and Rationalism," *Pres*, 9 Apr. 1925, 4–5; "Evolution and Religion," *Pres*, 25 June 1925, 5; D. J. Satterfield, "Christian Evolution?" *Pres*, 8 Dec. 1921, 10, 31; W. H. Griffith Thomas, Letter to the Editor, *Pres*, 22 Dec. 1921, 5; "The Evils of Evolution," *Pres*, 30 Mar. 1922, 3, 7; George McCready Price, "Outlaw Theories," *Pres*, 30 Mar. 1922, 8–11, 31. On George McCready Price, see Ronald L. Numbers, *The Creationists: The Evolution of Scientific Creationism* (Berkeley: University of California Press, 1992), 72–101. For Princeton Seminary's views on evolution, see Hart, *Defending the Faith*, 84–107.

143. John G. Hibben, "The Baccalaureate Address," *PAW*, 20 June 1923, 772–75. Professor Paul Van Dyke and trustees George B. Stewart and Charles Woods also signed the first draft of the Auburn Affirmation. *AN AFFIRMATION designed to safeguard the unity and liberty of the Presbyterian Church in the United States of America with all signatures and the Note Supplementary* (Auburn, N.Y.: Jacobs, 1924).

144. John G. Hibben to Charles W. Eliot, 9 Sept. 1924, Hibben Papers; Editorial, "In Closing," *DP*, 14 Apr. 1925, 2. See also Editorial, "An Abode of Bigotry," *DP*, 8 Apr. 1925, 2; Lewis Mack, "Religious Conference and Controversy," *PAW*, 15 Apr. 1925, 544.

145. *D.A.B.*, 16:111; Robert W. Rogers, *A History of Babylonia and Assyria*, 2 vols. (New York: Eaton and Mains, 1901); Ancient Oriental Literature examination, 26 May 1924; Ancient Oriental Literature examination, 2 June 1925, Examination File; *Catalogue, 1923–24*, 96; *Catalogue, 1927–28*, 60; Philip K. Hitti, Faculty File.

146. *Catalogue, 1924–25*, 5, 57, 98, 249–50; Norman Kemp Smith, an introduction to *Studies in the Philosophy of Religion*, by A. A. Bowman, 2 vols. (London: Macmillan, 1938), xix–xliv; Ethics of Christianity examination, 31 May 1922; Ethics of Christianity examination, 29 May 1924; Ethics of Christianity examination, 10 Feb. 1925, Examination File; A. A. Bowman, *The Absurdity of Christianity*, 2d ed. (London: SVM, 1932), 8, 13, 25–27.

147. J. David Hoeveler Jr., *The New Humanism: A Critique of Modern America, 1900–1940* (Charlottesville: University of Virginia Press, 1977), 3–5. In 1929, Hibben and Jacobus asked More to teach an undergraduate elective in the Origins of Christianity. On the invitation, More wrote A. A. Bowman, "I told [Hibben] that my interest lay strongly in the direction of Anglo-Catholicism, and that, however I might try to avoid any note of propaganda, still something of my views would come out; but he merely

said, Go ahead." Paul Elmer More to A. A. Bowman, 10 June 1929, as quoted in Arthur H. Dakin, *Paul Elmer More* (Princeton: Princeton University Press, 1960), 274.

148. Paul Elmer More, *The Christ of the New Testament* (Princeton: Princeton University Press, 1924), quote on 66; idem, *Christ the Word* (Princeton: Princeton University Press, 1927). On More's theology, see Hoeveler, *New Humanism,* 155–56, 160–64, 169–74; Francis X. Duggan, *Paul Elmer More* (New York: Twayne, 1966), 89–117. On More's thought and work at Princeton, see Whitney J. Oates, "Paul Elmer More: A Quest of the Spirit," in *The Lives of Eighteen from Princeton,* ed. Willard Thorp (Princeton: Princeton University Press, 1946), 302–17; Dakin, *More,* 177–387, esp. 321–22.

149. *Catalogue, 1924–25,* 98; Thomas S. Matthews '22, "Those Inflated 'Twenties,'" *PAW,* 13 Mar. 1931, 561.

150. TM, 10 Jan. 1924, emphasis added; 14 Jan. 1926, emphasis added.

151. "President Hibben's Alumni Day Address," *PAW,* 23 Feb. 1923, 430. On the epistemological neutrality of the academic study of religion, see Cherry, *Hurrying toward Zion,* 112–19; Marsden, *Soul of the University,* 413–14; Warren A. Nord, *Religion and American Education: Rethinking a National Dilemma* (Chapel Hill: University of North Carolina Press, 1995), 236–81, 304–19; D. G. Hart, "American Learning and the Problem of Religious Studies," in *The Secularization of the Academy,* ed. George M. Marsden and Bradley J. Longfield (New York: Oxford University Press, 195–233.

152. Editorial, "If This Be Logic," *DP,* 23 Oct. 1926, 2.

153. Ernest W. Mandeville, "The Collegiate Revivalists," *Churchman,* 9 Oct. 1926, 10–12; idem, "Buchman Method of Evangelization," *Churchman,* 16 Oct. 1926, 13–15; idem, "The Buchman Movement: Pro and Con," *Churchman,* 23 Oct. 1926, 11–13; Editorial, "Buchmanism—A Menace," *Churchman,* 30 Oct. 1926, 8–9; "Personal Work," *Time,* 18 Oct. 1926, 26–27.

154. "Undergraduate Opinion Damns Buchmanism as Result of Open Forum Investigations," *DP,* 22 Oct. 1922, 1. For student opinion regarding Buchman and the Philadelphian Society, see, for example, "Philadelphian Society Subject of Open Forum," *DP,* 20 Oct. 1926, 1, 6; Editorial, "The Philadelphian Society," *DP,* 20 Oct. 1926, 2; Editorial, "This Evening," *DP,* 21 Oct. 1926, 2; Editorial, "Between Brothers," *DP,* 22 Oct. 1926, 2; Editorial, "Aftermath," *DP,* 23 Oct. 1926, 2.

155. John G. Hibben to James R. Angell, 5 Oct. 1928, Box 14, Student Christian Association Records. The committee comprised trustees Edward D. Duffield, Melanchthon W. Jacobus, and Henry J. Cochran, professors Christian Gauss, William Gillespie, and John Colt, the secretary of the university H. Alexander Smith, chair of the Board of Directors of the Philadelphian Society John McDowell, and three members of the senior council. Purdy's invitation of Buchman to campus in May 1926 and the activities of the committee are described in their Report of the Special Committee, 31 Dec. 1926, 3–10, in TM, 13 Jan. 1927. This report was formally presented to the trustees at that date but released beforehand.

156. Meeting of the Special Committee, 9 Dec. 1926, 13, Box 14, Student Christian Association Records.

157. Report of the Special Committee, 31 Dec. 1926, 9, 10–12, emphasis added.

158. Ray Purdy to John G. Hibben, as cited in Lean, *Buchman,* 127–28.

159. Ray Purdy, Letter to the Editor, *DP,* 28 Jan. 1927, 2–3; Editorial, "Confessional," *DP,* 29 Jan. 1927, 2.

160. "Philadelphian Staff Will Quit March 1st," *DP,* 19 Feb. 1927, 1, 4; "Howard Resigns with Most of the Cabinet," *DP,* 24 Feb. 1927, 1, 3–4; Lean, *Buchman,* 128.

161. Editorial, "Election," *DP,* 4 Mar. 1927, 2. For a perspective on the controversy

sympathetic to Buchman, see Lean, *Buchman*, 125–28. For a complete examination of the controversy, see Dan Sack, "Disastrous Disturbances: Buchmanism and Student Religious Life at Princeton, 1919–1930." (Ph.D. diss., Princeton University, 1995).

162. Hart, *Defending the Faith*, 108–109, 128–32, 139–40, 147, 146–59; Richard W. Reifsnyder, "Managing the Mission: Church Restructuring in the Twentieth Century," in *The Organizational Revolution: Presbyterians and American Denominationalism*, ed. Milton J. Coalter, John M. Mulder, and Louis B. Weeks (Louisville: Westminster/John Knox, 1992), 55–66; James H. Moorhead, "Presbyterians and the Mystique of Organizational Efficiency, 1870–1936," in *Reimagining Denominationalism*, ed. Robert Bruce Mullin and Russell E. Richey (New York: Oxford University Press, 1994), 264–87.

163. TM, 14 Apr. 1927.

164. Merrimon Cuninggim, *The College Seeks Religion* (New Haven: Yale University Press, 1947), 156–57.

165. Melanchthon W. Jacobus to H. Alexander Smith, 31 Aug. 1927, Box 36, H. Alexander Smith Papers, Seeley G. Mudd Manuscript Library, Princeton University. Published with permission of Princeton University Library.

166. Robert R. Wicks, Faculty File.

167. TM, 12 Apr. 1928.

168. H. Alexander Smith to Melanchthon W. Jacobus, 13 Dec. 1928, Box 36, Smith Papers; Editorial, "Dean of Religion," *DP*, 23 Mar. 1928, 2.

169. Harry M. Gage, Charles A. Richmond, Marion L. Burton, "The Place of Religion in Higher Education in America," *Association of American Colleges Bulletin* 10 (1924): 83–106; Cuninggim, *College Seeks Religion*, 94; Marsden, *Soul of the University*, 338; Hart, "American Learning and the Problem of Religious Studies," 205–206.

170. Galen M. Fisher, ed., *Religion in the Colleges* (New York: Association, 1928), quotes on 5, 65, 71; "Required Attendance Upon Sunday Services Upheld by Large Poll," *DP*, 6 May 1926, 1. Another 1926 survey of 392 institutions revealed that 294 schools still had some form of compulsory religious exercises. A. P. Kephart, "The Problem of College Chapel Exercises," *ER* 71 (1926): 149.

171. Cuninggim, *College Seeks Religion*, 169.

172. "Mediaeval Ceremony Adopted Imparting Appropriate Spirit to Full Academic Procession," *DP*, 30 May 1928, 1, 4; John G. Hibben, "An Heritage of Holy Beauty," *PAW*, 8 June 1928, 1082.

173. John G. Hibben to Robert R. Wicks, 23 June 1928, Box 1, Dean of the Chapel Records, Seeley G. Mudd Manuscript Library, Princeton University. Published with permission of Princeton University Library.

174. "Philadelphian Society to Consider Changes," *PAW*, 6 May 1927, 889; Editorial, "Annual Meetings," *DP*, 6 Apr. 1927, 2.

175. Quoted in *Report . . . 1928*, 52.

176. *Bric-a-Brac (Princeton: Junior Class) 1931*, 296.

177. Minutes, Philadelphian Society Cabinet Meeting, 24 Jan. 1928; 14 Feb. 1928; as quoted in Matthew M. Coburn, "The Philadelphian Society: An investigation into the demise of an evangelical student Christian organization at Princeton University in the 1920s," (senior thesis, Princeton University, 1991), 90; Carolina Reitz, "Artwork Returns to Jadwin After Years of Travel," *DP*, 4 Feb. 1987, 1.

178. Robert R. Wicks, "Princeton and Religion," *PAW*, 1 Mar. 1929, 628.

179. *PAW*, 16 May 1930, 823.

180. "Religion in a Tactical Retreat," *Pres*, 1 May 1930, 8–9.

181. H. Alexander Smith to Frank L. Janeway, 13 Apr. 1929, Box 45, Smith Papers.

182. Jacobus to Smith, 31 Aug. 1927; Melanchthon W. Jacobus to H. Alexander Smith, 6 Nov. 1927, Box 45, Smith Papers.

183. Joseph C. Green to Robert M. Green 5 Apr. 1928, Box 29, Joseph C. Green Papers, Seeley G. Mudd Manuscript Library, Princeton University. Published with permission of Princeton University Library.

184. *Report . . . 1928*, 14.

185. Report of the Undergraduate Council to the Undergraduate Life Committee of the Board of Trustees of Princeton University concerning the religious situation at the University, in TM, 12 Apr. 1928; Henry Norris Russell to Melanchthon W. Jacobus, 27 Sept. 1927, Box 13, Henry Norris Russell Papers, Manuscript Division, Rare Books and Special Collections, Princeton University. Published with permission of Princeton University Library; Robert Garrett to Robert R. Wicks, 28 Nov. 1928, Box 1, Dean of the Chapel Records.

186. TM, 27 Oct. 1927; 12 Jan. 1928; 12 Apr. 1928.

187. "Dean Wicks Proposes New Chapel Plan," *PAW*, 7 June 1929, 1054; Robert R. Wicks, "Facing the Chapel Problem at Princeton," *PAW*, 14 June 1929, 1087–88, 1106; TM, 17 June 1929.

188. Robert R. Wicks, "Chapel Worship in a College," *PAW*, 25 May 1928, 984–86, quotes on 984.

Epilogue

1. George F. Thomas, "Religious Perspectives in College Teaching: Problems and Principles," in *Religious Perspectives in College Teaching*, ed. Hoxie N. Fairchild (New York: Ronald, 1952), 6.

2. Sir Walter Moberly, *The Crisis in the University* (London: S.C.M., 1948), 27. For a similar evaluation, see Howard Lowry, *The Mind's Adventure* (Philadelphia: Westminster, 1950), 62–98; Henry P. Van Dusen, *God in Education: A Tract for the Times* (New York: Scribner, 1951).

3. *College Reading and Religion: A Survey of College Reading Materials* (New Haven: Yale University Press, 1948).

4. Mark Silk, *Spiritual Politics: Religion and America since World War II* (New York: Touchstone Book, 1988), 23–107.

5. Merrimon Cuninggim, *The College Seeks Religion* (New Haven: Yale University Press, 1947), 95, 263, emphasis added, 188–92.

6. *Princeton University Catalogue: Undergraduate Instruction, 1955–56*, 414, 416.

7. *Bric-a-Brac (Princeton: Junior Class) 1955*, 138–40; Alexander Leitch, *A Princeton Companion* (Princeton: Princeton University Press, 1978), 87; H. Keith Bebee, "Faith and Practice at Princeton," *PAW*, 21 Mar. 1952, 11; Douglas Sloan, *Faith and Knowledge: Mainline Protestantism and American Higher Education* (Louisville: Westminster John Knox, 1994), 72–84.

8. Claude Welch, *Graduate Education in Religion: A Critical Appraisal* (Missoula: University of Montana Press, 1971), 175, 230.

9. Princeton University, Report of the Special Committee of the Faculty on Religious Education, 11 Apr. 1935, Box 1, George F. Thomas Papers, Manuscript Division, Rare Books and Special Collections, Princeton University. Published with permission of Princeton Uni-

versity Library. Melanchthon W. Jacobus links the events of the 1920s and the eventual hiring of Thomas in 1940. In their memorial to Jacobus after his death in 1937, the trustees recalled "his intense interest in religion and his unswerving insistence on the importance of religious instruction in the University. He had a distinct voice in the selection of the present Dean of the Chapel." Trustee Memorial, Melanchthon W. Jacobus, Alumni File.

10. Leitch, *Princeton Companion*, 403–404; Committee on Integration, 20 Aug. 1943, Box 1, Thomas Papers.

11. George F. Thomas to Roy Chamberlain, 5 Mar. 1951, Box 1, Thomas Papers. See also William A. Spurrier, "Religion," in *College Teaching and Christian Values*, ed. Paul M. Limbert (New York: Association, 1951), 144–64; Virginia Corwin, "The Teaching of Religion," in *Liberal Learning and Religion*, ed. Amos N. Wilder (New York: Harper and Brothers, 1951), 169–96; Seymour A. Smith, *Religious Cooperation in State Universities: An Historical Sketch* ([Ann Arbor]: University of Michigan Press, 1957), 74–105. On Protestantism role in the teaching of religion in the 1950s, see Dorothy C. Bass, "Ministry on the Margins: Protestants and Education," in *Between the Times: The Travail of the Protestant Establishment in America, 1900–1960*, ed. William R. Hutchison (Cambridge: Cambridge University Press, 1989), 58–60; Sloan, *Faith and Knowledge*, 86–104; George M. Marsden, *The Soul of the American University: From Protestant Establishment to Established Nonbelief* (New York: Oxford University Press, 1994), 394–96.

12. Thomas, "Religious Perspectives in College Teaching," 38.

13. Sloan, *Faith and Knowledge*, 84–86; J. Edward Dirks, "About the Journal," *Christian Scholar* 36 (1953): 4.

14. Thomas, "Religious Perspectives in College Teaching;" E. Harris Harbison, "History;" *Religious Perspectives in College Teaching*, 3–38; 67–97. In a similar study funded by the Hazen Foundation, Christian Gauss, Dean Emeritus of Princeton University, edited the work and provided the introductory essay, "Religion and Higher Education in America," *The Teaching of Religion in American Higher Education*, ed. Christian Gauss (New York: Press, 1951), 1–19. See also George F. Thomas, "Religion and the Universities," *PAW*, 28 Jan. 1955, 10–12; E. Harris Harbison, *The Christian Scholar in the Age of the Reformation* (New York: Scribner, 1956). For similar works, see Limbert, ed., *College Teaching and Christian Values*; Wilder, ed., *Liberal Learning and Religion*.

15. T. Guthrie Speers, "Princeton's Concern for Religion," *PAW*, 17 Jan. 1958, 8–9, 12, quote on 8.

16. Thomas, "Religious Perspectives in College Teaching," 17.

17. Reinhold Niebuhr, *The Contribution of Religion to Cultural Unity* (New Haven: Hazen Foundation, 1935), quoted in Marsden, *Soul of the University*, 398.

18. George F. Thomas, *Religion in an Age of Secularism* (Princeton: Princeton University Press, 1940), 16; idem, "Religious Perspectives in College Teaching," 17.

19. Hugh Halton, Letter to the Editor (paid advertisement), *DP*, 22 Mar. 1956, 4; "Text of the Statement Made by Father Halton," *DP*, 30 Sept. 1957, 1; James F. Ridgeway, "Carries his Case Across Country on 21-Stop Tour," *DP*, 25 Apr. 1957, 1.

20. John M. Cuddihy, *No Offense: Civil Religion and Protestant Taste* (New York: Seabury, 1978), 49–64; Silk, *Spiritual Politics*, 70–86; William F. Buckley Jr., *God and Man at Yale: The Superstitions of 'Academic Freedom'* (Chicago: Henry Regnery, 1951).

21. "Father Halton vs. Professor Stace," Editorial, *DP*, 9 May 1955, 2; Hugh Halton, Letter to the Editor, *DP*, 10 May 1955, 3; Halton, Letter to the Editor, *DP*, 10 May 1955, 3; James F. Ridgeway, "Priest Sets Up Aquinas Foundation as 'Open Forum,'" *DP*, 24 Sept. 1957, 4.

22. Philip Gleason, *Contending with Modernity: Catholic Higher Education in the*

Twentieth Century (New York: Oxford University Press, 1995), 105–66.

23. "Halton's Criticism Answered by SCA," *DP*, 5 Oct. 1955, 1; Hugh Halton, Letter to the Editor (paid advertisement), *DP*, 19 Oct. 1955, 8.

24. George F. Thomas, "The Meaning of Truth," *Christian Scholar* 36 (1953): 173–75. For a thorough discussion of the neo-orthodox theology and its epistemological commitments, see Sloan, *Faith and Knowledge*, vii–x, 1–71.

25. E. Harris Harbison, Letter to the Editor, *DP*, 11 Oct. 1955, 3.

26. Paul Blanshard, *American Freedom and Catholic Power* (Boston: Beacon, 1949). See also idem, *Communism, Democracy and Catholic Power* (Boston: Beacon, 1951). On Protestant anti-Catholicism in academia and American culture, see Patrick Allitt, *Catholic Intellectuals and Conservative Politics in America, 1950–1985* (Ithaca: Cornell University Press, 1993), 16–82; Gleason, *Contending with Modernity*, 261–82; Marsden, *Soul of the University*, 400–403; Donald F. Crosby, *God, Church, and Flag: Senator Joseph R. McCarthy and the Catholic Church 1950–1957* (Chapel Hill: University of North Carolina Press, 1978), 118–46; Barbara Welter, "From Maria Monk to Paul Blanshard: A Century of Protestant Anti-Catholicism," in *Uncivil Religion: Interreligious Hostility in America*, ed. Robert N. Bellah and Frederick E. Greenspahn (New York: Crossroad, 1987), 43–71.

27. E. Harris Harbison, "Christian Belief and Intellectual Freedom," *Christian Scholar* 36 (1953): 186.

28. Harbison, Letter to the Editor, 3.

29. Halton, Letter to the Editor, *DP*, 19 Oct. 1955, 8. On the place of neo-orthodox Protestantism within American higher education in the 1950s, see Marsden, *Soul of the University*, 397–400; Sloan, *Faith and Knowledge*, 72–110.

30. Willard Thorp, Letter to the Editor, *DP*, 17 May 1955, 3; Hugh Halton, Letter to the Editor (paid advertisement), *DP*, 20 May 1955, 8.

31. James F. Ridgeway, "Carries his Case Across Country on 21-stop Tour," *DP*, 25 Apr. 1957,1, 3; "Chaplain's Privileges," *PAW*, 4 Oct. 1957, 12; "Man of the Week," Editorial, *DP*, 14 May 1956, 2.

32. Frederick K. Poole, "Father Halton's Legitimate Complaint," Editorial, *DP*, 5 Oct. 1955, 2.

33. *Princeton University: The Graduate School, 1955–56*, 152–53.

34. Marianne Sanua, "Stages in the Development of Jewish Life at Princeton University," *American Jewish History* 76 (1987): 391–415.

35. George W. Elderkin published four pamphlets, which had the same title, *The Roman Catholic Controversy On The Campus of Princeton University* 4 parts (n.p., 1955–58). Each contained a ten- to sixteen-page essay by Elderkin and an exhaustive compendium of articles from the *Daily Princetonian* and other publications that chronicled the controversy.

36. Andrew H. Kesler, "Is God Alive?" *PAW*, 17 Nov. 1970, 9.

37. Robert Wuthnow, *The Restructuring of American Religion* (Princeton: Princeton University Press, 1988), 71–131; James Hudnut-Beumler, *Looking for God in the Suburbs: The Religion of the American Dream and Its Critics, 1945–1965* (New Brunswick: Rutgers University Press, 1994).

38. Donald A. Luidens, "Numbering the Presbyterian Branches: Membership Trends Since Colonial Times," in *The Mainstream Protestant "Decline"*, ed. Milton J. Coalter, John M. Mulder, and Louis B. Weeks (Louisville: Westminster John Knox, 1990), 43.

39. Peter L. Berger, *The Noise of Solemn Assemblies: Christian Commitment and the Religious Establishment in America* (Garden City, N.Y.: Doubleday, 1961). On main-

line Protestants' involvement in the civil rights movement, see James F. Findlay Jr., *Church People in the Struggle: The National Council of Churches and the Black Freedom Movement, 1950–1970* (New York: Oxford University Press, 1993). On the Protestant Establishment and the turmoil of the 1960s, see Sydney E. Ahlstrom, The Radical Turn in Theology and Ethics: Why It Occurred in the 1960s," in *Religion in American History: Interpretive Essays*, ed. John M. Mulder and John F. Wilson (Englewood Cliffs, N.J.: Prentice-Hall, 1978), 445–56; Dorothy C. Bass, "Revolutions, Quiet and Otherwise: Protestants and Higher Education during the 1960s," in *Caring for the Commonweal: Education for Religious and Public Life*, ed. Parker J. Palmer, Barbara G. Wheeler, and James W. Fowler (Macon, Ga.: Mercer University Press, 1990), 207–208, 223–26; Marsden, *Soul of the University*, 409–16; Leonard I. Sweet, "The 1960s: The Crises of Liberal Christianity and the Public Emergence of Evangelicalism," in *Evangelicalism and Modern America*, ed. George M. Marsden (Grand Rapids: Eerdmans, 1984), 29–43; Wuthnow, *Restructuring of American Religion*, 142–53.

40. Paul Tillich, *The Courage to Be* (New Haven: Yale University Press, 1952), 186–90.

41. Harvey Cox, *The Secular City: Secularization and Urbanization in Theological Perspective* (New York: MacMillan, 1965), 20–21, 217, 219, 234–35. On the collapse of neo-orthodoxy in the university, see Van A. Harvey, "On the intellectual Marginality of American Theology," in *Religion and Twentieth-Century American Intellectual Life*, ed. Michael J. Lacey (Cambridge: Woodrow Wilson International Center for Scholars and Cambridge University Press, 1989), 186–90; Sloan, *Faith and Knowledge*, 111–29. On secular theology and its rise, see Bass, "Revolutions, Quiet and Otherwise," 208–209; Langdon Gilkey, *Naming the Whirlwind: The Renewal of God-Language* (Indianapolis: Bobbs-Merrill, 1969), 107–46; Stanley J. Grenz and Roger E. Olson, *20th-Century Theology: God and the World in a Transitional Age* (Downers Grove, Ill.: InterVarsity Press, 1992), 145–69; Thomas W. Ogletree, *The Death of God Controversy* (Nashville: Abingdon, 1966); Marsden, *Soul of the University*, 417–19; Sloan, *Faith and Knowledge*, 129–49.

42. Bass, "Revolutions, Quiet and Otherwise," 211–12; Leitch, *Princeton Companion*, 529; Marsden, *Soul of the University*, 390–94; "A Survey of Princeton Freshmen," *PAW*, 23 Feb. 1971, 7, quoted in Marcia Graham Synnott, *The Half-Opened Door: Discrimination and Admissions at Harvard, Yale, and Princeton, 1900–1970* (Westport, Conn.: Greenwood Press, 1979), 224. For a fuller discussion of changes in Princeton's admissions policies in reference to gender, race, and religion, see ibid., 218–25.

43. Marsden, *Soul of the University*, 411–12; Leitch, *Princeton Companion*, 87. Mandatory attendance for juniors and seniors ended in 1935. Ibid.

44. John F. Wilson, "Introduction: The Background and Present Context of the Study of Religion in Colleges and Universities," *The Study of Religion in Colleges and Universities*, ed. Paul Ramsey and John F. Wilson (Princeton: Princeton University Press, 1970), 19.

45. D. G. Hart, "American Learning and the Problem of Religious Studies," in *The Secularization of the Academy*, ed. George M. Marsden and Bradley J. Longfield (New York: Oxford University Press, 1992), 195–96. On the persistence of the Protestant orientation in the academic study of religion in the early 1960s, see, for example, Paul Ramsey, ed., *Religion* (Englewood Cliffs, N.J.: Prentice-Hall, 1965).

46. Richard Schlatter, "Forward" to Clyde A. Holbrook, *Religion, A Humanistic Field* (Englewood Cliffs, N.J.: Prentice-Hall, 1963), ix.

47. John F. Wilson, "Mr. Holbrook and the Humanities," *Journal of Bible and Religion* 32 (1964): 253, 260.

48. Dwight Beck et al., "Report of the NABI Self-Study Committee," *Journal of Bible*

and Religion 32 (1964): 200. See also Welch, *Graduate Education in Religion*; Wilson and Ramsey, ed., *The Study of Religion in Colleges and Universities*. On the collapse of Protestant hegemony and the rise of the social scientific approach in the academic study of religion, see Hart, "American Learning and the Problem of Religious Studies," 195–233; Bass, "Revolutions, Quiet and Otherwise," 221–22; Marsden, *Soul of the University*, 415–16; Sloan, *Faith and Knowledge*, 179–211. On the scientific approach to the study of religion, see also R. Lawrence Moore, "Secularization: Religion and the Social Sciences," in *Between the Times*, 233–52; Murray G. Murphy, "On the Scientific Study of Religion in the United States, 1870–1980," in *Religion and Twentieth Century American Intellectual Life*, 136–71; Charles H. Long, "A Common Ancestor: Theology and Religious Studies," in *Religious Studies, Theological Studies and the University-Divinity School*, ed. Joseph Mitsuo Kitagawa (Atlanta: Scholars Press, 1992), 137–50.

49. Kesler, "Is God Alive?" 10.

50. Ibid., 8.

51. Student Christian Association Minutes, 26 Sept. 1966, Box 6, Dean of the Chapel Records; Annual Report to the President for the Year 1966–1967, University Chapel Records, Dean Ernest Gordon, Seeley G. Mudd Manuscript Library, Princeton University. Published with permission of Princeton University Library.

52. N. J. Demerath, III and Kenneth J. Lutterman, "The Student Parishioner: Radical Rhetoric and Traditional Reality," in *The Church, the University, and Social Policy: The Danforth Study of Campus Ministries*, ed. Kenneth Underwood, 2 vols. (Middletown, Conn.: Wesleyan University Press, 1969), 2:139. On the rise of evangelical campus ministries, see Ronald B. Flowers, *Religion in Strange Times: The 1960s and 1970s* (Macon, Ga.: Mercer University Press, 1984), 50–53; Keith Hunt and Gladys Hunt, *For Christ and the University: The Study of InterVarsity Christian Fellowship of the U.S.A., 1940–1990* (Downers Grove, Ill.: InterVarsity Press, 1991), 205–64.

53. Leitch, *Princeton Companion*, 87. For a full account of mainline campus ministries in the 1960s, see Sloan, *Faith and Knowledge*, 150–78. See also Bass, "Revolutions, Quiet and Otherwise," 211–21; Marsden, *Soul of the University*, 418–19; Ronald C. White Jr., "Presbyterian Campus Ministries: Competing Loyalties and Changing Visions," in *The Pluralistic Vision: Presbyterians and Mainstream Protestant Education and Leadership*, ed. Milton J. Coalter, John M. Mulder, and Louis B. Weeks (Louisville: Westminster John Knox, 1992), 126–42. On campus life in the 1960s, see Helen Lefkowitz Horowitz, *Campus Life: Undergraduate Cultures from the End of the Eighteenth Century to the Present* (New York: Knopf, 1987), 220–44.

54. On Protestant church-related higher education, see Christopher Jencks and David Riesman, *The Academic Revolution* (Garden City, N.Y.: Doubleday, 1968), 312–33; Robert Rue Parsonage, ed., *Church Related Higher Education: Perceptions and Perspectives* (Valley Forge, Pa.: Judson Press, 1978); Robert Wood Lynn, "'The Survival of Recognizably Protestant Colleges': Reflections on Old-Line Protestantism, 1950–1990," in *Secularization of the Academy*, 170–94; Bradley J. Longfield and George M. Marsden, "Presbyterian Colleges in Twentieth-Century America," in *Pluralistic Vision*, 99–124; Sloan, *Faith and Knowledge*, 203–206; Merrimon Cuninggim, *Uneasy Partners: The College and the Church* (Nashville: Abingdon, 1994). On Catholic higher education, see Jencks and Riesman, *The Academic Revolution*, 334–405; Gleason, *Contending with Modernity*; David J. O'Brien, *From the Heart of the American Church: Catholic Higher Education and American Culture* (Maryknoll, N.Y.: Orbis Books, 1994); James John Annarelli, *Academic Freedom and Catholic Higher Education* (Westport, Conn.: Greenwood Press, 1987), 27–56; Edward J. Powell, *Catholic Higher Education in America: A*

History (New York: Appleton-Century, 1972), 381–472.

55. Philip Gleason, "American Catholic Higher Education, 1940–1990: The Ideological Context," in *Secularization of the Academy*, 250–51; Richard T. Hughes and William B. Adrian, ed. *Models for Christian Higher Education: Strategies for Success in the Twenty-First Century* (Grand Rapids: Eerdmans, 1997); Albert Meyer, Memmo Simons Lectures, Bethel College, 1994 (unpublished lectures); Quentin Schultze, "The Two Faces of Fundamentalist Higher Education," in *Fundamentalism and Society: Reclaiming the Sciences, the Family, and Education*, ed. Martin E. Marty and R. Scott Appleby (Chicago: University of Chicago Press, 1993), 490–535; Thomas A. Askew, "The Shaping of Evangelical Higher Education Since World War II," in *Making Higher Education Christian: The History and Mission of Evangelical Colleges in America*, ed. Joel A. Carpenter and Kenneth W. Shipps (Grand Rapids: Eerdmans, 1987), 137–52.

56. *Princeton Weekly Bulletin*, 2 Oct. 1995, 5.

57. Clark Kerr, *The Use of the University* (Cambridge: Harvard University Press, 1963), 18–20.

58. Conrad Cherry, *Hurrying Toward Zion: Universities, Divinity Schools, and American Protestantism* (Bloomington: Indiana University Press, 1995).

59. For evangelical efforts, see, for example, Arthur Holmes, *The Idea of a Christian College*, rev. ed. (Grand Rapids: Eerdmans, 1987); Marsden, *Soul of the University*, 429–35; idem, *The Outrageous Idea of Christian Scholarship* (New York: Oxford University Press, 1997); Alvin Plantinga and Nicholas Wolterstorff, ed., *Faith and Rationality: Reason and Belief in God* (Notre Dame: University of Notre Dame Press, 1983); Roger Lundin, *The Culture of Interpretation: Christian Faith and the Postmodern World* (Grand Rapids: Eerdmans, 1993). For mainline Protestant efforts, see, for example, Mark R. Schwehn, *Exiles from Eden: Religion and the Academic Vocation in America* (New York: Oxford University Press, 1993); idem, "The Academic Vocation: 'Specialists without Spirit, Sensualists without Heart,'" *Cross Currents* 42 (1992): 185–99; William H. Willimon and Thomas N. Naylor, *The Abandoned Generation: Rethinking Higher Education* (Grand Rapids: Eerdmans, 1995); Sloan, *Faith and Knowledge*, 212–43; David Ray Griffin and Joseph C. Hough Jr., ed., *Theology and the University: Essays in Honor of John B. Cobb Jr.* (Albany: State University of New York Press, 1991); William C. Placher, *Narratives of a Vulnerable God: Christ, Theology, and Scripture* (Louisville: Westminster John Knox, 1995), 161–83. For Catholic efforts, see, for example, O'Brien, *From the Heart of the American Church*; Theodore M. Hesburgh, ed., *The Challenge and Promise of a Catholic University* (Notre Dame: University of Notre Dame Press, 1994). Warren A. Nord, who makes no religious self-identification, makes an argument for the inclusion of religiously informed perspectives, constructive theologians in religion departments, and moral education in state-supported higher education on educational and constitutional ground. *Religion and American Education: Rethinking a National Dilemma* (Chapel Hill: University of North Carolina Press, 1995).

Works Cited

Primary Sources

Unpublished Works

Alumni Files. Seeley G. Mudd Manuscript Library. Princeton University Library.

Blair and Lee Family. Papers. Manuscript Division. Rare Books and Special Collections. Princeton University Library.

Brown, Mary Dod. Papers. Seeley G. Mudd Manuscript Library. Princeton University Library.

Burgess, John Stewart. Papers. Manuscript Division. Rare Books and Special Collections. Princeton University Library.

Burr, Nelson R. Papers. Manuscript Division. Rare Books and Special Collections. Princeton University Library.

Cameron, Henry C. Family Papers. Manuscript Division. Rare Books and Special Collections. Princeton University Library.

Cooke Family Papers. MG 1031. New Jersey Historical Society.

Dean of the Chapel Records. Seeley G. Mudd Manuscript Library. Princeton University Library.

Dickinson, Jonathan. Papers. General Manuscripts (Miscellaneous). Rare Books and Special Collections. Princeton University Library.

Duffield, John T. Papers. Manuscript Division. Rare Books and Special Collections. Princeton University Library.

Eliot, Charles W. Papers. "What Place Should Religion Have in a College?" UA I 5.150. Box 334. Folder 36. Harvard University Archives.

Examination File. Seeley G. Mudd Manuscript Library. Princeton University Library.

Faculty Files. Seeley G. Mudd Manuscript Library. Princeton University Library.

Farrand, Wilson. Papers. Manuscript Division. Rare Books and Special Collections. Princeton University Library.

First Presbyterian Church of Princeton. Papers. Archives. Princeton Seminary Libraries.

Goodman, K. Sawyer. Scrapbook 1905–06. Seeley G. Mudd Manuscript Library. Princeton University Library.

Green, Joseph C. Papers. Seeley G. Mudd Manuscript Library. Princeton University Library.

Hall, Melvin. Papers. Seeley G. Mudd Manuscript Library. Princeton University Library.

Hibben, John G. Papers. Records of the Office of the President. Seeley G. Mudd Manuscript Library. Princeton University Library.

Hodge, A. A. Papers. Archives. Princeton Seminary Libraries.

Lowrie, Walter. Papers. Manuscript Division. Rare Books and Special Collections. Princeton University Library.

Machen, J. Gresham. Paper. Montgomery Memorial Library. Westminister Theological Seminary.

Mackenzie, J. C. Papers. John Dixon Library. Archives. Lawrenceville School.

Macloskie, George. Papers. Manuscript Division. Rare Books and Special Collections. Princeton University Library.

Marquand, Allan. Paper. Manuscript Division. Rare Books and Special Collections. Princeton University Library.

Martin, Paul. Papers. Manuscript Division. Rare Books and Special Collections. Princeton University Library.

McClure, Charles W. Papers. Manuscript Division. Rare Books and Special Collections. Princeton University Library.

McCosh, James. Papers. Seeley G. Mudd Manuscript Library. Princeton University Library.

McMurray, John V. A. Papers. Manuscript Division. Rare Books and Special Collections. Princeton University Library.

McPherson, Simon J. Papers. John Dixon Library. Archives. Lawrenceville School.

Medina, Harold R. Papers. Seeley G. Mudd Manuscript Library. Princeton University Library.

Miller, Lucius H. Papers. Manuscript Division. Rare Books and Special Collections. Princeton University Library.

Murch, Herbert Spencer. Papers. Manuscript Division. Rare Books and Special Collections. Princeton University Library.

Myers, William Starr. Papers. Seeley G. Mudd Manuscript Library. Princeton University Library.

Ordway, Smith. Diaries. Manuscript Division. Rare Books and Special Collections. Princeton University Library.

Osgood, Charles G. Papers. Manuscript Division. Rare Books and Special Collections. Princeton University Library.

Patton, Francis L. Letterpress Books and Papers. Records of the Office of the President. Seeley G. Mudd Manuscript Library. Princeton University Library.

Princeton Theological Seminary. Minutes of the Faculty of Princeton Theological Seminary. Archives. Princeton Seminary Libraries.

Princeton University. Minutes of the Faculty of Princeton University. Seeley G. Mudd Manuscript Library. Princeton University Library.

———. Minutes of the Trustees of Princeton University. Seeley G. Mudd Manuscript Library. Princeton University Library.

———. Papers of the Trustees of Princeton University. Seeley G. Mudd Manuscript Library. Princeton University Library.

———. *Report of the President of Princeton University*. Princeton: Princeton University Press, 1912–1928.

Records of the Dean of the Chapel. Seeley G. Mudd Manuscript Library. Princeton University Library.

Records of the Secretary. Seeley G. Mudd Manuscript Library. Princeton University Library.

Reid, Samuel J. Papers. Manuscript Division. Rare Books and Special Collections. Princeton University Library.

Russell, Henry Norris. Papers. Manuscript Division. Rare Books and Special Collections. Princeton University Library.

Scott, William Berryman. Papers. Manuscript Division. Rare Books and Special Collections. Princeton University Library.

Shields, Charles W. Papers. Manuscript Division. Rare Books and Special Collections. Princeton University Library.

Smith, H. Alexander. Papers. Seeley G. Mudd Manuscript Library. Princeton University Library.

Speer, Robert E. Papers. Archives. Princeton Seminary Libraries.

Steese, Edward. Papers. Manuscript Division. Rare Books and Special Collections. Princeton University Library.

Student Christian Association Records. Seeley G. Mudd Manuscript Library. Princeton University Library.

Sunday, William and Helen. Papers. Archives of the Billy Graham Center.

Tarkington, Booth. Papers. Manuscript Division. Rare Books and Special Collections. Princeton University Library.

Thomas, George F. Papers. Manuscript Division. Rare Books and Special Collections. Princeton University Library.

Trustees Files. Seeley G. Mudd Manuscript Library. Princeton University Library.

University Chapel Records. Seeley G. Mudd Manuscript Library. Princeton University Library.

Vail, William Penn. Examination Papers. Seeley G. Mudd Manuscript Library. Princeton University Library.

Van Dyke, Henry. Family Papers. Manuscript Division. Rare Books and Special Collections. Princeton University Library.

Warfield, B. B. Papers. Archives. Princeton Seminary Libraries.

Miscellaneous Materials

[Blair, Samuel]. *An Account of the College of New Jersey: in which are described the methods of government, modes of instruction, manners and expences of living in the same.* Woodbridge, N.J.: Printed by James Parker, 1764. Rare Books and Special Collections. Princeton University Library.

Bric-A-Brac (Princeton: Junior Class) 1897.

Bric-A-Brac (Princeton: Junior Class) 1931.

Bric-a-Brac (Princeton: Junior Class) 1955.

Catalogue of the College of New Jersey [Princeton University], 1869–1930.

College of New Jersey. *A General Account of the Rise and State of the College.* London, 1754. Rare Books and Special Collections. Princeton University Library.

Freshman Syllabus in Bible. Seeley G. Mudd Manuscript Library. Princeton University Library.

Hunt, Theodore Whitefield. "Woodrow Wilson's Attitude Toward Religion." [1924]. Archives. Princeton Seminary Libraries.

Notes on Junior-Senior Bible. Seeley G. Mudd Manuscript Library. Princeton University Library.

Patton, Francis L. *Syllabus on Ethics* [1903]. Seeley G. Mudd Manuscript Library. Princeton University Library.

———. *Syllabus of President Patton's Lectures on Ethics.* n.p., 1892. Seeley G. Mudd Manuscript Library. Princeton University Library.

"Princeton Inn Creates a Presbyterian Controversy." *New York Journal,* 12 Nov., 1897. E-File. Archives. Princeton Seminary Libraries.

Princeton Theological Seminary Catalogue, 1898–99.

Princeton University: The Graduate School, 1955–56.

Princeton University Catalogue: Undergraduate Instruction, 1955–56.

Sophomore and Freshman Bible Notes Second Term, 1898. Seeley G. Mudd Manuscript Library. Princeton University Library.

Syllabus on Junior-Senior Bible. Seeley G. Mudd Manuscript Library. Princeton University Library.

Published Works

AN AFFIRMATION designed to safeguard the unity and liberty of the Presbyterian Church in the United States of America with all signatures and the Note Supplementary. Auburn, N.Y.: Jacobs, 1924.

Alexander, Archibald. *Biographical Sketches of the Founder, and Princeton Alumni of the Log College.* Princeton: J. T. Robinson, 1845.

Alexander, James W. Jr. *Princeton - Old and New.* New York: Scribner, 1899.

Alexander, Samuel Davies. "Princeton College." *Scribner's Magazine,* May 1877, 626–27.

———. *Princeton College during the Eighteenth Century.* New York: A. D. F. Randolph, 1872.

Atwater, Lyman. *Ethics and Political Economy from Notes Taken in the Lecture Room of Lyman H. Atwater.* Trenton: Sharp, 1878.

———. "A Plea for Higher Education and Presbyterian College." *Biblical Repertory and Princeton Review* 34 (1862): 28–50.

———. "Proposed Reforms in Collegiate Education." *Princeton Review* 5 (1882): 100–20.

———. "Religion and Politics." *Report of Proceedings of the Second General Council of the Presbyterian Alliance, Convened at Philadelphia, September, 1880.* Ed. John B. Dales and R. M. Patterson, 323–29. Philadelphia: Presbyterian Journal Co., 1880.

———. Review of *Three Discourses upon the Religious History of Bowdoin College,* by Egbert C. Smith. *Biblical Repertory and Princeton Review* 31 (1859): 28–50.

Bacon, Benjamin W. "Courses Bearing on the Bible in Practical and Biblical Life." *The Religious Education Association. Proceedings of the Second Annual Convention, Chicago, March 2–4, 1904,* 131–35. Chicago: Executive Office of the Association, 1904.

Baird, Robert. *Religion in the United States of America*. Glasgow and Edinburgh: Blackie, 1844; reprint, New York: Arno Press, 1969.

Baker, Ray Stannard. *Woodrow Wilson: Life and Letters: Princeton 1890–1910*. Vol. 2. Garden City, N.Y.: Doubleday, 1927.

Baldwin, James Mark. *Between Two Wars 1861–1921: Being Memories, Opinions, Letters Received*. 2 vols. Boston: Stratford, 1926.

_____. *Development and Evolution*. New York: Macmillan, 1902.

_____. "James Mark Baldwin." In *History of Psychology in Autobiography*. Ed. Carl Murchison, 1–30. Worcester: Clark University Press, 1930.

_____. *Mental Development in the Child and the Race*. New York: Macmillan, 1894.

_____. *Social and Ethical Interpretations in Mental Development*. New York: Macmillan, 1897.

Berger, Peter L. *The Noise of Solemn Assemblies: Christian Commitment and the Religious Establishment in America*. Garden City, N.Y.: Doubleday, 1961.

Blanshard, Paul. *American Freedom and Catholic Power*. Boston: Beacon, 1949.

_____. *Communism, Democracy and Catholic Power*. Boston: Beacon, 1951.

Bowman, A. A. *The Absurdity of Christianity*. 2d ed. London: SVM, 1932.

Briggs, Charles A. *American Presbyterianism: Its Origin and Early History*. New York: Scribner, 1885.

_____. *Whither? A Theological Question for the Times*. New York: Scribner, 1889.

Bryce, James. *The American Commonwealth*, 3 vols. London: Macmillan, 1888.

Buckham, M. H. "The Place of Religion in a Liberal Education." *Religious Education* 2 (1907): 217–18.

Buckley, William F., Jr. *God and Man at Yale: The Superstitions of 'Academic Freedom'*. Chicago: Henry Regnery, 1951.

Butler, Joseph. *The Analogy of Religion, Natural and Revealed*. Ed. Joseph Cummings. New York: Phillips and Hunt, 1884.

Butler, Nicholas Murray. "Academic Freedom." *Educational Review* 47 (1914): 291–94.

Calderwood, Henry. *Handbook of Moral Philosophy*. 14th ed. London: Macmillan, 1888.

Canfield, James H. "Religion and Public Education." *Educational Review* 32 (1906): 453–60.

Chambers, Talbot W. "The Inauguration of Professor Briggs." *Presbyterian and Reformed Review* 2 (1891): 481–94.

Claus, Henry T. "The Problem of College Chapel." *Educational Review* 46 (1913): 177–87.

Clothier, Robert C. "Woodrow Wilson as Educator and Administrator: A Student's Perspective." In *Woodrow Wilson in Retrospect*. Ed. Raymond F. Pisney, 90–97. Verona, Va.: McClure Press, 1978.

College of New Jersey. *The First Centennial Anniversary of the College of New Jersey. Celebrated June, 1847*. Princeton: J. T. Robinson, 1848.

_____. *An Historical Sketch of the College of New Jersey*. Philadelphia: Joseph M. Wilson, 1859.

College Reading and Religion: A Survey of College Reading Materials. New Haven: Yale University Press, 1948.

Collins, Varnum Lansing. *Princeton*. New York: Oxford University Press, 1914.

Colwell, P. R., ed. *Duodecennial Record of the Class of Eighteen Hundred and Ninety-Seven Princeton University.* Princeton: Princeton University Press, 1907.

Conklin, Edwin Grant. "As a Scientist Saw Him." In *Woodrow Wilson: Some Princeton Memories.* Ed. William Starr Myers, 52–61. Princeton: Princeton University Press, 1946.

———. *The Direction of Human Evolution.* New York: Scribner, 1921.

Cope, Henry F. "Ten Years Progress in Religious Education." *Religious Education* 8 (1913): 137–43.

Corwin, Virginia. "The Teaching of Religion." In *Liberal Learning and Religion.* Ed. Amos N. Wilder, 169–96. New York: Harper and Brothers, 1951.

Cox, Harvey. *The Secular City: Secularization and Urbanization in Theological Perspective.* New York: MacMillan, 1965.

Craig, Hardin. *Woodrow Wilson at Princeton.* Norman: University of Oklahoma Press, 1960.

Craven, Elijah R. "The Log College of Neshaminy and Princeton University." *Presbyterian Historical Society* 1 (1902): 308–14.

Daniels, Winthrop M. *Recollections of Woodrow Wilson.* New Haven: Privately printed, 1944.

Darling, Timothy G. Review of *The Gospel for an Age of Doubt,* by Henry Van Dyke Jr. *Presbyterian and Reformed Review* 8 (1897): 348–55.

Dennis, Alfred Pearce. *Gods and Little Fishes.* Indianapolis: Bobbs-Merrill, 1924.

Dewey, John. "Academic Freedom." *Educational Review* 23 (1902): 1–9.

DeWitt, John. "Historical Sketch of Princeton University." *Memorial Book of the Sesquicentennial Celebration of the Founding of the College of New Jersey and of the Ceremonies Inaugurating Princeton University.* New York: Scribner, 1898.

———. *Ought the Confession of Faith to Be Revised?.* New York, 1890.

———. "Princeton College." In *Universities and Their Sons: History, Influence and Characteristics of American Universities.* Ed. Joshua L. Chamberlain. Vol. 1. Boston: Herndon, 1898.

Dirks, J. Edward. "About the Journal." *Christian Scholar* 36 (1953): 4.

[Dod, William Armstrong]. *History of the College of New Jersey, From Its Commencement, A.D., 1746 to 1783. [Prepared Originally for The Princeton Whig, Feb., 1844].* Princeton: J. T. Robinson, 1844.

Draper, John. *History of the Conflict between Religion and Science.* London: Henry S. King, 1874.

Duffield, John T. "Evolutionism Respecting Man, and the Bible." *Princeton Review* 1 (1878): 150–77.

———. *A Sermon Delivered in the Chapel of the College of New Jersey, Dec. 19th, 1876.* Princeton: Press Printing Establishment, 1877.

Edgar, Day. *In Princeton Town.* New York: Scribner, 1929.

"Education Bills before Congress." *New Princeton Review* 2 (1886): 131–34.

Elderkin, George W. *The Roman Catholic Controversy On The Campus of Princeton University.* 4 parts. n.p., 1955–58.

"Electives in College Studies." *New Princeton Review* 2 (1886): 284–85.

Eliot, Charles W. "Liberty in Education." In *Educational Reform: Essays and Addresses.* New York: Century, 1898.

_____. "The Religion of the Future." *Harvard Theological Review* 2 (1909): 389–407.

Encyclopedia of the Presbyterian Church in the United States of America. Ed. Alfred Nevin. Philadelphia: Presbyterian Encyclopedia Publishing Co., 1884.

Fisher, D. W. "Christianity in the College." *Princeton Theological Review* 1 (1903): 256–66.

Fisher, Galen M. *Religion in the Colleges.* New York: Association, 1928.

Fitch, Albert Parker. *Religion and the Undergraduate: Four Addresses Delivered at Princeton University, March 1915.* With an Introduction by John G. Hibben. Princeton: Published under the auspices of the "Daily Princetonian," 1915.

Fite, Warner. *A Complete Outline of Professor Fite's Lectures in Ethics.* Princeton: Printed by the Princeton Syllabi Co., [1917].

_____. *An Introductory Study of Ethics.* London: Longmans, 1903.

_____. *Moral Philosophy: The Critical View of Life.* New York: Dial, 1925.

Fitzgerald, F. Scott. *This Side of Paradise.* New York: Scribner, 1920.

Fleet, R. R. "The Religious Possibilities of the College." *Educational Review* 72 (1926): 392–96.

Fosdick, Raymond B. *Chronicler of a Generation.* New York: Harper, 1958.

Gage, Harry M., Charles A. Richmond, and Marion L. Burton. "The Place of Religion in Higher Education in America." *Association of American Colleges Bulletin* 10 (1924): 83–106.

Gauss, Christian. "Religion and Higher Education in America." In *The Teaching of Religion in American Higher Education.* Ed. Christian Gauss, 1–19. New York: Press, 1951.

Gilman, Daniel C. "Higher Education in the United States." *University Problems in the United States.* New York: Century, 1898.

_____. "The Shortening of the College Curriculum." *Educational Review* 1 (1891): 1–7.

Goodspeed, E. J. *A Full History of the Wonderful Career of Moody and Sankey, in Great Britain and America.* New York: Goodspeed, 1876.

Green, Ashbel. *Discourses, Delivered in the College of New Jersey; Addressed for the First Degree in the Arts; with Notes and Illustrations, including a Historical Sketch of the College, from its Origin to the Accession of President Witherspoon.* Philadelphia: Littell, 1822.

Guyot, Arnold H. *Creations; or The Biblical Cosmogony in the Light of Modern Science.* New York: Scribner, 1884.

Hageman, John F. *History of Princeton and Its Institutions.* 2 vols. Philadelphia: Lippincott, 1879.

Harbison, E. Harris. "Christian Belief and Intellectual Freedom." *Christian Scholar* 36 (1953): 183–88.

_____. *The Christian Scholar in the Age of the Reformation.* New York: Scribner, 1956.

_____. "History." In *Religious Perspectives in College Teaching.* Ed. Hoxie N. Fairchild, 67–97. New York: Ronald, 1952.

Harper, George M. "The New Program of Studies at Princeton." *Educational Review* 29 (1905): 140–50.

Harper, William Rainey. "What Can Universities and Colleges Do for the Religious Life of their Students?" *The Aims of Religious Education: The Proceedings of the Third Annual Convention of the Religious Education Association, Boston, February 12–16, 1905,* 110–13. Chicago: Executive Office of the Association, 1905.

Hibben, John G. *The Higher Patriotism*. New York: Scribner, 1915.

———. *Inductive Logic*. New York: Scribner, 1896.

———. *Logic: Deductive and Inductive*. New York: Scribner, 1905.

———. "The Philosophical Aspects of Evolution." *Philosophical Review* 19 (1910): 113–36.

———. *The Philosophy of the Enlightenment*. New York: Scribner, 1910.

———. "The Preceptorial System at Princeton University." *Journal of Pedagogy* 18 (1906): 249–56.

———. *The Problems of Philosophy*. New York: Scribner, 1898.

———. "Student Attitudes as an Administrator Sees Them." *Religion in the Colleges*. Ed. Galen M. Fisher, 3–5. New York: Association Press, 1928.

Hodge, A. A. "Church Action on Temperance." *Biblical Repertory and Princeton Review* 48 (1871): 595–632.

———. *Outlines of Theology*. New York: Robert Carter, 1860.

———. *Outlines of Theology*. Rev. ed. New York: Robert Carter, 1879.

———. "Religion in the Public Schools." *New Princeton Review* 3 (1887): 28–47.

———. Review of *Natural Science and Religion*, by Asa Gray. *Presbyterian Review* 1 (1880): 586–89.

Hodge, A. A., and B. B. Warfield. "Inspiration." *Presbyterian Review* 2 (1881): 225–60.

Hodge, Charles. *The Constitutional History of the Presbyterian Church in the United States of America: Part II, 1741–1788*. Philadelphia: Presbyterian Board of Publication, 1851.

———. "Parochial Schools." *Biblical Repertory and Princeton Review* 18 (1846): 433–41.

———. *Systematic Theology*. 3 vols. reprint, Grand Rapids: Eerdmans, 1986.

———. "Temperance Question." *Biblical Repertory and Princeton Review* 15 (1843): 461–69.

———. *What Is Darwinism?* New York: Scribner, 1874.

Hyde, William DeWitt. "The Place of Religion in a Liberal Education." *Homiletic Review* 58 (1909): 286–87.

Johnson, William H. Review of *Our Knowledge of Christ*, by Lucius H. Miller. *Princeton Theological Review* 13 (1915): 477–82.

Johnston, Alexander. *Lectures on Political Economy*. Trenton: Edwin Fitzgeorge, 1884.

———. *Syllabus in Jurisprudence*. Princeton: Princeton Press, n.d.

———. *Syllabus in Jurisprudence and Political Economy*. Princeton: Princeton Press, 1886.

Jordan, David Starr. *The Days of a Man*. 2 vols. Yonkers-on-Hudson, N.Y.: World, 1922.

Keener, Johyn H., ed. *Triennial Record of the Class of 1897 Princeton University*. New York: Grafton, 1900.

Kelsey, Francis W. "The Problem of Religious Instruction in State Universities." In *Education and National Character*, 128–49. Chicago: Religious Education Association, 1908.

Kent, Charles Foster. "The Bible and the College Curriculum." *Religious Education* 8 (1913): 453–58.

———. "Order and Content of Biblical Courses in College Curriculum." *Religious Education* 7 (1912): 42–49.

Kephart, A. P. "The Problem of College Chapel Exercises." *Educational Review* 71 (1926): 146–52.

Kerr, Robert P. *The People's History of Presbyterianism in all Ages.* Richmond: Presbyterian Committee of Publication, 1888.

Kirk, Harris E. *The Power of Religion.* New York: Doran, 1916.

Lambert, Gerald B. *All Out of Step: A Personal Chronicle.* New York: Doubleday, 1956.

Lieber, Francis. "The Necessity of Religious Instruction in Colleges." *Presbyterian Quarterly and Princeton Review* 2 (1873): 651–56.

Lowry, Howard. *The Mind's Adventure.* Philadelphia: Westminster, 1950.

Macloskie, George. "Common Errors as to the Relations of Science and Faith." *Presbyterian and Reformed Review* 7 (1895): 98–105.

_____. "Concessions to Science." *Presbyterian Review* 10 (1889): 220–28.

_____. "Mosaism and Darwinism." *Princeton Theological Review* 2 (1904): 425–51.

_____. "The Outlook of Science and Faith." *Princeton Theological Review* 1 (1903): 597–615.

_____. "Scientific Speculation." *Presbyterian Review* 8 (1887): 617–25.

_____. "The Testimony of Nature." *Presbyterian and Reformed Review* 1 (1890): 587–97.

_____. "Theistic Evolution." *Presbyterian and Reformed Review* 9 (1898): 1–22.

Matlock, William H. "Instruction in Religion in State Universities." *Educational Review* 40 (1910): 256–65.

McCosh, James. *Christianity and Positivism: A Series of Lectures to the Times on Natural Theology and Christian Apologetics.* New York: Robert Carter, 1871.

_____. "Growth in Grace Illustrated in the Life of Nicodemus." *Gospel Sermons.* New York: Robert Carter, 1888.

_____. *Inauguration of Rev. Jas. M'Cosh, D.D., LL.D., as President of Princeton College, October 27, 1868.* Princeton: Printed at the Standard Office, 1869.

_____. *The Life of James McCosh: A Record Chiefly Autobiographical.* Ed. William M. Sloane. New York: Scribner, 1896.

_____. "A Method of Teaching Religion in a College." *Biblical Repertory and Princeton Review* 41 (1869): 72–83.

_____. *The New Departure in College Education: Being a Reply to President Eliot's Defense of it in New York, Feb. 24, 1885.* New York: Scribner, 1885.

_____. "The Place of Religion in College." In *Minutes and Proceedings of the Third General Council of the Alliance of the Reformed Churches Holding the Presbyterian System, Belfast, 1884,* 465–70. Belfast: Alliance of Reformed Churches, 1884.

_____. "A Presbyterian College in America." *Catholic Presbyterian* 4 (1880): 81–87.

_____. *The Propriety of Acknowledging the Lord in All our Ways: The Baccalaureate Sermon Preached before the College of New Jersey, June 16, 1878.* New York: Robert Carter, 1878.

_____. *Psychology: The Cognitive Powers.* New York: Scribner, 1886.

_____. *Religion in a College: What Place It Should Have. Being an Examination of President Eliot's Paper, Read Before the Nineteenth Century Club, in New York, Feb., 3, 1886.* New York: A.C. Armstrong and Son, 1886.

_____. *The Religious Aspects of Evolution.* New York: G. P. Putnam's Sons, 1888.

Works Cited

————. "The Royal Law of Love." *Gospel Sermons*. New York: Robert Carter, 1888.

————. *The Scottish Philosophy, Biographical, Expository, Critical, From Hutcheson to Hamilton*. New York: Robert Carter, 1875.

————. "The Sifting of Peter." *Gospel Sermons*. New York: Robert Carter, 1888.

————. *Twenty Years of Princeton College: Being a Farewell Address Delivered June 20th, 1888 by James McCosh, D.D., LL.D., Litt.D.*. New York: Scribner, 1888.

————. *What An American University Should Be*. New York: J.K. Lees, 1885.

————. *Whither? O Whither? Tell me Where*. New York: Scribner, 1889.

————. *The World a Scene of Contest: The Baccalaureate Sermon Preached before the College of New Jersey, June 25, 1876*. New York: Robert Carter, 1876.

Mackenzie, John S. *Manual of Ethics*. 4th ed. London: University Tutorial Press, 1900.

Maclean, John. *History of the College of New Jersey, from its Origin in 1746 to the Commencement of 1854*. 2 vols. Philadelphia: Lippincott, 1877.

Miller, Lucius H. "The Authority of the Bible." *South Atlantic Quarterly* 9 (1910): 239–50.

————. "Modern Views of the Bible and of Religion." *South Atlantic Quarterly* 7 (1908): 309–19.

————. *Our Knowledge of Christ: An Historical Approach*. New York: Henry Holt, 1914.

————. "The Teaching of Ernst Troeltsch of Heidelberg." *Harvard Theological Review* 6 (1913): 426–50.

Minton, Henry C. Review of *The Scientific Evidences of Revealed Religion*, by Charles W. Shields. *Presbyterian and Reformed Review* 12 (1901): 453–54.

Moberly, Sir Walter. *The Crisis in the University*. London: S.C.M., 1948.

Moffat, James C. Review of *The Historically Received Conception of the University*, by Edward Kirkpatrick. *Biblical Repertory and Princeton Review* 35 (1863): 571–95.

More, Paul Elmer. *The Christ of the New Testament*. Princeton: Princeton University Press, 1924.

————. *Christ the Word*. Princeton: Princeton University Press, 1927.

"Mr. Lowell on Education." *New Princeton Review* 3 (1887): 131–33.

Norris, Edwin M. *The Story of Princeton*. Boston: Little, Brown, and Co., 1917.

Ormond, Alexander T. *The Concepts of Philosophy*. New York: Macmillan, 1906.

————. *Foundations of Knowledge*. New York: Macmillan, 1900.

————. "University Ideals at Princeton." *National Educational Associate. Journal of Proceedings and Addresses of the Thirty-Sixth Annual Meeting Held at Milwaukee, Wis., July 6–9, 1897*, 346–57. Chicago: University of Chicago Press, 1897.

Osborn, Henry Fairfield. *Creative Education in School, College, University, and Museum: Personal Observation and Experience of the Half Century, 1877–1927*. New York: Scribner, 1927.

————, ed. *Fifty Years of Princeton '77: A Fifty-Four Year Record of Princeton College and University*. Princeton: Printed at the Princeton University Press, 1927.

Ottman, Ford C. *The Devil in Cap and Gown*. New York: Arno C. Gaebelein, 1914.

Paley, William. *Natural Theology*. Ed. Francis Young. London: Ward, Lock, and Co., n.d.

Palmer, George Herbert. *Expenses at Harvard: An Address by Professor George Herbert Palmer Before Harvard Graduates, Commencement Day, 1887*. Cambridge: John Wilson, 1887.

_____. *The Field of Ethics*. Boston: Houghton Mifflin, 1901.

Patton, Francis L. *Addresses at the Induction of Rev. Francis L. Patton into "The Cyrus H. McCormick Professorship of Didactic and Polemic Theology," in the Presbyterian Theological Seminary of the North-West*. Chicago: Printed by order of the Board of Directors of the Seminary, [1872].

_____. "College or University? The Advantages of the Great University." *Saturday Evening Post*, 1 July, 1899, 5.

_____. "Contemporary English Ethics." *New Princeton Review* 1 (1886): 177–99.

_____. "The Dogmatic Aspect of Pentateuchal Criticism." *Presbyterian Review* 4 (1883): 340–410.

_____. "Dr. McCosh on the New Departure in College Education." *Presbyterian Review* 6 (1885): 341–47.

_____. *The Duty of Self-Control: An Address to the Students of Princeton University, in Marquand Chapel, Sunday Afternoon, January 30, 1898*. Princeton: Princeton University Press, [1898].

_____. "Evolution and Apologetics." *Presbyterian Review* 6 (1885): 138–44.

_____. "The Final Philosophy." *Princeton Review* 54 (1879): 559–78.

_____. *Inauguration of the Rev. Francis Landey Patton, D.D., LL.D., as President of Princeton College*. New York: Gray Brothers, 1888.

_____. "James McCosh: A Baccalaureate Sermon." *Presbyterian and Reformed Review* 6 (1895): 643–64.

_____. "The Letter and the Spirit." *Princeton Sermons*. New York: Revell, 1893.

_____. "The Meaning of Oughtness." *Presbyterian Review* 7 (1886): 127–50.

_____. *Pastors, Theology and the Age*. Philadelphia: Presbyterian Board of Publication, 1879.

_____. "The Place of Philosophy in the Theological Curriculum." *Princeton Review* (1882): 102–24.

_____. "The President's Address at the Opening of the College." *Princeton College Bulletin* 1 (1889): 1–11.

_____. "Religion and the University." *Memorial Book of the Sesquicentennial Celebration of the Founding of the College of New Jersey and of the Ceremonies Inaugurating Princeton University*. New York: Scribner, 1898.

_____. "Religion in College." *Princeton Sermons*. New York: Revell, 1893.

_____. "The Religious Life of the University." *Intercollegian* 22 (1899): 30–31.

_____. *The Revision of the Confession of Faith. Read Before the Presbyterian Social Union, N.Y., Dec. 2, 1889*. n.p., n.d.

_____. *Speech of Prof. Francis L. Patton, D.D., LL.D., President-Elect of Princeton College at the Annual Dinner of the Princeton Club of New York. March 15, 1888*. n.p., [1888].

_____. *A Summary of Christian Doctrine*. Presbyterian Board of Publication, 1875; reprint, Philadelphia: Westminster Press, 1928.

_____. *Syllabus of Prof. Patton's Lectures on the Anti-Theistic Theories*. n.p., n.d.

_____. *Syllabus of Prof. Patton's Lectures on Theism*. Princeton: Princeton Press, 1886.

_____. "Theological Encyclopedia." *Princeton Theological Review* 2 (1904): 110–36.

Patton, George S. "Beyond Good and Evil." *Princeton Theological Review* 6 (1908): 392–436.

———. "A Fruitful Method of Bible Study." *Bible Student* (1900): 209–12.

———. "At Princeton College." *Little Chap* 1 (1896): 49–51.

———. "Recent Works on Ethics." *Psychological Review* 8 (1901): 65–89.

———. Review of *Der Kampf un die Sittliche Welt*, by D. Wilh. Schmidt. *Princeton Theological Review* 5 (1907): 648–51.

———. Review of *Ethics Descriptive and Explanatory*, by S. E. Mezes. *Psychological Review* 9 (1902): 418–30.

———. Review of *A History of the Problems of Philosophy*, by Paul Janet and Gabriel Séailles. *Psychological Bulletin* 1 (1904): 166–69.

———. Review of *An Introductory Study of Ethics*, by Warner Fite. *Philosophical Review* 13 (1904): 379–81.

———. Review of *Les Fonctions Mentales dans les Sociétés Inferieures*, L. Lévy-Bruhl. *Philosophical Review* 21 (1912): 455–62.

———. Review of *Moral Evolution*, by George Harris. *Presbyterian and Reformed Review* 8 (1897): 531–41.

———. Review of *La philosophie pratique de Kant*, by Victor Delbos. *Philosophical Review* 15 (1906): 536–42.

———. Review of *A Study of Ethical Principles*, by James Seth. *Presbyterian and Reformed Review* 6 (1895): 578–81.

———. Review of *A System of Ethics*, by Friedrich Paulsen. *Presbyterian and Reformed Review* 11 (1900): 326–31.

Paulsen, Friedrich. *A System of Ethics*. Ed. and Trans. Frank Thilly. New York: Scribner, 1899.

Perry, Bliss. *And Gladly Teach: Reminiscences*. Boston: Houghton Mifflin, 1935.

Philadelphian Society. *One Hundred Years, 1825–1925: The Philadelphian Society of Princeton University Commemorates the 100th Anniversary of Its Founding*. n.p., [1925].

Pratt, Dwight M. Religious Life in our Colleges." *Homiletic Review* 58 (1909): 13–20.

Presbyterian Church, U.S.A. *Minutes of the General Assembly of the Presbyterian Church in the United States of America from its Organization, A.D. 1789 to A.D. 1820*. Philadelphia: Presbyterian Board of Publication, [1847].

———. *Minutes of the General Assembly of the Presbyterian Church in the U.S.A.*. New York: Presbyterian Board of Publication, 1871.

"President Hibben of Princeton." *Educational Review* 44 (1912): 107–108.

Princeton University. *General Catalogue of Princeton University, 1746–1906*. Princeton: Published by the University, 1908.

———. *Princeton in the World War*. Princeton: Princeton University Press, 1932.

———. *The World Peril: America's Interest in the War, by members of the faculty of Princeton University*. Princeton: Princeton University Press, 1917.

Pritchett, Henry S. "The Policy of the Carnegie Foundation for the Advancement of Teaching." *Educational Review* 32 (1906): 83–99.

———. "The Relations of Christian Denominations to Colleges." *Educational Review* 36 (1908): 217–41.

Reingold, Nathan, ed. *Science in the Nineteenth-Century: A Documentary History.* New York: Hill and Wang, 1964.

Report of Proceedings of the First General Presbyterian Council Convened at Edinburgh, July 1877. Ed. J. Thomson. Edinburgh: Thomas and Archibald Constable, 1877.

Reports on the Course of Instruction in Yale College; By a Committee of the Corporation, and the Academic Faculty. New Haven: Printed by Hezekiah Howe, 1828.

Review of *Philosophia Ultima*, by Charles W. Shields. *Biblical Repertory and Princeton Review* 33 (1861): 576.

Roberts, William C. "The American College." In *Minutes and Proceedings of the Third General Council of the Alliance of the Reformed Churches Holding the Presbyterian System, Belfast, 1884.* 472–76. Belfast: Alliance of Reformed Churches, 1884.

———. "Higher Education in the West." *Presbyterian Review* 9 (1888): 208–21.

Rogers, Fred B. "Cyrus Fogg Brackett: Physicist and Physician." *Journal of the Medical Society of New Jersey* 52 (1955): 452–56.

Rogers, Robert W. *A History of Babylonia and Assyria.* 2 vols. New York: Eaton and Mains, 1901.

Robinson, A. T. Review of *Our Knowledge of Christ*, by Lucius H. Miller. *Review and Expositor* 12 (1915): 610.

Root, Robert K. "Wilson and the Preceptors." *Woodrow Wilson: Some Princeton Memories.* Ed. William Starr Myers, 13–18. Princeton: Princeton University Press, 1946.

Scott, William Berryman. *Some Memories of a Palaeontologist.* Princeton: Princeton University Press, 1939.

Seth, James. *A Study of Ethical Principles.* New York: Scribner, 1898.

Shields, Charles W. *Directory for Public Worship and the Book of Common Prayer Considered with Reference to the Question of a Presbyterian Liturgy.* Philadelphia: Martien, 1867.

———. "The False Temperance Agitation." *Outlook*, 8 Oct. 1898, 377–79.

———. *The Final Philosophy, or System of Perfectible Knowledge Issuing from the Harmony of Science and Religion.* New York: Scribner, 1877.

———. "Historical Note on the Origin of Princeton University." *Memorial Book of the Sesquicentennial Celebration of the Founding of the College of New Jersey and of the Ceremonies Inaugurating Princeton University.* New York: Scribner, 1898.

———. *Introductory Lecture on the Relations of Science and Religion.* Philadelphia: Henry B. Ashmead, 1866.

———. *Philosophia Ultima.* Philadelphia: Lippincott, 1861.

———. *Philosophia Ultima or Science of the Sciences Vol. I. An Historical and Critical Introduction to the Final Philosophy as Issuing from the Harmony of Science and Religion.* Rev. ed. New York: Scribner, 1888.

———. *Philosophia Ultima or Science of the Sciences Vol. II. The History of the Sciences and the Logic of the Sciences.* New York: Scribner, 1889.

———. *Philosophia Ultima or the Science of the Sciences Vol. III. The Scientific Problems of Religion and the Christian Evidences of the Physical and Psychical Sciences.* With a Biographical Sketch by William M. Sloane. New York: Scribner, 1905.

———. "The Positive Philosophy of Auguste Comte." *Biblical Repertory and Princeton Review* 30 (1858): 1–27.

———. *The Scientific Evidences of Revealed Religion*. New York: Scribner, 1900.

Sinclair, Upton. *The Goose-Step: A Study of American Education*. Pasadena: Published by the Author, [1923].

Sloane, William M. "Princeton University." *Harper's New Monthly Magazine*, Nov. 1889, 886–900.

———. "The Renascence of Education." *Presbyterian Review* 6 (1885): 446–66.

Slosson, Edwin E. *Great American Universities*. New York: Macmillan, 1910.

Smith, Norman Kemp. *A Commentary to Kant's Critique of Pure Reason*. London: Macmillan, 1918.

———. Introduction to *Studies in the Philosophy of Religion*, by A. A. Bowman. 2 vols. London: Macmillan, 1938.

Smith, Seymour A. *Religious Cooperation in State Universities: An Historical Sketch*. [Ann Arbor]: University of Michigan Press, 1957.

Spurrier, William A. "Religion." In *College Teaching and Christian Values*. Ed. Paul M. Limbert, 144–64. New York: Association, 1951.

"Standardization of Biblical Courses." *Religious Education* 11 (1916): 311–23.

Starbuck, Edwin. "Religion in General Education." *Educational Review* 27 (1904): 53–59.

"Statistics of Higher Education." *Educational Review* 16 (1898): 402–404.

Stearns, Jonathan F. *Liberal Education a Necessity of the Church*. New York: John F. Trow, 1860.

Stearns, Wallace N. "Moral and Religious Education in the Universities and Colleges." *The Materials of Religious Education. Being the Principal Papers Presented at, and the Proceedings of the Fourth General Convention of the Religious Education Association Rochester, New York, February 5–7, 1907*, 53–57. Chicago: Executive Office of the Association, 1907.

Sturges, Jonathan. *History of the Class of '85, of Princeton College*. Princeton: MacCrellish and Quigley, 1885.

Synod of New Jersey. *Minutes of the Seventy-Fifth Annual Session of the Synod of New Jersey*. Trenton: MacCrellish and Quigley, 1897.

Thomas, David E. "Progress at State Universities." *Religious Education* 18 (1923): 237–40.

Thomas, George F. "The Meaning of Truth." *Christian Scholar* 36 (1953): 172–75.

———. *Religion in an Age of Secularism*. Princeton: Princeton University Press, 1940.

———. "Religious Perspectives in College Teaching: Problems and Principles." In *Religious Perspectives in College Teaching*. Ed. Hoxie N. Fairchild, 3–38. New York: Ronald, 1952.

Tillich, Paul. *The Courage to Be*. New Haven: Yale University Press, 1952.

Uphaus, Willard E., and M. Teague Hipps. *Undergraduate Courses in Religion at Denominational and Independent Colleges of America*. Ithaca: National Council on Religion in Higher Education, [1924].

Van Dusen, Henry P. *God in Education: A Tract for the Times*. New York: Scribner, 1951.

Van Dyke, Henry, Jr. *The Gospel for an Age of Doubt*. New York: Macmillan, 1897.

———. *A Plea for Peace and Work*. n.p., 1893.

———. "To a Young Friend Going Away from Home to Get an Education." *Educational Review* 26 (1903): 217–21.

Van Dyke, Henry, Sr. "The Charge." *Addresses at the Inauguration of the Rev. Francis L. Patton, D.D., LL.D., as Stuart Professor of the Relations of Philosophy and Science to the Christian Religion, in the Theological Seminary at Princeton, N.J., October 27, 1881*. Philadelphia: Sherman, 1881.

Walter, Howard A. *Soul Surgery*. New York: Association Press, 1919.

Warfield, B. B. "Calvin's Doctrine of Creation." *Princeton Theological Review* 13 (1915): 190–255.

———. "Charles Darwin's Religious Life: A Sketch in Spiritual Biography." *Presbyterian Review* 9 (1888): 575–602.

———. "Creation versus Evolution." *Bible Student* 4 (1901): 1–8.

———. "The One Hundred and Third General Assembly." *Presbyterian and Reformed Review* 2 (1891): 495–99.

———. *The Present-Day Conception of Evolution*. Emporia, Kans.: College Printing Office, n.d.

———. Review of *Darwinism Today*, by Vernon L. Kellogg. *Princeton Theological Review* 6 (1908): 640–50.

———. Review of *Philosophia Ultima Vol. III*, by Charles W. Shield. *Princeton Theological Review* 6 (1906): 541–42.

Warren, Howard C. "Academic Freedom." *Atlantic Monthly*, Nov. 1914, 689–99.

———. "Howard C. Warren." In *A History of Psychology in Autobiography*. Ed. Carl Murchison, 443–69. Worcester: Clark University Press, 1930.

Weber, Alfred. *History of Philosophy*. Trans. Frank Thilly. New York: Scribner, 1907.

Webster, Richard. *A History of the Presbyterian Church*. Philadelphia: Joseph M. Wilson, 1857.

Wertenbaker, Thomas Jefferson. "Woodrow Wilson and His Program at Princeton." In *Woodrow Wilson in Retrospect*. Ed. Raymond F. Pisney, 74–81. Verona, Va.: McClure Press, 1978.

West, Andrew F. "The Changing Conception of 'The Faculty' in American Universities." *Educational Review* 32 (1906): 1–14.

———. *The Proposed Graduate College of Princeton University*. Princeton: Princeton University Press, 1903.

———. "The Spirit and Ideas of Princeton." *Educational Review* 8 (1894): 313–26.

———. "The Tutorial System in College." *Short Papers on American Liberal Education*. New York: Scribner, 1907.

———. "What is Academic Freedom?" *North American Review* 140 (1885): 432–44.

White, Andrew D. *Autobiography of Andrew Dickson White*. 2 vols. New York: Century, 1905.

———. *A History of the Warfare of Science with Theology in Christendom*. 2 vols. New York: Appleton, 1896.

Wicks, Robert R. *The Reason for Living*. New York: Scribner, 1934.

Williams, Jesse Lynch. *Princeton Stories*. New York: Scribner, 1895.

———. "Princeton University." In *The University and Their Sons: History, Influence and Characteristics of American Universities*. Ed. Joshua L. Chamberlain. Vol. 1. Boston: Herndon, 1898.

Williams, John Rogers. *The Handbook of Princeton*. With an Introduction by Woodrow Wilson. New York: Grafton, 1905.

Woodrow Wilson. *A History of the American People*. 5 vols. New York: Harper and Brothers, 1902.

──────. Introduction to *The Handbook of Princeton*, by John Rogers Williams. New York: Grafton, 1905.

──────. *The Papers of Woodrow Wilson*. Ed. Arthur S. Link, John Wells Davidson, David W. Hirst, John E. Little et al. 69 vols. Princeton: Princeton University Press, 1966–94.

──────. "Princeton in the Nation's Service." *Memorial Book of the Sesquicentennial Celebration of the Founding of the College of New Jersey and of the Ceremonies Inaugurating Princeton University*. New York: Scribner, 1898.

Young, Charles A. *God's Glory in the Heavens*. Cranbury, N.J.: George W. Burroughs, 1894.

Youtz, Herbert A. Review *Our Knowledge of Christ*, by Lucius H. Miller. *Harvard Theological Review* 10 (1917): 105.

Periodicals

Alumni Princetonian, 1898.

Biblical World, 1904–1906, 1908, 1910.

Churchman, 1926.

Congregationalist, 1902.

Daily Princetonian, 1893–1894, 1896–1899, 1901–1928, 1955–1957, 1987.

Evangelist, 1896, 1898.

Herald and Presbyter, 1915.

Independent, 1886, 1902, 1912.

Nassau Herald, 1872, 1875–1897, 1988–1900.

Nassau Literary Magazine, 1890–1891, 1893–1894, 1900, 1902–1905, 1915, 1920–1923.

New-York Daily Tribune, 1885–1886.

New-York Evangelist, 1884.

New York Herald, 1898.

New York Times, 1885–1886, 1911, 1914, 1917.

New York Tribune, 1902.

New York Voice, 1897.

Philadelphian, 1904.

Philadelphian Bulletin, 1892.

Presbyterian, 1876, 1886, 1889, 1894, 1896–1898, 1902, 1904–1906, 1908–1910, 1912–1915, 1918, 1925, 1927, 1930.

Presbyterian Advance, 1925.

Presbyterian Banner, 1897, 1915.

Presbyterian of the South, 1915.

Princeton Alumni Weekly, 1900–1912, 1914–1925, 1927–1932, 1940, 1952, 1955, 1957–1958, 1970–1971.

Princeton Press, 1876, 1885, 1890, 1894, 1897–1898, 1902, 1915, 1917.

Princeton University Bulletin, 1898.

Princeton Weekly Bulletin, 1995.

Princetonian, 1876, 1881, 1883, 1885–1893.

The Voice Extra, 1897.

World, 1914.

Secondary Sources

Books

Abrams, Ray H. *Preachers Present Arms*. New York: Round Table Press, 1933; reprint, Scottdale, Pa.: Herald Press, 1969.

Ahlstrom, Sydney E. *A Religious History of the American People*. New Haven: Yale University Press, 1972.

_____. ed. *Theology in America: The Major Protestant Voices from Puritanism to Neo-Orthodoxy*. Indianapolis: Bobbs-Merrill, 1967.

Allitt, Patrick. *Conservative Intellectuals and Conservative Politics in America, 1950–1985*. Ithaca: Cornell University Press, 1993.

Altschuler, Glenn C. *Andrew D. White: Educator, Historian, Diplomat*. Ithaca: Cornell University Press, 1979.

Anchor Bible Dictionary. Ed. David Noel Freedman. New York: Doubleday, 1992.

Annarelli, James John. *Academic Freedom and Catholic Higher Education*. Westport, Conn.: Greenwood Press, 1987.

Bainton, Roland H. *Yale and the Ministry: A History of Education for the Christian Ministry at Yale from the founding in 1701*. 1957; reprint, New York: Harper and Row, 1975.

Balmer, Randall, and John R. Fitzmier. *The Presbyterians*. Westport, Conn: Greenwood Press, 1993.

Bledstein, Burton J. *The Culture of Professionalism: The Middle Class and the Development of Higher Education in America*. New York: Norton, 1976.

Bozeman, Theodore Dwight. *Protestants in an Age of Science: The Baconian Ideal and Antebellum American Religious Thought*. Chapel Hill: University of North Carolina Press, 1977.

Bragdon, Henry W. *Woodrow Wilson: The Academic Years*. Cambridge: Belknap Press of Harvard University Press, 1967.

Brown, Jerry W. *The Rise of Biblical Criticism in America, 1800–1870: The New England Scholars*. Middleton, Conn: Wesleyan University Press, 1969.

Burritt, Bailey B. *Professional Distribution of College and University Graduates*. Washington, D.C.: Government Printing Office, 1912.

Carter, Paul. *The Spiritual Crisis of the Gilded Age*. Dekalb: Northern Illinois University Press, 1971.

Cashdollar, Charles W. *The Transformation of Theology, 1830–1890: Positivism and Protestant Thought in Britain and America*. Princeton: Princeton University Press, 1989.

Chamberlain, Joshua L., ed. *Universities and Their Sons: History, Influence and Characteristics of American Universities with Biographical Sketches and Portraits of Alumni and Recipients of Honorary Degrees.* Vol. 2. Boston: Herndon, 1899.

Cherry, Conrad. *Hurrying Toward Zion: Universities, Divinity Schools, and American Protestantism.* Bloomington: Indiana University Press, 1995.

Clark, Norman H. *Deliver Us From Evil: An Interpretation of American Prohibition.* New York: Norton, 1976.

Clark, Walter H. *The Oxford Group: Its History and Significance.* New York: Bookman Associates, 1951.

Coben, Stanley. *Rebellion against Victorianism: The Impetus for Cultural Change in 1920s America.* New York: Oxford University Press, 1991.

Crosby, Donald F. *God, Church, and Flag: Senator Joseph R. McCarthy and the Catholic Church 1950–1957.* Chapel Hill: University of North Carolina Press, 1978.

Crunden, Robert M. *Ministers of Reform: The Progressives' Achievement in American Civilization, 1889–1920.* New York: Basic Books, 1982.

Cuddihy, John M. *No Offense: Civil Religion and Protestant Taste.* New York: Seabury, 1978.

Cuninggim, Merrimon. *The College Seeks Religion.* New Haven: Yale University Press, 1947.

————. *Uneasy Partners: The College and the Church.* Nashville: Abingdon, 1994.

Dakin, Arthur H. *Paul Elmer More.* Princeton: Princeton University Press, 1960.

Dictionary of American Biography. Ed. Allen Johnson et al. New York: Scribner, 1928–1937.

————. Supplement Five. Ed. John A. Garraty. New York: Scribner, 1977.

Dictionary of the History of Ideas. Ed. Philip P. Wiener. New York: Scribner, 1973–1974.

Duggan, Francis X. *Paul Elmer More.* New York: Twayne, 1966.

Fass, Paula S. *The Damned and the Beautiful: American Youth in the 1920.* New York: Oxford University Press, 1977.

Finke, Roger, and Rodney Stark. *The Churching of America 1776–1990: Winners and Losers in Our Religious Economy.* New Brunswick: Rutgers University Press, 1992.

Findley, James F., Jr. *Church People in the Struggle: The National Council of Churches and the Black Freedom Movement, 1950–1970.* New York: Oxford University Press, 1993.

Flowers, Elizabeth, and Murray G. Murphey. *A History of Philosophy in America.* 2 vols. New York: Putnam, 1977.

Flowers, Ronald B. *Religion in Strange Times: The 1960s and 1970s.* Macon, Ga.: Mercer University Press, 1984.

Frank, Thomas E. *Theological, Ethics, and the Nineteenth-Century American College Ideal: Conserving a Rational World.* San Francisco: Mellen Research University Press, 1993.

Furner, Mary O. *Advocacy and Objectivity: A Crisis in the Professionalization of American Social Science, 1865–1905.* Lexington: University Press of Kentucky, 1975.

Geiger, Roger L. *To Advance Knowledge: The Growth of American Research Universities, 1900–1940.* New York: Oxford University Press, 1986.

Gilkey, Langdon. *Naming the Whirlwind: The Renewal of God-Language.* Indianapolis: Bobbs-Merrill, 1969.

Gleason, Philip. *Contending with Modernity: Catholic Higher Education in the Twentieth Century.* New York: Oxford University Press, 1995.

Graham, Patricia A. *Community and Class in American Education, 1865–1918.* New York: John Wiley, 1974.

Grave, S. A. *The Scottish Philosophy of Common Sense.* Oxford: Clarendon Press, 1960.

Grenz, Stanley J., and Roger E. Olson. *20th-Century Theology: God and the World in a Transitional Age.* Downers Grove, IL: InterVarsity Press, 1992.

Griffin, David Ray, and Joseph C. Hough, Jr., eds. *Theology and the University: Essays in Honor of John B. Cobb, Jr..* Albany: State University of New York Press, 1991.

Haber, Samuel. *Efficiency and Uplift: Scientific Management in the Progressive Era, 1890–1920.* Chicago: University of Chicago Press, 1964.

Handy, Robert T. *A Christian America: Protestant Hopes and Historical Realities.* Rev. ed. New York: Oxford University Press, 1984.

_____. *A History of Union Theological Seminary in New York.* New York: Columbia University Press, 1987.

_____. *Undermined Establishment: Church-State Relations in America, 1880–1920.* Princeton: Princeton University Press, 1991.

Hart, D. G. *Defending the Faith: J. Gresham Machen and the Crisis of Conservative Protestantism in Modern America.* Baltimore: Johns Hopkins University Press, 1994.

Hawkins, Hugh. *Between Harvard and America: The Educational Leadership of Charles W. Eliot.* New York: Oxford University Press, 1972.

Heckscher, August. *Woodrow Wilson: A Biography.* New York: Scribner, 1991.

Herbst, Jungen. *The German Historical School in American Scholarship: A Study in the Transfer of Culture.* Port Washington, N.Y.: Kennikat, 1965.

Hesburgh, Theodore M., ed. *The Challenge and Promise of a Catholic University.* Notre Dame: University of Notre Dame Press, 1994.

Hoeveler, J. David, Jr. *James McCosh and the Scottish Intellectual Tradition: From Glasgow to Princeton.* Princeton: Princeton University Press, 1981.

_____. *The New Humanism: A Critique of Modern America, 1900–1940.* Charlottesville: University of Virginia Press, 1977.

Hoffman, Frederick J. *The Twenties: American Writing in the Postwar Decade.* New York: Viking Press, 1955.

Hofstadter, Richard, and Walter P. Metzger. *The Development of Academic Freedom in the United States.* New York: Columbia University Press, 1955.

Hofstadter, Richard, and Wilson Smith, eds. *American Higher Education: A Documentary History.* 2 vols. Chicago: University of Chicago Press, 1961.

Holifield, E. Brooks. *The Gentlemen Theologians: American Theology in Southern Culture, 1795–1860.* Durham: Duke University Press, 1978.

Holliday, Robert C. *Booth Tarkington.* Garden City, N.Y.: Doubleday, 1918.

Holmes, Arthur. *The Idea of a Christian College.* Rev. ed. Grand Rapids: Eerdmans, 1987.

Hordern, William E. *A Layman's Guide to Protestant Theology.* Rev. ed. New York: Macmillan, 1968.

Horowitz, Helen Lefkowitz. *Campus Life: Undergraduate Cultures from the End of the Eighteenth Century to the Present.* New York: Knopf, 1987.

Hovenkamp, Herbert. *Science and Religion in America, 1800–1860*. Philadelphia: University of Pennsylvania Press, 1978.

Howe, Daniel Walker. *The Political Culture of the American Whigs*. Chicago: University of Chicago Press, 1979.

———. *The Unitarian Conscience: Harvard Moral Philosophy, 1805–1861*. Cambridge: Harvard University Press, 1970; reprint, Middletown, Conn.: Wesleyan University Press, 1988.

Hudnut-Beumler, James. *Looking for God in the Suburbs: The Religion of the American Dream and Its Critics, 1945–1965*. New Brunswick: Rutgers University Press, 1994.

Hudson, Winthrop, and John Corrigan. *Religion in America*, 5th ed. New York: Macmillan, 1992.

Hughes, Richard T., and William B. Adrian. *Models for Christian Higher Education: Strategies for Success in the Twenty-First Century*. Grand Rapids: Eerdmans, 1997.

Hunt, Keith, and Gladys Hunt. *For Christ and the University: The Study of InterVarsity Christian Fellowship of the U.S.A., 1940–1990*. Downers Grove, Ill.: InterVarsity Press, 1991.

Hutchison, William R. *Errand to the World: American Protestant Thought and Foreign Missions*. Chicago: University of Chicago Press, 1987.

———. *The Modernist Impulse in American Protestantism*. Cambridge: Harvard University Press, 1976; reprint, New York: Oxford University Press, 1982.

Hutchison, William T. *Cyrus Hall McCormick: Harvest, 1856–1884*. New York: Appleston-Century, 1935.

Iggers, Georg G. *The German Conception of History*. Middletown, Conn.: Wesleyan University Press, 1968.

Jencks, Christopher, and David Riesman. *The Academic Revolution*. Garden City, N.Y.: Doubleday, 1968.

Kelley, Robert. *The Cultural Pattern in American Politics: The First Century*. New York: Knopf, 1979.

Kerr, Clark. *The Use of the University*. Cambridge: Harvard University Press, 1963.

Kuklick, Bruce. *Churchmen and Philosophers: From Jonathan Edwards to John Dewey*. New Haven: Yale University Press, 1985.

———. *The Rise of American Philosophy*. New Haven: Yale University Press, 1977.

Lean, Garth. *Frank Buchman: A Life*. Longdon: Constable, 1985.

Lears, T. J. Jackson. *No Place of Grace: Antimodernism and the Transformation of American Culture, 1880–1920*. Chicago: University of Chicago Press, 1983.

Leitch, Alexander. *A Princeton Companion*. Princeton: Princeton University Press, 1978.

Leslie, L. Bruce. *Gentlemen and Scholars: College and Community in the "Age of the University," 1865–1917*. State College: Penn State University Press, 1992.

Levine, David O. *The American College and the Culture of Aspiration, 1915–1940*. Ithaca: Cornell University Press, 1986.

Link, Arthur S. *Wilson: The Road to the White House*. Princeton: Princeton University Press, 1947.

Livingstone, David N. *Darwin's Forgotten Defenders: The Encounter Between Evangelical Theology and Evolutionary Thought*. Grand Rapids: Eerdmans, 1987.

Loetscher, Lefferts A. *The Broadening Church: A Study of Theological Issues in the Presbyterian Church since 1869.* Philadelphia: University of Pennsylvania Press, 1954.

_____. *Facing the Enlightenment and Pietism: Archibald Alexander and the Founding of Princeton Theological Seminary.* Westport, Conn.: Greenwood Press, 1983.

Longfield, Bradley J. *The Presbyterian Controversy: Fundamentalists, Modernists, and Moderates.* New York: Oxford University Press, 1991.

Lundin, Roger. *The Culture of Interpretation: Christian Faith and the Postmodern World.* Grand Rapids: Eerdmans, 1993.

Marsden, George M. *Fundamentalism and American Culture: The Shaping of Twentieth-Century Evangelicalism, 1870–1925.* New York: Oxford University Press, 1980.

_____. *The Outrageous Idea of Christian Scholarship.* New York: Oxford University Press, 1997.

_____. *The Soul of the American University: From Protestant Establishment to Established Nonbelief.* New York: Oxford University Press, 1994.

Marty, Martin E. *Modern American Religion, Volume 1: The Irony of It All, 1893–1919.* Chicago: University of Chicago Press, 1986.

_____. *Modern American Religion, Volume 2: The Noise of Conflict, 1919–1941.* Chicago: University of Chicago Press, 1991.

_____. *The Righteous Empire: The Protestant Experience in America.* New York: Dial, 1970.

Massa, Mark S. *Charles Augustus Briggs and the Crisis of Historical Criticism.* Philadelphia: Fortress Press, 1990.

May, Henry F. *The End of American Innocence: A Study of the First Years of Our Own Time, 1912–1917.* New York: Knopf, 1959; reprint, Chicago: Quadrangle Books, 1964.

_____. *The Enlightenment in America.* New York: Oxford University Press, 1976.

McCusker, John J. *How Much Is That in Real Money? A Historical Price Index for Use as a Deflator of Money Values in the Economy of the United States.* Worcester: American Antiquarian Society, 1992.

McLachlan, James. *American Boarding Schools: A Historical Study.* New York: Scribner, 1970.

_____. *Princetonians, 1748–1768.* Princeton: Princeton University Press, 1976.

Meyer, D. H. *The Instructed Conscience: The Shaping of the American National Ethic.* Philadelphia: University of Pennsylvania Press, 1972.

Miller, Donald G. *The Scent of Eternity: A Life of Harris Elliott Kirk of Baltimore.* Macon, Ga.: Mercer University Press, 1989.

Miller, Glenn T. *Piety and Intellect: The Aims and Purposes of Ante-Bellum Theological Education.* Atlanta: Scholars Press, 1990.

Miller, Howard. *The Revolutionary College: American Presbyterian Higher Education, 1707–1837.* New York: New York University Press, 1976.

Mizener, Arthur. *The Far Side of Paradise: A Biography of F. Scott Fitzgerald.* 2d ed. Boston: Houghton Mifflin, 1965.

Moore, James R. *Post-Darwinian Controversies: A Study of the Protestant Struggle to Come to Terms with Darwin in Great Britain and America, 1870–1900.* Cambridge: Cambridge University Press, 1979.

Mulder, John M. *Woodrow Wilson: The Years of Preparation*. Princeton: Princeton University Press, 1978.

Mulford, Roland J. *History of the Lawrenceville School, 1810–1935*. Princeton: Princeton University Press, 1935.

Noll, Mark A. *Between Faith and Criticism: Evangelicals, Scholarship, and the Bible in America*. San Francisco: Harper and Row, 1982.

———. *A History of Christianity in the United States and Canada*. Grand Rapids: Eerdmans, 1992.

———. *Princeton and the Republic: The Search for a Christian Enlightenment in the Era of Samuel Stanhope Smith*. Princeton: Princeton University Press, 1989.

Nord, Warren A. *Religion and American Education: Rethinking a National Dilemma*. Chapel Hill: University of North Carolina Press, 1995.

Numbers, Ronald L. *The Creationists: The Evolution of Scientific Creationism*. Berkeley: University of California Press, 1992.

O'Brien, David J. *From the Heart of the American Church: Catholic Higher Education and American Culture*. Maryknoll, N.Y.: Orbis Books, 1994.

Ogletree, Thomas W. *The Death of God Controversy*. Nashville: Abingdon, 1966.

Osgood, Charles G. *Lights in Nassau Hall*. Princeton: Princeton University Press, 1951.

Parsonage, Robert Rue, ed. *Church Related Higher Education: Perceptions and Perspectives*. Valley Forge, Pa.: Judson Press, 1978.

Perry, Lewis. *Intellectual Life in America: A History*. New York: Franklin Watts, 1984.

Piper, John F., Jr. *The American Churches in World War I*. Athens: Ohio University Press, 1985.

Placher, William C. *Narratives of a Vulnerable God: Christ, Theology, and Scripture*. Louisville: Westminster John Knox, 1995.

Plantinga, Alvin, and Nicholas Wolterstorff, eds. *Faith and Rationality: Reason and Belief in God*. Notre Dame: University of Notre Dame Press, 1983.

Powell, Edward J. *Catholic Higher Education in America: A History*. New York: Appleton-Century, 1972.

Primer, Ben. *Protestants and American Business Methods*. Ann Arbor: UMI Research Press, 1979.

Princeton Theological Seminary. *Biographical Catalogue of the Princeton Theological Seminary, 1815–1932*. Comp. Edward H. Roberts. Princeton: Published by the Trustees of The Theological Seminary of the Presbyterian Church Princeton, New Jersey, 1933.

———. *Necrological Reports*. Princeton: J.T. Robinson, 1899.

Princeton University. *General Catalogue of Princeton University, 1746–1906*. Princeton: Published by the University, 1908.

Ramsey, Paul, ed. *Religion*. Englewood Cliffs, N.J.: Prentice-Hall, 1965.

Ramsey, Paul, and John F. Wilson, eds. *The Study of Religion in Colleges and Universities*. Princeton: Princeton University Press, 1970.

Rich, Frederic C. *The First Hundred Years of the Ivy Club, 1879–1979: A Centennial History*. Princeton: The Ivy Club, 1979.

Ringenberg, William C. *The Christian College: A History of Protestant Higher Education in America*. With an Introduction by Mark A. Noll. Grand Rapids: Christian University Press and Eerdmans, 1984.

Roberts, Jon H. *Darwinism and the Divine in America: Protestant Intellectuals and Organic Evolution, 1859–1900*. Madison: University of Wisconsin Press, 1988.

Rothblatt, Sheldon. *The Revolution of the Dons: Cambridge and Society in Victorian England*. London: Faber and Faber, 1968.

Rudolph, Frederick. *The American College and University: A History*. New York: Vintage, 1962.

_____. *Curriculum: A History of the American Undergraduate Course of Study since 1636*. San Francisco: Jossey-Bass, 1977.

Russell, C. Allyn. *Voices of American Fundamentalism: Seven Biographical Studies*. Philadelphia: Westminster, 1976.

Sandeen, Ernest R. *The Roots of Fundamentalism: British and American Millenarianism, 1800–1930*. Chicago: University of Chicago Press, 1970; reprint, Grand Rapids: Baker, 1978.

Schmidt, George P. *The Liberal Arts College*. New Brunswick: Rutgers University Press, 1957.

_____. *The Old Time College President*. New York: Columbia University Press, 1930; reprint, New York: AMS Press, 1970.

Schmidt, Stephen A. *A History of the Religious Education Association*. Birmingham, Ala.: Religious Education Association, 1983.

Schwehm, Mark R. *Exiles from Eden: Religion and the Academic Vocation in America*. New York: Oxford University Press, 1993.

Selden, William K. *The Legacy of John Cleve Green*. Princeton: Printed by Office of Printing Services Princeton University, [1987].

_____. *The Princeton Summer Camp, 1908–1975*. Princeton: Printed at Princeton University Press, [1987].

Sewny, Vahan D. *The Social Theology of James Mark Baldwin*. New York: King's Crown Press, 1945.

Shedd, Clarence P. *The College Follows Its Students*. New Haven: Yale University Press, 1938.

_____. *Two Centuries of Student Christian Movements: Their Origin and Intercollegiate Life*. New York: Association Press, 1934.

Shepard, Robert S. *God's People in the Ivory Tower: Religion in the Early American University*. Brooklyn: Carlson, 1991.

Silk, Mark. *Spiritual Politics: Religion and America since World War II*. New York: Touchstone Book, 1988.

Sloan, Douglas. *Faith and Knowledge: Mainstream Protestantism and American Higher Education*. Louisville: Westminster John Knox, 1994.

_____. *The Scottish Enlightenment and the American College Ideal*. New York: Teachers College Press, 1971.

Smith, Gary Scott. *The Seeds of Secularization: Calvinism, Culture, and Pluralism in America, 1870–1915*. Grand Rapids: Christian University Press, 1985.

Smith, H. Shelton, Robert T. Handy, and Lefferts A. Loetscher, eds. *American Christianity: An Historical Interpretation with Representative Documents*. 2 vols. New York: Scribner, 1960–63.

Smith, Wilson. *Professors and Public Ethics: Studies of Northern Moral Philosophers before the Civil War.* Ithaca: Cornell University Press, 1956.

Stevenson, Louise L. *Scholarly Means to Evangelical Ends: The New Haven Scholars and the Transformation of Higher Learning in America, 1830–1890.* Baltimore: Johns Hopkins Press, 1986.

Synnott, Marcia Graham. *The Half-Opened Door: Discrimination and Admissions at Harvard, Yale, and Princeton, 1900–1970.* Westport, Conn.: Greenwood Press, 1979.

Szasz, Ferenc M. *The Divided Mind of Protestant America, 1880–1930.* University, Ala.: University of Alabama Press, 1982.

Thorp, Willard, Minor Myers, Jr., and Jeremiah Stanton Finch. *The Princeton Graduate School: A History.* Princeton: Princeton University Press, 1978.

Timberlake, James H. *Prohibition and the Progressive Movement 1900–1920.* Cambridge: Harvard University Press, 1963.

Trinterud, Leonard J. *The Forming of an American Tradition: A Re-examination of Colonial Presbyterianism.* Philadelphia: Westminster, 1949; reprint, New York: Books for Libraries Press, 1970.

Turner, James. *Without God, Without Creed: The Origins of Unbelief in America.* Baltimore: Johns Hopkins University Press, 1985.

United States Bureau of the Census. *Historical Statistics of the United States: Colonial Times to 1957.* Washington, D.C.: Bureau of the Census, 1960.

Van Dyke, Tertius. *Henry Van Dyke: A Biography.* New York: Harper, 1935.

Veysey, Laurence R. *The Emergence of the American University.* Chicago: University of Chicago Press, 1965.

Welch, Claude. *Graduate Education in Religion: A Critical Appraisal.* Missoula: University of Montana Press, 1971.

Wells, Jonathan. *Charles Hodge's Critique of Darwinism: An Historical-Critical Analysis of Concepts Basic to the 19th Century Debate.* Lewiston, N.Y.: Edwin Mellen Press, 1988.

Wertenbaker, Thomas Jefferson. *Princeton, 1746–1896.* Princeton: Princeton University Press, 1946.

White, Ronald C., Jr., and C. Howard Hopkins. *The Social Gospel: Religion and Reform in Changing America.* Philadelphia: Temple University Press, 1976.

Who's Who in the Clergy. Ed. J. C. Schwarz. New York, 1936.

Wiebe, Robert H. *The Search for Order, 1877–1920.* New York: Hill and Wang, 1967.

Wilder, Robert P. *The Student Volunteer Movement.* New York: SVM, 1935.

Willimon, William H., and Thomas N. Naylor. *The Abandoned Generation: Rethinking Higher Education.* Grand Rapids: Eerdmans, 1995.

Wilson, John F. *Public Religion in American Culture.* Philadelphia: Temple University Press, 1980.

Wind, James P. *The Bible and the University: The Messianic Vision of William Rainey Harper.* Atlanta: Scholars Press, 1987.

Wuthnow, Robert. *The Restructuring of American Religion.* Princeton: Princeton University Press, 1988.

Chapters in Edited Volumes

Ahlstrom, Sydney E. "The Radical Turn in Theology and Ethics: Why It Occurred in the 1960s." In *Religion in American History: Interpretative Essays*. Ed. John M. Mulder and John F. Wilson, 445–56. Englewood Cliffs, N.J.: Prentice-Hall, 1978.

Askew, Thomas A. "The Shaping of Evangelical Higher Education Since World War II." In *Making Higher Education Christian: The History and Mission of Evangelical Colleges in America*. Ed. Joel A. Carpenter and Kenneth W. Shipps, 137–52. Grand Rapids: Eerdmans, 1987.

Bass, Dorothy C. "Ministry on the Margin: Protestants and Education." In *Between the Times: The Travail of the Protestant Establishment in America, 1900–1960*. Ed. William R. Hutchison, 48–71. New York: Cambridge University Press, 1989.

_____. "Revolutions, Quiet and Otherwise: Protestants and Higher Education during the 1960s." In *Caring for the Commonweal: Education for Religious and Public Life*. Ed. Parker J. Palmer, Barbara G. Wheeler, and James W. Fowler, 207–26. Macon, Ga.: Mercer University Press, 1990.

Brooke, John H. "The Relations Between Darwin's Science and His Religion. In *Darwinism and Divinity: Essays on Evolution and Religious Beliefs*. Ed. John Durant, 40–75. Oxford: Basil Blackwell, 1985.

Carter, Paul A. "The Fundamentalist Defense of the Faith." In *Change and Continuity in Twentieth-Century America: The 1920s*. Ed. John Braeman, Robert Bremmer, and David Brody, 179–214. Columbus: Ohio State University Press, 1968.

Cherry, Conrad. "The Study of Religion and the Rise of the American University." In *Religious Studies, Theological Studies and the University-Divinity School*. Ed. Joseph Mitsuo Kitagawa, 115–35. Atlanta: Scholars Press, 1992.

Church, Robert L. "Economists as Experts: The Rise of an Academic Profession in the United States, 1870–1920." In *The University in Society*. Ed. Lawrence Stone, 2:571–609. Princeton: Princeton University Press, 1972.

Coben, Stanley. "The Assault on Victorianism in the Twentieth Century." In *Victorian America*. Ed. Daniel Walker Howe, 160–81. Philadelphia: University of Pennsylvania Press, 1976.

Demerath, N. J., III, and Kenneth J. Lutterman. "The Student Parishioner: Radical Rhetoric and Traditional Reality." In *The Church, the University, and Social Policy: The Danforth Study of Campus Ministries*. Ed. Kenneth Underwood, 2:88–118. Middletown, Conn.: Wesleyan University Press, 1969.

Durant, John. "Darwinism and Divinity: A Century of Debate." In *Darwinism and Divinity: Essays on Evolution and Religious Beliefs*. Ed. John Durant, 9–39. Oxford: Basil Blackwell, 1985.

Gleason, Philip. "American Catholic Higher Education, 1940–1990: The Ideological Context." In *The Secularization of the Academy*. Ed. George M. Marsden and Bradley J. Longfield, 234–58. New York: Oxford University Press, 1992.

Hart, D. G. "American Learning and the Problem of Religious Studies." In *The Secularization of the Academy*. Ed. George M. Marsden and Bradley J. Longfield, 195–233. New York: Oxford University Press, 1992.

_____. "Faith and Learning in the Age of the University: The Academic Ministry of

Daniel Coit Gilman." In *The Secularization of the Academy*. Ed. George M. Marsden and Bradley J. Longfield, 107–45. New York: Oxford University Press, 1992.

Harvey, Van. "The Intellectual Marginality of American Theology." In *Religion and Twentieth-Century American Intellectual Life*. Ed. Michael J. Lacey, 172–92. New York: Woodrow Wilson International Center for Scholars and Cambridge University Press, 1989.

Hawkins, Hugh. "University Identity: The Teaching and Research Functions." In *The Organization of Knowledge in America, 1860–1920*. Ed. Alexandra Oleson and John Voss, 285–312. Baltimore: Johns Hopkins University Press, 1979.

Higham, John. "The Matrix of Specialization." In *The Organization of Knowledge in America, 1860–1920*. Ed. Alexandra Oleson and John Voss, 3–18. Baltimore: Johns Hopkins University Press, 1979.

Hofstadter, Richard. "The Revolution in Higher Education." In *Paths of American Thought*. Ed. Arthur M. Schlesinger Jr. and Morton White, 269–90. Boston: Houghton Mifflin, 1963.

Hough, Joseph C., Jr. "The Marginalization of Theology in the University." In *Religious Studies, Theological Studies and the University-Divinity School*. Ed. Joseph Mitsuo Kitagawa, 37–68. Atlanta: Scholars Press, 1992.

Hutchison, William R. "Preface: From Protestant to Pluralist America." In *Between the Times: The Travail of the Protestant Establishment in America, 1900–1960*. Ed. William R. Hutchison, vii–xv. New York: Cambridge University Press, 1989.

———. "Protestantism as Establishment." In *Between the Times: The Travail of the Protestant Establishment in America, 1900–1960*. Ed. William R. Hutchison, 3–18. New York: Cambridge University Press, 1989.

Kevles, Daniel. "American Science." In *The Professions in American History*. Ed. Nathan O. Hatch, 107–25. Notre Dame: University of Notre Dame Press, 1988.

———. "The Physics, Mathematics, and Chemistry Communities: A Comparative Analysis." In *The Organization of Knowledge in America, 1860–1920*. Ed. Alexandra Oleson and John Voss, 139–72. Baltimore: Johns Hopkins University Press, 1979.

Link, Arthur S. "Woodrow Wilson: Presbyterian in Government." In *Calvinism and the Political Order*. Ed. George L. Hunt, 157–74. Philadelphia: Westminster, 1965.

Long, Charles H. "A Common Ancestor: Theology and Religious Studies." In *Religious Studies, Theological Studies and the University-Divinity School*. Ed. Joseph Mitsuo Kitagawa, 137–50. Atlanta: Scholars Press, 1992.

Longfield, Bradley J. "From Evangelicalism to Liberalism: Public Midwestern Universities in Nineteenth-Century America." In *The Secularization of the Academy*. Ed. George M. Marsden and Bradley J. Longfield, 46–73. New York: Oxford University Press, 1992.

———. "'For God, for Country, and for Yale,': Yale, Religion, and Higher Education." In *The Secularization of the Academy*. Ed. George M. Marsden and Bradley J. Longfield, 146–69. New York: Oxford University Press, 1992.

Longfield, Bradley J., and George M. Marsden. "Presbyterian Colleges in Twentieth-Century America." In *The Pluralistic Vision: Presbyterians and Mainstream Protestant Education and Leadership*. Ed. Milton J. Coalter, John M. Mulder, and Louis B. Weeks, 99–124. Louisville: Westminster John Knox, 1992.

Luidens, Donald A. "Numbering the Presbyterian Branches: Membership Trends Since Colonial Times." In *The Mainstream Protestant "Decline"*. Ed. Milton J. Coalter, John M. Mulder, and Louis B. Weeks, 29–65. Louisville: Westminster John Knox, 1990.

Lynn, Robert Wood. "'The Survival of Recognizably Protestant College': Reflections on Old-Line Protestantism, 1950–1990." In *The Secularization of the Academy*. Ed. George M. Marsden and Bradley J. Longfield, 170–94. New York: Oxford University Press, 1992.

Marsden, George M. "The Collapse of American Evangelical Academia." In *Faith and Rationality: Reason and Belief in God*. Ed. Alvin Plantinga and Nicholas Wolterstorff, 219–64. Notre Dame: University of Notre Dame Press, 1983.

_____. "Evangelicals and the Scientific Culture: An Overview." In *Religion & Twentieth Century American Intellectual Life*. Ed. Michael J. Lacey, 23–48. New York: Woodrow Wilson International Center for Scholars and Cambridge University Press, 1989.

_____. "Everyone One's Own Interpreter? The Bible, Science, and Authority in Mid-Nineteenth-Century America." In *The Bible in America: Essays in Cultural History*. Ed. Nathan O. Hatch and Mark A. Noll, 79–100. New York: Oxford University Press, 1982.

_____. "The Soul of the American University: An Historical Overview." In *The Secularization of the Academy*. Ed. George M. Marsden and Bradley J. Longfield, 9–45. New York: Oxford University Press, 1992.

Michaelsen, Robert. "Religion in the Undergraduate Curriculum." In *The Making of Ministers: Essays on Clergy Training Today*. Ed. Keith R. Bridston and Dwight W. Culver, 43–71. Minneapolis: Augsburg, 1964.

Miller, Glenn T., and Robert Lynn. "Christian Theological Education." *The Encyclopedia of the American Religious Experience*. Ed. Charles H. Lippy and Peter W. Williams, 3:1629–38. New York: Scribner, 1988.

Moore, R. Lawrence. "Secularization: Religion and the Social Sciences," In *Between the Times: The Travail of the Protestant Establishment in America, 1900–1960*. Ed. William R. Hutchison, 233–52. New York: Cambridge University Press, 1989.

Moorhead, James H. "Presbyterians and the Mystique of Organizational Efficiency, 1870–1936." In *Reimagining Denominationalism*, Ed. Robert Bruce Mullin and Russell E. Richey, 264–87. New York: Oxford University Press, 1994.

Murphy, Murray G. "On the Scientific Study of Religion in the United States, 1870–1980." In *Religion & Twentieth Century American Intellectual Life*. Ed. Michael J. Lacey, 136–71. New York: Woodrow Wilson International Center for Scholars and Cambridge University Press, 1989.

Neil, W. "The Criticism and Theological Use of the Bible, 1700–1950." In *Cambridge History of the Bible: The West from the Reformation to the Present Day*. Ed. S. L. Greenslade, 3:238–93. Cambridge: Cambridge University Press, 1963.

Noll, Mark A. "Christian Colleges, Christian Worldviews, and an Invitation to Research." Introduction to *The Christian College: A History of Protestant Higher Education in America*, William C. Ringenberg, 1–36. Grand Rapids: Christian University Press and Eerdmans, 1984.

Noll, Mark A., and David N. Livingstone. Introduction to *What is Darwinism? And Other Writings on Science and Religion*, by Charles Hodge, 11–47. Grand Rapids: Baker, 1994.

Oates, Whitney J. "Paul Elmer More: A Quest of the Spirit." In *The Lives of Eighteen from Princeton*. Ed. Willard Thorp, 302–17. Princeton: Princeton University Press, 1946.

Olbricht, Thomas H. "Intellectual Ferment and Instruction in the Scripture." In *The Bible in American Education: From Source Book to Text Book*. Ed. David L. Barr and Nicholas Piediscalzi, 97–119. Philadelphia: Fortress, 1982.

Oleson, Alexander and John Voss. "Introduction." In *The Organization of Knowledge in America, 1860–1920*. Ed. Alexandra Oleson and John Voss, vii–xxi. Baltimore: Johns Hopkins University Press, 1979.

Paul, Harry W. "Religion and Darwinism: Varieties of Catholic Reaction." In *Comparative Reception of Darwinism*. Ed. Thomas F. Glick, 403–36. Chicago: University of Chicago Press, 1988.

Porteous, A. J. D. "Biographical Sketch: Norman Kemp Smith (1872–1958)." *The Credibility of Divine Existence: The Collected Papers of Norman Kemp Smith*. Ed. A. J. D. Porteous, R. D. Maclennan, and G. E. Davie, 3–22. New York: St. Martin's Press, 1967.

Reifsnyder, Richard W. "Managing the Mission: Church Restructuring in the Twentieth Century." In *The Organizational Revolution: Presbyterians and American Denominationalism*. Ed. Milton J. Coalter, John M. Mulder, and Louis B. Weeks, 55–95. Louisville: Westminster/John Knox, 1992.

Richardson, Alan. "The Rise of Modern Biblical Scholarship and Recent Discussion of the Bible." In *Cambridge History of the Bible: The West from the Reformation to the Present Day*. Ed. S. L. Greenslade, 3:294–318. Cambridge: Cambridge University Press, 1963.

Ringer, Fritz K. "The German Academic Community." In *The Organization of Knowledge in America, 1860–1920*. Ed. Alexandra Oleson and John Voss, 409–29. Baltimore: Johns Hopkins University Press, 1979.

Ross, Dorothy. "The Development of the Social Sciences." In *The Organization of Knowledge in America, 1860–1920*. Ed. Alexandra Oleson and John Voss, 107–38. Baltimore: Johns Hopkins University Press, 1979.

Schlatter, Richard. "Forward." In *Religion, A Humanistic Field*. Clyde A. Holbrook, vii–x. Englewood Cliffs, N.J.: Prentice-Hall, 1963.

Schultze, Quentin. "The Two Faces of Fundamentalist Higher Education." In *Fundamentalism and Society: Reclaiming the Sciences, the Family, and Education*. Ed. Martin E. Marty and R. Scott Appleby, 490–535. Chicago: University of Chicago Press, 1993.

Shils, Edward. "The Order of Learning in the United States: The Ascendancy of the University." In *The Organization of Knowledge in Modern America, 1860–1920*. Ed. Alexandra Oleson and John Voss, 19–47. Baltimore: Johns Hopkins University Press, 1979.

Shiner, Larry. "The Meaning of Secularization." In *Secularization and the Protestant Prospect*. Ed. James F. Childress and David B. Harned, 30–42. Philadelphia: Westminster, 1970.

Sloan, Douglas. "The Teaching of Ethics in American Undergraduate Curriculum, 1876–1976." In *Ethics Teaching in Higher Education*. Ed. Sissela Bok and Daniel Callahan, 1–57. New York: Plenum, 1980.

Smith, James Ward. "Religion and Science in American Philosophy." *The Shaping of American Religion*. Ed. James Ward Smith and A. Leland Jamison, 402–42. Princeton: Princeton University Press, 1961.

Smith, Wilson. "Apologia pro Alma Matre: The College as Community in Ante-Bellum America." In *The Hofstadter Aegis: A Memorial*. Ed. Stanley Elkins and Eric McKitrick, 125–53. New York: Knopf, 1974.

Sweet, Leonard I. "The 1960s: The Crises of Liberal Christianity and the Public Emergence of Evangelicalism." In *Evangelicalism and Modern America*. Ed. George M. Marsden, 29–45. Grand Rapids: Eerdmans, 1984.

Turner, James. "Secularization and Sacralization: Speculations on Some Religious Origins of the Secular Humanities Curriculum, 1850–1900." In *The Secularization of the Academy*. Ed. George M. Marsden and Bradley J. Longfield, 74–106. New York: Oxford University Press, 1992.

Veysey, Laurence. "Higher Education as a Profession: Changes and Continuities." In *The Professions in American History*. Ed. Nathan O. Hatch, 15–32. Notre Dame: University of Notre Dame Press, 1988.

———. "Stability and Experiment in the American Undergraduate Curriculum." In *Content and Context: Essays on College Education*. Ed. Carl Kaysen, 1–63. New York: McGraw-Hill, 1973.

Welter, Barbara. "From Maria Monk to Paul Blanshard: A Century of Protestant Anti-Catholicism." In *Uncivil Religion: Interreligious Hostility in America*. Ed. Robert N. Bellah and Frederick E. Greenspahn, 43–71. New York: Crossroad, 1987.

White, Ronald C., Jr. "Presbyterian Campus Ministries: Competing Loyalties and Changing Visions." In *The Pluralistic Vision: Presbyterians and Mainstream Protestant Education and Leadership*. Ed. Milton J. Coalter, John M. Mulder, and Louis B. Weeks, 126–42. Louisville: Westminster John Knox, 1992.

Articles and Unpublished Papers

Ahlstrom, Sidney E. "The Scottish Philosophy and American Theology." *Church History* 24 (1955): 257–72.

Beck, Dwight, et al. "Report of the NABI Self-Study Committee." *Journal of Bible and Religion* 32 (1964): 200–201.

Broderick, Francis I. "Pulpit, Physics, and Politics: The Curriculum of the College of New Jersey, 1746–1794." *William and Mary Quarterly* 6 (1949): 43–57.

Brown, Ira W. "The Higher Criticism Comes to America." *Journal of Presbyterian History* 38 (1960): 193–212.

Bush, Sara. "The Princeton Chapels." (unpublished paper, April, 1994, Princeton University).

Cherry, Conrad. "Boundaries and Frontiers for the Study of Religion: The Heritage of the Age of the University." *Journal of the American Academy of Religion* 57 (1990): 807–27.

Christian Scholar's Review 21 (1991): 164–90.

Funk, Robert W. "The Watershed of the American Biblical Tradition: The Chicago School, First Phase, 1892–1920." *Journal of Biblical Literature* 95 (1976): 4–22.

Handy, Robert T. "The American Religious Depression, 1925-1935," *Church History* 29 (1960): 3-16.

Hart, D. G. "Poems, Propositions, and Dogma: The Controversy over Religious Language and the Demise of Theology in American Learning." *Church History* 57 (1987): 310–21.

Howe, Daniel Walker. "The Evangelical Movement and Political Culture in the North during the Second Party System." *Journal of American History* 77 (1991): 1216–39.

Humphrey, David C. "The Struggle for Sectarian Control of Princeton, 1745–1760." *New Jersey History* 91 (1973): 77–90.

McCormick, Richard P. "Alexander Johnston: An Appreciation." *Journal of the Rutgers University Libraries* 46 (1985): 12–22.

McGrath, Earl. "The Control of Higher Education in America." *Educational Record* 17 (1936): 259–79.

McLachlan, James. "The American College in the Nineteenth Century: Toward a Reappraisal." *Teachers College Record* 80 (1978): 287–306.

Meyer, Albert. Memmo Simons Lectures. Bethel College, 1994 (unpublished lectures).

Meyer, D. H. "American Intellectuals and the Victorian Crisis of Faith." *American Quarterly* 27 (1975): 585–603.

Moorhead, James H. "Henry Van Dyke, Sr.: Conservative Apostle of a Broad Church." *Journal of Presbyterian History* 50 (1972): 19–38.

Naylor, Natalie A. "The Ante-Bellum College Movement: A Reappraisal of Tewksbury's Founding of American Colleges and Universities." *History of Education Quarterly* 13 (1973): 261–74.

———. "The Theological Seminary in the configuration of American Higher Education: The Ante-Bellum Years." *History of Education Quarterly* 17 (1977): 17–30.

Olson, Alison B. "The Founding of Princeton University: Religion and Politics in Eighteenth-Century New Jersey." *New Jersey History* 87 (1969): 133–50.

Potts. David B. "American Colleges in the Nineteenth Century: From Localism to Denominationalism." *History of Education Quarterly* 11 (1971): 366–80.

Sack, Daniel. "'Refreshed in the Company of My Brethren': The Campus Religious Establishment and Student Agency at the College of New Jersey." *American Presbyterians* 73 (1995): 219–28.

Sanua, Marianne. "Stages in the Development of Jewish Life at Princeton University." *American Jewish History* 76 (1987): 391–415.

Schlesinger, Arthur M. "A Critical Period in American Religion, 1875–1900." *Proceedings of the Massachuesetts Historical Society* 64 (1932): 523–47.

Schwehn, Mark R. "The Academic Vocation: 'Specialists without Spirit, Sensualists without Heart.'" *Cross Currents* 42 (1992): 185–99.

Sloan, Douglas. "Harmony, Chaos, and Consensus: The American College Curriculum." *Teachers College Record* 73 (1971): 221–51.

Smith, Gary Scott. "Calvinists and Evolution, 1870–1920." *Journal of Presbyterian History* 61 (1983): 335–52.

Thorp, Willard. "The Founding of the Princeton Graduate School: An Academic Agon." *Princeton University Library Chronicle* 32 (1970): 1–30.

———. "When Merwick was the University's 'Graduate House,' 1905–1913." *Princeton History* 1 (1971): 51–71.

Urofsky, Melvin I. "Reform and Response: The Yale Report of 1828." *History of Education Quarterly* 5 (1965): 53–67.

Veysey, Laurence R. "The Academic Mind of Woodrow Wilson." *Mississippi Valley Historical Review* 49 (1963): 613–34.

Wallace, Peter, and Mark A. Noll. "The Students of Princeton Seminary, 1812–1929: A Research Note." *American Presbyterians* 72 (1994): 203–15.

Weeks, Louis. "The Incorporation of American Religion: The Case of the Presbyterians." *Religion and American Culture* 1 (1991): 101–18.

Wilson, John F. "Mr. Holbrook and the Humanities." *Journal of Bible and Religion* 32 (1964): 252–61.

Theses and Dissertations

Brill, Earl H. "Religion and the Rise of the University: A Study of the Secularization of American Higher Education, 1870–1910." Ph.D. diss., American University, 1969.

Coburn, Matthew M. "The Philadelphian Society: An investigation into the demise of an evangelical student Christian organization at Princeton University in the 1920s." Senior thesis, Princeton University.

Healy, Francis Patricia. "A History of Evelyn College for Women, Princeton, New Jersey 1887–1897." Ph.D. diss., Ohio State University, 1967.

Maxwell, Howard B. "The Formative Years of the University Alumni Movement as Illustrated by Studies of the University of Michigan and Columbia, Princeton, and Yale Universities, 1854–1918." Ph.D. diss., University of Michigan, 1965.

Sack, Daniel. "Disastrous Disturbances: Buchmanism and Student Religious Life at Princeton, 1919–1930." Ph.D. diss., Princeton University, 1995.

Snow, Louis Franklin. "The College Curriculum in the United States." Ph.D. diss., Columbia University, 1907.

Stewart, John W. "The Tethered Theology: Biblical Criticism, Common Sense Philosophy, and the Princeton Theologians, 1812–1860." Ph.D. diss., University of Michigan, 1990.

Index

347